THE CONTEST

THE CONTEST

The 1968 Election and the War for AMERICA'S SOUL

Michael Schumacher

University of Minnesota Press
Minneapolis
London

The publication of this book was assisted by a
bequest from Josiah H. Chase to honor his parents,
Ellen Rankin Chase and Josiah Hook Chase,
Minnesota territorial pioneers.

Published by the University of Minnesota Press
111 Third Avenue South, Suite 290
Minneapolis, MN 55401-2520
http://www.upress.umn.edu

ISBN 978-0-8166-9289-7 (hc)
ISBN 978-0-8166-9292-7 (pb)
A Cataloging-in-Publication record for this book
is available from the Library of Congress.

Printed in the United States of America on acid-free paper

The University of Minnesota is an
equal-opportunity educator and employer.

24 23 22 21 20 19 18   10 9 8 7 6 5 4 3 2 1

For Ken Ade

Contents

Preface

A political campaign is a dehumanizing rite. Its only purpose is
power, and tends to bring out the worst in men. Repetition, exhaustion,
anxiety, and pressure must be endured cheerfully. Instincts have to be
disguised. Sleep and privacy are elusive. Each day brings some new
temptation to compromise a little.

These words, written by journalist Jack Newfield in 1968, are as true today, in
the era of social media and cable television, as they were in days past when
campaign news was delivered by horseback, rail, sheets of newsprint, network
television, radio, and person to person. The election of 1968, in which Newfield's friend Robert Kennedy ran until he was assassinated in California on
the state's primary night, was one of the closest and most bitterly contested in
American history, conducted against a tumultuous backdrop that even today
seems impossible.

The world seemed poised for implosion. Soviet tanks and troops rumbled
through the streets of Czechoslovakia, using military might to quash a reform
movement. Thousands of Italian students, demanding reforms at the universities, battled with police. In France, students took over buildings at the Sor-
bonne, built barricades, fought with police, and touched off a national strike
involving more than seven million workers. In Japan, more than twenty-five
thousand students, demonstrating against the U.S. involvement in Vietnam,
touched off clashes with police.

The United States was the white-hot center of it all. During the 1968 election cycle, Martin Luther King Jr. and Robert Kennedy were assassinated, the
Tet Offensive erupted in Vietnam, President Lyndon Johnson decided not to
seek another term, George Wallace ran as a controversial third-party candidate,
students took over Columbia University, violence exploded across the country
in the wake of King's death, and the Democratic National Convention was
grotesquely disfigured by violent clashes between the city's police and youths
protesting the war and the old politics, among other issues.

When Senator Eugene McCarthy entered the race for the Democratic Party nomination, it was with great reluctance and little hope of success. Lyndon Johnson, despite his slippage in popularity among voters, was still very powerful, and it was a foregone conclusion that he would win the opportunity for reelection; his 1964 victory over Barry Goldwater had been the most dominant win in presidential election history. Still, there was a growing movement to unseat him, generated by antiwar groups. McCarthy knew, at least in the beginning, that he was likely to be a sacrificial lamb in his opposition to Johnson, but he agreed to run—no small act of courage—because he, too, felt strongly that Johnson needed to be challenged by a candidate dedicated to ending the bloodshed in Vietnam.

And so it began: McCarthy announced his candidacy late in 1967, and one of the most improbable presidential elections in modern U.S. history, continuously influenced by the events of the day, lurched out of the starting gate. Robert Kennedy joined the fray in late March—late enough to be accused of being an opportunist, as his entry came shortly after McCarthy's impressive, unexpected showing against Johnson in the New Hampshire primary. Hubert Humphrey committed to the race a few weeks after Kennedy. The campaign was contentious from the onset. McCarthy and Kennedy sniped at one another, despite their obvious similarities, and both attacked Humphrey, who, as vice president, represented the hated Johnson administration. On the Republican side, Richard Nixon ran virtually unopposed, with only token opposition from Nelson Rockefeller and Ronald Reagan; his greatest challenge was to defeat his loser's image. Former Alabama governor George Wallace, hoping to gain support for his segregationist agenda, became a surprisingly popular third-party candidate.

Each of these men had compelling résumés and campaign teams. McCarthy pieced together a grassroots campaign fueled mainly by youthful volunteers, who went "clean for Gene" by cutting their long hair, shaving their beards, and setting aside their blue jeans and miniskirts to dress in a style that made them look professional to the people they met while campaigning door-to-door; the amused media tagged the campaign "the Children's Crusade." Kennedy combined the older, more experienced people who had worked on his brother's 1960 campaign with younger, enthusiastic, idealistic staff members eager to reestablish a Kennedy legacy shattered so suddenly on November 22, 1963. Humphrey, entering the race too late to face the other candidates in the primaries, worked the caucuses, union halls, back rooms, and town halls, hoping to secure enough delegate support to win the nomination in Chicago. Nixon, a poor television presence, complemented his campaign team with a group of media specialists who would change the face of campaigning in the future.

Wallace, unburdened by the need for delegate votes, zigzagged cross-country, meeting supporters at state fairs, shopping-center parking lots, medium-sized halls, fish fries, and barbecues—anywhere the "common folk" gathered. Taken together, the candidates created a mosaic of every type of campaign strategy America had seen in its history.

Two issues—the Vietnam War and civil rights (which later morphed as an issue into law and order)—raced to the forefront of discussion and remained there throughout the election cycle. In researching and writing about the candidates and their attention to these issues, I found myself revisiting the historical events of the previous two decades and their connection to issues threatening to tear the nation apart in 1968. How could one write about civil rights without examining Hubert Humphrey's 1948 speech that divided the Democratic Party, the Southern states splitting away and forming what became known as the Dixiecrats? How could one write about George Wallace's segregationist politics without examining such seminal events as James Meredith's enrollment at the University of Mississippi, Wallace's attempts to bar two students from enrolling at the University of Alabama, the march on Selma, and Lyndon Johnson's groundbreaking civil rights legislation in 1964 and 1965? Could one write about Johnson's decision to step away from the presidency without looking at the events in the Vietnam War and the rise of the antiwar movement that led him to his decision? History is nothing if not a collection of antecedents, one leading to the next.

■ ■ ■ ■ ■

America's soul: when I thought about the subtitle for this book, I worried that might be hyperbolic, but the more I researched, the more I believed that, yes, the election was the culmination of a mighty struggle lasting for at least a decade, beginning with the early civil rights movement and continuing through the Vietnam protests, the battle waged over what America was and where it would be headed in the future. The continuum could be found in the history behind the development of the candidates and those who supported them.

The war for America's soul was generational, fought between those who served in (and lived through) World War II and their children, the skeptics and opponents of the Vietnam War, the two generations disagreeing vehemently on what constituted America's soul. Both sides offered valid points. The older generation had survived the Depression (or its remnants) and a global war. The 1950s, with the establishment of the middle class, homeownership, and movement in the way of travel and relocation, were a reward; the growth of the Soviet Union and its "empire," along with the budding space race, interrupted the calm and further engrained the nationalistic older generation with what it believed was the soul of the American way. These were principles worth fighting for, no matter the cost.

The younger generation—the baby boomers—wanted none of this. They were as interested as their parents in the political climate, but they were removed from the events that had shaped their parents' lives. They were too young to remember the Korean War, and World War II and the Depression were ancient history. They rejected blind nationalism. They demanded a voice in determining the direction America was taking. They had been weaned on television—the glass teat, as Harlan Ellison called it—and unlike their parents, their views were based on images. When they saw the newscasts of the battles for civil rights or the war in Vietnam, they insisted on action. When results were slow in coming, they took action. They *participated.* Not all of them were motivated by the purest of intentions, of course, but their numbers were significant enough to force a discussion between the two generations.

"None of us were raised as conspirators," Tom Hayden wrote in an afterword to *Conspiracy in the Streets,* an account of the Chicago Eight conspiracy trial. "We grew up in the fifties void, when McCarthyism seemed to have eradicated any trace of subversion from American culture. We were radicalized when our youthful dreams of reform encountered a systemic pattern of violent response."

Hayden, like so many young Americans, felt the split within his own family. Raised a Catholic and educated in Catholic schools, he felt a hard push against his natural inclination to rebel. "My father stopped talking to me, my mother couldn't understand me. She confused Indochina with Indonesia," Hayden recalled. "To protest the war meant breaking their hearts."

When Eugene McCarthy entered the 1968 presidential election as a peace candidate and promised to challenge the old way of doing business in the political world, the younger generation embraced a new opportunity. Oddly enough, the values held by the two groups were essentially the same; they differed in their views on how those values should be pursued. In the 1968 election, Eugene McCarthy and, to a lesser degree, Robert Kennedy represented the new politics; the old politics were represented by Richard Nixon, Ronald Reagan, George Wallace, and Hubert Humphrey.

Humphrey was the wild card in this group. He was as beholden to the old politics as anyone on Capitol Hill, yet he was a dyed-in-the-wool liberal, often at odds with those seeking to preserve tradition, dating back to his days as mayor of Minneapolis, when he had battled organized crime and anti-Semitism. His progressive views on civil rights were unassailable. He preferred to work within the system he had followed his entire career, but not at the cost of defeat while battling for causes and issues he held dear. His engaging personality, his powers of persuasion, his unflappable will, his ability to work both sides of the aisle—all aided him when he pushed through some of the traditional ways of conducting business in Washington, D.C., especially in the Senate.

Then came the vice presidency. After an unsuccessful run for the presidency in 1960, Humphrey concluded that his chances of being elected to the office depended on his serving as a vice president. He would have to be patient. John Kennedy was immensely popular, and odds favored his serving two terms. This, of course, did not happen, and Humphrey found himself serving as Johnson's vice president when LBJ ran for reelection in 1964. The office came with a price: before announcing Humphrey as his running mate, Johnson forced Humphrey to vow complete, unquestioned loyalty. Humphrey readily agreed. Johnson had been his mentor in the Senate, they had worked well together over the years, and Humphrey could see no circumstance in which he couldn't at least discuss any disagreements he might have with LBJ. He was wrong in this assumption, especially when it came to their disagreements about the escalating war in Vietnam. Johnson punished Humphrey whenever his vice president went public with his differences.

This placed Humphrey in an awkward position when he decided to run for the presidency in 1968. Johnson's last-minute decision not to run for reelection, based on his inability to end the extremely unpopular war, forced Humphrey into a difficult decision. He wanted to run, but he was still vice president and tied to Johnson. He had his own ideas about working toward an ending to the war, ideas differing from the president's, but as his vice president he was bound to stand by LBJ's decisions. His silence was especially mandated when Johnson announced that the United States was attempting to negotiate an end to the war through peace talks in Paris. The negotiations, which involved trying to get both sides to agree with the peace talks, were too sensitive for Humphrey to stray, even in the slightest way, from the president's position.

None of the other candidates faced this critical limitation. Eugene McCarthy and Robert Kennedy hammered away at Humphrey for his support of Johnson's policies, as did the various antiwar groups now regularly demonstrating against the war. The gulf between the old and new politics widened; the battle of words between the two generations heated up. Although it was tempting to place Humphrey, with his defense of the White House position or his silence, in the old school or criticize him for selling out his old liberal values, Humphrey was, in fact, caught somewhere between the two groups, trapped by his position and reluctance to split from his boss on the central issue of the campaign. He, more than any other candidate, had become a symbol of the country itself, a casualty in the war for America's soul. It might be argued that he was doomed unless he resigned his vice presidency, and that wasn't going to happen.

His plight was in full view during the week of the Democratic National Convention, when McCarthy and his hopes for a new direction were crushed by the forces of the old politics and Humphrey, as leader of those traditional standards, accepted his nomination, while outside the convention hall, the youths of America were beaten senseless by the forces of law and order. Television cameras captured the essence of America's soul, and it was ugly.

■ ■ ■ ■ ■

"Television's influence in covering the Democratic National Convention is likely to be a subject of study for years," Jack Gould of the *New York Times* wrote in "TV: A Chilling Spectacle in Chicago," an analytical piece published on August 29, the day after delegates nominated Hubert Humphrey as the Democratic Party's presidential candidate, the same day as the nation's second-most-populated city faced irrepressible brutality in its streets. "Untold millions of viewers, as well as the delegates in the hall, saw chilling TV tape recordings of Chicago policemen clearing the streets in front of the Conrad Hilton Hotel," Gould wrote, offering a convention floor/city streets juxtaposition that the television networks had exploited during their previous evening's coverage.

By 1968, television had replaced radio and newspapers as America's primary source of news, and news producers were exploring ways in which to use the tools at their disposal to their advantage. Photographs still captured the moment frozen in time; the motion of the television camera made an event seem more *real*. I remember the shock of seeing Jack Ruby gun down Lee Harvey Oswald on live television, and, one day later, the sorrow of seeing little John Kennedy Jr. saluting the casket bearing his father's body as it passed in the funeral procession. Both of these became iconic photographic images. The same might be said about the images of war: memorable photos of Vietnam, such as the image of the Vietcong soldier being shot in the head at point-blank range, and of the young Vietnamese girl running hysterically down the road after her village had been napalmed, remain firmly in memory, although one might argue that the footage of the fighting and casualties in Vietnam, shown on television every night, changed the way people felt about a war being fought thousands of miles away.

Television, although still relatively new in 1968, had a profound effect on electoral politics. Television—and, more specifically, the televised Nixon–Kennedy debates in 1960—swayed public opinion, and sometimes for the wrong reasons. Voters were taken by the younger Kennedy image, not his experience. The use of television for campaigning was staggering; the sight of a candidate delivering his message on-screen or as a voice-over in an ad using film to create a collage of photos or film brought the candidate into living rooms across America.

Richard Nixon, always suspicious of the news media, complained bitterly in his 1962 book, *Six Crises,* about the lessons that television taught him in his 1960 race against John Kennedy. He wrote, "I believe that I spent too much time in the last campaign on substance and too little time on appearance: I paid too much attention to what I was going to say and too little to how I would look. Again, what must be recognized is that television has increasingly become the medium through which the great majority of the voters get their news and develop their impressions of the candidates." Nixon would not repeat this "mistake" in 1968, and as cynical as the remark might have been, it was grounded in truth. Voters tended to believe what they saw more than what they read.

Jack Gould, in his *Times* piece, wondered how the view of the violence in the Chicago streets, seen on small television screens throughout the convention hall, might have influenced the voting. "The arrests, disturbances and unofficial total injuries around the hotel illustrated how television was able to relay information to the delegates and affect the convention's mood," he wrote.

Gould was especially disgusted by the way the three main television networks—CBS, in particular—made a major news story out of what was a minor story, if a story at all. It was no secret that some of the most powerful Democrats had little use for Humphrey or McCarthy when the convention opened. Ted Kennedy's popularity was soaring, despite his repeated denials that he would be a candidate for either the presidency or vice presidency, and his absence from the convention itself. In what Gould termed "excessive emphasis," the networks pumped up the rumor of a draft-Kennedy boom, despite flimsy evidence of Kennedy interest. Was television, rather than reporting the news, trying to influence it—or, worse yet, create it?

Of course, there was always pressure not only to be the best but to be the first. So the rush was to be expected. What was not expected was the mutation of a new combination of the news and entertainment, a type of programming that would become a staple on future television coverage of political conventions.

ABC, badly trailing the other two networks in its news division, came up with the idea of staging a debate between two politically savvy, highly entertaining, controversial individuals representing the liberal and conservative wings of the spectrum. The two would debate the issues of the day, especially those influencing the election. Sparks would fly, viewers would be entertained. This could not be a one-night stand. Instead, there would be a different debate every night of the two conventions. If word got around and the momentum built, a ratings spike might ensue.

ABC chose two ideal candidates— two intellectuals famous enough to attract a large audience and, to sweeten the deal, known to loathe each other: William F. Buckley Jr. and Gore Vidal. Both were quick with a retort, and neither shied away from the slashing remark. The setting was crucial: the men were seated so closely together that they were all but rubbing up against each other.

Buckley, who wrote a nationally syndicated newspaper column, was possibly the best-known conservative voice in the country. He had founded *National Review* magazine in 1955 and hosted *Firing Line,* a popular television interview program. He had run for mayor of New York in 1965, representing the Conservative Party. Vidal, whose best-selling books included the controversial satire *Myra Breckinridge,* published earlier in 1968, had written for the screen and stage. He, too, had run for political office, losing a congressional race in 1960.

The debates were testy from the onset, but both men held their tempers. Then, on August 28, the most violent day of the Democratic Convention week, when television cameras had presented Humphrey's nomination backlit by the battles in the streets, the Buckley–Vidal debate, the eleventh in the series, nearly came to blows. The discussion had turned to the topic of how some of the young demonstrators were carrying and waving the Vietcong flag, an action the moderator likened to displaying a Nazi flag in America during World War II. Buckley agreed with the comparison and felt that Vietcong sympathizers should be treated the way Nazi sympathizers were treated during "The Good War." Vidal disagreed immediately. "As far as I'm concerned," he shot back, "the only sort of pro- or crypto-Nazi I can think of is yourself." Buckley, accustomed to pushing others to extremes, lost his cool. "Now, listen, you queer," he began, knowing that Vidal was an open homosexual, "stop calling me a crypto-Nazi, or I'll sock you in the goddamn face and you'll stay plastered."

The exchange became water-cooler material in offices across the country and would be remembered for decades after the confrontation. Cursing was not common on television at that time, nor was it common to see Buckley lose his composure. A congenial man known for smiling as he tossed bon mots at his opposition, Buckley now represented the hair-trigger temperament of a nation split by tense disagreement. It made for entertaining television, but Buckley regretted the confrontation for the rest of his life. The two men went to their graves without resolving their hostilities.

The debates were not without their political value, and they served their medium well. Future election coverage would offer the offbeat to counter the often staid analysis on the convention floor and in the television studio. Did they sway voter opinion? It is hard to tell, but it is noteworthy that a survey conducted in 2015 discovered that a large percentage of young viewers claimed they got their news from Comedy Central's *The Daily Show* and that Donald Trump, embattled by uncomplimentary news coverage, has labeled major television networks' content as "fake news."

■ ■ ■ ■ ■

A word or two about the opposition. In writing this account, I hoped to set the record straight about the groups that opposed the war, fought for civil rights, and set the agenda for other important social changes breaking through in the late 1960s. It was easy to dismiss such organizations as the Students for a Democratic Society, the National Mobilization Committee to End the War in Vietnam, and, perhaps more than any, the Youth International Party as groups of radical, attention-seeking, disruptive cranks whose sole intention was to make trouble. One cannot dispute this to some degree: many of those clashing with the police during the Chicago Democratic Convention had traveled to the Windy City with the goal of creating trouble. This simplification, however, was a grotesque journalistic failure. Historian Theodore White, for instance, waved off many of the actions as the work of "crazies" and refused to even mention Abbie Hoffman or Jerry Rubin by name in his book *The Making of the President 1968*. Worse yet, he accused David Dellinger and the Mobe of seeking out violent confrontations with the police—a fatuous accusation, at the very least. Anyone knowing Dellinger and his lifetime devoted to nonviolent demonstration, or anyone witnessing his attempts to keep peace during convention week, knows that this just wasn't the case. All too often, the press chose cliché and oversimplification in its reportage of what happened in Chicago, a fact underscored by its portrayal of the violent confrontations between the police and young people in Lincoln and Grant Parks. The kids, too many in the press opined, had *asked* for the police response when they disobeyed orders prohibiting their assembly in the park after curfew and their demonstrations, without permit, in the city's streets; they were being disorderly, regardless of the merits of their cause. The tone of such coverage, it might be noted, changed when the police removed their badges and attacked reporters and photographers covering the events in the parks.

Perhaps it was unavoidable. The overheated rhetoric and violence of 1968 backed one into dark, unexplored regions of the mind. A negotiated settlement to the Vietnam War, for all the hope those prospects engendered, was not happening; Martin Luther King, the most compelling example of nonviolent protest the country had ever seen, had been gunned down. The reaction to these and other events had been immediate and forceful, and those reactions had been grounded in American history, in what we had been as a country and who we believed we were. The Black Panthers, the Student Nonviolent Coordinating Committee, and other activist groups had ushered in, as far as white America was concerned, a form of aggressive politics that the country had never experienced in its long, shameful history of dealing with the heirs of those stolen from Africa. The sight of Black Panther cofounder Bobby Seale, one of eight "coconspirators" (a misnomer if there ever was one) on trial for his participation in the 1968 protests during the week of the Democratic National Convention, bound and gagged in the courtroom for the offense of demanding his right to an attorney of his choosing, was a disturbing example of America's inability to address the realities of its history. Seale was the only African American in the group being tried, and he was silenced, symbolically and in fact, for speaking out in a circus of a trial in which everyone spoke out. I wondered at the time if this was a matter of giving America a choice: would we listen to James Baldwin, as eloquent an essayist as black America ever encountered, or would we be forced to contend with Eldridge Cleaver and a much more forceful argument? *The Fire Next Time* minced no words; *Soul on Ice* took words to the streets.

Those witnessing the events of the Chicago convention, as well as the other significant events of the year, filtering what they saw through their own experiences, expectations, knowledge of American history and politics, and sense of morality, reacted to the violent collision between past and present in predictable ways. The forces of protest were demonized, ridiculed, and misrepresented in too many reports. It was the easy, but less than honest, way out. And the public, weary from facing the newspaper accounts and nightly reports on television, were content to believe that all of this was true.

This inspired me when I was writing the "Resistance" chapter of this book. I chose four leaders—Abbie Hoffman, Jerry Rubin, David Dellinger, and Tom Hayden—because they were leaders of the three largest groups (Yippies, Mobe, and SDS) present in Chicago during the convention. At the time, they were dismissed as outside agitators with very little to contribute when, in fact, they spent their adulthoods as dedicated activists in the civil rights and antiwar movements. All were educated; all had given a great deal of thought to the best ways to advance their causes. Tom Hayden had written *The Port Huron Statement,* a twenty-five-thousand-word document that historian Michael Kazin, author of *America Divided: The Civil War of the 1960s* and *American Dreamers: How the Left Changed a Nation,* would call "the most ambitious, the most specific, and the most eloquent manifesto in the history of the American left."

These men came to symbolize the rift between the old and the new politics, the Establishment and what came to be known as the Movement. Their presence at the convention changed history: voters would associate Hubert Humphrey and the Democratic Party with the New Left, and Republicans would occupy the White House for twenty of the following twenty-four years. The Democratic Party was fractured for that long as well. To those who would dispute the significance of the battle for Chicago, I respectfully ask: Would history be different if the Democratic National Convention had been as listless and *safe* as the Republican National Convention in Miami a few weeks earlier?

I think we know the answer.

■ ■ ■ ■ ■

The more I researched, the more I came to believe that the election of 1968 represented a marker, a turning point in American electoral history. It is a story of faith—and the loss of it. It is a story of change. Today, there are more primaries, with a much greater number of voters participating in the nominating process, and there is substantially more news coverage than there was in the past; the cult of personality has discolored the process as well. There was a greater sense of politesse in the past than we see today, when negative campaigning dominates the primary and general election campaigns. Information is parsed out in sound bites and video clips more easily digestible to a nation that seems to lose more of its attention span each year. The gulf between the two parties' ideologies appears to widen with each election, and there are no indications that this is going to change. Electoral College votes, more important than ever, determine how and where candidates campaign.

This is not to say or imply that all of this is new since the 1968 election; most of the elements listed here have been present, in one form or another, since the beginning of presidential politics. It is, however, a matter of prevalence.

THE CONTEST

Introduction

A War, Wise Men, and a
Speech That Changed History

1 In those final moments before he would be signaled that he was on live
television in front of a national audience, President Lyndon Baines Johnson had the opportunity to reconsider what he was about to say. Every presidential address makes history, one way or another—such is the nature of the
office—but only a few during any term of office have the potential to seriously
alter the course of history. Johnson, widely known for his flair for the dramatic,
realized that this speech, on March 31, 1968, would be one of those occasions.

As far as the nation knew, Johnson would be speaking about the Vietnam
War and his plans, as commander in chief, for its immediate future. Recent
public opinion polls indicated that he had lost the country's faith in the way
he was handling a war that dragged on with no end in sight. A Gallup Poll
released earlier that same day indicated that only 36 percent of those polled
viewed favorably the job the president was doing; worse yet, only 26 percent
supported the way he was handling Vietnam. In Johnson's mind, these figures
only underscored the decision he was about to announce.

Johnson, never foolish enough to manipulate numbers in his favor when
history was on the line, had been clinging for months to the recommendations of his most trusted advisors, a group of senior advisers known simply as
the "Wise Men." In a November 1967 conference with this small, inner-circle
group of former statesmen, military leaders, businessmen, and elder advisors, Johnson had received what he viewed to be an important vote of confidence. The public opposing the war did not have all the pertinent information
and, therefore, was not seeing the entire picture of the Vietnam War; Johnson,
the Wise Men said, was doing the right thing and should stay the course in
Vietnam.

But what was that course? Greater troop commitment, with the inevitable
loss of human life and the escalating monetary expense? Relentless bombing

1

of North Vietnam with little evidence of its having any effect on the enemy? Every day brought more bad news and strong reaction from those opposing the war. Antiwar demonstrations erupted on college campuses, in front of draft induction centers, and near military installations. In November 1967, Eugene McCarthy, a relatively unknown senator from Minnesota and open critic of the war, had announced his candidacy for the Democratic Party nomination in opposition to a sitting president, his candidacy gaining traction in early 1968.

By the beginning of 1968, Johnson was so embattled that he seriously considered denouncing his candidacy for reelection during his State of the Union address in January. He had typed the announcement and slipped the page into his suit jacket pocket, only to have a change of heart while delivering his speech; once again, he chose to hang on. Abandoning his candidacy, he reasoned, would damage the bills he hoped to push through Congress.

A fierce but brief offensive against South Vietnam, staged by the North Vietnamese Army and Vietcong, signaled the beginning of the end of the president's dwindling support of the status quo in Vietnam. The Tet Offensive, as it came to be known, commenced on January 30, the Indochinese lunar New Year, with Communist troops storming South Vietnam and battling American and South Vietnamese troops in almost every major city. U.S. military intelligence had noted troop movements and North Vietnamese infiltration into South Vietnam and anticipated a military charge from North Vietnam, and the U.S. and South Vietnamese troops had emerged with a resounding military victory, but it was a public relations catastrophe for Johnson and the military. The images on television and in newspaper reports bespoke of a war effort much different from the one being presented by the Johnson administration.

What came out of the Tet Offensive was nothing less than very troubling. In Saigon, the South Vietnamese capital and supposedly a U.S.–South Vietnamese stronghold, enemy troops blew a hole in the wall protecting the U.S. embassy and stormed into the compound; they were defeated within hours of the invasion, but the mere thought of their initial success brought into sharp focus the credibility gap between what Americans were hearing about the war and what was actually taking place. "Only a few months ago we were told that 65 percent of the population was secure," Eugene McCarthy said while campaigning in Manchester, New Hampshire. "Now we know that even the American Embassy is not secure."

The bloodiest and most protracted fighting took place in Hue, the ancient capital of Vietnam, a cultural center and one of South Vietnam's most beautiful cities. Hue was taken with only token resistance, and over the following twenty-four days the National Liberation Front flag flew over the Citadel while the Vietcong systematically butchered nearly three thousand civilians specifically targeted for execution. By the time the city was pacified on February 25, the Communist forces had lost 5,113 men, while the South Vietnamese had lost 384, and the Marines, 142.

By this point, Americans had grown numb from the figures and statistics. They had been hearing them on the evening news or reading them in the newspapers for months, accompanied by the latest photos and television news films of the fighting. Tet, however, produced some of the most memorable quotations and images to rise out of the war.

Ben Tre, a city of thirty-five thousand, was the setting for an observation that would play on the front pages and in stateside conversation for weeks. After taking the city, the Vietcong dug in and sustained heavy losses from artillery shelling and air attacks. By the time the American and South Vietnamese troops were able to regain control of the city, Ben Tre was in ruins, nearly half of its buildings reduced to rubble. "It became necessary to destroy the town to save it," an American major told Peter Arnett, the acclaimed war correspondent covering the war for the Associated Press. The quote, repeated ad nauseum, became a symbol of American futility.

One of the most notorious images from the war was taken on the fourth day of the offensive. AP photographer Eddie Adams and NBC correspondent Howard Tuckner were walking in Saigon when they witnessed an astonishing scene. A Vietcong guerrilla fighter, his hands bound behind his back, was confronted on the street by General Nguyen Ngoc Loan, the national police chief. After waving off troops standing nearby, Loan pointed his pistol at the prisoner's head. Adams lifted his camera and clicked its shutter at the precise moment when Loan squeezed the trigger, and the resulting photograph of the prisoner grimacing as he was being executed, his executioner's arm fully extended and a hand gripping the gun inches from his head, became one of the enduring images of the war. The photo would go on to win a list of awards, including the Pulitzer Prize. The magnitude of the photograph, as well as the horror that people felt when seeing it, was lost on General Loan. The executed man, as a leader, had ordered the executions of many others. "Many Americans have been killed these last few days, and many of my best Vietnamese friends," Loan said. "Now do you understand? Buddha will understand."

While the world reacted to the absurdity and horror of the war, President Johnson and military higher-ups attempted to lessen the impact of the reports and images. Before requesting an additional 206,000 troops, General William Westmoreland, the four-star general in charge of the American military in Vietnam, proclaimed the Tet Offensive to be a solid American victory. "The enemy's well-laid plan went afoul," he said laconically after inspecting the damage to the American Embassy in Saigon. "They lost as many people at Tet as we have lost in the entire war," Johnson declared, as if this would mollify the American public. General Maxwell Taylor would later deem Tet to be "the greatest victory we ever scored in Vietnam."

Such pronouncements were being met with skepticism, if not outright derision. Americans, who would be casting their ballots in the very near future, were uninterested in hearing about victories in a faraway country, in a war that made less sense every day when they heard the latest reports; they wanted the troops to return home. The war, an increasing number of Americans believed, could not be won. Further, it had become a national obsession.

"Vietnam had become a second consciousness, coexisting with that which was concerned with 'normal' things," Harry McPherson, Johnson's top speechwriter, wrote in his memoirs. "One thought of friends, and Vietnam; raising a family, and Vietnam, investing in the market, writing a letter, visiting a university, watching television, and Vietnam."

"The credibility of the American strategy of attrition died during the Tet offensive; so too did the credibility of the man who was by now Johnson's most important political ally, General Westmoreland," wrote David Halberstam in *The Best and the Brightest,* his acclaimed account of the men who ran the Vietnam War. "If Westmoreland's credibility was gone, then so too was Johnson's. The Tet offensive had stripped Johnson naked on the war, his credibility and that of his Administration were destroyed."

CBS Evening News anchor Walter Cronkite, whose reputation as the most trusted newsman in America had been forged by his even, clear-headed, unbiased delivery of the news, had his own crisis of faith on the very first day of the Tet Offensive, when he arrived at work and examined the teletype reports in the newsroom. "What the hell is going on?" the fifty-one-year-old anchor fumed, genuinely confused and disturbed by the news. "I thought we were winning the war!"

Cronkite had been dissatisfied with the war reports and the official explanations of what was going on in Vietnam for months, but he had dutifully reported the official government and military statements as they were issued. He was losing his patience with those who called opposition to the war unpatriotic. CBS held firm on neutrality and objectivity in reporting. But what if, in doing so, the network was passing on misleading or false information to its viewers? Cronkite felt that he needed to see the war firsthand. "I proposed to our news president, Dick Salant, I should go to Vietnam as quickly as possible," Cronkite wrote in *A Reporter's Life,* his autobiography, "and try to present an assessment of the situation as one who had not previously taken a public position on the war. Salant agreed."

On February 6, Cronkite left the safety of New York for the battle-torn topography of Vietnam. After several delays in Tokyo, he arrived in Saigon on February 11.

2 On the morning of March 31, after attending church services, President Johnson and his wife, Claudia "Lady Bird" Johnson, dropped by the apartment of Vice President Hubert H. Humphrey. At first, the visit was difficult for Humphrey to comprehend. Johnson didn't just pop in on the spur of the moment, even if he was about to deliver an important speech on the biggest issue of the day. Johnson was aware that Humphrey was flying to Mexico in a couple of hours, so his visit had to be very important—and brief.

Johnson and Humphrey had been at loggerheads over the Vietnam War since 1965, when Humphrey had offered Johnson his unsolicited opinions about the war in a lengthy memorandum offering a number of suggestions about how the war might be better conducted. Angered by the memorandum, which he considered to be a sign of disloyalty, LBJ had frozen Humphrey out of almost all subsequent conferences and discussion about Vietnam until a depressed and contrite Humphrey made clear that the president would have his unconditional backing in the future. Humphrey was particularly troubled by the bombing of North Vietnam, which he considered to be a hindrance to setting up negotiations for peace, but he chose his words cautiously whenever the subject came up with Johnson.

Now, as it turned out, Johnson wanted Humphrey's appraisal of the speech—in private, with only the president's assistant, Jim Jones, present in the room.

Humphrey ushered his two visitors into his study and closed the door. There are two accounts of what happened next. One has Johnson reading the text of his speech to Humphrey, the other has Johnson handing the pages to Humphrey, who read the speech himself. There were two versions of the peroration, the second of which Johnson withheld until the vice president had absorbed his thoughts on Vietnam.

Regardless of how the message was delivered, the vice president's reaction was same. He was pleased by the speech, which he judged to be "one of [Johnson's] better ones," "the best thing I ever heard you say." Humphrey believed that Johnson's proposed bombing halt would be welcomed by the North Vietnamese and South Vietnamese leaders, as well by Johnson's television audience. The president disagreed. It would probably be interpreted as election-year politicking, he argued. He handed Humphrey his alternate ending to the speech, one written earlier in the day by Horace Busby, under LBJ's directive. In this alternate ending, Johnson would announce that he would be leaving office at the end of his current term.

The ending caught Humphrey by surprise. His face flushed, and his eyes filled with tears.

"Mr. President, are you really going to do that?" he asked.

"As of now, I'm almost certainly going to," Johnson replied.

Humphrey pleaded with Johnson to reconsider, but the president held firm. There was a remote possibility that he might change his mind, he allowed, but it was very unlikely. If he was campaigning for reelection, he insisted, the public would question his motives for trying to end the war.

"I've got to become totally non-political. I just don't see any way out of it," he said of his refusal to run for reelection.

There was another reason, Johnson went on, for his withdrawing from the race: his family's medical history. "Even if I should run and be re-elected, I most likely would not live out my term," he told Humphrey.

Health problems had struck down the men in the Johnson family well before they reached old age. Lyndon Johnson's father, Sam Ealy Johnson, had suffered a heart attack at fifty-five and had died less than two weeks after his sixtieth birthday. An uncle's heart had given out when he was fifty-seven. Lyndon himself had barely survived a massive heart attack in 1955, at the age of forty-six, and he had had other health issues since then. He was convinced to the core that he would follow the path of his predecessors. Robert Caro, Johnson's biographer, described a time when Lady Bird Johnson tried to convince her husband that this was not necessarily the case. "He looked at her scornfully and said flatly, 'It's a lead-pipe cinch,' " Caro reported.

There was no question that after all the stress he had been through during the years of his vice presidency and presidency, he looked older than his actual age. He had been a tall, sturdy, imposing figure, and he used his physical presence as an advantage when he needed to dominate an opponent in a disagreement, whether he was stepping into that individual's space and using his six-foot-three-inch frame to tower over him during a discussion, or crushing his hand with his own massive hand when he was greeting him.

This was not the LBJ of early 1968.

Theodore White, whose *Making of the President* books chronicled each presidential election from 1960 to 1972, was shocked when Johnson received him for a conversation in the Oval Office. White had not seen him since his work on *The Making of the President 1964,* when he was energetic and cruising through the election. The man now greeting him looked utterly exhausted:

> His eyes, behind gold-rimmed eyeglasses, were not only nested in lines and wrinkles, but pouched in sockets blue with a permanent weariness. His forehead was creased, not only in the red wrinkles of elevenses, which never unknit, but with layer upon layer of brow wrinkles above them, which kept folding and unfolding as he spoke. He spoke with an undertone, with a softness, a tiredness that did not begin to lift until the very end of the hour-long conversation.

Johnson would later admit that his health concerns weighed heavily on him, that they had become "a question of how much the physical constitution could take. I frankly did not believe that I could survive another four years of the long hours or unremitting tensions I had just gone through."

Johnson had never been one to sleep more than an average of five hours per night, but recent months had found him unable to sleep—or, when he did sleep, he was tormented by a recurring nightmare that dated back to his childhood. In his nightmare, he was paralyzed, unable to help himself or influence events taking place around him. The dream took on additional significance after he took up residence in the White House, when he thought about Woodrow Wilson and how, after his stroke, he had been tucked away in the outer reaches of the White House, his true condition hidden from the public. Johnson was tortured by the possibility of this happening to him. As he told Doris Kearns, then a trusted White House aide and, later, author of the best-selling portrait *Lyndon Johnson and the American Dream,* he would awaken from the nightmare and, unable to fall back to sleep, grab a small flashlight and shuffle down the halls of the White House until he reached the place where Woodrow Wilson's portrait hung. "He found something soothing in the act of touching Wilson's picture; he could sleep again," Kearns (later Doris Kearns Goodwin) wrote. "He was still Lyndon Johnson, and he was still alive and moving; it was Woodrow Wilson who was dead."

Hubert Humphrey undoubtedly knew some of this history, but as Johnson stood before him and worried about his health, the vice president knew something else: when the president left office after the election in November and the swearing in of the new chief executive the following January, he, the vice president, would also be out of a job. Humphrey coveted the presidency and had even made a very unsuccessful primary run against John F. Kennedy in 1960, but after accepting the position of vice president in 1964, he had set his sights on 1972, after Lyndon Johnson had served his second full term and the Democratic field was wide-open. Humphrey believed that Johnson would triumph over Richard Nixon, the Republican Party's likely choice in 1968, and he stated as much to the president.

Johnson wasn't budging.

"If you're going to run, you'd better get ready damn quick," he instructed Humphrey.

"There's no way I can beat the Kennedy machine," said Humphrey, who had been overwhelmed by the Kennedy money, charisma, and campaign strategy in 1960.

"You've got to get moving," Johnson advised.

As the three men prepared to leave Humphrey's study, Johnson turned to Humphrey and ordered him not to say a word about their conversation to anyone, including his wife, Muriel. He suspected the talkative Humphrey of leaks in the past, and he wanted Humphrey's word that he wouldn't let his wife in on their secret.

Humphrey gave his word and kept it.

3 To anyone who saw him regularly, Lyndon Johnson was as complex a human being as could be imagined, seemingly capable of every human emotion and foible, possessed of good and evil in constant conflict, a bigger-than-life figure and living, breathing caricature, a man of endless contradictions.

Jack Valenti, a Johnson aide and confidant, wrote that it was possible that Lady Bird Johnson was the only person to truly know the man. "His mind was honeycombed with contradictions." Valenti declared. "He was terrifying, kind, hyperenergetic, ruthless, loving; a lover of land, earth water, and animals; patient, impatient, restless, caring, petty, clairvoyant, bullying, compassionate, tough, devious, generous, and full of humor and wit. I have often said that almost anything you could say about Lyndon Johnson good or bad, had at least a hint of truth to it."

Joseph Califano, a Johnson insider and aide, bluntly stated that Johnson "gave new meaning to the word Machiavellian." He said,

> The Lyndon Johnson I worked with was brave and brutal, compassionate and cruel, incredibly intelligent and infuriatingly insensitive, with a shrewd and uncanny instinct for the jugular of his allies and adversaries. He could be altruistic and petty, caring and crude, generous and

petulant, bluntly honest and calculatingly devious—all within the same few minutes. He had a marvelous, if often crude, sense of humor. Once he made up his mind, his determination to succeed usually ran over or around whoever and whatever got in his way.

Johnson's dynamic, hyperbolic personality had taken him a long way, from modest beginnings in rural Texas to the nerve center of world politics. He was, to a great extent, self-made. Born on August 27, 1908, Johnson was precocious enough to have graduated from high school at sixteen but poor enough to have college at an expensive, prestigious university evade him. He attended Southwest Texas State Teachers College and, while a student, taught at a Mexican American school that exposed him to the inequalities imposed upon those of impoverished, nonwhite backgrounds. The experience affected him for the rest of his life, as did his need to prove himself to those educated at storied universities.

The initials "LBJ" became an important part of his identity. His wife, the former Claudia Alta Taylor, was known as Lady Bird, and his daughters, Lynda Bird and Luci Baines, also bore the same initials. Johnson would joke that the similar initials meant that the family could share the same luggage, but he imagined it in a much larger context. As reported by Robert A. Caro in the second volume of his massive, multibook Johnson biography, the future president told his friend Horace Busby that he fashioned his three-initial name after the way Franklin D. Roosevelt used FDR as a kind of shorthand for his identity. "What I want is for them to start thinking of me in terms of initials," Johnson told Busby. "He was just so determined that someday he would be known as LBJ," Busby recalled.

The LBJ initials became commonplace, even legendary, when he served, first, in the House of Representatives, from 1937 to 1949, and then in the Senate, from 1949 to 1961. An indefatigable worker, Johnson used the force of his personality and a native, uncanny understanding of political machinations to forge important, early alliances with President Franklin D. Roosevelt, Vice President John Nance Garner, Speaker of the House Sam Rayburn, and Senator Richard Russell, the powerful Georgia senator and future adversary on civil rights legislation. He established his leadership skills early in his senate career, leading to his being chosen majority whip in 1951, and, two years later, after Republicans assumed control of the Senate, setting a record after being selected the youngest minority leader in Senate history. Robert Caro would refer to him as the "Master of the Senate," and you would have been hard-pressed to find disagreement. Fellow senators and historians alike would agree that he might have been the most effective senator in U.S. history. He eyed the presidency and considered a run in 1960, but he wound up serving—unhappily—as John Kennedy's vice president.

His elevation to the presidency following Kennedy's assassination led to some of the highest and lowest points of his political career. He followed through on some of Kennedy's highest priority projects, including sweeping civil rights legislation that Kennedy had only just begun to explore at the time of his death. His signature vision for a Great Society in America, which seemed to include and absorb all aspects of contemporary living, from social structure to infrastructure, became his country's most progressive step forward since the New Deal. His legacy, by all indications, had been assured.

Then came the escalation of the Vietnam War, a conflict he had inherited from Kennedy but which he was unprepared to handle. It would be his undoing.

4 Johnson's speech was the product of a kind of evolution, taking weeks to complete and going through so many permutations that Harry McPherson, the address's main architect, lost track of how many drafts he had written. This wasn't unusual in the case of a major address, with tempers fraying over what seemed like a simple phrase or thought, the process a matter of constant honing. The speech on Vietnam was exponentially more difficult because suggestions on how to construct solutions to growing problems in the Southeast Asian country varied so widely that a consensus was hard to reach. Opinions shifted, sending the latest draft back for more revision.

What made this evolving script so noteworthy was Johnson's amazing, eleventh-hour shift of position. The first draft, begun in early February and completed in early March, written while Johnson was still angry and frustrated over the events of the Tet Offensive, was essentially another plea for public patience and support of the war effort. Secretary of Defense Robert McNamara, at one time an outspoken proponent of Johnson's Vietnam policies but recently critical of the bombing of North Vietnam, had been dismissed, replaced on March 1 by Clark Clifford, whom LBJ hoped would be more supportive of his plans. Johnson still stubbornly believed in what he called the light at the end of the tunnel; he maintained that victory was possible, but it would require more sacrifice, money, and troops.

This stance changed when Johnson came to the slow realization that his position had little support among the American people, news media, elected officials on Capitol Hill, and even members of his cabinet. Johnson's credibility took a huge blow when Walter Cronkite returned to the States after nineteen days in Vietnam and prepared a special television news report titled "Report from Vietnam: Who, What, When, Where, and Why," which aired on CBS at 10:00 p.m. EST on February 27.

Cronkite's trip to Vietnam had been eye-opening to the newsman, disturbing enough to convince him that, for all the optimism offered by the military and the Johnson administration, the idea of a victory in Vietnam was a lost cause. "It seems now more certain than ever, that the bloody experience of Vietnam is to end in a stalemate," he declared.

He had visited Saigon first. In a meeting with William Westmoreland, he listened as the general assured him that all was going well, that the assault on Saigon had ended with a convincing victory for the U.S. and South Vietnamese troops. The enemy had been driven out. It was that way throughout South Vietnam, the general said: the Communist forces were driven out, at the cost of enormous enemy casualties. It was the same story in Hue, Westmoreland said. The enemy had been defeated and expelled from the city. When Cronkite attempted to visit Hue, he saw that this was anything but the case. Intense fighting was still taking place, and Cronkite was endangering his safety by even attempting to enter the city. He was evacuated from the area by a helicopter carrying twelve marines in body bags.

Cronkite and his CBS crew patched together a powerful half-hour report that spelled out the differences between the rosy picture the American public was being fed by the military and what was actually happening. Cronkite interviewed everyone possible, putting a face on the war, from orphans to political leaders. He listened to the observations of the war correspondents writing about Vietnam. His talks with soldiers revealed their feelings of hopelessness, despair, and frustration.

"My decision was not difficult to reach," he wrote. "It had been taking shape, I realized, since Cam Ranh Bay. There was no way that this war could be justified any longer—a war whose purpose had never been adequately explained to the American people, to a people whose conscience burned because of the terribly, the fatally unequal sacrifice of the troops and the home front."

Cronkite didn't need to employ hyperbole or stacked statistics in his report; the interviews and images were more than enough. Although admitting that his conclusions were "speculative, personal, and subjective," Cronkite reported as authoritatively as one who had witnessed the truth and felt honor bound to deliver it to others. To believe that victory was possible was to buy a bill of goods from optimists. To believe that the United States, with all its military might, would win the war was equally misguided. Cronkite could draw only one logical conclusion. "It is increasingly clear to this reporter that the only way out will be to negotiate, not as victors, but as an honorable people who lived up to their pledge to defend democracy and did the best they could," Cronkite asserted at the closing to his report.

The devastating report left Lyndon Johnson in the position of competing with someone who enjoyed greater public respect and credibility than he could ever muster. He could no longer hope that the antiwar demonstrators would be depicted as radical nihilists, that writers disagreeing with his policies could be dismissed as voices without all the facts. As Johnson himself admitted, he could not stand up to Cronkite. "If I've lost Cronkite, I've lost Middle America," he supposedly said to Bill Moyers, then working for Johnson in the White House.*

Damaging though it was, the Cronkite report was only a continuation of what was looking to be LBJ's dark night of the soul, in which even victories looked like defeats. On Tuesday, March 12, Johnson won the New Hampshire primary, garnering 49.4 percent of the Democratic vote to 42.2 percent for Eugene McCarthy—and Johnson, who had refused to enter his name on the ballot and who had not personally campaigned in the state, had won as a write-in candidate. Only two months earlier, McCarthy was virtually unknown in New Hampshire, and in an Elmo Roper Poll conducted for *Time* magazine and published the last week of February, only 11 percent of the respondents said they intended to vote for McCarthy. A poll conducted by the White House had McCarthy at 18 percent. But the Minnesota senator had run an aggressive campaign featuring a small army of young volunteers blanketing every corner of the state. Their work, McCarthy's public appearances, and the plunging national numbers of those supporting the war elevated McCarthy's popularity significantly.

Johnson might have taken some solace in his victory, but the ballots cast for McCarthy were interpreted as an antiwar vote—or, worse yet for the president, an anti-Johnson vote. The press painted the primary figures as a Johnson defeat; *Newsweek* labeled it an "astonishing political upset." Johnson, whose love affair with the press had ended long ago, shrugged off the analysis. "New Hampshire," he harrumphed, "is the only place where the candidate can claim twenty-five percent as a landslide, forty percent as a mandate, and sixty percent as unanimous."

Then, the day after the New Hampshire primary, Robert Kennedy announced his candidacy. Johnson and Kennedy's intense dislike for one another,

---

* There were other published variations of this quote, including "If I've lost Cronkite, I've lost the country" and "If I've lost Cronkite, I've lost the war."

nationally known and dating back to the John Kennedy administration and the younger Kennedy's role as attorney general and his brother's chief advisor, had been one of the major reasons contributing to Robert Kennedy's refusal to enter the 1968 race. Voters, he insisted, would interpret his candidacy as an undisguised affront to the president, and he would have no part of that. In addition, RFK speculated that his running against Johnson would divide the Democratic Party. McCarthy's strong showing in New Hampshire indicated an already existing division.

Kennedy's candidacy was another sizable blow to Johnson. Kennedy, a vocal critic of Johnson's handling of the Vietnam War, might have looked opportunistic in the wake of the New Hampshire primary, but the bottom line could not be denied: Kennedy was young, intelligent, good-looking, charismatic, well financed, and, unavoidable to overlook, the brother of the man Johnson had replaced. Robert Kennedy's candidacy, Johnson admitted, was "the thing I had feared from the first day of my presidency."

Kennedy sensed his fear, long before announcing his candidacy, and he even foresaw the possibility of the president's bowing out of the race. Kennedy had been discussing Johnson and Vietnam with friends. Journalist Jack Newfield, present at the meeting, remembered Allard Lowenstein, a Kennedy confidant and strong opponent of the war, suggesting that Johnson might opt out of running for reelection if antiwar candidates fared well in the early primaries. The others at the meeting disagreed, but Kennedy saw Lowenstein's point.

"I think Al may be right," Newfield remembered Kennedy saying. "I think Johnson might quit the night before the convention opens. I think he is a coward."

5 Johnson was no coward, but he was susceptible to dark, sometimes prolonged bouts of self-pity, usually when his methods of having things his way failed. He would ask, demand, cajole, negotiate, humiliate, threaten—anything that worked—and if he still failed to reach his desired results, he would do his best to make his opponent feel sorry for him. His adversaries, he would complain, were people he thought of as friends, or people who benefited the most from his Great Society legislation.

"How is it possible," he asked Doris Kearns, "that all these people could be so ungrateful to me after I had given them so much?" He had fought for equal rights for all Americans, yet he was repaid by rioting in the streets. He had pushed for legislation assisting students with scholarships, loans, and grants, and they showed their appreciation by demonstrating on campus against him and the war.

"I remember once going to visit a poor family in Appalachia," he went on. "They had seven children, all skinny and sick. I promised the mother and father I could make things better for them. They seemed real happy to talk to me, and I felt good about that. But then as I walked toward the door, I noticed two pictures on the shabby wall. One was Jesus Christ on the cross; the other was John Kennedy. I felt as if I'd been slapped in the face."

He was in need of some reinforcement as March was winding down when, on the recommendation of Clark Clifford, his secretary of defense, he brought in the Wise Men for another consultation on Vietnam. In the past, Johnson had been in general agreement with this group of senior advisors, who tended to be more hawk than dove when the issue was national defense, and he probably figured he would maintain their support for his unraveling Vietnam policies this time around. Four months earlier, on November 2, 1967, he had approached them for their advice on five basic questions:

1. What could we do that we are not doing in South Vietnam?
2. Concerning the North, should we continue what we are doing, shall we mine the ports and take out the dikes, or should we eliminate bombing of the North altogether?
3. Should we adopt a passive policy of willingness to negotiate, should we aggressively seek negotiations, or should we bow out?
4. Should we get out of Vietnam?
5. What positive steps should the administration take to unite and better communicate with the nation?

These same questions were appropriate in March 1968. If anything, they were more pressing after the Tet Offensive and the deepening loss of the public's confidence in America. In November, Johnson received their support, although during that meeting, he had withheld opinions and documents that might have affected the group's decisions. The day before that November meeting, Secretary of Defense Robert McNamara had offered the president a detailed memorandum with recommendations that the United States take a different approach in Vietnam; Johnson did not offer a copy of the memorandum or a detailed report of it to the Wise Men. Nor did he share Rear Admiral Gene La Rocque's pessimistic report stating that a military victory in Vietnam was unlikely, or CIA Director Richard Helm's opinion that the United States could disengage from Vietnam with minimal risk.

McNamara's memo represented an almost complete turnabout from his position in the past. At one time, in his earlier years as secretary of defense,

McNamara had almost slavishly endorsed the military's strategies in Vietnam. He had been the ultimate hawk. His views had changed significantly over time, as the war continued endlessly, the casualties mounted, the bombing of North Vietnam seemed as unsuccessful as it seemed brutal, the reports from the military didn't jibe with what was actually going on, and the unrest in the United States divided the nation. McNamara found himself in a quandary. The president demanded complete loyalty from his cabinet members and other subordinates, and McNamara struggled to be supportive in light of his shifting feelings about the war. He hoped his memo would detail his opinions in a sense of positive criticism. The popular criticism, from Johnson and others in his administrations, was that opponents to the war offered nothing but negatives; they complained but offered no solutions. McNamara's memo was packed with ideas for future solutions.

In his cover letter to his memorandum, McNamara warned Johnson that "continuation of our present course of action in Southeast Asia will be dangerous, costly in lives and unsatisfactory to the American people"—words that sounded prophetic in the aftermath of the Tet Offensive. Although Johnson claimed to have "studied McNamara's memo carefully," judging it to be worthy of "thoughtful attention," he turned it over for review by McGeorge Bundy, Walt Rostow, Clark Clifford, and others inclined to agree with the course of action at that time. McNamara was ultimately treated as if he was losing his nerve. From that point, McNamara's tenure on LBJ's cabinet was on the clock. In mid-November, Johnson announced that McNamara would be leaving his post for a position as president of the World Bank. "I do not know to this day whether I quit or was fired," McNamara remarked years later. "Maybe it was both."

In that November 1967 meeting, the Wise Men wound up encouraging Johnson to continue his course in Vietnam, but their position had changed dramatically a few months later, when they reassembled in Washington, D.C. The group members varied from meeting to meeting, depending on the topic under discussion and the availability of the members; this one included former secretary of state Dean Acheson; General Omar Bradley; national security advisor McGeorge Bundy; Arthur Dean, negotiator of the Korean War settlement; former secretary of the treasury Douglas Dillon; Supreme Court Associate Justice Abe Fortas; former deputy secretary of defense Cyrus Vance; General Maxwell Taylor; United Nations ambassador Arthur Goldberg; Henry Cabot Lodge, a former senator and diplomat to Saigon; John J. McCloy, a former high commissioner to West Germany; General Matthew Ridgway, a commander during the Korean War; diplomat Robert Murphy; and former deputy secretary of defense George Ball. The group arrived on March 25, and for the better part of the next two days, they were briefed on Vietnam, how the war was presently being fought, and what lay in store in the future.

The credibility gap between the optimism from those running the war and what the public was being told became apparent early on. Their first formal meeting took place after dinner on March 25, when they met Deputy Secretary of State Philip Habib, who spoke about the political climate in Vietnam; Major General William E. DePuy, who briefed the men on the military situation in the country; and George Carver of the CIA, who talked about the North Vietnamese and the pacification efforts. Each of the three brought a different level of expertise to the table, and each had a differing opinion on what the United States should do in the future in Vietnam. DePuy, who had commanded troops in Vietnam and now acted as a special assistant to the Joint Chiefs of Staff, spoke of the Tet Offensive and its aftermath, his presentation declaring a victory in the Tet battles. His optimism about the fighting going forward was marred by his citing the kind of statistics that had caused the public to be distrustful of the numbers offered by the military.

Arthur Goldberg set off a tense exchange when General DePuy said the forces of North Vietnam had lost 45,000 troops during the Tet Offensive. Goldberg inquired about the killed-to-wounded ratio of the U.S. troops.

"Seven to one," DePuy estimated, "because we save a lot of men with helicopters."

"What was the enemy strength as of February 1, when Tet started?"

"Between 150,000 and 175,000," DePuy stated.

"What is their killed-to-wounded ratio?" Goldberg asked.

"We use a figure of three and a half to one."

"Well, if that's true they have no effective forces left in the field," Goldberg concluded.

George Carver, though supportive of the war effort, offered a bleak view. The pacification program, he allowed, was taking longer than anticipated, and in all likelihood it would be slow going in the future.

Philip Habib presented the most pessimistic outlook of the three. By his estimation, the United States could expect another five to seven years' commitment to Vietnam if it continued with its current military operations.

Clark Clifford, who was growing more and more convinced that the war could not continue as an action with a goal of victory in mind, bluntly asked Habib, "What would you do if the decision was yours to make?" After an extended pause, Habib answered, "Stop the bombing and negotiate."

The next day, President Johnson invited the Wise Men to confer with

General Creighton Abrams, Westmoreland's deputy commander in Vietnam, and General Earle Wheeler, chairman of the Joint Chiefs of Staff. Johnson expected the two military higher-ups to put more of a positive spin on post-Tet Vietnam than the previous evening's reports, and the two generals did not disappoint him. The morale among American troops, they said, was improving. Both favored further escalation of the war: more troops, more bombing, and, if necessary, ground troops moving into Laos, Cambodia, and North Vietnam. According to Abrams, the training of the South Vietnamese soldiers was looking up.

As planned, Johnson met with the Wise Men after their briefing with the generals. If he expected the kind of endorsement he had received from them the previous November, he quickly learned otherwise. McGeorge Bundy spoke first, saying that there had been a "significant shift" in the group's position since their November gathering. It was time to disengage if, as others suggested, there was no hope in reaching the original goals set when the United States became involved in Vietnam. As each of the men offered his opinion, Johnson came to understand that he no longer had a majority backing. Fortas and Murphy backed him without qualification. Bradley favored future involvement in Vietnam, though he was against further escalation. The others wanted a dramatic change of course, including a bombing halt and peace negotiations.

Johnson left the meeting angry and defeated. "Your whole group must have been brainwashed," he said to George Ball, "and I'm going to find out what Habib and the others told you." He let Arthur Goldberg know how angry he was with the talk of a bombing halt. "Let's get one thing clear," he raged. "I am not going to stop the bombing. I have heard every argument on the subject and I am not interested in further discussion. I have made up my mind, and I am not going to do it."

Johnson, not surprisingly, remembered the meeting in more favorable terms. "I thanked the advisers for their views and their counsel and asked them to continue to be available to me," he wrote in *The Vantage Point,* his memoirs of his presidency. The advisers, he proposed, were influenced by the gloom-and-doom media, and they had not been privy to all available information regarding Vietnam. Nevertheless, their conclusions bothered him. "If they had been so deeply influenced by the reports of the Tet offensive, what must the average citizen in the country be thinking?" he wondered.

Clark Clifford, for one, had a strong idea about what people were thinking. In his travels across the country, the defense secretary witnessed the nation's continually growing disenchantment with Johnson's war policies. Johnson held his ground. Rather than show any recognition of the public pressure on him to change the U.S. course in Vietnam, he made two "hard-nosed" speeches in mid-March, prior to his consultation with the Wise Men—speeches that Clifford characterized as being "stern . . . facing up to the commitment that we had made."

"They were, in effect, something of a restatement of our intention to seek and achieve military victory in Viet Nam," Clifford remembered. "I was deeply concerned about those two speeches." Clifford's feelings about Vietnam policies now leaned strongly toward negotiated settlement. He hadn't seen the early drafts of Johnson's forthcoming March 31 speech, and when he finally did, he was very unhappy with what he read. During a lengthy formal discussion about the latest draft of the address, Clifford put his feelings on the table. The speech, he said, set the wrong tone, and he said as much. "I recall making the statement that this was a speech about war, and what I thought the President should do was make a speech about peace," he said.

For all his vitriol over his lack of support, Johnson had little recourse but to change. Prior to his meeting with the Wise Men, his Vietnam speech said nothing about a bombing halt or negotiating a settlement. It still contained strong language about pursuing the old course in Vietnam. Johnson continued to cling stubbornly to the original intent of helping South Vietnam hold on to its independence against North Vietnamese aggression. He wanted peace but loathed the idea of the North Vietnamese dictating any of the terms. In the days following his consultation with the Wise Men, the topic of Vietnam heated up even more than before. The wording of the forthcoming speech eventually became less heavy-handed, but not until it had been debated, often angrily.

One other serious consideration now entered the picture: dropping out of his reelection. In recent months, the thought had never been far from Johnson's mind, but he now found himself sounding the idea with his advisers. He enjoyed creating drama, which was one reason his advisers often found it difficult to take him too seriously; he now appeared to be searching for someone to provide him with a good reason to continue.

On March 27, the day after his disastrous conference with the Wise Men, and only four days before his scheduled Vietnam speech, Johnson posed the idea of his not running to Joseph Califano, one of his senior aides on domestic policy. He asked Califano who would win the Democratic nomination if he pulled out of the race. "Bobby Kennedy," Califano said, knowing how distasteful that prospect would be to the president. Kennedy, Califano surmised, would steal some of McCarthy's supporters and, in the long run, capture the nomination.

"What about Hubert?" Johnson wondered.

"I don't think he can beat Kennedy."

Johnson's next remark caught Califano off guard. "What's wrong with Bobby?" Johnson asked. "He's made some nasty speeches about me, but he's never had to sit here. Anyway, you seem to like his parties."

The president, Califano realized, was serious.

"Bobby would keep fighting for the Great Society programs," Johnson continued. "And when he sat in this chair he might have a different view on the war."

On another occasion, while talking with Califano and Harry McPherson about the speech and new language being inserted into it, Johnson brought the subject of his dropping out of the race back into play. "What do you think about my not running for re-election?" he asked.

The two did not immediately respond. McPherson finally broke the silence. "Of course you must run," he said.

"Why?" Johnson responded. "Give me three good reasons why."

McPherson, who had sympathized with Johnson's recent struggles, admitted that if he were Johnson, he wouldn't run. The job was "murderous," and he could see nothing in the near future that suggested that it would be less difficult. "But I'm not you," he finished. "You have to run."

"That's a conclusion, not a reason," Johnson countered. "What would be so bad about my not running? What would happen?"

Johnson waved off McPherson's suggestion that none of the candidates would be able to push their bills through Congress. As a senator and majority leader, Johnson had been a master at seeing his favored legislation meet winning votes. As president, he had succeeded in seeing his Great Society plan passed into law. In Johnson's opinion, any of the leading candidates—Nixon, McCarthy, or Kennedy—would fare better than he would at this point.

"They'd be new," he explained, "and Congress always gives a new man a little cooperation, a little breathing room. I'd be the same old Johnson coming back to the well again, beggin' and pushin' 'em to give me a better bill than last year. No, Congress and I are like an old man and woman who've lived together for a hundred years. We know each other's faults and what little good there is in us. Give me another reason."

Califano and McPherson were spared further discussion when the conversation was interrupted by Marvin Watson, who needed the president's immediate attention. Once out of Johnson's earshot, the two aides discussed what had just occurred, and they concluded that Johnson wasn't truly serious, that he had only been thinking out loud.

They were not alone in making this assumption. Johnson seemed to be preparing for another run, despite the negativity swirling around him. Postmaster General Lawrence O'Brien, dispatched to Wisconsin to check on Johnson's standing in the state's upcoming April primary, reported the grim news. Johnson was in deep trouble in the Dairy State, overmatched by Eugene McCarthy in the number of his campaign offices, volunteers, and, most importantly, voter support; the odds were that he would be soundly defeated, maybe by as large a margin as two to one. Johnson listened to O'Brien's report and read the press's commentary on his chances, but still showed no signs of dropping out. More notably, he gave no hint of his thoughts about withdrawal to O'Brien, James H. Rowe Jr., and others working on his campaign. He had yet to meet Terry Sanford, the former governor of North Carolina, just brought onboard to manage the campaign.

If he was orchestrating every angle of a major announcement, as he often did, Johnson was outdoing himself. On Saturday, March 30, the day before he was to deliver his address, Johnson spent much of the day in the Cabinet Room, going over every word of the speech with advisors. An announcement of a bombing halt was a new addition to the text, though there was disagreement over the wording. No one wanted the North Vietnamese—or the American people, for that matter—to misinterpret the unilateral decision to cease the controversial bombing north of the demilitarized zone. The president sat at the meeting, jacketless, his tie undone and sleeves rolled up, considering every suggestion until, around nine in the evening, agreement was reached by all parties on the speech—with one exception: the ending to the address. McPherson, hearing that the original peroration no longer applied to this most recent draft, had excised it. He had intended to replace it but hadn't had the time prior to the meeting. He promised to have a new one ready for the president as soon as possible. He said he would keep it brief, since the speech was already running long.

"That's O.K.," Johnson assured him. "Make it as long as you want. I may even add one of my own."

As McPherson recalled in his memoirs:

When he left, I turned to [Clark] Clifford, who was gathering up his papers.

"Jesus, is he going to say sayonara?"

"What?"

"Is he going to say goodbye tomorrow night?"

Clifford looked at me with pity, as if I were too tired to be rational.

6 Hubert Humphrey was deeply troubled by the president's visit to his apartment. By Johnson's orders, he couldn't speak to anyone, including his wife, about Johnson's plans, but this was too big a revelation for him to process alone. When he arrived at Andrews Air Force Base and stepped aboard Air Force Two, two hours late for his flight, he brushed past the flight crew, his friends and aides, a smattering of dignitaries, and the press, offering very little but a cursory greeting. For Humphrey, who could talk the paint off a wall, this was highly unusual behavior. Instead of chatting with those gathered around him, he walked to his office at the front of the plane and stayed there for the duration of the flight.

Humphrey replayed his conversation with Johnson in his mind. He found it hard to accept that the president was serious. Johnson had talked of leaving office almost four years earlier, after one of his greatest triumphs, his landslide victory over Barry Goldwater.

"He told me immediately after the 1964 election, I think it was the day after, when Muriel and I were at the [LBJ] Ranch, that he wasn't going to run for re-election, but I just didn't take him seriously," Humphrey said years later. "And I don't doubt that he ran it in and out of his mind a hundred, maybe a thousand times. He liked to test every idea, especially one as important as that, on everyone within hearing distance."

Once in Mexico City and checked into the Maria Isabella Hotel, Humphrey ate a light lunch with a few of his staff before deciding to go for a walk with his friend and personal physician Dr. Edgar Berman. He walked at a brisk pace, all but ignoring the waves and shouts of those recognizing him. Berman had inquired about Humphrey's mood during their flight, but Humphrey had dismissed his questions with a few words about how the president had visited, wanting to show him his speech. Berman knew better than to press him for more.

"You know, Johnson's a strange man," Humphrey said when they arrived back at the hotel. "He takes delight in keeping people dangling."

"So, what else is new?" Berman disliked Johnson and resented the way he had mistreated Humphrey over the years. Rumors had been circulating recently about the possibility of Johnson's replacing Humphrey as his vice president. Berman wondered to himself if this was what troubled Humphrey.

Humphrey's uncharacteristic behavior continued that evening during his dinner with Mexico's president Gustavo Díaz Ordaz at the U.S. embassy. Johnson's speech overlapped the dinner, and as the time approached for Johnson to begin, Humphrey asked if anyone would object to his listening to the speech as it was being broadcast on Armed Forces Radio. Humphrey, Ordaz, and other

American and Mexican dignities crowded into the ambassador's study. A radio was switched on.

When the president began his speech, Humphrey still was not certain which ending Johnson had chosen.

7 Deputy Press Secretary Robert H. Fleming, supervisor of the Johnson broadcast, was stunned when he read the ending to Johnson's speech on the TelePrompTer only a few minutes before the broadcast. Although Johnson told the Army Signal Corps man setting up the TelePrompTer that he was still unsure of whether he would be using the ending, he was now absolutely certain that, in less than an hour, he would have announced that he would not be running for another four years in the White House.

His wife and two daughters sat nearby, out of camera view. Regardless of what Johnson said, someone he loved was going to be disappointed. Lady Bird Johnson felt that her husband would be better off by leaving office; Lynda and Luci, who had husbands serving in Vietnam, disapproved. That very morning, Lynda had returned from California, where she had seen her husband, Charles Robb, leave for Southeast Asia. The president had risen early to greet her when she returned. A tearful, distraught Lynda asked her father why the fighting had to continue, prompting what Lady Bird said was "such pain in his eyes as I had not seen since his mother died."

Johnson worried about how his decisions might affect his sons-in-law. In a sense, the war had become as personal to the commander in chief as it was to a pipefitter in Detroit, yet Johnson was the one who heard the angry chants asking how many babies he had killed today. The war, he knew, was going to be his lasting legacy. He bore the weight of knowing that everything he had accomplished in his Great Society, all the health, education, and welfare reform, the groundbreaking civil rights legislation—arguably the most important social legislation in American history, other than Franklin D. Roosevelt's—might be wiped out by the memory of an unpopular war that he had not started but seemed incapable of finishing.

At 9:01 EST, President Johnson, seated at his desk in the White House's Oval Office, looked directly at the television camera and began his address. He looked tired but relaxed.

"Good evening, my fellow Americans," he opened. "Tonight I want to speak to you of peace in Vietnam and Southeast Asia.

"No other question so preoccupies our people. No other dream so absorbs the 250 million human beings who live in that part of the world. No other goal motivates American policy in Southeast Asia."

It was a strong opening, a shift in tone from war to peace. In fact, the word *war* was not uttered in the early portion of the speech. Johnson spoke of failed attempts to set up peace talks and the Tet Offensive, reassuring Americans, those listening in from abroad, and, most importantly, the Vietnamese people, North and South, that another, similar offensive mounted by the North would not be successful. The inevitable bloodshed, Johnson continued, was not necessary. "There is no need to delay the talks that could bring an end to this long and this bloody war."

In the past, the North Vietnamese had insisted on a cessation of the bombing as a condition to negotiation. The United States had balked at the condition. The bombing, it was believed, would act as an incentive encouraging negotiation. It didn't. The Tet Offensive had illustrated, among other things, the North Vietnamese's willingness to absorb enormous casualties and just dispatch more troops to continue. Although Johnson resisted the bombing halt until the final days leading to his televised address, he sounded convincing in selling the measure as a "first step to deescalate the conflict."

All bombing of North Vietnam would cease, Johnson announced, except in the area of the demilitarized zone, where enemy troops had amassed and posed a threat to American and South Vietnamese forces in the area. Johnson calculated that roughly 90 percent of North Vietnam would now be safe from the bombing—a reduction of violence that he hoped would induce a peaceful settlement through peace talks. Johnson extended one warning: "If peace does not come now through negotiations, it will come when Hanoi understands that our common resolve, and our common strength is invincible."

The bombing halt would be debated well into the future, and as time would show, it would not bring a hasty conclusion to the war. Johnson went on to talk about South Vietnam's responsibilities in taking more control in the war and in determining its destiny, and he spoke of sending an additional 13,500 American troops to Vietnam over the following five months. He offered no timetable for U.S. withdrawal from Vietnam. Instead, he addressed the lengthy commitment the United States had made to that point—a commitment that had involved three presidents and great costs in lives and money. He repeated U.S. objectives in the war and even invoked John Kennedy's inaugural address in asking Americans to "pay any price, bear any burden, meet any hardship, support any friend, oppose any foe to assure the survival and the success of liberty."

At one point in the middle of his lengthy speech, Johnson raised his arm as a signal to his wife. It was a very subtle motion but one with a message: he would be using the second peroration to the speech. He had not changed his mind.

He built up to his announcement slowly, noting that throughout his thirty-seven years in public service, he had "put the unity of the people first . . . ahead of any divisive partisanship." The country, he said pointedly, was presently divided.

"What we won when all of our people united just must not now be lost in suspicion, selfishness and politics among any of our people.

"Believing this as I do, I have concluded that I should not permit the Presidency to become involved in the partisan divisions that are developing in this political year.

"With America's sons in the fields far away, with America's future under challenge right here at home, with our hopes and the world's hopes for peace in the balance every day, I do not believe that I should devote an hour or a day of my time to any personal partisan causes or to any duties other than the awesome duties of the office—the Presidency of your country.

"Accordingly, I shall not seek, and I will not accept, the nomination of my party for another term as your President."

The final three sentences of the president's address were probably lost on a nation in collective shock. Throughout the day and during the speech itself, the White House phone lines were busy as Johnson's inner circle, already in on the ending to his speech, called his closest friends and aides and informed them of his decision. In making his announcement at the end of an important speech on Vietnam, Johnson had found a way of upstaging himself: in the days to come, more people would be talking about his walking away from the presidency than analyzing his plans for Vietnam.

Walking out of the Oval Office with his family, Johnson felt more refreshed than he had felt in months. "In forty-five minutes I had finished," he would remember. "It was all over and I felt better. The weight of the day and the weeks and the months had lifted. . . . Now it was history and I could do no more."

8 Hubert Humphrey wept when he heard Johnson state that he would not be running, as did Humphrey's wife, Muriel. "Why didn't you tell me?" she asked her husband.

"I've tried to prepare you for it all day, but I didn't know myself," Humphrey said. The hours—and days and weeks—ahead were bound to be hectic. In the embassy, people flooded into the room and insisted that Humphrey immediately announce his candidacy. If he didn't, they warned, the nomination was all but certain to go to Robert Kennedy. Humphrey refused the bait. He had to consider all his options before making any announcements. If he chose to run, he had to assemble a campaign staff, find financing, and make plans for campaigning in almost no time. He needed to talk to the president before joining the fray. Would the unpredictable Johnson support his candidacy, now that he had said that he wanted to keep partisanship out of his future? Or, as impossible as it might have seemed to those watching his address, would LBJ change his mind at the last minute and reenter the race, riding in like a Texas cowboy on a charging white steed? There was no saying what he would do.

Among the other candidates running for the presidency, the reaction to Johnson's announcement was respectful. Eugene McCarthy, at Carroll College in Waukesha, Wisconsin, preparing for the state's April 2 primary, was giving a speech when Johnson announced his intentions of not running for reelection. When McCarthy finished his speech, reporters rushed up to the platform and gave him the news. The hall erupted in cheers when the candidate relayed the news to his supporters. He departed quickly for his Milwaukee headquarters, where his campaigners were literally dancing in the street.

Richard Goodwin, a one-time Johnson aide now working as a media specialist for McCarthy, was in Milwaukee, watching LBJ's speech on television with Blair Clark and Theodore White. Goodwin, after joining the McCarthy camp because of his opposition to the Vietnam War, was eager to hear the president's latest plans for the war.

"As he began to talk about Vietnam, I felt somber, sorrowful," Goodwin recalled. "I had worked against him, wanted to keep him from the presidency, but not this: this beaten, melancholy man, so little like the massive, unquenchable figure I had served." Despite these feelings, he leaped up in celebration when Johnson made his announcement. "I thought it would take another six weeks," he said to White.

Eugene McCarthy was restrained in his remarks about Johnson. Shortly after hearing about Johnson's speech, he had turned to a friend and said, almost regretfully, "I feel as if I've been tracking a tiger through long jungle grass, and all of a sudden he rolls over and he's stuffed." He was somber and accommodating at his press conference, praising Johnson's decision as one "clear[ing] the way for the reconciliation of our people."

"I took no personal satisfaction in the victory over President Johnson," McCarthy declared. "Withdrawal was a personally sad and difficult moment for a man who had given so many years in the service of his country. It seemed to me that Lyndon Johnson might in fact feel liberated by his withdrawal."

Abigail McCarthy, the senator's wife, shared these feelings: "I was genuinely moved and I believed that he had come to the decision sorrowfully, nobly, because he thought it best for the country." She impulsively called the White House, hoping to say a few words to Lady Bird Johnson, but LBJ came to the phone first. McCarthy told him that she admired him for making a difficult decision, but Johnson, who spoke in what McCarthy described as "suppressed triumph," in "the voice of a man who operated in the supreme confidence that he could outmaneuver anyone," seemed to dismiss the idea that he had sacrificed much in abandoning another term in office. "Honey," he told her, "I'm just one little person. It's not important what happens to me." Lady Bird Johnson, unenthusiastic about talking to the wife of a man largely responsible for driving her husband from office, was nonetheless gracious as always when she picked up the phone. She had two sons-in-law in Vietnam, and as she advised Abigail McCarthy, "When you have two guys out there, you know what Vietnam is about."

Robert Kennedy was in the air, on a flight from Phoenix to New York, during the president's speech. John Burns, New York State Democratic chairman, rushed onto the plane when it rolled to a stop at John F. Kennedy International Airport. Kennedy, in the process of leaving his seat when Burns arrived, dropped back in his seat and fell silent when Burns delivered the news. He sat motionless, unwilling to talk to reporters gathered at the gate. He had no idea what to say. He decided to schedule a press conference for ten o'clock the following morning, and hurried back to his Manhattan apartment. He sat silently throughout the forty-minute drive, muttering only one quiet thought: "I wonder if he'd have done this if I hadn't come in."

Richard Nixon was also on a plane during Johnson's address. Ironically, Nixon had canceled a nationally televised speech on Vietnam when the president asked for national time for his own speech on the war. In deference to Johnson, Nixon canceled his speech and attended a campaign rally in Milwaukee instead. He had asked his press secretary, Patrick Buchanan, to listen to the speech and brief him on it when he returned to New York. Buchanan, along with a large group of reporters, was waiting for him at LaGuardia Airport. Buchanan bolted ahead of the reporters to give Nixon the news. Pressed for a statement, Nixon offered a flippant response about the current election cycle's being "the year of the dropout. First Romney, then Rockefeller, and now Johnson." George Romney and Nelson Rockefeller, two early challengers for the Republican nomination, had already left the field, leaving Nixon the presumptive nominee. Nixon would regret the tone of his statement. "While the dropout label might have been apt for the first two," he would confess, "I was justifiably criticized for thus characterizing Johnson's action."

On April 1, the day after Johnson's speech, Johnson's announcement dominated the front page of every major newspaper in the United States. The last few sentences of the president's address, rather than his in-depth discussion about Vietnam, became the *lead* of the stories, with Vietnam either relegated to secondary status or separate sidebar reports. This could have been expected, in the sense that a president's voluntarily leaving office would be an attention-grabbing report at any time, but it also underscored Johnson's great political acumen: his announcement deflected, or at least put off, immediate analysis of his new Vietnam policy. There would be plenty of opportunity to closely examine his plans for Vietnam, but for the time being, a stunned nation wanted answers to why he refused to accept another Democratic Party nomination for the presidency.

His friends and former colleagues, including old foes, weighed in favorably. Georgia Senator Richard Russell, one of Johnson's long-standing friends in the Senate and a man who had vigorously opposed Johnson's landmark civil rights bills, saluted his decision, saying that it "proved the sincerity of his overwhelming desire to end the war in Vietnam and bring peace to the whole world." Arkansas Senator William Fulbright, a vocal and highly visible opponent of the war, called Johnson's renunciation "an act of a very great patriot." Idaho Senator Frank Church, another critic of Johnson's standing on the war, called the speech "Lyndon Johnson's finest hour."

"By removing himself as a target and a symbol, the President did much to cleanse the political atmosphere of the poison which had been filling it," wrote *New York Times* political columnist Tom Wicker. It was an important point. The public, so critical of Johnson prior to the speech, was now upbeat in response to the president's message. A Gallup Poll, conducted six days after the speech and published in mid-April, showed a substantial recovery in Johnson's standing among voters. Of those questioned, 41 percent approved of the way Johnson was handling the war, up from a miniscule 26 percent a month earlier. Not surprisingly, 64 percent favored his decision to halt the bombing of North Vietnam. His overall approval rating jumped from 36 percent to 49 percent.

"Mr. Johnson is, indeed, a freer man than ever before," observed Max Frankel in a newspaper piece titled "The Liberation of Lyndon Johnson," "free to do his job as he sees fit and free even of the abuse and antagonism that contributed so much to his decision to withdraw from Presidential politics only a fortnight ago."

So it ultimately came down to faith: despite the fact that the war continued to rage on in Southeast Asia, Americans believed—or at least wanted to
believe—that Lyndon Johnson was moving in the right direction toward finding an end to the war, and Johnson, enjoying a spike in his popularity after
months of watching it plummet, believed that he had curried enough favor
from his national constituency to once again exert his will in whatever direction his ambition might take him. He had just over seven months between the
moment he rejected another run for the presidency and the general election. He
had said that he would avoid partisan politics in the months ahead, but anyone
who knew him would be skeptical of his honoring that vow. It would simply
be too far out of character.

Indeed, Lyndon Johnson would cast an ominous shadow over what would
turn out to be one of the hardest-fought presidential elections in American history, played out against the old and new politics, a young generation and their
parents, the hopeful and the cynical, and a backdrop of events that made 1968
one of the most turbulent years in the country's history.

Book One
THE CANDIDATES

1 Hubert Humphrey
The Long Road to Contention

Lyndon Johnson's decision to drop out of the presidential race affected Hubert Humphrey's career in more ways than the vice president would have imagined only a few weeks earlier. Humphrey knew, perhaps as well as anyone, that Johnson faced a protracted, difficult battle in a campaign for reelection, and he had heard Johnson's own talk of bowing out of the race, but he expected the president to run—and win. He anticipated another four years as the country's second-in-command, just as he figured he would be running for the presidency four years hence, after LBJ had served his second full term in office. He had spent two decades in national office, working a plan he had been developing since the days of his youth, when he had brashly predicted that he would be president one day; he reasoned that he still had the capacity to attain that goal, but his immediate future demanded that he make decisions without his usual deliberation in planning.

This was not his style. In the days following Johnson's announcement, he had avoided reporters' questions about his plans for the immediate future mainly because he didn't know what he would be doing. He felt confident that he could defeat Eugene McCarthy and Robert Kennedy in a battle for the Democratic nomination, but he would be on a stony path all the way. For one, it was too late for him to enter the primaries. Only two—South Dakota and California—were still open to him. South Dakota, he felt, offered few rewards in the large delegate picture, and as for California, he doubted that he could throw together the organization and money required to seriously compete in the state.

He also had issues with opposing McCarthy and Kennedy. He liked both men, and they had worked well together when they were all in the Senate. He and McCarthy had not only served in the Senate together; they represented the same state and generally shared the same views. As vice president, he took exception to some of McCarthy's remarks about Johnson and Vietnam; those disagreements would inevitably be raised during their respective runs for the presidency. Humphrey had been brutalized by Kennedy when Humphrey briefly ran against John Kennedy for the presidency in 1960, but time had healed those wounds. Humphrey had cordial relationships with both Kennedys when Jack occupied the White House, and he and Bobby had gotten along in the Senate when Bobby was a senator and Humphrey was, first, a senator and then vice president. However, Humphrey did not relish the thought of running as RFK's opponent. "I said after the 1960 campaign that I never wanted to get into a political battle with the Kennedys again," he said, "and I meant that both respectfully and in a sense of just my personal life. When it came down to 1968, I just thought, 'Gee whiz, here we go again.' And I had some real doubts about it."

1 Humphrey's career path had taken him through strongly defined victories and defeats, strengths and weaknesses, and a steady rise to prominence. He was, in every respect, a son of the prairie, a gregarious progressive lacking the cynicism of standard Washington, D.C., politics, an issues-oriented advocate possessing great modesty yet also a self-confidence that served as a driving wheel for his political vision. He took pride in his humble origins and the lessons they taught him. He had grown up in Doland, South Dakota, a tiny town of six hundred, in which his father, Hubert H. Humphrey Sr., owned a drugstore. The elder Humphrey was passionate about politics and served as the town's mayor. These simple beginnings had a marked effect on a life destined to reach the highest level of American life. "The kind of public man I am," Humphrey would summarize, "has been overwhelmingly shaped by two influences: the land of South Dakota and an extraordinary relationship with an extraordinary man, my father."

As Humphrey's younger sister, Frances Humphrey Howard, would recall, Hubert was viewed as special from the beginning. It wasn't a matter of his receiving preferential treatment from his parents; he was simply seen as having qualities that set him aside from his siblings. Frances spoke of how her mother glowed when she spoke about her second son. "He, according to my mother, was the happiest child, even from birth. Always fixing things up. Always making amends so that nobody was getting hurt. This endeared him 'cause parents naturally love children who are cooperative."

He was nicknamed Pinky because of his healthy complexion, and he kept the nickname until he graduated from high school. If anyone was going to be called Hubert, it was his father. At the drugstore, however, the elder Humphrey was known almost exclusively as H.H.

Contrary to what one might assume, Doland was a land of great opportunity for someone as ambitious as the younger Humphrey. One could thrive in a small town where competition was limited and participation encouraged. Humphrey's intelligence glowed in the small classroom, his limited athleticism overlooked by coaches desperately trying to find kids to fill out their rosters. Despite his slight physique, he played guard on his high school football team, and he also ran track and was a member of the basketball team. He turned out for and starred in school plays. He was well known in neighboring schools, as well in his own; it was virtually impossible to see him in action and forget him.

Julian Hartt, son of a preacher and one of Humphrey's closest friends in high school, remembered seeing Humphrey on the sideline of a football game, talking nonstop and walking up and down the sidelines in front of the stands, exhorting the Doland football fans into rowdy cheers. Hartt, attending eighth grade at Gordon, the school competing against Doland, listened to Humphrey's taunts until he could stand it no more. "I finally yelled at him to shut up or I'd knock his block off," Hartt recalled. "He grinned at me and took his cap off and waved it and then went tearing up the line. He did stay out of reach, however, the rest of the game."

The next year, Hartt's family moved to Doland, when his father took over the Methodist ministry at the town's only church. Humphrey was one of the first kids he met on the first day of high school. "He stepped up, took his cap off, and said, 'I'm Pinky Humphrey. Glad you moved to Doland.'" To Hartt's amazement, the Humphrey kid remembered their confrontation at the football game. "He was just indestructibly cheerful," Hartt said of Humphrey. "If he had a severe critic, let alone a real enemy among his peers, I don't know who in the world it would have been."

Pinky Humphrey inherited this quality from his father. Thought to be the only Democrat in town—his own wife consistently voted Republican—Hubert Senior was intelligent and engaging enough to be one of Doland's civic leaders. His drugstore served as an informal meeting place where, with H.H. usually in the center of the fray, politics were debated until exhaustion brought it all to an end. The most well-read inhabitant of Doland, with a massive library that included books on everything from music to political biography, H.H. held an opinion on just about every conceivable topic, and he wasn't the least bit reluctant about expressing it. It was said that he dispensed advice or an opinion with every pill going over the counter. Pinky was often a very interested bystander when the debates ensued, and he learned much about arguing a case from what he saw and heard. His father's pleasant temperament, maintained even during the most passionate of arguments, set an example that he would follow throughout his political career.

Empathy and compassion became the younger Humphrey's most important boyhood lesson. Doland required rigorous spirits among its townsfolk. The agricultural community based its hopes on the weather, particularly rainfall, and the dust bowl era nearly brought the region to its knees. Crops floundered; the air was so saturated with dust that people had to cover their mouths and noses with damp cloths, even to breathe inside. Locusts descended in biblical proportion, destroying all plant life in their paths, and when the greenery was gone, they ate the paint off the buildings. The Depression hit; the town's two banks failed. The Humphreys hung on like their neighbors, but H.H.'s empathy cost them dearly. Humphrey extended credit to his drugstore customers, but hard times made it impossible for them to pay their bills. H.H. canceled their debts—$13,000, as his son recalled—money the Humphrey family needed to cover their own bills.

"I can remember as clear as I'm sitting here when he canceled out all the bills that the farmers owed him," Frances said. "He said to my brothers, Hubert and Ralph, 'Look, I can't collect their bills then they won't have any money to buy anything from me. Plus that, I have lost their good will.'"

They lost their house. Hubert Junior would never forget the day in 1927 when he came home from school and saw his parents standing in the front yard with a strange man. Mrs. Humphrey was crying. They were signing over the deed to their house to pay their bills. "My father talked to the man for a short time, signed a paper, and then the man went away," Humphrey wrote in his autobiography. "Afterward, Dad wept." The sight left the fifteen-year-old boy badly shaken, but this, too, offered a lesson useful later in his life. Rather than accept defeat, the elder Humphrey, without the slightest hint of shame, rented a house, resumed his work at the drugstore, and never looked back.

The store did not just provide the family with an income and H.H. with a place to meet and greet neighbors; it was engrained in the family's identity. H.H. stocked his shelves with items that he liked but could never sell. His sons worked beside him—Pinky when he was so young that his father had to build a lift that enabled Pinky to reach across the counter or reach the soda fountain spigots.

■ ■ ■ ■ ■

The Depression years affected Humphrey's life in ways he could have never foreseen. After graduating from high school, Humphrey attended the University of Minnesota until his father needed help at the family drugstore, which he had relocated to Huron, South Dakota, a much larger city but one that meant more competition. The struggle continued. Figuring that his career would probably wind up in his father's store, Humphrey took time away from Huron long enough to secure a pharmacist's degree at the Capital College of Pharmacy in Denver. Throughout his life, Humphrey would speak somewhat nostalgically about his time working at his father's pharmacy, but this was selective memory. He was unhappy much of the time, convinced that this wasn't his calling. He missed the bustle of activity he had encountered in Minnesota, and he was more interested in politics than in preparing Humphrey homemade concoctions to treat farmers' hogs. He met Muriel Buck, a young bookkeeper, and they married on September 3, 1936. He returned to the University of Minnesota in 1937.

A degree in political science offered little in immediate employment opportunities, so Humphrey decided to work on a master's degree, with the hope of using it to teach, probably on the university level. His choice of university—Louisiana State University—boiled down to a matter of good timing meeting good time. The school offered a $450 fellowship, plus tuition, to a student from the northern part of the United States. Its purpose was more than mere scholarship. In the North, Southern life was treated as if it was foreign; the fellowship would give a northerner a different perspective.

"There was a special business of the Negro population and the southern white man's attitude toward, and treatment of, the Negro," Charles Hyneman, chairman of LSU's Political Science Department, recalled. "I figured one would never understand what that was, unless he lived in it and saw it. I thought the offer was a really good experience."

Hyneman knew Everon Kirkpatrick, a former student now teaching at the University of Minnesota, and Kirkpatrick recommended Humphrey as the ideal candidate for the fellowship. Grateful for the offer, Humphrey moved, along with Muriel and their infant daughter, Nancy, to a rooming house near the campus in 1939.

Humphrey's education, as Hyneman hoped, took place more outside the classroom than in it. Humphrey, of course, had heard about the South, but he had never been immersed in its culture. Politics—much of it still part of the old, corrupt Huey Long populist tradition—dominated day-to-day life and conversation. Humphrey, who intended to write his thesis on Roosevelt's New Deal, was drawn into it. He met and befriended Russell Long, son of Huey Long and a future colleague of Humphrey's in the Senate, and they spent hours debating the South and its politics. Deeply disturbed by what he saw on the street, where strict segregation divided blacks and whites, where whites lived in beautifully painted houses with large green lawns while blacks existed in unpainted shacks with open sewers running in the yards, Humphrey not only felt sickened by what he saw but was also outraged by the northerners' perception of the South. "My abstract commitment to civil rights was given flesh and blood during my year in Louisiana," he would confess.

His studies were a miserable experience. He and his dissertation advisor, a PhD candidate at Harvard, did not see eye to eye on the direction of his dissertation, and Humphrey feared that he was going to fail. Fortunately for Humphrey, the advisor returned to Harvard, and he passed his defense of the dissertation. During one awkward but humorous moment, one of the three-man panel stated that he was going to fail Humphrey—and for a strange but, as time passed, prescient reason. "If we gave you a degree," he told Humphrey, "you'll just as likely not end up a college professor, and if we flunk you right now, you are more likely to go back to Minnesota and run for the United States Senate, and you'll amount to something."

Humphrey passed by a unanimous decision.

■ ■ ■ ■ ■

Humphrey was not ready for a Senate run just yet, but his political career was on the horizon. His effervescent personality, intelligence, ability to make a quick study out of almost any topic, ambitions, moral conviction in public policy, powers of persuasion, and growing list of political connections—they all moved him to a short list of up-and-coming players in the Minnesota political galaxy. Both sides of the aisle saw him as a force of nature in the future. Change was in the air. Minneapolis had a well-earned reputation for its organized crime and corruption in government. When the mayoral election arrived in 1943, Humphrey was approached by a group of civic leaders and asked if he would be interested in running. Humphrey barely gave it a second thought.

His first run for public office exposed strengths and weaknesses that would remain with him throughout his life. His extraordinary energy and people skills propelled him to succeed where others, particularly unknowns, might have failed; his drugstore experiences, watching his father and eventually dealing with customers himself, led to a natural ease with people of all types. Expressions such as "pleased as punch" and "by golly," cornball when coming from others, became a charming part of his repertoire. And when he gave a speech, from formal oration to informal talk at a coffee meeting, he left an impression connected to only the upper echelon of politicians. He didn't have to sell himself.

These qualities carried him through the mayoral primary. Five candidates entered the nonpartisan contest, and when the votes were counted, Humphrey and the incumbent mayor, Marvin Kline, received the most votes and would run against each other in the general election. Humphrey's weaknesses—a disorganized staff and a shoestring budget—slowed him down in his campaign against Kline. More disturbing, perhaps, was his inability to unite two distinct groups—the academic community and labor unions—on his behalf. Humphrey moved comfortably in both groups, but they hated each other, and as a result, he lost votes when members of one group felt he was catering to the other. Humphrey was fortunate to have Arthur Naftalin, a former reporter for the *Minneapolis Tribune,* assisting him with press relations and media contacts; Naftalin proved to be invaluable in getting the Humphrey name in front of people who might otherwise have missed it.

Humphrey came up short in the June 14 general election, losing to Kline, 60,075 to 54,350, but he did not consider it a defeat. The experience taught him much about Minneapolis, the power structure and political players, fundraising, and the organization of a campaign. He had taken a learn-as-you-go approach to his first campaign, and he had suffered for his disorganization, especially in the utilization of volunteers and door-to-door canvassers. He would run for the office again, and when he did, he would be much better prepared. In the meantime, he taught political science classes at Macalester College in St. Paul and led a drive to unite the Democratic and Farm-Labor parties in Minnesota. The unification, he felt, was necessary if a liberal agenda had any chance of taking hold in the state.

The seasoning paid dividends when Humphrey and Kline squared off in the next mayoral election. The incumbent realized that Humphrey was going to give him a tough race, and the resulting campaign was one of the nastiest in Minnesota history. The Kline campaign attempted to tie Communist money into the Humphrey campaign and, worse yet, brought Humphrey's lack of military service into play. Humphrey had attempted to enlist on several occasions, but he always flunked the physical. When he eventually passed, he was issued a uniform and placed on a waiting list, but he failed yet another physical before he was inducted. The results of the physical were a matter of public record, but this was an issue that would bother Humphrey in future elections.

It didn't matter in this election. Humphrey won, 86,377 to 55,263, in the largest vote spread in the city's mayoral election history.

▪ ▪ ▪ ▪ ▪

Humphrey's term as mayor of Minneapolis completed the learning curve of his early education in politics. The city's strong council–weak mayor system of government, in which Humphrey had no final say over anything but the police department, placed him in the position of trying to develop a coalition of power brokers, individual businesses, well-informed private citizens, and knowledgeable intermediaries, all in at least semiagreement about the direction the city needed to take. Humphrey's enthusiasm helped. If given the chance, he could be very passionate. Minneapolis, burdened by corruption, dysfunction, in-fighting among liberals, and social inequality and prejudice, needed a thorough cleansing and, in some cases, rehabilitation. Humphrey, it turned out, was the man for the job.

He began with the police department. In all probability, the Minneapolis department suffered from the same problems one found in most big-city departments. The graft and protection money, the ignoring of such vices as gambling, prostitution and after-hours drinking establishments—none of it was unique to Minneapolis. But the new mayor in town was having none of it. He had campaigned on the promise that he was going to clean up the city, and he intended to make good on the promise. He replaced the police chief with Ed Ryan, a no-nonsense, straight-arrow, tough Irish cop who had trained at J. Edgar Hoover's academy. The results were immediately noticed by both sides of the law. The organized crime syndicate dispatched a representative to city hall with the simple query of what Humphrey would demand to let things slide back to the old status. Humphrey sent him packing. Late one night, when returning from work, Humphrey heard a gunshot near his home. He ignored the warning.

Troubled by Minneapolis's reputation as "capital of anti-Semitism in America," and by the lack of opportunities for African Americans in the city, Humphrey took the initiative to work on a fair employment practices ordinance. He faced resistance but recognized the debt that he owed both groups. Jews had contributed heavily to his mayoral campaign, and Arthur Naftalin, his chief administrative assistant (and future Minneapolis mayor), was Jewish. The ordinance eventually passed, after an avalanche of meetings, hearings, and studies.

Humphrey needed all of his formidable stamina to pursue his goals. Naftalin recalled his boss's long days and nights at city hall. Humphrey's ambitions ate away at his time until one day slipped into the next. "He would come in late at night, after he'd made a round of evening meetings, dinners, and whatnot," Naftalin said, "and [he] came back to the office at 12:30 or 1:00 in the morning 'cause his mail basket was crowded with stuff. It would all wind up in my basket the next morning, all marked rush, everything was marked *rush*."

Orville Freeman, a Humphrey contemporary who would eventually reach the heights of Minnesota and national politics, brought into the Humphrey administration to spearhead the housing for veterans efforts, summed up Humphrey's early days as mayor as "action, peripatetic action." "He was pressing us and pushing us and driving us just all the time," Freeman remembered. "The police department [was] just all over the place. We had strikes and dealing with people and making speeches and people coming in and veterans' problems and rebuilding the city."

Such was the beginning of Humphrey's lifetime of public service—and he looked at choices that way: he was a servant of the public. But even in those early days, he trained his eye on a larger future, and like most career politicians with inflated ambitions, he constructed his future out of wisely chosen and executed opportunities. His building blocks were memorable.

2 Humphrey gained his first significant national exposure on Wednesday, July 14, 1948, when he delivered a rousing, historically significant address at the Democratic National Convention. Oppressive ninety-three degree heat suffocated everyone in Philadelphia's Convention Hall; this would be the last convention that either party would hold in a hall without air-conditioning. Given the topic of his address—civil rights—Humphrey would have preferred to avoid overheated and irritable listeners; the delegates from the South, more accustomed to these conditions, tended to be overheated on the topic in any case.

Neither party had a taste for the issue. Every so often, a legislative scrap would be tossed in the direction of those seeking programs to engender equal rights for a race that had suffered inequality since the first slavers had plied their trade centuries earlier, but powerful, binding legislation since the days of Lincoln had been slow in arriving. Most recently, on December 5, 1946, President Harry Truman, a proponent of meaningful civil rights legislation, had appointed a fifteen-member commission to study the issue. The commission's 178-page report, *Secure These Rights,* delivered on July 14, 1947, called for improvements that went far beyond the transparent generalizations that found their way into the party platforms every four years. The commission studied civil rights issues from multiple angles, from education and employment injustices to the lynchings still prevalent in Southern states. The report proposed fifteen detailed recommendations designed to move the country forward— solutions that were bound to infuriate leaders in the South.

Humphrey, with his eyes set on a 1948 Senate run, was pleased. As mayor of Minneapolis, he had been indefatigable in his efforts to shatter the city's reputation as one of the worst anti-Semitic metropolitan centers in the United

States. He had succeeded, and now, in Philadelphia, he was primed for battle on a larger stage. He was part of his party's platform committee, and he intended to raise his voice in favor of meaningful wording, based on the report, in the party's civil rights portion of the plank.

He was stunned to learn that he had very little support among his fellow platform committee members. The obstacles ahead were imposing. Truman's popularity was declining, and it was beginning to look as if he had little or no chance against Thomas Dewey, his Republican opponent, in the November general election. A strongly worded Democratic platform would lose him the South and, in all probability, the election. The Democrats intended to insert a civil rights statement into the platform, but the party was fractured on the approach to take. The Southern delegation, threatening to walk off the convention floor if the plank's language promised wide-sweeping changes to the Dixie tradition, demanded wording that favored states' rights in dealing with civil rights matters—in short, no movement from business as usual. Committee members from the rest of the country preferred a statement favoring the admission of problems and a vow to work on these problems in the future, but there was strong disagreement over the wording, especially if it endangered Truman's already troubled candidacy. Truman himself waffled on his previously tough stance on civil rights.

The Republicans complicated the dispute when, in the party's earlier held convention, the subject of civil rights was addressed in its platform. The Republicans specifically attacked lynching and mob violence, calling them "a disgrace to any civilized state" and demanding legislation putting an end to them. In addition, the plank called for an end to poll taxes and segregation in the armed forces. The platform read,

> One of the basic principles of this Republic is the equality of all individuals to life, liberty, and pursuit of happiness. The principle is enunciated in the Declaration of Independence and embodied in the Constitution of the United States; it was vindicated in the field of battle and became the cornerstone of the Republic. The equal opportunity to work and to advance in life should never be limited to any individual because of race, religion, color, or country of origin. We favor enactment and enforcement of Federal legislation as may be necessary to maintain this right of all times in any part of this Republic.

The proposed Democratic platform, which offered almost the same wording as its plank four years earlier, looked weak in comparison. Other than stating that "racial and religious minorities must have the right to live, the right to work, the right to vote, [and] the full protection of the laws," and "call[ing] upon the Congress to exert its full authority to the limit of its Constitutional powers," the Democratic platform was soft, with no specific issues addressed—certainly nothing in the wake of the Truman commission report's findings and recommendations.

Humphrey, after hearing the different proposals for the platform, was in no frame of mind for compromise. Prior to leaving for the convention, he had consulted with colleagues in Minneapolis about the direction to take, and he had arrived in Philadelphia with a goal of seeing a significant civil rights platform presented at the convention. He was not a strong Truman supporter, but he admired the president's commitment to moving progressively in civil rights legislation. Now he, too, was waffling from his previous position. In addition, Humphrey feared "the Republicans might have seized the issue by default."

The deliberations over the three proposed planks quickly degenerated into open hostility. It was generally believed that the states' rights platform, proposed by former Texas governor Dan Moody and backed by delegates from eight other states, was doomed from the start; only three members outside the South had any use for it. The fight came down to strong disagreement between the innocuously worded plank, endorsed by Truman and thought by the majority to be workable with the South, and the more pointedly worded plank presented by Humphrey and Wisconsin congressman Andrew Biemiller. Humphrey, always a persuasive speaker, presented his case passionately, gaining a few votes but not nearly enough to win the day. Tempers boiled over during the debate. Humphrey and Biemiller labeled the milder plank a "sellout to states' rights over human rights." Illinois senator Scott Lucas angrily countered that Humphrey was trying to "redo Franklin D. Roosevelt's work and deny the wishes of the present President of the United States."

"Who does this pipsqueak think he is?" Lucas fumed, using a word he would apply to Humphrey on a dozen occasions during the skirmish.

When the Humphrey–Biemiller proposal was put to a vote, it was badly defeated, seventy to thirty. But Humphrey and Biemiller weren't finished. They were entitled to present the minority plank to the convention delegates, but Humphrey, as leader of the charge and the man designated to present it, would be doing so at considerable risk. To this point, the bickering had been restricted to the privacy of the Bellevue-Stratford Hotel and was unknown to the public; taking the minority plank to the convention floor meant the entire country would see how splintered the Democratic Party had become. Humphrey himself did not believe the minority plank stood a chance when the assembled delegation voted on it, and some of his closest confidants, such as Orville Freeman and Eugenie Anderson, agreed. By pursuing the minority plank further, Humphrey might be placing his senate race—and perhaps his entire political future—on the line. Humphrey's ambitions were no small matter. Only a month before the convention, he had mulled over the idea of having his name entered as a vice-presidential candidate, and he was not alone in seeing himself as a player in the national political game. David K. Niles, Truman's advisor on minority matters, approached Americans for Democratic Action leader Joseph Rauh and warned him that Humphrey's dogged pursuit of the minority plank might end his political career. "Joe," he advised, "you won't get fifty votes for your minority plank and all you'll do is ruin the chances of the best liberal product to come down the pike in years." President Truman, after being briefed about Humphrey's plans, offered a gruff response. As far as he was concerned, Humphrey and his cohorts were just a bunch of "crackpots."

Humphrey agonized over his dilemma. Aside from his consultations with friends and advisors, he sought the counsel of the two people he trusted most: his wife and his father. Muriel Humphrey, aware of her husband's convictions, encouraged him to finish what he had started; he was doing the right thing, she assured him. "Her strong faith once again calmed my fears," Humphrey would recall.

Hubert Humphrey Sr., part of the South Dakota delegation, recognized the battle between the pragmatic and ideal taking place in his son's mind. He, like the majority of others, believed that the minority plank had no chance of passing in a floor fight, and he had been around long enough to recognize the perils his son was facing in rebelling against the wishes of the most powerful figures in his party. "This may tear the party apart," he said, "but if you feel strongly then you've got to go with it. You can't run away from your conscience, son."

"What do you think will happen?"

"I don't know," the elder Humphrey answered. "But you'll at least have the eight votes of the South Dakota delegation."

In Humphrey's hotel room, Minnesota delegates talked through the night. It was nearly sunrise when Humphrey dismissed them, announcing that he had a speech to write and a few hours of sleep to catch before he addressed the convention later in the day. His decision was final. "If there is one thing I believe in this crazy business," he told his fellow Minnesotans, "it's civil rights. Regardless of what happens, we're going to do it."

Eugenie Anderson called Humphrey's decision "very courageous." "I think it was very important that Humphrey himself made the final decision," she declared, "not because he thought he would win it, but because he had really wrestled with it and came to the conclusion that he would do it because it was the right thing to do."

The protocol was set. Biemiller would deliver the plank, and Humphrey would deliver the speech supporting it. Biemiller called Sam Rayburn, Speaker of the House of Representatives and chairman of the convention, and made arrangements for Humphrey and him to speak during the convention's afternoon session. Dan Moody had already called Rayburn on behalf of the other minority report, so Biemiller and Humphrey would follow this presentation. It promised to be a long, very hot day in the convention hall, culminating that evening with Harry Truman's appearance to accept his party's nomination for a run at his first full term in the White House.

While Biemiller took care of the formalities, Humphrey and Milton Stewart, head of the New York chapter of the Americans for Democratic Action, worked on the final draft of Humphrey's speech. The usually verbose Humphrey would be very restricted in the amount of time he would be allotted—he estimated a maximum of fifteen minutes—so he had to be brief and precise. The two men conferred as activities in the hotel room swirled around them. Eugenie Anderson observed the extreme pressure that Humphrey was feeling—he was as tense as she had ever seen him, she would recall—and completing the speech was becoming very difficult. Biemiller and Joseph Rauh had written a new paragraph they hoped to have inserted into the speech—a paragraph listing the four main points of Truman's Commission on Civil Rights—but Humphrey was having trouble finding a place to insert it in the text. He did not wish to upstage the president or imply, even in the most subtle way, that these points had been his idea, and he didn't want to just drop the new paragraph into the text. Anderson suggested a solution. Why not add a line that praised Truman for his civil rights efforts in the past? Humphrey liked the idea, and the rest of the writing came easier.

His doubts, however, persisted as the hours passed, and he eventually found himself on the stage, awaiting his time to address the assembly. He still felt strongly about what he was doing, but he worried about the ramifications of the speech. He was wandering into a no-man's-land, unfamiliar with the political topography and working without a map, stating, in simple terms, what should have been obvious, but uncertain about the response. What if the plank received very few votes from the delegates? Or the Southern delegation followed up on their threat to walk out of the hall in the middle of his speech? Or, as was suggested, he was hooted off the stage and sent packing, a political pariah with no future in the party? Humphrey, seated on the dais, a yellow Truman button standing out on the right lapel of his dark suit, shuffled through the pages of his speech and wondered.

Ed Flynn, the powerful party boss from the Bronx, sat nearby. He was aware of Humphrey's intentions, and Humphrey offered him a look at the text, with the hope that the more experienced politician might give him some advice. The wording of the speech, he said rather defensively, was not too strong or demanding. "I'm sure we don't really have much chance to carry it," Humphrey admitted, perhaps as a preemptive strike, "but we ought to make the fight."

Flynn examined the speech and came away impressed. "You go ahead, young man," he told Humphrey. "We should have done this a long time ago. We've got to do it. Go ahead. We'll back you." When Humphrey worried about the Southern delegates storming out and perhaps forming their own splinter party, Flynn waved off the threat. "Let them," he said. "Some of them should have been out of the party a long time ago." He promised Humphrey the New York delegate votes, and said he would find more. They were going to win the fight. And with that, he was off to work the floor and secure as many votes as he could.

Flynn's assurances boosted Humphrey's confidence, and when it came time to speak, after Dan Moody's plank had been proposed, and Biemiller had entered the Humphrey–Biemiller plank on the record, Humphrey was ready to deliver his first major address to a national audience. By that time, word had circulated about what to expect from the speech, and an otherwise hot, listless assembly was poised to listen.

The speech, in turns fiery, hopeful, provocative, persuasive, and, at times, understated, interrupted repeatedly by applause and ovations, took roughly eight minutes to deliver, marking it as one of the briefest speeches Humphrey would ever deliver. Delegates wept; others rose to their feet and urged him on. Humphrey, sweating profusely, his dark hair glistening under the hot klieg lights, was in total command, from the early portion of the speech, when he acknowledged that he was addressing an emotionally charged issue that elicited polarized responses, to his final lines, when he evoked Harry Truman's name and exhorted the delegates to endorse his progressive but long overdue line of thinking. Although he read the written speech to make certain he stated exactly what he intended to say, he was occasionally inspired by the delegates' reaction and improvised to play into their emotional responses.

"It was the greatest speech I ever heard," Illinois delegate and future senator Paul Douglas remembered. "He was on fire, just like the Bible speaks of Moses. His face was glowing and his sentiments were marvelous." Others would later compare the speech to William Jennings Bryan's "Cross of Gold" speech, and Lincoln's Gettysburg Address was also brought up. The consensus, then and in years to come, was that it was one of the greatest speeches in American history:

I realize that I am dealing with a charged issue—with an issue which has been confused by emotionalism on all sides. I realize that there are those here—friends and colleagues of mine, many of them—who feel as deeply as I do about this issue and who are yet in complete disagreement with me.

My respect and admiration for these men and their views was great when I came here.

It is now far greater because of the sincerity, the courtesy, and the forthrightness with which they have argued in their discussions.

Because of this very respect—because of my profound belief that we have a challenging task to do here—because good conscience demands it—I feel I must rise at this time to support this report—a report that spells out our democracy, a report that the people will understand and enthusiastically acclaim.

Let me say at the outset that this proposal is made with no single region, no single class, no single racial or religious group in mind.

All regions and all states have shared in the precious heritage of American freedom—all people, all groups have been the victims of discrimination.

The masterly statement of our keynote speaker, the distinguished United States senator from Kentucky, Alben Barkley, made that point with great force. Speaking of the founder of our party, Thomas Jefferson, he said:

"He did not proclaim that all white, or black, or red, or yellow men are equal; that all Christian or Jewish men are equal; that all Protestant and Catholic men are equal; that all rich or poor men are equal; that all good or bad men are equal.

"What he declared was that all men are equal, and the equality which he proclaimed was equality in the right to enjoy the blessings of free government in which they may participate and to which they have given their consent."

We are here as Democrats. But more important, as Americans and I firmly believe that as men concerned with our country's future we must specify in our platform the guarantee which I have mentioned.

Yes, this is far more than a party matter. Every citizen has a stake in the emergence of the United States as a leader of the free world. That world is being challenged by the world of slavery. For us to play our part effectively, we must be in a morally sound position.

We cannot use a double standard for measuring our own and other people's policies. Our demands for democratic practices in other lands will be no more effective than the guarantee of those practiced in our own country.

We are God-fearing men and women. We place our faith in the brotherhood of man under the fatherhood of God.

I do not believe that there can be any compromise on the guarantee of civil rights which I have mentioned.

In spite of my desire for unanimous agreement on the platform there are some matters which I think must be stated without qualification; There can be no hedging—no watering down.

There are those who say to you—we are rushing this issue of civil rights. I say we are a hundred and seventy-two years late.

There are those who say to you—this issue of civil rights is an infringement on states' rights. The time has arrived for the Democratic Party to get out of the shadow of states' rights and walk forthrightly into the bright sunshine of human rights.

People—human beings—this is the issue of the twentieth century. People—all kinds and sorts of people—look to America for leadership—for help—for guidance.

My friends—my fellow Democrats—I ask you for a calm consideration of our historic opportunity. Let us forget the evil passions, the blindness of the past. In these times of world economic, political, and spiritual—above all, spiritual—crisis, we cannot—we must not, turn from the path so plainly before us.

That path has already led us through many valleys of the shadow of death, and now is the time to recall those who were left on that path of American freedom.

For all of us here, for the millions who have sent us, for the whole two billion members of the human family—our land is now, more than ever, the last best hope on earth. I know that we can—I know that we shall—begin here the fuller and richer realization of that hope—that promise of a land where all men are free and equal, and each man uses his freedom wisely and well.

My good friends, I ask my party, and I ask the Democratic Party to march down the high road of progressive democracy, I ask this convention to say in unmistakable terms that we proudly hail and we courageously support our President and leader, Harry Truman, in his great fight for civil rights in America.

When he had finished, Humphrey looked down from the dais at a spontaneous eruption breaking out below him. Douglas began an impromptu march through the hall, his Illinois delegates hoisting the state standard behind him. California followed, then Wisconsin, New York, New Jersey, and Ohio. Other state standards bobbed with the rhythmic clapping and shouting. The delegations from the Southern states, stung by what they considered to be a sharp rebuke of their traditions and beliefs, remained in their seats, refusing to so much as acknowledge the speech. They would have their say, but later.

Sam Rayburn allowed the celebration to go on for eight minutes before gaveling it to a halt in order to take a vote. Despite the festive atmosphere in the hall, a vote in favor of the minority platform was anything but assured—a fact made clear when Alabama, Arizona, and Arkansas "nays" put the plank in a deep hole in the early going. A California approval helped bring the tally close to even, and from then on, the voting see-sawed between approval and rejection. Ed Flynn, it turned out, had done his work. Support from Illinois, New Jersey, New York, and Pennsylvania gave Humphrey hope that the impossible just might take place. When the time came for South Dakota to add its numbers to the tally, Hubert Humphrey Sr., as promised, declared: "I am Hubert Humphrey Sr., I cast South Dakota's eight votes for the plank." Appropriately enough, given Andrew Biemiller's work on the plank, the votes assuring the minority plank the victory came from Wisconsin.

The final count, formally announced by Rayburn, favored the minority plank, 651½ to 582½. A roar swept through the convention hall. The Southern delegates prepared to walk out, but before they could stage their demonstration, Rayburn called for a recess. When the convention reconvened, the entire Mississippi delegation and half of the Alabama delegates fulfilled their promise and formally walked out. In its reportage, *Time* magazine added a dramatic flair to the story: "They all plodded, stony-faced, through the crowd, tripped over Truman signs stacked in the aisle, walked out the doors into a pelting rainstorm. As they emerged, a thunderclap split the air."

As feared, four Southern states broke away from the Democratic Party and formed what came to be known as the Dixiecrat Party, which nominated South Carolina governor J. Strom Thurmond as its own candidate. The projections of the South's defection destroying Truman's chances would prove to be mistaken.

Twenty years later, while making his own run for the presidency, Humphrey would look back and state that his civil rights speech was his proudest achievement to that point. In an interview with David Frost, he used the speech to frame a discussion about the role of a public servant. "I think that a man in public life ought to be an educator and a persuader," he said. "This is his first duty, to teach, to educate, to persuade, to convince, to develop a public attitude and a public opinion." There was still a lot that needed to be done to reach the equality he envisioned, he admitted, but the speech had opened the door to the possibilities.

■ ■ ■ ■ ■

The convention concluded, and Humphrey took the train back to Minneapolis. The ride took a day, giving Humphrey ample time to consider what he had accomplished in Philadelphia and what lay ahead in the upcoming months, when he would be running for the Senate against Joseph Ball, the Republican incumbent. His job was formidable: no Democrat had ever won a Senate seat in Minnesota.

When his train arrived in Minneapolis, Humphrey received a hero's welcome from two thousand friends, acquaintances, and supporters gathered at the station. Humphrey was hoisted on the shoulders of several men and carried two blocks to an area where an eighty-car caravan awaited to parade him to city hall. The reception had been organized by Humphrey's friend Fred Gates, who would be playing a prominent role in Humphrey's campaign for the Senate.

Joseph Ball, a former journalist, had been appointed to the Senate by Governor Harold Stassen in 1940, to complete the term of Ernest Lundeen, who had been killed in a plane crash. The moderately liberal Joe Ball had won a full term in 1942, but in the years that followed, his political philosophy shifted to the right. Political analysts believed that two specific decisions made him vulnerable in his run for reelection: he voted for the Taft-Hartley Act and was one of only sixteen senators who voted against the Marshall Plan. Both votes fell squarely into Ball's fiscally conservative line of thinking, though they came at a time when Minnesota's labor influence was strengthening and liberalism was on the rise.

"I figured that the sources of my support were the businessmen and the prosperous farmers," Ball would say when recalling his Senate contest against Humphrey. "I pitched my 1948 campaign on the dangers of inflation and the trend toward state socialism. I had become a conservative. The people, I guess, were further left than I was."

Humphrey was indeed more liberal, and his recent wave of publicity propelled his image in a race that Ball might have been favored to win. In terms of personality, the two man were opposites. Ball exuded a low-key, low-energy, soft-spoken style, whereas Humphrey came on like a dynamo in his speech and actions. The one time the two debated face-to-face, someone counted the words spoken, and it turned out that Humphrey uttered three times the number of words as did his opponent. Of course, this would have come as no surprise to anyone who knew Humphrey, but to those who didn't, the combined forces of Humphrey's intellect and energy struck like a wrecking ball.

Humphrey needed to accentuate these traits if he was going to have any chance of winning. At first glance, Ball appeared to hold an advantage. He was the incumbent, with strong financial backing and endorsements from a majority of the state's larger newspapers. Financially strapped (a condition that would plague him throughout his career), Humphrey had no choice but to defeat his opponent through hard work and hustle. His daily schedule, dividing his time between his mayoral obligations and relentless campaigning that might find him visiting up to ten cities a day, was a grueling test that Humphrey, with his genuine affection for people, somehow managed to enjoy. Big or small, the events and cities appealed to him. With Fred Gates accompanying him and doing most of the driving, Humphrey sped from town to town, stowing bread and cheese in the car's back seat for sandwiches consumed on the fly, engaging in endless meet and greets and small-town gatherings, talking so much that he occasionally had a doctor waiting at the next stop to spray his overburdened throat. The summer festival season found him visiting such events as the Sauerkraut Festival in Springfield, Watermelon Day in Sanborn, the Bohemian Dance in Owatonna, and a full lineup of others. He consumed twenty-five ears of corn in a contest at the Ortonville Corn Feed and downed fifteen cups of coffee at the Kaffeeklatsch in Willmar.

"I visited all the county fairs, shaking hands and eating hot dogs until I had hot dogs coming out of my ears," he told a reporter from *Time*. "I used to be razzed for it. People said it was not dignified to campaign for the U.S Senate in that way. But when I'd go down a midway, the barker would stop and point me out, saying: 'Hey, there's my friend who is going to be the new Senator from Minnesota.'"

Humphrey relished his everyman background and how it provided him insight into his constituents. In every small town he visited, he made a point of bringing up his humble origins, and it became the backbone of his campaign strategy. "It's like running a drugstore," he said of campaigning. "When people come in, you've got to do things for them, show an interest in them, take them to the door."

Joseph Ball could hear the Humphrey bandwagon marching down the street, picking up new members in every town, gathering momentum. Humphrey, he would state nearly two decades after the race, was a "giant killer," and he, Senator Joe Ball, was not a giant. The election was slipping away, and he had no way of stopping the Minneapolis mayor: "He was all over the state and he was a good campaigner."

Humphrey's final campaign numbers were impressive. In slightly over three months' time, from late July until the early-November election, Humphrey visited 450 communities in Minnesota, which included 31,000 miles of driving to every county in the state and giving 691 speeches. He hammered away at Ball's Taft-Hartley and Marshall Plan history, assuring himself a strong labor vote. Farmers, fearing a loss of their farms under Ball's tough economic stances, rushed over to Humphrey as well. On election night, Humphrey collected 729,494 votes to Ball's 485,801—a victory margin of just under a quarter of a million votes.

Humphrey basked in his newfound glory. What had begun with a controversial speech threatening his very future in politics had morphed into his becoming a nationally known figure with a promising future that few would have predicted.

3 Humphrey learned, soon enough, that there was a vast difference between how business was conducted in Minnesota and how it transpired in Washington, D.C. The Senate reveled in its slow, deliberate traditions, and the hyperkinetic, loquacious new senator from Minnesota was slow to recognize—or accept—it.

Humphrey's early days in the Senate were not happy ones. He arrived in Washington with a head full of ideas and energy that belied his thirty-seven years, but he learned that his open, forceful ways as mayor in Minneapolis, what established him as a giant on the state and local levels, were not appreciated in the Senate, where he was just another freshly scrubbed face in an extraordinary rookie group that included Lyndon Johnson of Texas, Estes Kefauver from Tennessee, Paul Douglas from Illinois, and Russell Long from Louisiana. The Southern senators, in control of some of the most important committees in the Senate, still harbored deep resentment of Humphrey's leading the civil rights charge at the 1948 Democratic Convention. Humphrey had barely settled into his desk in the back of the Senate chambers when Richard Russell of Georgia, a venerable figure in the Senate, said, loud enough for Humphrey to hear, "Can you imagine the people of Minnesota sending that damn fool down here to represent them?" Humphrey, stung by the remark, was reduced to tears.

And if all this wasn't enough, *Time* magazine profiled Humphrey in the cover story of its January 17, 1949, issue, fresh off the presses when Humphrey was sworn into office. The cover photo of Humphrey, staring with determination and backed by a tornado sweeping into town, along with the story, portrayed Humphrey as the eager new kid in town, a tough new voice ready to shake up the quiet ways on Capitol Hill. The generally favorable piece had sharp teeth, and while Humphrey enjoyed the publicity and the pride that it raised within his family, he also had to contend with the effect the piece had on his fellow senators, veterans and novices alike. There weren't too many senators likely to appreciate *Time*'s depicting Humphrey as a "glib, jaunty spellbinder with a listen-you-guys approach" with "the cyclonic attitude of an ad salesman."

Humphrey brought much of his misery on himself. He knew the unwritten maxim that freshmen senators kept their thoughts to themselves while they learned the ins and outs of the Senate, but he would honor it only to a point. He also intended to contribute. Before he had even taken office, he confided in the press, telling reporters that the Senate might be ready to act on civil rights legislation. This, predictably, went over poorly with the Southern senators, who had had more than their fill of him a few months earlier, and it wasn't likely to gain him much elevation in a city still largely segregated. Given the derisive nickname, The Voice, Humphrey pressed on, making himself heard far more than Senate custom favored. There was merit to much of what he had to say, but it mattered little to a legislative body chained to its old ways. Frozen out, Humphrey tried to find a way to fit in. "Never in my life have I felt so unwanted as I did during those first months in Washington," he would remember.

The Minnesota senator crossed the line on February 24, 1950, just over a year after he had taken office, when he delivered a devastating critique of the Joint Committee on Reduction of Nonessential Federal Expenditures—a committee that, in Humphrey's view, was as nonessential as any in the Senate. In hindsight, Humphrey would admit that his declaration had been in very poor judgment for two reasons. First, the committee was chaired by conservative Virginia Democrat Harry Byrd, one of the most powerful and highly respected figures in the Senate. Second, Byrd was absent from the Senate chambers, attending to his sick, aging mother, on the day that Humphrey dropped his bomb. If Humphrey had any doubts about how his thoughts would be received, he didn't have to wait long for an answer. The next day, senator after senator, Republican and Democrat alike—twenty-five, by Humphrey's estimate—stood up and supported Byrd and assailed Humphrey on the Senate floor. Humphrey sat there silently and absorbed the punishment. Afterward, a mortified Humphrey left the chambers and tried to catch the elevator out. When the doors swung open, Humphrey found himself face-to-face with Harry Byrd. Humphrey extended his hand. "Senator," he said to Byrd, "I know when I've been licked."

4 By the time he was reaching the end of his first decade in the Senate, Hubert Humphrey had built a résumé that he hoped would be sufficient for a successful run at the presidency. He made no secret of his ambitions, and it was a foregone conclusion that he was on a short list, along with Senators Lyndon Johnson, Stuart Symington, John Kennedy, and perhaps a few others, for a White House run when Eisenhower's second term ended in 1960. Humphrey was confident that he had earned the respect of his colleagues in Washington, D.C., and though his name and image had appeared in just about every major media source over the years, he still figured he needed more national exposure if he was going to compete against better-known candidates with bigger war chests.

The exposure he sought came from a most unexpected source. Near the end of 1958, he flew overseas on a number of missions in the Soviet Union and eight European countries. His main objective, as he described it, was to use his positions as an Eisenhower appointee to the General Assembly of the United Nations and a member of the Senate Foreign Relations Committee "to encourage international co-operation in science and medical research." With the possible exception of a stop in Geneva, where he witnessed United Nations Disarmament Committee negotiations over a nuclear test ban agreement, his work, although high profile and important in government circles, was not newsworthy enough to seize the attention of the average American. He started in Paris, where he attended a UNESCO conference and met with future Nobel Prize winners Jacques Monod and André Lwoff. In West Berlin, he consulted with cancer specialists and visited with Mayor Willy Brandt on the sensitive topic of German–Soviet relations in the divided city. He visited children's hospitals, consented to interviews in some cities, and, in general, acted as a goodwill ambassador and devoted tourist. Humphrey viewed his busy schedule as nothing less than a mission for international peacekeeping: a spirit of cooperation between nations in research and treatment of health issues that went a long way toward holding agreeable relations between countries in political matters. On a personal level, any media exposure helped Humphrey feather his résumé.

His fortunes changed in Moscow, where he was scheduled to meet with national health officials. While in Germany, he had run into Vasily Kuznetsov, a Soviet acquaintance from the days when they were both delegates to the UN General Assembly. Humphrey told Kuznetsov that he wanted to see Nikita Khrushchev while he was in Moscow. Humphrey expected nothing to come of the request—Khrushchev, though hoping to thaw the cold relations between his country and the United States, was unlikely to meet with an American so low ranking as Humphrey—but on the afternoon of December 1, Humphrey was informed that Khrushchev would see him. Humphrey had no time to prepare: the call came at two thirty, and the meeting was to take place at three.

Humphrey anticipated a relatively brief meeting, telling his wife that he would be back at the hotel in time for dinner. The meeting lasted eight and a half hours and found the two men jousting over a variety of topics. Both men enjoyed the debate, even if it caught them at opposite ends of sensitive topics. Khrushchev greeted Humphrey warmly in his spacious but spartanly furnished Kremlin office, and after posing for photographs, Humphrey, speaking through an interpreter, the only man besides the two in the room, opened the conversation by trying to engage the Soviet premier in a discussion about the health and medical issues that had brought him to Moscow in the first place. It was an innocuous place to begin—a place where they might find agreement and ease into more controversial subjects—but Khrushchev, although listening carefully to Humphrey, showed only marginal interest in the discussion. As Humphrey later remarked, Khrushchev preferred to let the American do most of the talking, "as if to take my measure," but his responses to the health and medical topics impressed Humphrey as the "reaction of a man discussing things normally left to others."

After an hour of almost tepid conversation, Humphrey felt he had taken up enough of the Soviet leader's time. Khrushchev, however, wanted to continue, and their exchanges became more lively when they bantered back and forth on Berlin, U.S. foreign policy, and other topics of international affairs. With Khrushchev's permission, Humphrey took detailed notes of their conversation, filling more than twenty pages with quotations and observations. Khrushchev became more forceful and animated when talking about the arms race, the division of Berlin, and a nuclear test ban. He was unhappy about America's military presence in Berlin, which he called "a bone in my throat." He accused the United States of arming West Berlin with nuclear weapons for potential use against the Soviet Union, and assured Humphrey that his country would reciprocate if the United States initiated any bombing. Then, as if to take some of the edge off the discussion, he told Humphrey that he respected Eisenhower, whom he viewed as a man of integrity and peace. He could not say the same for Secretary of State John Foster Dulles; much of the rest of the world, including some of America's European allies, had no use for him either. Humphrey suspected that many of Khrushchev's comments were issued with the tacit understanding that they would be brought to Eisenhower's attention, and he dismissed some of Khrushchev's statements as so much posturing.

Humphrey was nobody's delivery boy. He refused to back down from Khrushchev's remarks, and he defended the U.S. position on every point. The two had been parrying for four hours when Khrushchev excused himself to use the toilet. Humphrey used his absence to tell the interpreter that he was worried that he was taking too much of Khrushchev's time. This was not the case, the interpreter insisted: Khrushchev would call an end to the meeting when he was ready.

It was after seven, and both men were hungry. Khrushchev ordered a veritable banquet—caviar, beef, chicken, pheasant, fish, and fresh fruit, preceded by appetizers of crabmeat and small pork sandwiches. While they were being served, Humphrey endeared himself to Khrushchev by narrating a story about a fierce debate between Winston Churchill and Clement Attlee in Parliament. After their debate, Churchill and Attlee headed to a nearby men's room, continuing their spirited conversation as they walked. Attlee continued to talk as he walked up to a urinal, only to be angered when he looked up and discovered that he was talking to himself. Churchill was standing at a urinal across the room. "Look, Winston," Attlee fumed, "your behavior is atrocious! We can be partisans in the House, but once we leave it we are gentlemen and friends. To leave me talking to myself is outrageous."

Khrushchev laughed uproariously and asked Humphrey to slowly repeat the story so his interpreter could write it down. The story, Khrushchev decided, would be sent to Russian ambassadors around the world.

After dinner, Khrushchev invited Anastas Mikoyan, his deputy premier, to join them for a discussion about foreign trade relations. Three hours later, Mikoyan excused himself, and the three men decided to end the meeting— until Humphrey remembered that he had yet to question Khrushchev about China. This was not a topic that Khrushchev cared to discuss, other than to say that his country and China were allies. Humphrey pressed ahead by asking about the Chinese communes.

Khrushchev's remarks stunned Humphrey.

"They are old-fashioned," he said of the communes. "They are reactionary. We tried that right after the revolution. It just doesn't work, not nearly as good as the state farms and the collective farms. You know, senator, these communes are based on the principle—to each according to his ability, to each according to his need. Well, you know that won't work. There is no incentive. You can't get production without incentive."

"That's rather capitalist," Humphrey observed.

"Call it what you will, it works."

The meeting, Humphrey would say, was not only important for the publicity it gained him, as he considered a run for the presidency; it convinced him that he was capable of dealing with heads of state.

5 Humphrey's meeting with Khrushchev unofficially ignited his candidacy for a 1960 presidential run. He would be coy about making it official, saying nothing substantive about it in public, but in retrospect, there can be no doubt that the Khrushchev meeting would be the launching pad for an already ambitious man. Upon his return home from the Soviet Union, Humphrey saw his image, complete with heavy winter coat and fur hat, smiling off the cover of *Life* magazine, which included Humphrey's lengthy written account of his audience with Khrushchev. His office phone rang off the hook with interview requests from newspapers, magazines, and television news programs. There seemed to be no bottom to the well of invitations—one estimate placed the number at a hundred a week, at the peak—for public appearances and speeches. Humphrey could not have scripted a better way to boost his public profile. For a fleeting moment, he considered a similar meeting with China's Mao Zedong, but he ultimately rejected it.

But for all the urging from his friends and colleagues, Humphrey resisted the temptation to formally announce his candidacy. It was simply too early. He had no worries about Richard Nixon, the presumptive Republican nominee, whom Humphrey believed could be defeated by any good Democratic candidate. As for the Democrats, John F. Kennedy told Humphrey and anyone else listening about setting his sights on the 1960 election, and Lyndon B. Johnson, despite his claims of having no interest in campaigning for the presidency, was well positioned to walk straight to the front of the line of presidential hopefuls if he ever changed his mind. If Humphrey announced too early, he risked being microscopically examined and discarded before the primary season began in early 1960. He had his strong supporters, mostly from Minnesota, but he had no money or campaign organization.

He spent most of 1959 in quiet planning. Running for office on a national scale required organizational skills that Humphrey had never tested. In the past, he had worked almost exclusively with Minnesota organizers, and one in particular, Orville Freeman, elected the state's governor in 1954, was no longer available to contribute the hours and effort necessary for an endeavor of this nature. Humphrey, seven years Freeman's senior, had met Freeman when he was teaching political science in St. Paul and Freeman had been his student. A strong friendship developed, and Freeman had worked as a secretary to Humphrey when Humphrey became Minneapolis's mayor. Both shared liberal politics and believed this was the direction the country as a whole ought to be taking.

Freeman was present on July 4, 1959, when a group of the Humphrey brain trust assembled at a Duluth hotel for a serious discussion about Humphrey's potential as a presidential candidate. Congressmen John Blatnik and Joseph Karth and a handful of others strongly favored his candidacy. The conversation ran the gamut of topics related to a presidential run, including whether Humphrey's liberal agenda would be embraced on a national level; how Humphrey, strapped for cash, might be expected to fatten his coffers; and when the optimum time to announce his candidacy might be. No final, definitive answers were forthcoming. They agreed that Humphrey would be a long shot for the nomination—Humphrey placed his odds at ten to one—and that it would take a superior effort to win over the influential, big-city party bosses, so crucial at convention time; they also agreed that a formal announcement of his candidacy should be put on hold. Instead, Freeman and McCarthy formed an exploratory Humphrey-for-President committee.

Humphrey's staff would be learning on the job. James Rowe, a longtime friend, was one exception. Rowe had worked in the Roosevelt White House, and he was closely connected to Lyndon Johnson. When Rowe learned that Johnson would not be running in 1960, he joined the growing Humphrey campaign team. In one of his early contributions, Rowe drew up a twenty-six-page document, "The Strategy of Hubert Humphrey," that outlined, point by point, everything he felt Humphrey would have to do if he were to have even a remote chance of competing in the race. The main focus, Rowe decided, would have to be on the primaries—a route that Humphrey strongly resisted. Primaries were physically and psychologically grueling, expensive, and inconclusive; one could win every primary and still not be guaranteed the nomination. The rules varied from state to state. One never knew what to expect, from one city to the next. Humphrey balked at taking this approach, but Rowe remained adamant in his claim that Humphrey stood absolutely no chance if he didn't participate in at least a few key states. Wisconsin, as a border state to Minnesota, would be a good choice, and South Dakota, with Humphrey's old ties to the state, might work as well. Oregon looked promising, as did West Virginia, which was likely to give Kennedy problems.

Humphrey, with some hesitation, agreed to enter a handful of primaries, beginning with the Wisconsin primary on April 2, but he refused to compromise when Rowe instructed him to totally dedicate himself to the campaign, at the cost of his duties in the Senate, if necessary. By Rowe's thinking, a decision such as this was out of Humphrey's hands. "In politics," he argued, "your strategy is never based on choice—it is forced on you."

"You'd better make up your mind," Rowe told him. "If you're going to run for president, run for president. Quit being a senator. You can't be shuttling back and forth between one speech and another and getting back to the capitol. Look at John Kennedy; he's doesn't worry about that. He's made a commitment. He is going to do this. Everything is being designed that way.

"And with you, you're doing a half-baked job, you know. You're spending a little time at it and not enough time, and the time that you're going at it is not well worked out."

Humphrey would not be convinced. He felt a strong obligation to his Minnesota constituents and to his duties in the Senate, and though he would eventually admit that Rowe was right, he spent his campaign moving between Washington, D.C., and wherever he was campaigning.

The sharp differences between the Humphrey and Kennedy styles were clear from the onset. Humphrey looked ill prepared and disorganized— which, to a large degree, he was—while the Kennedy campaign ran like a well-functioning machine. Humphrey's announcement of his candidacy was botched when his plans were leaked to the press, forcing Humphrey to move before he was ready. He called a hasty press conference that looked poorly timed and almost whimsical. The announcement was made in Minnesota on December 30, 1959, and by Humphrey's own assessment, "it was simply a lousy way to become a candidate."

"By announcing in Minnesota," he wrote in his autobiography, "we seemed to be ignoring the national press, neither involving them nor exciting them, and indeed, almost insulting their self-view as arbiters of who shall be considered a serious candidate. Had we done it on purpose, it would have been stupid. Doing it by accident was worse."

Kennedy, conversely, stood in the hallowed hall of the Senate Caucus Room on January 2, surrounded by the national press and delivering a polished speech that demonstrated why he had been the early favorite in the race. For the past year, his face had been seen in every important mass-circulation magazine, and his byline had appeared over stories that seemed only to complement his best-selling, Pulitzer Prize–winning *Profiles in Courage*. To Humphrey's dismay, Kennedy was the overwhelming darling of an indulgent press. "It was quite obvious that he had the national attention," Humphrey said of Kennedy. "He had the publicity, he had the attraction, he had the 'it.'"

The disparity between the Humphrey and Kennedy campaigns became all the more visible while they campaigned in Wisconsin, their first head-to-head competition. The Kennedy entourage flew about the state in the *Caroline,* Kennedy's private Corsair named after his daughter, while Humphrey slid on snowy roads in a rental bus with poor heating and in questionable repair. Kennedy could stretch out and nap on his plane between campaign stops, while Humphrey tried to catch some sleep on an army cot stashed in the back of the bus. Humphrey's envy of Kennedy peaked one morning in the predawn darkness, when a plane flew over the Humphrey campaign bus and Humphrey, fully dressed yet shivering on his bed, called out, "Come down here, Jack, and play fair."

Humphrey tried to present himself as an average Joe, but the strategy backfired. Voters, he discerned, were endlessly fascinated by the Kennedy mystique—by JFK's war hero image, by the sight of a young, attractive couple with their two kids, by the possibility that they could turn Washington, D.C., upside down. Humphrey could compete with none of this. Although he and Kennedy shared many of the same views and Humphrey had greater experience in politics, this was an election where image, rather than issues, was high currency. "I cannot win by competing in glamour or public relations," he complained. "The Kennedy forces are waging a psychological blitz that I cannot match. I'm not the candidate of the fat cats."

Humphrey's lack of funding crippled his campaign efforts in Wisconsin. Kennedy had eight offices in the state to Humphrey's two. Humphrey's first office in Wisconsin, opened in Milwaukee in 1959, was shut down due to a lack of money, then reopened, only to lose its telephone when the campaign couldn't pay the bill. Finding the money needed for advertising was a constant challenge. "I feel like an independent merchant competing against a chain store," Humphrey said when comparing his campaign funding to Kennedy's.

And so there he was, patrolling a state full of people who liked him and appreciated his efforts on their behalf, but who might or might not surrender him their votes. The situation was not unlike the way Wisconsin had endorsed Fightin' Bob La Follette's Progressive movement and had recently voted in such Democratic liberals as Gaylord Nelson for governor and William Proxmire for Senate—the same state that had sent Joseph McCarthy, he of the supersized ego and paranoid politics, to the halls of the Senate. The state oozed diversity, the differences often divided by geography. Those living in the northern part of the state, the survivors of bitterly cold winters, began stacking firewood before summer had ended, while in the southeast, on the shore of Lake Michigan, in a maven of blue-collar municipalities and new, fresh-scrubbed suburbs, people kept close watch on the Milwaukee Braves and wondered among themselves whether the likes of Henry Aaron, Eddie Mathews, and Warren Spahn could conjure up another World Series appearance capable of keeping a midsized Milwaukee on the map. Milwaukee was a city known for its beer, with such labels as Schlitz and Miller High Life, while Madison was famous for its politics. The big state holiday lasted for two weeks every November, when folks of all ages, armed with shotguns, migrated to the north woods with dreams of eight-point trophies and a year's supply of venison.

Hubert Humphrey understood these people much more, he could claim, than his opponent. His home state boasted of many similarities in lifestyle and politics, and if Kennedy's Massachusetts possessed a rich history that dated back to the colonies and Revolutionary War, Wisconsin (and Minnesota) had witnessed the revolution of immigrants moving west—Poles and Germans and people from the Scandinavian countries settling in, plying their trades, and keeping their traditions on the fires. Yes, this should have been Humphrey territory.

Kennedy had declared himself the underdog at the beginning of his tour of Wisconsin, but this was really a matter of his trying to shout down reality. Humphrey owned the farm vote, but that made up only 15 percent of the overall count; his strong favor with labor was more problematic for Kennedy, cutting into his popularity in the larger urban areas in the southeastern corner of the state. But it still wasn't enough for Humphrey. Kennedy led in all other major demographics and looked to be in good shape with the religious vote, generally believed to be a weakness. According to a *Time* magazine breakdown of the candidates' strengths and weaknesses, "Kennedy might figure an automatic advantage with the 1,200,000 fellow Roman Catholics who make up 30% of the total population." Humphrey had been accurate in his assessment of the Kennedy blitz. Aside from his father and sister, Kennedy had every family member, including his wife, brothers and sisters, in-laws, and even his aging mother blanketing the state. The Kennedy strategy for Wisconsin had been simple: don't just win, win big. Kennedy, running unopposed, had already won the New Hampshire primary; a huge win in Wisconsin might create a snowball effect imposing enough to convince Humphrey to bow out.

But it wasn't going as planned. When the polls showed Humphrey faring better than expected, the candidates turned up the heat in their rhetoric. Humphrey accused Kennedy of being a weak liberal and trying to buy the vote; Joseph Kennedy's friendship with Joe McCarthy, and his support of Richard

Nixon, bubbled to the surface as well. Kennedy, in turn, asserted that his Senate voting record stacked up to Humphrey's at any time. Along with the tougher banter came accusations of dirty tricks. Word circulated that Jimmy Hoffa, the powerful yet controversial union leader despised by the Kennedys, was financially backing Humphrey. Worse yet, a vicious, anti-Catholic flyer made the rounds in heavily Catholic districts. The Humphrey camp cried foul; the flyer, it was hinted, might have originated in a Kennedy group trying to discredit Humphrey. A bitter exchange between the two candidates' campaigns ensued, led by Humphrey's angry denials of contributing in any measure to the anti-Catholicism.

April 5, election day, arrived with very little decided. Both candidates took cautiously optimistic stands, Kennedy that he would win, as Louis Harris, his private pollster, predicted, Humphrey that he would not be embarrassed by the final vote count. A last-minute rumor claimed that in a state where party crossover votes were permitted, Kennedy would enjoy a spike in support when Republican Catholics jumped party lines and voted for him. Kennedy was un-impressed. He was already tired of the emphasis placed on his religious be-liefs, and he knew it was only going to intensify in West Virginia, where only 5 percent of the population was Catholic.

The two opponents were in distinctively different frames of mind as they watched the returns come in. Voter turnout was the heaviest for a Wiscon-sin primary since World War II, and while Kennedy won, 476,024 to 366,753 (or 56.5 percent to 43.5 percent of the vote), it was not the blowout that Kennedy had been banking on. The mood in his hotel suite, where he and his team watched the numbers roll in, was far from festive. Jack Kennedy sulked; Bobby Kennedy glowered. Humphrey, they knew, would not be going away.

Humphrey, on the other hand, did everything but step out a victory dance in the hall of his Milwaukee hotel. This was a moral victory—an indication, he gushed, that he was being taken seriously as a candidate. He was about the only one to feel this way. His campaign staff and advisers, almost to the man, encouraged him to drop out of the race. They had run out of money, and the staff was in disarray. Humphrey might have come closer than expected in Wis-consin, but Kennedy had ultimately held serve.

Humphrey would not consider the advice. He had already paid his filing fee for the West Virginia primary, and he would borrow whatever seed money he needed to start up in the state. He had won four of Wisconsin's ten congres-sional districts, and he had narrowly lost one other; he now had delegate votes to use as bargaining chips at the Democratic National Convention in July. He would eventually see the wisdom in his advisers' words, but for the moment, he felt "a little intoxicated with the belief that [he] was an outside possibility."

Kennedy, meanwhile, prepared for another battle. When one of his sisters asked what the Wisconsin primary really meant, he was quick with a response. "It means," he stated, "that we have to do it all over again. We have to go through every [primary] and win every one of them—West Virginia and Maryland and Indiana and Oregon, all the way to the Convention."

■ ■ ■ ■ ■

In the West Virginia primary, the brawl between Humphrey and Kennedy escalated into an open war. Both flew to the state with a new sense of purpose, Humphrey to exploit what he considered to be strong advantages over his opponent, Kennedy to put the Catholicism issue to rest, once and for all. Both felt that these were keys to success in a state that neither understood.

Humphrey was $17,000 in the hole—a substantial amount in 1960—when he first set foot in West Virginia. He had borrowed start-up money from friends, which he complemented with money of his own, and while he was still struggling, he was encouraged by the knowledge that he wouldn't be needing nearly as much money to campaign in West Virginia as he had been forced to spend in Wisconsin.

Or so he thought. West Virginia had a practice of "slating" candidates in its elections—providing voters with a list of approved candidates whose names might be lost otherwise in the lengthy list of names running for various offices in the state. It cost money to gain a listing on the slate, and for someone like Humphrey, paying off each of the state's fifty-five counties was cost prohibitive, whereas Kennedy had no difficulty in seeing that his name appeared among the favored. Slating was lawful throughout the state, but it only added fuel to Humphrey's growing belief that the Kennedys were buying the primaries.

"Politics in West Virginia involves money—hot money, under-the-table money, open money," wrote Theodore White, who called the political environment "sordid"—a word also chosen by JFK biographer Michael O'Brien. "West Virginia had the most sordid election system of any state in the country," he wrote. "It practically invited corruption."

The Kennedys added to Humphrey's woes by seeing that the sources of some of his campaign financing dried up. Adlai Stevenson's New York supporters had been donating money to the Humphrey campaign; when the Kennedy campaign heard this, they placed calls to the Stevensonians. Continue to support Humphrey, they were told, and Stevenson stood no chance of being considered for secretary of state, if Kennedy won. The money stopped coming.

(When the primary was over and the candidates reported their campaign expenditures, Humphrey listed a meager $23,000 spent in West Virginia; Kennedy assigned more than that to his television budget alone. Kennedy officially claimed that he had spent $100,000, but observers found that figure pathetically low. One estimate placed the final figure at $1.5 million.)

Humphrey felt, and rightfully so, that his modest background and New Deal politics would work to his advantage in a state with a nation-high 15 percent unemployment rate, blue-collar environment, and down-to-earth politics; voters would appreciate his homespun manner and speeches spiced by an occasional "by golly" or "by cracky," the familiar colloquialisms that Humphrey would trot out, whether he was addressing his colleagues on the Senate floor or mixing with the locals at a spaghetti dinner in a town far removed from Washington, D.C. His heavy labor involvement would play well with the state's coal miners. Finally—and not to be underestimated—he was not what John Kennedy was: a Catholic.

He was well received wherever he went. On the night he addressed his followers following his defeat in Wisconsin, his naked exuberance gushing into every corner of the hall, Humphrey had winked at the press with a "I always told you fellows that politics could be fun, didn't I?"—and he had meant it. His "Happy Warrior" nickname stuck with him for good reason. And it was fun in the early weeks in West Virginia. "Every town we went to, it was great," he recalled, saying that he could not remember any time in his career when he was better received than during his early days of campaigning in West Virginia. "I said one tine that I felt like a conquering Caesar returning home. It was just magnificent! Crowds of people. Enthusiasm. Just marvelous."

Kennedy had arrived in the state in a sour and curdled mood. The Wisconsin primary left a hangover that was compounded when Lou Harris gave him the unwelcome news that he was losing his popularity in West Virginia. When Harris polled the state in January, he found Kennedy to be enjoying a commanding 70 percent to 30 percent lead over Humphrey. Harris took another poll and discovered that Humphrey had taken the lead. It didn't make sense. Kennedy had made a few brief jaunts to the state prior to his coming in for good, and nothing he had said or done should have caused his numbers to drop. Harris dug around for answers, and what he determined was disconcerting: the original poll had been conducted before the average citizen in West Virginia knew that Kennedy was Catholic. Influential Protestant ministers had sounded warnings that Kennedy, as president, might be more beholden to the Vatican than to the people he was supposed to be representing as chief executive. The thought disappointed, angered, and distracted Kennedy. He had allowed that he would have to address his Catholicism at some point during his campaigning in the state, but he had hoped that the main emphasis of his campaign stops would be on the differences between him and his opponent, not on an issue out of his control.

Kennedy complained, with plenty of evidence to support him, that the press was obsessed with the religion angle and ramped up its coverage accordingly. Kennedy would not accept that his Catholicism, rather than his positions on the economic issues faced by West Virginia, would determine the vote. "Is anyone going to tell me that I lost this primary 42 years ago on the day I was baptized?" he asked at a campaign stop in Fairmont.

He drove home the point in a number of his West Virginia stops. His aggressive stance challenged religious bigotry head-on. His religious faith, he stated, hadn't mattered when he had enlisted in the navy; it hadn't mattered in anything else he had done in his life. He wasn't running for the highest office in the land in order to push a religious agenda on the country of many faiths. Yes, he was a Catholic, but that had nothing to do with his politics. If elected, he would be taking an oath on a Bible; to ignore that oath would be both a sin and an impeachable offense. He did not say it openly, but his message couldn't be misunderstood: a vote against him because of his religious faith was a vote for bigotry.

In West Virginia, the Kennedys understood firsthand just how privileged their lives had been. They knew the word *poverty,* but they could not have begun to define it until they had wound their way down the Mountain State's back roads and encountered human beings living so desperately that *poverty,* as Jack and Bobby might have defined it, was a major improvement. Jack could not imagine a child who had never tasted milk, or who might take his government-provided lunch home to help feed his family. The men and women had Walker Evans faces, and those fortunate enough to be employed worked with the knowledge that their jobs could be temporary. In the mining towns, laborers were lowered deep into the earth, where, in artificial light and oppressive air, they toiled life-abbreviating and physically dangerous jobs—at a time when the demand for coal was dropping precipitously. The Kennedys struggled to accept that this was happening in the United States. Pierre Salinger, Kennedy's press secretary, observed the effect that this had on the candidate. "West Virginia brought a real transformation of John F. Kennedy as a person," he said.

The campaign grew bitter when the candidates became more acerbic in their attacks on each other. Neither, by nature, was a negative campaigner. In Wisconsin, Kennedy had been bruised by some of Humphrey's references to his wealth, but when supporters with damaging information about Humphrey approached him, he turned them down. "He didn't believe that he could improve his chances by tearing down the personal character of the opposition," observed Myer Feldman, a Kennedy administrative assistant in the Senate and an ombudsman specializing in digging up information on Nixon for JFK in 1960. Humphrey, likewise, refused to become involved in negative discussion about Kennedy's Catholicism. Both, however, were in chippy moods as the weeks passed in West Virginia. Kennedy was disgusted by Humphrey's continuous public complaints about his campaign spending. One particular statement galled him. Humphrey, upset by the state's slating practices, had lashed out in public: it was, he implied, a case of buying the vote. "I can't afford to run throughout this state with a black suitcase and a checkbook," he said, obviously referring to his well-funded opponent.

Although offended by such remarks, Kennedy held his temper, and even found a way to respond with some humor. His father, he joked, had wired him with very strict instructions. "Don't buy one vote more than necessary," Joseph Kennedy instructed his son. "I'll be damned if I'll pay for a landslide."

Humphrey and Kennedy traded barbs at stops throughout the state, each accusing the other of nasty campaigning. "I never expected it to become so bitter," Humphrey allowed. "This is just cheap, low-down, gutter politics." "I have never been subject to so much personal abuse," Kennedy groused.

The acrimony dipped to its nadir when Kennedy, acting on the advice of his father, invited Franklin D. Roosevelt Jr. to stump for him in the state—a decision that at first glance looked like brilliant strategy. President Roosevelt had offered badly needed assistance to the impoverished state, and he was revered in West Virginia more than three decades later; his son, who bore the same name and a remarkable resemblance to his father, by endorsing Kennedy, provided powerful ammunition to use against Humphrey. To strengthen the connection, the Kennedy campaign mailed fifty thousand letters, individually addressed and bearing the former president's Hyde Park, New York, postmark, to West Virginia homes. The letters, talking up Kennedy and asking for support, had been signed by FDR Jr. Humphrey liked to use his liberal, New Deal talking points in his campaign appearances, but he couldn't compete with this.

But it didn't stop there. In what had to be the most savage maneuver launched against Humphrey to that point in his career, FDR Jr. praised Kennedy's war heroism while making certain that the public understood that Humphrey had never fought for his country. An anonymous package from Minnesota had supplied the Kennedys with unsubstantiated documentation—letters supposedly exchanged between Humphrey and his draft board—painting Humphrey to be a draft dodger. Humphrey had always been extremely sensitive about the subject. He had attempted to enlist in the army and navy on three occasions during World War II but had been turned away for medical reasons.

Bobby Kennedy saw the war record issue as a means to inflict serious damage in a state with the highest percentage of Medal of Honor recipients in the United States. Roosevelt initially resisted Bobby's insistence that he speak of this in his campaign stops, but after about ten days of Bobby Kennedy's badgering, along with supporting phone calls from Lawrence O'Brien, one of JFK's top campaign officials, Roosevelt gave in. "He's a good Democrat," Roosevelt said of Humphrey, "but I don't know where he was in World War II."

An enraged Hubert Humphrey demanded an apology and retraction. His story, he insisted, was already on the record, and Roosevelt knew it. There was no estimating how much damage had been done. Franklin D. Roosevelt Jr. would apologize after the primary, as would John Kennedy, who apparently was unaware of the war-record plan and was appalled when he heard the news about it. Kennedy might have been bothered by this negative campaigning, but he did nothing to set the record straight. "Frank Roosevelt is here making his speeches, and I'm making mine," he told David Broder, then working as a young reporter for the *Washington Star*, when Broder questioned him about FDR Jr.'s remarks. Half a century later, in 2010, Broder still recoiled from Jack Kennedy's remark, describing it as "super-cool, almost cold-blooded."

Humphrey's upbeat disposition and forgiving nature failed him on this occasion. He accepted Jack Kennedy's explanation about not knowing about the subject prior to FDR Jr.'s speeches, but he never forgave Roosevelt or Bobby Kennedy. "It was a dishonest and politically unnecessary thing to do," he charged, incredulous and angry that the Kennedy campaign had stooped to such measures.

The animosity between Humphrey and Kennedy was such that both camps felt uneasy about a televised, hour-long debate scheduled for May 4. It might not have happened at all had Kennedy been more confident in his position in the primary. He had turned down Humphrey's challenge to a debate in Wisconsin, but in light of the final voting results in the Dairy State, he concluded that he might have been overconfident. He could improve his uncertain standing in West Virginia by doing well in a debate. Herb Waters and Lawrence O'Brien, representing Humphrey and Kennedy, respectively, met at the Charleston Press Club on more than one occasion and tried to negotiate an agreement for a peaceful debate. They finally agreed that the best approach would be to limit their attacks to the Republicans rather than each other.

Kennedy upended Humphrey in a debate that ran long in discussion of issues and short on fireworks between the candidates. Kennedy, whose debating acumen would be on national display a few months later during his historic televised confrontations with Richard Nixon, rocked Humphrey during an exchange about West Virginia's depressing unemployment and poverty conditions. Kennedy's heartfelt empathy based on all he had witnessed in his extensive traveling throughout the state came through convincingly in his talk about how the government had to be more active in helping the poor. Kennedy underscored his case with a prop: the contents of the government-issued food rations for the poor, a package that included powdered milk, cornmeal, and cans of beans. This, he said, would be improved if he were elected president. Humphrey could legitimately point to his many achievements in helping the poor, but Kennedy's "artful presentation," as he called it, left him looking like the weaker of the two candidates. "It was dramatic and effective," Humphrey conceded.

As in Wisconsin, Humphrey was well aware of the differences between him and his opponent, whether it involved their bankrolls, the size of their campaign staffs and volunteers, or even their campaign songs. Kennedy used a recording of Frank Sinatra's 1959 hit "High Hopes," rerecorded with new lyrics tailored for the Kennedy campaign. Humphrey had a song written especially for the primary, "I'm Gonna Vote for Hubert Humphrey," sung to the tune of "Give Me That Old Time Religion" and performed by Jimmy Wolford, a local country singer who accompanied Humphrey on the bus.

Humphrey faced the disparity between his and Kennedy's campaign styles one more time in the final days leading to the primary. Both wanted to present last-minute, televised events amounting to little more than summations of their primary pitches, Kennedy via a half-hour, documentary-style program, Humphrey through the more traditional telethon, in which he could connect more directly with voters. Humphrey nearly missed the opportunity: when he directed Herb Waters to write a check to pay for the television time, Waters informed him that it couldn't be done; they didn't have enough money. Humphrey, beaten down and exhausted by the rigors of the campaign, pitched a fit. Find the money, he ordered Waters, who broke down in tears over the situation. When he had calmed down, Humphrey placed numerous calls to potential donors. He added some of his own money—funds earmarked for his daughter's wedding the following week—and the telethon was on.

Unfortunately for Humphrey, the telethon was a disaster. He had spent so much time raising money and was so exhausted from the relentless campaigning, that he had no time to prepare prior to his arrival at the television studio. He stumbled on some questions and offered canned responses to others, none of it strengthening his standing with voters. The callers weren't screened for the nature of their questions, leaving Humphrey dealing with bizarre messages, such as a woman who kept repeating that he should leave the state.

Kennedy offered a masterful presentation, tightly assembled to provide biographical highlights and concise information on where he stood on key issues in West Virginia. By now, his compassion for the state's impoverished families and malnourished children was well established, exceeding anything Humphrey could say; as exit polls at voting locations showed, the profoundly moving segment in Kennedy's program moved some voters to change their vote.

The tight race originally projected never materialized. Humphrey had seen his lead in the polls dwindle over the weeks to nothing, but he still led on the drizzly morning when West Virginians headed to the polls. In the end, Kennedy had won the day. Humphrey watched the tabulation of the votes on the television in his Charleston hotel room, while Kennedy, who had returned to Massachusetts earlier in the day, leaving his Charleston headquarters in the charge of his brother, enjoyed the results in the comfort of his home. The final count was lopsided. Kennedy won, 61 percent to 39 percent, with support coming from all over the state; he won forty-eight of West Virginia's fifty-five counties.

For Humphrey, one important question needed to be considered. There was no disagreement about whether Humphrey could defeat Kennedy; it was just a matter of *when* Humphrey should drop out of the race. West Virginia delegates were not obligated to follow the primary results, and Humphrey, running unopposed, had taken the District of Columbia primary. James Rowe argued that if Humphrey dragged his feet in leaving the race, he might be able to broker his meager delegate count into some influence at the Los Angeles convention. Joseph Rauh disagreed. Remaining in the race, he argued, would reinforce the charge, aimed at Humphrey in Wisconsin and West Virginia, that his candidacy was not serious, that he was merely a stalking horse for Lyndon Johnson or Stuart Symington. Humphrey listened to the arguments and conferred with his wife. Muriel Humphrey preferred that he drop out and work at being reelected in the Minnesota senatorial race.

Humphrey wondered how a quick defeat in 1960 might affect his presidential ambitions in the future. He concluded, while he watched the West Virginia results coming in, that he would probably have to serve as vice president before standing any chance of winning the presidency. He simply did not have the money or national reputation to defeat some of the Democratic Party's better-known names. The vice presidency, however, was a long way in the future—1968, at the earliest—if Kennedy won the election and was reelected

in 1964. He had already told JFK, in no uncertain terms, that he was not interested in being Kennedy's running mate.

After reviewing his options, he reached what he felt was his only conclusion: he visited his headquarters and announced to supporters gathered there
that he was suspending his candidacy. The next day, he was back on the floor
of the Senate.

6 Hubert Humphrey believed that learning from failure was a crucial com-
ponent of success. His first presidential bid had taught him much about
organizing and financing a campaign, both weaknesses in the primaries, and
he promised himself that he would not make the same mistakes when the time
came to run again.

Humphrey won his reelection to the Senate six months after his West Virginia primary defeat to Kennedy, who, on the same day, emerged victorious in
his bid for the presidency against Richard Nixon. Kennedy had chosen Texas
senator Lyndon Johnson as his running mate—a decision that helped him secure the South in a very close general election. Humphrey, expecting Kennedy
to win, was already training his sights on a 1968 presidential run. In the meantime, he settled into his role as the Senate's Democratic whip.

His plans changed abruptly when Kennedy was assassinated on November
22, 1963. At the time of his death, Kennedy had been gearing up for his reelection campaign the following year. His replacement, Lyndon Johnson, faced
the extremely difficult challenge of soothing a nation in mourning, continuing
the programs of a popular president, assembling his own reelection staff, and
running for office in a way that established his own identity while dimming
the notion that he was a surrogate. At some point—probably at the Democratic
National Convention—he would have to announce his choice of running mate.

Humphrey jumped at the opportunity to let Johnson know that he was interested in the job. He spoke to a friend about his interest at JFK's funeral, and
over the ensuing weeks, he mined the opinions of his friends and political colleagues. He took nothing for granted. He still had painful memories of his push
to become Adlai Stevenson's running mate in 1956. At the time, he wasn't sure
about Stevenson's ability to defeat the incumbent, Dwight D. Eisenhower, in
the future. After a long conference with Stevenson, he concluded that he was
going to be offered the job, and he jabbered to all and sundry that he would
be the vice-presidential candidate, only to learn otherwise at the convention,
when Stevenson decided to let the delegates decide the candidate. The delegates barely gave Humphrey serious consideration. Estes Kefauver was se-

lected, and Humphrey suffered great humiliation. It was a mistake he wouldn't be repeating with Johnson—at least not as flagrantly.

Some of Humphrey's friends voiced concern about the wisdom of Humphrey's becoming a vice president under Johnson. The president could be temperamental and difficult; he micromanaged everything. John Nance Garner, who served as thirty-second vice president under Franklin D. Roosevelt, had famously said that the vice presidency wasn't worth a bucket of warm shit—or "spit," as the cleaned-up quotation went—and there was no denying that it was an underappreciated position. When asked to list Nixon's contributions as his vice president, Eisenhower had paused, then joked, "Give me a minute and I'll think of one." Johnson had relinquished his powerful position of Senate majority leader to serve as Kennedy's vice president, and the experience left him miserable and depressed. The Kennedys—particularly Bobby—had treated him with thinly disguised disdain, and he had often been left out of the loop in important decisions. Johnson, one of the most forceful personalities in Washington, D.C., could make Humphrey just as miserable. LBJ, Humphrey was warned, would "cut his balls off."

Humphrey assured his confidants that he was aware of all this, that he felt confident in his abilities to serve in a meaningful way. He believed that his connections with labor, the midwestern states, and the liberals in the northeastern states could be supplemental strengths in Johnson's presidential campaign. He and Johnson had worked well together in the past, and he could, he intimated, use their working relationship to implement change in the ways in which the vice presidents operated. "You'll be surprised," he told a friend. "My vice presidency is going to be more than just four years of mothballs and doldrums."

Humphrey based his self-assurance on his recent work with Johnson on historic civil rights legislation—a sweeping new law that all but guaranteed Johnson's presidential legacy. John Kennedy had introduced comprehensive civil rights legislation in the House shortly before his assassination, and Lyndon Johnson had vowed to continue the quest. The bill passed in the House on February 10, 1964, by a 290 to 130 vote. The real test would be in the Senate. Johnson believed he might be able to rustle up a majority vote in the Senate—public sentiment, on high alert in the wake of the civil rights struggles in the South over the past several years, seemed to support a change—but bringing the bill to that vote was going to be next to impossible. The Southern senators were certain to filibuster, and no civil rights filibuster in U.S. history had ended in cloture. Johnson had his doubts. He had to maintain a distance from day-to-day activities, and Mike Mansfield, the Senate majority leader, wanted nothing to do with leading this particular charge. Instead, he decided that Hubert

Humphrey was the right man for the job. As majority whip, Humphrey had worked extensively with his colleagues on diverse legislation. He was effective, persuasive, well liked by both parties, and ambitious enough to understand the importance of successful civil rights legislation to his résumé.

Humphrey seized the opportunity. Nearly sixteen years had passed since he had taken the podium at the 1948 Democratic National Convention in Philadelphia and lit a charge into the dormant discussion about civil rights legislation. Nothing much had happened since that night. A noteworthy law had been passed here and there, and the courts had handed down a few significant decisions—enough for opponents of civil rights legislation to declare that progress, slow as it was, was being made, that you didn't overturn old laws and behavior overnight, that more patience was required. There would be change but only in due time.

Humphrey knew his history, and he knew about time—and not just the time that had passed since his civil rights speech at the convention. A Constitutional amendment had abolished slavery on January 31, 1865—slightly more than ninety-nine years ago—and the Fourteenth Amendment had passed a few years later, in 1868, followed by the Fifteenth Amendment in 1869. These amendments should have ended it, but there were always loopholes, always ways to allow states to avoid enforcing them. And Humphrey needed no reminders of how many times, over the course of all those years, further legislation had either fallen by the wayside before passing or had been ignored when it was passed into law. The lynchings, murders, beatings, and intimidations continued as always, and the evidence of open, institutionalized racism could be found everywhere, at lunch counters, in public transportation, and in shacks erected within walking distance of fine white dwellings. Humphrey had recently thumbed through two travel guidebooks and learned that in some Southern hotels it was easier to register a pet than find a room for an African American. In Columbus, Georgia, six hotels and motels allowed dogs in rooms, but none allowed African Americans. In Charleston, South Carolina, ten establishments permitted dogs but would not permit blacks. No, there would be no more patience. It was time to close the loopholes and end the foot-dragging.

Johnson called Humphrey in for a talk before the debating began. Using reverse psychology, which Humphrey quickly recognized, Johnson predicted defeat. Reaching cloture on the filibuster, he chided Humphrey, was going to demand around-the-clock vigilance and commitment. Liberal senators paid lip service to their favorite causes, but they couldn't be counted on to back up their talk with the tough work required.

"You have this great opportunity now, Hubert, but you liberals will never deliver," Johnson said. "You don't know the rules of the Senate and your liberal friends will be off making speeches when they ought to be present. You've got a great opportunity here but I'm afraid it's going to fall between the boards. . . . No, your bomb-throwing friends will be out making speeches to the already-converted—for a fee."

The motivational tactics worked. Humphrey, who would later confess that he might have been angry with Johnson if he hadn't been correct in his assessment, resolved to prove him wrong. He calculated the votes needed and saw the task before him. The Democrats had fifty-nine senators, but eighteen were Southern Dixiecrats unmovable in their opposition to the bill. Add two Republicans—Texas senator John Tower and Arizona senator Barry Goldwater—to the opposition and Humphrey needed to convince sixty-six of the remaining eighty senators into voting to end a filibuster. Even if the non-Southern Democrats voted as a bloc, Humphrey would have to persuade twenty-five Republicans into crossing party lines. During their meeting, Johnson had advised Humphrey that Minority Leader Everett Dirksen was the key to gaining the necessary Republican support. Touch base with Dirksen—often—Johnson suggested; massage his ego, appeal to him as an influential leader, talk him up in the press, speak to him as a confidant, do whatever was needed to gain his trust and support.

Humphrey organized. He wanted to know before the filibuster where his colleagues stood. Johnson had made it known that he had no intention of compromising on a bill that had evolved into a proposed law more rigid and detailed than Kennedy's; it was going to be all or nothing. The Senate, a haven for compromise, would demand compromise. For any hope of success, Humphrey had to know the major points of contention before the two sides came out swinging. He spoke extensively with Minority Whip Thomas Kuchel, Dirksen's appointed Republican floor leader for the bill. He appointed seven "captains" in charge of debating the bill's seven main titles. He drew up schedules to assure that there would always be a quorum, day and night. He created a daily newsletter to keep all interested parties, including the press, up to date on the bill's progress.

Senator Richard Russell, the sixty-six-year-old segregationist from Georgia, led the filibuster. A personal friend and occasional political foe of Lyndon Johnson, Russell was as organized, dedicated, and popular on both sides of the aisle as Humphrey. He came prepared to debate the constitutionality of the bill, point by point, for as long as it took to defeat it. He understood the stakes: lose the filibuster and the game was over. He had men willing to take the debate into their old age, so it all came down to endurance.

Humphrey insisted on congeniality—not an easy accomplishment as the filibuster stretched from weeks to months, and frustration mounted. "I made up my mind early that I would keep my patience," for a cloture vote, he would recall. "I would not lose my temper and that if I could do nothing else, I would try to preserve a reasonable degree of good nature and fair play in the Senate."

Ironically, Humphrey did not fear angry or disrespectful retorts from his Southern opponents; they were known for their patience and decorum. The liberals, however, were notorious for their contentious behavior—with other liberals. One of Russell's strategies was to extend the filibuster until the bill's proponents grew impatient and began to argue among themselves. Humphrey kept Johnson's observation in mind. While wooing uncommitted colleagues for a cloture vote, he pushed for continual unity among those already in his stable. The newsletter helped. All sides were presented in the daily reports.

Humphrey followed LBJ's advice and buttered up Dirksen at every opportunity. He spoke of Dirksen's sense of duty, of his commitment to what was right, regardless of party affiliation. Despite Johnson's statements against compromise, he encouraged Dirksen to submit his alternatives to the bill, as written, never promising to change but hinting that it might be possible. Dirksen objected to two provisions in the bill: the article calling for equal access to public accommodations, and the one demanding equal opportunity for employment. Humphrey asked Dirksen to submit his ideas for compromise. Dirksen stalled.

"I continued to make every effort to involve him," Humphrey remembered. "I was his Jiminy Cricket, visiting with him on the floor, in the cloakroom, in the corridors and on the elevators. I constantly encouraged him to take a more prominent role, asked him what changes he wanted to propose, urged him to call meetings to discuss his changes."

As the weeks passed, the Republican leadership found themselves hamstrung. Their original strategy of stretching out the filibuster until frustrated Democrats wanted it to end and fought among themselves backfired. Uncommitted, open-minded Republicans switched, one by one, to the pro–civil rights side. Humphrey, although pleased with this development, held back on any celebratory words. This legislation was too important to take anything for granted. He needed to be certain.

Religious groups reinforced the support. A nondenominational group of priests, nuns, ministers, and rabbis, a constant presence at the Senate gallery, wrote letters to the senators, placed calls to their offices, and held prayer vigils, to great effect. Russell complained that these activists hardly represented all of their congregations' memberships, but it was a hollow cry. The sight of religious figures on television, ignoring the differences in their faiths in favor of preaching the equality of all people, regardless of color, packed a wallop that could not be easily avoided. "It made all the difference in the world," Joseph Rauh remarked.

Dirksen remained uncommitted, though the midwestern states were mostly in favor of killing the filibuster. If cloture wasn't a sure thing, it was close. Russell and the more rigid Southern senators, still arguing the constitutional points in the wording of the bill, showed signs that they were willing to dump their no-compromise position. It was now boiling down to a matter of saving face. The Southern senators still had to answer to their constituents, who weren't interested in excuses. Dirksen struggled to understand how the Justice Department could interfere with the hiring practices of private businesses or with hotels' accommodations policies. Dirksen, Humphrey, Attorney General Robert Kennedy, Mike Mansfield, and others chewed over these points until they reached a compromise: the states would be allowed to exercise the enforcement of these issues until it became clear that the states were not acting by the law's intentions; at that point, the Justice Department would intervene.

Dirksen, over Russell's objections, was ready to stand behind the bill, and a number of senators fell in behind him. Humphrey, the first to engineer cloture in a civil rights filibuster, stood back while Dirksen basked in the credit for his role of passing historic legislation. On June 10, the filibuster ended with a seventy-one to twenty-nine vote; nine days later, the bill was adopted by a seventy-three to twenty-seven vote.

Johnson received the lion's share of the credit for the passing of the law, and he was happy to receive it. Such legislation was a cornerstone to a political legacy. Humphrey, too, glowed in the aftermath of the passing of the Civil Rights Act of 1964. His vision, expounded in 1948, had come to pass. He was now back on the national stage, if not front and center, at least close enough for people to notice him. In working so closely with Johnson, he had positioned himself at the front of the line when the time arrived for Johnson to select a vice-presidential candidate in his run for reelection. This was what Humphrey was hoping for, and he couldn't have been more satisfied.

■ ■ ■ ■ ■

Humphrey was by no means Johnson's sole choice for the vice presidency. A running gag in Washington, D.C., was that Johnson would have preferred to be his own vice president—he knew and could trust himself—but since he had to choose someone, he had a wealth of qualified candidates. His soundings included conversations with advisers, members of both bodies of Congress, labor leaders, the press, and potential candidates themselves; he followed the tradition of searching for a candidate to fill out the presidential ticket for the forthcoming election. He liked Mike Mansfield, his replacement as Senate majority leader, but Mansfield rejected him as soon as he brought it up. Orville Freeman briefly crossed Johnson's mind. Johnson deemed Adlai Stevenson, another highly qualified candidate, to be too old to serve for two full terms. Secretary of Defense Robert McNamara, another Johnson favorite, leaned toward the Republican Party. Bobby Kennedy, a favorite in the public opinion polls, wanted the job and was thought to be a leading candidate for it, and while he didn't initially eliminate Kennedy as a candidate, Johnson's rocky past with the attorney general and his strong desire to escape the Kennedy influences on his presidency made Bobby more of a problem than a solution. Sargent Shriver, head of the Peace Corps and someone Johnson liked and trusted, might have fulfilled some of LBJ's advisers' recommendation that he choose a Catholic, but Shriver was Bobby Kennedy's brother-in-law and, as Richard Goodwin remembered, "Johnson had no intention of putting Bobby Kennedy, or any Kennedy, or any relative of any Kennedy on the ticket." Eugene McCarthy, junior senator from Minnesota, another Catholic, and an up-and-comer on the national scene, intrigued Johnson. McCarthy presented a problem of some substance: could Johnson overstep Humphrey and offer the vice presidency to a senator (and Humphrey protégé) from the same state?

McCarthy was flattered that the president would consider him. It had never crossed his mind that he might be a candidate, and after talking to Johnson about it, he found himself, quite unpredictably, wanting the job. He had a few things favoring him. His track record in the Senate, although nowhere near as impressive as Humphrey's, was a good moderate to liberal record, he had given a memorable nominating speech for Adlai Stevenson at the 1960 Democratic Convention, and his wife, Abigail, was a friend of Lady Bird Johnson. Like so many others, McCarthy had just assumed that Humphrey was going to get the nod, but if Johnson was serious about considering him, he would go along with it and see how the selection process played out.

Johnson took his time in vetting the possibilities, and when he had concluded his search, three candidates were still in the public eye: Humphrey, McCarthy, and Kennedy. Johnson eliminated Kennedy by publicly declaring that no one in his cabinet would be considered for the vice presidency. Kennedy was not pleased. Johnson's decision was aimed at singling him out, and their final meeting involving his candidacy had gone poorly. A dejected Bobby Kennedy left the meeting with the feeling that there was nothing left for him in Washington, D.C.—at least not for the time being. Johnson took great pleasure in reenacting their conversation, which included a devastating imitation of RFK's shock at getting the news, for friends and aides. In a city like Washington, which seemed to sustain itself on gossip, innuendo, leaks to the press, and titillating news stories, word of Johnson's behavior was bound to make the rounds. When Kennedy heard about Johnson's cruel skit about their meeting, he angrily confronted Johnson. Their well-documented feud hit a new low.

Kennedy had company in his displeasure over the way Johnson was handling the naming of his running mate. Eugene McCarthy also felt as if he was being toyed with by the president. McCarthy's objection was not to Johnson's game itself—McCarthy enjoyed pulling one off on someone as much as the next guy—but instead to the boorish and transparent nature of the game, the sheer unattractiveness of it, not unlike the president's skinny-dipping parties in the White House pool and his invitations to dignitaries to shoot, kill, and mount the heads of animals on his Texas ranch—two activities that LBJ seemed to enjoy to no end. (Although invited to participate in both of these activities, McCarthy declined, having neither the interest nor patience for them.) What rankled McCarthy was the lack of communication. As the days to the convention approached, McCarthy reasoned that Johnson was going to choose Humphrey, and that the president was simply using him to build interest and suspense in a convention that was offering very little of either. If this was the case, McCarthy still had no problem with it. He did, however, want to be let in on the plan. The press was still bandying his name around as a candidate, and McCarthy didn't want any last-minute embarrassments. The White House, however, refused to return his calls. "When we got to Atlantic City," McCarthy recalled, "it got down to about the day before and I said, 'Call again. I don't want to look silly. Let us know,' because we were reliable, we could play their game."

McCarthy ended the charade a day before the Democratic National Convention commenced in Atlantic City. McCarthy sent the White House a telegram, withdrawing his name from consideration and saying that Humphrey was the best candidate, and read the telegram to reporters before Johnson had the opportunity to respond. When the president eventually reached McCarthy by phone, he made a point of telling the senator that he had settled on Humphrey before he read the telegram. McCarthy, running for reelection to the Senate, didn't flinch. The publicity circulating around his candidacy for the vice presidency had benefited him.

Humphrey figured he had the nomination locked up. Johnson had put him through the paces over weeks heading up to the convention, and Humphrey felt he had passed every test. On Johnson's orders, James Rowe had visited

Humphrey and subjected him to a grueling interview. Rowe's queries, highly personal and direct, were designed to ascertain that Humphrey had no secrets in his background that the news media would unearth after Johnson named Humphrey his running mate. What was the state of Humphrey's financial affairs? To whom did he owe money and under what circumstances? Was there anything in his background, such as a mistress or past extramarital affair, that might embarrass the president or jeopardize Humphrey's candidacy? Humphrey protested some of the questions. He had been in public service long enough, he told Rowe, that he couldn't possibly have any secrets. Rowe assured him that the questions were a formality, that they were the type of questions the Republicans would be asking of any vice-presidential candidate.

Over recent months, Humphrey had consciously avoided any discussion about the vice presidency with Johnson; they spoke often, but the civil rights voting bill dominated their conversations. Humphrey's success at breaking the filibuster proved his acumen in working with both parties on controversial, high-stakes legislation. This might have been enough to convince Johnson that Humphrey was a good choice for vice president, but Humphrey saw that Johnson was kept informed of anything pertinent to the discussion.

The Sunday before the opening of the convention, Hubert Humphrey and Eugene McCarthy appeared separately on *Meet the Press*. Both acquitted themselves well. Although not standoffish in his appraisals of the vice presidency and his candidacy for the office, McCarthy spoke of the "matter of obligation, apart from any personal feelings" that he faced as a serious candidate for the vice presidency. This was pure McCarthy: smooth, almost noncommittal, the good soldier awaiting orders. He believed he was qualified and was ready to answer the president's call, but he would not force Johnson's hand. In fact, he said, he had not spoken to Johnson about the vice presidency.

Humphrey's half hour came after McCarthy's, and Humphrey, in contrast to McCarthy, openly campaigned for the job. He had spoken to Johnson about the vice presidency on two occasions, but he, like McCarthy, did not want the president to feel pressured in making his decision. Johnson knew Humphrey well; he was aware of his work in the Senate, his midwestern background, and his liberal politics. With the Atlantic City convention directly ahead, Humphrey made his final pitch, knowing that Johnson would be watching—and, indeed, he was: immediately after the program Johnson called both candidates to congratulate them on their appearances.

The convention opened without an announcement from Johnson. *Time* predicted that the nod would go to Humphrey, but the magazine also noted that another candidate, such as Mike Mansfield, might still be under consideration. "The mounting suspense—the vice-presidential choice—was just the sort of emotion that Lyndon Johnson likes to provoke," *Time* noted. Johnson had asked the major television and radio broadcasting companies to hold open three minutes immediately following his nomination; the companies presumed that Johnson would make his vice-presidential announcement at that time. "By just keeping mum until then," *Time* concluded, "he will have succeeded also in keeping the spotlight on himself; he enjoys that sort of thing immensely."

That was to be on Wednesday of convention week. McCarthy lost his patience between his *Meet the Press* appearance on Sunday and the following Tuesday. Humphrey, doing his best to keep Johnson's unpredictability in perspective, heard again from James Rowe on Tuesday. The president had reached a decision: Humphrey would be his running mate. The news, however, came with all kinds of attachments. Johnson still wanted to maintain the air of uncertainty surrounding his choice, so Humphrey was sworn to secrecy and could tell no one, not even his wife, of LBJ's final decision; if word leaked out, the deal was off. Humphrey protested—"This is ridiculous: a man can't even tell his own wife"—and he was eventually allowed to give Muriel the news. Rowe had brought along a copy of the morning's *Washington Post,* in which appeared an article that Johnson demanded Humphrey read. During his interview with the *Post* reporter, Johnson explained what he expected from his vice president. Humphrey skimmed the article while Rowe summarized it, point by point. The vice president, Johnson asserted, was allowed to disagree with him until he had reached a decision; once the president had made up his mind, the vice president was expected to totally support him. Humphrey consented to this provision, though he would later regret it. Finally, Humphrey was to fly to Washington, D.C., that evening for a private, eleventh-hour conference with Johnson. Humphrey agreed, and his eventful day seemed to be over.

But there was more. Walter Jenkins, a Johnson White House aide, called with the news that the airport in Washington was fogged in; Humphrey and his group would have to fly the next day. Jenkins nixed the suggestion that the group drive to the capital—Washington was only a couple hours away—stating that the president, for reasons he was keeping to himself, insisted that they fly. Humphrey, as agitated as Rowe had ever seen him, let everyone in the room know just how angry he was about the tomfoolery connected to LBJ's secrecy. "Hubert," Rowe said after Humphrey's diatribe, "you'll be a candidate for vice president and we can both tell Johnson he's a shit."

But there was still more. The next morning, while eating breakfast before his flight to Washington, Humphrey learned that another senator, Thomas Dodd of Connecticut, would be a passenger on the same flight. Johnson had summoned him to the White House as well. Humphrey boiled over. Was Dodd being considered? he fumed. Rowe, who must have been as exasperated by Johnson as anyone, explained that Dodd was just a decoy, a part of the ruse: with Eugene McCarthy no longer part of the discussion, Johnson needed a new face to keep the press guessing. Dodd was that face.

Johnson's micromanagement of the convention had everyone on edge—and should have been a strong hint to Humphrey about what lay in store for him as vice president. When Humphrey and the rest arrived in Washington, they were greeted at the airport by Jack Valenti, who announced yet another delay. Lady Bird Johnson was arriving at the convention center in Atlantic City, and the president wanted to ensure that the national news coverage would focus on her rather than Humphrey and Dodd at the White House. Valenti took Humphrey and Dodd on a meandering, hour-long drive through the city, eventually stopping the limousine at the White House. The men waited in the car until Johnson sent for Dodd. An exhausted Hubert Humphrey fell asleep in the limo.

He was awakened by a knock on the window. The president was ready to see him. The two met in the Cabinet Room, and Johnson came right to the point: "Hubert, do you want to be Vice President?" After Humphrey answered in the affirmative, Johnson offered up a rambling dissertation about the office, much of it repeating what Humphrey had read in the *Post* interview, some depicting the position in such negative terms that one would have wondered who in his or her right mind would ever consider it. Taking the job, Johnson said, would damage their friendship; the new relationship, he declared, would be "like a marriage with no chance of divorce." There could be no question of his fealty, no question of whether he had Humphrey's support when times got tough. Humphrey had known Johnson long enough to know the answers the president was seeking, and in the unlikely event that Johnson had any doubts about Humphrey prior to the meeting, he knew, after listening to Humphrey, that he had his vice-presidential candidate.

The rest was formality, from Johnson's announcing Humphrey as his running mate at the convention to a general election that found Johnson pasting Barry Goldwater by an unprecedented margin. Humphrey's ascendancy continued.

7 The marriage was rocky from the beginning, causing one of Humphrey's closest allies to remark that "Hubert's was probably the shortest presidential–vice presidential honeymoon on record." Humphrey took the oath of office on January 20, 1965. He had barely had time to hang pictures in his

office and arrange his desk to his satisfaction when he faced his first crisis as vice president.

On February 7, in the central highlands of South Vietnam, the Vietcong launched a mortar attack on an American barracks in Pleiku, killing eight Americans (a ninth would die later) and wounding more than one hundred others. Twenty U.S. aircraft were destroyed or heavily damaged. The middle-of-the-night attack, the first to date on a specifically American target, indicated a new, bold, aggressive approach to the U.S. presence in Vietnam. Special Assistant for National Security Affairs McGeorge Bundy, already in Saigon for consultations with top army brass, rushed to Pleiku the next day. He visited the injured troops. His immediate reaction to the attack had been to recommend immediate and powerful retribution by bombing key North Vietnamese targets, which would send an unmistakable message to the leadership about the consequences of such actions. Seeing the wounded Americans affected him deeply and strengthened his resolve. Ambassador Maxwell Taylor backed his recommended course of action.

Back in the States, Johnson called a meeting of the National Security Council. Humphrey would have attended a meeting of this nature, but he was out of town; Senator Mike Mansfield replaced him. Also in attendance were Secretary of Defense Robert McNamara, his assistant Cyrus Vance, Assistant Secretary of State George Ball, and others. From the onset, Johnson indicted that he supported Bundy's recommendations, and most at the meeting agreed. Mansfield stood alone in opposition to the bombing. He feared that bombing North Vietnam, even if in this case it was to be a onetime response, signaled a dangerous escalation to a war that to this point the United States and South Vietnam, for all their superior firepower, had been unable to win. The bombing, Mansfield suggested, might bring the estranged Soviet Union and China closer together, and a unification of those two powerhouse Communist countries was the last thing that anyone wanted. Further, Soviet premier Aleksei Kosygin was presently in Hanoi, which made the timing of the reprisal bombings look bad. Perhaps something could be accomplished through negotiation.

Johnson listened to his old friend and ally, but he had already made up his mind. American troops would target three North Vietnamese locations while the South Vietnam air force hit another. The attacks would occur as soon as the details were worked out. Johnson, concerned about the safety of American women and children in Saigon and other locations throughout South Vietnam, ordered their immediate evacuation. The United States, the president told those seated at the table around him, had been holding the peace for too long. "They are killing our men while they sleep in the night," he said. "I can't ask our

American soldiers out there to continue to fight with one hand tied behind their backs."

Heavy fog reduced the retaliatory strikes from four to two, one by the United States and one by the South Vietnamese. Johnson's hopes that these strikes might back the North Vietnamese down were unfounded. On February 10, just three days after the Pleiku attack, the Vietcong staged another attack on an American military installation, this one an enlisted men's barracks in coastal Qui Nhon. Twenty-three American and seven Vietnamese soldiers lost their lives, and an additional twenty-one Americans were wounded. To Johnson, this indicated a new enemy commitment to violence; he was now prepared to meet force with force. He called another National Security Council meeting, and this time Humphrey was present.

Humphrey's position on affairs in Southeast Asia had been consistent over the years, dating back to his first term in the Senate. He subscribed to the popular theory that the fall of one country would lead to the fall of others until, like dominos, they had all toppled and were under Communist control. His stance on Communism stretched back to his days as mayor of Minneapolis and his role in cofounding the liberal yet decisively anti-Communist Americans for Democratic Action, and he had a long history of being very vocal, even by his standards, about what he felt were the destructive forces of Communism in America. His anti-Red stance, however, had its limitations. One did not race recklessly into battle. This had been Senator Joseph McCarthy's problem: his bullying and overheated rhetoric had ultimately sabotaged his mission. One had to enter warfare, whether on the floor of the Senate or in the fields of foreign countries, with a measure of reason.

He held strong opinions about Pleiku and the events in the aftermath of the attack. While he did not oppose a retaliation for the Vietcong aggression, he opposed the bombing in North Vietnam while Kosygin was in the country. He discussed his feelings with Robert McNamara and Dean Rusk, and they seemed to support his position that the United States hold off on the bombing until the Soviet leader was out of the country. They said nothing, however, at the National Security Council meeting. Humphrey had the support of George Ball, Johnson's foil on all things Vietnam, and Ambassador Llewellyn Thompson, but all the others at the meeting favored another strong answer to this latest attack. Johnson was furious with Humphrey: the vice president, less than a month in office, had already reneged on his promise to support the president once he had made up his mind on a policy or action.

Humphrey failed to register the point. He mistakenly thought Johnson was soliciting ideas and solutions, and he further felt that his and Johnson's long history in the Senate allowed him to speak directly and frankly with him. Johnson, of course, disagreed. He was the president and commander in chief, and the Gulf of Tonkin resolution gave him extraordinary authority in matters pertaining to the Vietnam War. He had already reached a decision based on extensive consultation with civilian and military advisors on the way the United States should answer the Pleiku and Qui Nhon attacks. What Humphrey failed to grasp was what the others seated around him already knew: when Johnson asked your view, it was always in your best interests to give him the answer he was looking for.

Humphrey compounded his problems with Johnson a few days later, on February 15, when he submitted a detailed memo to the president, in which he addressed his own feelings about Vietnam and the policies the United States might employ in the future. At the beginning of the memo, before offering his observations and advice, Humphrey noted his and Johnson's new professional relationship, and he approached the president with proper humility. He recognized the agreement they had entered into when Johnson approached him about being his vice president, and he would continue to be loyal and supportive. He had no interest in second-guessing Johnson or his advisers, and he acknowledged that he was not an authority on Vietnam.

What followed—a presentation stated in fifteen points—was bound to make Johnson unhappy, but Humphrey, true to his long history of speaking his mind, however controversial the topic or difficult the consequence of addressing it, plowed ahead, the wording of his text indicating that he recognized the likelihood of his upsetting the president. Humphrey opened by reminding Johnson that in the general presidential election of only a few months ago, Goldwater had been the one pushing for a military solution to Vietnam through escalation of the war, which only led to a "trigger-happy bomber image" that voters rejected. The Democrats, Humphrey argued, "never stood for military solutions alone," which might not have worked in Vietnam in any event. "We have always stressed the political, economic, and social dimensions," Humphrey wrote.

This was an important point, and Humphrey constructed his argument around it. Americans, he observed, strongly backed war efforts if they believed in the reasons behind the U.S. involvement in the military action. This had been the case in World War I, World War II, and, to some extent, Korea. The conflict in Korea lost public support when Americans quit believing that involvement in the country was in the national interest. The same held true in Vietnam: "We have not succeeded in making this national interest interesting enough at home or abroad to generate support." It might have helped, he proposed, if the public felt better about South Vietnam. The country's corrupt government, along with its inability to train an army capable of defending the country, undermined that confidence. "People can't understand why we would run grave risks to support a country which is unable to put its own house in order," Humphrey concluded.

Humphrey worried that the Vietnam War was nudging the United States closer to a war with China. Americans had already demonstrated a distaste for such a war a dozen years earlier in Korea, and there was no reason to suspect this attitude had changed. The Cold War had been thawing ever so slowly over the past few years, but that could change if the Soviet Union felt compelled to back China for any reason. The Soviet Union certainly wouldn't stand by while the United States chose to use the nuclear option against China.

Humphrey concluded his memo with points addressing the future— predictions that in retrospect look downright prophetic. He warned Johnson of the consequences that might rise from escalating the U.S. involvement in the war—problems that might affect the president's prized domestic policies. "We now risk creating the impression that we are the prisoner of events in Vietnam," Humphrey asserted. "This blurs the Administration's leadership role and has spillover effects across the board. It also helps erode confidence and credibility in our polices." In one of his memo's more prescient statements, Humphrey noted that the political problems arising as a result of escalation were from "new and different sources" typically friendly to the Democratic Party—"Democratic liberals, independents, [and] labor."

Humphrey was too shrewd a politician to dump on a president known for his sensitivity to criticism. He softened his blows by praising Johnson's "political ingenuity" and stating that he was quite capable of applying his considerable talents to resolving the war in a way that didn't include escalation; this was his opportunity to extend "his unrivaled talents as a politician" to an international stage. It would benefit the world, the United States, and Johnson's legacy.

Humphrey offered one final cautionary note—a warning given with only a few months of the future in mind, but which, as time would show, applied to years in the future: "If, on the other hand, we find ourselves leading from frustration to escalation and end up short of a war with China but embroiled deeper in fighting in Vietnam over the next few months, political opposition will steadily mount."

The memo ended as it began, with Humphrey vowing to support Johnson whatever his final decision; the memo, he stated, simply represented his feelings.

As time would prove, Humphrey was spot-on in his memo, but its timing was poor. He was proposing a slow, measured, peaceful approach to handling the Vietnam War at a time when the president and almost every one of his advisers were looking at an escalation of the U.S. presence in the country. Any action short of the deployment of nuclear weapons appeared to be on the table; a large-scale ground war seemed to be a certainty. Johnson felt confident that he had the public's backing on this dramatic change of direction. Humphrey expected resistance, perhaps even angry opposition, to some of the points in his memo; he and Johnson had gone back and forth on contentious issues in the past, when both were senators and, more recently, when LBJ was in the White House and Humphrey was working as majority whip in the Senate. This was not going to be the case with this memo. Johnson exploded when he read it, and Humphrey was surprised by the depth of his anger. In his memoirs, Johnson characterized himself as the reasonable leader willing to listen to all advice; in reality, he had a plan—escalation—and you either fell in behind him or you were outside looking in.

The memo placed Humphrey on the outside. He was frozen out of the president's inner circle, uninvited to meetings in which Vietnam was discussed. From February through July 1965, Johnson excluded Humphrey from any significant meeting regarding Vietnam. Ironically, Humphrey, a supporter of America's military presence in Southeast Asia, was silenced at a time when Johnson made the decision to escalate the war. Miserable and chastised, Humphrey stood by while the direction of the war changed into a military action that, in time, would bring down the Johnson administration, Humphrey included. In an effort to earn his way back into the president's favor, Humphrey spoke openly in support of LBJ's new direction in Vietnam. Johnson relented eventually, when he sent Humphrey on a fact-finding trip to Southeast Asia. Humphrey had learned his lesson about second-guessing his boss. He would never do it again.

2 Eugene McCarthy
Making of a Grassroots Candidacy

One could easily understand how Lyndon Johnson might not have regarded Eugene McCarthy as a serious presidential candidate. McCarthy's muscular intellect, his apparent lack of ambition, his athleticism, his spirituality and even temper—all were traits that Johnson might admire in an educator but not in the leader of the free world. Their differences made them almost polar opposites. One could not imagine LBJ lacing on a pair of ice skates any more than one would find him reading William Blake. McCarthy did both.

McCarthy was as much a product of his region as Johnson was of his. Born in the small town of Watkins, Minnesota, on March 29, 1916, Eugene Joseph McCarthy inherited his most notable characteristics from his mother, a devout Roman Catholic and even-tempered woman of German heritage, whose ancestors had arrived in Minnesota as part of a German agricultural settlement in Minnesota shortly after the Civil War. Michael McCarthy, Gene's father, was a tough, cynical cattle buyer, whose long absences from home left Anna in charge of raising their four children.

The influence of Catholicism on Eugene McCarthy's life should not be underestimated. From his grade school years at St. Anthony's in Watkins through his high school and college years at St. John's Abbey and University in Collegeville, Minnesota, McCarthy's studies were fortified by a spirituality that he carried with him throughout his life. He was a good student to begin with, and he was well read long before he began his early years of college, but the Benedictine monks stretched his intellectual growth into such studies as philosophy and poetry. McCarthy briefly considered studying for the priesthood, but he was too restless to pursue it for long, and a stint in the army ended the thought. An excellent athlete, McCarthy rounded off his education by participating in baseball and ice hockey.

He might have settled into a career as a university professor—he taught at the College of St. Thomas in St. Paul, Minnesota, after his return from the service—but his attention gravitated to politics. He won a seat in the U.S. House of Representatives in 1948, and ten years later, he moved on to the Senate. His cool intellectual and calm demeanor disguised any ambitions he might have had, which was fine with McCarthy. He had always been a quiet one. He was interested when he became a finalist in Johnson's search for a vice-presidential candidate in 1964, and he cared, more than he let on, when he was bypassed. It was probably just as well: he objected openly to Johnson's escalation of the Vietnam War, and when peace activists began looking for a candidate to oppose LBJ in 1968, he was on a short list of possibilities.

1 Eight months before President Johnson stunned the country with his decision to drop out of the presidential race, a formal "Dump Johnson" campaign was announced at a National Student Association conference at the University of Maryland. At the center of the small movement was a hyperkinetic young activist/organizer named Allard K. Lowenstein, an avowed liberal whose growing opposition to the Vietnam War ultimately led him to believe that the best way to end the fighting would be to replace the hawkish president with a dove.

Lowenstein, thirty-eight, never stayed in one place for any length of time. His impressive résumé included, among many entries: college at the University of North Carolina; the presidency of the National Student Association; the national chair of Students for Stevenson; jobs working for Eleanor Roosevelt and Hubert Humphrey; study in South Africa, where he saw the brutal effects of apartheid, leading to his involvement in the civil rights movement in the United States; a law degree from Yale; an unsuccessful run for Congress; and the cofounding of the National Conference of Concerned Democrats. He was a reformist, ideologically left of center but caught between the radical Left, which far too often, he felt, alienated the targeted public and stood little chance of success, and the liberals adhering to the old ways. He resisted the pull of the frustrated, anti-American rhetoric of the radical faction, just as he disliked Communism and its appeal to some intellectual circles. Lowenstein strongly supported the traditional democratic process; he just wanted more people involved in it.

"The hard-driving Lowenstein had a knack for galvanizing bright, competent, earnest, well-placed young men and women—student government presidents, college newspaper editors, seminarians, Peace Corps returnees," wrote Todd Gitlin. "By upbringing, training, and ambition these children of affluence were winners. They had been raised to believe in the promise of America and they hated the war partly because it meant that the object of their affections, the system that rewarded their proficiency, was damaged goods."

The Dump Johnson campaign was not Lowenstein's first order of business in designing his plan to force the hands of those making the decisions regarding the war. He began much more modestly. He had gone the petition route, imploring signatures from the predictable groups of students and liberals, some of the petitions finding their way to the White House, but he quickly determined that this was a dead end, not unlike the efforts of Joseph Rauh, the influential leader rising out of the ranks of Americans for Democratic Action. Rauh favored the construction of a strong party peace plank for the 1968 Democratic National Convention. Lowenstein rejected the idea outright. The convention would be President Johnson's moment of glory, and there was no way the Democrats could successfully launch a platform that angered, embarrassed, attacked, or otherwise displeased him. Rauh, for his part, was looking for a way to goad Johnson into action.

Curtis Gans, a cofounding member of the Students for a Democratic Society and a Lowenstein friend since their college days at the University of North Carolina, currently the editor of the *ADA World,* a magazine for Americans for Democratic Action, agreed with Lowenstein that somebody—or some group—had to find a way of forcing the president into de-escalating the war. He agreed that the petition route was ineffective. Gans, using a pseudonym, wrote an article ("The Issue: Vietnam; The Target: Johnson") in the July 1967 issue of the *World,* suggesting that "the most effective strategy must be for liberals to work within the Democratic Party for a change of policy if possible and for a change of leadership if necessary." Gans suggested that a candidate to push Johnson in the primaries might be effective in addressing the need for change.

Lowenstein liked the idea, but he and Gans disagreed over the best way to go about finding a candidate. Lowenstein preferred running a well-known third-party candidate—someone like Martin Luther King or pediatrician/antiwar activist Benjamin Spock—while Gans believed a nationally known Democrat running head-on against Johnson would be more effective. The Dump Johnson strategy grew as 1967 wore on, when there was no sign of a change in the Johnson administration's war policy. Rioting burned the inner cities in some of America's biggest metropolitan areas, antiwar demonstrations picked up in number and intensity, and, on the other end of the spectrum, the "Summer of Love" indicated a youth movement crying out for change.

To say that the Dump Johnson effort was a modest endeavor would be an understatement—at least in the beginning. Lowenstein, Gans, and a third activist, Harold Ickes, went to work, operating on a budget of a thousand dollars and out of a headquarters consisting of the living room in Gans's Washington, D.C., townhouse. Gans and Lowenstein traveled almost nonstop, crossing the country, visiting a total of twenty-two states, spreading the word, picking up whatever support they could muster. Ickes manned the phone when he wasn't traveling with the other two. The media ignored them, but the message was getting out nonetheless. The growing momentum gained support from such large groups as the Dissenting Democrats, the Coalition for a Democratic Alternative, and the California Democratic Council. Lowenstein and Gans proved to be an effective duo. Gans would act as Lowenstein's advance man, visiting towns, gathering names and numbers, and setting up speeches for Lowenstein. Although they could be wordy at times, Lowenstein's passionate speeches recruited more followers, many of them college students willing to work as volunteers.

Lowenstein and Gans began their pursuit of a candidate to run against Johnson in the presidential primaries. Their short list of potential candidates included General James Gavin, John Kenneth Galbraith, Robert Kennedy, Frank Church, George McGovern, Don Edwards, and Eugene McCarthy, but they all were unwilling or unable to run. Gavin, a former warrior now opposed to the Vietnam War, was interested, but he was eliminated from consideration when he said he would only run as a Republican. Galbraith, an economist, college professor, writer, and former ambassador to India under Kennedy, would have happily signed on as a candidate, but he had been born in Canada and was ineligible. Kennedy declined, saying that voters would interpret his candidacy as a personal vendetta against Johnson. McGovern, who viewed a run against Johnson as a losing endeavor, might have been inclined to enter the race if he hadn't already been engaged in a tight senate race in his home state of South Dakota; he didn't even want to be on the ballot as a favorite son. Other senators up for reelection begged off for the same reason. Edwards felt that, as a congressman, he was too inexperienced to be taken seriously.

Eugene McCarthy's name had come up on several occasions during the search. He wasn't up for reelection, and his antiwar position was well established. He also had a personal reason for opposing Johnson. He had never forgiven Johnson for stringing him along on his vice-presidential decision. Still, when Lowenstein approached McCarthy about running against the president in the Dump Johnson campaign, the senator declined. "I think Bobby should do it," he insisted. Robert Kennedy, he submitted, had a better chance of winning.

Lowenstein visited Kennedy at Hickory Hill, Kennedy's home in McLean, Virginia, and tried to talk the senator into changing his mind. Kennedy's advisors were divided on his prospects. One had to go back to 1884 to find an upstart candidate who had successfully unseated a president for his party's nomination; Chester Arthur had been president then, and James Blaine had seized the Republican nomination from him. Kennedy figured on waiting his turn. Johnson could have another four years, and Kennedy would run in 1972. War or no war, he wasn't about to be a sacrificial lamb, especially if it meant being beaten by someone he disliked as much as he loathed Johnson. Kennedy strongly believed that a run against Johnson would divide the Democratic Party, which would only damage his standing in the party.

Lowenstein boiled over. The "honor and direction" of the United States were on the line, he reminded Kennedy. "We're going to do it without you, and that's too bad," Lowenstein said, his frustration and anger rising, "because you could have become president of the United States."

"Well, I hope you understand I want to do it, and that I know what you're doing should be done, but I just can't do it," Kennedy said.

Earlier in the year, when explaining his commitment to his ideology, Lowenstein had told Kennedy that "you need a movement before you can get a candidate." But now he found himself in precisely that position: the Dump Johnson movement was snowballing as the weeks passed, but by fall 1967, the cause was still looking for the candidate.

Lowenstein returned to Eugene McCarthy for another round of persuading. Lowenstein didn't have to persuade McCarthy about a need for change. McCarthy was bored with the Senate and some of what he considered to be its outdated traditions. He was restless, ready to move on. As his friend and fellow Minnesotan Hubert Humphrey observed: "Basically, Gene disdains whatever peer group he is in. If he was teaching college students, he found most of his colleagues dull. When he was in the House, he grew tired of congressmen. In the Senate, he found few senators or senatorial duties that interested him."

In making a decision about entering the race, McCarthy faced a split in his own family. His wife, Abigail, was dead set against it, but his children wanted him to run. His daughter, Mary, a Radcliffe student active in the antiwar protests, begged him to run, even if it meant his forsaking his career as a senator.

"Mary, I know somebody should challenge the President," Abigail McCarthy agreed with her daughter during one of their frequent telephone conversations. "Something must be done. But does your father have to be the one to do it?"

"Mother, that is the most immoral thing you ever said," Mary answered, reminding her mother that her question flew in the face of everything she had taught her.

Mary McCarthy had her father's attention. Gene McCarthy was very aware of the two big issues—the war and racial inequality—on college campuses across the United States. He had lectured on university campuses and listened to what students had to say. He was especially concerned that these young voices were not being heard or, worse, were experiencing the sense of rejection and powerlessness one feels when being ignored by those in power.

"Meeting with these students re-enforced my belief that it was vitally important that the young people be given a chance to participate in the politics of 1968," McCarthy stated in *The Year of the People,* his account of his bid for the Democratic Party nomination for the presidency. McCarthy had high hopes for what might rise out of this participation. "This, I felt, would not be the more-or-less traditional student participation," he said. "If given a chance, their activities would be of a much higher political order."

On October 20, McCarthy met with Lowenstein and Gerald Hill for breakfast in Los Angeles. McCarthy had been dropping hints that he was seriously considering a run for the presidency. Earlier in the month, he had bounced the idea off Robert Kennedy in a seven-minute meeting in the Senate cloakroom. He told Kennedy, "I'm not worried as to whether I'm a stalking horse for you," leaving Kennedy with the impression that there would be no hard feelings if at some point Kennedy changed his mind about entering the race. As McCarthy would later recall, Kennedy remained noncommittal during their meeting. If he objected to McCarthy's bid for the nomination, he didn't show it.

McCarthy's breakfast with Lowenstein and Hill, informal and often punctuated by laughter, concluded with a mutual understanding. After inquiring about fund-raising, rounding up volunteers, and obtaining endorsements from labor groups, McCarthy put the matter of his candidacy to rest. There had been a list of others considered, McCarthy noted, but "I guess you can cut it down to one."

The group considered the best date to make a formal announcement. The optimum time, they decided, would be at the Conference of Concerned Democrats convention in Chicago on December 2. In the meantime, no one was to say a word about McCarthy's candidacy.

2 In *Miami and the Siege of Chicago,* his book-length account of the 1968 Republican and Democratic National Conventions, Norman Mailer, an avowed Robert Kennedy supporter, grumbled after meeting with McCarthy that the senator "did not look nor feel like a President." McCarthy, Mailer averred, presented himself "more like the dean of the finest English department in the land."

It was a valid observation. McCarthy was unlike any candidate in recent memory. If one can judge by McCarthy's own statements, the presidency seemed to mean little. "I didn't say I want to be president," he told a television interviewer. "I'm willing to be president." When he told Hubert Humphrey, his friend and colleague—and, perhaps most notably, the vice president, with strong presidential aspirations of his own—that he was considering a run for the office, he did so in a way that surprised Humphrey. "He spoke so casually as he usually does," Humphrey said, "that I felt that it was just sort of a lark on his part."

It was not a lark, but it was not a run for the *presidency,* either. The campaign, in McCarthy's eyes, was the vehicle for a message. The presidency had never been a goal of McCarthy's, and the appearance of reluctance on his part was an accurate depiction. In the early weeks of his candidacy, from the moment he decided to run until he actually began campaigning in New Hampshire, he was reluctant to even say that he was running for the office.

McCarthy's break with the Johnson administration occurred on August 17, 1967, when Undersecretary of State Nicholas Katzenbach appeared before the Foreign Relations Committee on U.S. Commitments. Katzenbach's testimony rankled McCarthy. If one were to believe Katzenbach, the president was entitled, by the Gulf of Tonkin Resolution, to follow the course of action he deemed best in Vietnam—without running every detail past Congress. The resolution, Katzenbach said, was a declaration of war, even if a formal declaration of war had not been made in Vietnam. In the middle of his hearing, an infuriated McCarthy rose and walked out of the room. "This is the wildest testimony I have ever heard," he told E. W. Kenworthy, a *New York Times* reporter in the hall outside the hearing room. "There is no limit to what he says the president can do. There is only one thing to do—take it to the country."

McCarthy had grown tired of trying to be a team player. He distrusted Johnson's motives and his freewheeling ways of dominating both bodies of Congress. Shortly after taking office after the assassination of John Kennedy, Johnson had attempted a power play. He was rebuffed. McCarthy strongly disapproved of how Johnson, in the executive branch, still maneuvered to manipulate the legislative bodies. Katzenbach's appearance before the Foreign Relations Committee, in McCarthy's view, was just another example of the type of abuse of power contributing to the alienation of Americans from the political process.

McCarthy's harsh words about Vietnam and the war's effect on the country's moral center represented a significant turn in the senator's thinking. His voting record, if scrutinized, indicated a senator willing to go along with the majority in approving revenues earmarked for financing the war. He had joined ninety-seven other senators in endorsing the Gulf of Tonkin Resolution. He had backed LBJ in his programs. His changes had occurred within the past year, when he began questioning the U.S. involvement in the Vietnam War and the way it was being reported by the president, the generals, and even the press. It was time to fight back.

"If I have to run for president to do it," he told E. W. Kenworthy after walking out of the Senate Foreign Relations Committee hearing, "I'm going to do it."

3 Eugene McCarthy and Allard Lowenstein were destined for a falling out. They were totally different personalities, with differing methods of attaining their goals. McCarthy was subtle, Lowenstein a sledgehammer. McCarthy objected to the "Dump Johnson" expression, which, he told the *New York Times,* "has never been one of my words." The Dump Johnson terminology, McCarthy felt, misdirected the focus of discussion—in this case, from the war itself to an individual. He was willing to abandon his candidacy in the unlikely event that Johnson agreed to unconditionally stop all bombing of North Vietnam, immediately initiate peace talks, and work on creating a coalition government in South Vietnam. Lowenstein's hot rhetoric could alienate moderate voters who might otherwise agree with the principles of his proposals. Lowenstein was dedicated, extremely industrious, perceptive in his analysis, and persuasive; these assets, if applied too aggressively, could lead to the questioning of his motives. In addition, McCarthy was acutely aware that Lowenstein preferred Kennedy as his candidate.

McCarthy wondered what lay ahead in the Conference of Concerned Democrats gathering in Chicago. He was not interested in hearing incendiary or confrontational words, no matter how well intended, from leaders or attendees, nor did he want his name too tightly affiliated to any specific interest group. Announcing his candidacy at the conference could have just that effect. McCarthy still perceived himself as more of a representative of a major cause than the traditional candidate, and he was concerned that his message might be lost in overheated anti-Johnson sentiment.

He decided to announce his candidacy earlier than planned, on the morning of November 30, two days before he was scheduled to address the convention. The press conference, held at ten o'clock in the Caucus Room of the Old Senate Office Building, offered a sneak preview of what voters could expect to see in the months ahead. True to character, McCarthy was relaxed and low-key, and also true to character, he left what he had on his mind open to interpretation.

Rather than state specifically that he was entering the race as a candidate, he opened with "I intend to enter the Democratic primaries in four states: Wisconsin, Oregon, California, and Nebraska. The decision with reference to Massachusetts and also New Hampshire will be made within the next two or three weeks."

(The reasons for choosing these primaries, he would later say, were purely geographic: "Our first plan was to concentrate on four 'critical primaries' regionally distributed: Massachusetts in the Northeast, Wisconsin in the Midwest, Oregon in the Northwest, and California—with the possibility of adding New York, a primary different from all others. New Hampshire was added later, under urging from Democrats in New Hampshire and some pressure from restless troops.")

McCarthy went on to say that he believed "the issue of Vietnam and the issues related to it should be raised in the primaries." He had been talking to Democratic leaders across the country, covering at least half the states, and he had also spoken to students on college campuses and to voters everywhere, and what he found was "a deepening moral crisis in America—discontent and frustration and a disposition to take extralegal if not illegal action to manifest protest."

McCarthy devoted much of the press conference to the sources of all that discontent and frustration. He offered statistics about the costs, in lives and money, of the war. He condemned the spending on the war when the money could be earmarked for domestic needs, on poverty and other constructive programs. The war had spiked inflation. On college campuses, students were becoming alienated from the political process, with "a tendency to withdraw from political action, to talk of non-participation, to become cynical and to make threats of support for third parties or fourth parties or other irregular political movements."

McCarthy was clear in noting that his entry into the primaries was an attempt to offer voice to those alienated Americans. He said nothing about the Dump Johnson campaign, however, though he stated at the onset of his announcement that the president was the figurehead of the war and, as such, directly responsible for "my decision to challenge the President's position and the Administration position . . . to intensify the war in Vietnam." The president and his best and brightest, to borrow journalist David Halberstam's expression, gave no "positive indication or suggestion for a compromise or for a negotiated political settlement." Yes, McCarthy wanted peace but not at any price, rather, in "an honorable, rational" way that would enhance the United States' standing in the world.

The press conference was a head-scratcher. What, exactly, was McCarthy saying? Could he possibly have been more vanilla in the delivery of his message? If this man, standing at the podium and reading from a two-page typed script, could not garner any real enthusiasm from a bevy of reporters looking for something to write about, how was he going to play on television in front of millions of viewers?

McCarthy's announcement received a lukewarm response from the press. *Newsweek,* in an article titled "The McCarthy Bomb," was not impressed. "Within the political fraternity McCarthy's own explanation of what he is up to is too lofty to be credited," Kenneth Crawford wrote. The *Washington Post* cautioned that "his entry may channel into the political process dissent that often has been aimless and sometimes destructive." In an unsigned editorial, the *New York Times,* characterizing McCarthy as a "thoughtful, responsible man," predicted that he could be "expected to clarify the alternatives in Vietnam."

Jeremy Larner, who would work as McCarthy's principal speechwriter throughout the campaign, quipped that the speech had "none of the punchiness of the contemporary press release," but he admired McCarthy's substance-over-style approach. "If McCarthy came on flat and cautious, it might just be because he tried to say only what he knew," Larner suggested. "Where other politicians worked to make themselves an 'image,' to see themselves as others saw them, McCarthy seemed to cherish a private sensibility, to struggle with a refined and exacting conscience."

The Conference of Concerned Democrats gathering in Chicago confirmed McCarthy's fears. Thousands of attendees from forty-two states converged on the Conrad Hilton Hotel, braving a cold, blustery Windy City day for a series of meetings and caucuses and a look at the new Democratic Party candidate. More than four thousand lined up and poured into the main conference hall, with another estimated two thousand placed in a nearby overflow hall, where the speeches were piped in. Many others, unable to find a place in either hall, shivered on the sidewalks outside.

When McCarthy arrived, tardy but not much more than fashionably late, he was treated to the sight of Allard Lowenstein on the podium, delivering a fiery speech like one might find at a call-and-response tent-show revival, his anti-Johnson invective drawing roars of approval from the conference attendees. "When a President is both wrong and unpopular," Lowenstein said in the most memorable line of his speech, "to refuse to oppose him is both a moral abdication and a political stupidity." This kind of talk might not have been unusual or out of line at a conference rally, but it was not the tone that McCarthy wished to set for his campaign. Nor could he have been happy about having to follow Lowenstein's speech with his own subdued address.

McCarthy stewed while he waited in the back of the hall for his turn to speak. If Lowenstein was aware of McCarthy's arrival, he gave no indication of it. While he charged ahead, believing that he was merely filling time until McCarthy arrived, the angry senator stood in the rear of the hall, repeatedly kicking a paper cup against a wall. Curtis Gans finally made his way to the platform and told Lowenstein that McCarthy was present and waiting to speak. Lowenstein would later insist that he had stopped his speech in the middle of a thought, "as soon as I had word that he was in the hall," but in in a conflicting account, Lowenstein supposedly held up his notes and declared that he was almost finished, and then proceeded to talk on. "Al was confused about who was running for president," Gans remarked later.

Whatever the case, McCarthy was in a sour state—not an optimum mental place for delivering an important speech to a mass of would-be supporters. Accounts of the speech described it as "dull and uninspired," "flat," "the speech of a college professor, not a candidate." McCarthy took exception to the criticism. The speech, he judged, was "rather a good speech" that probably seemed too restrained when following, as it did, Lowenstein's overstated diatribe. It was going to be a long campaign, McCarthy reasoned, and the right pacing and tone were required. "It was not time for storming the walls, but for beginning a long march," he said.

In his speech, McCarthy traced back over much of what he had stated at his Washington press conference two days earlier. He opened by dropping the names of Adlai Stevenson, who had won the Democratic Party nomination for the presidency in 1952 and in 1956 in Chicago, and John F. Kennedy, who had been heavily influenced by Stevenson's ideas. From there he was off to his condemnation of the Vietnam War. Entering the primaries, he said, was a way to "test the mood and spirit" of the country. As in his press conference, he avoided personal attacks on the president. Lowenstein had done enough of that already.

The events at the conference extended the widening gap between McCarthy and Lowenstein. McCarthy had to assemble his campaign staff in the near future, and while Lowenstein wanted to work as McCarthy's campaign manager, McCarthy had already privately rejected that idea. McCarthy and Lowenstein distrusted each other after the fiasco in Chicago. McCarthy appreciated all that Lowenstein had done for him so far—and stated as much to Lowenstein in a letter—but he was looking for someone who shared his philosophy on how a campaign should be conducted. Lowenstein had spoken McCarthy's name only once during his tirade in Chicago, and while McCarthy never would have exposed his ego by expressing his displeasure in public, he was irked by being upstaged at his first important campaign speech. Aside from disliking McCarthy's speech, Lowenstein took issue with McCarthy's detached demeanor: he was not behaving like a serious contender. "I saw him as a candidate," Lowenstein said. "He saw himself as a moral protester for a cause."

The most significant development to rise out of the conference was McCarthy's meeting with David Hoeh, a young Dartmouth professor and antiwar protester from New Hampshire, and Gerry Studds, a Yale graduate and teacher at St. Paul's School in Concord, New Hampshire. The two men approached McCarthy with the hope of changing his mind about not running in the New Hampshire primary. McCarthy could see no point in the venture. New Hampshire tended to vote Republican, and as a result of the state's many defense contracts, the state's Democrats would in all likelihood cast their ballots for Johnson. If asked to choose, McCarthy preferred the Massachusetts primary, where he could at least expect an encouraging share of the liberal vote, especially now that Ted Kennedy had decided against placing his name on the ballot as a favorite son.

Hoeh and Studds conceded that the going would be rough, but they argued that this might be a good reason for McCarthy to enter the primary. Since McCarthy wasn't expected to win, any kind of respectable showing could benefit the opening of his campaign. Hoeh and Studds believed that McCarthy and his message would fare better than expected.

McCarthy listened but would not make a commitment. He agreed to meet with them in December, when he would be giving a speech in the state.

4 Eugene McCarthy left the convention with the CCD endorsement but very little else in terms of advancing his candidacy. The press remained skeptical, seeing it as either a matter of an ideologue tilting at windmills, or as someone holding a space until someone with a chance of beating LBJ—that is, Robert Kennedy—got around to entering the race. McCarthy, who could be thin-skinned when doubted or criticized, was going to need every last bit of his wit and intelligence when addressing the perceptions of his candidacy.

The specter of a Robert Kennedy candidacy haunted him from the day he announced his intentions of entering selected primaries. In the question-and-answer session following his announcement, the press quickly brought Kennedy into the discussion. McCarthy admitted that he had spoken to Kennedy about his opposing Johnson in the primaries, and if this had bothered Kennedy, he had given no indication of it. "I would have been glad if he had moved early," McCarthy said of the possibility of Kennedy's entering the race. "I think if he had, there'd have been no need for me to do anything." Texas governor John

Connally, a friend and strong supporter of the president, dismissed McCarthy as nothing more than a stalking horse for Robert Kennedy. Kennedy himself sounded less than convincing when he insisted he was not running and that McCarthy's candidacy would be beneficial to the Democratic Party.

Allard Lowenstein had entered the fray the day after McCarthy's announcement, when he appeared on *Meet the Press*. Lawrence Spivak, the program's host, noting that Lowenstein was generally regarded to be a Kennedy man, asked, "What is your answer to those who say that you and Concerned Democrats are using Senator McCarthy as a stalking horse for Senator Robert Kennedy?"

Lowenstein, accepting the inevitability of the question, served a generic response. "I think it is flattering to be called the loyal and experienced operative, whatever an operative is, and Senator Kennedy wouldn't be a bad person to be loyal and experienced on the behalf of. I think he is one of the great men around, but the fact is, I don't work for Senator Kennedy or for Senator McCarthy. I would like to see all the Democrats in the country who feel discontented with the direction of the party and the country rally behind an alternative who can win, and I think that alternative is Senator McCarthy."

Unhappy with the response, Spivak prodded Lowenstein to be more specific. Did Lowenstein think that a strong showing by McCarthy in the primaries might lead to Kennedy's eventual nomination at the Democratic National Convention?

Lowenstein allowed that it was very likely that a strong showing by McCarthy in the primaries would lead to an open convention, and that Kennedy could benefit from it. But he also said pointedly that any good Democrat would offer "a distinct improvement" over Johnson. As far as he knew, Kennedy was not a candidate, which left McCarthy as the alternative for Democratic voters. There was no telling what would happen in a head-to-head match between the president and his challenger.

The emphasis on Robert Kennedy was rooted in the political realities of the moment. Even though he repeatedly denied his candidacy, Kennedy was nevertheless seen as the front-runner in the Democratic nomination race. A December 5 Harris Poll found McCarthy far behind Johnson, 63 percent to 17 percent, with 20 percent of the respondents undecided. That same survey found Kennedy preferred to Johnson by 52 percent to 32 percent. If nothing else, the poll revealed Johnson's vulnerability.

Throughout November and December, McCarthy acted like a candidate, even if he did come up short in detailing his specific plans. He now had a press following, and he answered their questions about issues often enough to keep his name on the pages of the *New York Times, Washington Post,* and other influential newspapers. He obliged interview requests and offered the kind of esoteric responses that led even the most cynical of reporters to believe that there was more substance to this man than mere opposition to the president and his war. Reporters and news analysts wondered why he was avoiding the New Hampshire primary, which to this point had no enthusiastic candidates. Even the president was mum about his entering the primary.

Although he still dragged his feet about entering the primary, which, he believed, offered a potential pitfall (and should he make a good showing, a golden opportunity for Robert Kennedy to step in), McCarthy was weakening in his resolve to stay out. His visits to the state and meetings with David Hoeh, Gerry Studds, and others were cordial and informative. Beginning with the CCD conference in Chicago and extending through the following weeks, McCarthy's New Hampshire supporters had prepared a sales pitch that they hoped would be enough to convince McCarthy to enter the primary. They planned a campaign itinerary that plotted the most efficient course of campaigning to give McCarthy maximum exposure in minimal time. They gathered press clippings of New Hampshire's coverage of the McCarthy campaign. They estimated budgets and considered staffing in the state. They prepared a detailed memorandum with campaign strategy. "At each step in the preplanning from Chicago onward," remembered Hoeh, "we were reassured that we were being perceived as experienced and creditable—advantages that were valuable to the process of creating the proper political climate for McCarthy in New Hampshire."

The McCarthy campaign was gaining momentum. McCarthy finally appointed a campaign manager on December 12. Blair Clark, a fifty-year-old New Yorker, had extensive media background but virtually no campaign experience—a strong positive, given McCarthy's unorthodox views about running for office. As Clark would notice from day one on the job, McCarthy had an almost infuriating disinterest in the workings of his campaign machinery. The chain of command was uncertain, and job descriptions ill defined; communications between national, state, and local groups were a disaster. McCarthy would stand aside while his variant staffs worked out the logistics. "It is impossible ever to make a neat diagram of the McCarthy campaign," writer Theodore White observed. "He was not that kind of man, nor was it that kind of organization."

Clark, a Harvard classmate and friend of John F. Kennedy, had an extensive background as a journalist, first with the *St. Louis Post-Dispatch* and then as an editor of the *New Hampshire Sunday News.* He had worked for CBS News, eventually advancing up the ranks to the position of general manager and vice president. He was friends with Mary McCarthy, who shared his opposition to the Vietnam War, and who introduced him to her father at the CCD convention in Chicago and pressed him into finding work for Clark on his campaign.

Clark set up the national McCarthy-for-President headquarters on the fifth floor of an office building within easy walking distance of the White House. When he started adding staff, youth seemed to be a requirement. None of his assistants had prior experience on a national campaign, and almost all were less than thirty-five years old. Clark enlisted Curtis Gans's organizational skills, putting him in charge of securing delegates. Seymour Hersh, a thirty-year-old investigative reporter, was given the job of press secretary, and Peter Barnes, twenty-five, a former reporter for *Newsweek* and member of Senator Walter Mondale's staff, became a researcher and writer for McCarthy. Sam Brown, twenty-four, was brought onboard to coordinate McCarthy's student volunteers.

Clark played a significant role in McCarthy's decision to enter the New Hampshire primary. The holiday season arrived without an announcement, with McCarthy still uncertain about the importance of the primary. Clark disagreed, and during a train ride from Washington, D.C., to New York, he presented his case to McCarthy. Clark felt it imperative that McCarthy face the tough contest in New Hampshire; the voting public needed to know him. If he was at all serious about challenging Johnson, he needed to do so in hostile territory. It was the best way to gauge his strengths and weaknesses.

McCarthy agreed, and on January 3, he formally announced that he would be entering the primary.

3 Richard Nixon
Reboot

On paper, Richard Nixon appeared to be an ideal presidential candidate. Happily married, the father of two grown daughters, a period of working for one of the most successful laws firms on the East Coast, a lifetime in public service that included stints in both bodies of Congress, capped by his two-term vice presidency under Eisenhower . . . it was a strong résumé. Further, his autobiography was the story of the American Dream, an appealing rise from a modest beginning to the heights of power that might give Americans hope.

But there was something Shakespearean about him, an almost sinister aura that could make one believe that, in the end, he would impale himself on his own foibles.

His main objective, as the election season approached, was to find the themes to his candidacy, and to assemble the perfect team to implement them into an unbeatable force within his party and, ultimately, the electorate.

In short, he would have to reinvent himself.

1 How do you shed the loser's image? Such was the challenge for Richard Nixon when he began planning another run at the presidency. He had been narrowly beaten by John Kennedy in his 1960 presidential bid, and two years later, while taking on Governor Edmund "Pat" Brown in the California gubernatorial race, he had not only been defeated but in a postelection press conference he had bitterly declared an end of his life in electoral politics. "Just think how much you're going to be missing," he lashed out at the press. "You won't have Nixon to kick around anymore, because, gentlemen, this is my last press conference."

Nixon, it turned out, was not only a loser; he was a poor loser.

To television interviewer David Frost, he admitted that, in hindsight, he felt he had made a mistake, but he was not prepared to totally write off everything he had said. He told Frost,

> I was convinced that I was not the man for the times at that point and I was willing to accept that decision. Then events changed that. As a result of the Republican division in '64 and as a result, too, of the great foreign policy crises, what I stood for seemed to be what the country needed. Now, when I say "country," that sounds like a self-serving statement, and maybe it's intended to be, but what I really mean is that a great number of people in the country felt that I had a point of view and a type of experience that the nation might need for leadership at this point. And if those events hadn't occurred, I wouldn't be here today. Nothing that I could have done would have changed it.

"I have never regretted what I said at the 'last press conference,'" Nixon wrote in his memoirs. "I believe that it gave the media a warning that I would not sit back and take whatever biased coverage was dished out to me." The result, Nixon professed, was "much fairer treatment" from the press in years to come. "From that point of view alone, it was worth it."

The media lacerated Nixon after the press conference. "Barring a miracle, his political career ended last week," *Time* magazine declared. Five days after the election, ABC television ran a scathing half-hour special titled "The Political Obituary of Richard Nixon," hosted by newsman Howard K. Smith and including, as one of its prominent voices, Alger Hiss, a man Nixon had helped convict of perjury in one of the century's most infamous legal cases. The battering Nixon took on the ABC program resulted in the network's receiving thirty thousand letters protesting Nixon's rough treatment.

Nixon had hoped that a victory in California would serve as the starting block to another presidential bid in 1968, but aside from the strange form of political self-immolation that his press conference turned out to be, he would have history, along with the changes of direction within his own political party, working against him. The 1968 election would mark the end of John Kennedy's two terms as president, leaving Nixon, if chosen as his party's candidate, open to a battle with someone who had not beaten him in a previous election. Kennedy's assassination changed that. Lyndon Johnson, if he chose, could run for the presidency, and if he won and proved to be popular, he would occupy the White House until 1972.

It had never been easy to market Nixon, despite his strong political résumé. He had served in public office since 1946, first as a congressman, then as a senator, and, most recently, as a two-term vice president under Eisenhower. An energetic, effective campaigner, he inevitably managed to look bad on paper—and, to the regrets of his supporters, on television. His 1960 presidential debates with Kennedy stood as undeniable proof: after the first debate, polls found that a majority of those watching it on television felt Kennedy had won the debate, whereas those listening to it on the radio believed Nixon had prevailed. On television, still a new medium to presidential politics, style scored as heavily as substance. Both candidates presented their views convincingly, but JFK looked relaxed, confident, and knowledgeable compared to Nixon, who never fully conquered the medium. Nixon appeared uncomfortable in front of the television cameras. He perspired heavily, looked awkward and angular, and, to the delight of those who disliked him, he was shifty eyed when he read from a teleprompter. Campaign strategy was changing in the advent of television campaigning. Onscreen, Nixon came across as stodgy in comparison to Jack and Jackie Kennedy, the young, attractive, energetic glamour couple. In radio, you listened; on television, you watched. And viewers could not take their eyes off the Kennedys.

Nixon was fully aware of his shortcomings on television, and in his perfect world, he would have curtailed his appearances on television. His hatred of the medium did nothing to advance his cause. Television, to Nixon, was artificial, from the makeup they applied to you before an interview, to the studio setting used to record your appearance, to the canned questions asked by every sincere-looking interviewer. Still, he had no choice. If he expected to beat, first, his Republican challengers for the party nomination, and, eventually, LBJ in the November election, he would have to employ television to his advantage.

But first he had to overcome his image as a loser.

Patrick Buchanan, a leading voice of conservatism in the late-twentieth century and advisor to three presidents, viewed Nixon's reputation as a loser as the former vice president's personal Sisyphus, just as he believed that Nixon was the "inevitable" Republican candidate for the presidency in 1968. Nixon was respected for his loyalty and willingness to fight for what he believed, and the national Republican Party would have favored him as their presidential candidate if not for one drawback. "Their hesitancy in supporting him could be summed up in three words: 'He can't win,'" Buchanan recalled. "We love him, the rank and file would say, we just can't elect him. 'Nixon is a loser.'"

Buchanan, all of twenty-seven when he sought out and introduced himself to Nixon at a cocktail party in Belleville, Illinois, in December 1965, had attended Georgetown University in Washington, D.C., as an undergraduate student, and Columbia University's School of Journalism for his master's. He joined the staff of the *St. Louis Globe-Democrat,* working as an assistant editorial writer, but his heart was in politics. He had strongly supported the rise of Barry Goldwater conservatism after Nixon's unsuccessful bid for the presidency in 1960. At the time of his 1965 meeting with Nixon, Buchanan was more conservative than his future boss, and before hiring him, Nixon grilled him on his political stances and asked him how he felt about William F. Buckley, editor of the *National Review* and perhaps the most highly regarded conservative voice in the media. "You're not as conservative as Bill Buckley, are you?" Nixon wanted to know. Buchanan, in the best tradition of the politician, judiciously replied, "I have great respect for Bill Buckley." Nixon, impressed by Buchanan's analytical capabilities, hired him as the first member of what would evolve into his presidential campaign team. His primary duties would be as a researcher and speechwriter. He was assigned an office at Nixon's 20 Broad Street law office building in Manhattan and put to work.

2 Leonard Garment, a young litigator at the Nixon, Mudge, Rose, Guthrie and Alexander law offices in New York, played an invaluable role in helping Nixon shed his loser image and stage a successful television campaign. In the beginning, Nixon and Garment were an unlikely pairing. Garment, a former jazz clarinetist, was by his own self-definition "a more or less conventional inactive liberal Democrat practicing law," with the "conventional notions of a negative sort about Richard Nixon that came out of that time," when he first met Nixon at a cocktail party a short time after Nixon joined the law firm in 1963. Despite what he perceived to be their differences, he was pleased to have Nixon's name added to the law firm's roster. When he had his initial in-depth, one-on-one conversation with Nixon, Garment was impressed that Nixon seemed open to him, even though Garment was candid with him about his political beliefs. After talking to Nixon and hearing him discuss his life as a public servant, Garment became convinced that the former vice president was restless and ready to run for the presidency again.

The two worked together on a high visibility case, *Hill v. Time Inc.,* an invasion of privacy case that had slowly and tediously worked its way to the U.S. Supreme Court. The case focused on a September 9, 1952, Philadelphia suburban home invasion by three escaped convicts who held a family captive in their home for nineteen hours but left without harming anyone. However, the family—particularly Elizabeth Hill, the wife of James Hill and mother of three teenaged daughters and four-year-old twins—was traumatized by the event, and the subsequent attention and notoriety led to the Hill family's selling their house and moving to Connecticut, where they eschewed all requests for interviews and offers from publishers for their story. They strenuously objected when a new Broadway play, *The Desperate Hours,* premiered and was advertised as a work based on true crime events. Not surprisingly, the play added dramatized events that had not taken place, adding to the emotional and mental distress the family had been trying to overcome. They saw lawyers after a February 28, 1955, issue of *Life* magazine ran a review of the play. The magazine never mentioned that some of the scenes in the play were fictionalized; instead, it ran a pictorial with photos of the Hills' former house, which the magazine rented from its current owners, in which the actors and actresses were photographed in scenes from the play. The Hills had repeatedly stressed there had been no violence, drug use, or profanity—all in the play—during their ordeal. They had been treated decently, they told the press; all these elements and more were added to the play for dramatic effect. The family found itself back in the spotlight when the *Life* piece appeared.

Garment represented the Hills in the trial. He initially requested that the magazine publish a retraction, but the editors refused. *Life* argued that it was protected by the First Amendment, but Garment was able to show that the magazine had deliberately published material that its editors knew to be false. The jury awarded the family a $175,000 settlement, and an appellate court upheld the verdict. Time Inc. filed for a Supreme Court hearing. Nixon joined Mudge Rose in the period prior to the Supreme Court hearing, and Garment felt that he would be the ideal attorney to argue the case before the justices. Nixon, although bothered by misgivings, agreed.

Nixon worked tirelessly in researching and planning his argument, "reading and virtually committing to memory the *Hill* trial record, the state court decisions, and copious quantities of background material, including federal and state case law, law review articles, and philosophical writings on libel and privacy." Garment was impressed. "His behavior," he later said of Nixon, "was a sign not only of professional pride but of his determination not to let recent defeats drive him from the public arena."

The court reversed the previous verdict on a five to four vote, ruling that *Life* magazine was indeed protected by the First Amendment. Abe Fortas, one of the dissenting justices, encouraged Nixon to retry the case. Time Inc. avoided another trial by offering the Hill family a settlement. Nixon moved on.

Garment, reflecting on the case in 2007, believed that the case ultimately— and ironically—helped dispel Nixon's image as a loser. "The net effect of the Hill case," he proposed, "was to establish his credentials and to bring him back into the public eye in a surprising and favorable way."

A single court case, however, was not going to change public perception. If Nixon expected to change his loser image, he had to accomplish one task: win at the polls. Nixon had not tasted victory in an election since being part of the Eisenhower ticket in 1956, and he had not won on his own since his 1950 Senate run.

By mid-1967, it was evident to anyone paying the slightest attention that Nixon was gearing up for another run at the presidency. He had been very busy and visible in the nearly five years passing since what he announced as his final press conference following his defeat in California. He had worked to unify the Republican Party in the aftermath of Barry Goldwater's historic loss to Lyndon Johnson in the 1964 presidential election. He had stumped for Republican candidates across the country in 1966. He traveled to Europe, Asia, the Middle East, and elsewhere, engaging in high-profile meetings with world leaders. He remained neutral in public when asked about his plans, but in private, when meeting with influential Republicans and even potential rivals in the 1968 primaries, he admitted that he was all but certain that he would be entering the presidential race. He quietly began gathering a campaign staff.

In June 1967, his old friend and close advisor H. R. "Bob" Haldeman volunteered a lengthy, unsolicited memorandum addressing the ways Nixon might use the media to his advantage in his forthcoming presidential bid. Haldeman had managed Nixon's 1960 presidential and 1962 gubernatorial campaigns; he had seen Nixon at his best and worst. He was well acquainted with Nixon's almost paranoid suspicion of reporters and disaffection for television. This did not concern the hard-nosed forty-two-year-old former advertising executive in the least: he was interested only in how to market Nixon to voters who had been previously unenthusiastic about what he might offer as president. By nature, Haldeman had little time for lollygagging. He presented his case directly and, when necessary, forcefully.

And so it was in his memo to Nixon. The nature of a national campaign, Haldeman wrote, had changed. A presidential candidate could hit the campaign trail, engaging in an endless string of public appearances, and he would not begin to reach the size of an audience that he would reach on a single television program. Haldeman remembered all too clearly Nixon's campaigning in 1960: "We started Nixon off in 1960 sick and under medication and then we ran his tail off." The overwhelming pace and demands of traditional campaigning mentally exhausted a candidate, leaving him mentally dull, despite his will to continue. A candidate needed time to relax, recharge, and revisit his strategies. "The time has come," Haldman argued in his memo, "for political campaigning—its technique and strategies—to move out of the dark ages and into the brave new world of the omnipresent eye."

The best procedure, Haldeman suggested, was to use television in ways that reached an optimum number of viewers and allowed the candidate to cut back on his standing at factory gates and in school auditoriums, shouting himself hoarse from platforms hastily set up in parking lots, stumping in several cities on the same day, subjecting himself to oppressive weather that held crowds down even as it ate up a candidate's time and money.

This was what Nixon needed to hear. He could easily recall the onrushing wave of fatigue that engulfed him during his race against Kennedy, how, for just one example, he had been ill the night of the first debate and looked worn and dull next to Kennedy's fresh, camera-friendly face. Television—the omnipresent eye—had drawn a cold sketch of Nixon back then. Haldeman was now suggesting an approach capable of sculpting a new image. It wasn't just a matter of dispelling the prevailing loser image, or that of "Tricky Dick," the man who would sell you a bad used car. Intelligent use of television was capable of making people believe they had had Nixon all wrong in the first place.

So, yes, television: viewers tended to believe what they saw more than what they read or heard, and as long as there were none of the hated gimmicks obvious to either Nixon or his viewers, he would use television to project him into future victory.

One communiqué, one of the most compelling and unexpected letters Nixon would receive, suggested that Nixon's loser image could be a plus. Rose Mary Woods, Nixon's longtime secretary and one of the few people he trusted implicitly, had run across the letter while she was performing her brand of triage on the candidate's mail, and she had strongly recommended that Nixon give it his consideration. William Gavin, a thirty-one-year-old high school English teacher from suburban Philadelphia, began his letter by asking Nixon to run for the presidency, but his reasoning had to have caught Nixon's attention: Nixon, he said, had lost in his recent past, but his losing worked to his advantage. "Nothing can happen to you, politically speaking, that is worse than what has happened to you," Gavin wrote. "Run," he went on, "You will win."

This might not have gone any further had Gavin not continued with concrete suggestions that the Nixon camp would eventually modify for television. "Be bold," he exhorted Nixon. "Why not have live press conferences as your campaign on television? People will see you daring all, asking and answering questions from reporters, and not simply answering phony 'questions' made up by your staff. This would be dynamic; it would be daring. Instead of the medium using you, you would be using the medium."

The letter impressed Nixon—so much so that he asked Leonard Garment to look into it. Garment contacted Gavin and met him for lunch. In a matter of weeks, Gavin was on Nixon's staff.

Nixon agreed that he needed a new image to be marketed to the voting public, but he made a point of saying that he wanted no advertising agencies involved. If television would help, so be it. Nixon favored Garment as a recruiter for his advertising staff. With almost no experience in advertising, Garment wouldn't be hindered by any preconceptions about the professionals he would be seeking. He would be following his instincts as a television viewer.

Garment's first hire, Frank Shakespeare, had a strong television background on his résumé. He had been creative vice president of CBS's New York affiliate. During his initial meeting with Garment, Shakespeare offered "an illuminating two-hour lecture on the impact of modern television" on politics and how television influenced the way viewers perceived candidates. Shakespeare and Garment, along with several other Nixon advisors, then gathered in a CBS screening room and watched hours of recorded Nixon television appearances. They concluded that Nixon excelled in loose, informal settings, coming across as "surprisingly congenial." Conversely, the more formal the setting, the less favorably he presented himself. Ray Price, a Nixon speechwriter present at the screening, spoke for the group when he said, "It's not the man we have to change, but rather the impression."

The group discussed options for presenting Nixon in television ads. They concluded that the ideal format for catching Nixon at his best would be a town-hall, question-and-answer presentation, although, unlike the William Gavin suggestion that Nixon use a press conference setting and ignore the usual canned questions, the group believed that Nixon certainly should see the questions beforehand. He could practice his responses and appear spontaneous. Good editing would take care of the rest.

Garment had a summer-home neighbor, Harry Treleaven, a former vice president of the prestigious J. Walter Thompson advertising agency, whom he hoped to enlist in the Nixon campaign effort. He had broached the subject with Treleaven on one previous occasion, but Treleaven seemed uninterested. Now, a few months later and faced with a new sense of urgency, Garment decided to give it another try. Treleaven, a native Chicagoan, had worked in Los Angeles before heading to New York for a career change. He had been writing radio scripts on the West Coast; he made television commercials in New York. More important, as far as Garment was concerned, was Treleaven's experience working on a congressional campaign in Texas. The candidate, a forty-two-year-old named George H.W. Bush, was attempting something no one had ever achieved before: win an election as a Republican in a strictly Democratic district in Houston. Bush was trailing badly in the polls when Treleaven signed on, and that, along with Bush's failure to win the office in a previous election, presented a heavyweight challenge. Treleaven was unfazed.

"We can turn this into an advantage by creating a 'fighting underdog' image," he believed. "Bush must convince voters that he really wants to be elected and is working hard to earn the vote. People sympathize with a man who tries hard: they are also flattered that anyone would really exert himself to get their vote."

It was all about image: Bush came from a wealthy family, studied at Yale, and hardly came across as a working-class hero. This perception had to change. Treleaven went to work. Off came Bush's suit coat; up rolled his shirt sleeves. Television viewers saw him down on the street, toiling to gain voters' trust, a visual contrast to his opponent. When election day arrived, Bush not only came out on top, he won convincingly.

Treleaven and Garment discussed the ways that Treleaven might contribute to the Nixon campaign, and Garment learned that Treleaven had strong opinions on how Nixon could be marketed, first, as the best candidate in the Republican field, and, second, as a candidate capable of defeating a sitting president. Garment offered Treleaven the position of creative director of advertising. His responsibilities would include "[devising] a theme for the campaign, [creating] commercials to fit the theme, and [seeing] that they were produced with a maximum of professional skill." Treleaven accepted the offer.

Roger Ailes, the third major participant in the Nixon television effort, joined the campaign as the result of an encounter with Nixon in a Philadelphia television studio. The twenty-eight-year-old Ailes served as executive director of *The Mike Douglas Show,* a talk show snowballing in popularity in the daytime television schedule. An Ohio native, Ailes had quickly ascended the ranks at the program when he started on the show as a prop boy in 1965. By the time Nixon ran into him two years later, he had been promoted to a position where he was in charge of overseeing the Monday-thru-Friday, ninety-minute production. The future creator of Fox News did not reach his position by withholding opinion. He had been blessed with intelligence and charm to supplement his ambition. When Nixon was in the green room at *The Mike Douglas Show,* awaiting his turn before camera, Ailes was on hand to talk to him and keep him loose. When Nixon complained that "it's a shame a man has to use gimmicks like this to get elected," Ailes pushed back. "Television is not a gimmick," he declared.

Ailes had little use for Nixon, who impressed him as the kind of guy who as a child received a briefcase on Christmas morning. Ailes had very little use for politics in general. "I don't even know if I was registered to vote back then," he would remember.

What irritated him was Nixon's casual dismissal of a medium that meant everything to him. Nixon's future, Ailes told him, depended on savvy use of television, and if he didn't understand that, he would never make it to the White House.

Nixon liked the brash response. He asked Garment to find something for Ailes to do for the campaign. After meeting with Garment for breakfast in New York, Ailes was hired to produce Nixon's television spots. Nixon's television team was now in place.

3 Nixon did not have to look long or far to find someone to manage his campaign. He would have preferred Bob Haldeman, with his experience in running a campaign, or John Ehrlichman, who had served as his advance man in the California governor's race, but neither wanted the job. So, after some deliberation, he turned to John Mitchell, a fifty-four-year-old attorney with extensive political connections across the country. A former PT-boat commander during World War II, Mitchell had been practicing law since 1938 and was now a highly touted, nationally known municipal bond attorney, whose firm, Caldwell, Trimble and Mitchell, had merged with Nixon Mudge at the beginning of 1967. The gruff, cynical, stoic, pipe-smoking, detail-minded Mitchell had no significant experience in electoral politics prior to his agreeing to work on Nixon's campaign. However, his experiences in the bond cases had involved his working closely with powerful state and local figures, connections that promised to be invaluable when the election season heated up.

Mitchell was a force. He loathed the press and avoided contact with reporters whenever possible. The press, he assured anyone around him, was the enemy. He tolerated no criticism or disagreement. When one Republican congressman questioned Mitchell's qualifications to work as Nixon's campaign manager, he was quickly offered an appraisal of the situation. "I'm his campaign manager and I'm running the show," Mitchell told the astonished congressman. "When I tell Dick Nixon what to do, he listens. I'm in charge. So, if you have questions about the campaign call me. But you won't be able to reach me because I'll be busy electing a president of the United States. I'll get your message. But call *me,* don't call *him,* because *I'm* running this campaign."

Mitchell established his value to Nixon as soon as he went to work for him. He called or reconnected with contacts in Wisconsin—a key state in the Nixon plan—and in no time a Nixon organization, headquartered in Madison, had fanned out to include every county and every major city in the state. Mitchell's organizational skills, Nixon learned, were phenomenal, and his ascent into Nixon's tightest inner circle moved rapidly. "Within a few months I was beginning to turn increasingly to him for advice and counsel on political matters," Nixon recalled.

Journalist Theodore White went a step further in assessing Mitchell's importance to Nixon, ranking him in the top five individuals holding "critical influence on his thinking" (Pat Nixon, Rose Mary Woods, H. R. Haldeman, and Robert Finch being the other four), adding that "Mitchell became not only an educational force in Nixon's life but a friend to be trusted almost more than any other." Nixon, upon convincing Mitchell to run his campaign, characterized Mitchell as "the heavyweight."

Bob Haldeman and John Ehrlichman joined the campaign staff early on, Haldeman as Nixon's chief of staff, Ehrlichman as the campaign's advance man and tour director.

Haldeman's association with Nixon dated back to 1956, when Haldeman served as a volunteer advance man during Nixon's campaign for reelection as vice president under Eisenhower. "I was impressed with Richard Nixon the man; I was interested in him," Haldeman would recall, adding that four years earlier he had written Nixon and offered to work in any useful capacity. At that point, he had been working in advertising for twelve years and was looking for a way to add to his experiences. "There was no great ideological thrust or noble ambition involved in this, and no thought at all of becoming permanently involved in either politics or government," he admitted. "It was a thing where I felt it would be an interesting side experience where I could make a contribution that would be worthwhile, something [that] would be a learning experience and an interesting experience for me."

There had been no work for him in 1952, but Haldeman persisted in volunteering his services, and from 1956 on he had an increasingly vital role in Nixon's political life. They grew closer when Nixon's second vice-presidential term ended and Nixon moved back to California. Their personal friendship deepened, and with that came a greater level of trust on Nixon's part. As Nixon associates would attest, breaking into Nixon's tight inner circle was extremely rare. For Haldeman, it was a matter of personality and efficiency. As he would demonstrate over the years, he was willing and able to take on any task, no matter how difficult or unseemly, if he felt it would benefit Nixon's cause. His loyalty, like that of John Mitchell, was beyond reproach, although, like Mitchell, he did not back down from the occasional disagreement with the strong-willed Nixon.

When reflecting on his times on the campaign trail with Nixon leading up to 1968, Haldeman viewed each election cycle as a learning experience, not simply as a matter of the ins and outs of running a campaign, but also in terms of discovering Nixon's strengths and weaknesses. The 1960 run against Kennedy had been physically and mentally exhausting, a barn burner of a race that, turning out as agonizingly close as it did, taught Haldeman how a detail here or a detail there might lead to invaluable votes necessary for a victory. Nixon had been difficult, micromanaging details that might have been better left up to others, and this, combined with the constant activity, the nights of very little sleep, the anxiety, the banter with the press, and all the other factors present in every national campaign, had contributed in Haldeman's mind to Nixon's downfall. By his own account, Haldeman saw Nixon every day in 1960 leading up to election night. He believed that he knew the inner workings of the man.

So he was disappointed two years later, in 1962, when Nixon, after relocating from Washington, D.C., to his native California, decided to oppose Pat Brown in the gubernatorial race. "I never felt that he should run; told him so right up to the time he was walking down that corridor to announce he was going to run," Haldeman said in 1988. "My argument there was that he shouldn't run for Governor because he didn't want to be Governor." According to Haldeman, Nixon ran because he was advised that he needed to keep a public profile and maintain a political base if he ever intended to run for national office again. "That was the reason he was running for Governor," Haldeman said. "It was not because of any burning desire to do anything for the State of California. I had the belief that politically you don't have a chance of winning an election that you don't really want to win for the purpose of serving in that office."

Nixon surprised him, as he surprised many of those close to him, when he decided to leave California for New York after his defeat. Nixon had very little interest in practicing law, and New York, in terms of his political future, meant a new turf to conquer. Haldeman watched as Nixon rebuilt his reputation by stumping for Republican candidates and trying to hold the fracturing party together in the 1964 and 1966 elections. When he sent his memo to Nixon in 1967, he had no doubt that Nixon would be running again for the presidency, and while he was reluctant to serve in his previous position of campaign manager, he was willing to work as Nixon's chief of staff.

John Ehrlichman had known Haldeman dating back to when they both had been undergraduate students at UCLA. They had maintained their friendship after graduation, when Haldeman took a job in an advertising agency in San Mateo, California, and Ehrlichman attended law school at Stanford and eventually moved his family to Seattle. When Haldeman approached Ehrlichman in 1959 and asked if he would be interested in working as an advance man on Nixon's presidential campaign, Ehrlichman was, as he described it, "feeling an itch." He had no special interest in Nixon or the Republican Party, but he was intrigued by the prospects of working for the vice president and helping him in his quest for the presidency.

This, of course, did not work out, but Ehrlichman learned a great deal about the parameters of campaigning—and about Nixon. Nixon could be standoffish, demanding, and impatient, but as Haldeman also noted, he ran himself to exhaustion. He had vowed to visit all fifty states during his 1960 run, which not only wore him down but also led to his making such questionable choices as visiting Alaska as time ran out and he found himself behind in the polls, when he might have concentrated his time in trying to secure states with larger numbers of voters and, ultimately, Electoral College votes. Ehrlichman shrugged off Nixon's razor-thin defeat and returned to Seattle.

Two years later, he answered Haldeman's call again when Haldeman asked him to handle the scheduling in Nixon's California gubernatorial race against Pat Brown. It was a contentious, uphill battle, complete with dirty tricks and mudslinging, with Nixon an underdog despite his high-profile past as vice president. That history worked against him: a large number of California voters viewed Nixon's run as little more than a preliminary to another presidential bid in 1964. On election night, Nixon was soundly defeated, leading to his press conference announcing his retirement from politics.

Ehrlichman, present at that press conference, offered a different assessment on what actually took place. Nixon, aware of his sliding numbers in the polls and prepared to concede defeat, had been drinking heavily on election night as he watched the returns in his Beverly Hills Hilton suite. As Ehrlichman would note, "it didn't take much alcohol under the best of circumstances" to put Nixon in a weakened state, and on election night, "Nixon had begun greeting defeat with lubrication but without grace." He got very drunk, and the next morning, he was badly hungover and in no condition to meet the press. Haldeman arranged to usher him out a side door without his addressing reporters, but Nixon, looking horrible and in one of the darkest moods of his political life, decided at the last minute to vent before the gathered press.

The episode bothered Ehrlichman enough that he confronted Nixon about his drinking before agreeing to work as part of his 1968 campaign staff. Nixon agreed that Ehrlichman had every right to expect him to stay in "the best of condition in a campaign," and Ehrlichman left their meeting with the understanding that Nixon would avoid alcohol during the grueling months ahead. "As far as I'm concerned," he wrote in his memoirs, "he kept that bargain during the 1968 campaign."

4 Nixon needed opposition. His party needed to know that he was the best man for the nomination, and the public needed to be convinced that he could win the election in November. In Michigan governor George Romney, Nixon found a way to satisfy those needs.

Romney had risen from the rubble of the 1964 election to hold the leading position in the early polls on the presidential election to follow. Romney's background offered much to recommend him. He was a self-made man. He had guided American Motors through a huge developmental period that found the automobile manufacturer building compact cars like the American and Classic—models that influenced the direction taken by Detroit's Big Three. His adventure into politics found him on the fast track to the governor's mansion. In 1966, while Nixon was stumping for Republican candidates in an effort to rebuild his party, Romney was storming through Michigan, running for reelection to the state's top office. He overwhelmed his opponent in the general election.

Nixon did not consider Romney a serious contender in the presidential race. It had been easy for him to win over his home state, but Romney would be facing a lot tougher challenge when he faced the national press, hungry for stories, looking for angles, ready to pounce on the first sign of a gaffe. Romney, Nixon felt, couldn't handle "big-league pitching."

Romney, the front-runner in the very early weeks of the campaign, long before Nixon began to make his move, had the bad habit of spontaneously speaking in ways that required further explanation after his words appeared in print. "He was particularly vulnerable to charges of indecisiveness and was forever making observations off the cuff that later had to be 'clarified' to get him out of hot water," wrote journalist Jules Witcover, who traveled with Romney on the campaign trail.

Romney struggled with questions about the Vietnam War, leading Witcover to observe that he was building "a public impression that he was a businessman out of his element in politics." This was bad news for Nixon, who wanted the public to believe that Romney was a strong candidate and thus, for Nixon, a worthy opponent. If that were the case, beating Romney in the New Hampshire primary, as Nixon expected, would represent a notable victory.

Unfortunately for Nixon and his plans, Romney sabotaged his own campaign with his statements about the war. Romney, initially a strong supporter of American involvement in Vietnam, had shifted his stance. He was now critical of the Johnson administration's handling of the war. The news media peppered him with questions about Vietnam, which he managed to deflect until the end of August, when he agreed to appear on a news and features program in Detroit.

It could not have gone more poorly. During the taping of the interview on August 31, 1967, when asked about the inconsistencies in his position on the war over the years, Romney made statements he would never live down. He and nine other governors had visited Vietnam in 1965, and during that trip he had received what he called "the greatest brainwashing that anyone can get when you go over to Vietnam, not only by the generals, but also by the diplomatic corps over there, and they do a very thorough job." Since returning to the States, he had been researching the history of Vietnam. "As a result I have changed my mind," he told the television reporter. "I no longer believe it was necessary for us to get involved in South Vietnam to stop aggression in Southeast Asia and to prevent Chinese Communist domination in Southeast Asia."

The statement was not only frank; it revealed Romney to be no different than the steadily increasing percentage of Americans who, at one time supportive of the war, had changed their views. Unfortunately for Romney, *brainwashed* was a word that resonated in an extremely negative way. Without access to the kind of information available to elected officials, voters could be forgiven if they felt they were being deceived by the government or military. However, someone running for the position of commander in chief, a man capable of traveling to Vietnam and being received by some of the highest ranking officials and military personnel . . . well, he just couldn't appear in front of the American people and claim brainwashing. Further, the trip had occurred in 1965. Why had it taken two years for him to make such a strong public statement? "How long does a brainwashing linger?" smirked the *Detroit News,* which demanded that Romney withdraw from the race and leave the field open to Nelson Rockefeller. When asked about how the brainwashing remark might have affected Romney's candidacy, Eugene McCarthy, rarely at a loss for words when an occasion arose for a pithy remark, shrugged it off with, "I think in that case a light rinse would have been sufficient."

The blowback from Romney's remark was immediate and devastating. Romney dropped sixteen points in the next Harris Poll; he was ridiculed across the country, the butt of comedians' jokes and editorial cartoons. Despite the damage his brainwashing statement had inflicted on his candidacy, Romney stood fast to the statement. "I was not misunderstood," he insisted two days after making the statement, while addressing the press, when asked if his remarks might have been misunderstood. "If you want to get into a discussion of who's been brainwashing who, I suggest you take a look at what the Administration has been telling the American people." Hoping to rehabilitate his image, he refused to drop out of the race.

No one else seemed to be willing to step up. Charles Percy, young and popular after his 1966 Senate victory in Illinois, was not interested, nor was John Lindsay, New York City's charismatic liberal mayor. New York governor Nelson Rockefeller, a liberal Republican thought to be a contender, adamantly insisted that he was not a candidate, to the extent of openly financing Romney's campaign. Newcomer Ronald Reagan, who had defeated Nixon's nemesis Pat Brown in the 1966 California gubernatorial election, seemed alternately interested and disinterested—not exactly the stance the nation wanted to see in a presidential candidate.

Rockefeller's reluctance to run puzzled Republican liberals and moderates. Aside from Nixon, he had the best name recognition of viable GOP candidates, and his liberal social views might woo moderate to conservative Democrats seeking an alternative to LBJ. His credentials sparkled. He served the Roosevelt administration as an assistant to the secretary of state and as coordinator for Latin American affairs. He worked as the secretary of health, education, and welfare under Eisenhower, leaving when he was elected governor of New York in 1958. As governor, he had overseen sweeping changes.

A divorce and subsequent marriage to a younger woman made him gossip-sheet fodder, while his candidacy for the 1964 Republican presidential nomination had placed him on one side of a bitter party struggle. Goldwater supporters had shouted him down as he tried to challenge the party platform at the 1964 Republican National Convention in San Francisco; he had countered their opposition with open scorn. The liberal side of the party, led by Rockefeller and Pennsylvania governor William Scranton, had attempted—and failed—to wrestle the nomination from Goldwater and the Far Right, but as they stood in the ashes of the campaign, knowing full well that Barry Goldwater stood no chance against Lyndon Johnson, they refused to support the nominee, party unity be damned. Goldwater's defeat had been sour vindication of their pessimism.

Four years later, Rockefeller was not enthusiastic about another run, despite all the talk and encouragement. In any event, he would not force himself to approach party bigwigs, tail between his legs, contrite, begging for their support. He didn't relish a battle with Nixon, which was all but assured. George Romney, who held many of the same beliefs, would make a good surrogate—and he *wanted* the job. (Of course, Rockefeller coveted it as well, but he found it easy to deny it in public.) Rockefeller shoveled money into the Romney campaign; he advised the Michigan governor on how to run a national campaign, set him up with volunteers, and praised Romney's merits to the press. He continued to support him through the missteps and misstatements, including the *brainwashed* disaster.

Despite all this, reporters and pundits expected him to declare his candidacy, and over the months Rockefeller fed the speculation by saying that he might run as a favorite son in New York. He took it a step further a few months later when he admitted that he would accept the nomination if he was drafted. He did not discourage Maryland governor Spiro T. Agnew from setting up a Draft Rockefeller movement.

But there was one inescapable problem, a contradiction that Rockefeller could not overcome: he was popular with voters but still disliked by his party. He might have been strong enough to win the general election, but it was highly unlikely that he would find his way onto the ballot. The public opinion polls told the cold truth. He consistently ran ahead of Johnson (53 percent to 35 percent in early November, which was much better than Nixon), but Nixon thrashed him by as great as a five-to-one margin when county chairmen were asked about their preference. The blunt reality was, as concluded by the Harris pollsters: "Nixon today would sweep a nationwide G.O.P. primary, but Rockefeller would be a much more likely winner against Mr. Johnson."

Neither Nixon nor Rockefeller appealed to the Republican Party's conservative voters. Ronald Reagan, positioned much farther to the right than the more moderate Nixon and Rockefeller, was their choice. Reagan lagged far behind the other two in experience in public office, but his national exposure as an actor in movies and television closed the difference in name recognition. His criticism of the 1964 and 1965 violence in the Watts section of Los Angeles, along with his strong views about how antiwar protests should be handled, brought into sharp focus the increasing concern about law and order in contemporary urban America. People were buying guns and talking about how they would use them to defend their homes; counterdemonstrations to antiwar rallies led to skirmishes on the streets. Californians blamed Democratic leadership for the liberal legislation and the kid-gloved law enforcement that seemed connected to the mayhem. The 1966 election, Reagan's first dip into electoral politics, was going to focus on moral issues: "crime, drugs, and juvenile delinquency." Reagan, ever the professional, played to the cheap seats. He could address these issues with generalities guaranteed to mollify the masses. His leading-man looks, easygoing demeanor, soft-spoken but firm public statements, and take-back-the-night beliefs won him the 1966 gubernatorial election and projected him, as governor of a huge state, as a strong player in the 1968 presidential race. If nothing else, running in the California primary as a favorite son might find him holding enough delegate votes to eventually influence the Republican Party at the August 1968 national convention in Miami.

Reagan and the possibilities of his entering the race concerned Nixon and

his campaign staff. Reagan could divide the party and cause all kinds of problems in an election that still figured to favor Lyndon Johnson, despite his un-
popularity. A strong swing to the far right might lead to the same type of mess
that had brought the party down over the past four years. As a candidate, Reagan was no Barry Goldwater, but their politics shared common denominators.
According to Nixon, "Reagan's views were as conservative as Goldwater's,
but he had what Goldwater lacked: the ability to present his views in a reasonable and eloquent manner."

Hoping to sound out the California governor's intentions, Nixon flew to
California and met with Reagan in July 1967. Both were cagey in what they
revealed about their plans. Nixon told Reagan that he had "tentative plans" for
entering the primaries. Reagan, acting surprised that he himself would even be
considered presidential material, informed Nixon that he had no intention of
entering the primaries, but held out the option of running as a favorite son in
the California primary, mainly, he said, "to assure party unity in California." It
is unlikely that either man, savvy as he was, was fooled by the other's explanation. In the months ahead, they would circle one another in an awkward dance,
each wary of the other, Nixon rightfully confident that his lead in the polls
would carry him through.

5 In its October 20, 1967, issue, *Time* magazine ran a lengthy cover story
that attempted to identify and sort through the putative candidates for the
1968 Republican presidential nomination. Titled "Anchors Aweigh," the article
framed its assertions with a mention of the upcoming National Governors'
Conference, an annual taxpayer-supported bash that mixed business with pleasure, with heavy emphasis on the latter. The 1967 rendition would be an eight-
day cruise to the Virgin Islands, attended by forty-two governors, twenty-one
from each party, and a mass of seven hundred aides, journalists, wives, and
various hangers-on, all primed for days and nights filled with eating, drinking,
dancing, partying, lounging in the sun, and, whenever the mood struck, politicking. Nelson Rockefeller, George Romney, and Ronald Reagan were in attendance, along with "enough potential vice-presidential candidates to create a
traffic jam on the promenade deck." Since this was a cruise for governors only,
Richard Nixon was notably absent from the roster of presidential aspirants, as
was Illinois senator Charles Percy, whose name was bandied about in circles of
election watchers, but who emphatically denied any interest in running.

Time had been tracking potential Republican candidates for the better part
of a year, its objective being twofold: to parse out the candidate with the best

chance of coming out on top for the nomination, and to then identify which candidate offered the strongest challenge of unseating Lyndon Johnson in the presidential election. They were not necessarily the same man. Although unpopular, LBJ was a shoo-in for the Democratic Party nomination, and even in his weakened position, he would be difficult to beat in the general election. There was an outside chance that Johnson might follow in Harry S. Truman's steps and drop out of the race, but Truman had only done so after his approval rating had plunged to 23 percent in November 1951 and he had lost the New Hampshire primary to Estes Kefauver a few months later. Nixon might have summed up the current situation best when he noted that in 1964 the Republicans had been at a disadvantage because they were running against Johnson's campaign promises. "Now we can run against his performance," an optimistic Nixon declared.

Nixon, *Time* projected, was the front-runner and man to beat. Romney, by virtue of his misstatements, was out. One intriguing possibility would be a "dream ticket" pairing Nelson Rockefeller with Ronald Reagan, who would grab the delegates from New York and California, respectively, as well as northern and western states. Reagan's conservatism, appealing to voters who might otherwise favor George Wallace, would balance Rockefeller's liberal leanings, making a strongly balanced ticket. The current Gallup Poll, pitting a Rockefeller–Reagan pairing against Johnson–Humphrey, had the Republican candidates comfortably ahead of the incumbents, 57 percent to 43 percent.

That neither Rockefeller nor Reagan was interested in running did little to quell the speculation. It was early in the season, and campaign watchers reasoned that either or both would probably be open to the party's call. Rockefeller, aboard the *SS Independence* bound for the Virgin Islands, responded irritably to queries about the *Time* story. "I wouldn't be human if I didn't appreciate a nice remark," he told reporters, "but I'm not a candidate, I'm not going to be a candidate, and *I don't want to be President.*" And just in case he hadn't been heard or wasn't believed by the press corps, he repeated himself: "I *said* I don't want to be President."

While the states' chief executives worked on their tans and glutted on lobster, a massive antiwar demonstration, one of the largest in American history to that point, commenced in Washington, D.C., on October 21, capping a "Stop the Draft" week of nationwide demonstrations. The Washington event was the jewel of the week, and depending on whom you were talking with, between fifty thousand and one hundred thousand protesters assembled in the nation's capital to have their feelings heard. Organized by David Dellinger and the National Mobilization Committee to End the War in Vietnam, the March on the Pentagon, as it came to be known, featured a day of speeches, music, demonstrations, civil disobedience, and, in one of the most prominent displays of political theater in its time, an attempt to levitate the Pentagon and exorcise its demons. It all began at West Potomac Park near the Lincoln Memorial and concluded in the parking lot of the symbol of American military might. Antiwar activists Jerry Rubin and Abbie Hoffman led a list of well-known Vietnam opponents that included pediatrician and activist Dr. Benjamin Spock, novelist Norman Mailer, folk music trio Peter, Paul, and Mary, singer/songwriter Phil Ochs, and poet/musician Ed Sanders and his band, the Fugs. Defense Secretary Robert McNamara urged restraint from army personnel, federal marshals, military police, and other law enforcement on hand to stand between the demonstrators and the Pentagon. In the early going, the event was peaceful. Skirmishes broke out when a few dozen demonstrators attempted to storm the Pentagon office building, and the following morning when authorities attempted to clear the area of protesters. In all, 683 protesters were eventually arrested, but the event was mostly the nonviolent confrontation the organizers envisioned. Less than 50 demonstrators and law enforcement officials were injured. Mailer's prizewinning account of the events, *Armies of the Night,* recorded the drama, tension, action, and absurdity of what the *Washington Post* would call "a touchstone event in American history."

The event bore importance not for what it accomplished but for what it represented. The antiwar demonstrations were snowballing in number and effect; young people of draftable age were being seen and heard, and seizing at least temporary control of the national consciousness, whether government officials approved of it or not. The sight of a young, long-haired youth placing a daisy in the barrel of a National Guardsman's rifle was both moving and, to a large portion of America, unsettling. The Pentagon march was the crowning touch to a summer's worth of events—and rebellion. The Summer of Love had brought forth *Sgt. Pepper* and the Grateful Dead, air spiked with acrid hints of marijuana smoke, acid trips and Dr. Timothy Leary, free and open sex, kids hopping in cars or microbuses and discovering America, and mass protests against the violence and death in Southeast Asia. The youth movement was going to unseat its parents' generation—the Establishment—and replace it with its own version of utopia, beginning with peace in Southeast Asia. The Establishment, however, was pushing back. An enormous June 1967 antiwar rally in Los Angeles, featuring appearances by Dr. Benjamin Spock, Muhammad Ali, H. Rap Brown, Phil Ochs, and others, erupted in violence. Television images captured film of rioting, baton-swinging police beating unarmed demonstrators, including some in wheelchairs. People were beaten senseless. Ochs, who had earlier sung his new antiwar song "The War Is Over," was transfixed by the sight of a war being fought in the streets of his city. "Phil thought it was the beginning of something really big and really bad," his friend artist Ron Cobb remembered. "It was like a movie to him, a Fellini movie."

What he was seeing was only the beginning.

Out of the mayhem rose a sliver of hope for the Republican would-be candidates, who, to the man, preferred to avoid any discussion about Vietnam, especially after the Romney affair. The disruptive assemblies on the college campuses and in the streets offered a chance to deflect the Vietnam issue to a discussion about law and order. Indeed, those living in or around large urban areas still associated the law-and-order problems with the racially motivated rioting, but now that the demonstrations were commanding headlines in some of these large cities, the war and racial tensions could be bundled into a convenient general discussion. For Republicans, this was very good news. Law and order hit voters in the gut; Vietnam, at this stage of the discussion, when voters didn't know whom or what to believe, could only appeal to a deteriorating sense of patriotism.

Talk of the war was at the center of an episode onboard the *Independence*. President Johnson had directed Marvin Watson, one of his top aides, to send a telegram to Price Daniel, a former governor of Texas, who was operating as Johnson's eyes and ears on the *Independence* cruise. Johnson, feeling the heat from the opposition to his policies in Vietnam, was seeking a vote of confidence from the governors onboard the ship, and his telegram specifically listed the governors who needed persuading to vote in Johnson's favor. Watson sent the telegram, and the *Independence* received it, but what happened next was one of those incidents that, had it been more important, might have been assigned a place in political lore. The telegram was either misdelivered or stolen outright—and there were disputes about this—but in any event, it wound up in the Republicans' hands. Someone ran off copies on the boat's mimeograph machine and saw that they were properly distributed, and before long, everyone onboard, including the press, was in on Johnson's now very embarrassing directive. Of the potential presidential candidates onboard, Rockefeller said very little, while Reagan, whose press aide, Lyn Nofziger, had initially briefed the press about the existence of the telegram, seemed content to sit back, sip crème de menthe through a straw, and chuckle at the brouhaha. Predictably, George Romney had the most to say. Romney, believing that LBJ already had more than enough power in the decision-making in Vietnam, had been a vocal opponent of this kind of resolution in the past; this latest message, he insisted, was typical of the "news manipulation, snow job, hogwash, and attempts at brainwashing" that one could expect from the Johnson administration, especially in its handling of the war.

The president would have to wait for that vote of approval.

6 In his public statements and interviews with the press, Nixon remained noncommittal about his plans, even as he went about assembling what proved to be one of the most formidable campaign staffs in recent memory. To exorcise his loser image, Nixon needed more than strong showings in upcoming primaries; he required a strong media team to see that the point was not lost on the public. While his television team pondered the best ways to make him presentable on the tube, Nixon had others join Pat Buchanan in researching, writing speeches, and addressing reporters daily. Each seemed to have a fancy title, but the jobs all pointed in the direction of recasting an old image into something that appealed to skeptical voters.

Everything was going Nixon's way. Although he had yet to formally announce his candidacy as 1967 drew to a close, it was a foregone conclusion among the pundits, even though Nixon and the Republican Party still fought off a nagging uncertainty about Nixon's ability to beat Johnson in the general election. Nixon's popularity within his own party was undeniable. An October Gallup Poll placed Nixon far ahead of the Republican field, with 42 percent of the respondents saying they would favor him on the Republican ticket. Nelson Rockefeller placed second in the poll, with 18 percent of the vote. Reagan followed at 14 percent, and Romney, still stinging from his "brainwashed" statement, had dropped to 13 percent. More significantly, the poll placed Nixon ahead of Johnson in a head-to-head match, 49 percent to 45 percent. That lead slipped away in the next poll, but Nixon was encouraged. He appeared to be well positioned for the upcoming primary season.

Then came the shocker: shortly before Christmas, offering no indication of what led to his decision, Nixon confided with his family and closest friends that he was almost certain he would be dropping out of the race. He had been depressed in recent weeks, though he said nothing about the root of the downturn in his mood. Perhaps it was an understanding of the enormity of what he was about to undertake, the prospects of having the press yapping at his heels for months on end, the innumerable meals on the road, all the flights and airports, the cities and towns, large and small, the speeches, and the sea of outstretched hands. His wife was lukewarm at best about his running; that much Nixon already knew.

On December 22, following a busy day of lunching with his law partners, conferring with his campaign advisers later in the afternoon, and in the evening hosting a Christmas party at his apartment, an exhausted Richard Nixon spent the late hours of his day in his home office, sitting by a fire and weighing the pros and cons of the decision he had to make. He pulled out a yellow legal pad and under the heading of "I have decided personally against becoming a candidate," he drew up a list of reasons leading to that decision. Almost all of them sprang from past campaigns. The memories of his losses in 1960 and 1962 continued to haunt him, and there was no predicting how his family might respond to another painful loss. He hated the idea of going through the fundraising process. He questioned whether he had the heart or zeal necessary for a successful campaign. "Personally, I have had it," he wrote. "I want nothing else." And the harshest entry of all: "I don't give a damn."

He was torn by conflict. "Had I come all this way to avoid the clash?" he wondered. "I *did* want to run. Every instinct said yes. But now, on the brink of that decision, I was surprised to find myself procrastinating."

It is unclear how serious Nixon was about abandoning his quest. He had been working and planning for two years. He had assembled a very strong staff and group of advisors for the battles ahead. He had had a lot of time to think about his plans. What had changed?

Nixon discussed his feelings with his wife and daughters on Christmas Day. Julie and Tricia tried to talk their father into changing his mind, while Pat stayed noncommittal, stating that she would support his final decision. On December 28, Nixon flew to Key Biscayne, Florida, for some time to think away from his family. He conferred with Rev. Billy Graham, who listened to his ruminations and advised him to run. "I think it is your destiny to be President," he told Nixon.

Nixon returned to New York on January 9, in time to celebrate his fifty-fifth birthday. He had reached a decision that he was now prepared to share with his family. Whether his difficulties amounted to eleventh-hour self-doubts before he dedicated himself to the tough months ahead, or if they were simply a "charade," an exercise calculated to assure himself that he had "a secure home front," as historian Stephen E. Ambrose suggested in his biography of Nixon, the final result remained the same. He would run.

George Wallace
Politics of Race

Can a former truck driver who is married to a former dime-store clerk and whose father was a plain dirt farmer be elected President of the United States?

This was the question, repeated often, posed by the George Wallace camp from the beginning of Wallace's unlikely run for the presidency. Although it appeared to be a modest, self-effacing query, it was in reality a stiff challenge: If you dare, vote for someone outside the boys' club in Washington, D.C. This is not a man rising from privilege; he comes from peasant stock. A vote for him is a tally for Everyman.

George Corley Wallace seemed to have been placed on this planet to be a politician. He enjoyed interacting with people; more important in terms of his political career, he instinctively knew how to manipulate them. He had studied law and even served as a judge for a while, but this was not his calling, any more than it had been Richard Nixon's. Although he had risen from modest means and never seemed to have enough money for his next sandwich, let alone luxury, his life had been on a collision course with high-level politics. It was said that he would walk across a huge stretch of farmland in order to shake hands with a sweaty farmer seated on a tractor, or cross a busy street to greet two voters standing alone on a sidewalk. He not only did it, he did it happily.

Short and wiry, Wallace looked like a prizefighter in one of the lower weights—which he had been for a brief time in his youth. As often as not, he wore an expression caught somewhere between a sneer and a snarl. He reveled in his image as a scrapper. He would need every one of these qualities if he was to have any hope of making headway in a race stacked against him.

1 George Wallace seized the national news spotlight on a sweltering afternoon of June 11, 1963, when he blocked the entrance to the University of Alabama's Foster Auditorium in an attempt to deny two young African Americans, James Hood and Vivian Malone, the opportunity to register for classes. The scene, as carefully crafted as a scene from a Broadway play, right down to the markings on the pavement indicating where the key players were to be standing, would be recorded by the estimated four hundred reporters and cameramen jockeying for position and hoping to escape a sun that bore down on them relentlessly. A few months earlier, Wallace had been elected to his first term as Alabama governor on his promise to keep his state segregated, and this was his chance to make good on his vow.

Throughout his life, Wallace would insist, unconvincingly, that he was not a racist. He proudly admitted to being a segregationist, but he drew a distinct line between being a racist and a segregationist. He meant no harm to blacks, he would say; he just didn't want them sharing his space in restaurants, schools, churches, and other public facilities, nor did he want blacks marrying his state's white daughters. It was what *they*—the blacks—wanted as well. Or so he said. It had been the way of the South from the day Lee surrendered to Grant, and the only time there seemed to be any trouble now was when outsiders—liberal agitators, Communists, or Communist sympathizers, in Wallace's book—interfered in matters that were none of their concern. Wallace vehemently maintained, as did the governors of all the Southern states, that racial issues were not to be decided by the federal government; these were state matters best decided by the individual states.

President John F. Kennedy and his younger brother, Attorney General Robert F. Kennedy, strongly disagreed. JFK wanted to see new federal legislation guaranteeing equal rights in employment, housing, and voting, but bills of this nature always failed in Congress, if they even managed to make it out of committee for debate and a vote. Enforcing existing laws, particularly those already ruled upon by the Supreme Court, was another matter. The civil rights movement, gaining momentum in recent years through the activities of the Freedom Riders, voter registration drives, sit-ins, civil disobedience, and marches led by Rev. Dr. Martin Luther King Jr., Ralph Abernathy, and other black leaders, had addressed the gross inequalities between whites and blacks, and the Kennedys decided that the time had arrived to enforce laws habitually ignored by segregationists in the South.

The first big test had gone poorly, when James Meredith, a twenty-nine-year-old African American, attempted to enroll at the University of Mississippi. The air force veteran's efforts had begun in 1961, when he applied for admission to the university, only to be denied by university officials. Recent attempts had been thwarted by Governor Ross Barnett, an outspoken segregationist, who personally blocked an entranceway to the Oxford, Mississippi, campus. The Kennedys refused to buckle. Meredith, they stated, was going to register. Fearing a violent altercation between those protecting Meredith and those fighting his admission, the Kennedys attempted to broker a peaceful solution with Barnett. The deal would have allowed Meredith to register while Barnett and the university gave all the appearances of putting up strong resistance before giving way to the inevitable. Unfortunately, Barnett, who offered a number of suggestions, including a preposterous scenario that called for armed marshals drawing guns on him while he blocked the entrance to the school, hesitated until it was too late to firm up a final arrangement.

"I had been involved in the various plans which kept shifting and changing in what, looking back on it, was a sort of unconscionable way," Nicholas Katzenbach, the deputy attorney general, said in an interview two years later. Katzenbach had flown to Oxford to oversee Meredith's registration, and he was frustrated by the way both sides handled the matter. "I mean, you had a plan at 2 o'clock, and at 3 o'clock, after a conversation with the Governor, this was changed. There were all these efforts."

Governor Barnett seemed to have no clue as to how to properly address the trouble ahead. He would say that he wanted no trouble, that he would cooperate with those trying to register Meredith, but his actions said otherwise. At a packed Ole Miss football game, he delivered a fiery speech defending segregation and his state's honor; he relented only when the infuriated Kennedys threatened to brief the press about their secret negotiations.

On the evening of Sunday, September 30, 1962, the night before Meredith was scheduled to register at the university, a mass of more than one thousand angry students, citizens, and outsiders, armed with shotguns, rifles, baseball bats, eggs, Molotov cocktails, rocks, bricks, and bottles, converged on the campus. A force of highway patrolmen, state police, and U.S. Marshals stood guard over the campus, and President Kennedy had federalized the state's National Guard; federal troops were on standby in Memphis. When night fell, Barnett dismissed the state police, leaving only the marshals to defend the campus. Tensions were further stretched when the president addressed the nation on television at ten o'clock and urged people to obey the law. The gathered masses erupted in rage when it became known that Meredith was hidden away somewhere on campus. The U.S. Marshals assigned to protect Meredith and the campus, badly outnumbered but ordered not to shoot unless Meredith's life was in peril, tried to control the crowd with tear gas, and for five hours, the two sides battled. By the time federal troops were called in to restore order, 28 marshals had been shot, 166 overall had been injured, and 2 people—a French journalist and a local jukebox repairman—had lost their lives. The arrival of the troops worked against the government: there were so many that it looked like an invasion or occupation. Meredith registered without further violence, but he would require an armed escort to classes throughout the school year.

Wallace, on the campaign trail and yet to be elected governor of Alabama at the time of the rioting, used Ole Miss as a means of propping up his own anti-integration rhetoric. After praising Barnett's stand, Wallace offered a statement linking himself to the Mississippi governor. "I, like Governor Barnett, am tired of being pushed around by the Justice Department and the irresponsible, lousy federal courts," he declared. "I am going to stand up against those who would try to take over our school system."

Wallace's own defiance of integration laws could be traced back four years, to 1958, when he had made his initial run for governor of Alabama. He had not made segregation a campaign issue, and he had been beaten by a vocal segregationist named John Patterson. When analyzing his defeat, Wallace estimated that being soft on the school segregation issue had cost him the election. "John Patterson out-niggered me," he complained bitterly to friends. "And boys, I ain't going to be out-niggered again!"

When he ran again in 1962, he dramatically altered his approach. Segregation burned at the molten core of his campaign speeches, and to connect more directly with his voters, he shelved the kind of flowery language associated with the campaign stump, replacing it with the earthier, plain speech that one heard on the street, in the factories, in farm country. Wallace had always preached a populist message; now he sounded like the good ol' boys he would share a Dr. Pepper with at the corner drugstore. He handily won the general election and never looked back. In his inaugural address, he delivered a battle cry that would be remembered and repeated by supporters and detractors alike: "In the name of the greatest people ever trod this earth, I draw a line in the dust and toss the gauntlet before the feet of tyranny. And I say, Segregation now! Segregation tomorrow! Segregation forever!"

Wallace's swagger masked his grave safety concerns over the enrollment of two students at the University of Alabama. He feared a reprise of the University of Mississippi violence, which would greatly tarnish his message and place much of the responsibility for the injuries or deaths on his shoulders. In Wallace's perfect world, he would win the day if the Kennedys overreacted by sending in federal troops to keep order, casting Wallace, the university, and the State of Alabama in their all too familiar role of the little guy being intimidated by a big, brutish bully. Wallace figured that someone in the Justice Department—presumably Deputy Attorney General Nicholas Katzenbach—would fly to Tuscaloosa to handle the showdown. On the day of the confrontation, Wallace would make a grand gesture of blocking the entrance and delivering a speech before standing aside and allowing the two students to pass. His countrymen would praise him for taking a courageous stand and living up to his campaign promises.

This plan, with a few tweaks here and there, would have constituted the Kennedys' perfect world as well. They had no intention of legitimizing Wallace's grandstanding by sending in federal troops. Nor did they plan to lead Wallace away in handcuffs, as the governor privately feared. The Kennedys made it very clear to Wallace that the two students were going to register, regardless of the measures taken to oppose it. According to Nicholas Katzenbach, the Kennedys figured that Wallace would willingly capitulate if the Justice Department allowed him the opportunity to save face. "If we went through the symbolic business, Wallace would give up," Katzenbach remembered later. "We really had to give him his little show."

For the Kennedys, the past year had been an explosive learning experience on just how little they understood about the South and its traditions. Law and reason meant nothing when dealing with a racist monster like Eugene "Bull" Conner, the police commissioner of Birmingham, who used high-powered fire hoses, police dogs, and nightsticks on any black who dared to defy his orders. Men, including well-respected citizens, still slipped on white robes and hoods, and meted out their brand of vigilante justice after sundown. The Kennedys had been insulated from all this when they were growing up. They certainly knew about the Civil War and Reconstruction and Jim Crow; they were familiar with the words *poverty* and *segregation.* But they had never encountered it, firsthand, until they entered adulthood and, more specifically, politics. They were stunned, for instance, when Jack was campaigning in West Virginia in 1960 and they encountered the squalid living conditions and dangerous working environments in the state. Jack and Bobby Kennedy had entered the state with the belief that their Catholicism would be their main obstacle to overcome, when, in fact, voters had much more basic needs on their minds.

The South and the civil rights movement represented a continuation of their on-the-job education. They, like so many northern whites, could not fathom how an entire region of the country could still seethe from battlefield defeats suffered a century earlier. Further, they could not understand or accept how civil rights laws could be so blatantly abused. And, as Jack Kennedy had discovered when he submitted a new civil rights legislation package to Congress on February 23, 1963, no region of the United States had the inclination to push for further inroads.

This alone frustrated the Kennedys, but what drove them to the brink was the pressure they felt from the black community to do more. Martin Luther King wasn't satisfied with the slow progress the Kennedy administration was carving into civil rights legislation and enforcement, and more militant black activist groups talked about taking action into their own hands. Recent demonstrations in Birmingham had become more destructive and violent, with young African Americans willing to go to combat with the police. King risked his life any time he made a public appearance. The Kennedys moved forward with as much authority as they could muster, but progress was painfully slow and unacceptable to an oppressed race of people all too familiar with the cry for patience—an excuse that had been a century in the making.

Ironically, Wallace would have preferred to avoid a schoolhouse confrontation—at least in early 1963. He pleaded for more time, at least until the fall of 1963, to sort through the intricacies of school desegregation—despite his campaign promises—but the ploy had grown old and tired. The battle line was drawn on May 21, when a federal judge ordered the University of Alabama to admit two black students to summer classes. Wallace responded that he personally would see that it would not happen. A registration date of June 11 was set.

In the weeks leading up to the confrontation, Wallace toyed with Robert Kennedy. He baited him over the telephone. On one occasion, he refused to talk to Kennedy; instead, he turned the call over to one of his friends, who frustrated Kennedy to no end while everyone in Wallace's office listened in on a speakerphone. When Kennedy flew down to Alabama to meet with Wallace, the governor made a big point of tape-recording their conversation, as if to show Kennedy that he did not trust him. Kennedy was furious with Wallace and his cohorts, but that was the effect that Wallace wanted to elicit.

The showdown at the University of Alabama, in retrospect, was almost anticlimactic. Wallace delivered on his promise of keeping the campus clear of possible troublemakers, and the meeting was carefully staged, to the extent of marks being chalked on the pavement to indicate where the media were to stand and where security was to assemble. An estimated 150 state patrolmen encircled the Foster Auditorium, with a mass of state troopers, clad in riot gear, lined up on a path leading to the building. The Kennedys were similarly cautious. The two students, decked out in their Sunday best, were instructed to stay in the car while Nicholas Katzenbach negotiated with Wallace; they would not be entering the building to register but instead be driven to their respective dormitories. This meant that Wallace would not be arrested for defying a court order by physically obstructing their entrance to the building. Had there not been the violence at the University of Mississippi a year earlier, the pageantry in Alabama might have been waved off as overkill.

A podium for Wallace had been set up behind another white line, strategically placed so Wallace would benefit, at least minimally, from the shade while Katzenbach stood in the oppressive heat and sun.

Wallace emerged from an air-conditioned auditorium when Katzenbach, the two students, and others in their entourage arrived. The governor, looking every bit as defiant as he felt, waited for the associate attorney general to begin.

"I have President Kennedy's proclamation," Katzenbach began. "I have come to ask you for unequivocal assurance that you or anyone under your control will not bar these students. I have come here to ask now for unequivocal assurance that you will permit these students who, after all, merely want an education in the great University—"

Wallace interrupted him before he could finish.

"Well, you make this statement, but we don't need for you to make a speech," he said. "You made your statement."

Katzenbach, visibly angry, continued. He wanted Wallace's assurance that he would step aside and allow James Hood and Vivian Malone to enter the building.

Instead of responding, Wallace, speaking into a microphone hanging from his neck, declared that he had a statement of his own to make. He produced a four-page, typed speech attacking the federal government for offering "a frightful example of oppression of the rights, privileges, and sovereignty of this state by officers of the federal government." This was Wallace's big moment, and he was determined to milk it for all it was worth. He condemned the government's actions, claiming that "millions of Americans will gaze in sorrow upon the situation."

Wallace made certain that the nearly four hundred members of the press in attendance knew that without his efforts and intervention there might have been a violent confrontation. He—Wallace—stood as the representative of "thousands of other Alabamans."

Katzenbach stood rigidly, arms crossed tightly around his chest, sweat coursing down his face, trying to hold his growing anger while Wallace went on. When Wallace finally concluded his statement, Katzenbach asked him to stand aside and allow the students to enter the building, even though Hood and Malone were still seated in a car. Wallace refused to respond. He held his position in front of the door, maintaining an uncomfortable silence while Katzenbach waited. Katzenbach repeated his order twice more, but Wallace refused to budge. The students, Katzenbach said, *would* be registering with the university, with or without Wallace's cooperation, but for the time being, they would go to their dormitories and check in.

A few hours later, at three o'clock that afternoon, Wallace was again standing in front of the auditorium door. Katzenbach was nowhere to be seen. This time, Wallace faced a handful of armed soldiers, commanded by National Guard General Henry V. Graham, who stood before Wallace in full uniform, complete with a Confederate flag patch stitched on his breast pocket. Another group of federalized troops were on the way. Wallace had spoken to Graham earlier in the afternoon and had promised to offer no resistance if he were allowed to give one final statement. As promised, he stepped aside and allowed the two black students to enter the auditorium, but not before declaring that the state was winning the bigger battle because "we are awakening the people to the trend toward military dictatorship in this country."

■ ■ ■ ■ ■

President Kennedy had no time to savor a victory in Alabama. With almost no time to prepare, he decided to deliver a nationally televised address that same evening, a speech calling for sweeping new civil rights legislation in Congress. The confrontation with Wallace had convinced him that the time was ripe for making a strong commitment to federal laws ensuring equal rights to all Americans, and he did not wish to waste a single day in introducing his program. At one o'clock in the afternoon, before he had even had the chance to see the playback of the Wallace encounter or hear any of the analysis of it, Kennedy called a meeting with Republican leaders Senator Everett Dirksen and Congressman Charles Halleck. He outlined his plans and asked them to help the bills come to a vote. The new legislation faced obstacles in the months ahead. An extended filibuster was certain.

Not everyone around the president agreed with his decision to give the speech that night. Bobby Kennedy, for one, believed that the president needed more time to prepare the content and wording of a speech of this magnitude, but Jack Kennedy insisted on riding the events of the day. Footage of Alabama and Wallace, along with hastily prepared analysis, was preempting regularly scheduled television programming. The nation's collective mind was on civil rights. This was the time to strike.

The text of the speech was a jumbled mess, full of strikeovers, marginal notes, and thoughts not fully developed when Kennedy faced the television camera that evening, but one wouldn't have known it. Kennedy's passion for the subject carried the day. After opening with a mention of the events in Alabama earlier in the day, Kennedy challenged every American to "stop and examine his conscience."

He built his case deliberately. Nonwhite Americans, he pointed out, were asked to serve in the military in such places as Berlin and Vietnam, yet those same Americans were denied entrance to public places and institutions of higher learning. The facts were disturbing: a black American had only half the chance of completing high school and one-third the chance of completing college as a white American born on the same day; he had twice the chance of being unemployed. He could expect to live seven years less than a white person.

The speech gained momentum with each new sentence. Although clearly outraged by the inequality, Kennedy kept his tone even and nonaccusatory. This, he said, was a "moral issue," and he challenged white viewers to put themselves in the position of their nonwhite counterparts. "If an American, because his skin is dark, cannot enjoy the full and free life which all of us want, then who among us would be content to have the color of his skin changed and stand in his place? Who among us would then be content with the counsel of patience and delay?"

This was Kennedy at his best, delivering a speech on the same level as his historic inaugural address. As in that address, he was now asking Americans to become involved. "It is time to act—in the Congress, in your state and local legislative body, but, most of all, in all our daily lives."

Kennedy carefully avoided accusing any particular region or group for the confrontations and violence of the recent past; instead, he blamed the existing laws (or the need for more specific laws) as the cause of so many of the problems. This needed to be changed, and Kennedy's proposed legislation struck a heavy blow to the social traditions in the South. "I am therefore asking the Congress to enact legislation giving all Americans the right to be served in facilities which are open to the public—hotels, restaurants, theaters, retail stores and similar establishments." This much, Kennedy judged, was "an elementary right."

Kennedy's address, in retrospect, was significant as much for how it further defined the president as it was for its commentary on civil rights and call to action. Kennedy's heartfelt feelings had never been manifest in this way, and he had been criticized for not extending stronger leadership in civil rights issues. The speech, coming on the heels of the events in Alabama, offered the hope that a new day might be arriving for Americans of all colors.

■ ■ ■ ■ ■

But this long day in civil rights history was not over. The president's speech still echoed in the minds of millions when, shortly after midnight, NAACP organizer Medgar Evers drove into the driveway of his home in Jackson, Mississippi. Evers had spent the evening in a strategy meeting. He was aware of the events at the University of Alabama but had not heard Kennedy's speech. He had just left his car and was reaching his kitchen door when a shot rang out and he was struck in the back by a .30-06 bullet fired by a white fertilizer salesman hiding nearby. Evers's wife and children, awaiting his arrival inside the house, rushed out to his side. The bullet had torn a gaping exit wound in his chest. He died less than an hour later.

2 As the years separated him from the event and a would-be assassin's bullet put him permanently in a wheelchair and gave him pause to consider some of the decisions he had made in his life, George Wallace would say that he regretted taking his stand at the University of Alabama:

> It will probably be my legacy that this sensational thing we pulled at the University of Alabama will probably obliterate all the good we've done since those days. I made a very bad mistake in saying "segregation forever"—[and] that day at the University of Alabama, carried nationwide [on radio and television] gave me a bad image and was not good for the state's image. If I had to do it over, I would not have stood in the schoolhouse door at all; I would have prevented violence on the campus in some other manner.

He harbored no such regrets in the years immediately following his attempt to block integration at the school. He had an audience larger than he ever dreamed possible. His office was flooded with cards, letters, and telegrams from across the country—more than forty thousand in the three days following his actions, according to Wallace biographer Dan T. Carter—and the majority of those were favorable. Wallace might have expected encouragement from the South, but the support from other regions of the country led him to believe that he was delivering a message about widespread discontent over the federal government's telling the individual states what to do.

He tested his theory when, as a Democrat, he entered three presidential primaries in 1964, with surprising results. Although a prohibitive underdog, Wallace received 30 percent of the Indiana vote, 34 percent of the Wisconsin vote, and a very surprising 43 percent of the Maryland tally. Although he would eventually reject the notion of running in the general election, Wallace deemed the high numbers he received in the primaries to be a victory, proof that his states' rights message was reaching the people. He had forced both major parties to consider the issue. "I was the instrument through which the message was sent to the high councils of the parties," he crowed.

Theodore White, analyzing Wallace's popularity, attributed the unexpectedly high percentages to a "backlash" vote. According to White, the term had been coined in 1963 by economic columnist Eliot Janeway "to describe what he feared might happen if automation and economic downturn combined to squeeze factory employment down in the near future. In any competition between Negro and white workingmen for jobs in a shrinking market, Janeway feared that white workers might 'lash back' at Negro competitors."

Wallace, White proposed, fell into this line of thinking. Lower- to middle-class whites, fearing a black encroachment on their way of life, embraced the candidate who might protect what they considered to be their interests. In the Wisconsin primary, Wallace enjoyed a spike in popularity from the blue-collar, largely Polish, Italian, and Serb voters on Milwaukee's South Side; he won every white district in Gary, Indiana. Wallace was not a threat as a candidate in 1964, but he had seen enough to believe that he might make serious inroads if he ran again in 1968.

Wallace thrived on being underestimated, and far too often the media were happy to oblige. It was easy to judge him as a loudmouth redneck with a weak agenda, which led to his intelligence and political savvy being underestimated. Wallace proved his formidability on June 2, 1963, nine days before his stand at the University of Alabama, when he appeared on NBC's *Meet the Press,* the most prestigious television news program at the time. NBC's preparations for the program were extraordinary. Rather than face interviewers in Washington, D.C., which was customary with the program, Wallace was flown to New York under an assumed name and greeted at the NBC studios by the heaviest security force the studio had employed since Nikita Khrushchev had appeared on the program. The four-man panel questioning Wallace was formidable: *Meet the Press* producer Lawrence Spivak, Frank McGee of NBC News, Anthony Lewis of the *New York Times,* and Vermont Royster of the *Wall Street Journal.*

Wallace was exceedingly nervous as he waited to go on the program. He had traveled to New York with Bob Ingram, a friend and political reporter for the *Montgomery Advertiser.* Ingram tried to calm Wallace, with very little success. Wallace fidgeted and looked totally unready to appear in front of the biggest television audience of his career. He sensed an ambush by hostile questioners—a reasonable enough assumption—and he worried that he might be undermining his presidential aspirations by taking questions he might not be able to answer. He had no foreign policy stance, he complained to Ingram; what would he look like with no position at a time when the world roiled with international tension? Ingram, frustrated by Wallace's mounting tension, handed the governor a *Wall Street Journal* and instructed him to read an article and come up with a position. Wallace went over the article like a college student cramming for an exam.

Such performance anxiety was not uncommon when Wallace was appearing on television or in front of large crowds. He would worry about every little detail, only to pull himself together and stage his event as if it was the easiest task he would be performing that day.

This was the case when Wallace was finally led into the studio and cameras began recording the *Meet the Press* interview. Wallace showed no sign of apprehension. He appeared to be relaxed, and, in the eyes of one observer, an Associated Press reporter covering the appearance, he looked "in total command of himself and at least partial command of his audience." Viewers expecting the rantings of a frothing racist saw a man prepared for pointed questions and ready to answer them, all in a way that made him look cool and earnest, if not reasonable. "Hold your temper, even if they spit on you," Ingram had counseled Wallace just before he went on the air, and Wallace took the advice to heart. The questions, as one might have expected, were razor sharp and often leading, but Wallace parried as if he had been shown a list of questions prior to the interview. Wallace repeatedly stated that his forthcoming actions at the university were a matter of trying to assert states' rights in the face of what he considered to be federal malfeasance. No, this was not a simple case of discrimination. No, there would be no violence at the university, and, yes, if he were to be arrested, he would surrender peacefully and without incident. His concerns about the panelists treating him like a future presidential candidate and asking about his foreign policy ideas were unfounded. "All they wanted to know about was niggers," Wallace told Ingram after the program, "and I'm the expert."

Backlash: the enormous positive response to the *Meet the Press* engagement and Wallace's stand at the University of Alabama a short time later, coming from all across the United States, not only nosed Wallace forward toward his testing the presidential waters in 1964; perhaps more important, it indicated a sullen mood running counterpoint to the civil rights movement and the effects to force-feed desegregation to its opponents. The economics aspects of the backlash might have been visible to those observing the desperate poverty in such states as Alabama or Mississippi, where blacks were easy scapegoats among impoverished whites desperate to pay their bills and put food in front of their children. These aspects were less obvious, yet still very real, on the streets of Baltimore and Boston, in the working-class neighborhoods of Chicago and St. Louis, in the inner city of Washington, D.C., in the Bronx and Queens boroughs of New York City, in Cleveland and Los Angeles and so many others. Wallace possessed a native understanding of this; his role, as he conceived it, would be to stir the proverbial pot. So it was in 1964 when he tested the voters' temperaments in a handful of states. Even then, he was looking ahead to 1968. By then, he would have had additional time to prepare, and he would be ready to strike.

3 Despite sweeping civil rights legislation passed by the U.S House of Representatives and Senate, and signed into law by President Johnson in 1964, African Americans were still being denied their basic right to register to vote throughout the Southern states. Jim Crow was still alive and well. Black men and women attempting to register to vote were ignored, treated with hostility, forced to pay oppressive poll taxes, or subjected to "literacy" tests that would have challenged even a PhD from an Ivy League school. Whites viewed this as a means of political self-preservation: their elected officials—and their racist policies—would remain in power as long as the black vote was denied. The voter registration drives of recent years had cut inroads into this inequality but not enough to matter. Johnson wanted a new voter registration bill passed into law, but he preferred to let the 1964 legislation sink in before pressing for more.

In early 1965, Martin Luther King, always adept at focusing media attention on specific events symbolizing a much larger problem, announced that he intended to stage a fifty-mile walk from Selma to Montgomery, Alabama, the walk designed to raise national awareness of the outrageously disproportionate ratio of white to black registered voters in George Wallace's state, as well as protest the recent murder at the hands of the police of an unarmed African American protester in nearby Marion, Alabama.

The voting issue would have been reason enough. In Selma, blacks outnumbered white citizens, but the city, once a hub in the slave trade, had one of the worst black voter registration records in the country. Of the city's 15,000 voting-age black citizens, only 325 were registered to vote, whereas 67 percent of the city's 14,000 prospective white voters were registered.

King's decision was not without controversy. The Student Nonviolent Coordinating Committee (SNCC) had been working exhaustively on the voter registration campaign in Selma, and members felt that Dr. King's involvement would be tantamount to his jumping out in front of an existing parade. Only a few months earlier, he had won the 1964 Nobel Peace Prize, which meant a lot in credibility currency—perhaps too much so, in the minds of other groups. Worse than the ego-deflating was the reality that King would make his appearance and move on, leaving the repercussions of the march on the shoulders of the SNCC and their black following in Selma. There was no questioning King's leadership or abilities to command national attention, but the SNCC felt slighted enough to drop out of the march altogether.

King's plan of leading a large number of people—rumor had it that there would be at least a thousand—in a march destined to place King directly before the governor in the state capital bothered Wallace. He had been keeping as low a profile as possible in racial matters in recent months. He had taken his share of praise and criticism since the University of Alabama confrontation, but his 1968 presidential aspirations, along with the reality that he needed to keep the federal government content if he expected to see badly needed funds for some of his programs, had dictated that he dial down some of his public appearances and statements. He had delegated tasks that might lead to racially charged hostilities. He didn't have to look far to find someone more than willing to shoulder the dirty work. King, however, was bringing the voter registration issue directly to him.

Wallace decided that King and his followers could not be permitted to complete their march to Montgomery. How this would be accomplished became the subject of great discussion. Wallace insisted that there could be no violence, but a new surge of militancy among blacks, especially the younger ones, made it impossible to predict a peaceful march, even with King in attendance. Wallace listened as Bill Jones, one of his most trusted aides, offered a suggestion that might lead to a logical solution. King and his leadership group, Jones suggested, did not expect the march to continue all the way through to Montgomery; they figured they would be stopped long before they reached the shadow of the state capitol. What would happen if they were allowed to walk the entire distance without incident? Fifty-four miles was a long, long way, and a large percentage of the marchers were in no physical condition to walk it. Wallace could order Highway 80 closed for safety reasons, preventing King's marchers from driving into Montgomery. In the end, the march would fall apart, and King would be nationally embarrassed.

Wallace liked the idea and was prepared to go along with it, until another of his advisors chipped in the possibility that there could be violence along the way. The logistics of providing adequate law enforcement protection were all but impossible. Then, as time wound down to the day of the march, King announced that he would not be leading the march. The threat of assassination was too great, plus he was needed to tend to his church in Atlanta.

After rejecting Bill Jones's plan, Wallace considered other options. He stubbornly maintained that the march could not go on, but he was now walking a very narrow plank between maintaining his tough public image and maintaining the peace. He chose a way designed to contain the marchers while holding down the possibility of violence. The protesters would be cleared to progress as far as the Edmund Pettus Bridge, but they could not be allowed to proceed any farther. The bridge, which spanned the Alabama River, would bottleneck the walkers, who would be confronted by law enforcement on the other side of the bridge. Wallace specifically stated that there was to be no violence, that the police and troopers were to stand still, their billy clubs in a defense posture in front of them, while the marchers were ordered to turn around and head home. If the marchers refused, the police were to fire tear gas canisters but only enough to break up the crowd. Wallace was adamant: there could be no violence.

This, of course, was what he said behind closed doors. In public, at a press conference held the day before the march, Wallace took a more assertive stance, designed no doubt to appease constituents. There would be no march, he said; the bridge would be closed to traffic as a matter of public safety. This stated, Wallace went on to contradict the orders he had given in his private meetings. Albert Lingo and his state troopers, he said, had been ordered to use "whatever methods necessary to prevent a march."

With King no longer participating, there was some disarray over leadership roles in the march. Prior to King's announcement, the Student Nonviolent Coordinating Committee chose to officially drop out of the march, with some members, including SNCC chairman John Lewis, opting to march as private citizens rather than as representatives of the organization. On the day of the march, three of King's Southern Christian Leadership Conference leaders— Andrew Young, Hosea Williams, and James Bevel—drew straws to determine who would be the official SCLC leader in King's absence. Williams drew the shortest straw. John Lewis was asked to co-lead, even if the SNCC was not endorsing the march.

On Sunday morning, after a service and meeting at the Brown Chapel, the marchers lined up in twos and, walking silently along the city sidewalks, made their way to the bridge. The Edmund Pettus Bridge was an arching structure; one could not see across the bridge to the other side. When the first line of marchers reached the apex of the bridge, they could see what lay between them and the twelve miles they were scheduled to walk that day. Blue-jacketed and white-helmeted state troopers, along with a large posse of young men deputized by Sheriff Jim Clark, later described by Lewis as "a mean, vicious man" given to using an electric cattle prod on demonstrators, were assembled, many on horseback, at the end of the bridge. Townsmen lined both sides of the bridge. "John, can you swim?" Hosea Williams asked John Lewis as the two looked down at the Alabama River below. "No, Hosea, can you?" "Yes." "We're not going to jump," Lewis declared. "We're not going back. We're going forward."

The marchers advanced until Major John Cloud, the acting commander of the state troopers, lifted a megaphone and announced that the demonstrators were participating in an unlawful march and had two minutes to break up and return to their church. "May we have a word with the major?" Hosea Williams called out.

A minute passed. Cloud repeated his orders that the marchers disperse. When they didn't, Cloud ordered his troopers to advance.

The carnage began as soon as the troopers reached the marchers. Men, women, and children were shoved into each other until they tripped and fell to the ground. Tear gas canisters were fired, batons employed mercilessly. Horses charged into the screaming multitude. Civilians lining the bridge cheered every blow delivered.

John Lewis, knocked to the ground and beaten on the head by a club-wielding trooper until he was badly bleeding and his skull fractured, was certain this demonstration would be his last. Nearly five decades later, when recalling what would become known in civil rights history as "Bloody Sunday," Lewis was amazed that he had survived. "I still don't remember how I made it through the streets of Selma back to the Brown Chapel that evening."

The blunt force of the cruelty was reinforced by the immeasurable weight of hatred. One of the attackers used a length of rolled rubber wrapped in barbed wire; others used clubs and bats. A young boy, screaming for help, was snapped repeatedly by a trooper's bullwhip. "March, nigger," the trooper demanded. "You wanted to march and now I'm gonna help you." Another child, an eleven-year-old girl, recalled the terror of seeing horses trampling people on the ground. "The last thing I remember seeing on the bridge that day was this lady," she would recall many years later. "I don't know did the horse run over her? Did the guy hit her with the billy club as she fell? But I do know the sound of her head hitting that pavement, and I'll never forget it." "I remember seeing a horse, a white horse, and then I saw several other horses," another said. "One of the officers came to me, a state trooper, and he hit me across the back of my neck. I made a slight turn and he hit me again, and I fell to the ground."

The marchers retreated as quickly as they could, given the extent of their injuries and the blinding clouds of tear gas. The police pursued them. Fallen demonstrators lay wherever they fell, surrounded by backpacks, bedrolls, bags of personal possessions, shoes, and other clothing.

John Lewis: "I saw people rolling, heard people screaming and hollering. We couldn't go forward. If we tried to go forward we would've gone into the heat of battle. We couldn't go to the side, to the left and to the right, because we would have been going into the Alabama River, so we were beaten back down the streets of Selma, back to the church."

Ambulances, gathered at the end of the bridge, halted where the road was blocked off before the march, administered to the most seriously wounded. In all, seventeen demonstrators were injured badly enough to require overnight hospitalization; forty others were treated and released at the hospital. Dozens of others were treated at the Brown Chapel.

News cameras recorded the violence. ABC television broke into its regularly scheduled Sunday-night movie presentation to offer footage of the scene on the Pettus Bridge; the movie, *Judgment at Nuremburg,* was a dramatization of the crimes against humanity trials following World War II, and of evil that could prevail if people stood silently and did nothing while a group such as the Nazis gained power and slaughtered innocent people because of their heritage and religious beliefs.

When Martin Luther King learned of the bloodshed in Selma and saw the coverage on television, he regretted his decision to return to Atlanta rather than participate in the march. "I shall never forget my agony of conscience for not being there when I heard of the dastardly acts perpetrated against nonviolent demonstrators that Sunday, March 7," he wrote later. "As a result, I felt I had to lead a March on the following Tuesday."

But King's concerns extended beyond his anguish over those beaten in the demonstration: he also worried that his message of nonviolence was being eroded by recent events. He was already waist deep in criticism shaped by frustration. A growing number of blacks, especially youthful ones, saw no reason not to offer resistance when their heads were being cracked. When state troopers had chased demonstrators back into residential neighborhoods following the events of Bloody Sunday, angry blacks had thrown rocks, bottles, and anything else at their disposal at the troopers. In recent months, such militant leaders as Malcolm X and Stokely Carmichael had urged their followers to fight back. Then, on February 21, two weeks prior to Selma, Malcolm X had been murdered, further frustrating the African Americans subscribing to his message.

King's appeals to the White House for voting rights legislation were being stonewalled. President Johnson promised such legislation, but he asked King to stay patient. The 1964 civil rights laws had involved a protracted, hard-fought battle. LBJ was uncertain that he could win again so soon after his previous struggles. He had other pressing bills that he hoped to pass as part of his Great Society program, and he could see no reason to compromise his position in influencing the passage of these bills by aggressively pursuing civil rights legislation so closely following the package from the previous year. He had told King as much at a private White House meeting prior to Selma, but the bloody events accompanying the march, coupled with a national reaction that included demonstrations in some of the nation's large cities, including outside the White House, turned up the heat over passing a comprehensive voting rights act. In the aftermath of Selma, Attorney General Nicholas Katzenbach's office faced liberal demonstrators demanding more Justice Department involvement in the South. Demonstrators piled up outside the White House gates, demanding that Johnson take some kind of meaningful action.

George Wallace might have found all this amusing had he not been facing troubles of his own. As in all his confrontations, he claimed a victory in Selma, saying that halting the march, even in the way it was stopped, saved lives and injuries. He anticipated an excoriating national press reaction to Selma, and he received exactly what he expected. "He has written another shameful page in his own record and in the history of Alabama," declared a *New York Times* editorial. "The brutality is the inevitable result of the intolerance fostered by an infamous state government that is without conscience or morals," wrote the *Washington Post* in an especially damning editorial published two days after Bloody Sunday.

Wallace, of course, saw it differently.

"The Selma bridge was an unfortunate incident," he conceded in a 1974 interview, although in that same conversation, he tried to convince his interviewers that no one had been hurt or hospitalized in Selma. When corrected, he backpedaled to admit that he was unhappy with the way the troopers and posse had clashed with the marchers. "The bridge confrontation could have been handled differently, and I'm sorry it was handled exactly as it was," he allowed. "But actually the troopers were worried about them getting across the river, where there was a group of . . . people . . . antagonists on the other side. . . . They thought if they did get over there and got tied up, they couldn't get them separated."

Wallace's account would vary over the years, but he was consistent in declaring that he wanted to avoid violence. Now he was facing another march, led by King, forty-eight hours after the first. King had implored other civic and church leaders to travel to Alabama for the march, and they poured into Selma from all across the country. Newspapers and magazines dispatched reporters and photographers to give the march complete coverage. In an effort to avoid additional violence, King asked a Montgomery court to prohibit Wallace from interfering with the second march. The Justice Department did the same. But Judge Frank Johnson did not rule in the way they had hoped he would. Instead of granting them the opportunity to march unimpeded, he blocked all activity until he had the chance to review the case. He promised a decision Thursday, two days after the scheduled second march.

The judge's decision backed King into an awkward position. He did not wish to buck a court order, particularly one issued by a federal judge like Frank Johnson, who was known to be sympathetic to the civil rights movement, nor did he want to risk another melee similar to the one on March 7. Still, an esti-mated 450 clergymen had traveled to Selma to show their support and, if nec-essary, risk their personal safety. Wallace, likewise, hoped to avoid any further altercations after the nationally condemned first march.

Fortunately for both men, LeRoy Collins, director of the national Com-munity Relations Service and a former governor of Florida, flew to Alabama and spent hours negotiating with King and Lingo about a potential solution to the problem—a solution that would allow symbolic victories to both sides. The march, as he proposed it, would begin as planned, and when the demonstrators reached the point where the violence had erupted during the previous march, they would again encounter troopers assembled in their path. As before, Ma-jor John Cloud would announce that the march was illegal and the partici-pants would have to disassemble. This time, however, the troops would stand down and allow the marchers to continue. In exchange, King would pause for a prayer before leading the marchers back to Selma. If the plan was carried out without incident, there would be no violence, and both sides could claim a vic-tory. The arrangement, however, had to be kept secret. The president himself would not be briefed on the plan.

On Tuesday afternoon, March 9—"Turnaround Tuesday," as it would be known in civil rights history—King led a huge assembly of marchers, estimat-ed at two thousand, from the Brown Church toward the Pettus Bridge. All but a few of those in attendance believed that this would be the first leg of a four-day, three-night trek ending with a meeting with Governor George Wallace in Montgomery. When King and the frontline marchers reached the bridge and encountered troopers assembled in their path, King listened as he was ordered to leave, then dropped to his knees to pray. After several prayers and a singing of "We Shall Overcome," King and the other leaders, without uttering a word of explanation, turned and walked back through the masses before them, heading back to Brown Church. King's deal, when it became public, was harshly criticized by some of his most ardent supporters. The decision drew an even bigger wedge within the growing disenchanted in the SNCC. King remained convinced that he had done the right thing. Civil disobedience of the court order was not advisable in this case, he said, and he confessed to have been very worried about the likelihood of great bloodshed if the march had continued. There would be a Selma-to-Montgomery march in the very near future, he vowed, but it would be better to see that all the legal issues were addressed and the march planned thoroughly before they set out.

Turnaround Tuesday did not end with the return of the marchers. Later that same night, the murder of another out-of-stater graphically proved that the violent forces of racism would not be deterred by the courts, the presence of the country's best-known civil rights leaders, or the masses of black and white activists gathering in Selma. Three white Unitarian clergymen from Boston had traveled to Selma for the second march, and after the day's events, they had gone to a black diner for a bite to eat. It was dark when they left to walk back to the Brown Church, but they lost their way. They wound up in a rough white neighborhood, where they were confronted by three white racists. The three clergymen were chased down and beaten. Rev. James Reeb, a social worker and church pastor, absorbed a blow to the head from a club or baseball bat; he died in a hospital two days later.

Reeb's death received national headline attention. President Johnson and Vice President Hubert Humphrey called the Reeb family to offer condolences. Media response was deafeningly negative; in Washington, D.C., senators and congressmen weighed in, barely measuring their words in response to still another murder. Wallace realized, perhaps for the first time, he had lost control of the battle. He could still muster the firepower needed to put down any insurrection, but this was no longer the point. The country had grown tired of all the posturing, threatening, bullying, and—yes—killing, and Wallace stood to lose the sum of his political resources if strong measures weren't taken to stop the violence. He obviously could not be held responsible for the insane actions of redneck Klansmen or townsfolk with torch-and-pitchfork mentalities, but he had to control his own law enforcement agencies and state troopers. Failing that, what could he do?

Instead of continuing the status quo and risking a loss of an unknown national audience sympathetic to a 1968 presidential bid, Wallace took a bold move: he contacted the White House and requested a formal meeting with the president—the sooner, the better. Johnson blocked out three hours on Saturday, March 16.

Wallace had no idea that he had played into LBJ's hand. Prior to the events in Selma, the president had aides quietly and methodically working on a voter registration rights bill that he had hoped to spring on both bodies of Congress sometime in the months ahead, presumably after other Great Society bills had been pushed through. He had been clear about this with King when the two had met earlier in the year. Selma, however, demanded an acceleration of the process while offering a window of opportunity that might not have existed before: senators and congressmen alike seemed moved enough—*angry* enough—over the recent carnage in Alabama to actually pass voting rights legislation with minimal resistance. The timing of the Wallace visit was exquisite. Here was a man who had spent years railing against federal interference in what he considered to be state issues, visiting the White House with a plea for help in his state. Johnson recognized Wallace to be craftier than many allowed—"he's a lot more sophisticated than your average southern politician," he told aides— but he delighted, as LBJ could when he held the upper hand over the enemy, in the irony of Wallace's predicament. "It's his ox in the ditch," Johnson noted, using the colorful backroom imagery for which he was known, "let's see how he gets him out."

According to Johnson speechwriter and aide Richard Goodwin, who was present for much of the Johnson–Wallace meeting, the time the president spent with the Alabama governor "might have been Lyndon Johnson's finest performance." Johnson, a formidable physical presence under the most casual of circumstances, seated Wallace on a couch, and positioning himself in a rocking chair and leaning in until he was inches from Wallace's face, asked Wallace why he had asked to see him. Wallace, visibly uncomfortable, stumbled over his words as he ran through his old spiel about states' rights versus federal intervention. For the purpose of their discussion, Wallace spoke of how it was a state's obligation to protect its citizens, ideally without federal intervention. Alabama, he told the president, was being overrun by outside agitators, Communist sympathizers, and other out-of-state groups threatening the security of the state's good people. Huge demonstrations such as those in Selma, Wallace intimated, had to stop.

When Wallace finished, Johnson leaned back in his chair and, speaking firmly yet almost casually, went on the offensive. Showing Wallace a news clipping illustrated by a photograph of a trooper kicking a black man on the ground, Johnson demanded an explanation about how that kind of violence had taken place under Wallace's watch. He then addressed Alabama's poor record of registering black voters. When Wallace protested that he was powerless to order the county registrars to register black voters, Johnson found his patience slipping away. "Don't shit me about your persuasive power, George," Johnson countered. "Why, just this morning I was watching you on television . . . and you were attacking me."

"Not you, Mr. President, I was speaking against federal intervention—"

"You were attacking me, George. And you know what? You were so damn persuasive that I had to turn off the set before you had me changing my mind. Now, ordinarily I'm a pretty strong-minded fellow, just like those registrars. Will you give it a try, George?"

The onslaught continued. The demonstrations, Johnson remonstrated, were the result of a large group of Americans being denied a constitutionally guaranteed right to vote; give them that right and the demonstrations would cease. There could be no conditions either—no intimidation tactics from the likes of Jim Clark, no poll taxes, no ridiculously difficult literacy tests. Johnson favored the use of anecdote, the more homespun the better, to bolster his arguments, and in addressing the literacy tests, he spoke of a recent visit from a black Alabaman with a PhD. The man could not pass the test and was denied his right to register to vote. "He didn't know how to read and write well enough to vote in Alabama," the president scoffed. "Now, do all your white folks in Alabama have Ph.D.'s?"

(Wallace would later remark that Johnson's aggressive tactics had been more than a little persuasive. "Hell, if I'd stayed in there longer," Wallace quipped, "he'd have had me coming out *for* civil rights.")

Thoroughly defeated, Wallace flew back to Alabama with nothing from Johnson but a promise to help keep the forthcoming Selma-to-Montgomery march safe, should Wallace indicate that he needed help. To make matters even more humiliating, before departing for home, Wallace appeared with Johnson at a jam-packed press conference in the Rose Garden. Johnson briefed reporters on the specifics of his meeting with Wallace, stating that additional violence in Selma would not be tolerated. Wallace, he said, needed to publicly come out in support of voting rights for *all* people. Before turning the microphone over to Wallace, the president unloaded his big announcement: in two days, on Monday, he would be bringing a voting rights bill to Congress; the issue would be put to rest, once and for all.

Wallace had very little to add to Johnson's statements. The meeting, he allowed, had been a cordial one, even if they still disagreed on "a variety of issues."

When the press conference ended, the president returned to the White House and met with his attorney general. He instructed Nicholas Katzenbach to draft a voting rights bill—and have it on his desk the next day.

■ ■ ■ ■ ■

Johnson had good reason to feel a sense of urgency about the bill. There was limited shelf life on the national attention span, and today's outrage would be forgotten tomorrow. "I knew that it would probably not take long for these aroused emotions to melt away," he admitted later. "It was important to move at once if we were to achieve anything permanent from this transitory mood."

The day after his humbling at the White House, Wallace was at it again, this time on *Face the Nation,* where he attempted to solicit national empathy by placing the blame for the country's feelings about Alabama at the feet of media-created misconceptions. Black Alabamans could register to vote, Wallace insisted; it was the press that, through "unmitigated falsehood," led the public to believe that racist Alabamans, rather than the infiltration of Communists and other rabble-rousers, caused the problems in the civil rights movement. In fact, if one were to look carefully at the demonstrations in such cities as Washington, D.C., and New York, one would judge Alabama to be more tolerant of its demonstrators.

In short, nothing had changed.

At nine o'clock on the evening of March 15, eight days after Bloody Sunday, Lyndon Johnson addressed a joint session of Congress with a speech titled "The American Promise." The brainchild of Richard Goodwin, who managed to compose it under intense pressure over a period of roughly eight hours, the speech was spring-loaded to include references to the recent trouble in Selma, LBJ's call to action through a comprehensive voter registration bill, a strong reminder that civil rights was not limited to one single group or the opposition of any one individual group or region of the country, that denying a group the right to vote addressed the bedrock upon which the nation had been founded, and that there could be no future excuses or delays in correcting these wrongs. Johnson had even contacted Goodwin at one point during the writing and asked him to include an anecdote about his teaching days after his graduation from college, when, in Cotulla, Texas, he encountered young Mexican American kids who attended classes without having eaten before school and who felt, even if they couldn't understand it, the impact of racism on their daily lives.

The speech was a masterwork, by far the most powerful statement on civil rights that Johnson would issue during his presidency and, arguably, one of the strongest statements offered by *any* president in U.S. history. There had not been enough time between the completion of the text and Johnson's delivery of the speech to put it on a teleprompter, so the president read it from pages in a binder. Under other circumstances this might have made the words seem less personal, but the words themselves, along with Johnson's passionate delivery of them, were riveting to those listening to the speech in person and the millions watching it on television.

"At times," Johnson said near the opening of the speech, "history and fate meet at a single time in a single place to shape a turning point in man's unending search for freedom. So it was at Lexington and Concord. So it was a century ago at Appomattox. So it was last week in Selma, Alabama.

"There, long-suffering men and women peacefully protested the denial of their rights as Americans. Many were brutally assaulted. One good man, a man of God, was killed."

Johnson was only warming up. He went on to speak of the promise that the United States made to every one of its citizens ("that he should share in the dignity of man . . . that he should share in freedom, he shall choose his leaders, educate his children, and provide for his family according to his ability and his merits as a human being"); America, Johnson said, was failing in this promise in many areas of the country, where "every device of which human ingenuity is capable has been used to deny this right [to vote]." The problem, he continued, was that "no law that we now have on the books—and I have helped put three of them there—can ensure the right to vote when local officials are determined to deny it."

Wallace, watching the president's address on television in Alabama, must have felt the disintegration of his age-old states' rights argument with each of Johnson's words. This was Johnson at his most persuasive, and as he outlined the legislation he would be sending to Congress in two days, there could be no doubt that the game would be significantly changed when the bill passed—and it was going to pass. Martin Luther King, watching the presidential address on television in Montgomery, where he awaited a court decision on a Selma-to-Montgomery march, viewed the speech as a "victory like none other . . . an affirmation of the movement."

Johnson's speech gained momentum, aided by frequent interruptions caused by applauding senators and congressmen, and reached its apex after Johnson had completed his call for legislation and insisted that it be passed with "no delay, no hesitation, and no compromise with our purpose."

Johnson continued:

But even if we pass this bill, the battle will not be over. What happened in Selma is part of a far greater movement which reaches into every section and State of America. It is the effort of American Negroes to secure for themselves the full blessings of American life.

This cause must be our cause too. Because it is not just Negroes, but really it is all of us, who must overcome the crippling legacy of bigotry and injustice.

Johnson paused briefly before delivering the penultimate line in an already memorable speech:

"And . . . we . . . shall . . . overcome."

For a moment, the chambers were silent, as if all in attendance had to absorb what they had just heard. Then, in one spontaneous cry of support, relief, and determination, the building was filled with sound, from those on the floor and those in the gallery. Senator Mike Mansfield of Montana wept. Manny Celler, a seventy-seven-year-old congressman, jumped to his feet and cheered. Richard Goodwin, standing in the well and listening to the reaction to the words he had written, was overwhelmed by the thought of being "a part of something greater and more noble than oneself." "God, how I loved Lyndon Johnson at that moment," he would write in his memoirs.

In Alabama, King and his colleagues erupted in a cheer. "I looked over toward Martin," said C. T. Vivian, "and Martin was very quietly sitting in the chair, and a tear ran down his cheek."

For Johnson, it was an unforgettable moment, one that caught him thinking that, whether he planned it or not, he had become a part of history: "I remember the ride home from the Capitol that night. As we circled the reflecting pool, I looked toward the Lincoln Memorial. There had always been something haunting for me in that statue of Lincoln—so life-like and so clear-cut a reminder of the persistent gap between our promises and our deeds. Somehow that night Lincoln's hopes for America seemed much closer."

4 Lyndon Johnson signed the Voting Rights Act into law on August 6, 1965. He would call the law the most important piece of legislation passed during his administration.

George Wallace had watched his state in the national spotlight, suffering defeat after defeat in civil rights cases that he opposed. Three days after Johnson's speech before the joint session of Congress, Judge Frank Johnson delivered his decision on the Selma-to-Montgomery march, ruling that the march could go forward. In one final, desperate measure of opposition, Wallace refused to finance the protection of the protesters, saying that his state could not afford the heavy expense. President Johnson ordered the Alabama National Guard to handle it. The march commenced, with Martin Luther King leading, on March 21, 1965, arriving in Montgomery on March 25. Wallace watched from a statehouse window as thousands of demonstrators and marchers assembled at the capitol building, but he refused to meet with King or anyone else. Doing so, he argued, would be tantamount to endorsing the march. In the wake of all that had occurred in recent weeks, the march was relatively uneventful—until it was over. On the evening of the protestors' arrival in Montgomery, Viola Liuzzo, a white, thirty-nine-year-old Detroit housewife, mother of four, and Selma volunteer, lost her life while transporting a young black participant between Selma and Montgomery. A carload of Klansmen pulled alongside her on a rural strip of highway in Lowndes County and opened fire. The youth escaped unharmed.

Wallace, enough of a realist to conclude that he had nothing to gain and much to lose by continuing his hard-line confrontation with the federal government, retreated to safer ground. Five days after refusing to meet King and others in Montgomery, he agreed to host a group of civil rights leaders and advocates in the capitol, signaling the first time in Alabama history that a governor had agreed to meet a group of this nature. The hour-and-a-half gathering broke no new ground, other than to symbolize a possible thawing in Wallace's long-standing opposition to civil rights groups. More significantly, Wallace ordered the state's county registrars to open on ten additional days per month to register voters. Whatever bones he had to pick with the federal government over the interference with state laws—and there were many—would have to be set aside until his run for the presidency in 1968.

But there was a hitch—and a substantial one, in Wallace's mind: when he would begin making his overtures to a presidential run, he would no longer be the governor of Alabama. The state had strict term limits prohibiting any governor from serving consecutive terms, which mandated Wallace's leaving office after the completion of his term in 1966. Wallace felt strongly that he needed to show continuity in his state as a prerequisite for a presidential candidacy, but it wasn't going to happen under current law. He called a special legislative session and attempted to have the constitution amended in time to run for reelection, but he didn't have the support.

Wallace decided that he needed a surrogate, and he could think of no better candidate than his wife, Lurleen. She would follow his directions to the letter. Such a move was not unprecedented in American history, although in this case Lurleen Wallace appeared to be an unlikely and reluctant candidate. Wallace's friends and advisers discouraged the move, but George was adamant about it.

Lurleen Wallace impressed her husband's biographer as being "an obscure and rather lonely figure, pleasant enough on public occasions, but essentially a private person, unassuming and unprepossessing." She tolerated politics rather than reveling in them, as her husband did, and where he loved to plunge into campaign crowds, bathing in the glow of their support, Lurleen's nirvana was a silent boat on a good fishing hole. She had no political experience, other than fulfilling her meager obligations as the state's First Lady. She placed more value on her role as a mother of four than she placed on politics.

The Wallaces had met in the summer of 1942, while George was working as a twenty-four-year-old dump truck driver for the Alabama Highway Department. George had stopped in at a Kresge's five-and-dime store in Tuscaloosa for a sandwich at the lunch counter and spotted Lurleen working behind a nearby cosmetics counter. Lurleen, a sixteen-year-old high school graduate with aspirations of becoming a nurse, was immediately attracted to George when he sauntered over to buy a bottle of hair oil—"brilliantine," as he called it. He struck Lurleen as being funny, intelligent, and a Southern gentleman with a rakish style. She did not share George's obvious interest in politics— "Politics was something Daddy discussed at the house with other people, not with me," she would tell Marshall Frady, a George Wallace biographer—but it didn't matter to George. He was smitten with her from their first date—lunch at a competing drugstore lunch counter when she was on a break from work— and they married on May 21, 1943, shortly after George received his notice for induction into the service.

This particular gubernatorial campaign promised to be a spirited one. The leading candidate, Ryan DeGraffenried, had been arduously working to build a power base among politicians, businessmen, the media, and voters, and while George Wallace probably would have defeated him in a head-to-head contest, Lurleen had a strenuous, demanding battle ahead of her. But fate intervened one evening, when DeGraffenried, bound for another campaign stop, was killed just after his small plane had lifted off on a stormy, windy evening.

Lurleen Wallace had barely entered the race when serious health issues threated to derail her campaign. A few years earlier, in 1961, while delivering the Wallaces' youngest child by caesarean section, doctors had detected a small mass attached to Lurleen's uterus. The tumor had been removed and, as was often the custom of the day and by George Wallace's orders, Lurleen had been told nothing of the true nature of the tumor.

Now, just as Lurleen prepared for her campaign, she fell ill again, and another tumor was discovered. Doctors ordered a hysterectomy to be performed the second week of January 1966. George braced himself to abandon the campaign, but Lurleen insisted on continuing. Doctors removed the tumor, which proved to be malignant, but they told Lurleen that they had caught the cancer in time and assured her that "she was able to run for governor."

The Wallaces succeeded in keeping the entirety of Lurleen's medical history from the public, and after a brief period of recovery, they hit the campaign trail together. Lurleen opened each stop with a brief statement before turning the proceedings over to George. The true nature of the campaign was transparent from the onset: a vote for Lurleen was a vote for George. While George stood before crowds, exulting in the whooping and hollering, Lurleen sat off to the side, all but shrinking into her turtleneck and blazer, her eyes set not on her husband or the mass of people in front of them, but on something in the distance, an object, real or imagined, that gently occupied her attention until it was time to pack up and move on. Life with George had been different from what she had expected. It wasn't that he was abusive in any way; he was always off on his own somewhere, pursuing his passions, while she waited and waited. She had considered divorce on occasion but inevitably fell back into the marriage for their children and her invisibility. She could be defensive about her run for office, arguing that she really wanted the job, but when the votes were eventually tabulated and she was installed as the next governor of Alabama, it all boiled down to one undeniable truth: she had done it for George.

5 Lurleen Wallace occupied her husband's old office while George took over his own work space in a room nearby. Lurleen proved to be efficient in carrying out George's directives, and Alabama operated the way it always had.

Lyndon Johnson's assessments of George Wallace's abilities had been on the mark: he was no ordinary Southern politician. During his term in office, Wallace had pursued programs so progressive that LBJ, during his meeting with Wallace, muttered in exasperation: "You came into office a liberal—you spent all your life wanting to do things for the poor. Now, why are you working on this? Why are you off on this black thing?"

Wallace strove to improve Alabama's poor standing in such issues as poverty, education, medical care for the poor, and assistance for the elderly. He saw that teachers' pay was increased; he pushed for a free textbook program and led the effort to expand the number of the state's junior colleges and trade schools. Under his watch, more people received welfare benefits and public assistance. Workman's compensation benefits increased. These programs benefited blacks as well as whites, and they required vigilance to maintain, especially after Lurleen Wallace took office.

Wallace's *black thing,* as LBJ referred to Wallace's battles with civil rights advocates, was directly tied into his political ambitions, in both his state and nationwide. George *needed* Alabama. His presidential campaign would depend on Alabama contributions almost exclusively for funding in the early goings, and with this in mind, all the while he stumped with his wife, Wallace looked to strengthen his position throughout the state. His enemies—most notably those opposing his proposed term limits changes in the constitution—were effectively wiped out, some choosing not to run again, others being crushed in the election. By the time Lurleen delivered her inaugural address on January 16, 1967, George had reached a level of power unlike any ever achieved in his state.

While he sat in his office, smoking cigars and directing activities, he plotted strategy for his 1968 presidential campaign. He had informally launched his campaign while he was on the road with Lurleen, when he included a sequence in his speeches where he spoke about the greatness of Alabama and its citizens and concluded by speaking of "the Alabama Movement," as he was calling his candidacy. "An Alabaman would make as good a President as one from Ohio or New York," he told cheering crowds, "and a darn sight better than one from Texas, I tell you that."

"It's the working man in this country that's got 'em all shook up," he said. "It's the working man that's going to change this country." This was the old, familiar Wallace, harping on the old, shopworn underdog theme, firing up those attending his rallies by instructing his supporters that they were just as good and capable as any of the smug, self-congratulatory "eggheads" from the North and East. And now that he had their attention and approval, he made certain that his audiences understood that *he* was the Alabaman ready to take on the opposition. He would be going it alone, outside the two major parties, which he deemed to be politically, socially, and morally bankrupt.

"You can put LBJ in the sack," he told a throng of supporters in October 1966, just before the general election.

You can put HHH in the sack. And you can put Robert "Blood-for-the Vietcong" Kennedy in the sack. You can put Earl Warren in the sack: Warren doesn't have enough legal brains in his whole head to try a chicken thief in my home county. You can put wild Bill Scranton and the left-wing Governor Romney and Nelson Rockefeller, that socialist governor, in the sack. Put 'em all in the same sack, shake up I don't care which one comes out, you stick him back in—because there isn't a dime's worth of difference in them.

This kind of talk was well received in fairgrounds, gymnasiums, village squares, and other gathering places throughout Alabama, and Wallace was willing to gamble that it would play well elsewhere in the country, wherever disgruntled Americans assembled to hear something outside the political talk du jour. But stepping outside the Republican and Democratic circles presented logistical problems for his campaign organizations. He would not be receiving any support or assistance from national or state parties outside his home state. The task of getting his name placed on ballots in all fifty states, with their specific and often quirky requirements, would amount to a herculean effort. Some states seemed to go out of their ways to discourage third-party candidates, and it would take a roster of attorneys just to read through the requirements. Some states, for instance, required only a few hundred signatures for a candidate to be placed on the ballot. In California, a candidate needed sixty-six thousand signatures, roughly 1 percent of the state's population, but each person signing had to be a registered member of Wallace's American Independent Party, and the filing deadline, the earliest in the country, was December 31, 1967. It was a daunting task for Wallace's shorthanded campaign staff, and Wallace was none too happy about what he perceived to be intentional roadblocks set in front of third-party candidates.

"The law was written to make you fail," he complained. "In my judgment, that was the intent of the law. They couldn't comprehend anybody having enough support to convince 100,000 voters . . . to go to an official of the State and sit down and fill out forms and re-register and swear to it and so forth. That is almost impossible to do."

A much bigger challenge lay ahead. Lurleen Wallace was feeling poorly, and during a visit to the Anderson Clinic in Houston, she learned that her cancer had returned.

5 Robert Kennedy
Shadows of Indecision

When describing Robert Francis Kennedy—known by family, friend, and foe by the more familiar nicknames of Bob or Bobby (or RFK, to Kennedy followers)—there seemed to be only one agreement: he was a man of powerfully conflicting characteristics. He could be kind, mean, competitive, temperamental, gentle, hostile, ruthless, sensitive, ambitious, opportunistic, judgmental, driven, tender, and empathetic—not unlike Lyndon Johnson, whom Kennedy deeply disliked. Arthur M. Schlesinger, longtime family friend, confidant, and adviser, simply stated, "He was a divided man." "He was not just complex but contradictory," wrote his friend journalist Jack Newfield. "His most basic characteristics were simple, intense, and in direct conflict with each other. He was constantly at war with himself." Wrote another journalist, "The inescapable truth about Robert Kennedy is that the paradoxes are real, the conflicts do exist."

In *Remembering America,* Richard Goodwin, calling Kennedy "a constellation of contradictions," recorded an anecdote that offered a subtle yet telling example of Kennedy's divided nature. Kennedy, an avid skier, was out on the slopes one day when he saw his nephew, John Kennedy Jr., then a little boy, take a hard fall. As he skied over to where his brother's son sat in the snow, he noticed that John-John, as he was called, was crying. "Kennedys don't cry," Bobby lectured as he helped the boy to his feet. "This Kennedy cries," John-John responded. And so, wrote Goodwin, did RFK, "although one rarely saw the tears."

> It was his most tenaciously maintained secret: a tenderness so rawly exposed, so vulnerable to painful abrasion, that it could only be shielded by angry compassion at human misery, manifest itself in love and loyalty toward those close to him, or through a revelatory humor.

These traits began to manifest themselves when, as the third son of a demanding Joseph Kennedy, he had to scrape and claw for any recognition in a family of strong, dominating personalities. The elder Kennedy, whom Bobby worshiped, had huge plans for his two older sons, Joe Jr. and Jack, but not for Bobby, who was tiny and slightly built—the "runt," as Joseph Kennedy called him—and who was clearly his mother's favorite. Mental and physical toughness were required if one expected to be noticed in a family known for its competitiveness and ambition. Bobby had to assert himself if he ever hoped to be heard at the spirited dinner-table discussions about politics and the events of the day. Joseph Kennedy expected the older two boys to go into public service and work their way up the political ladder as adults; he harbored no such hopes for Bobby, who might excel, but as an attorney for a good law firm.

Joseph Kennedy's designs for his oldest son ended when Joe Jr. was killed during World War II, signaling the beginning of Jack's ascension in Joseph Kennedy's and, ultimately, the public's eye. While Jack entered politics and quickly worked his way up through the House of Representatives and the Senate, Bobby practiced law, gaining some notoriety when he worked for Senator Joseph McCarthy, a friend of his father's. More than one analyst portrayed Robert Kennedy as a quick study, learning more and better from experience than from textbooks; he painted in broad strokes, which often brought his personality traits, positive and negative, into sharp focus.

When Jack decided to run for the presidency in the 1960 election, Bobby followed, and from that point until Jack's assassination on November 22, 1963, Bobby would maintain his identity through the actions of his brother. He ran Jack's campaign, served as his attorney general, and acted as his most trusted adviser. He was not only noticed; in time, he was viewed to be his brother's successor in a Kennedy White House dynasty that would include Jack, Bobby, and the youngest brother, Ted. That changed when Jack was murdered in Dallas. "The assassination punctured the center of Robert Kennedy's universe," Jack Newfield observed. "It made Robert Kennedy, a man unprepared for introspection, think for the first time in his life, what *he* wanted to do, and what *he* stood for."

"I suppose up to November of 1963 that my whole life was built around President Kennedy," Robert Kennedy admitted.

What was important to me and what I felt strongly about was not just the dedication to an individual and not a dedication to my brother, but just the fact that I thought through him that we could make a contribution and remedy injustices and change the direction of the United States and accomplish some good. So my life was dedicated to that, not so much as to what I was going to be or what role I was going to play. . . . I expect that after November, 1963, that perhaps I was looked upon with different eyes, and obviously I had to play a different role because what existed for me before that period of time didn't exist afterward.

His role, he felt, would be in the White House, but he was projecting ahead to 1972, when Lyndon Johnson had completed what figured to be his second full term in office. When Kennedy decided to run for the Senate in 1964, as a prerequisite for that run for the presidency, he set himself up for all kinds of criticism. He was running in New York, rather than his home state of Massachusetts, and the old accusations of his being opportunistic and ruthless echoed from the chambers of his past. Still, he ran and he won, and then from his early days in the Senate, he refused to follow the traditional be-seen-and-not-heard protocol. He spoke out against the Vietnam War and Johnson's apparent refusal to settle it at the negotiating table with representatives from both North and South Vietnam. He considered a run for the presidency in 1968, setting off the ultimate battle within himself. Or as John Nolan, an attorney friend and advisor, noted, "From the neck down he wanted to go; from the neck up it just didn't make sense to him."

1 Kennedy's inner turmoil pushed him in every direction. He was being brutally frank when he told Allard Lowenstein, when Lowenstein visited him in late 1967 and tried to convince him to oppose a sitting president, that he could not run for the presidency because he did not want to divide the party; that he felt that his running would be interpreted as a vicious affront to Lyndon Johnson; that it was unlikely that he could defeat LBJ, the incumbent, in the race for the Democratic nomination. All but a tiny few of his friends and political allies held the same view. The timing just wasn't right.

Not that there weren't dissenting opinions or long, soul-searching (and occasionally heated) discussions about his running. Ethel Kennedy, Bobby's wife, pushed for his entering the race, whereas Ted Kennedy, Bobby's closest confidant, argued against it. Most of the old guard—those who worked on John Kennedy's election and served as members of his White House team—felt that Kennedy would be making a big mistake by running against an incumbent president. The young Turks on Robert Kennedy's Senate staff believed that he had an obligation to contest Johnson because of the Vietnam issue alone. Adam

Walinsky, one of RFK's closest confidants, left him a note that simply stated, "Lyndon Johnson is a lame duck president."

Kennedy understood and respected both sides, which only made his decision all the more difficult.

The debate over Kennedy's candidacy began in earnest in the fall of 1967, during a series of informal meetings at Kennedy's home in Virginia, at his apartment in New York, and in the residences and offices of his friends and advisors, sometimes with Kennedy present, sometimes not. On September 23, Kennedy sat in on one of the early discussions at Hickory Hill, his residence in McLean, Virginia. The debate on that occasion was between Kennedy speechwriter and friend Arthur Schlesinger Jr. and publisher James Loeb, who opposed the idea of Kennedy's candidacy, and Allard Lowenstein and Jack Newfield, who urged him to run. As Schlesinger remembered, much of the meeting focused on Vietnam and how current policy should nudge Kennedy into the race. Lowenstein argued that the war had made Johnson extremely vulnerable, and recent polls supported his case. A Gallup Poll released in July had Johnson leading Kennedy, 45 percent to 39 percent; in a mere two months, Kennedy had blown past Johnson, with a 51 percent to 39 percent lead at the time of the Hickory Hill meeting. That margin would widen in the months ahead. The Dump Johnson movement thrived as well.

Lowenstein, who had pulled off his shoes and sat cross-legged on a chair during the meeting, looking nearly two decades his junior, his passion and convictions evident to all in attendance, pushed hard, arguing "in fevered language" that Kennedy could defeat Johnson in the primaries.

Schlesinger disagreed. The polls, he thought, could be misleading. He favored an approach proposed by Joseph Rauh, a powerful Democrat who suggested that the war issue could be addressed in a strong platform at the Democratic National Convention in the following August. None of the others agreed. The Vietnam issue, Newfield reminded Schlesinger, had been approached in the 1964 platform, and while it was weak, it had been ignored. Kennedy, remaining mostly silent during the meeting, listening with a "bemused smile on his face," expressed his skepticism. "How do you run on a plank, Arthur?" he asked Schlesinger. "When was the last time millions of people rallied behind a plank?"

As far as Kennedy was concerned, voter perception was an enormous roadblock to his running. A large percentage of voters would dismiss the notion that he was opposing an incumbent because he hoped to change the direction of the war and the problems in the inner cities; instead, he would be perceived as the ruthless opportunist driven by the desire to oust his enemy, the usurper of the Kennedy White House.

"I think Al is doing the right thing," he said of Lowenstein's search for a candidate to oppose Johnson, "but I think someone else will have to be the first to run. It can't be me because of my relationship to Johnson."

Nothing was decided that night, as very little would be decided during subsequent meetings, with different names arguing essentially the same points. This, however, did not mean that Kennedy wasn't listening or carefully considering everything he heard. As John Nolan, an administrative assistant to Kennedy when RFK was attorney general, observed, Kennedy needed information for a decision. "He was probably better at getting information from people than most other people I know," Nolan said. "He was usually very sparing about expressing his own opinions. He was a good questioner and, I always felt, able to get more information and take more advantage of information, the knowledge of people who were working for him or working with him, or people he would just meet some place, just by asking a simple direct question."

2 The precise origins of the Robert Kennedy–Lyndon Johnson feud will never be known. Neither of the combatants could remember what started it, though their mutual dislike was as clear and resounding as the ringing of a ship's bell on a silent night. One of Johnson's earliest memories of his eventual antagonist was of Robert Kennedy's service as assistant counsel to Joseph McCarthy when the Wisconsin senator was browbeating his way to the public eye during his Communist witch hunts. LBJ loathed McCarthy, and he was not inclined to like anyone attached to him. Johnson and Kennedy came from almost polarized backgrounds, and at least one authority on the feud, Jeff Shesol, author of *Mutual Contempt,* an in-depth study of the sour relationship, felt that their backgrounds made them almost inevitable enemies. "It was as if one was designed to confound the other," Shesol wrote.

Kennedy could not help but notice Johnson, whose mercurial rise to power and influence in the Senate made him the focus of national attention. Content to work in the Justice Department, Kennedy had very little interest in electoral politics, at least in the 1950s; his brother John, however, was entirely different, and as a member of the Senate prior to his run for the presidency in 1960, he watched Johnson operate daily. Johnson had his own designs on running in 1960, but he hedged on announcing his candidacy until it was too late.

Most accounts of the Robert Kennedy–Lyndon Johnson hostilities agree that the 1960 election cycle contributed mightily to the split between the two men. Johnson believed that Robert Kennedy opposed and tried to discourage his brother's choosing him as his running mate—a charge that RFK denied—

and he felt that Kennedy's opposition stemmed from disparaging remarks he made about Joseph Kennedy during the 1960 Democratic National Convention. This would have made sense, since RFK would brook no criticism of his father. Bobby said nothing about it at the time, but Johnson refused to let it go. Johnson's service as Jack Kennedy's vice president, difficult from the onset, found Johnson frozen out of discussions involving important executive decisions. Johnson liked John Kennedy and deeply respected his office, and he felt that Bobby Kennedy was largely responsible for his distance from the president. Johnson confronted Bobby in 1961, after a White House dance for General James Gavin, when a small group gathered for scrambled eggs in an upstairs kitchen at the White House.

"Bobby, you do not like me," Johnson said in the presence of the others. An embarrassed Robert Kennedy tried to extricate himself from the conversation. "Your brother likes me," Johnson continued, referring to the president. "You sister-in-law likes me. Your Daddy likes me. But you don't like me. Now, why? Why don't you like me?" The awkward scene played on for an excruciatingly long time, Johnson unwilling to let Kennedy terminate the conversation by ignoring his questioning. Finally, Johnson pressed the issue of Joseph Kennedy. "I know why you don't like me," he said. "You think I attacked your father. But I never said that. Those reports were all false. . . . I never did attack your father and I wouldn't and I always liked and admired you. But you're angry with me and you've always been upset with me."

Johnson's words rattled Kennedy. Was he telling the truth when he insisted so forcefully that he had been misquoted in the papers? The day after the kitchen encounter, Kennedy cornered John Seigenthaler, a Kennedy friend and White House aide who had witnessed Johnson's remarks at the convention when he was working as a reporter for the Nashville newspaper *The Tennessean*. Seigenthaler remembered Johnson's words well. "He's not telling the truth," he said of Johnson's claims of being misquoted. Seigenthaler later took the additional measure of looking up copies of the newspaper write-ups of LBJ's speech. The articles confirmed his memory He then sent copies of the articles to Robert Kennedy with a note stating, "There can't be much doubt . . . that he was vicious." Kennedy hated lying more than just about any other character flaw, and by his estimation, Johnson was a man incapable of telling the truth. He would never fully trust Johnson again.

The assassination of John F. Kennedy altered the dynamics in the LBJ–RFK relationship. The man that the Kennedys had left on the outside was, in the wake of shots fired on a sunny Friday morning in Dallas, the new chief executive and commander in chief at the zenith of worldwide politics. In an effort to maintain stability and continuity, Johnson asked many of the slain president's staff and cabinet members, including Robert Kennedy, to stay on. Kennedy remained for what was bound to be an unhappy tenure. He and Johnson stood side by side during the civil rights struggles, but they avoided each other as a matter of practice. Johnson had virtually no time to establish his administration before he had completed John Kennedy's term and was running in the 1964 election. The naming of his vice-presidential candidate placed him in still another awkward position with Robert Kennedy—the "Bobby problem," as Johnson called it. Kennedy was widely regarded as a good vice-presidential candidate, but Johnson balked at the idea. He wanted to escape all things Kennedy and establish his own identity in the Oval Office. Kennedy, however, wanted the position. Johnson resolved his dilemma by announcing, publicly and in direct conversation with Kennedy, that he would not be considering any members of his cabinet for the vice-presidential position. A forty-minute meeting on July 29, 1967, during which Johnson detailed why he wouldn't be naming Kennedy as his vice-presidential candidate, was especially brutal for Kennedy because Johnson was essentially delivering a transparent declaration: no one else in the cabinet would be considered, but none would have been considered in any event. For Johnson, it was a long-awaited moment: his Bobby problem had disappeared.

Johnson's landslide victory over Barry Goldwater in the general election established LBJ's dominant presence apart from the Kennedys. When Robert Kennedy chose to leave his job as attorney general and run for the U.S. Senate, Johnson wholeheartedly endorsed him, going as far as to campaign for him in New York City and elsewhere around the state. This might have seemed like a strange move to those following the enmity between the two men over the years; in reality, it illustrated the complexity of their professional relationship.

"Bobby's relationship with Johnson was more complicated than you are led to believe," said Walt Rostow, National Security advisor under Johnson. "It is true there were elements of real cross-tension. On the other hand, there are letters in which Bobby wrote how he understood the burdens Johnson was carrying. He offered to be ambassador in Saigon. Johnson did not want Bobby to be vice president, but he felt he had a duty to help him get elected to the Senate, so he went up to New York and campaigned with him. And Bobby wanted this."

Any thaw in the feud in the aftermath of LBJ's campaigning for Kennedy evaporated as the war in Vietnam continued to escalate. Kennedy's support of the war had been falling away, almost in direct proportion to Johnson's escalation of the war. He joined the growing group of skeptics who believed that the United States could not win the war by using conventional weapons and strategy. By the time Robert McNamara had been replaced and Allard Lowenstein had accelerated his Dump Johnson movement at the end of 1967, the feud between Kennedy and Johnson had reached a point beyond reconciliation. Kennedy's opposition to the administration's handling of the war, becoming more open and critical with each new speech, infuriated Johnson. He would understand Kennedy's opposition to the war—those numbers were climbing nationwide—but he hated Kennedy's acting as if he was taking the moral high ground in a war that had been advanced by Kennedy and his brother. Johnson might have dreaded a face-off with Kennedy in a presidential race, but at the beginning of 1968, with still no candidacy announcement, Johnson believed he was safe.

Then came Tet.

3   On January 31, Robert Kennedy addressed questions from a large group of journalists at an eagerly anticipated breakfast meeting at the National Press Club in Washington, D.C. Aware of the persistent skepticism surrounding his statements about his noncandidacy, Kennedy hoped to use the occasion to set the record straight. The setting had an informality to it that encouraged frank answers to even the most pointed questions: Kennedy's answers were for background only. His remarks could not be attributed for publication unless Kennedy himself gave the reporters permission to quote him. Even so, Kennedy gave a lot of thought to the kind of questions he would be asked, and he and his press secretary, Frank Mankiewicz, discussed the best ways to answer the most probing queries.

"There was a deep political instinct in him that said he shouldn't run," Mankiewicz recalled. "He was getting a lot of sober political advice from people he believed to be good political advisors, saying that he should not run. And if he was not going to run, then clearly it was in his interest to cut off all speculation as early as possible."

The press arrived with questions about Kennedy's candidacy, the Vietnam War, recent unrest in the inner cities, Lyndon Johnson, Eugene McCarthy, and the Democratic Party's odds in the November election. Kennedy, relaxed and forthright, gave them much to consider. The Vietnam War, he told them, was "one of the greatest disasters of all time for America." Despite these strong feelings, Kennedy believed that McCarthy was making a tactical error in running solely as a peace candidate. In this regard, McCarthy was playing into Johnson's hand. The war had divided the country, generation pitted against generation, but, in Kennedy's opinion, "Gene McCarthy hasn't been able to stop the unrest in the country. You have to be able to touch this uneasiness."

Unstated in his critique of McCarthy was Kennedy's disapproval of the Minnesota senator's stance on urban and racial distress. McCarthy wasn't a racist by anyone's definition, and his votes in the Senate certainly favored all steps forward in civil rights issues, but his campaign all but ignored some of the most pressing domestic issues dividing the country. These were not times for neutrality or inaction. Kennedy reserved his harshest criticism of Johnson in this regard. Johnson, Kennedy charged, was "on the side of repression now," largely for political reasons: there were more white voters than black voters.

McCarthy, Kennedy averred, was failing as a candidate because he was unable to connect with Americans' general sense of decency and generosity: "If someone could appeal to the generous spirit of Americans to the race question, this is what the campaign should be about." Hidden in the remark was Kennedy's belief that he was just the type of person to do this.

As expected, the reporters were most interested in the prospects of Kennedy's opposing Johnson and McCarthy in the presidential race. Kennedy stood his ground on his noncandidacy. He would not divide his party and hand the office to a Republican, nor would he engage in a losing campaign that could weaken his standing in the Senate. "If I ran, a lot of states would be split down the middle," he stated. "I not only would take the risk of weakening my opportunity to talk and have an effect on the issues, but I could bring down a good many other Democrats as well." Although he did not offer any names his candidacy might harm, it was well known that such peace candidates as George McGovern, J. William Fulbright, and Frank Church faced stiff challenges in their campaigns for reelection to the Senate.

The reporters pressed Kennedy, but he wasn't taking any bait. When asked if he would endorse Johnson if he won the Democratic nomination as expected, Kennedy answered that he would but without enthusiasm. Frustrated, the journalists asked if there was anything they could place on the record about Kennedy's refusal to run. Kennedy responded that they could quote him as saying that he would not enter the campaign "under any conceivable circumstances." Frank Mankiewicz cut in with a suggestion. It might be better, he said, if the quote read "under any foreseeable circumstances." Kennedy agreed.

Even as Kennedy stood in the Press Club and denounced a run for office, reporters in attendance were receiving and passing around wire tapes with very troubling news: South Vietnam, including Saigon, was under attack by North

Vietnamese troops flooding into major cities in the country. The extent of the offensive was unknown, but within the next twenty-four hours the world would realize that the onslaught eventually labeled the Tet Offensive had begun. Kennedy would wonder if he had spoken too soon at the backgrounder breakfast.

4 The Tet Offensive was one of those news items with the capacity to change minds, emotions, and overall dispositions. Prior to Tet, the majority of Americans supported Johnson's actions in Vietnam; the number of vocal critics in high places was increasing, but the overall numbers hanging in with Johnson were notable. Those protesting the war were more disillusioned than angry; Tet changed that. Walter Cronkite, perhaps *the* voice of Middle America, was hurrying to Vietnam to see the war firsthand. Some of Robert Kennedy's most loyal supporters, men encouraging him to run—Adam Walinsky, Peter Edelman, and Richard Goodwin, for instance—hinted that they would join the McCarthy forces if Kennedy refused to enter the race.

After reading news articles about the Tet Offensive in the newspapers the day after his breakfast at the National Press Club, Robert Kennedy wrestled with his thoughts, many conflicting, about what he should do. His brother Ted had recently returned from Vietnam after spending parts of December and January in the country with harsh words about the war and the plight of the country's refugees—words that did not jibe with the official line coming from the White House and the generals—and Ted's observations, along with the newspaper accounts, led Bobby to another decision: in the past, he had criticized the war but, with only a rare exception, not Johnson personally. He was of a different mind now. Johnson was lying, and Kennedy was not going to tolerate it—not with so many lives hanging in the balance.

On February 8, Kennedy delivered a scorching indictment of the war in a speech in Chicago. His book *To Seek a Newer World* was fresh in bookstores across the country, and Kennedy visited the Windy City as a guest of a book-and-author luncheon hosted by the *Chicago Sun-Times*. Before the luncheon, Kennedy met with Chicago mayor Richard J. Daley, one of the country's true Democratic power brokers. Daley disfavored anyone competing with a sitting president, for essentially the same reasons that had given Kennedy pause for the better part of a year. However, Kennedy found an ally in his opposition to the war. Daley hated the war on general principles, but it had become personal after a friend's son, a young man Daley had helped gain admittance to Harvard a few years earlier, was killed in action in Vietnam. Daley suggested that rather than run against Johnson, Kennedy might accept a compromise: he could help form a panel to study the war and recommend ways to end it; Kennedy, in fact, might chair the panel himself. Daley promised to make a few calls and see how others responded to the idea.

Kennedy wasn't in a compromising frame of mind at the luncheon. In a speech marking his break with the Johnson administration on the war, Kennedy spoke of Vietnam in general, the Tet Offensive in specific, the official line on the war, and how the public should regard the official explanation on how the war was going. He contradicted the White House position on almost every turn.

He opened by addressing the Tet Offensive, now receiving extensive coverage in newspapers and on television and radio: "Our enemy, savagely striking at will across all of South Vietnam, has finally shattered the mask of official illusion with which we have concealed our true circumstances, even from ourselves. But a short time ago we were serene in our reports and predictions of progress." Kennedy predicted—correctly, as it turned out—that the North Vietnamese would be driven back after sustaining heavy losses, but he cautioned that this should not be misconstrued as a military victory. If the Tet Offensive had proved anything, it was that no place in South Vietnam was safe, even though the United States and South Vietnamese forces greatly outnumbered the enemy and possessed more and vastly superior firepower. It was time, Kennedy said, "to seek out the austere and painful reality of Vietnam, freed from wishful thinking, false hopes and sentimental dreams."

One can imagine Lyndon Johnson's immediate response to these words. Johnson and the highest leadership in the military had been trying to reassure the public that the Tet Offensive was a crushing victory for the U.S. and South Vietnamese troops, but here was a senator and highly visible, trusted figure—but one who had not served in the armed forces—claiming that they were lying to the public, that, like skillful magicians, they were successfully misdirecting the public's attention through a series of illusions.

And Kennedy had traveled to Chicago with a list of what those illusions were. He had already spoken of the first: the belief that the Tet Offensive represented a military victory for the U.S. and Vietnamese troops. The problem, he said, could be tied in to a misconception that the United States believed it could win a war that was not supported by the South Vietnamese people. The second illusion was directly related to the first: "the illusion that we can win a war which the South Vietnamese cannot win for itself." The disconnect between the people and their corrupt government was such that the people felt no urge to risk their lives for it. "We support a government without supporters. Without the efforts of American arms that government would not last a day."

Kennedy's third illusion cut to the core of the reason for the United States' involvement with Vietnam—a principle necessary for American citizens to continue to support the war: "that the unswerving pursuit of military victory, whatever its costs, [was] in the interest of either ourselves or the people of Vietnam." The people in Vietnam, Kennedy said, had suffered immeasurably since the United States had escalated the war in 1965. More than two million Vietnamese were without homes as the result of American forces dropping twelve tons of bombs for every square foot in the country. "It is the people we seek to defend who are the greatest losers," Kennedy stated. If anything, the Tet Offensive seemed to show how morally bankrupt the war had become. For an example, Kennedy chose the recent photograph, appearing in newspapers everywhere, of the South Vietnamese chief of Vietnamese Security Services executing a prisoner of war that U.S. troops had handed over to him—an open violation of the Geneva convention that the rest of the world would witness and rebuke. "The photograph of the execution was on front pages all around the world," Kennedy told his audience, "leading our best and oldest friends to ask, more in sorrow than in anger, what has happened to America?"

Finally, Kennedy continued, there was the illusion that

> this war can be settled in our own way and in our own time on our own terms. . . . We have not done this, nor is there any prospect we shall achieve such victory. Unable to defeat our enemy or break his will— at least without a huge, long and ever more costly effort—we must actively seek a peaceful settlement. We can no longer harden our terms every time Hanoi indicates it may be prepared to negotiate, and we must be willing to foresee a settlement which will give the Vietcong a chance to participate in the political life of the country.

Of all of Kennedy's statements, this might have been the one that rankled Lyndon Johnson the most. It was fallacy to suggest that the United States, with all its military might, could not defeat the North Vietnamese in conventional warfare. The generals had convinced him that this was so. He had considered a negotiated settlement to end the war, but certainly not with the Vietcong setting any terms of the negotiations or life in Vietnam after a cease-fire.

Kennedy might have concluded his speech on this final illusion, but he couldn't resist the temptation to lecture. The war, he intimated, had presented a lot of lessons, and the United States would do well to heed them, painful as they were, even at this late date. "Our nation," Kennedy stated, "must be told the truth about this war, in all its terrible reality, both because it is right—and because only in this way can any Administration rally the public confidence and unity for the shadowed days which lie ahead."

5 One of the most influential arguments favoring RFK's entering the race came in the form of a letter written by Kennedy's friend the journalist and novelist Pete Hamill. Hamill was out of the country, in Ireland, finishing a novel, at the beginning of the new year. He had written the letter before the Tet Offensive, but Kennedy didn't see it until February 9, the day after his speech in Chicago. Hamill had read of Kennedy's decision not to run in the *Irish Times,* and he was driven to speak out. The letter appealed to Kennedy's sense of history and responsibility; Hamill rejected the idea that Kennedy's entry into the race would split the Democratic Party. The party, Hamill argued, would be divided if Johnson served four more years in the White House. "I wanted to say that the fight you might make would be the fight of honor," Hamill wrote. "I wanted to say you should run because if you won, the country might be saved. . . . If we have LBJ for another four years, there won't be much of a country left."

Hamill saw the JFK presidency as a significant "historical moment, some moment when it all seems to have been put together as an idea." It was a time of idealism:

> I wanted to remind you that in Watts I didn't see pictures of Malcolm X or Ron Karenga on the walls. I saw pictures of JFK. That is your capital in the most cynical sense; it is your obligation in another, the obligation of staying true to whatever it was that put those pictures on those walls. I don't think we can afford five summers of blood. I do know this: if a 15-year-old kid is given a choice between Rap Brown and RFK, he *might* choose the way of sanity. It's only a possibility, but at least there is that chance. Give that same kid a choice between Rap Brown and LBJ, and he'll probably reach for his revolver.

Hamill's letter seemed to have stirred a new determinism in Kennedy. He carried it around in his briefcase, reread it and reread it, and showed it to friends and advisors.

If Robert Kennedy needed an event to jump-start his presidential campaign, it occurred in late February, with the arrival of a disturbing fifteen-hundred-page document analyzing the deepening chasm between black and white America in the wake of the civil rights movement and recent rioting in the country's biggest cities. For three consecutive summers, beginning in Watts in 1965, there had been a cacophony of violence, looting, burning, and vandalism, the turbulence increasing each year in size, numbers of cities involved, and scope.

On July 28, 1967, Lyndon Johnson created a blue-ribbon panel, known as the National Advisory Commission on Civil Disorders, chaired by Illinois governor Otto Kerner, to study the unrest and file a report on its findings. The panel, which also included New York mayor John V. Lindsay as its vice chairman, spent seven months on the study, interviewing civil rights advocates, law enforcement personnel, witnesses to the violence, members of the press, social scientists and scholars, and anyone else deemed capable of contributing to an understanding of the riots and events leading up to them. Johnson wanted three basic questions answered: *What happened? Why did it happen? What can be done to prevent it from happening again?* Between August and November, 130 witnesses appeared before the board in Washington, D.C. Board members visited eight of the cities heavily affected by the riots. When the report was finally written and submitted, it represented the most comprehensive document ever offered on urban black America and the violent response to the hopelessness of inner-city ghettos.

Johnson boiled over when the report was delivered to the White House on February 28, two days before it was scheduled to be released to the public. The panel, while acknowledging the Johnson administration's significance in establishing long overdue measures guaranteeing the most basic civil rights to African Americans, declared that America still practiced a double standard when dealing with the black and white citizens. The sentence "Our nation is moving toward two societies, one black, one white—separate and unequal," stated on the document's opening page, became the report's most memorable and hotly debated statement.

"Great sustained national efforts were required to combat racism, unemployment, and poverty," explained Senator Fred R. Harris, a member of the panel, years later. "There was no doubt about that. We said: It is time to make good the promises of American democracy to all citizens—urban and rural, white and black, Spanish surname, American Indian and every minority group."

The panel recommended numerous steps that the government might take to address the inequities and send the country along a better path in its racial relations, the recommendations addressing four particular categories: employment, education, the welfare system, and housing. The guidelines offered by the report included suggestions for both the immediate and near-distant future.

"Unemployment and underemployment are among the most persistent and serious grievances of our disadvantaged minorities," the panel declared. "The pervasive effect of these conditions on the racial ghetto is inextricably linked to the problem of civil disorder."

Commission recommendations for addressing this included the goals of creating a million new jobs in the public sector and a million jobs in the private sector, with an emphasis on new black businesses in the inner cities, within the next three years. Job education and training ranked high on the panel's list of priorities.

Johnson objected to the report in both principle and particulars. Relations between whites and blacks, he countered, were improving, and he wasn't shy about taking some of the credit for it. After all, he had been the president to push through the most historic civil rights legislation in a century. It was under his watch that archaic and racist practices were struck down in the South. This was why he took the recent urban disturbances almost personally: didn't African Americans realize how much better off they were because of his efforts? He would never shake the sorrow the riots had caused him, and he would bristle whenever Jack and Robert Kennedy were credited as pioneers in civil rights improvements. He was displeased enough with being saddled with the Vietnam War after JFK's death; he would be damned if his Great Society efforts would go unappreciated, undercut by a document like the Kerner report.

Further complicating matters was the indisputable truth that present budgetary concerns made the panel's recommendations impossible to achieve. As it was, Congress was demanding cuts to LBJ's current budget—cuts that threatened the futures of existing Great Society provisions. The war was bleeding the budget dry, and there was continual demand for more money to fund the ever-escalating effort. The panel's suggestions might have been worthy ideals under other circumstances; they were unthinkable now. What galled Johnson was the certainty that *he* would be the one held accountable for failure to follow the panel's guidelines. *He* would be the one blamed for dragging his feet and continuing the tradition of requesting more time while those most affected by the inequities watched their years passing by.

In his memoirs, when offering his side of the story for posterity, LBJ would see his reaction to the report on even terms—he called the report "constructive and helpful" when he finally addressed it after weeks of silence, and in *The Vantage Point,* he wrote that the panel's "analysis reflected extremely close agreement between the Commission's proposals and the administration's program"—but those behind the scenes saw a much more negative reaction. Joe Califano, who read an advance copy of the report before Johnson and feared that the president would "erupt" when he saw it, spoke privately with Johnson and offered suggestions on how he could publicly respond to it. His worries about LBJ's reactions proved to be justified. After trying to cool the president off and listening to Johnson's negative response to the report, Califano predicted the worst case scenario: Johnson would either "ignore or demean the commission." Johnson chose the former, to the extent of refusing to accept his bound presidential copy when Executive Director David Ginsburg tried to present it to him.

The report struck other major figures in different ways. Martin Luther King was ecstatic with the panel's conclusions and began working some of them into his speeches. George Wallace similarly decided to include points from the report in his public statements, but for entirely different reasons. The report, he said, only boosted some of the remarks he had been making in his law-and-order statements. Richard Nixon agreed. The report, he scoffed, "blames everybody for the riots except the perpetrators of the riots."

A few weeks after the release of the report, with Johnson still maintaining his silence on it, Vice President Hubert Humphrey acted as a proxy for the president, addressing the heart of the president's unstated objections in the keynote address to the Triennial Convention of B'nai B'rith Women in Washington, D.C. "Let us maintain some historical perspective," he urged his audience, undoubtedly aware that his words would be considered the official White House stand. "Let us be clear that we have already traveled a considerable distance. We are not just starting out."

Humphrey vigorously objected to the report's suggestion that whites were largely to blame for the creation and maintenance of inner-city ghettos—and, by extension, the violence erupting from them as blacks, mired in hopelessness, expressed their rage. This, Humphrey contended, came "dangerously close to a doctrine of group guilt." He conceded that there was a movement toward two separate societies, as the Kerner report charged, but he argued that this was "part of the picture, and . . . not the main part." Ever the optimist, Humphrey called separatism "the backwash of the past, not the wave of the future."

To Robert Kennedy, the White House response fortified his contention that Lyndon Johnson and his administration were not fit to govern. The war in Vietnam represented a misguided failure in foreign policy, while the reaction (or, in Johnson's case, the refusal to react) to the Kerner report indicated an administration out of touch with the most compelling issue on the domestic front. Four more years of Johnson would mean four additional years of the kind of policies now dividing America. "This means," Kennedy remarked, "that he's not going to do anything about the war and he's not going to do anything about the cities, either."

Kennedy had no faith in Eugene McCarthy's ability to unseat Johnson in the primaries, even after hearing from Allard Lowenstein, who projected a strong McCarthy showing in New Hampshire and a McCarthy victory in Wisconsin.

Polls projected weak overall numbers for McCarthy, and Kennedy doubted McCarthy's staying power over the long haul. Kennedy felt that the Minnesota senator was lazy—not a characteristic conducive to presidential ambitions and the grueling process of a drawn-out campaign.

Kennedy decided to enter the presidential race in early March (March 7, according to Jack Newfield), when Johnson, still free-falling in the national polls, made it clear that he would not be addressing the Kerner report in the near future, if ever. The chore now was finding the proper date for the announcement.

6 Mayor Richard Daley delivered on his promise to speak to the president about the creation of a commission to study the Vietnam War. Johnson listened to Daley's suggestions about the panel, including the recommendation that Robert Kennedy act as its chairman. Johnson expressed interest in such a commission, but he stalled on acting on it.

The weeks passed, and the New Hampshire primary loomed in the very near future. Despite urgings from his closest advisors that he announce his candidacy, Kennedy held back. For all that had occurred, pushing him to his decision to run, he still believed in the reasons that had kept him from entering the race over the past six months, and he believed that he would probably be beaten by Johnson in a head-to-head contest for the Democratic nomination. He held out the slightest hope for the Vietnam commission: if it was created and the president was serious about it, he might be able to avoid the prospects of dividing his party and damaging his future prospects of a White House run.

"That was Bob, the politician, trying to have his cake and eat it, too," said Fred Dutton, an RFK advisor and skeptic of the commission. "He was trying to get the war over with, which he felt very strongly about at that time, have great influence, and yet not necessarily have to challenge the President. But I always felt—and I wrote him a memo at the time—that was a totally unrealistic operation, which nothing would come of and he would look absurd to the extent it got out."

Potential RFK supporters, particularly youthful ones, unaware of Kennedy's inner turmoil, lost their patience with his indecision. Boobirds and hecklers attended his speeches, interrupting them with catcalls. He was especially stung by a sign—HAWK, DOVE, OR CHICKEN—at an appearance at Brooklyn College. Worst of all, he was being abandoned by young voters turning to Eugene McCarthy and joining his "children's crusade." One painful split found

Richard Goodwin, who had edited and polished Kennedy's Chicago speech, heading to the McCarthy camp. To Goodwin, Vietnam was too great a priority to wait for Kennedy to make up his mind.

Johnson's first response to the Vietnam commission proposal came during a meeting with Ted Sorensen. The president had invited Kennedy's aide and speechwriter to a meeting at the White House. Johnson had known Sorensen from his days in John Kennedy's administration, and he was one of a very few RFK insiders with whom he felt he could confide. The meeting was set up for March 11, the day before the New Hampshire primary, and as far as Sorensen knew, it was simply going to be "a five-minute thing . . . a social meeting."

It turned out to be much more. Before his White House meeting, Sorensen dropped by Robert Kennedy's Senate office, and the two men discussed the Vietnam commission. Kennedy asked Sorensen to broach the subject with Johnson, but without mentioning his or Richard Daley's names.

"I had no idea what the meeting with the President was going to be like— whether I would have any chance to discuss Vietnam in any substance," Sorensen would recall. "My own guess is the President had no such meeting in mind, either."

When Sorensen arrived at the White House, Johnson relocated the meeting from the Oval Office to a much smaller study, and the five-minute courtesy meeting that Sorensen envisioned turned into a "wide-ranging" conversation that found the president in prime form, offering opinions about such present and former cabinet members as Dean Rusk, Robert McNamara, and Clark Clifford; his reasons for not running in the forthcoming Massachusetts primary; his observations about Eugene McCarthy's campaign in New Hampshire; and, of course, the Vietnam War. He hinted, on a couple of occasions, that he might not run for reelection, but Sorensen didn't take him seriously. He sounded quite the opposite: "To me," Sorensen wrote in his memoirs, "the president sounded like a presidential candidate, talking about the upcoming campaign." Sorensen dismissed Johnson's talk of not running as a matter of LBJ's resorting to his melodramatic ways.

The conversation eventually turned to the Vietnam War and the proposed commission. Sorensen suggested that Secretary of State Dean Rusk, under intense pressure and criticism for his part in handling the war, be replaced, but Johnson wouldn't consider it. When Sorensen, without mentioning names, suggested the creation of a Vietnam commission similar in structure to Otto Kerner's National Advisory Committee on Civil Disorders, the president admitted that he had received a similar thought from Richard Daley. Johnson seemed warm to the idea. "If it could be done without looking to the Communists as though we're just throwing in our hand, that might be useful," Johnson told Sorensen. "I'll think about that." Johnson ended the discussion by asking Sorensen to draw up a list of candidates to sit on the commission, flattering Sorensen by saying that he might make a good member. Sorensen left the meeting feeling upbeat: maybe there was still a way to move forward toward peace in the Southeast Asian country while, at the same time, keeping Robert Kennedy out of the presidential race.

Book Two

THE PRIMARIES

6 New Hampshire
Victorious Losers

1 Richard Nixon arrived in New Hampshire on February 1, relaxed and confident, eager to begin a campaign that would bring him back to national political relevance. The signs were good. The sitting president was like a gored animal, badly injured by the events of recent months. As for the competition within his own party, Romney still refused to give in to the obvious indications of a doomed campaign, and Nelson Rockefeller still vacillated on whether he would actually run. Nixon would win the New Hampshire primary; the only question was by how much. Recent polls had him leading Romney by 40 percent, and Rockefeller by 14 percent. Nixon knew better, however, than to place his faith in polls. Voters could be very fickle from one month to the next.

There was no fanfare to his arrival. He had yet to formally declare his candidacy, and he literally arrived in the state under cover of darkness, ending a travel day that began in New York, proceeded on with a flight to Boston, and ended with Nixon's being driven to Nashua, New Hampshire, arriving around midnight and surprising an unwitting hotel keeper with his small entourage's unexpected check-in. No one outside the Nixon group knew he was in the state—just the way Nixon wanted it. As the forthcoming weeks would demonstrate, the campaign was choreographed down to the simplest step.

Nixon had scheduled a press conference for the following afternoon, but most of New Hampshire would know about his candidacy before he stepped forward to make it formal. On the day of his late-night drive into the state, the U.S. Mail delivered 150,000 letters from Richard Nixon to New Hampshire homes. Nixon announced his candidacy in the letter, telling voters that their responsibilities were "greater than ever," that the next president would have tough decisions to make at home and abroad. "I believe I have found some answers," he informed his readers.

This was a reinvented Nixon, and he wanted voters to know it. This wasn't Tricky Dick, the used-car salesman, the poor loser, the politician who had stumbled away from the public with the vow to never return. The Richard Nixon voters were now seeing was *presidential;* he would lead the country in its time of crisis.

This, of course, was all part of the plan Nixon's handlers were developing. The main thrust of the plan involved a bit of misdirection: Nixon was to look open and available, although, in reality, his time with the public, particularly the press, was to be restricted. He would avoid the old standard operating procedures, now a campaign-trail cliché, such as hanging around factory gates, attending a glut of fish fries and luncheons, kissing babies, and haunting shopping centers, high school gymnasiums, and bowling alleys. He would give the same speech wherever he went—no point in risking misstatement resulting in the loss of his big lead. New Hampshire was a Republican state, and the voters there knew of and liked Richard Nixon. The primary, Nixon's campaign officials believed, was Nixon's to lose. Overexposure was the enemy. The last thing Nixon needed was to look desperate. That was George Romney's turf.

And he wouldn't make the mistake of overworking, as he had in 1960. There would be no reprise of his first debate debacle with John Kennedy, when he had arrived at the television studio exhausted and feeling the painful effects of a bad knee, a miserable counterpart to a man who understood the intricacies of television image. This time around, Nixon's daily schedule would be lighter, and he would spend scheduled weekends in Florida, where he could relax and work on his tan. With any luck, he would look younger and more vibrant than the Nixon of eight years earlier.

His media team had created a marketing plan that proved to be remarkably effective. Nixon, they had determined months earlier, while watching hours of film of the candidate in motion, was more appealing to voters in an extemporaneous setting.

In Hillsborough, Nixon was filmed in a town-hall setting, answering questions posed by about two dozen cherry-picked local citizens. The press, not appraised of the taping, protested the exclusion afterward but to little avail. Nixon was at his finest, handling the queries "with an old-timer's ease," "relaxed and informal." The lengthy tape was cut down and edited into five-minute segments earmarked for television viewing throughout the primary season. Similar tapings followed. In a compromise, the press was allowed to listen to the question-and-answer sessions in a room outside of the taping room and to meet Nixon later for other questions, but by then, the real work had been completed. Nixon found television, at least in this format, easy and accommodating. His other obligation—taping voice-overs for one-minute spots—was better yet. He could record these in the privacy and comfort of his hotel room.

"There were different pieces of information that were assembled," Leonard Garment said of the tapings. "It worked really well because it was really quite loose, and we're very open. And Nixon understood that that was the way it was going to go, if it was going to go successfully for him." The ads, intended to project a new image of the candidate, achieved their intended goal. The "new Nixon," Garment said, "was essentially the same Nixon, but one who was open to new possibilities, like any intelligent person."

His speeches and meetings with the press went smoothly. It helped that William Loeb, editor of the *Manchester Union Leader,* the state's largest and most conservative daily newspaper, not only endorsed Nixon; the paper's straight news coverage dropped any pretense of objectivity. NIXON'S THE ONE, the campaign slogan proclaimed, and it would have been difficult to dispute the claim. Nixon's stump speeches were heavy on generalities and one-liners ("You can't handshake your way out of the kind of problems we have today") and lean on specifics. Nixon spent three days in New Hampshire before flying to Wisconsin for some campaigning in the second major primary. In his brief time in the state, he left a huge footprint.

2 While Nixon coasted, George Romney continued to struggle. One could not criticize his determination or dedication, but he simply could not find a way to connect with the New Hampshire voters. He was better looking, more engaging, and more forthright in detailing his plans than Nixon, but no one seemed to notice. If anything, his numbers were getting worse. When he arrived in New Hampshire on January 12, he already had months of soft campaigning behind him. He was the only declared Republican candidate, yet he was falling in the polls to Nixon, who had yet to announce his candidacy, and to Nelson Rockefeller, who insisted that he had no intention of running. Romney hadn't recovered from his "brainwashing" remarks of the previous year, and it looked as if he never would. If that wasn't enough, he had to contend with the rumor, innuendo, and other nonsense common to the campaign trail. A pamphlet making the rounds questioned whether he could run for office, since he had been born while his parents were visiting Mexico. He was accused of indulging in too much alcohol, even though Romney, a devout Mormon, assured the public, "I've never had a drink in my life."

His work ethic was beyond the pale. No stop was too small, no weather conditions too prohibitive to pull him away from the task. One morning—his first of campaigning in New Hampshire—he pulled himself out of bed before dawn and braved twenty-below-zero temperatures to stand, hatless and freezing, at a factory gate in Nashua. According to Jules Witcover, a journalist covering the primary, many first-shift workers looked at him as if he were crazy. In an appearance that seemed to symbolize the sad futility of his efforts in New Hampshire, Romney visited a Franklin bowling alley and conversed with a league of women bowlers. When he tried his hand at bowling, Romney learned it wasn't his sport. He managed to knock down nine pins, but he wasn't going to quit until he made a spare. He rolled ball after ball at the lone pin standing until he finally succeeded on his thirty-fourth attempt, ending his embarrassing lesson on persistence.

According to one report, the typical Romney campaign day found the candidate "outside of a factory greeting workers at 6:30 A.M., an 8:00 A.M. breakfast meeting/speech, mid-morning opening or visiting home headquarters, a high school or college speech, a noon luncheon with a service club, more home headquarters meetings in the afternoon accompanied by street campaigning, a radio interview, a meeting with a local newspaper editor, perhaps a break from campaigning for dinner or a dinner speaking engagement, and often a speech or meeting with workers in the evening with the campaign day ending for him after 11:00 P.M." Romney, known for his great physical conditioning and stamina, particularly for his jogging, needed every bit of it to maintain his schedule.

Romney's campaign was probably buried before he set foot in New Hampshire. One of Romney's own polls found him running worse against Nixon than he had been a year earlier, another had him trailing Nixon 70.3 percent to 11.3 percent. His bad habit of stating an opinion before he had thought the stance through, only to have to clarify (and reclarify) his position later, made him look indecisive. The Tet Offensive, breaking out in Romney's early days in the state, might have offered him the opportunity to solidify his position on Vietnam had he been at all clear in his position, but after delivering a strong, well-conceived speech at Keene State College, in which he called for a negotiated settlement to end the war, he found himself backtracking on some of his statements the very next day. Even his slogans failed to pass muster. His billboard ads telling viewers that his way to reduce crime was to fight moral decay were pulled when Romney's advisors suggested that this sounded like something one might hear in a dentist's office.

Funding was drying up as well. Romney had spent a million dollars on the campaign to that point, and he figured that he would need at least twice again that amount just to limp into the Miami convention. Rockefeller had sunk money into the Romney coffers, but if Rockefeller were to announce his own candidacy, as expected, contributors had little to gain by investing in what amounted to little more than an endorsement of a stalking horse. One of Romney's own campaign officials might have pushed Romney to the brink when he suggested that Romney might not have enough New Hampshire votes to defeat a Rockefeller write-in tally.

Romney challenged Nixon to a debate when Nixon opened his campaign in New Hampshire, but Nixon brushed him off. A debate, Nixon tried to explain, would not be in the best interests of either candidate. It certainly wouldn't have served Nixon well. He had failed miserably in his debates with Kennedy in 1960, and it probably cost him the election; he had nothing to gain and a lot to lose by debating Romney, who trailed by such a large margin that he could only hope to gain from a Nixon misstatement. "The great debate of 1968 will be, or should be, between the Republican nominee and Lyndon Johnson," Nixon said, still convinced that Johnson would be the Democratic nominee.

Romney was assailed by the press—when anything was written about him at all. He made good copy. When he stumbled on his words, the press delighted in passing along his latest gaffe. The *Manchester Union Leader*'s William Loeb, notorious for his signed, front-page editorials, attacked Romney at every opportunity. A Nixon supporter, Loeb went so far as to criticize Romney's state-of-the-art computer system, which tracked voter demographics and voting trends. "When all this personal data is coupled with opinion surveys and behavioral studies," Loeb wrote, "the potential for manipulating the electorate of New Hampshire is enormous." In case the reader might have missed the message, Loeb drove home his point in capital letters: "NEW HAMPSHIRE IS TO BE THE TESTING GROUND OF THIS KIND OF A 'PROGRAMMING POLITICS' AND YOU THE VOTERS OF THIS STATE ARE TO BE THE GUINEA PIGS."

For all his time and effort, Romney had to concede that he was beaten. He officially dropped out of the race on February 28, while attending a governors' conference in Washington, D.C. He had not found the Republican support needed to continue, he told reporters, and he would be much more effective in working for another candidate. Significantly, he volunteered no names of candidates he might find worthy of an endorsement.

Romney's announcement left New Hampshire an uncontested victory for Nixon, a last-minute addition to the ballot. Nixon was unhappy with the hollow victory.

"I was disappointed by Romney's withdrawal," he would remember. "Even though I had knocked him out of the ring, now I would win without having actually defeated an opponent in the election—and the test of the election was, after all, the reason I had decided to enter the primaries in the first place."

3 Had he not been as self-confident as he was, Eugene McCarthy might have expected New Hampshire to be difficult, perhaps even hostile. This was a state with important defense contracts vital to its economy, and voters tended to vote Republican. Even the wind and snow of the typical New England winter seemed to conspire against campaign volunteers slogging door-to-door through the slop. Homeowners were unlikely to ask them into their homes and less likely yet to stand out on their porches for a campaign spiel. McCarthy had no idea what to expect. His campaign staff was inexperienced and his door-to-door campaigners were college kids, graduate students at best. Still, he began his campaign with the belief that, while perhaps hawkish and patriotic in belief, the typical voter was probably unhappy with the way the Vietnam War was being conducted.

From its opening days in the Granite State, the McCarthy campaign defied conventional campaign wisdom and practice. The candidate, his staff and army of volunteers, the day-to-day operations—all seemed to operate on their own set of rules. To those with experience working on campaigns or, in the case of reporters, following them closely, McCarthy came across as detached, unwilling to lead and happy to delegate, and disconnected with the people devoted to his bidding. His demeanor suggested that he was running on cool intelligence at the cost of political savvy and elbow grease. He could be impatient, as if he believed that he deserved to be getting better than he was receiving.

His staff and volunteers, on the other hand, were willing to make any sacrifice or carry out any task, no matter how menial, to advance the cause. They had cut their hair or shaved their beards, and tuned down what they chose to wear, all in an effort to "Get Clean for Gene." While McCarthy, his family, and his campaign lieutenants slept in comfortable hotel beds, volunteers packed themselves into sleeping bags and slept on any available floor. They subsisted on peanut butter sandwiches and soft drinks. And yet their numbers expanded, from students from nearby East Coast colleges to youthful volunteers from as far away as the Midwest. There might be two or three thousand fanning out around New Hampshire on weekdays; the numbers swelled to five thousand on weekends, when college kids would abandon their studies for a couple days and join a cause that promised, if successful, to change the course of history. You couldn't place a price on their energy.

Ben Stavis, a graduate student pursuing a Ph.D. in Chinese studies at Columbia University, worked on McCarthy's staff as a map designer. A staff member, by his definition, "was essentially anyone who worked during the week. He prepared materials to be used on weekends, then supervised the people who came on weekends." A staff member didn't even have to work but a day or two. What he or she learned in that limited time would be enough to supervise the volunteers.

No one on the McCarthy staff—or the candidate himself, for that matter—knew what to expect from the volunteers. Never in the history of U.S. presidential elections had such emphasis been placed on extensive canvassing. Dubbed the "children's crusade" by the media, the youthful volunteers faced obstacles that older campaign workers never had to confront, largely as a result of a generation gap dividing young activists and their parents. How would these young, idealistic workers be received by older, more worldly, perhaps cynical voters? What could they really know, given their relative inexperience? Would they be helping or hindering McCarthy? Sam Brown and John Barbieri, his top assistant in New Hampshire, had to deal with these and other questions with the arrival of each new wave of volunteers, and in the early weeks of the New Hampshire effort, they discovered that misconception could be a major roadblock. According to Ben Stavis, "students were thought, in January and February of 1968, to be indifferent, incapable, and ineffective in 'constructive' politics."

The volunteers canvassing neighborhoods were under strict orders about how to conduct their business. Their job was to distribute McCarthy campaign materials and answer any questions the voter might have about the candidate. They were not to engage in drawn-out discussions about the issues, particularly Vietnam. The ideal conversation would draw the voter into expressing views that would give the volunteer an indication of how that voter felt about McCarthy and the issues. The visits would be as educational for the volunteers as for the voter. It was imperative to dress conservatively, stay friendly, and move along as quickly as the circumstances allowed. All candidates used canvassing as part of their campaigning, but McCarthy was setting a precedent in his use of volunteers in this way. He wanted every registered Democrat or independent to be called upon—more than once, if they showed interest.

The plan worked better than expected. If the college undergrad was perceived as being a loud, long-haired, poorly dressed, angry, protesting, antiestablishment troublemaker, the canvassers proved otherwise. They believed in the system and wanted to be a part of it. These were kids from another time, another generation. The Tet Offensive had forced New Hampshirites to reconsider their support of Lyndon Johnson and the Vietnam War, and they were listening to an alternative from friendly young people backing a senator they didn't know.

This perception supported McCarthy's low-key style of campaigning. His witty intelligence enchanted rally attendees—"That's like choosing between vulgarity and obscenity, isn't it?" he responded when a woman bemoaned the possible election-night face-off between Johnson and Nixon—but it did not seem forced or artificial. He avoided using a desultory tone, which, like slogans, could sound simplistic, condescending, or insulting to a public that liked to think it was smart and discerning when the voting booth curtain closed behind them. Loudmouths were not presidential; a calm, reasoned divining of issues and possible solutions separated the leaders from the pretenders.

Aside from a twenty-minute hockey exhibition, during which McCarthy laced on ice skates and played with a semipro hockey team, and an early photo session, which found McCarthy standing out in frigid weather conditions to pose in the precise location where John F. Kennedy had begun his campaign in New Hampshire in 1960, McCarthy stayed away from obvious photo ops and eschewed the use of private polls. He gave speeches, attended luncheons, stood at factory gates, and visited radio and television stations but was known to turn down, sometimes out of sheer petulance, opportunities that might have helped his campaign. He waved off an appearance on *Meet the Press,* miffed because he wasn't the news program's featured guest. On election day, he bypassed an early interview on the *Huntley-Brinkley Report* on NBC—he deemed their studio set to be too elaborate and "ostentatious"—in favor of a visit with CBS and David Schoumacher.

Celebrity endorsements and appearances boosted his profile in the state. Actors Paul Newman, Myrna Loy, Robert Ryan, and Tony Randall, and *Twilight Zone* creator and writer Rod Serling, turned up at pro-McCarthy rallies. Newman, who possessed all the charisma that McCarthy seemed to lack, was especially effective. At one stop, he was asked why he felt the need to help McCarthy. The actor responded, "I didn't come here to help Gene McCarthy. I need McCarthy's help. The country needs it." The quote made its way into all the daily papers.

Robert Lowell traveled with McCarthy and, for better or worse, exerted considerable influence on McCarthy's thinking. The highly acclaimed poet held strongly stated antiwar opinions, and he could be abrasive while talking to some of McCarthy's staff and supporters. McCarthy, a poet himself, valued the intellectual muscle that Lowell brought to the campaign, and their discussions about poetry, literature, religion, and philosophy pulled the candidate out of the drudgery of daily campaigning.

McCarthy, whose hands-off approach to dealing with his staff was occasionally interpreted as aloofness, preferred to give his workers the leeway to work through prickly problems, which led to tensions that dogged his campaign from the beginning. Local organizers who had logged countless hours in setting up the New Hampshire campaign events resented the appearance of national staffers who, the locals felt, barged in and tried to take control of a situation already under control. Miscommunication was inevitable, bruised egos a common malady. The locals thoroughly appreciated the arrival of Richard Goodwin, whose credentials were impeccable, and whose self-confidence was contagious. ("With these two typewriters," he reportedly said to Seymour Hersh upon his arrival in New Hampshire, "we're going to overthrow the government.") They were less impressed with others, who resisted giving access to McCarthy when his attention was needed. McCarthy, aware of the difficulties, stayed outside the fray. It was going to be a long campaign; the staffs in the individual states would have to learn to work with the national staff. They would smooth out the organizational roughness of the campaign, while the volunteers did the heavy lifting. "My campaign may not be organized at the top," he cracked on election night, "but it is certainly tightly organized at the bottom."

4   The Johnson write-in campaign in New Hampshire, through a series of colossal blunders and poor decisions, boosted the McCarthy effort in unanticipated ways and acted, in its own peculiar manner, as a template on how to sabotage a candidate's chances. With the early polls indicating what appeared to be an unsurpassable Johnson lead over McCarthy, the LBJ campaign officials underestimated McCarthy's ability to cut the distance between the two candidates. The three main figures in the write-in campaign—New Hampshire governor John King, Senator Thomas McIntyre, and campaign manager and businessman Bernard Boulin—were far more experienced in conducting a campaign than the McCarthy team, but they misjudged the disposition of the state's voters. McCarthy was deemed to be a one-issue candidate, when, as postprimary analysis would conclude, McCarthy represented a strong alternative to a very unpopular president. McCarthy was a presence, standing out in the cold, flooding the state with a well-conceived media plan, playing hockey with a semipro team, commanding an army of volunteers knocking on doors and talking up their candidate in telephone cold calls. Compared to McCarthy's efforts, Johnson looked disinterested.

By the time the Johnson camp finally accepted the notion that McCarthy was a powerful presence in New Hampshire and that he was going to be running over the long haul, desperate measures were required if Johnson hoped to avoid embarrassment at the voting booths. Two courses of action—pledge cards and negative campaigning—were poor choices and nearly sank the campaign, causing voters to turn to McCarthy because of their displeasure with the president.

The pledge cards were Boulin's idea. Each registered Democrat in the state was sent a card asking for a pledge of support. The numbered cards were divided into three parts, the first to be submitted to the White House, the second to be sent to the state's Democratic committee, the third portion, presumably as a reminder to vote for Johnson, whose name was not on the ballot, was to be retained by the voter. In return, the voter received a signed photograph of Lyndon and Lady Bird Johnson, as well as a note of gratitude from King and McIntyre. Henry Cabot Lodge had used a similar approach four years earlier when he was running for the presidency. It had worked for him, but it backfired on Johnson, precipitating a stormy round of criticism. The McCarthy group denounced the pledge cards as an infringement on the secret ballot, with McCarthy quipping that it was "not at all inconsistent with administration policy to kind of put a brand on people." Newspaper editorials worried that there was possible retaliation in store for any voter failing to vote for Johnson. The cards were quickly pulled from circulation, but the damage had been done. One McCarthy campaign poster advised voters that *You Don't Have to Sign Anything to Vote for Gene McCarthy.* According to Arthur Herzog, a McCarthy campaign volunteer, some Democrats maintained that the pledge card debacle "might have cost them up to ten thousand votes."

The negative advertising, called "intensive and intemperate" by the *New York Times,* along with the personal attacks on McCarthy by McIntyre, King, and others, might have caused even more damage—an irony that would not escape the notice of analysts after the primary's votes were counted. Prior to his campaign blitz in the state, McCarthy was unknown by three out of five state residents, and even after McCarthy made his campaign known in New Hampshire, the polls gave him no chance of winning. Yet the passage of time and the growth of McCarthy's popularity spooked the men running the campaign of a president who, four years earlier, had retained his office by the largest voter margin in history. The negative campaigning tarnished Johnson's image at a time when his approval ratings needed a boost.

King and McIntyre took the offensive, choosing to attack McCarthy's stance on the Vietnam War and, by extension, his patriotism—a dubious approach, given the recent Tet Offensive and the revelation, published in the *New York Times* two days before the primary, that General Westmoreland was requesting an additional 206,000 troops to prop up the war effort. A year earlier, New Hampshire voters might have been persuaded by this type of advertising; now, the issue wasn't the war itself but Johnson's handling of it.

The attacks were vicious. King called McCarthy "a champion of appeasement and surrender"; ads claimed that Hanoi was closely watching the primary, hoping for a McCarthy victory, because a vote for McCarthy would be a vote for Ho Chi Minh. A radio ad warned voters that to support McCarthy would be disastrous: "To vote for weakness and indecision would not be in the best interests of our country." McCarthy was especially offended by a charge, issued by McIntyre on the day before the election, that McCarthy's position on conscientious objection and amnesty for those leaving the country rather than submitting to the draft would "let American draft dodgers return home scot-free without punishment." This, McCarthy charged, constituted "a gross misinterpretation of what I had proposed."

McCarthy refused to engage in a bitter exchange over the negative advertising. The cheap shots were winning him sympathy votes that might otherwise have gone to Johnson. A calm, rational approach appealed to the electorate. New Hampshire voters liked to think of themselves as independent thinkers who, despite their tendency to vote Republican, were beholden to no one. McCarthy tried to appeal to that independence in his radio ads running in the final days before the election. He had begun his campaign with a simple challenge ("New Hampshire Can Help Bring the Nation Back to Its Senses"), and he was closing it with an extension of the idea: "Think how it would feel to wake up Wednesday morning to find out that Gene McCarthy had won the New Hampshire primary—to find that New Hampshire had changed the course of American politics." Once guarded in his assessments of his chances against Johnson, McCarthy felt optimistic about his chances in the final days leading to the primary; he was "euphoric," as his wife described him. The Johnson campaign, measuring its losses over the weeks, made a preemptive strike by announcing that McCarthy would consider his campaign a failure if he didn't collect at least 30 percent of the vote.

When night fell on New Hampshire the evening before the voting, McCarthy was not inclined to disagree. It was long-shot thinking, backed by weeks of proving that he really did belong in the race.

5 New Hampshire awoke to heavy snowfall on March 12, but the weather had little noticeable effect on the McCarthy campaign volunteers, who gathered for one last day of work, or on Democratic voters, who turned out for the primary in record numbers. Richard Goodwin regarded the heavy voter turnout as "a welcome signal that indifference had yielded to interest, apathy to engagement." He could remember a time, only a few weeks earlier, when

he and McCarthy had been able to dine in public without getting any attention. Now, as he walked through the Sheraton-Wayfarer Hotel on election day, he witnessed a remarkable transformation: newspaper and television reporters busied themselves by interviewing anyone connected to the McCarthy campaign, television cables snaked down the hotel corridors, and McCarthy supporters and volunteers filled "every vacant space, sitting against the walls [and] standing in crowded rooms." People believed they were witnessing the birth of a movement. Or maybe it was the new groundbreaking of a seedling of hope.

Whatever it was, the exit polls gave reason for optimism. McCarthy was faring very well in the state's smaller cities and towns and holding his own in the bigger municipalities. A festive mood lifted exhausted campaign volunteers. McCarthy allowed himself a dash of relief. Maybe this would all turn out, if not in his favor, at least better than he might have anticipated when he began his campaign in New Hampshire. By sundown it was confirmed: he was going to do much better than the political prognosticators forewarned. Going into the day, Governor King was still holding fast to his belief that McCarthy would be fortunate to pull one out of four voters; a CBS poll, released on election night, placed McCarthy at 29 percent.

As he had throughout his stay in New Hampshire, McCarthy scoffed at the gloomy numbers and overall reportage. "Reporters and political experts were so wrong about much of the campaign of 1968 that many, had they professional integrity, would have put away their typewriters and written no more on politics," he would write later.

The final numbers produced the kind of contradiction that can only happen in politics: the winner was viewed as the loser, and the defeated was crowned the victor. Johnson's write-in candidacy netted the president 49.4 percent of the votes cast by Democratic voters; McCarthy pulled 42.2 percent. The numbers narrowed considerably when the Republican crossover vote was tallied. McCarthy wound up 230 votes shy of claiming an upset victory over the incumbent president. Further, due to poor filing for delegate count by the LBJ campaign team, McCarthy would be receiving twenty of the state's twenty-four delegates at the Democratic National Convention in August.

McCarthy greeted his jubilant staff, volunteers, and followers later on election night. Amid chants of *Chi-ca-go, Chi-ca-go,* McCarthy thanked the thousands who had labored for him, calling them the best, most intelligent campaigners in history. "People have remarked that the campaign has brought young people back into the system," he said. "But it's the other way around. The young people have brought the country back into the system."

The press almost unanimously deemed McCarthy's New Hampshire showing as a condemnation of Lyndon Johnson. *Time* magazine, in a cover story on

McCarthy published a week after the primary, reported that an NBC poll of Democratic voters showed that more than 50 percent of those polled said they had no knowledge of McCarthy's position on Vietnam. "Clearly," the magazine concluded, "the vote was as much anti-Johnson as antiwar." The war, reporters and editors agreed, played a major role in the final vote. "McCarthy's big vote," a *Washington Post* editorial said, "is a demonstration of significant opposition to the war." While lauding McCarthy's efforts, the press was still skeptical of presenting McCarthy as a serious contender for the Democratic Party nomination. The consensus was that Johnson, despite his shrinking popularity, would be facing Richard Nixon in November. McCarthy's unexpected success in New Hampshire was a signal, not an imposing entrance into the race. "Senator McCarthy was not a candidate in the conventional sense," declared a *New York Times* editorial, "because, as a practical matter, he cannot prevent President Johnson's renomination."

Richard Goodwin, aware of Johnson's strengths and weaknesses, was not going to concede the nomination to his former boss, but he was cautious in his assessment of the primary's effects on the campaign. "The least you did was to prove Johnson is vulnerable," he told a group of McCarthy volunteers. "And by that you made a major contribution to national politics that will change the policies of the Republican party as well as the Democratic."

■ ■ ■ ■ ■

Richard Nixon surprised no one. He had run a tight, disciplined campaign in New Hampshire, and when the votes were tabulated, he, as the only declared candidate on the ballot, had been a roaring success, gathering more than eighty thousand votes—the largest count in New Hampshire primary history, and more than all Democratic candidates combined. On the Republican ticket, he demolished runner-up Nelson Rockefeller, a write-in candidate, by a seven-to-one margin. Three days before the primary, Nixon had sounded a lot like McCarthy when appealing to New Hampshirites to send a strong message to the nation about Johnson's inadequacies in leadership. "Here is your chance to give a signal to the nation that the people of New Hampshire say we have had enough of the policies of failure," he said.

The final vote total satisfied Nixon. The press, however, demanded more convincing. After all, how difficult was it to run up big numbers when he was running unopposed? The *New York Times,* while complimenting Nixon's strong campaign, needed more proof of the former vice president's strength. Getting the big vote totals without competition could "hardly be taken as the conclusive victory he would like to make it appear."

This was unarguably true, but Nixon and his campaign staff had reason to celebrate. The number of voters supporting him was impressive, especially under the circumstances. In coming to New Hampshire, he was essentially starting from scratch, striving to overcome the loser label and two high-profile losses in a row. After years away, he had shown that he was still popular with voters. Further, he had established a campaign style that he would maintain throughout his run for the presidency. If the rumor mill turned out to be correct, he would be facing Nelson Rockefeller at some point in the near future, or perhaps Ronald Reagan, who had curried the favor of the GOP's Far Right. If so, he would be prepared.

6 The New Hampshire primary eliminated Robert Kennedy's lingering doubts about a decision to enter the presidential race. He had agonized over it for months, returning endlessly to the same barriers blocking his desire to run. New Hampshire proved, if there ever had been a question, that the Democratic Party was badly fractured with or without Kennedy's entry into the race. McCarthy's strong showing indicated powerful opposition to Johnson and the Vietnam War. If McCarthy performed as well as projected in the Wisconsin primary, there was a realistic possibility that he could unseat the president.

Kennedy still awaited Johnson's response to his proposed commission to study the war, and there was no telling how LBJ's narrow victory in New Hampshire might influence his decision. The senator viewed Johnson's decision as all-important: in Kennedy's mind, it was the president's final chance to end the war an acceptable way while saving face with the Americans who had voted him into office. Time was becoming critical. Kennedy needed to make a formal announcement within the next day or two.

He had no one but himself to blame for his predicament, first by procrastinating for months about entering the race, and, in recent days, for opening the door a sliver in his dealings with the press. The day after the primary, upon returning to Washington, D.C., after a brief visit to New York, he was greeted at the airport by reporters demanding his reaction to the New Hampshire vote. Rather than offer a generic response to give journalists something to insert in their stories, Kennedy offered up an explosive statement that reopened conjecture about his intentions. He would be "actively reassessing" his position on running against the president, he said. The press, already convinced that Kennedy intended to run, jumped on his statements.

Voters, perhaps a majority of them, were going to find Kennedy's remarks—and the timing of them—inexcusably insensitive. McCarthy hadn't had a day to savor his showing in New Hampshire, and here was Robert Kennedy elbowing his way into the headlines. To anyone unaware of the difficulties Kennedy experienced in making a decision on whether to run—and that would have been most of the country—Kennedy would look as if he had been standing back, watching McCarthy do all the heavy lifting in New Hampshire, waiting to see if the Minnesota senator could put up any kind of fight against Johnson, and then changing his mind about running when McCarthy proved Johnson's vulnerability. These were the ruthless and opportunistic characteristics Kennedy had been working to shed.

Kennedy had little time or inclination to give this much thought. On the afternoon of his comments at the airport, he taped an interview with Walter Cronkite, slated for viewing on that evening's news. He repeated the statements he had made at the airport, listing the reasons for his reconsidering his position. After the Cronkite taping, he met with Eugene McCarthy, and over the course of a frosty conversation, he demonstrated to McCarthy that while he wasn't 100 percent certain, he would probably run.

The meeting involved some skullduggery on the part of both men. Reporters had staked out McCarthy's office, and rather than deal with their questions, the two men agreed to meet in Ted Kennedy's senate office. To reach the office undetected, McCarthy walked through the senate gymnasium, where reporters were not allowed; he then stepped outside, reentered the building, and took a back way to Ted Kennedy's office. Robert Kennedy awaited, alone.

The ensuing conversation was punctuated by long, awkward periods of silence. The meeting opened with a discussion about Kennedy's airport statements earlier that morning, with Kennedy trying to explain what he meant by his comments. McCarthy, justifiably upset by the timing of Kennedy's statements, did little to assuage Kennedy's uneasiness. As McCarthy would later attest, the twenty-minute conversation—the longest ever between the two—was noteworthy more for what was not said than for what was actually stated. Kennedy never volunteered his decision to run. Instead, he tried to explain away his airport statements with the rationalization that he had not entered the New Hampshire primary because he feared a party split; the vote had indicated that the party was already divided. The main point was to defeat Johnson and end the war. McCarthy, buoyed by the results of the New Hampshire primary, told Kennedy that in the unlikely event that he defeated Johnson, he only intended to serve one term. "I did not ask Senator Kennedy for his support in return for my stepping aside in 1972, nor did I promise to support him in 1972," McCarthy would remember. "I simply said I was interested only in one term."

When the meeting broke up, neither man had changed position. McCarthy fully expected Kennedy to run, and Kennedy still intended to run. The meeting had been an ugly formality.

All that stood between Kennedy and an announcement was the Vietnam commission, and in all likelihood Kennedy knew that Johnson would never go for it. Still, he asked his brother Ted to set up a meeting with Secretary of Defense Clark Clifford for the next morning, March 14, while promising his family, advisors, aides, and supporters that he would make a formal definitive announcement concerning his candidacy within the next thirty-six hours.

It was all or nothing on the issue of the commission. The day of the New Hampshire primary, Secretary of State Dean Rusk had gone before the Senate Foreign Relations Committee and made it clear that there were to be no significant changes in the administration's policy on the war in the near future. Kennedy, disturbed by Rusk's statements, must have known that Johnson was not going to fire Rusk, as a number of higher-ups hoped, nor would he be contradicting Rusk by announcing any differences from Rusk's statements.

The 11:00 a.m. meeting at Clifford's Pentagon office, remembered by both Clifford and Ted Sorensen (who surprised Clifford by accompanying Kennedy) as being cordial, stayed on point, with both sides adhering to their respective positions. Kennedy did not know that Clifford, at one time a hawk on the Vietnam War, was slowly but dramatically changing his position on how the war was being handled, nor would he learn about this evolving disposition during the meeting. Clifford listened carefully as Kennedy, with occasional input from Sorensen, laid out his position. Johnson's Vietnam policies were no longer acceptable, and Kennedy felt it imperative that he become more involved in changing them. One option, he told Clifford, would be for him to run for the presidency. If he won, he would change things himself. The other option would be to persuade Johnson to change things himself. "Ending the bloodshed in Vietnam is far more important to me than starting a Presidential campaign," Kennedy said.

Sorensen brought up his earlier conversation with the president about the creation of a Vietnam commission and offered a list of thirty-nine names of potential candidates for the board. The list included prominent names in the military, Congress, academia, and the media and even the candidates for the current presidential election. Sorensen took the offensive in the discussion by stating that in publicly announcing the creation of the commission, all Johnson had to do would be to admit that he had been mistaken in his policies on Vietnam.

That would never happen, Clifford stated.

"The statement does not need to go that far," Kennedy interjected. "If the

President would issue a statement that the time had come to reevaluate, in its entirety, our policy in Vietnam, this language would be sufficient for me, if coupled with the appointment of a board consisting of persons recommended by us."

Kennedy did not issue a direct ultimatum, but Clifford understood that Kennedy wasn't in a bargaining mode.

Kennedy, Clifford would recall in an interview a year later, "felt that if the President would agree to do that, then Senator Kennedy would have met his obligation to his country and he could advise all these people who are urging him to run that there was now no occasion for him to run because President Johnson was going to go ahead on a plan which he felt could very well lead to peace."

Clifford, of course, was not authorized to approve or disapprove Kennedy's list of potential board members, but he promised to present it to Johnson.

It was now his turn to speak. Prior to the meeting, Johnson had warned him that Kennedy might be up to some tricks, and though Clifford did not see that in Kennedy, he did recognize an aggression that might not be realistic in Kennedy's ultimatum. Johnson's approval rating among voters was sliding, but this didn't mean that he was unelectable. Clifford reminded Kennedy that he had seen a similar circumstance in 1948, when Harry Truman had been abandoned by liberals enamored with Henry Wallace. Truman had prevailed. Clifford strongly felt that Kennedy had no chance of defeating Johnson, and he told Kennedy as much. Besides, the president, Clifford said, could change his Vietnam policies before the Chicago convention, leaving Kennedy without his prime issue. Finally, Clifford brought forth the certainty, now shopworn from all the discussion, that by dividing the Democratic Party, Kennedy would be guaranteeing the election to the Republicans.

Kennedy assured Clifford that he had considered all this, but he was standing firm: he would enter the race if Johnson turned down his proposal. The meeting ended with Clifford convinced that "a confrontation could no longer be prevented." Kennedy and Sorensen didn't know what to expect. They had entered the meeting with Clifford under the mistaken impression that the creation of the commission was a done deal; the three of them were gathering, Sorensen thought, "to talk about the mechanics, to see whether it was a realistic alternative and whether it really did signal a change in Vietnam policy that would cause Robert Kennedy to change his mind about the presidency." When discussing it in the future, Clifford insisted that he had not been appraised of the pending commission, so Kennedy's and Sorensen's words were a revelation to him.

Whatever the case, Kennedy was unsure about what to expect from Johnson, but he learned, soon enough, shortly after Clifford met with the president, along with Vice President Hubert Humphrey and close LBJ aide Abe Fortas. When Clifford met with the president and the other two at three thirty that same afternoon, Johnson quickly rejected the Kennedy proposal, for four reasons. First, it would be seen as a political deal, no matter how the commission was presented. Second, Johnson considered it a matter of giving comfort to North Vietnam. Third, he felt that it was an attempt to seize some of his authority as president and commander in chief—a power grab he would never permit. Finally, the names on the list of possible board members were, by Johnson's estimation, people already opposed to the war. Johnson was also miffed that a similar commission hadn't been created to study the Bay of Pigs, but as Robert Kennedy pointed out in his conversation with Clifford, such a committee had indeed been created to study the botched operation. Whatever Johnson felt about a tie-in between the commission and his feud with Kennedy, he kept to himself.

Every man in the room agreed with Johnson's position, which might have been predicted: Humphrey was LBJ's vice president and inclined to support Johnson's views, and Fortas, one of the president's closest friends, was one of the biggest hawks on Capitol Hill.

Clifford called Kennedy immediately after the meeting and, with Johnson listening in on another line, informed him of the president's decision. Kennedy asked if it would matter if he wasn't connected in any way to the commission; Clifford responded that it would not.

Kennedy had only one direction to take. He had stayed out of the race until he had exhausted every reason to enter it. He would run.

■ ■ ■ ■ ■

On Saturday, March 16, Robert Kennedy stood before reporters in the Caucus Room of the Old Senate Office Building, on the very same spot where his brother had announced his candidacy in 1960.

Two days had passed since the call about Johnson's decision, and they had been two eventful ones. Hickory Hill had been overrun with guests, all eager to contribute to Kennedy's fledgling campaign. Kennedy had huddled with Ted Sorensen, Arthur Schlesinger, Adam Walinsky, and others, all haggling over the proper wording for the announcement of his candidacy. Others placed calls to Democratic Party dignitaries, to announce the news of Kennedy's running and seek advice and feedback. Mayor Daley in Chicago still opposed Kennedy's entry into the race.

Despite all the activity, Kennedy seemed somewhat morose about his decision. He openly admitted that the timing of his announcement made him look ruthless, but he could find no way around it. He had already frittered away the chance to enter the New Hampshire primary, and the deadline had passed for his entering other primaries as well. If he didn't immediately enter the race, his already slim hopes of defeating Johnson would dwindle to nothing.

Ted Kennedy was dispatched to Wisconsin to deliver the news of his brother's pending announcement and to offer an unusual eleventh-hour proposal. The brainchild of Richard Goodwin, now working for Eugene McCarthy, the proposal suggested that there might be a way for Eugene McCarthy and Robert Kennedy to work together in a tandem effort to defeat Lyndon Johnson. Goodwin ran the idea past Blair Clark, McCarthy's campaign manager, and after receiving an affirmative response, he called Ted Kennedy. This might not have been an ideal scenario for his brother, but Ted Kennedy, resigned if not totally enthusiastic about Bobby's candidacy, knew intimately of Bobby's dilemma over McCarthy. Bobby had held a fleeting hope that McCarthy would drop out of the race after he entered it—McCarthy had suggested as much at one time—but McCarthy's numbers against Johnson in New Hampshire eliminated that option. Still maintaining that McCarthy stood no chance against Johnson in the marathon of primaries and campaigning for delegate votes outside the primaries, Robert Kennedy felt that his only realistic strategy would be to bulldoze McCarthy in every head-to-head primary contest, eliminating McCarthy by the sheer force of the vote and his momentum. Those prospects brought him no joy.

The Ted Kennedy–Eugene McCarthy meeting almost failed to materialize. Kennedy's flight from the East arrived in Chicago too late for his connecting flight to Green Bay, and McCarthy, exhausted from his hectic first day in Wisconsin, and not wanting to see Kennedy in the first place, grew tired of waiting; at eleven o'clock, with still no sign of Kennedy, he went to bed. Meanwhile, Kennedy booked a charter flight to Green Bay. When he arrived at the Northland Hotel, it was after one o'clock in the morning. McCarthy, no longer interested in talking to Kennedy, had to be talked into dressing and attending the meeting. Suddenly, McCarthy's suite became a very busy place. Blair Clark and Curtis Gans, McCarthy's national organizer, both accompanying Kennedy on his flight, joined Eugene, Abigail, and Mary McCarthy, as did McCarthyites Richard Goodwin, Jerry Eller, Sam Brown, and several others. In what had to have been one of the most awkward, unusual meetings one could imagine, Kennedy discussed everything but the purpose of his mission. McCarthy would recall their discussing "the campaign and the way it was developing, the public opposition to the Administration's policy, his [Ted Kennedy's] recent trip to South Vietnam to investigate corruption in the civil government, and . . . the St. Patrick's parade in Boston, in which we were both scheduled to march."

Kennedy eventually brought up the topic of his brother's candidacy. McCarthy had already heard the news: Walter Cronkite had spoken of Robert Kennedy's forthcoming announcement on the six o'clock evening news. Bobby was free to do as he chose, McCarthy said; it wouldn't alter his plans. He was grateful, though, that Ted had flown out to deliver the message in person.

Kennedy continued by broaching the topic of the two candidates working together to reach their mutual goals of defeating Johnson and ending the war. The Kennedy camp would be willing to help out in Wisconsin.

McCarthy wasn't interested. "From all the indications we have, we are doing very well in Wisconsin," he told Kennedy. "We need no help, and I think it is better to have the primary here clear cut."

Nor was he enamored with the idea of the two candidates dividing the primaries between them. In theory, it might have been beneficial for only one of them to oppose Johnson in any given primary, rather than both entering and splitting the vote, and had RFK proposed it earlier, McCarthy might have been willing to go along with it. Now, with New Hampshire behind them and Bobby Kennedy unable to enter the Wisconsin, Pennsylvania, and Massachusetts primaries, McCarthy had the opportunity to collect a sizable number of delegate votes on his own. McCarthy wouldn't be handing over California, and he had just announced his plans to add the Indiana primary to his list. Ted Kennedy had come to the meeting with a written plan in his briefcase, but he didn't bother to take it out for review. The conversation wound down, and Kennedy left with the feeling that he had accomplished little more than pay McCarthy a courtesy call.

The next day, Robert Kennedy, backed by his wife and nine of their children, faced more than four hundred reporters, staff members, well-wishers, and colleagues in the Senate Caucus Room. "I am announcing today my candidacy for the presidency of the United States," Kennedy began, and from there he went on to state that he meant no disrespect of Lyndon Johnson, but that their differences ran so deep that he felt compelled to oppose him for what he believed to be the good of the country. "I run because it is now unmistakably clear that we can change the disastrous, divisive policies only by changing the men who make them. . . . For the reality of recent events in Vietnam has been glossed over with illusions. The report of the riot commission has been largely ignored. The crisis in gold, the crisis in our cities, the crisis on our farms and in our ghettos, all have been met with too little and too late."

Kennedy would offer better and more impassioned addresses in the weeks

NEW HAMPSHIRE ■ 193

ahead, when he would be less concerned about sounding ruthless and opportunistic than on this occasion, but the speech prepared for him hit on all the important points. A number of reporters would comment on how he resembled his brother, right down to his Bostonian accent. He repeated verbatim some of the same phrases that Jack had used eight years earlier. Likewise, the differences were noteworthy. Jack had been smooth and relaxed; Bobby, always the more emotional of the brothers, occasionally came across as ill at ease. After all, he was taking on the task of unseating a president; this had not been the case with Jack.

Kennedy spoke of Gene McCarthy and how he hoped to work with him on changing the leadership in the White House. It was too late for Kennedy to oppose McCarthy in three of the upcoming primaries, and he intended to support McCarthy in them. "It is important now that he achieve the largest possible majority next month in Wisconsin, in Pennsylvania, and in the Massachusetts primaries," he stated. He and McCarthy would be squaring off in Nebraska, Oregon, and California—and possibly Indiana.

The response to Kennedy's announcement was predictable. The outcry against the timing of his entry into the race came through loud and clear. McCarthy, rather than show pique, quipped that "an Irishman who announces the day before St. Patrick's Day that he's going to run against another Irishman shouldn't say it's going to be a peaceful relationship." Johnson masked his true feelings by shrugging off Kennedy's candidacy as a matter of the senator's "speculating." Richard Nixon, aside from wondering how Kennedy's opposition might affect his own candidacy, feared for the senator's safety. "Very terrible forces have been unleashed," he said, speaking in private to John Ehrlichman. "Something bad is going to come of this. God knows where this is going to lead."

Others had similar fears, though they dared not voice them in public. Kennedy's views were bound to unleash the hatred and vitriol in the darker sectors of society, and it was no stretch of the imagination to envision Kennedy's encountering an unstable enemy on the campaign trail. Kennedy himself held such fears, but he kept them to himself. Like his brother before him, he felt an urgency to maintain a strong physical contact with the public. This was the risk of campaigning. He would establish as strong a security force as possible, but that did not guarantee his safety. He admitted his concern during a conversation with Rev. Walter Fauntroy, the Washington, D.C., representative of the Southern Christian Leadership Council. He felt confident in the possibility of winning the nomination, he told Fauntroy, but there was "one problem" standing in his way.

"I'm afraid there are guns between me and the White House," he said.

7 Robert Kennedy's announcement enraged Lyndon Johnson. He had been expecting it, but that didn't make it any easier to accept. The final years of his public service career were being walled in by Kennedys—first, by John, whose tragic death had handed him the office he had always craved but in circumstances that found him chasing the ghost of a martyr, then by the younger brother, who would use his charisma and family name to take back the office. It was humiliating. The public would cheer Kennedy's entrance even as they forgot all that he, LBJ, had done for his country. His legacy would be Vietnam, a war dumped in his lap by his predecessor, a Kennedy. Johnson couldn't even escape Robert Kennedy in his sleep. In one recurring nightmare, he found himself cornered and driven to the edge by a mass of "rioting blacks, demonstrating students, marching welfare mothers, [and] squawking professors," all eager to finish him off. In the nightmare, "Robert Kennedy had announced his intention to reclaim the throne in the memory of his brother," and "the American people swayed by the magic of the name, were dancing in the streets."

Johnson wondered if he could physically bear up under the weight of recent events, including the North Korean capture of the *Pueblo,* an American spy ship caught in Korean waters; the Tet Offensive and the resulting public relations entanglement; the Kerner Report and recommendations that short-circuited the hard work he and his administration had accomplished in pushing equal rights forward; and the disappointing conclusions of his most trusted loyalists, the Wise Men. He had already lived through one heart attack, and his family history suggested another might be in the future. There was no way, in his mind, that he could mount a vigorous campaign for reelection *and* oversee solutions to the troubles facing his country. Johnson, quite possibly the most adept vote counter in U.S. Senate history, could also count delegate votes. He had only four delegate votes in New Hampshire, and since he had refused to enter the Massachusetts primary, McCarthy would get all of that state's votes. It looked like McCarthy was going to win by a landslide in the forthcoming Wisconsin primary as well. These were not insurmountable numbers, of course, and Kennedy's entry into the race might split future delegate votes with McCarthy, but Johnson had to ask himself: was another four years in the White House worth the present and future aggravation?

He decided that it was not, and began preparing for the announcement he would be televising on March 31.

7 Wisconsin

A Reward for the Challenger

1 By any measure, the Wisconsin primary should have been an easy contest for Eugene McCarthy. Lyndon Johnson's name was still on the ballot, assuring the president at least a minimal vote from stubborn supporters, and Robert Kennedy, whose name was not on the ballot, would receive a showing in write-in votes. At the beginning of the year, Johnson had been a prohibitive favorite, with McCarthy expected to draw less than 20 percent of the vote, but the president's popularity had dropped precipitously in the weeks following the Tet Offensive. Before his March 31 television address, Johnson had been appraised of his pathetic numbers in Wisconsin: McCarthy was expected to carry the state by a 60 percent to 40 percent margin, maybe even as high as two out of three Democratic votes. The Wisconsin primary came with one caveat: the crossover vote. Since Republicans could cross over and vote for a Democratic candidate on the ballot (and vice versa), one could not be assured of one's strength in the state, even when the poll figures were factored in. With this in mind, the McCarthy campaign officials decided the safe approach would be the ambitious goal of visiting or contacting every household in the state. With campaign contributions pouring in after the strong McCarthy showing in New Hampshire, anything seemed possible.

If McCarthy felt any joy in seeing two of his fellow Minnesotans—Vice President Hubert Humphrey and Secretary of Agriculture Orville Freeman—campaigning for Johnson in Wisconsin and facing increasing voter apathy, he kept it to himself. When he formally began his Wisconsin campaign on March 15, with Johnson still in the race, he had set a goal of defeating the president and seeing his campaign attain a new legitimacy among voters—a legitimacy that would carry him through the other primaries. At one time he had imagined Johnson dropping out after the California primary and Robert Kennedy's entering at that point, but Kennedy's entering the race in mid-March and Johnson's televised announcement in the final days changed McCarthy's strategy. Rather than gain momentum by focusing on Wisconsin and campaigning lightly in Indiana, as he originally intended, McCarthy now had to concern himself with facing off against Kennedy in the Hoosier state.

The McCarthy campaign, using the same organizational template that had worked so well in New Hampshire, showed signs of weakening in Wisconsin. The national, state, and local organizations clashed; communications misfired. Most of this occurred behind the scenes, well out of view of the public, who saw or read reports focusing on the thousands of young volunteers blanketing the state, as they had in New Hampshire, or stuffing envelopes at McCarthy headquarters spaced throughout the state.

One disagreement received unwanted national scrutiny. No one in the senator's Milwaukee headquarters had scheduled a McCarthy appearance in Milwaukee's black neighborhoods—an omission that upset a sizable number of McCarthy workers and volunteers and led to an angry gathering in Curtis Gans's hotel room on March 25.

Milwaukee had a reputation for racial discord and upheaval. Father James Groppi, a white, Roman Catholic priest from one of the city's most impoverished inner-city parishes, had led numerous civil rights marches and demonstrations protesting, among other issues, the city's fair and open housing laws. Black groups, led by Groppi and others, demonstrated for two hundred consecutive days. White Milwaukeeans, most notably the large concentration of Poles living on the city's south side, fought back. The combustible confrontations between blacks and whites, intensified by Milwaukee's iron-willed police chief, boosted Milwaukee's reputation of being one of the most racist cities in America.

The reasons for McCarthy's staying away from the black neighborhoods varied, depending on whom you were talking to. For some, including Curtis Gans and Jeremy Larner, it was a practical issue: McCarthy needed Milwaukee's white vote, and there was no reason to risk it by trying to appease a smaller, marginalized voting bloc. McCarthy's senate voting record, Gans and others insisted, had been progressive and favorable to civil rights legislation; as a presidential candidate, he had made his position well known in one of his New Hampshire speeches.

Those disagreeing with this stance insisted that McCarthy reinforce his position on civil rights, not just for the Wisconsin primary but for future primaries as well. With Kennedy in the race, civil rights issues would inevitably climb in prominence, beginning in Indiana, with its large concentration of black voters in the northern part of the state. Wisconsin's total African American population was only 2 percent of the state's overall population, but the vast majority lived in Milwaukee, comprised 12 percent of the city's population, and suffered the same hardships common to black residents in any large U.S. city.

McCarthy, for his part, saw no reason for whipping up a tempest over the small number of blacks working for his campaign, his not placing greater emphasis on issues affecting black communities, or his not visiting the black neighborhoods in Milwaukee. This, he said, was only the second primary of the season, and the first, New Hampshire, didn't have a ghetto. He was strapped for time and had very little for tromping through any neighborhood, black or white. He felt he had been forthcoming about his position about civil rights in his speeches and in his interviews with reporters; he was on record as a supporter of the president's civil rights commission's report. The press, he argued, was always on the lookout for an angle to explore in stories, and with Kennedy now in the race, comparisons between the two contenders were inevitable, even if analyzing McCarthy's avoidance of the ghettos was, in the candidate's opinion, a "pointless" exercise. "I couldn't get the Negro vote away from Bobby Kennedy," he stated, adding that he couldn't have gained the black vote if he had "moved into the ghetto and stayed in there this whole campaign."

Other factors clouded the decision-making process. Henry Maier, the incumbent mayor, was exceedingly popular in Milwaukee, and he was up for reelection and on the ballot. The only question about his reelection was how big a margin of victory he would achieve. An outspoken critic of the black demonstrations in his city, Maier presented a problem to McCarthy: the public would be voting for Maier on primary day, and McCarthy didn't want to damage his chances by looking like a Maier opponent.

Those attending the informal meeting in Curtis Gans's hotel room argued these points, often in heated debate. This was not a time for McCarthy to act like a politician, his critics maintained; this issue was too important for that. Gans, Jeremy Larner, and Richard Goodwin countered in favor of the badly needed white vote. The meeting, Ben Stavis recalled, featured a lot of "highly technical and symbolic" back-and-forths on such topics as whether McCarthy should walk or ride through the black section of Milwaukee, whether he should deliver a major civil rights address in front of a black or white audience, and how the McCarthy campaign members might comport themselves in front of an audience that was itself divided between pacifists following Martin Luther King and activists supporting more militant black leaders. Gans, more concerned that McCarthy defeat LBJ in the primary, ruled in favor of the white vote, setting off a storm of protest and accusations that the McCarthy higher-ups were racists. The meeting broke up without a resolution to the split.

Had things ended there, the meeting might have remained an internal matter hidden from public scrutiny and comment, but it became a national news item when Seymour Hersh, McCarthy's press secretary, and his assistant, Mary Lou Oates, resigned following the meeting. They claimed they were leaving for "personal reasons," with no further explanation, but someone in the McCarthy camp leaked the story to a *New York Times* reporter, saying that they were leaving as a result of decisions made at the meeting. *Times* reporter Donald Janson broke the story on March 30, setting off a hastily arranged McCarthy five-mile walk and drive through Milwaukee's inner city. But, as McCarthy himself would admit, the damage had been done. His commitment to civil rights would be questioned for the remainder of his candidacy. "I couldn't say anything that would do as much damage as that story has done," he said.

McCarthy's problems went beyond black and white. The Hersh and Oates defections, had McCarthy been paying closer attention, stood as a stark commentary on the sometimes dysfunctional relationship between McCarthy and his staff. McCarthy claimed that he and Hersh split on good terms, but that was probably wishful thinking voiced by a candidate who loathed any kind of confrontation or disagreement with members of his staff. Hersh would later admit that his differences with McCarthy over campaigning in Milwaukee's inner city was not the sole reason for his leaving. By his own admission, he had grown weary of the "tremendous power fight" within the McCarthy organization, of the same tired questions from reporters, of a position that really didn't suit him. "I was dying to get out of the job. I hated it," he would recall. "I'd much rather have gone off to be a speech writer, or helped organize something because I believed in the campaign."

There were noticeable inequities that were bound to bother a professional like Hersh. The McCarthy press corps stayed at the swank Sheraton-Schroeder Hotel, apart from the student operation at the much more modest Wisconsin Hotel. Those subsisting on peanut butter and jelly sandwiches while others dined on steak were bound to notice, as were the campaign officials doling out the money financing the arrangements. Tensions mounted when Curtis Gans pulled back on the financial reins and the press officials found themselves on the outside looking in, both in terms of standards of living and meaningful access to the candidate. Hersh had a tough job keeping reporters happy and informed about a candidate who seemed to have little use for the press, and losing any of the few perks the job had to offer was not going to sit well with him.

But such was the nature of the McCarthy campaign. McCarthy's lack of steady, day-to-day involvement with his staff was noticed but rarely commented on by reporters now accustomed to the candidate's easygoing demeanor, but the Hersh and Oates resignations forced them to reevaluate the divisions within the ranks. *Time* magazine, in a critique of the McCarthy campaign officials, noted that "for all its intelligence and enthusiasm, the McCarthy organization suffers severely from a lack of professionalism." Three British journalists, following the campaign for a book they intended to write about the 1968 election, viewed the skirmish in Gans's hotel room as a manifestation of a rift between the political idealists and pragmatists—a battle that would be waged in the McCarthy camp throughout the campaign: "What had happened, for the first time but not the last, was that the McCarthy *crusade,* last hope within the system of the militants for peace and civil rights, had come into contact with the McCarthy *campaign,* a political operation aimed at winning the Democratic Presidential nomination."

2 Richard Nixon's campaign was as carefully planned as McCarthy's seemed occasionally serendipitous. Part of this rose out of lessons learned from defeat, part from Nixon's naturally suspicious nature. No detail, however small, could be overlooked; no public appearance, regardless of significance, overplanned. New Hampshire had gone a long way in convincing voters that a new Nixon was on the prowl, but it had not dispelled every last vestige of his losing image. New Hampshire had been a lot of shadowboxing. President Johnson, still in the race when Nixon began campaigning in Wisconsin's slushy confines, still stood in the way of the White House. Nixon still needed a strong show of strength, and running unopposed in Wisconsin wasn't going to accomplish it. Nixon needed a Republican opponent in the primaries.

To find one, Nixon had only to look to New York, where Nelson Rockefeller was still presiding over his flaccid refusal to enter the race. Young, liberal Republicans wanted him to represent their interests, and the national polls indicated an increasing interest in Rockefeller as an alternative to the moderately conservative Nixon or the ultraconservative Ronald Reagan. A January Harris Poll, in which respondents were asked to pit Rockefeller against Johnson, as well as Republican possibilities, found Rockefeller running dead even with LBJ, while Nixon, Romney, and Reagan trailed the president by nine to fourteen percentage points. A similar poll conducted in March was encouraging to Rockefeller backers: Rockefeller now led Johnson 41 percent to 34 percent, while Nixon and Johnson were knotted up at 39 percent each. There was one significant catch: Rockefeller couldn't get his own party to support him. An early February Gallup Poll gave Nixon a fourteen-point lead over Rockefeller in head-to-head competition, and the spread increased to a 24 percent Nixon lead a short time later. Analysts attributed this to the Republican Party leadership's lingering displeasure over Rockefeller's refusal to endorse Barry Goldwater in 1964. "If Rocky reaches for the mountain," a Republican state representative told a *Time* reporter, "a thousand people will try to cut off his hand."

Rockefeller learned this firsthand at a Republican breakfast in Washington, D.C. Of the thirty-six Republican senators invited, only seventeen turned up, and only two voiced open support for Rockefeller. The Republican governors offered better numbers—eighteen of twenty-six supported Rockefeller, at least privately—but it was clear that the senators and governors favored Nixon as the party's choice for the presidential nomination.

Rockefeller had his GOP backers, including New York mayor John V. Lindsay, at one point considered a possible candidate for the 1968 presidential race; William E. Miller, Goldwater's running mate in 1964; Tom McCall, governor of Oregon; and Spiro T. Agnew, Maryland's first-term governor, whose moderate liberalism matched Rockefeller's. Agnew had been pushing for Rockefeller's candidacy for more than a year, with no help or encouragement from Rockefeller, until the reluctant New York governor finally gave him approval to chair an exploratory "Rockefeller for President" committee—on condition that this did not declare or imply his formal candidacy for the Republican nomination.

To hear Rockefeller tell it, he suffered from the same malady as Robert Kennedy on the Democratic side: he didn't want to divide his party. He was burdened by the memory of how, only a few years earlier, when the Republican Party required a supreme effort to stand any chance of ousting Johnson, he had stood apart from the fray, unwilling to negotiate his political standing by supporting a candidate who was little more than a sacrificial lamb. Nixon, on the other hand, had labored to keep the party united. Rockefeller was determined to avoid this in the 1968 election. "I am not going to create dissension within the Republican Party by contending for the nomination," he said in early March, "but I am ready and willing to serve the American people if called."

This was the attitude that set Agnew to work. Rockefeller's conceit that he wouldn't disrupt the party's machinations by running against a favored candidate like Nixon, but would accept the burden of candidacy if offered to him, was not likely to elicit enthusiastic responses from Republican officials and voters seeking a candidate totally dedicated to the marathon task ahead, but it was a stance Rockefeller had been taking since late 1967. The nay-saying did nothing to convince party officials or the press that Rockefeller was not going to run; for that, there were too many rumors, too many instances in which Rockefeller appeared to be softening his position. The timing of an announcement was critical. Since it was unlikely that he would beat Nixon in

New Hampshire, and it was certain that he would be annihilated by Nixon in Nebraska, and with the filing date for New Hampshire long passed and the one for Nebraska looming in the very near future, Rockefeller could cut his losses in the two primaries and still meet the filing deadlines for primaries in which he could adequately compete. In the meantime, he had Agnew and others drumming up support and keeping the news media interested.

Agnew championed Rockefeller's candidacy at every turn; he was, in the words of journalist Jules Witcover, "the New Yorker's John the Baptist." Agnew was utterly certain that Rockefeller would run. With time for primary filing dates running out, Rockefeller scheduled a press conference for March 21. As soon as he heard of Rockefeller's plans, Agnew, ready to take his bows for all the work he had put into the Rockefeller cause, set up a press conference in his office for just prior to the Rockefeller announcement. He said nothing to the press about Rockefeller: he would have unsuspecting reporters watching on his office television when Rockefeller made his announcement of his candidacy. Agnew maintained the ruse to the moment that Rockefeller's press conference opened. When asked if he knew what Rockefeller was going to say, Agnew responded truthfully that he did not.

When Rockefeller stood at the microphone in the ballroom of the New York Hilton, he had a surprise of his own. "I have decided today to reiterate unequivocally that I am not a candidate campaigning directly or indirectly for the Presidency of the United States," he declared. He then proceeded to warm up the reasons he had dished out in previous statements. The party, he said, had made clear its dedication to Nixon, and he would not divide the Republicans by challenging the candidate of their choice. Rockefeller had nothing new to offer, other than his appreciation to the people laboring on his behalf. He would keep the Draft Rockefeller door ajar and would run if his party beckoned, but he would do nothing to encourage such a movement.

Agnew watched the screen of his black-and-white television in embarrassed silence. What he had hoped would be a personal triumph in front of the press had turned into a devastating, humiliating beat-down. Why hadn't Rockefeller called and personally appraised him of his decision prior to the press conference? Wasn't he owed at least that much, after all of his months of talking him up to anyone willing to listen? No, he had to learn in front of a group of reporters studying his face for any twitch of reaction, to be followed by questions that would only deepen his humiliation.

(In the future, Rockefeller would refuse the accept any of the blame for either Agnew's misunderstanding of his intentions or the mix-up about the phone call. He allowed that he probably should have called Agnew, but at the time he had reason to keep his decision to himself. Two days before the press conference, the *New York Times* had published a report claiming that Rockefeller had made the decision to run, even though, as Rockefeller explained, he had reached the opposite conclusion; the *Times* story, Rockefeller said, made it look like he was vacillating more than he was. Staying mum between then and his announcement, he decided, was the best policy. As for Agnew's being let down by his decision, Rockefeller insisted that he had consistently warned Agnew that his candidacy was never a certainty.)

Agnew suffered as well as he could through his ordeal with the reporters in his office. It was impossible to disguise his shock, but he managed to hide his anger toward Rockefeller. He remained gracious in his assessment of the press conference. Yes, he admitted, he was "tremendously surprised" and "disappointed" by what Rockefeller had to say, but that did not alter his belief that Rockefeller was "clearly the best possible candidate."

Richard Nixon, of course, followed the Rockefeller announcement with great and very mixed interest. He believed that he could defeat Rockefeller, although Rockefeller would have been a worthy opponent—certainly a test of Nixon's strength. Agnew intrigued him. There was probably no chance of Agnew's defecting to his side—not in the near future, anyway—but he wanted to know more about the man. He asked his staff to arrange an informal meeting.

3   Lurleen Wallace's health deteriorated throughout the later months of 1967 and into 1968, eventually limiting her ability to govern and her husband's opportunities to campaign. Her cancer had returned. Now in constant pain, she initially tried to hide the worst of it from George, though she confided in aides that she didn't think she would survive this time around. Hoping to shrink the tumor in her abdomen, doctors suggested an aggressive betatron radiation treatment. She soldiered on, trying to balance her treatments with her duties as governor, mother, and companion on a small number of her husband's campaign appearances.

George had no delusions about winning the general election in November. He pinned his hopes as a third-party candidate on winning as many states as possible and denying the two major party candidates the required majority of Electoral College votes needed to win the presidency. This, he felt, was a reasonable goal, obtainable by his winning the Southern states and a couple of others elsewhere. If that happened, he would gain the bargaining chips needed to influence the eventual outcome in the House of Representatives: he could gain support of his favorite bills by offering to surrender his Electoral College votes to the candidate most willing to work with him. "If it goes into the House, that will mean many states will have voted for me," he told conservative columnist John J. Synon. "Their congressmen will think twice before they vote against the wishes of their people."

There was precedent for a House vote. In 1800, the race between Thomas Jefferson and Aaron Burr was decided in the House; twenty-four years later, John Quincy Adams received the House vote in a five-candidate race. Wallace claimed that he was in the race to win, but he was up-front about his role as a "spoiler." "That's exactly what I'm trying to do, to spoil the chances of both national political parties," he said. "After all, they've spoiled all the chances for the people." He meant to show voters that the two parties were equally inept, that their issues and solutions were essentially the same.

Since he had no knowledge of the Vietnam War, the election's big issue, or a detailed plan for how to win or end it, he said very little about it in his speeches other than to offer generalizations that were light on solutions and heavy on patriotism. "I believe in my country right or wrong," he would say. "As long as American servicemen are committed between life and death in southeast Asia, then I'm for standing with them." He was able to tie the war in with his big issue—law and order—in a way that drew enthusiastic response. Authorities, he said, had to be free to curb the disruptions at the antiwar demonstrations and college campus rallies; they were a threat to the public welfare. Wallace found a lot of support for this position, including endorsement from law enforcement officers and agencies weary of trying to suppress nasty confrontations between those protesting and those supporting the country's actions in Vietnam.

Wallace was a master of enflaming his followers. He had a list of ideas and catchphrases that he used almost everywhere he went, knowing the response they would get. Blue-collar audiences hooted in derision whenever he peppered his speeches with talk of *pseudo-intellectuals, Communists, anarchists,* and *bureaucrats,* bearded more often than not, often being one and the same. Dropping a name like folksinger/antiwar activist Joan Baez earned him thunderous applause. It didn't matter that no protester had ever blocked a presidential limousine by lying down on the road in front of a presidential motorcade; crowds whooped whenever Wallace declared that if that happened after he was elected, "it'll be the *last* car he'll ever lie down in front of."

Wallace's campaign had begun long before he formally declared his candidacy, dating back to when his wife was running for his governor's seat in 1966, and gaining momentum throughout the next year. Lurleen accompanied him when possible, until her health declined. There had been frightening moments. She had been rushed to the Anderson Clinic in Houston after she had fainted during one of her husband's appearances in Long Beach, California. At the christening of the George Wallace campaign headquarters in Houston, she was overcome by the heat and the effects of her treatment; it would be her last public appearance on the campaign trail.

That had been early January 1968. She had lost a noticeable amount of weight and was ghostly pale, but she assured everyone but her closest aides that she was on the road to recovery. She returned to Alabama and tried to fulfill her duties as governor. George, trying to balance campaigning with time with Lurleen, became a behind-the-scenes, de facto governor, helping Lurleen in what was now the endgame stage of her illness. He volunteered to suspend his campaign; she told him she would be disappointed if he did. Whenever he left for a campaign jaunt, he would go through the motions of saying that he should stay, and she would tell him to go. There was nothing he could do for her at home, though staying by her side kept the critics at bay. The campaign trail, with its bare energy, constant attention for throngs of supporters, and the empowerment he felt from it all, became his refuge.

4   Jay Sykes, a journalist and college professor from Milwaukee, directed the Wisconsin effort for Eugene McCarthy. The origins of the statewide campaign, Sykes learned, had gone largely the way the national campaign had gone: a few, well-paced progressive seeds had germinated into a full-blown grassroots campaign. What surprised Sykes was the ease in which it had been accomplished.

The Wisconsin campaign started out the way the national effort had begun, with a handful of dreamers striving to find a peace candidate to oppose Johnson in the forthcoming election. The small, Madison-based group of organizers originally hoped to stage a "vote no" campaign that encouraged citizens to vote against Johnson; there was no expectation of actually running a candidate against an incumbent president. Like those pushing the Dump Johnson movement, the Wisconsinites aimed at forcing Johnson's hand on the war. But once the idea of running a candidate was proposed, things moved along quickly. Wisconsin, as Sykes liked to point out, was an "isolationist state" known for its maverick politics and politicians. This was the state responsible for both the liberal Senator Fightin' Bob La Follette and the hyperconservative Senator Joe McCarthy. Anything could happen in Wisconsin—and often did.

The overwhelming majority of initial organizers came from academic backgrounds, and according to Sykes, rather than being frowned upon by their higher-learning institutions for participating in partisan politics, they were encouraged to work on the campaign. Antiwar sentiments ran deep at the University of Wisconsin, already known for its liberal politics, and no one seemed to find anything objectionable about a one-issue candidate.

But as far as the group was concerned, this wasn't going to be a matter of a candidate's making a statement in the Dairy State and disappearing; the ideal candidate would be in it for the long haul. Two names received the most attention: Robert Kennedy and Eugene McCarthy. Sykes rigorously opposed Kennedy, whom he felt was unsuited as a presidential candidate. When toward the end of 1967, McCarthy announced his candidacy, the group knew they had their man. "When McCarthy said he was going to run," Sykes would recall, "we held this meeting in Madison. And, without giving it really too much thought, we decided to change the Concerned Democrats and their 'vote no' campaign to a McCarthy for President campaign."

Time—or the lack of it—became the big issue. Wisconsin's McCarthy for President leaders had yet to meet the candidate as 1967 was drawing to a close. This meant they would have roughly three months to mount a campaign, to introduce McCarthy to a majority of voters who knew little or nothing about him. McCarthy's national team would be in the state, of course, but its members were uneducated about the state's peculiarities. Madison, along with Milwaukee, Racine, and Kenosha in the southeast corner of the state, generally voted Democratic, and McCarthy would find little resistance in winning over voters there. The rest of the state was a crapshoot.

The group moved quickly, and since there was very little money and those involved had scant experience in political campaigns, they learned as they went along. Their first check bounced. With no way of affording fancy digs in an upscale downtown Milwaukee hotel, they set up a headquarters on the fourth floor of the Wisconsin Hotel, a modest but well-maintained establishment located in the thick of it all. Phones were installed, a stenciled McCarthy Headquarters sign hung outside, and the organization opened to the public. Finding volunteers to work the desks was no problem: so many volunteers turned out that the leaders had to strain to find something to occupy their time. Making voter lists became a popular endeavor.

The most pressing goal in those early days prior to the official opening of the McCarthy campaign in Wisconsin was to find a way to place that candidate in front of the people. The news media, Sykes knew from his own experience, loved the kind of grassroots candidacy that McCarthy represented, but aside from a scheduled appearance at the University of Wisconsin in Milwaukee, he had no plans to visit Wisconsin before his national organization opened in the state in March. The Wisconsin organization hoped to get him to Milwaukee, which had affiliate television stations with all three major networks, and two daily newspapers, the *Milwaukee Sentinel* in the morning and the *Milwaukee Journal* in the evening.

"We thought it would be nice if he stopped here in Milwaukee just for a few minutes," Sykes would recall. "We called up his office, and Jerry Eller told us he didn't think they could do it. He wouldn't have the time. And we said, 'Well, we only need five or ten minutes. We could make a lot of hay out of that time.' He agreed [to] set down here in Milwaukee and then before he took a small plane from Milwaukee to Madison, we'd have a press conference."

This was a notable victory. Those running the McCarthy for President campaign in Wisconsin had no delusions about their position. As a challenger to an incumbent president, McCarthy was not yet taken seriously as a candidate; he was tilting at windmills. An appearance in Milwaukee, along with the attendant news coverage and the existence of McCarthy headquarters in Madison and Milwaukee, would afford him much higher regard, not to mention continuous coverage, when he eventually arrived in the state to campaign.

Sykes believed the media coverage turned the state in McCarthy's favor. "If I can attribute McCarthy's eventual [primary] victory to anything, in addition to the condition at the Vietnam War, it's the press, which, while not always favorable to him, probably gave him as much coverage as they gave any candidate in the state. It's just part of the Wisconsin tradition. They take their politics very seriously. And, of course, they're always interested about an intra-party dispute."

The press might not have embraced the McCarthy campaign with unfettered enthusiasm, but the candidate was appealing enough to bear watching and reporting. The campaign gave the Wisconsin for McCarthy organization a sense of legitimacy it craved. From the beginning, the group had fought off an overshadowing doubt about its legitimacy. Did McCarthy and his national organization accept the Wisconsin outfit as the state's true representation of the senator's candidacy? Would the Wisconsin group be cast aside when the McCarthy national effort invaded the state for the big push to the primary? McCarthy's brief visit to the state, appearance on television, and meeting with several Wisconsin for McCarthy representatives had settled some of the concerns, as did seed money advanced by the national organization.

5   The April 2 Wisconsin primary results reflected the predictions of the syndicated polls: a record number of votes had been cast, and Richard Nixon and Eugene McCarthy won by considerable margins. Nixon captured

79.4 percent of the Republican vote; Ronald Reagan, on the ballot but not as an announced candidate, pulled 11 percent, and Nelson Rockefeller netted 2 percent as a write-in candidate. Nixon, who had spent only seven days campaigning in the state, came away pleased and confident. "We have months to go and many days of hard work," he said, "but the road ahead points to victory in November."

Johnson's withdrawal from the race two days before the primary deprived McCarthy of the satisfaction of defeating a sitting president in straight-on competition, but he was very happy with the final results. He had won his first primary, earning 56 percent of the Democratic vote to Johnson's 35 percent, with Robert Kennedy taking 6 percent as a write-in candidate. "We have demonstrated our ability here in Wisconsin to win the election in November," he told supporters in Milwaukee after being declared the victor in the primary. "I am sorry my principal opponent didn't last out the home stretch, but by any interpretation this is a most significant victory." As for the Indiana primary ahead, McCarthy had no worries about taking on Kennedy. "I think that after Indiana there will be only one candidate," he predicted to the press the day after his Wisconsin win.

For a candidate like McCarthy, whose candidacy, not that long ago, had been scorned as the endeavor of ideologues fighting for a cause they couldn't possibly win, this optimism was potentially dangerous territory. With his taste of victory and newfound belief in his candidacy, McCarthy was moving into a place where faith could be as punishing as it could be rewarding: in New Hampshire, he had been cautious about revealing too much about himself and his desire to be president; if he had been as soundly beaten as the early polls projected, he could have walked away with a shrug, the defeat wouldn't have been personal. In fact, it was easy to overlook voting totals that placed him on the losing end in New Hampshire. In celebrating his proximity of victory, he and those working for him had stepped up to the threshold of self-belief. *Was victory possible? Or, more importantly, was it possible that McCarthy wanted to be president?* Prior to election night in New Hampshire, he had behaved as if he believed he had been drafted as a candidate; he could take the presidency or leave it. He had been moved by the events in New Hampshire, but when he entered Wisconsin, he still maintained a distance between the office and his desire for it.

"If you're in politics fifteen or twenty years, you kind of respond to circumstance," he told a reporter in Milwaukee. "And then you're willing to have a try at it. Do I want it for myself? No. There's no personal need driving me toward it. But if the situation compels you and you're in politics, you go."

He permitted himself more hope, more of a connection to the goal of his campaign, after the votes were tallied in Wisconsin and he had established himself as the man to beat, at least for the time being.

6 On April 3, the day after the Wisconsin primary, Lyndon Johnson altered the dialogue of the campaign, even if temporarily, when he announced that North Vietnam had agreed to meet with the United States in peace talks. Johnson had hoped for this eventuality when he announced the bombing halts during his March 31 denunciation speech, but some of his closest aides, including George Aiken and Abe Fortas, were skeptical. In the past, on a number of occasions, the United States had attempted to bring North Vietnam to the negotiating table by using temporary bombing halts as an inducement, but it had never worked. Johnson himself was surprised by how quickly the enemy had responded to his latest bombing halt.

It hadn't arrived without a struggle. Two highly respected newspapermen, Harry Ashmore, former executive editor of the *Arkansas Gazette,* and William Baggs, editor of the *Miami News,* were in Hanoi, meeting with Hoang Tung, editor of *Nham Dan,* a Communist Party newspaper. Ashmore and Baggs had met with Ho Chi Minh on a previous visit to Hanoi, and Ho had trusted them as if they were emissaries to the State Department, telling them that he wouldn't consider peace talks without a bombing halt. The two sides never reached agreement.

The two Americans and Tung were talking again when Johnson delivered his March 31 speech. The Americans told Tung that Johnson was earnest in the bombing halt and his decision to negotiate, even though the most recent stoppage had been violated by the United States in an air strike of Thanh Hoe, a town that Johnson described as "a major transfer post for men and supplies, moving toward South Vietnam—either due south toward the demilitarized zone or westward into the infiltration routes through Laos." Thanh Hoe was seen by the North Vietnamese as part of the no-bombing zone—Senator J. William Fulbright angrily accused Johnson of violating the terms of his own speech—but Johnson felt his speech had exempted the city from the bombing halt.

Ashmore and Baggs urged Tung to convince Ho Chi Minh that Johnson was serious in his hopes of resolving the conflict through negotiation, rather than militarily. This was a sincere effort. "I don't know if we had any effect on the final decisions or not," Ashmore would recall. "They blew hot and cold for two or three days; finally we were given an *aide-memoire* in which they accepted the proposition."

8 Torrents of Rage and Sorrow

1 On Thursday, April 4, two days after the Wisconsin primary, Martin Luther King Jr. was murdered on the balcony outside his hotel room in Memphis. His death would signal a dramatic shift in the presidential campaign, with the candidates, in the violent, bloody aftermath of the assassination, shifting their focus from the Vietnam War to civil rights, urban decay, and law and order in a nation as divided as the Kerner Commission deemed it to be. The King assassination came at a time when King was at a crossroads in his own life, when he was brooding more than ever over not only the racial division in his country but also the divisions among African Americans. The violence was escalating to such an extent that his message of nonviolent protest was being rejected by a growing number of his onetime followers, now considering other methods of fighting back against injustice and discrimination.

The first three months of 1968 had been brutal. On February 8, in Orangeburg, South Carolina, a march protesting segregation in a bowling alley disintegrated into a violent altercation with law enforcement officers when highway patrolmen opened fire on the marchers, killing three and wounding another twenty-seven. Confrontations raked the states, north and south. More recently, at a King-led march down Beale Street in Memphis, the police had clashed with more than twelve thousand marchers; a sixteen-year-old, described as a looter by the police, was killed, sixty others were wounded, and more than two hundred were arrested. King was badly shaken by the knowledge that this had occurred during one of his supposedly nonviolent events. He also witnessed enough to know that vandalism by blacks had to shoulder at least some of the blame for the violence.

The bloodshed led him to ruminations about his own mortality. His outspoken opposition to the Vietnam War had expanded his enemies list beyond racists resisting civil rights; his safety was in danger whenever he appeared in public. On this most recent trip to Memphis—his third in a month—his flight from Atlanta had been delayed while the plane was searched for explosives, despite the fact that it had been under armed guard overnight. He was embarrassed when the pilot informed the plane's passengers that the delay was due to King's being onboard. Depressed, King wondered if his message was drowning in the events of the day. He surprised Ralph Abernathy, one of his top lieutenants, by saying, "Maybe we just have to admit that the day of violence is here . . . maybe we have to just give up and let violence take its course."

His mission in Memphis was to offer support to the city's striking sanitation workers, the majority being black and, not surprisingly, receiving less in benefits than their white counterparts. The strike, more than seven weeks old when King landed in Memphis on April 3, had the city on edge. King hoped to use this jaunt to Memphis to organize another mass rally/march, this one better planned and more peaceful than its predecessor.

He had a speech at the Bishop Charles Mason Temple scheduled for the evening of April 3, but his heart wasn't in it. He was exhausted from his nonstop activities, and he figured the attendance for the speech would probably be less than optimum, due to the torrential rain pounding the Memphis streets throughout the day. When the time arrived for King's entourage to depart for the temple, King asked Ralph Abernathy to speak in his place; he would remain at the hotel. At the temple, Abernathy looked out on the mass of people who had braved the nasty weather and assembled to hear King's speech. He placed a call to the Lorraine Motel and told Martin Luther King that a lot of people were going to be terribly disappointed if he didn't appear. King relented.

His decision to speak that evening turned out to be a historic one: the last speech he would ever deliver, while not on the level of his famous March on Washington "I Had a Dream" oration, was memorable, catching the civil rights leader at his most human and vulnerable, yet also at his powerful and inspirational best. The speech began slowly, not much more than the typical address he had given on countless occasions, but it gained emotional momentum as King went on, his mind locked on his mortality, as it had been in recent days. He spoke of the difficulties on his flight to Memphis; he dug back in time, to 1958, when he had been stabbed by a mentally disturbed woman in Harlem. The letter opener she had used in the attack had come so close to his heart that he would have died if he had sneezed before the surgeon removed the blade from his chest.

He accepted the danger and constant threats against him as part of his mission. "I don't know what will happen now," he admitted to an audience now hanging on his every word. "We've got some difficult days ahead. But it really doesn't matter to me now, because I've been to the mountaintop." His voice rose. "Like anybody, I would like to live a long life. Longevity has its place. But I'm not concerned about me now. I just want to do God's will. And he's allowed me to go up to the mountain, and I've looked over, and I've seen the promised land. I may not get there with you. But I want you to know tonight that we, as a people, will get to the promised land. And so I'm happy tonight. But I'm not worried about anything. I'm not fearing any man. Mine eyes have seen the glory of the coming of the Lord."

The next day, a man named James Earl Ray, calling himself John Willard, checked into a fifth-floor room of a flophouse across the courtyard of the Lorraine Motel. He brought with him a 30.06 Remington rifle he had purchased a few days earlier in Birmingham. His prey, Martin Luther King, did not stray from his motel room on the afternoon of April 4, but just before six that evening, a car drove into the courtyard, and King appeared on the balcony outside his room three floors below Willard's position in the rooming house bathroom across the way. King, about to leave for dinner at a local minister's house, to be followed by an appearance at a rally at a church, called down to the men in the car. They exchanged pleasantries. While they chatted, the assassin braced his rifle on the bathroom window and placed King in the sights of his weapon's scope. One of the men below the balcony advised King to bring a coat; Memphis was going to be chilly.

A shot rang out, and King dropped to the floor of the balcony, a huge cut tearing the right side of his face. Ralph Abernathy, still in the hotel room, rushed through the sliding glass door leading to the balcony and looked down at the wounded civil rights leader. The men below sprinted up. King, although conscious, never uttered another word. It was a minute after six.

The ambulance seemed to take an eternity to arrive. While waiting for it, Abernathy pressed a towel to the wound, hoping to stop the bleeding. King was taken to St. Joseph's Hospital, and despite the efforts of surgeons, Martin Luther King Jr. was pronounced dead at five after seven, less than twenty-four hours after he had spoken so eloquently about his mortality.

In a matter of hours, some of the nation's largest cities, including Washington, D.C., would be in flames.

2 Robert Kennedy was in Muncie, Indiana, boarding a charter plane bound for Indianapolis, when he learned that Martin Luther King had been shot. Details were sketchy. King, Kennedy was told, was still alive, but he had been very badly wounded, presumably by a white gunman reportedly seen leaving the area. Those around Kennedy advised him to cancel the speech he was scheduled to give in Indianapolis's inner city later that evening. It might not be safe.

Kennedy slumped in his seat, stunned by this recent turn of events. This was the beginning of his campaign for the Indiana primary, his first day in the state, and he had just completed an appearance at Ball State University in Muncie. His speech had been well received. Near the end of a question-and-answer segment following his address, a young black man had asked Kennedy a question that haunted him as he considered the news about King. "You seem to believe in the good faith of the white people toward the minorities in this country," the young man stated without a strain of rancor. "Do you think that faith is justified?" "Yes," Kennedy responded without hesitation. Now, an hour later, seated on a plane next to *Newsweek* correspondent John J. Lindsay, he agonized aloud over his answer. He had called for black America's faith, and now their "spiritual leader" had been wounded, perhaps mortally, by a white man. Lindsay, listening to Kennedy, was convinced that the senator was also thinking about his brother.

While Kennedy was en route to Indianapolis, people on the ground in Indianapolis discussed the best course of action to take. Walter Sheridan, one of Kennedy's campaign coordinators, and one of those responsible for arranging the Indianapolis appearance, had heard from Kennedy's press aide Pierre Salinger that King had been shot and that he was in a hospital, fighting for his life. Salinger felt that the event should be canceled, but Sheridan, at the site of the evening's speech, opposed the idea.

"I went out into the crowd and tried to get a feeling of the crowd; it seemed pretty good," Sheridan remembered. "There were about six or seven of the militant leaders there, and we had agreed they'd be on the stage with the Senator. And so I called them all into a room in a school nearby and told them about Martin Luther King, which they did not know, and asked them what I should do. And they unanimously said that he should come and there would be no trouble, which I agreed with. I thought he had to come."

Kennedy learned, as soon as his plane had taxied to a stop in Indianapolis, that Martin Luther King had not survived. Kennedy, covering his eyes with his hands, moaned, "Oh, God, when is this violence going to stop?" The discussion turned to Kennedy's plans for the evening. His wife urged him to cancel his speech and go directly to the hotel; others feared for his physical well-being as well. When he heard from the police chief, Kennedy was advised that riots were likely, and there were no guarantees of his safety. Kennedy listened, but he had already reached his decision: he was going to speak. He asked an aide to take Ethel to the hotel and stay with her until he arrived after his speech.

He scribbled notes on a legal pad while he was being transported to the rally site. He had to choose his words carefully, but time did not allow him to fully compose, revise, or rehearse what he had to say.

He would be speaking from a flatbed truck at the corner of Seventeenth Street and Broadway—the worst neighborhood in the black section of town. When he arrived at the site, he faced a large crowd, comprised mainly of African Americans, waiting to see him. Many had been waiting for hours. The mood was festive, meaning they had yet to hear of Martin Luther King's death; it would be Bobby Kennedy's terrible duty to inform them. When he climbed onto the back of the truck, he was wearing his dead brother's long, black topcoat. Two spotlights shone down on him. A wet drizzle saturated the air.

Kennedy's voice did not carry the tone one was accustomed to hearing at campaign rallies. He was somber and quiet, and the crowd fell silent in an effort to hear him. He opened by stating that he was only going to speak for a minute. "I have some very sad news for all of you, and I think some sad news for all of our fellow citizens and people who love peace all over the world," he said, his voice shaky. "And that is that Martin Luther King was shot and killed tonight in Memphis, Tennessee."

The crowd responded with a loud collective gasp. People wept, moaned, prayed, dropped to the ground, cursed, covered their faces with their hands. A group of black youths, who had arrived at the last minute and gathered at the edge of the mass of people, shouted, "Black power!" Kennedy paused briefly before continuing, and when he spoke, he did so very slowly, gathering his thoughts carefully and allowing the crowd to absorb each word before hearing more:

> Martin Luther King dedicated his life to love and to justice between fellow human beings. He died in the cause of that effort. In this difficult day, in this difficult time for the United States, it's perhaps well to ask what kind of a nation we are and what direction we want to move in. For those of you who are black—considering the evidence evidently is that there were white people who were responsible—you can be filled with bitterness, and with hatred, and a desire for revenge.
>
> We can move in that direction as a country, in greater polarization— black people amongst blacks, and white people amongst whites, filled with hatred toward one another. Or we can make an effort, as Martin Luther King did, to understand and to comprehend, and replace that violence, that stain of bloodshed that has spread across our land, with an effort to understand, compassion and love.

Kennedy underscored his point by addressing, for the first time in public, his brother's assassination:

> For those of you who are black and are tempted to be filled with hatred and mistrust of the injustice of such an act, against all people, I would only say that I can also feel in my own heart that same kind of feeling. I had a member of my family killed, but he was killed by a white man. But we have to make an effort in the United States, we have to make an effort to understand, to get beyond, or go beyond those rather difficult times.

John Lewis, the civil rights worker badly beaten during the Selma march in 1965, a Kennedy aide in Indianapolis and co-organizer of this appearance, would remember the effect that Kennedy's speech, particularly his poignant mention of his brother, had on the crowd. "It was an amazing speech," Lewis recalled three decades later. "I knew he had to have thought of his brother when he got this news, but I never dreamed that he would talk about him. That was something Bobby Kennedy never, ever did in public—he never talked about the murder of his brother. To do it that night was an incredibly powerful and connective and emotionally honest gesture. He stripped himself down. He made it personal. He made it real."

"Bob gave the most moving talk I ever heard," said RFK aide Fred Dutton. "It came from a heart that hurt and knew the meaning of what had happened that night as only a handful of people could really feel it."

Kennedy's speech lasted for seven minutes. He clutched his notes throughout but never consulted them. Borrowing a page from his literary past, he recited a poem when making his appeal for the nonviolence that Martin Luther espoused:

> My favorite poem, my favorite poet was Aeschylus. And he once wrote: "Even in our sleep, pain which cannot forget / falls drop by drop upon the heart / until, in our own despair, / against our will, / comes wisdom through the awful grace of God."
>
> What we need in the United States is not division; what we need in the United States is not hatred; what we need in the United States is not violence and lawlessness, but is love and wisdom, and compassion toward one another, and a feeling of justice toward those who suffer within our country, whether they be white or whether they be black.
>
> So I ask you tonight to return home, to say a prayer for the family

of Martin Luther King—yeah, it's true—but more importantly to say a prayer for our own country, which all of us love—a prayer for understanding and that compassion of which I spoke.

We can do well in this country. We will have difficult times. We've had difficult times in the past. And we will have difficult times in the future. It is not the end of violence; it is not the end of lawlessness; and it's not the end of disorder.

But the vast majority of white people and the vast majority of black people in this country want to live together, want to improve the quality of our life, and want justice for all human beings that abide in our land.

Let us dedicate ourselves to what the Greeks wrote so many years ago: to tame the savageness of man and make gentle the life of this world. Let us dedicate ourselves to that, and say a prayer for our country and for our people.

The speech was emotionally naked, a tribute to Kennedy's ability to bravely address a highly volatile topic in its essence. He didn't ask his listeners to forgive their leader's assassin; that would have been too much to expect, and inappropriately so. He wanted them to stand back and examine the source of their rage and, in their actions, avoid the reactionary hatred that might define them for the rest of their lives. Martin Luther King demanded racial equality and justice but not at the price of the social and religious principles to which he was ordained. Kennedy's eyes brimmed with tears as he spoke: he knew, all too well, the terrible relationship between anger and grief.

He left immediately after completing his speech, but his difficult day was far from finished. He was driven to his hotel, where he placed a call to Coretta Scott King, the slain leader's widow. After expressing his condolences, he asked Mrs. King if there was anything he could do for her. He was familiar with the role. After his brother's death, he had personally overseen the details of tasks, large and small, confronting Jacqueline Kennedy over the next few days. His sister-in-law was as strong and resolute as they came, as was Coretta Scott King, but grief has the power to paralyze.

Mrs. King asked Kennedy to supervise the return of her husband's body to Atlanta. Bobby saw that a chartered flight would bring King home from Memphis—an action that brought criticism from those who viewed it as a politically motivated move. Mrs. King, grateful for the assistance, disagreed with the criticism. "There was some concern within the organization as to whether or not this was quite the proper thing to do," she would recall. "I said that 'I don't really see anything wrong, period; [it was] one friend to another friend.'"

Kennedy's speech in Indianapolis had a powerful effect on the aftermath of the murder of Martin Luther King: the rioting predicted by the city's police chief did not occur. The city remained peaceful. King's death dramatically changed Kennedy's campaign. It didn't take the death of a beloved black leader to arouse Kennedy's empathy; inequality between whites and blacks had been at the front of his mind since the release of the Kerner Report and his eventual entry into the presidential race. It had been Vietnam, however, that pitted him against Johnson. King's death shifted his priorities. He would still be a vocal opponent of the war in Southeast Asia, but the thrust of his campaign would now be on a war against poverty and injustice in his own country.

Said Jack Newfield, journalist and friend of Robert Kennedy: "Martin Luther King's assassination was, I believe, a significant turning point not only in Robert Kennedy's campaign, but also in the way he thought about himself. It altered his own consciousness.

"Kennedy sought the Presidency in 1968, he said and believed, because of the war in Vietnam. But Dr. King's murder, preceded as it was by Johnson's abdication and the start of peace talks, enabled Kennedy to glimpse the deeper roots of America's internal disease, and to imagine himself as the possible healer of that disease."

3 Cities across America erupted in a seething, bloody response to Martin Luther King's assassination. When the rioting had ceased, more than a week after King's death, the numbers would vary on how many cities were involved, and how many citizens had been killed, wounded, or arrested. One thing was certain: very few major cities were exempt from the violence, and scores of smaller cities had problems as well. Washington, D.C., was one of the hardest hit. Chicago, New York, Detroit, Baltimore, Oakland—cries of "Burn, baby, burn!" became an existential imperative.

Lyndon Johnson, a champion of civil rights but now a lame-duck president, implored the public to remain peaceful. "We can achieve nothing by lawlessness and divisiveness among the American people," he said. "It is only by working together that we can move toward equality and fulfillment for all of our people." His words were ignored. King had been struggling to preach the message to those who had grown, first, cynical of his message and, later, angered by his willingness to accept what they considered to be empty promises; they weren't about to listen to reason from a white president.

And so the rioting began. In Washington, D.C., it escalated at breathtaking speed. Black activist Stokely Carmichael, a handgun tucked in his belt, led a group of young African Americans through a black business district along Fourteenth Street NW, past grocery stores, restaurants, movie theaters, and other retail stores. Carmichael and his group visited every establishment along the way, asking owners and managers to shut down their businesses out of respect for King. Most places closed. Carmichael had another message: blacks were now prepared to fight violence with violence. "If you don't have a gun, go home," he encouraged people assembling in the street. "When the white man comes he is coming to kill you. I don't want to see any black blood in the street. Go home and get you a gun and then come back because I got me a gun."

Carmichael's plans, whatever they were, were of no significance to those around him in the street. He had no control of them. Glass shattered, Black Power slogans were shouted, small fires were set, and looters stormed into stores. As had been the case in the rioting of recent years, most of the violence began in the inner city, where black businesses were vandalized, looted, or destroyed. It fanned out from there, the violence overwhelming anything in its path and spreading until, on April 5, the day after King's assassination, it had reached an area two blocks from the White House. No one was safe. The president called in four thousand federal troops. Some of the iconic government structures in the nation's capital were transformed into armed camps.

Troops were stationed in strategic posts on the White House lawn and on the steps of Congress; machine guns looked out from the steps leading to the congressional building. Barricades were set up, armed troops walked the streets.

In New York, Mayor John Lindsay, attending a Broadway play, had his evening interrupted by the news of rioting in Harlem. In a move that was either very brave or very foolhardy, he attempted to walk the Harlem streets amid the mayhem, before attention focused on him and he had to be rescued by Percy Sutton, Manhattan's black borough president. Nearby Newark, New Jersey, was ablaze. More than a thousand fires were set in Baltimore, and by the time Governor Spiro Agnew had called in six thousand National Guardsmen and an additional five thousand federal troops to restore order, the ghetto sections of the city were battle zones, six people had died, and five thousand had been arrested.

On the West Coast, rioting engulfed San Francisco and, to a lesser extent, Oakland. In Oakland, violence was held to a minimum by the Black Panthers, who, fearing the slaughter of blacks creating a disturbance, patrolled the streets and discouraged any type of aggressive actions. Ironically, the Black Panthers bore the brunt of Oakland's negative news coverage when a ninety-minute gun battle broke out between police and members of the group. Three police officers were wounded. The Panthers fled in all directions. Two members, El-dridge Cleaver and Bobby Hutton, two weeks shy of his eighteenth birthday, holed up in a house and were trapped in its basement. The police turned their weapons on the house for thirty-nine straight minutes and finally launched tear gas at it, leaving Cleaver and Hutton with an awful choice: they could stay in the house and almost certainly perish, or they could attempt a surrender, knowing that the odds were good that they would be gunned down as soon as they stepped out of the building. They chose to surrender. Hutton was the first out, and the police opened fire on him when, according to Deputy Police Chief Robert Cazadd, Hutton "crouched over and officers could not see his hands." Seeing what had happened to Hutton, Cleaver stripped before stepping outside; the officers could see that he was unarmed. He was shot in the leg, but other than being roughed up by the police when he was taken into custody, he came away from the confrontation relatively unharmed. Who provoked the confrontation and who shot first would be debated for years, with Cleaver claiming that he and Hutton had discharged their weapons in self-defense, the police countering that they had been ambushed. Cleaver, in 1980, confessed that the Black Panthers had instigated the confrontation.

The rioting represented the worst fighting between Americans on American soil since the Civil War. The sheer numbers were staggering: thirty-nine dead over a stretch of more than a hundred cities, countless wounded, nearly twenty thousand arrested, and more than fifty thousand National Guardsmen and federal troops brought out to quell the violence. The Cleaver-Hutton story received continuing press attention in the aftermath of the Oakland shoot-out and was boosted by a letter supporting the Black Panthers, submitted to the *New York Review of Books* and signed by such literary luminaries as Norman Mailer, Susan Sontag, Grace Paley, and James Baldwin, among many others. But the biggest news story to emerge from the rioting—a story that would have direct bearing on the 1968 Democratic National Convention in August—came out of Chicago.

The rioting in the city had been a ramped-up reprise of the violence engulfing the nation in preceding summers. The burning, looting, and destruction, according to some reports, were the worst of any city in the nation. The main thrust of the violence was in the city's South and West Sides; perhaps even more alarming, as far as Chicago's white citizens were concerned, was the storming of the city's "Loop," the main business district in downtown Chicago. Mayor Richard J. Daley counterattacked with all the muscle he could muster: the full extent of the police force, the National Guard, and federal troops. He set a curfew, which under the circumstances seemed like a hollow edict. The arrests piled up, but the rampage went on. Firefighters, trying to extinguish fires set at the rate of one every two and a half minutes, had to deal with snipers shooting at them and mobs intent on stopping them. Sanitation workers, brought out to clear the streets, were bombarded with rocks, bottles, and bricks. An angry Richard Daley, already aware of plans to disrupt the Democratic National Convention in August, issued an order to the superintendent of police that would reverberate nationwide in the months to come: "I said to him very emphatically and very definitely that an order be issued by him immediately, to shoot to kill any arsonist or anyone with a Molotov cocktail in his hand, because they're potential murderers, and shoot to maim or cripple anyone looting."

Daley's words were stunning, and not just because he uttered them. In the days following his dictum, his office received tremendous response, with one report estimating that fifteen out of sixteen respondents favored his decision. Daley's orders struck a chord in the minds of a huge percentage of the population that believed that the terrible violence was a symptom of a society that had gone soft on crime. Ronald Reagan spoke for frustrated conservatism when he asserted that the death and destruction in the big cities were tragedies that resulted "when we began compromising with law and order, and people started choosing which laws they'd break."

A quiet would eventually settle over Chicago, but its mayor could stand confident of public support in the future.

4   The candidates suspended their campaigns immediately following the news of Martin Luther King's death. Robert Kennedy honored one prior commitment, an appearance in Cleveland, where he delivered a heavy-hearted speech addressing King's message and the "mindless menace of violence" in response to his loss. "This is a time of shame and sorrow," he told his audience.

Kennedy intended to fly to Atlanta to see Coretta Scott King and attend King's funeral, but before doing this, he returned to Washington, D.C., where he walked the streets and surveyed the devastation that had left portions of the city in burned-out ruins. This was a private moment, void of politics or speechifying or even a protective entourage. The sight of the wreckage depressed him, not unlike the way he had felt eight years earlier, when he and his brother toured West Virginia and witnessed the effects that poverty had on those living desperate lives that they had no chance of escaping. It was an awkward moment of truth, wounded by its own conflicts: Kennedy could not condone the actions that had reduced the city to this mess, but he could understand the fury that had led to it.

Eugene McCarthy harbored similar emotions. Like Kennedy, he supported the law, but as he watched the reports of King's assassination and the ensuing violence in the cities on television, he conceded that he had no idea how he would react if he were black. He resisted making a commitment to attend King's funeral in Atlanta: it was going to be a media event, which would only chip away at the solemnity of the occasion. Given the choice, McCarthy would have preferred a symbolic but meaningful gesture such as attending a closed service in a black community. Blair Clark, arguing that McCarthy's absence in Atlanta would not be understood, talked him into attending King's funeral.

McCarthy's concerns about the funeral services were well founded. In one ironic moment, a recording of King's voice, carrying in over the church's loudspeakers, urged his funeral planners to keep his funeral brief. "If you get somebody to do the eulogy," he instructed them, "tell him not to talk too long." King's genuine modesty was ultimately trumped by the enormity of his life and influence. There were two separate ceremonies on the same day, one at his Ebenezer Baptist Church, and another, three and a half miles away, at Morehouse College, King's alma mater. The services ran long, and the stifling heat made them seem even longer. Eugene McCarthy sat directly behind Robert Kennedy at the Baptist church. The brevity that King hoped for in the speeches was ignored. Ralph Abernathy delivered an eloquent but lengthy address eulogizing his teacher and friend.

Jacqueline Kennedy, invited to the funeral by Coretta Scott King, wore a black silk suit similar to Mrs. King's, the two widows sharing the suffering that rises from martyrdom and public grieving. Jackie Robinson, a civil rights leader by example, was in attendance, as were Aretha Franklin, Stevie Wonder, and Sammy Davis Jr. from the entertainment world. Lyndon Johnson was the most prominent of the nonattendees; the Secret Service warned him that it would not be safe. Hubert Humphrey went in his place. George Wallace, who never disguised his contempt for King, was the only presidential candidate to skip the funeral.

The ceremony was followed by a massive procession to Morehouse College. King's body was transported on a farm wagon pulled by two mules. Tens of thousands of mourners walked in the procession, stood on the side of the road and watched it pass, and sang "We Shall Overcome" and hymns. Robert Kennedy walked the entire route; Eugene McCarthy and Richard Nixon joined for portions of the procession. By the time the second service ended and King was taken to the South View Cemetery for burial, nearly seven hours had been devoted to honoring Martin Luther King and his legacy. "No coffin can hold his greatness," Ralph Abernathy intoned at the conclusion of the services, "but we submit his body to the ground."

Indiana

Killing Floor

1 Neither Eugene McCarthy nor Robert Kennedy embraced the prospects
of campaigning in Indiana. The state had a Democratic governor and, in
Vance Hartke and Birch Bayh, two liberal Democrats in the U.S. Senate, but
history dictated that, come November, the vote for president would go to whoever was representing the Republican Party. The state had supported Richard
Nixon in the 1960 general election, and it was almost a certain bet that voters would be supporting him again in 1968. The Kennedy name carried little
magic in the Hoosier State, and Robert Kennedy would experience strong anti-
Kennedy sentiments on many of his campaign stops in the state.

Indianans might have found their ideal leader in Roger Branigin. The
sixty-five-year-old, Harvard-educated governor took pride in a provincialism
his constituents could admire. He distrusted outsiders, especially those determined to tell him how to run his state. Fiscally conservative—"I do not believe
that solvency is a sin"—Branigin and his right-hand man, state chairman Gordon St. Angelo, bore the standard for social conservatism as well. On close
examination, Branigin looked nothing like the typical northern Democrat. He
did, however, represent the typical Indiana Democrat. "A large majority of the
one million-odd Democrats in the state," observed the *New York Times,* "tend
to fit in one or more of these categories: organization-oriented, conservative,
hawkish on Vietnam, Southern in outlook, rural or resentful of Negro social
and political advances."

Branigin would be squaring off against McCarthy and Kennedy in Indiana's
primary. He had agreed to run as a stand-in for Lyndon Johnson, but he was only
lukewarm on the idea. He didn't care for the president, whom he deemed to be
"a selfish, opinionated man of considerable mediocrity," and he only agreed
to run after Johnson promised concessions benefiting the state. When Johnson
dropped out of the race, Branigin, already on the ballot, decided to continue on
as a favorite son. A primary victory, he felt, was preferable to turning Indiana's

delegates over to another candidate. "I believe that only a Hoosier can express a Hoosier's view at the Democratic national convention," he said.

Branigin promised to be a formidable opponent. At the beginning of the campaign in Indiana, Branigin held a lead in the polls, with Kennedy running second and McCarthy third, and it wasn't difficult to see why. Branigin's folksy, homespun demeanor was a statewide hit, whether he was jokingly accusing the media of "trying to put words into my oral cavity" or accusing Robert Kennedy of being a wealthy tourist attempting to buy an election; no one seemed to notice or care that the man speaking had received a law degree from an Ivy League school and had earned millions over the years. Branigin fit the image, right down to the design of his campaign headquarters, which was built to resemble a country store, cracker barrels and all.

It didn't hurt, either, that Branigin had the backing of Eugene C. Pulliam, the influential publisher of the right-wing *Indianapolis Star* and other newspapers in the state. In the *Star,* Pulliam had the state's most popular newspaper, which he used to advance his ultraconservative agenda. Branigin and Pulliam had known each other for years. Pulliam had endorsed Branigin in his successful 1964 gubernatorial run, but Branigin took nothing for granted four years later. He had met with Pulliam and sought his blessing before agreeing to run as a stand-in for Johnson.

Pulliam not only backed Branigin in the 1968 Indiana primary but also went out of his way to attack his opposition, particularly Robert Kennedy, with negative news stories, editorials, and editorial cartoons that drove Kennedy to complain that the *Indianapolis Star* was the worst newspaper in the United States. "The *Indianapolis Star* was the bane of our existence," sighed Lawrence O'Brien, who resigned his cabinet position as postmaster general to join the Kennedy campaign in Indiana. "It bordered on the obscene, but not quite."

Finally, Branigin enjoyed the benefits of Indiana's patronage system, which found state appointees kicking in 2 percent of their salaries to the state treasurer, the money to be designated for any number of projects, including the financing of a campaign like Branigin's. With a vested interest in the candidate, Branigin could expect the backing of counties throughout the state.

2 On April 5, Richard Goodwin visited Eugene McCarthy with the sole purpose of informing him that he was leaving McCarthy's campaign in favor of joining Robert Kennedy's. Getting to McCarthy's residence had been difficult. The rioting near Goodwin's hotel in Washington, D.C., had subsided, replaced by an eerie silence. Federal troops moved along streets lined with

burned-out buildings. Goodwin learned that he had to obtain a pass authorizing him to leave his hotel and walk around in public.

Goodwin had given his decision a lot of consideration. As he would recall, he had "enjoyed the McCarthy campaign, working with the kids, the whole atmosphere, open, freewheeling, relatively free of the usual infighting, [and] maneuvering for position." The Kennedy campaign would be different. But Kennedy was a close friend, and Goodwin had no wish to have any part in defeating him. Those were the personal reasons. On a larger scale, the historic events of the past week—Johnson's renunciation of his candidacy and Martin Luther King's assassination—had nudged the decision-making process along, even if it made it no easier. McCarthy was aware of how close Goodwin was to the Kennedys, and that Goodwin had joined his campaign mainly because he wanted to see an ending to the war; when he had come onboard, McCarthy had declared his candidacy and Kennedy had not. Now, with King dead, Johnson out of the picture, and Kennedy in the running, Goodwin had to consider the best candidate for ending the war and restoring some order between blacks and whites. "McCarthy would be a good president," Goodwin believed. "Bobby had the possibility of greatness."

McCarthy received the word graciously. He knew, even before hearing the news, why Goodwin was visiting him. Goodwin had brought his campaign badly needed credibility in the early goings, and now he would be taking his considerable skills to the opposition. The two parted unhappily.

Goodwin's decision, along with Lawrence O'Brien's decision to leave his postmaster general position to join Kennedy, represented a shift in attitude in working for a Kennedy. Both had worked for Jack Kennedy eight years earlier, and both had been caught up in the whirlwind of idealism and hope, in the belief that John F. Kennedy would lead the United States into a new political frontier. Goodwin and O'Brien, like so many attracted to Kennedy, had been political neophytes, unaware of the toll that the Washington, D.C., grind could—and would—extract.

It would be different in 1968, in Indiana and the overall campaign.

"I can't say I was a hard-charging young tiger rushing into action," O'Brien would recall of his work on the Kennedy campaign.

To some extent, my feeling was, "Well, here we go again." I'd spent a lot of time in Indiana for Jack Kennedy in 1960 and there I was, going over the same ground eight years later for another Kennedy. I can't say I felt the same enthusiasm I had felt the first time. A lot had happened in those eight years. I had held major responsibilities in Washington, yet

here I was, back in Indiana, organizing get-out-the-vote drives. I did my
job the best I could, but it was a job, not the adventure it once had been.

O'Brien had another reason for such feelings. While considering the idea of
leaving his Johnson-appointed cabinet position, O'Brien heard from Hubert
Humphrey, who had yet to make a final decision on running for the presidency
but who was sounding out O'Brien about the possibilities of his coming to
work for him. O'Brien and Humphrey were friends, and O'Brien had always
enjoyed a good working relationship with the vice president. The war issue
helped tip the scale in Kennedy's favor. Humphrey was still too tethered to
Johnson's Vietnam policies, and O'Brien wanted the war to end more quickly
than seemed likely under Johnson or Humphrey. Robert Kennedy appeared to
be the better option.

Goodwin, although closer personally to Robert Kennedy, shared many of
O'Brien's thoughts. He, too, was older and more experienced. But working for
a Kennedy was different this time around, and not just because Robert Kennedy was not his brother. The eight years that had passed between the election
of Jack Kennedy and the candidacy of Bobby Kennedy had redefined the mission: Vietnam, the civil rights movement, the Cold War, and other historical
events had placed Robert Kennedy in the uncomfortable position of confronting the ghosts of his brother's presidency.

O'Brien and Goodwin needed the benefit of their experience. When they
arrived in Indiana, they had roughly four weeks to work before the primary.
In trying to organize the volunteer effort throughout the state, O'Brien was up
against a reality he hadn't faced in 1960. Young Indianans, whom O'Brien had
counted on as a strong base of support, were lining up behind Eugene McCarthy, and older, traditional Democrats were committed to Branigin. Without the
support of the state's Democratic machine and contending with a hostile press,
the Kennedy campaign could not count on sources of support that had been
crucial in 1960. To O'Brien, success depended on broadening Kennedy's base
of support while the candidate proved that he was not limited to a single issue.

Goodwin, as Kennedy's media consultant, figured prominently in crafting
Kennedy's image. His responsibilities included working with local television
stations, developing campaign ads, and assembling a television documentary.
John Frankenheimer, the Hollywood director of such films as *The Birdman
of Alcatraz, The Manchurian Candidate,* and *Seven Days in May,* offered to
help, and Goodwin put him to work on a documentary focusing on Kennedy's
informal, relaxed side, an aspect of his life rarely seen by the public. Since
the Pulliam-owned papers made a practice of ignoring Kennedy when they

weren't attacking him, the television spots, although expensive to air, became vital in keeping Kennedy's image in front of the public.

Kennedy, of course, was all too acquainted with the importance of image in electoral politics. He had to find a way to address the important issues of his campaign in a manner that didn't alienate voters. Indianapolis was home to the national headquarters of the American Legion, and the state backed Johnson's Vietnam War policies. The urban disturbances following the assassination of Martin Luther King increased the already substantial interest in law-and-order issues while decreasing sympathy toward poverty and inner-city life; this was especially true in the state's southern counties, which had been a stronghold of the Ku Klux Klan. Kennedy modified his stump speeches from stop to stop, fine-tuning his campaigning in a way that might reach otherwise hostile audiences without compromising his principles. The modifications were subtle, but they were noticeable to those who had been following Kennedy closely. When campaigning in front of an African American audience, he spoke directly about the inequalities and poverty conditions that had led to the recent civil unrest. An address to a largely white, conservative assembly found him framing these remarks with a commentary about law and order. "I was the nation's chief law enforcement officer for three and a half years," he would say, "and no one knows better than I the importance of law enforcement. We have to make it clear we're not going to have lawlessness in the United States, we're not going to accept violence."

Kennedy's words were largely based on advice he had received from John Bartlow Martin, an Indiana writer, historian, Adlai Stevenson speechwriter and biographer, and authority on Indiana's politics and history, whom Kennedy hired as an adviser and speechwriter. Martin argued that Kennedy had to take a pragmatic approach if he ever hoped to defeat Roger Branigin in the primary— he had to appeal to those inclined to vote for the Indiana governor. Martin traveled with Kennedy throughout the state, advised him on what he might expect at each stop, and while Kennedy was speaking, stood on the outer fringes of the crowds and eavesdropped on what people were saying. The crowds, Martin reported, responded with great enthusiasm when Kennedy spoke for law and order and against the violence, even if they rejected his talk about the cause of and solutions to inner-city problems. The blacks, too, accepted Kennedy's condemnation of lawless behavior; many of them had been victimized by the rioting and vandalism.

When speaking to white audiences about poverty, unemployment, poor education, and squalid conditions of the ghetto, Kennedy spoke of the necessity of creating jobs that allowed blacks to succeed on their own. He added, however, a condemnation of "the welfare system, the handout system and the idea of the dole" that imprisoned blacks to a lifelong sentence of misery. "The welfare system in the last analysis destroys the family and destroys the idea of a man running the family," Kennedy said. "Some welfare is going to be necessary for the people, but we have to move away from the welfare system and establish a substitute." These ideas were consistent with what he had been suggesting all along, but the wording sounded surprisingly Nixonian.

Kennedy softened his tough stance on Vietnam, as well. Some of his advisors felt he should shy away from any in-depth discussion on the topic, but Kennedy rejected the idea. Instead, he backed away from his strong antiwar stance and focused on how the United States might be able to disengage with honor. Critics assailed the approach as transparent politicking, but it made very little difference: in post-primary surveys, the Kennedy vote was split almost equally between the pro-Vietnam and antiwar voters.

Perhaps most surprising of all, Kennedy attacked Big Government bureaucrats as a source of the frustrations of people like Indianans; the individual states, he felt, needed a greater say in determining their direction. This statement, a transparent concession to Indiana's provincialism, was one Kennedy would never have made in the past, when he was working under his brother or Lyndon Johnson and arguing about government intervention in civil rights issues. In a blistering assessment of Kennedy's campaign statements, the *New York Times* criticized Kennedy for jeopardizing his liberal credentials by "making noises like a conservative." He now sounded, said the *Times,* like George Romney.

The debate about how much Kennedy should adapt his speeches to his audiences' beliefs boiled over among Kennedy's campaign staff. Adam Walinsky and Jeff Greenfield, two of Kennedy's principal speechwriters, were furious. Kennedy's passion for the poor, the overlooked or forgotten, the minorities stepped on by white America, those incapable of standing up for themselves— Kennedy had been their advocate in Washington, D.C.; this new stance seemed watered down and impotent. John Bartlow Martin disagreed. Kennedy was still hitting these points, but it all boiled down to doing so in a manner that won votes. "It was a matter of emphasis, not substance," Martin insisted. Kennedy, he pointed out, always spoke about injustice *and* law and order. This did not appease the dissenters. As Fred Dutton would remember, disagreement led to "the most explicit debate of some substance that we had in the campaign."

Kennedy's first presidential primary campaign was marked by highs and lows, but it picked up steam as it went along. Supporters, sometimes smaller in numbers than Kennedy would have liked, were joined by the curious, out to see one of the famous Kennedys in the flesh. Family members chipped in, as they had when Jack ran eight years earlier, making appearances at luncheons, meetings, coffee klatches, and other gatherings; Ethel Kennedy and several of the Kennedy children always seemed to be nearby. Rose Kennedy caused a minor stir when she took exception to a reporter's question about the amount of money being sunk into the campaign and answered, "It's our own money, and we're free to spend it any way we please. It's part of the campaign business. If you have the money, you spend it to win."

And spend, they did. Although the Kennedy campaign was no different than any other campaign in its efforts to disguise the final dollar amounts devoted to a primary, estimates had them spending two million dollars in Indiana, including a quarter of a million on television time and handouts that featured an information packet designed to look like a newspaper, the figures generally exceeding the amounts attached to the Branigin and McCarthy campaigns. If Kennedy couldn't buy the vote, it wouldn't be for lack of effort.

One of the most intriguing investments was the conversion of the famous Wabash Cannonball train into a single-day whistle-stop vehicle. The five-car train stopped in Logansport, Peru, Wabash, Huntington, and Fort Wayne, and Kennedy enjoyed the experience as the highlight of his time in Indiana. Thousands of people, including children held out of school for the chance to see the candidate, packed the platforms and areas around the train stations. In Wabash, the world's first city lit by electricity, cheering supporters held signs reading "Socket to 'em Bobby," while the city's mayor, a Republican, offered him the key to the city. It was a box of petunias in Huntington, nicknamed the "City of Petunias." Officials from the different cities jumped onboard and, as the train rumbled on between stops, conferred with Kennedy in an informal, relaxed environment. Kennedy delivered a speech at each stop, concluding each with a paraphrase of a George Bernard Shaw line in *Back to Methuselah:* "Some men see things as they are and say, 'Why?' I dream things that never were and say, 'Why not?'" The line became so associated with Kennedy that a large percentage of the population believed he was the author of the expression.

3 Eugene McCarthy would have bypassed the Indiana primary if Robert Kennedy had not entered the race. The conservative state held very little promise, especially on the war issue, and McCarthy might have been better served by concentrating his efforts on other primaries on his list. McCarthy declared his intentions of entering the Indiana primary the day Kennedy entered the presidential race and announced that he would be running in Indiana.

McCarthy wasn't concerned about Roger Branigin's entry as a favorite son—a Branigin victory would have little bearing on the ultimate outcome of the Democratic campaign—but he was not about to allow Kennedy to waltz into the state and claim other, uncontested delegate votes. Instead, he entered the primary and over the course of four weeks saw his campaign's greatest weaknesses exposed.

McCarthy did not expect to win in Indiana—not with a favorite son and a new candidate named Kennedy stranding in his way. Analysts projected him to earn just under 20 percent of the vote, at best. The press was playing up the primary as a head-to-head confrontation between McCarthy and Kennedy, which, of course, it wasn't, not with a third contestant involved, but McCarthy and Kennedy were both treating it as an important face-off. In interviews, Kennedy liked to compare the Indiana primary to the 1960 West Virginia primary, with the obvious implications: his brother had entered the West Virginia primary as an underdog, and his unexpected victory had sent Hubert Humphrey packing; Robert Kennedy now hoped that a convincing victory in Indiana would have the same effect on McCarthy. His counterpart, still the leader in the race for the nomination, hoped to weather the storm with a respectable showing that set up a direct confrontation in Nebraska.

It wouldn't be easy. The Wisconsin victory had come at a high price to his organization and funding. The children's crusade, with its college kids and young adults eagerly awaiting orders, was still alive and healthy, although its numbers had diminished due to defections to the Kennedy campaign. Bickering between the national and local McCarthy campaign officials further widened the schism that began in Wisconsin. Skirmishes were the norm within any campaign organization, but the in-fighting in McCarthy's led to serious problems with scheduling, event organization, the establishment of McCarthy storefront headquarters throughout the state, and general disagreement over who was to be doing what. McCarthy's funds were so low that flyers couldn't be printed—or, if they were, they sat stacked in offices, awaiting money necessary for postage. Rental cars and buses stayed parked for a lack of gasoline money. The main headquarters in Indianapolis—the first two floors of the Hotel Claypool, which had lost the six floors above to a fire—was scheduled to be razed; it was so miserable that it came to be known as the Hotel Cesspool.

"For all its style, energy, and charm, the McCarthy campaign was not coming off," wrote Arthur Herzog, a staff member. "Overshadowed by Kennedy, it lacked cohesion and a focus. The candidate, in the lull in Vietnam discussion following the President's announcement of a bombing halt, seemed to have no real issue."

McCarthy created or exacerbated many of his problems. At the onset of his campaign in Indiana, he downplayed the significance of the primary in his overall quest for the nomination, which Jeremy Larner interpreted as a defense mechanism, "a fear of looking bad—like certain athletes who would rather lose than go all out to win. If one goes all out and loses, then one is without excuse."

Even if this were not the case, if it was merely another manifestation of his normal, reserved demeanor, McCarthy left a trail of confusion in his wake. His serendipity, such as the occasion when he missed an appearance because he decided to play in a baseball game, was not appreciated by his overworked, beleaguered advance team, so understaffed and inexperienced that it seemed miraculous that any appearances came off without a hitch. The college-aged volunteers, the backbone of McCarthy's success in New Hampshire and Wisconsin, fulfilled the same roles in Indiana, but between the doors slamming in their faces and McCarthy's apparent indifference, they suffered from a "perpetual identity crisis," as Larner put it. "At two in the morning," he would recall, "my hotel room would fill with lost souls who had slaved all day but weren't sure if they were really wanted or if they had any business being there."

McCarthy's disconnect and lethargy might be partially attributed to concerns about Robert Kennedy that bordered on obsession. The concerns were not without merit. McCarthy knew, going in, that he was going to be outspent and outhustled by a fresh, charismatic candidate who moved about as freely and easily in the "old politics" as he did in the "new politics." Kennedy would receive very little from the press, but he was more than adequately prepared to defend himself by advertising in newspapers and on television. McCarthy was prepared for all that. What he was not prepared for were the personal attacks designed to set the two candidates apart and illustrate that Kennedy was more liberal on social issues, more in touch with the American people, and better equipped to lead America through turbulent times. The approach was similar to the one taken by the Kennedys against Hubert Humphrey in West Virginia in 1960: make sure the attacks were not coming directly from the candidate, act surprised when the target objected to the attacks, and promise to set things straight, even if that was never adequately done. Robert Kennedy had been behind Franklin D. Roosevelt Jr.'s attacks on Humphrey; McCarthy would learn that Pierre Salinger, the Kennedy press secretary, was behind the attacks aimed at him.

McCarthy's voting record was the focus of the attack. A "fact sheet," the handiwork of a New York City–based group calling itself Citizens for Kennedy, made its first appearance before the Indiana primary and was distributed across the United States. It was available in the Kennedy storefronts as well. The group saw that the media were supplied with this material, which charged McCarthy with taking a less than liberal position on such issues as a minimum wage bill, Social Security, and civil rights. McCarthy complained that the fact sheet, which appeared in several permutations, distorted, mispresented, or falsified his voting record—a claim eventually backed by the *New York Times*. Kennedy disavowed any connection to the attack sheet, but it ultimately didn't matter. A year after the election, McCarthy would still be defending himself from the information published about his record. "The experience of these attacks, misrepresentations, and distortions was the most disappointing part of the entire campaign," McCarthy allowed.

Despite the disappointments and setbacks, McCarthy discovered much to enjoy in Indiana. He and his closest staff advisers had decided to concentrate their campaigning on the state's smaller towns and rural areas, particularly where Roger Branigin might be vulnerable, which the poet in McCarthy found inspiring. He wrote a handful of new poems as he tooled around the state. Small as they occasionally were, the crowds coming out to see the candidate were enthusiastic. McCarthy, who generally looked upon Indianans as intellectual rubes, nevertheless found their more relaxed way of life, which seemed to be a throwback to a less hectic era, similar to what he experienced while growing up in Minnesota. Celebrities—Rod Serling, Myrna Loy, Garry Moore, Dustin Hoffman, and Simon and Garfunkel—traveled to the state to stump for him, reprising their roles in New Hampshire. Then there was Paul Newman, who appeared at fifteen stops, attracting huge gatherings of swooning women, many following him from city to city. Newman turned out to be a godsend to the financially strapped McCarthy campaign. "We started auctioning off things he had touched, and doing a little fund raising in that way," Tony Podesta, one of Newman's bodyguards, remembered years later. The actor, who would later make hundreds of millions for charity from his "Newman's Own" grocery products, learned that even the remnants of his lunches weren't exempt from the fund-raising effort. "It was somewhat unorthodox," Podesta said, "but, given the money we had versus the money Kennedy had, we had to resort to almost anything, and so we began to auction chicken bones."

Like Kennedy, McCarthy adjusted his campaign message for Indiana. The Vietnam War was still an integral part of his campaign agenda, but he was now taking a deliberate approach in his criticism of Lyndon Johnson, lest he knock a dent in the delicate peace negotiations that Johnson was promoting. McCarthy encouraged the peaceful settlement to the conflict and suggested the possibility of a coalition government in Vietnam that included the Communists.

He also proposed that the South Vietnamese government become more active in determining its fate, be it in the fighting or the negotiating. The *New York Times*, noting that the candidates were largely uninformed about the negotiations regarding the peace talks, pointed out the difficulty that McCarthy and the others encountered while talking about Vietnam on the campaign trail: "The dangers are that the candidates may inadvertently make remarks or suggestions in public which will interfere with the peace negotiations, or even commit the candidates, through ignorance or misinformation, to policies they may not want to live with next year after one of them finally gets to the White House."

Perhaps it was for this reason, or maybe because Robert Kennedy chose to make domestic issues the crux of his speeches, that McCarthy tilted the focus of his Indiana campaign speeches to big-city problems, racial strife, and economic issues. He had no misconceptions about where he stood: Kennedy would easily capture the state's black vote. Still, he was tired of hearing, as he had in Wisconsin, that he had little connection to minorities, and he was especially touchy about it under some of the fire he was receiving from the Kennedy campaign. In addition, he attacked Dean Rusk and J. Edgar Hoover, central figures in the Vietnam War and the law-and-order issues: it was time, he said, for them to be relieved of their jobs.

He changed his earlier dismissal of the primary's importance. During an appearance at the George Rogers Clark Memorial in Vincennes, he spoke of the value he now placed on the forthcoming primary: "I hesitate to say that this is the most important primary, but it is the critical one at this point," he declared. "As far as I am concerned, as Indiana goes, I think that's the way the Democratic Party will go in Chicago. And the way the Democratic Party goes in Chicago, is the way the country will go next November."

The turnabout in McCarthy's attitude might have been prompted by his primary victory in Pennsylvania on April 23. Prior to his entry into it, the nonbinding primary had meant little to McCarthy, who disregarded it as a "popularity contest." But after considering the possible gains he might make if he won the primary, he changed his mind. Kennedy, Johnson, and Humphrey were not listed on the ballot, and McCarthy hoped to pick up about 200,000 votes in the primary. He campaigned for two days in the state, keeping hectic schedules in Pittsburgh and Philadelphia. It paid off on election day. McCarthy received 428,259 votes, a huge 71.6 percent of those cast for Democrats—an affirmation of his candidacy that he could not ignore. He had now won four primaries; no one else in the running had won a single one. A victory in Indiana would continue momentum that he would need in Nebraska, Oregon, and California.

"If I win here," he said in Indiana, "I'll win in Chicago."

4 Nixon's proselytizing on law and order, a practice that allowed him to ignore talk about Vietnam, about which he had little to say, profited substantially when, on April 23, a group of radical student activists, both black and white, seized control of Hamilton Hall at Columbia University. The nationwide violence following Martin Luther King's assassination had barely cooled to a simmer when the confrontation between authorities and protesters flared up again, relocating the media focus from the ghetto to the halls of a venerable university in the nation's largest city. Located on Manhattan's Upper West Side, Columbia had long been a jewel in New York City's educational and cultural history. The Ivy League school, founded in 1754, had strong connections to the city and, by some measure, the national government, but these relationships sparked student demonstrations, a national student strike, and ultimately a takeover that quickly became part of the dialogue between the presidential candidates.

Up against the wall, motherfucker.

This line, lifted from a LeRoi Jones poem, a rallying cry, a challenge, a threat, a shout of rage, a command, a zygote of racial venom blowin' in the wind, was revolutionary speak, and talk of revolution was anthemic in 1968, especially in the fiery streets after the assassination of Martin Luther King. The expression was loaded with questions, to be debated in a land of dualism, between blacks and whites, young and old, wealthy and poor, educated and uneducated, Republican and Democrat, in the hands of academia and the ghetto sidewalks strewn with glass. How much of the anger and violence was the grave, perhaps overdue response from centuries of oppression, and how much was basic criminal behavior? How long should the blowback be allowed to continue, and what kind of force should be used to contain or eliminate it? What were the limits to actions rising from the powerless now becoming empowered? What kinds of precedents were being set, and where would they stand in history? What was legitimate protest, and what was the shouting of anarchy? In the past, these and other questions had been answered by those holding power, position, wealth, and, ultimately, might backed by weaponry. But this had been changing in recent years, and in an election year such as 1968, the voters demanded leaders who could protect and reassure them.

Grayson Kirk and Mark Rudd, the leading opponents in the Columbia confrontation, were by nature forceful and extremely stubborn players in the drama that unfolded at the end of April. Kirk, the sixty-one-year-old president of Columbia, ruled over the university in an authoritarian manner bound to infuriate campus activists hell-bent on change. A board member at a number of corporate and banking institutions, including Con Edison, IBM, and Mobil

Oil, Kirk expected unchallenged student compliance to his orders at all times, and he made no secret about the direction he saw the student activists taking. "Our young people, in disturbing numbers, appear to reject all forms of authority, from whatever source derived," he said in a speech delivered in Virginia on April 12, "and they have taken refuge in a turbulent and inchoate nihilism whose sole objectives are destruction."

He might have been describing Mark Rudd when he noted that "the gap between the generations has never been wider or more potentially dangerous." He was aware of Rudd's strengths as a leader, dedication as an activist, and commitment to a number of national causes; what probably worried him most was Rudd's fearlessness. Early in 1968, Rudd, a native of an upscale community in New Jersey, traveled to Cuba, where he studied the revolution and its leaders, and returned, as he described it, "fired up with revolutionary fervor." As the leader of the local chapter of the Students for a Democratic Society (SDS), the twenty-year-old Rudd constantly searched for ways to convert all the talk taken from the seemingly endless number of SDS and other campus meetings into meaningful action—he and his energetic group came to be known as the "action faction" by other SDS members—and Grayson Kirk was well aware of his activities around the campus. Kirk had a standing order prohibiting indoor demonstrations on the Columbia campus; Rudd thumbed his nose at the decree by leading a demonstration against the Institute for Defense Analysis (a group of university officials examining, among many things, the distribution of weapons research projects to universities) in Columbia's Low Library. Kirk responded by sending Rudd and his cohorts to their respective deans, who placed them on academic probation. At a Columbia memorial service for Martin Luther King at the St. Paul's Chapel, Rudd walked up to the pulpit, seized the microphone from the speaker, and dressed down Columbia officials for their hypocrisy in paying tribute to King while dismissing the needs and interests of the residents of nearby Harlem. Rudd even made his disagreement with Kirk a personal issue when, in an open letter to Kirk, "Reply to Uncle Grayson," he ridiculed Kirk's Virginia speech and let the Columbia president know, in no uncertain terms, that a revolution was taking place on his campus.

"We will take control of your world, your corporation, your university, and attempt to mold a world in which we and other people can live as human beings," he wrote. Rudd viewed Kirk as a despot whose rigid control of the university symbolized a much larger, more troubling menace: a potential police state, run by a government unwilling to consider the will of the people. "There is only one thing left to say," he said in conclusion to his letter. "It may sound nihilistic to you, since it is the opening shot in a war of liberation. I'll use the words of LeRoi Jones, whom I'm sure you don't like a whole lot: 'Up against the wall, motherfucker, this is a stick-up.' Yours for freedom, Mark."

When criticizing Columbia for its relationship to Harlem, Rudd was specifically targeting a plan to build a new gymnasium in a section of nearby Morningside Park, a tract of land on the boundary of Harlem owned by the city but leased to Columbia for a nominal fee of $3,000 per year. Neighboring Harlem residents were outraged. Columbia had expanded in the past, and the encroachment into Harlem had cost 7,500 residents their homes. The new gym would displace more families, plus it would be cutting into a park where the area children liked to play. As the topper, the new gym would be open only to Columbia students. The drama played out over a period of years, with no dirt being bulldozed around the project. Columbia eventually offered to build another, much smaller gym open to the public. This had been rejected on principle, and in February 1968 ground was finally broken, setting off another round of protests that had no effect whatsoever on the construction.

The battle was ideal for the kind of action Rudd envisioned: not only would he and his group be locking horns again with the Columbia University administrators, but his actions would also be impacting a community, and if the police became involved, useful media coverage would be gained. Rudd scheduled a meeting for April 23. Demonstrators would gather at the sundial in the middle of the campus, there would be speeches, and afterward everyone would head to Low Library for another prohibited demonstration and to plot further activities.

The early portion of the planned activities commenced without a problem. Nearly 300 people, including a smattering of professors, assembled at the sundial, and speeches were delivered. A group of about 150 conservative counter-demonstrators—short-haired jocks, as they were derisively called by Rudd's group—gathered nearby, some carrying signs critical of Rudd, SDS, or the protesters. The demonstration at the library, however, was not going to happen: the building had been locked down. Angry demonstrators looked for guidance, and someone suggested a march to the site of the new gym. The scene at the construction site was chaotic. Demonstrators tried to tear down the fence guarding the site, but they were unsuccessful. The police arrived, one SDSer was arrested, and tempers boiled over. As he would later admit, Rudd felt as if he was losing control of a situation calling for some kind of meaningful improvisation, and when that failed to materialize, the protesters decided to return to Columbia.

Rudd estimated a gathering of 500 near the sundial. This, he believed, was the time for action. His biggest objection against the SDS was the members' tendency to talk rather than act. At the very least, the action now should be the occupation of a building and a mass sit-in. Rudd likened it to taking a hostage. They selected nearby Hamilton Hall, one of the campus's main classroom buildings and home to the office of Henry Coleman, the college dean. The building was seized with no resistance, and the students trapped Coleman in his office, taking him prisoner until Columbia officials met their list of demands, which included halting the gym construction, amnesty for those on probation for previous demonstrations, and the cessation of the university's research for the Defense Department.

The early hours of the occupation of Hamilton Hall were marked by indecision over what to do next. The taking of the hall had been a spontaneous coup, with no thought about the future. The young revolutionaries found themselves staring down a racial divide when the white students argued that Hamilton Hall should remain open for classes the next day, while black activists, who had joined those storming the hall, felt it should remain shut down as a statement supporting Harlem's interests. Talk of revolution and Black Power did not lift the discussion from the mire. Meanwhile, university officials and the police weighed their options. The standoff was volatile, but it had been mainly peaceful. Grayson Kirk felt that the university had taken a restrained approach to the student occupation, but he was eager to end the impasse. David Truman, Columbia's vice president, argued against any police intervention in the immediate future. All sides realized that they were dealing with the unfamiliar: sit-ins were commonplace on and off college campuses in 1968—there were 101 sit-ins or demonstrations on college campuses in the spring of that year alone—but no one had ever taken this approach at a university. "We were still really middle-class kids, and suddenly we were in a different league from the student protest we had begun that morning," Rudd would remember.

Night fell, and after being asked to leave by the blacks, who wanted to make a statement separate from the others, Rudd and the white students and SDSers left Hamilton Hall. They broke a window in the Low Library building and let themselves in. They wandered through the administration offices and settled into Kirk's office, with its priceless art that included Rembrandt's *Portrait of a Dutch Admiral.* The rifled through his file cabinets, smoked his cigars, and tried to sleep.

The siege did not end the next day, or the day after that; a week passed before it concluded. During that time, three additional buildings were commandeered, classes were shut down, work was halted on the gym, and such noteworthy figures as SDS founder Tom Hayden, activist/provocateur Abbie Hoffman, and Black Power leader Stokely Carmichael arrived on campus.

Hamilton Hall was rechristened Malcolm X University. A student couple were married. The takeover generated national media attention, though there was little of significance to report. The students issued mimeographed news releases to the press. Students and Columbia officials offered their side of the stories to reporters. Each occupied building formed a committee to negotiate with officials. In this unusual setting, in which principle carried as much weight as actual movement, the students and activists were breaking new ground.

"I had never seen anything quite like this," Tom Hayden wrote.

> Students, at last, had taken power in their own hands, but they were still very much students. Polite, neatly attired, holding their notebooks and texts, gathered in intense knots of discussion, here and there doubting their morality, then recommitting themselves to remain, wondering if their academic and personal careers might be ruined, ashamed of the thought of holding an administrator in his office but wanting a productive dialogue with him, they expressed in every way the torment of their campus generation.

Everyone was resigned to the truth that this all had to come to an end, and that the conclusion was likely to be violent. Despite their revolutionary bravado, those holding the buildings captive had only to look at the police presence on the campus to know, in their souls, that they were in charge for only as long as the powers that be permitted it. What would happen if the authorities started blocking the students on the outside from bringing provisions and food to those barricaded in the buildings, or, more to the point, if the police, acting on orders, stormed the five buildings? There were rumors that some of the blacks in Hamilton Hall were armed, but everyone else was defenseless against the firepower the police possessed. The best they could do was to find a way to slow down the assault.

Shortly after midnight on Tuesday, April 30, an estimated mass of a thousand police began assembling at Columbia. The electricity and phone lines were cut. Warned that a police charge was imminent, those in the occupied buildings built barricades near stairwells, on elevators, and in entrances to offices; according to the plan, no one was to resist arrest. None of that mattered when the police moved, in military formation, at two thirty in the morning. The police broke through the barricades and confronted anyone in their path not wearing a uniform. Students were beaten relentlessly and mercilessly with billy clubs, blackjacks, flashlights, and, according to one report, brass knuckles. Students, professors, innocent bystanders gathered on the campus—no one was exempt. Some of the students were taken to police wagons or city buses marked "Special" destined for the police station; others were taken to hospitals. It would be noted that not all of the police were involved in the brutality, and that, in comparison to the violence in the street confrontations during inner-city violence, the brutality was relatively light, but to the public, which supported the taking back of the university but not the violence employed in doing so, Columbia had become a bloody symbol of the deepening chasm between protesters and authorities, of a generation gap widening and becoming more contentious by the month. The numbers were sobering: 772 arrested (including 524 students), 148 injured (including 20 police), and 120 charges of police brutality filed against the police—the largest number in the department's history.

Life magazine gave the Columbia takeover extensive, fourteen-page coverage in its May 10 edition, complete with photographs of the students occupying the offices and the police storming the campus. "In the end," the magazine concluded, "the rebellion caused two kinds of casualties at Columbia—the wounds suffered by those who were caught up in it and the scars inflicted upon the prestige and spirit of a great institution of learning."

Richard Nixon followed the Columbia strike with great interest. The American people, he felt, would disapprove of the actions against Columbia, which he labeled a "national tragedy and a national disgrace." It fit neatly into his expanding law-and-order stance, and by working it into his statements, he could not be accused of racism in his proclamations about the need for tougher stands against civil violence. After all, this involved a large percentage of white protesters, and it occurred on a highly regarded university campus, not the streets of the ghetto. Patrick Buchanan, a Columbia alumnus, wrote for Nixon a gloves-off statement in which the candidate called Columbia "the first major skirmish in a revolutionary struggle to seize the universities of this country for radicals and vehicles for revolutionary and political goals."

5 As the candidates were discovering, student skepticism and opposition could be found anywhere. Robert Kennedy faced a hostile audience when he appeared at the University of Indiana Medical School on April 26. He might have known what was in store for him when he entered the auditorium and a black janitor called out, "We want Bobby!" and a number of students shouted, "No we don't!" Kennedy's speech antagonized them further. Aware that he was speaking to students from affluent families, students preparing for affluent careers, Kennedy used the occasion to criticize the medical community for

failing to provide badly needed services to the poor. "Decent medical care," he said, had to be "something more than a luxury of the affluent."

The students gave the twenty-one-minute address a frosty reception. They did not applaud at the conclusion of the speech, and the question-and-answer session that followed, usually a Kennedy favorite, was tense. Kennedy liked to use his interaction with his audiences as a tool for persuasion; his attempts on this occasion were not well received by the medical students, who seemed more concerned about the costs of the programs Kennedy was proposing than in the benefits they would provide impoverished communities. The tone of the questions bothered Kennedy, but he held his temper. He finally let his irritation show when a student, essentially repeating what others had said, asked, "All these programs sound very fine and nice and all that, but where's the money gonna come from?"

"From you!" Kennedy shot back, stabbing the air with an index finger. He turned the index finger toward others in the audience. "And you . . . and you . . . and you."

He gathered his thoughts before continuing. "Let me say something about the tone of these questions," he went on. "I look around this audience, and I don't see many black faces, or black men who are going to become doctors. For the poor, it's very difficult to get into the medical profession." This was the core of Kennedy's anger toward the racial injustice in the United States: while white America prospered, minorities were held back from attaining similar success. It was even more pathetic when one thought of the connection between Vietnam and the medical profession. Affluent young students received deferments while attending medical school; those unable to afford a university education were drafted and shipped off to war. "You white students sit here in your medical schools while black people are carrying the burden in Vietnam," Kennedy charged.

Afterward, a still shaken Kennedy turned to journalist David Halberstam. "They were so comfortable," he said of the students in disgust, "so comfortable."

One of Kennedy's great disappointments to date had been his inability to secure the youth vote. McCarthy's antiwar position won him the hearts and minds of the young in the early goings, before Kennedy had announced his candidacy, but Kennedy felt that his stance on Vietnam was as solid as McCarthy's and that his civil rights record was superior to McCarthy's. Yet he struggled to make headway into this voting bloc. He was reminded of this late one evening while out for a walk with Richard Goodwin, when he passed a McCarthy headquarters and encountered a handful of McCarthy volunteers seated on the steps outside. Viewing this as an ideal opportunity to pick the brains of his young opposition, Kennedy asked if they would mind if he sat down with them. The volunteers knew who he was, of course, but they invited him to sit on the steps with them. As Goodwin would later write, the brief, ensuing conversation caught Kennedy's attention. The volunteers, a bit uneasy at first, told Kennedy that they were working for McCarthy in an effort to end the war, and when Kennedy responded that he, too, was trying to end the war, one of the volunteers reminded Kennedy, and not so gently, that he hadn't been around when she joined the McCarthy forces in New Hampshire; she would be staying with McCarthy to the end. Kennedy asked the others, almost all of whom had left good jobs or school to join the McCarthy campaign, if they felt the same way. They did. "I want you to know that you make me proud to be an American," Kennedy said. "You've done a wonderful thing. I'm only sorry that we couldn't have done it together." And with that, he was off. When out of earshot of the volunteers, Kennedy expressed his regrets to Goodwin. These young people, he told Goodwin, were his people, and he would have loved to have them on his side. "Well," he concluded, "it can't be helped. If I blew it, I blew it."

6   While the Democratic Party candidates campaigned for their chunk of the Indiana vote, Hubert Humphrey dragged his feet on officially entering the race. He did nothing to deflate the persistent rumors about his candidacy, and at times he seemed to be teasing the public about his intentions. He had been in constant motion since Johnson's denunciation. He and his advisors had placed a steady stream of calls to party and labor leaders with mixed but overall encouraging results. Those closest to him urged him to declare before the Kennedy juggernaut wrapped up the nomination; others favored a more measured approach. Before donning any Humphrey straw boaters, some bigwigs wanted to see how the Kennedy–McCarthy skirmish played out in Indiana. Overall, Kennedy was the major threat. Still, very few discouraged Humphrey from running. Labor leaders in particular were enthusiastic. Humphrey huddled with the president, who offered advice but reiterated his position of remaining uncommitted to any candidate. Humphrey came out of the meeting with the impression that LBJ favored him over McCarthy and Kennedy, which was really not much of an endorsement, given Johnson's dislike of the two senators.

Humphrey believed he could beat Kennedy and McCarthy, with or without LBJ's blessing, and he felt that he could do it without boosts from primary victories. He could do it the old-fashioned way, by gathering delegate votes in backroom meetings and caucuses in nonprimary states, by relentless campaigning and favorable press coverage. He had actually been ready to declare his candidacy within days of Johnson's dropping out, but Martin Luther King's assassination had put any thoughts of that announcement on hold. Humphrey traveled to Atlanta, attended King's funeral as the White House's official representative, and avoided making the kind of statement about his plans that might be regarded as disrespectful of the slain civil rights leader.

The days—and weeks—passed, and the press, always in queue for a new angle on a story, grew restless. Reporters and pundits still believed that Humphrey's candidacy was inevitable, though Humphrey gave them nothing definitive, even if his public appearances and behind-the-scenes maneuvering pointed to a presidential run. A Citizens Committee for Humphrey, headed by such financial powerhouses as John Loeb, John Conner, and Sidney Weinberg, was formed. Humphrey began piecing together a campaign staff—an imperative decision given some of the staffing problems he had dealt with in 1960. Humphrey astutely recognized the need to infuse youthful talent into his campaign staff—people who could offset the ascent of youth in the McCarthy and Kennedy campaigns, as well as the vice president's counter to LBJ and the old politics—and his selection of Senators Fred Harris and Walter Mondale to codirect his campaign was a strong move in that direction.

Harris was an impressive catch. A close friend of both Robert Kennedy and Hubert Humphrey, Harris, thirty-seven, was one of the most promising up-and-comers on Capitol Hill, an agreeable legislator who seemed to be on the fast track to an upper-level government position. "*Time* magazine once said that I was the only person who could have breakfast with Lyndon Johnson and lunch with Hubert Humphrey and dinner with Robert Kennedy," he would remember years later, and in 1968 both Kennedy and Humphrey had him on their short lists for vice-presidential possibilities. Harris and Johnson fell out over the Kerner Commission report—Harris was a member of the board—but Harris had promised to assist the Johnson–Humphrey effort as their chairman of Rural Americans for Johnson and Humphrey. When LBJ dropped out, he agreed to stay on with Humphrey as cochair of his campaign staff.

In "Fritz" Mondale, Humphrey was returning to his Minnesota roots, and to someone he had worked with extensively in the past. Mondale's résumé belied his thirty-nine years. He had been appointed to Humphrey's senate seat when Humphrey won the vice presidency in 1964, but he had established his credentials well before that. At seventeen, he had worked as a bell-ringer on Humphrey's mayoral reelection campaign, and two years later, he was a congressional district manager for Humphrey's senatorial campaign. He was a progressive voice in the Democratic-Farmer-Labor Party, and as Minnesota attorney general at the ripe old age of thirty-two, he had proven his mettle in a number of important cases. Similar to Harris, Mondale had the reputation of being a major new player in Washington, D.C., and he was quick to cite Humphrey as his political mentor.

Mondale had been initially skeptical of Humphrey's chances in an all-out campaign against the other two Democratic candidates. He had watched Johnson's televised March 31 announcement with Washington senator Henry "Scoop" Jackson, and when Humphrey's name came up as a possible candidate, Mondale had not been enthusiastic. He could see no way that Humphrey could beat Kennedy. He changed his mind over the ensuing weeks, when Kennedy looked strong but beatable. If anyone was being left behind, it was Eugene McCarthy.

Mondale, of course, knew McCarthy, and he approved of McCarthy's opposition to the Vietnam War; he admired his intellect. He was bothered, however, by his unpredictability and found him a difficult presidential candidate to support. "He had great aspirations and great confidence in his talent," he observed. "But Gene also had a way of fading when it came to the heavy lifting, as if he were tuned out from the expectations of the people around him. He was also something of a lone wolf."

Harris and Mondale represented two of the highest-placed candidates on Humphrey's wish list, but he was not as fortunate in acquiring the talents of others. He wanted Lawrence O'Brien, with the postmaster general's successful track record of working on campaigns, to oversee his campaign, but O'Brien had already committed to Bobby Kennedy. Joseph Rauh, another influential old friend, adamantly opposed the administration's position on the Vietnam War and would not endorse, let alone work for, Humphrey. The former cofounder of Americans for Democratic Action supported Eugene McCarthy instead.

Humphrey kept a running tabulation of his probable delegate votes. By his thinking, he was in very good shape—maybe good enough to win the nomination on the convention's first ballot. During Humphrey's meeting with Johnson, the president had suggested that the key to a Humphrey victory would be found in six states: New Jersey, Illinois, Pennsylvania, Indiana, Ohio, and Michigan. Humphrey immediately scheduled appearances in these states. A numbers game commenced in the news media as well. There was, as there always was, disagreement on the candidate's strength. Writing for the *Washington Post,* David Broder agreed that Humphrey was probably the Democratic front-runner and that Humphrey had a reasonable chance of securing the nomination on the first ballot. But nothing, he noted, was assured. By Broder's calculation, Humphrey had roughly 900 delegate votes—412 votes shy of the 1,312 needed for the nomination. Like Johnson, Broder listed Pennsylvania, Ohio, Michigan, Illinois, and New Jersey as the key states that Humphrey needed to win. A Kennedy blitz through the primaries—a very real possibility—could damage Humphrey's standing. As Broder saw it, "the ideal outcome, from Humphrey's viewpoint, would be for McCarthy and Kennedy to fight each other to a standoff in the primaries, leaving Humphrey as the unity candidate unscarred by any defeats."

Humphrey was ready. The campaign marked the beginning of the fulfillment of a lifelong dream, and he felt confident that it was within his grasp. With his enthusiasm boiling over, he scheduled the announcement of his candidacy for Saturday, April 27, assuring him maximum coverage in the nation's Sunday newspapers and television news programs.

More than fifteen hundred supporters squeezed into the ballroom of the Shoreham Hotel in Washington, D.C., with another thousand waiting outside, all gathered to hear the Happy Warrior announce his plans for what would now be a closely contested three-way race, with Humphrey offering a more traditional alternative to Kennedy and McCarthy. Introduced by Fred Harris as the experienced politician "unmatched in American political life," Humphrey, smiling broadly and speaking in a heavily emotional voice, offered his audience the upbeat message that everyone expected.

"Here we are, just the way we ought to be—the politics of happiness, the politics of joy, the politics of purpose—that's the way it's going to be all the way from here on out," Humphrey opened, his statement to be dissected—and soundly criticized—in the weeks to come. He was obviously addressing the frenzied supporters in front of him, employing the optimism that was his political calling card, but the pundits bristled at the "politics of joy" expression, coming, as it did, at a time when darkness seemed to shroud the United States' political and social landscapes. Over the past few weeks, the most respected civil rights leader of the twentieth century had been slain, cities across the country had erupted in violence in response, and an Ivy League school had been commandeered by protesting students; the body counts in Vietnam, America's most unpopular war to date, continued to rise. Where was the joy in any of that? Angered and hurt by the criticism, Humphrey stuck by his remarks over the ensuing weeks, when attacks came at him from all angles, from newspaper editorial cartoons to the Robert Kennedy camp. His happiness, he said, was in being an American, in being part of a system that had given so much to so many and continued to work at becoming better. "You bet, I'm happy," he insisted. "I'm happy to have a chance to do something about this country, happy that I have a chance to speak up for this country, happy that I have a chance to help somebody else to be happy in this country. That's what it's all about."

(In his autobiography, published in 1976, Humphrey would concede that his politics of joy statement, although not the first time the expression had been used by a politician, was, in this instance, "an unfortunate statement" that "failed to get my message across." The media scorn still hurt eight years later, but Humphrey admitted that he might have found a better way to state his case. "I simply meant that the right to participate in democratic processes was, in part, 'the pursuit of happiness' of which our founding fathers spoke," he explained.)

Humphrey's twenty-minute speech, a mere outline in comparison to the avuncular orator's usual style, composed by a team of speechwriters, touched on all the important points, from Humphrey's stating of his qualifications to his hopes for America. He praised Johnson ("I believe Lyndon Johnson's Presidency will loom large in history for its dramatic leadership toward social progress, human opportunity and peace"), and he paraphrased Victor Hugo ("The future has several names. For the weak, it is the impossible. For the fainthearted, it is the unknown. For the thoughtful and the valiant, it is ideal."). He spoke of American ideals and how they might be attained. His supporters interrupted him repeatedly, with applause and shouts of encouragement. Humphrey acknowledged that the campaign ahead was going to be difficult, but he declared that his role was that of a unifier, both within his party and throughout the country. His campaign would reflect that concern:

> For 1968 is not the year for frenzied or inflammatory rhetoric, or for finding scapegoats for our problems. It is a year for common sense.
>
> It is a time requiring in every person, in every post, in every level of leadership, maturity, restraint and responsibility.
>
> I will resist the temptation to deceive either the people or myself. I have been too close to the Presidency to believe that the solutions are simple and the answers are easy.
>
> What concerns me is not just winning the nomination, but how it is won.

Reaction to Humphrey's announcement was positive but subdued. Newspaper and television reporters welcomed Humphrey's entry into the race, not only for the experience he was bringing to the table, but for his contrast to the other candidates. Humphrey represented the current administration, and much had been accomplished during Johnson's tenure, despite the missteps in Vietnam. Mary McGrory, in a *Washington Star* column, called Humphrey the "safe" candidate, "the man in the middle for those who find Bobby Kennedy too wild and Gene McCarthy too irreverent." In an editorial titled "Humphrey Takes Responsible Course," the *Fort Worth Star-Telegram* praised Humphrey's candor and refusal to sugarcoat solutions to the Vietnam War. "By saying he would run on the record of the Johnson administration but 'not rest on it,' the Humphrey candidacy adds a new dimension to the race, which up to now has been a popularity contest between two candidates with, so far, one issue and one way of thinking about it."

Lyndon Johnson responded to Humphrey's announcement by exerting a measure of control in subtle but typical fashion. He made it publicly known that he considered the presidency to be more than just a single individual holding the country's highest office. The presidency, he said, included the president, his cabinet members, and other appointees, and since, as per his March 31 statement, he refused to enter into partisan packages, he expected the others to do the same. This was a strong rule, with consequences, said press secretary George Christian, who briefed the press in lieu of Johnson's addressing reporters in person. "I wouldn't think they could partake in partisan activities and hold positions they have and still stay in keeping with the spirit of [the president's] statement," Christian said, adding that no actions would be taken against three cabinet members (Secretary of Agriculture Orville Freeman, Secretary of Labor W. Willard Wirtz, and Secretary of Health, Education and Welfare Wilbur J. Cohen) who had already publicly announced their support of Humphrey, and Undersecretary of Agriculture John A. Schnittker, who was supporting Kennedy.

William Connell, speaking for Humphrey, shrugged off the edict, stating that Humphrey was more concerned about gaining delegate support than in collecting endorsements.

7 Robert Kennedy's uncertainty regarding his standing among Indiana voters was merited. A Gallup Poll, conducted nationally and published on April 28, nine days before the primary vote, revealed confusing, inconclusive information about Kennedy's base of support. McCarthy, as one might have expected, drew his highest percentages among the educated anti-Vietnam voters. Humphrey enjoyed his biggest numbers among older voters supporting Johnson's Vietnam policies. Kennedy, who easily won the African American vote, seemed stagnant on the war issue, with 28 percent of those opposing

LBJ's handling of the war supporting him, and an equal 28 percent of those supporting the president supporting him.

But interpreting polls could be like reading tea leaves, and Indiana voters didn't necessarily reflect the national mood, as Kennedy, McCarthy, and Branigin determined when Indiana voted on May 7. Kennedy, in a surprising vote, carried 42.3 percent of the Democratic vote, with Branigin tallying a disappointing 30.7 percent; McCarthy pulled 27 percent, a last-place finish but better overall than expected.

A scent of accomplishment hung in the air on election night at McCarthy headquarters. McCarthy had lost his first primary since New Hampshire, but the numbers, like those in the New England state, were encouraging. The Nebraska primary loomed in the near future, and McCarthy felt the Indiana primary had prepared him for his first one-on-one contest against Kennedy. "We've tested the enemy now and we know his techniques," McCarthy told his cheering supporters, "We know his weaknesses."

Kennedy, watching McCarthy's speech on a television in his hotel room, dismissed his opponent's bravado. He was enjoying a very good day. In the Washington, D.C., primary, which McCarthy hadn't entered and Kennedy had all but ignored in favor of campaigning in Indiana and elsewhere, Kennedy had bested Humphrey, 62.5 percent to 37 percent. The win in Indiana had kept the Kennedy undefeated election streak intact. Regardless of McCarthy's spin on the primary, there had been only one winner.

"Senator McCarthy says it's just another step in a series of steps, and this isn't a defeat," Kennedy said in his Indianapolis headquarters. "I don't know whether people think it's so good to be second or third. That's not the way I was brought up. I was always taught that it was much better to win. I learned that when I was about two."

8 In the very early morning hours following election night, Robert Kennedy encountered two exhausted young McCarthy workers at the Indianapolis airport. Both were awaiting flights back to their homes. Kennedy approached them and asked if he could buy them breakfast, and he somehow found someone willing to open shop and serve them. Their conversation was similar to, but much longer and more detailed, than his previous chat with the volunteers in front of the McCarthy headquarters. They talked about Vietnam, the inner city, and McCarthy's inability to win over black Americans. One of the two, Taylor Branch, who would go on to win a Pulitzer Prize for his book *Parting the Waters: America in the King Years, 1954–63*, told Kennedy that he

had his draft physical coming up, but that he had no intention of serving if he passed. Kennedy felt that he should serve if he were drafted but added that he opposed the war as much as the young man. Branch, who admitted to being "bowled over" by Kennedy and his honest, direct approach to the conversation, nevertheless informed Kennedy that he was going to remain with McCarthy. His coworker, a young woman named Pat Sylvester, said the same. Kennedy told them that while he was disappointed, he admired them for their commitment.

Kennedy's powers of persuasion, although not totally successful, left a profound mark on the two. They composed a long letter to Kennedy, saying that they admired Kennedy and further explained their loyalty to McCarthy, and saw that Kennedy received it. Kennedy, equally impressed with these two young people, talked about them for days after the encounter. These were the kind of young voters he would have to win over to win the nomination.

10 Nebraska

Expectations, High and Low

1 So the Indiana primary had settled nothing, other than to establish Robert Kennedy as a formidable candidate—if there had been any doubt of that. The Nebraska primary lay ahead, but Kennedy wasn't invincible. In a Gallup Poll published on April 27—the day of Humphrey's entry into the race, and ten days before the Indiana primary—Democratic voters questioned nation-wide preferred Kennedy to McCarthy and Humphrey, though Kennedy placed third when Republican and independent voters were factored in. Further, when those polled were asked whom they would vote for if one of the candidates dropped out, McCarthy supporters preferred Humphrey to Kennedy, 42 per-cent to 31 percent, and Humphrey supporters preferred McCarthy, 54 percent to 28 percent. This might have been disconcerting news to Kennedy, whose brother had scored his lowest vote in Nebraska in 1960, if not for his oppo-nents' weaknesses in the state. Humphrey was not on the ballot, and McCarthy, with only a skeletal organization outside Lincoln, was a nonpresence who had designated only four days for campaigning in Nebraska.

Richard Nixon, in what was deemed to be one of his strongest states, faced competition in Nebraska as well. Ronald Reagan, still denying his candidacy but adding that he was willing to listen to the voters, was on the Nebraska ballot; he would be providing an option for Republican voters finding Nixon too liberal. The big surprise was Nelson Rockefeller, who backtracked on his March 21 statements and entered the Republican race on April 30.

Rockefeller had been insisting, rather coyly, that he was not a formal can-didate but would run if drafted, but as the days ticked off in March and April and he consulted with influential politicians and businessmen and made public appearances before enthusiastic audiences, he became convinced that he was, in fact, being called upon to run. The events of the day dictated it. Nixon, he felt, held an advantage in foreign policy experience—not to be taken lightly at a time when Vietnam was never far from the national dialogue—but he also believed that he held the upper hand on domestic experience, especially in urban areas. The job ahead was monumental. Nixon already had great momentum; he had moved effortlessly through the primaries and had amassed a large number of delegate votes. Rockefeller had just over three months to persuade the Republican power brokers that he was the right man for the nomination, and the Republican leadership had not forgotten (or forgiven) his steadfast refusal to endorse Goldwater in 1964. His strategy for victory depended on his ability to convince his party that he, rather than Nixon, stood the best chance of defeating the Democratic candidate in November.

"The dramatic and unprecedented events of the past weeks have revealed in most serious terms the gravity of the crisis that we face as a people," he stated in his announcement of his candidacy, referring to the assassination of Martin Luther King, the rioting in the cities, and the law-and-order posturing that followed. "In the new circumstances that confront the nation I frankly find that to comment from the sidelines is not an effective way to present the alternatives."

2 The end was quickly approaching for Lurleen Wallace. She knew she was dying, but she tried to remain positive for the sake of her family. Her husband and children remained in various degrees of denial, even though, by the end of April, she had dropped to sixty-eight pounds, she was receiving morphine to block her pain, and she talked frequently to her husband and close friends about death, to which she was resigned. The cancer had metastasized, spreading to her liver and lungs, and doctors had to all but plead to get George to acknowledge the truth about her condition. He knew but just refused to accept it. One day, he broke down in tears when he walked into her hospital room and saw medical personnel inserting an IV into her neck; Lurleen assured him that this was not an uncommon practice. On another occasion, George tried, without success, to pay for doctors to fly to Japan and learn about a radical treatment that he felt might work. Lurleen tried to comfort George by telling him that if all failed, they would meet in heaven.

Aside from the terrible prospect of losing his wife, Wallace had practical matters to address. His campaign for the presidency had been interrupted more times than he cared to consider. Despite mounting criticism from those who knew about Lurleen's declining condition—newspapers continued to publish reports about her pending recovery—Wallace squeezed in some campaigning, such as a three-day, five-city jaunt to Texas, whenever it seemed that Lurleen had stabilized and there was no threat of anything drastic occurring in his absence. As for Lurleen's state business, the hospital installed a small office in a room across the hall from Lurleen's room. George would conduct his wife's official business, and when it was called for, he would take her papers to sign.

The enormity of Lurleen's suffering and final days weighed heavily on him. Whatever their marital problems in the past, the two had become extremely close over the past few months, Lurleen encouraging her husband to go about his campaigning, George reluctant to leave her side. He also had to deal with their children, who couldn't understand the severity of her illness or the inevitability of her death. On April 13, she had left St. Margaret's Hospital in Montgomery and returned to the governor's mansion to be with her daughter Lee on her seventh birthday. She would never leave. With medical personnel attending to her twenty-four hours a day, she stayed at the mansion for the rest of her days.

On May 5, with his wife deteriorating to such an extent that doctors advised Wallace that Lurleen was down to her final days, George canceled a brief campaign trip to be with Lurleen at her request. "I feel like something's going to happen to me," she told him. "Please stay with me." Her condition worsened throughout the day until by midnight she had lapsed into a coma. She died, a short time later, on May 6, her husband and children at her bedside.

George's life changed dramatically. With Lurleen gone and Alabama law prohibiting him from taking over her role as governor, Wallace left the mansion and moved into a ranch-style house. Lurleen's death had left George so dejected that he couldn't imagine living in the governor's mansion again. In the weeks following his wife's funeral, he canceled his campaign appointments and kept to himself, occasionally receiving guests or visiting Lurleen's gravesite. He would eventually resume his campaign, but he had no plans on when that might be.

3 Eugene McCarthy arrived in Nebraska with the same ambivalent attitude about campaigning as he had had at the beginning of his campaign in Indiana. The Nebraska primary, he told several reporters dining at a hotel restaurant in Omaha, wasn't all that important—nor were any of the primaries, for that matter, except possibly California. Rather than hang around Nebraska, a state all but certain to vote Republican in November, and a state where Kennedy was predicted to win the primary, McCarthy decided to spend his time and money elsewhere. Better to get a head start in Oregon, where he had at least a fair chance of defeating Kennedy, than to try to cram intense campaigning in the prairie state, when only seven days separated the primaries in Indiana and Nebraska.

"Although I hoped that I would not do too badly in Nebraska, I had no real reason to expect that I would run very well," he allowed in *Year of the People,* his account of his run for the nomination in 1968. "Oregon was the critical state and we had to concentrate our money, time and effort there, giving Nebraska little more than a quick once-over and hoping for the best."

Jules Witcover, one of the reporters seated at the table with McCarthy in Omaha, felt there might have been other reasons for McCarthy's dismissal of the Nebraska primary. Shortly after his defeat in Indiana, McCarthy had complained of the Kennedys "poisoning the well in Indiana," an indication, Witcover wrote, "of a growing bitterness on McCarthy's part." McCarthy had talked up a big confrontation with Kennedy in Nebraska, but McCarthy seemed to lose interest in the primary when Kennedy rejected his invitation to debate.

Most perplexing, perhaps, was McCarthy's decision to skip Nebraska's biggest annual Democratic event, the Jefferson-Jackson fund-raising dinner on May 10. Although Hubert Humphrey was the guest of honor and the dinner's keynote speaker, McCarthy and Kennedy had been allotted time to speak as well. This was a prime opportunity, invaluable in terms of exposure and publicity, and the closest McCarthy would come to a face-to-face confrontation with Kennedy. Witcover and the other reporters sat in disbelief as McCarthy told them he was flying to Oregon the night before the event.

There was at least one other reason for McCarthy's apparent disinterest in campaigning in Nebraska: he simply did not have the soldiers needed to go to battle. The number of volunteers, so strong in New Hampshire, was dwindling, especially at the local level. The Indiana primary had stretched McCarthy's resources as far as they would go, and the westward move was a challenge they weren't prepared to meet. "These workers were strong but they needed more resources—more staff, more money, more of the Senator's time. None was available," remarked Ben Stavis, who was now acting as a kind of personnel director for staff moving from state to state. Some staff were dispatched directly from Indiana to Oregon, where McCarthy hoped to set up a strong command post and organization to compete with Kennedy in two western states.

"Nebraska was Indiana only worse," said Arthur Herzog, who had been part of the McCarthy campaign since New Hampshire. "Indiana had been a vampire, sucking the blood from the McCarthy organization—every cent, every volunteer, every moment of the candidate's time, and for Nebraska there was nothing left."

It was not all gloom and doom for McCarthy during his brief tour of Nebraska. He enjoyed the sights and smells of the freshly plowed and planted farmland, which reminded him of what he had read in Willa Cather's *O Pioneers!* The people, regardless of their party affiliation, were friendly. He would remember one particular luncheon, hosted by a father-and-son team of farmers, both men Republicans, both intending to vote Republican in the primary, the son saying that in lieu of a vote, he was offering McCarthy "the next best thing . . . a typical Nebraska lunch—roast beef and strawberries." Such seemingly small encounters inspired McCarthy more than rallies in the state's larger cities.

The McCarthy presence in Lincoln, home to the University of Nebraska, was considerable, reinforcing his standing as the preferred candidate on college campuses—a status that McCarthy regarded so seriously that he told reporters, with a straight face, that he considered the national student vote a primary victory unto itself. McCarthy might have made a better impression outside of Lincoln and Omaha if he had shown enthusiasm elsewhere, but he was characterized as "tired, dispirited, and sometimes peevish," by E. W. Kenworthy of the *New York Times:* "His speeches were disjointed and dull. His humor was edged with sarcasm."

McCarthy chose the wrong time for all this. Robert Kennedy set up his Nebraska campaign with a single purpose: to defeat McCarthy so convincingly that the Minnesota senator would simply give up the fight.

And he had the staff and volunteers, the money, and the ambition, along with his victory in Indiana, to give it a good run.

4 The early polls gave Bobby Kennedy a twenty-point lead over McCarthy in Nebraska, but Kennedy was not totally convinced that this was the case. He liked his chances, but the state's demographics did not line up in his favor. Nebraska's population was only 5 percent black and 15 percent blue-collar—two groups that Kennedy could always count on—and the farming population, the few that voted Democratic, might be drawn to McCarthy, who was from a nearby state and who, as a congressman, had been on the Agriculture Committee. This was a state of few densely populated urban areas and a lot of wide-open spaces occasionally dotted with small towns; the logistics of personal appearances were going to be a headache. Published reports rumored Kennedy to be planning a whistle-stop tour similar to his Wabash Cannonball whistle-stop in Indiana, but Kennedy dropped the idea in favor of the traditional motor vehicle tour. His time in Nebraska was eroded by plans for a daylong trip to South Dakota, where he planned to make a few cursory appearances in support of the state's June 4 primary, and a quick stop in Ohio, where he hoped

to meet with the state's delegates and convince them to hold off on supporting Humphrey with their votes. His entry into the Nebraska primary had originally come as a sort of nod to his speechwriter, Ted Sorensen, a native Nebraskan who convinced him that it would be a worthy endeavor.

Sorensen's brother, Philip Sorensen, a former lieutenant governor and recent candidate in a failed campaign in Nebraska's gubernatorial race, helped Kennedy substantially in the organization of his campaign, setting him up with his Democratic connections throughout the state. Not that it was all that much—Nebraska had fewer than 200,000 registered Democratic voters—but once he had committed his name to the ballot, Kennedy went all out, as always, in his efforts to win. The rancor between Kennedy and McCarthy had escalated to the point where they were sniping at one another in public appearances and interviews with the press, although Kennedy made it clear that he now considered Hubert Humphrey to be his chief competition in the race.

While tooling through Nebraska, Kennedy found another group to add to his list of overlooked, underappreciated, struggling people. Small farmers, squeezed out or disappearing due to the growth of corporate farms, caught Kennedy's attention and sympathy. He was already aware, if somewhat vaguely, of the plight of the small farmer as a result of his friendship with Cesar Chavez, the Mexican American leader of California's National Farmworkers Association, who was leading a strike on behalf of the migratory grape pickers. Kennedy had initially been reluctant to become involved in the senate subcommittee hearings on migratory labor, but after meeting with Chavez and others, and hearing testimony about how law enforcement and other officials addressed the strikers and workers, Kennedy found himself deeply sympathetic with a large group of people who lived difficult lives involving overwork, chicken-feed pay, and disrespect from people permanently settled in a grape-growing region.

The conditions were not exactly the same in Nebraska, but the small farmers were being pinched out by forces much larger than they, working long hours in conditions out of their control, and quite often earning just enough to keep the farm from going under for another year. Kennedy loved the state's rural expanses, and he addressed some of the problems of farming in his speeches. It wasn't all Vietnam and big urban centers. He offered a lighthearted comment about losing his farm plan when the wind blew a sheet of paper out of his hand; on another occasion, he quipped that he was doing more for the farmers than any other candidate based on the sheer amount of eggs and milk that his family was consuming.

Peter Edelman, a Kennedy speechwriter and advisor who traveled with the

Kennedy entourage, noticed a huge change in Kennedy when he was in a rural setting. "With a huge, frenzied crowd he tended to be more emotional and to be a hotter kind of speaker," Edelman observed. "With a smaller, more laconic crowd he could tend to be sort of quieter and more playful. . . . The place where he could really be closest to himself—and he said this sometimes—was with rural people. He really felt that they, in a romantic kind of way, were his kind of people, particularly the farmers in Nebraska. . . . He saw them as a kind of forgotten and alienated American, another person who thought that this system had just left him behind."

Astronaut John Glenn, in Nebraska with Kennedy, felt that Kennedy's love for rural Nebraska stemmed from "the plain physical beauty of the countryside and square fields and plow patterns, and the greenness. . . . Spring out in the Midwest is a beautiful thing, and he was quite impressed with it. He remarked about it many times."

Whatever the reason, Kennedy was as relaxed as he would ever be on the campaign trail—and much more so than he would be in upcoming weeks. On Mother's Day, he posed with his mother for photographers in Omaha. In Bellevue, when a rowdy heckler was led away by police, Kennedy promised to spring him from jail if he was elected president. When the mayor of Beatrice presented him with a deed for an inch of the city's land, Kennedy caused a stir when he joked that he would bring his wife and eleven children to the city if he lost in Nebraska; the Kennedys had ten children, and RFK's quip confirmed a rumor that Ethel Kennedy was expecting another child.

For as smoothly as the campaigning was going in Nebraska, Kennedy could still be goaded into a confrontation. On the day before the primary, during an appearance at Creighton University in Omaha, Kennedy lost his patience with a student, similar to the way he had dressed down the students at the medical school in Indiana. During the question-and-answer portion of his appearance, Kennedy spoke of the disproportionate number of impoverished African Americans being drafted when a student asked if the military wasn't "one way of getting young people out of the ghettos." Kennedy responded in barely concealed irritation. The students at Creighton and elsewhere were able to use their deferments as protection against combat service in Vietnam—and these students would argue that they deserved those deferments—and yet it was acceptable for minorities unqualified for or unable to afford a university education to be drafted as fodder in the immoral war?

"Look around you," Kennedy said. "How many black faces do you see here, how many American Indians, how many Mexican-Americans?" He grew more outwardly angry as he went along. "The fact is, if you look at any regiment or division of paratroopers in Vietnam, forty-five percent of them are black. How can you accept this? What I don't understand is that you don't even debate these things among yourselves. You're the most exclusive minority in the world. Are you just going to sit on your duffs and do nothing, or just carry signs and protest?"

In an irony that Kennedy would have appreciated, he delivered his message to Creighton students in the hot, midday sun; then while addressing a large group of blacks in Omaha's inner city in what was to be his final speech of the Nebraska campaign, he had to cut his speech short when torrents of rain soaked everyone, including Kennedy, in the open air. Even nature seemed to be playing favorites.

5 At the onset of his campaign in Nebraska, Eugene McCarthy predicted that he would pull 30 percent of the vote: Kennedy, he projected, would not receive a majority. McCarthy's figures turned out to be largely accurate. At 31 percent in a heavy turnout, he exceeded his expectations far better than the polls had projected, and while Kennedy's 51 percent meant a majority vote tally, and a twenty-point margin of victory, it was not enough to force McCarthy out of the race. However, McCarthy did concede that Kennedy's win in Nebraska was a "significant victory." As expected, Nixon rolled over the competition, garnering 70 percent of the vote.

The surprises came elsewhere. The write-in effort for Hubert Humphrey took a beating, winning only 9 percent of the vote. That, along with Lyndon Johnson's 6 percent (he was on the ballot because the ballots had been printed before his withdrawal), indicated a sound rejection of the administration. On the Republican side, the Nelson Rockefeller write-in campaign netted a paltry 5 percent. Ronald Reagan, whose name appeared on the ballot despite his continuous insistence that he was nothing more than a possible favorite son candidate, collected 43,203 votes—21 percent of the Republican total—more than double what he had anticipated. "I don't know what political meaning this vote may have," he said, calling the vote total a "happy surprise."

Reagan was much too crafty to reveal his strategy. He had been governor of California for less than two years, and while he had shown a remarkable ability to learn on the fly while imposing his brand of conservatism on the state, he was not well known nationally, other than by face and name recognition arising from a television and motion picture career, and even then one had to wonder how much currency he could gather from such movie appearances in *Bedtime for Bonzo, Sergeant Murphy,* and *Knute Rockne, All-American.* Reagan could put his photogenic qualities to good use: TV spots showing Reagan the politician in California could be shown in Nebraska and elsewhere, with very little risk to Reagan's political future. "If this home-screen politicking stirs up a nice vote for him in Nebraska and Oregon," wrote columnist Tom Wicker, "it will embarrass Nixon and enhance the Reagan vote-getting reputation. If it flops, Reagan can always point out that he never set foot in either state."

Wicker also pointed out that candidates in 1968—most notably Reagan and Rockefeller—were using the polls more than ever as part of their campaign strategies. Neither Reagan nor Rockefeller could beat Nixon with delegate votes collected in the primaries—they were both entering the picture far too late for that—but favorable polls, especially those showing them defeating Democratic candidates in a general election, might convince delegates at the Republican National Convention to support their candidacy. It was a long, but perhaps their best, shot.

McCarthy, trotting out his customary nonchalance after the votes were counted, said that he was already looking ahead to Oregon. Others in the McCarthy campaign found the decisive Nebraska loss reason for alarm. The Kennedy Express was firing on all cylinders, and McCarthy's primary contests with him had produced discouraging results, with no signs for improvement. The surprise of New Hampshire and the victory in Wisconsin were out of the minds of all but the most strident McCarthy supporters. He badly needed to win in Oregon. McCarthy, announced Pierre Salinger, Kennedy's press secretary, was no longer "a credible candidate."

Or, more bluntly, in the view of Arthur Herzog, "the McCarthy campaign was on the mat and the referee was counting."

11 Oregon
McCarthy's Big Stand

1 Robert Kennedy believed that he had to win every primary he entered if he hoped to win the Democratic nomination. It was a tall order but a reasonable analysis of his standing in the race. He could realistically expect to pass McCarthy in delegate votes at some point, but the same could not be guaranteed about his chances against Hubert Humphrey, whose connection with the old politics ran much deeper than Kennedy's. It wasn't just about delegate votes, either. What Kennedy needed was the sense of inevitability that he might gain from a string of victories. No Kennedy had ever lost an election, primary or otherwise. A continuation of that unbeaten streak could be very influential, come convention time, not to mention its effect on the American public.

Oregon spelled trouble, though Kennedy didn't realize it at first. He entered the state so confidently that he assigned some of his top staff to work elsewhere. Larry O'Brien was in New York, Steve Smith and others in California. Although the polls indicated a tight race, Kennedy figured to beat McCarthy. "If I get beaten in a primary, then I'm not a very viable candidate," he said in a statement that he would soon regret.

But the campaign was poorly organized in Oregon. A month before the primary, Kennedy's headquarters in Portland, the state's largest city, consisted of two desks and three workers. Kennedy entrusted the state organization of his campaign to Congresswoman Edith Green, whose ties to the Kennedy family ran back to 1960, when she had managed John Kennedy's Oregon campaign. This time around, she was not nearly as effective.

According to Green, Kennedy faced difficult, almost impossible hurdles to overcome. First, and the obstacle most affecting Green and the state organization, was time. Kennedy's late entry into the race gave state officials only two months to prepare for the primary date. This abbreviated period of time was also affected by Green's having to divide her time between her duties in the House of Representatives and the Kennedy campaign. "It was understood that

I could not personally spend a great deal of time on it," she said, "but I would take over the chairmanship in name and do whatever I could in terms of persuading others to become actually involved, and will be involved as much as I could. But there was no chance of any day-to-day work on it, and, therefore, they would have to get other people."

When Green ran John Kennedy's campaign in 1960, she had had many months to introduce the candidate to a state that knew almost nothing about him. He had arrived with no press interest, and his early appearances were less than stellar in terms of attendance; he was well known by the time the primary rolled around. Bobby was well known when he arrived eight years later, but he came with baggage that would take time to work through. Jack had been seen as engaging, whereas Bobby was considered ruthless, especially in the eyes of the state's unions. (Portland's current mayor had been investigated for corruption and had been exonerated.) Further, Kennedy faced a backlash from Oregonian voters already committed to McCarthy, voters who believed that Kennedy's late entry in the race had been opportunistic. These perceptions would be difficult to change in short order.

This wasn't Kennedy's kind of state in any event. African American voters made up only 1 percent of the state's population, Hispanic voters even less. The state was white, middle-class, college educated, left-leaning independent, and comfortable. There were no ghettos, unless you counted a five-block section of Portland. The universities in the state, including the University of Oregon and Oregon State, favored McCarthy, as did Oregon's two senators, Wayne Morse and Mark Hatfield, two longtime, vocal opponents of the Vietnam War. (Morse had actually tried to talk Kennedy out of entering the Oregon primary, but even if he had been successful in convincing Kennedy that he would struggle in Oregon, the state's election laws stipulated that, as an announced candidate, Kennedy's name had to be on the ballot unless RFK signed a document stating he was not a candidate.) The labor unions, scrutinized by Kennedy when he was attorney general, had long memories and wouldn't be endorsing him. He would have to claw his way for votes.

He received a cruel education about his predicament throughout his first day of campaigning in the state. His appearances were greeted politely but with little apparent enthusiasm. He had a smorgasbord of appearances scheduled, from a business luncheon to a visit to a nursing home, from a chain saw factory to a high school. A visit to an antipoverty center was so poorly attended that Kennedy joked that he was grateful that the police were present to hold back the crowd. He was not going to have much luck with his standard poverty and inner-city speeches.

Pierre Salinger, Jack Kennedy's press secretary and on the campaign trail with Bobby, sensed trouble from the beginning. "The first twenty-four hours in Oregon I really had the sense that we were down the tubes in Oregon," he remembered. "It was very depressing, to arrive in Oregon. The thing was that nobody could figure out anything to do to change it because if you were going to carry on the central theme of Bob's campaign, which had to do with poverty and blacks and people, this subject was absolutely falling on deaf ears in Oregon."

After a few days of campaigning, Kennedy admitted that he was in serious trouble. "Let's face it," he said, "I appeal best to people who have problems." On another occasion, while dining in Portland, he complained that his audiences were "too comfortable" for his message. "I can't get a foothold here in Oregon."

His campaign style didn't help. Oregonians were straightforward, practical citizens with their own ideas about how a campaign should be run. They had little use for the soirees, teas, and luncheons hosted by Kennedy's mother and sisters; these gatherings might have gone over on the East Coast, but Oregonians found them a waste of time and money. Nor were they interested in photo ops or what they considered to be political grandstanding, as Kennedy discovered when he stripped to his shorts and took a spontaneous swim in the cool May waters of the Pacific. This was considered utterly foolish by folks who never considered swimming in the ocean until after August 1.

By Edith Green's assessment, Robert Kennedy's popularity, as indicated in the polls, slipped almost daily while he was in the state. He wasn't trying to antagonize people; they simply did not understand him. Kennedy, by necessity, split his time between Oregon and California, a key state with a primary one week after Oregon's, and Green believed that Oregonians were turned off by the newscasts of Kennedy in California, surrounded by masses of people tugging at his clothing and jockeying for positions that could bring them closer to the candidate. This was the kind of behavior they might have expected from their teenaged daughters, who just a few years earlier had packed the Portland Coliseum and screamed their lungs out when the Beatles sang "Twist and Shout." It was not appropriate for a man running to be president of the United States.

"I'm just absolutely convinced that the demonstrations over TV at night from California appearances, stirring up frenzy, pulling off cuff buttons and ties!—this just did not go over with Oregonians," Green explained. "I'd watch the L.A. crowds, where there was this frenzy sort of thing going on. It was just killing us up here."

2 Eugene McCarthy thought he could beat Robert Kennedy in Oregon. A casual observer might have wondered if he had taken leave of his senses. After all, Kennedy had schooled McCarthy in two consecutive primaries, and there were times when Kennedy's dog, Freckles, his state-to-state companion, seemed to be gathering more media attention. But McCarthy was no more accustomed to losing than Kennedy. Primary losses were temporary setbacks, not to be confused with the much larger picture. A victory in Oregon could be a gateway to an ever bigger one in California. There was no telling what could happen if he won these two states.

McCarthy's state organization in Oregon was much better organized than Kennedy's—and, in some ways, more organized than McCarthy's national organization. The state's two major organizers, Howard Morgan and Blaine Whipple, had a deeper understanding of Oregon's electorate than Edith Green, and they had had a lot more time to prepare strategies than Green. Morgan, the Democratic Party's state chairmen at one time, and Whipple, a real estate broker, had begun their quest in late October 1967, when they met with a group of seventy-five Oregonians and tried to hash out the ideal candidate to run as an antiwar candidate. McCarthy was their choice. A meeting with McCarthy in Washington, D.C., produced no commitment from the still-reluctant senator, but they had McCarthy's ear. The group had already begun to put together a presentation when McCarthy announced his candidacy less than a month later.

When McCarthy flew to Portland on February 1, he seemed just as disinterested in his candidacy as he had been with the Oregon contingent in October. Yes, he was now officially a candidate, but he wasn't about to change to accommodate the process. McCarthy reminded the Oregonians that they had been the ones to approach him about running, rather than the other way around, and that their decisions had to be based on what they already knew about him. "It's all up to you," he told them. "You must accept me for what I am or forget this romance right now."

This, of course, was before McCarthy's strong showings in New Hampshire and Wisconsin, before he saw what was possible and gained some enthusiasm about his candidacy. He was being forthright about not changing—he never did change his style or manner during the campaign—but he became more cooperative after he accepted the fact that he was being taken seriously as a candidate, that he wasn't simply a sacrificial lamb with a cause. Not that his attitude would have mattered much: the Oregon group worked tirelessly on its own, setting up fifty headquarters in cities throughout the state and organizing student volunteers to canvass every corner of the state—including some targets so remote that they were approached on horseback. These efforts illustrated a statewide resolve: to beat Kennedy, one had to outwork him.

This was uplifting news, coming at a crucial time. For all of McCarthy's optimism after the Nebraska primary, his national organization was torn and frayed, running low in money, plagued by skirmishes with the state and local organizations, in need of stronger leadership and direction. McCarthy, preoccupied with a tough campaign schedule, expected the warring factions in his own camp to work out their grievances among themselves. He was too busy to micromanage his campaign.

His campaign had lost its shine. It could no longer surprise people as it had in New Hampshire, or energize them as in Wisconsin. He was currently running like a thoroughbred that had led for three-quarters of the race, only to see the favorite charging ahead on the third turn: he could still win the race, but he would have to find renewed strength, determination, stamina, and commitment. The favorite now was Hubert Humphrey, and McCarthy knew that he would have to eliminate Robert Kennedy—just as Kennedy felt he had to eliminate McCarthy—for any plausible chance against the vice president.

Although he was adept at disguising it, there was an air of desperation in McCarthy's campaign style. His civility toward Kennedy had burned off somewhere between Indiana and Nebraska, and his open attacks became more frequent and intense. Worse yet, there was a personal animosity that McCarthy made no attempt to disguise. Allard Lowenstein, friend to both candidates, was put off by what he felt was McCarthy's open hatred toward Kennedy, a feeling that began early and deepened as the primary season went along. "It became clear as it went along that he did have a very profound hate for Kennedy, which was shared," Lowenstein asserted. "There was no less hate by Kennedy for McCarthy, but Kennedy, partly because of a lot of us that preached at him about it, behaved following his entrance into the race much better about McCarthy than his feelings would have indicated and certainly better than McCarthy did about Kennedy."

McCarthy deeply resented Kennedy's statements that only he, Robert Kennedy, could win the November election, that McCarthy wouldn't stand a chance against a Republican rival. "If there was one argument that was designed to make people stay with McCarthy, and that was designed to make people furious, it was that," Lowenstein noted. "It was the one argument that, when I heard it, I blew up over. I said that I just could not believe anybody would say that. I said, 'We started a movement to stop Lyndon Johnson, when you people wouldn't have a damn thing to do with it. And the argument that you people made then was that we couldn't stop Lyndon Johnson. Now don't come back to us and use that same horseshit now.' It was completely . . . apart from the fact that it was stupid, I mean, it was wrong, it was politically stupid because it had to make everybody angry. And, until it was too late, they never stopped saying that.'"

There was more, however. The "fact sheets" were still making the rounds, though not as widely as in Indiana, and McCarthy complained bitterly about the inaccuracies and cheap shots. The animosity had deepened to such an extent that McCarthy was taking the offensive in the battle of words. On his first night in Oregon, in what was not his finest moment in the campaign, he told a Corvallis audience that educated people voted for him, while the undereducated voted for Kennedy—a knock that offended some of McCarthy's own people. It got worse. On a flight to one of his campaign stops, when asked whom he might support, Kennedy or Humphrey, if he was eliminated from the race, he stated that he might support Humphrey if his fellow Minnesotan changed his position on Vietnam. The remark ignited a firestorm of protest within his own ranks, when staff members and volunteers objected to his potential backing of a member of the Johnson administration and an outspoken proponent of Johnson's war policies. McCarthy initially protested that he had been misquoted, but his statement had been taped; he dug himself in a deeper hole when he tried to explain that he had "no preference between Humphrey and Kennedy." This was no more acceptable than his original remark. McCarthy tried to mollify his critics by attacking both Kennedy and Humphrey during a speech in San Francisco's Cow Palace the evening after he made his original statement, but Jeremy Larner, for one, felt that McCarthy's misstep was a manifestation of McCarthy's personal dislike for Kennedy running out of control.

"It was a political necessity at this point for McCarthy to dramatize his differences with Robert Kennedy," Larner wrote in his memoir of the McCarthy campaign, "but we were surprised to see the pleasure he took in deriding Bobby and the power with which he began to play with his audience." Larner continued:

> Some of the attacks were legitimately scornful of Kennedy's "old politics" techniques. But the mockery began to take on a disturbingly personal edge. He talked as though Bobby were a fake and nothing more. He developed a whole new bit ridiculing Bobby's dog Freckles. Audiences egged him on, either from hatred for Kennedy or from a guilty need to feel they were on the right side in a contest of good vs. evil.

McCarthy's attacks, tame in comparison to the negative campaigning that would become the standard of electoral politics over the decades to come, were as personal as the rigidly self-controlled McCarthy allowed himself to be. He and Kennedy shared similar views on Vietnam, but McCarthy could chip away at his opponent by bringing up his past, when he had been part of his brother's administration. Some of the foreign policy decisions made at that time, McCarthy asserted, had led to "disastrous adventures" such as the Vietnam War. "These policies were not merely the product of specific misjudgments," McCarthy insisted. "Rather, they grew from a systematic misconception of America and its role in the world. I am not convinced that Senator Kennedy has entirely renounced that misconception."

It was a thorough, claws-out trashing. McCarthy ripped Kennedy for not denouncing the military, the CIA, and the Department of State, and he decried his silence about the policies of such leaders as Dean Rusk and Robert McNamara.

If McCarthy intended to use his criticism as a means of flushing Kennedy out into an open debate, it didn't work. He had challenged Kennedy to debate before the Indiana and Nebraska primaries, and Kennedy had rejected him, just as he was turning him down in Oregon. Kennedy felt that he had too much to lose and not enough to gain in a head-to-head exchange. He had no desire to antagonize McCarthy's followers in a debate or any other public exchange. He still hoped to gain a large number of McCarthy's disciples in the event that McCarthy dropped out of the race.

3 Richard Nixon was in the enviable position of being able to campaign in Oregon without the baggage and vitriol that plagued his Democratic counterparts. The polls had him leading the field by a considerable margin. In the primaries that he entered, nearly seven in ten Republicans voted for him. Any other candidate in any other election would have been coasting.

But not Nixon. He took nothing for granted. He would not be on the ballot in California—he refused to enter a primary with a favorite son candidate, and Ronald Reagan was California's—so he campaigned harder in Oregon than he had campaigned in any other state. He had competition in Oregon—he was up against Rockefeller and Reagan—and he did not regard them lightly. Rockefeller, he felt, was very beatable, despite the fact that Rockefeller had upset Barry Goldwater in the 1964 Oregon primary. Reagan was the opponent to keep an eye on. If Reagan won or did well, he might parlay his Oregon numbers with the delegates he would be winning in California and conceivably block a first-ballot nomination at the convention.

Rockefeller's indecision over his candidacy wound up hurting him in Oregon. When he announced that he was not a candidate, he also signed an affidavit to that effect in Oregon, guaranteeing that his name would not be on the state's primary ballot. Now that he was in the race, he would have to run as a write-in selection. This was going to be very difficult. Rockefeller had won the Republican vote as a write-in candidate in Massachusetts, but Nixon had not run in that contest, and the only candidate there was a favorite son. It would be much different in Oregon, where Rockefeller was far removed from his East Coast base of support, and where Nixon and Reagan were listed on the ballot. Rockefeller's only chance stood in a media blitz involving mass mailings and heavy exposure on television and radio and in newspaper ads. Since he had no intention of campaigning in person in the state, his campaign was all but assured of minimal to no coverage.

Ronald Reagan was essentially the same story but with one huge exception: his name would be included on the ballot. Reagan held firm to his position that he was not a candidate, that he was merely a favorite son in California, but he was steadily gaining support from the Republican conservatives, and for someone who insisted that he wasn't a candidate, he was certainly acting like one. He was sinking a lot of money into advertising in Oregon, and he seemed to be giving a speech or issuing a statement every day in California.

Rockefeller and Reagan's positions placed Nixon in the ideological and political center of his party. Nixon was comfortable here, away from the fringes, positioned in the middle of the big government versus minimal government debate, addressing people looking for a sensible change from the Johnson years. As the campaign wore on, he became more and more adept at avoiding reporters' questions that might cause trouble. He dodged queries about Vietnam, saying that his opinions meant nothing next to the larger goal of ending the war before the election. He skillfully maintained his law-and-order position without making it a black-and-white issue. His Oregon campaign might have been written off as just another yawn-producing exercise if not for a May 16 speech that added a new wrinkle to Nixon's centrist position in his party. In a speech titled "A New Alignment for American Unity," Nixon spoke of a new group of Americans—a "new majority"—that went largely unheard in the din of the country's turbulent times.

The core of this new majority, the "silent center," was made up of "the millions of people in the middle of the political spectrum who do not demonstrate, who do not picket or protest loudly," Nixon said, stating the obvious but doing so in a way that might be embraced by the millions who gasped at the images they saw on the evening news or complained bitterly at the breakfast table at the latest offerings in the morning newspaper—people who spoke at the ballot box. "As this silent center has become a part of the new alignment," Nixon continued, "it has transformed it from a minority into a majority."

A Silent Majority, as it would come to be known.

"This was hardly sensational new dogma," wrote William Safire, who worked on the speech and admitted that he borrowed the idea from a speech given by Paul Douglas, a former senator, "but it did show some thoughtful commentators that the man likely to be the next President was aware of some unifying common denominator in a society then appearing to be coming apart at the seams."

The idea was both simple and powerful: Nixon, standing square in the middle of his party, recognized (and would lead) a majority in the middle of America—a group silently searching for someone to give them a voice.

4 On May 24, just four days before the Oregon primary, syndicated columnist Drew Pearson and his assistant, future muckraking luminary Jack Anderson, teamed up in Pearson's "Merry-Go-Round" column, alleging that Robert Kennedy, while attorney general, had ordered the wiretapping of Martin Luther King's telephone. The timing of the revelation could not have been accidental. Pearson, a friend of Lyndon Johnson, was no fan of the Kennedys, and the release of this information, while perhaps not terribly damaging in Oregon, was bound to anger African Americans in California. Kennedy, wrote Pearson, had initially ordered the wiretap on July 16, 1963, but he dropped it when the FBI objected, arguing that King traveled too much for the wiretap to be effective and that blacks would have a "bad reaction" if it was discovered. Kennedy was supposedly concerned about King's association with Communists. Pearson, writing that Kennedy again ordered a wiretap in October 1963, claimed that these reports, along with Kennedy's denial of issuing these orders, were "very important in gauging Kennedy's qualifications to be President, and whether he is telling the truth."

When questioned about the story, Jack Anderson admitted that it was the brainchild of Lyndon Johnson. He had been vice president at the time of the tapping, and five years later, with his avowed enemy running for the office he was currently holding, Johnson was prepared, despite his public proclamations to the contrary, to interfere behind the scenes if it meant keeping Robert Kennedy out of the White House. "Drew got it from Lyndon," Anderson told RFK biographer Evan Thomas, speaking of the backstory to the Drew Pearson column. "Drew got me to confirm it with the FBI. Of course it was timed."

Kennedy did, in fact, issue a limited wiretap order, supposedly in the interests of national security, and he expected his actions to surface someday in the news. But a blunder by Pearson gave him enough wiggle room for a denial. At one point in the column, Pearson mistakenly substituted the word "bugging" for "wiretapping." There was a big difference between the two, and the FBI could bug without permission from the Department of Justice but could not wiretap without it. Kennedy consulted with a legal advisor, and they decided that a little misdirection might help defuse what could have been an explosive revelation: Kennedy would avoid addressing the issue, while his campaign staff would offer across-the-board denials, with Kennedy saying nothing to set the record straight. In addition, Pierre Salinger, Kennedy's press secretary, would firmly deny Kennedy's authorizing any "electronic eavesdropping." To the public, the different terms all sounded alike. Salinger ended the discussion by telling the press, "Senator Kennedy has never discussed individual cases and isn't going to now."

Eugene McCarthy used the controversy to continue his call for the removal of J. Edgar Hoover as director of the FBI. The attorney general, McCarthy stated, without specifically mentioning Kennedy or the column, often acted as a rubber stamp for FBI requests, including wiretapping. "Everybody knows that in a formal sense the FBI is subject to the Attorney General," McCarthy said, "but you allow someone like J. Edgar Hoover—it's as though he's not to be challenged. And if the Attorney General says that 'the head of the FBI asked for it and therefore I did it,' you have a complete inversion really of how the line of authority and responsibility should run."

McCarthy was not about to let Kennedy escape without a withering rebuke, and it came in the form of a radio ad in which a black narrator said, "I used to be for Robert Kennedy, but then I learned about how he bugged my brother Martin Luther King's phone."

To the great relief of Kennedy's campaign staff, the controversy never gained much traction. The press seemed to accept the denials and explanations, and reporters lost interest.

Kennedy wasn't alone in dealing with a public relations quagmire. Hubert Humphrey had problems of his own. *The Drugstore Liberal,* a Humphrey biography, was dropped by its publisher shortly before its scheduled publication date.

"We didn't publish because we didn't think it was a very good book," explained a senior vice president at McGraw-Hill, the publisher originally set to issue the book. "There wasn't any pressure from anyone."

The biography, eventually picked up by Grossman Publishers, was essentially a hatchet job, heavy on the negative analysis of Humphrey's career and light on the reportage of his achievements. The book's flap copy and back-cover copy made it clear to anyone picking up the book that this was not going to be hagiography. Its two authors, Robert Sherrill, a Washington-based correspondent for *The Nation,* and Harry W. Ernst, director of publications at West Virginia University, portrayed Humphrey as a political opportunist willing to say anything or step over anyone to advance his career. A quotation lifted from the biography, printed on the back cover of the Grossman edition of the book, alerted readers as to what to expect: "Humphrey is a very responsible and intensely sincere guy. He just happens to be unstable. He wishes everyone so much good that he is quite capable of promising everything to everyone, and as a consequence one side gets misled and hurt. It is lying in a way, but it is Humphrey's way, so it is not quite lying."

Unstable—not exactly a description a presidential candidate hoped to see connected to his character, although the word would be bandied about in future elections. Humphrey stayed mum on his feelings about the book, even when suspicions arose after McGraw-Hill advertised it and then dumped it. McGraw-Hill's spokesman explained that some ads had to be submitted to periodicals well before the cover date to accommodate lead times, but something didn't add up. *The Accidental President,* an earlier Sherrill book, had been very critical of Lyndon Johnson. Didn't McGraw-Hill wonder if he would be taking the same approach with Humphrey? In addition, book manuscripts are read by editors and vetted by publishers' legal departments before they are placed in production. At what point, then, did the publisher decide that it wasn't a very good book?

These questions were never answered, and the biography, when released, was a sales disappointment. By the time it hit the streets, Humphrey had moved on.

5 Oregon rejuvenated McCarthy and his campaign. If he had lost enthusiasm in Nebraska, he regained it as he made his way throughout Oregon, stepping up his schedule of appearances, putting more bite into his speeches, and presenting himself, possibly for the first time since Wisconsin, as the man to beat. The polls showed McCarthy and Kennedy in a very close sprint to the finish line, but both candidates knew that the Oregon primary was McCarthy's to lose. He was the aggressor, and he scored heavily in his attacks on Kennedy and Humphrey, whom he scorned as just more helpings of the old politics; he dismissed media analysis claiming he and Kennedy held very similar views. Kennedy and Humphrey, McCarthy told a large audience in Portland, were in a

sense chained to their own personal histories: "Each of them in a particular way has obligations to the past and is under some pressure to defend old mistakes."

He sensed a fear in the Kennedy camp. Kennedy refused all challenges to debate, including McCarthy's public announcement that he had purchased a half hour of television time for such a confrontation. Kennedy seemed to be avoiding him. Then, if he needed proof, there was a strange near-confrontation at the Portland zoo two days before the primary. The two candidates were greeting zoo guests in separate parts of the facility, neither aware of the other's presence, when Jeremy Larner spotted the Kennedy press bus parked nearby. He alerted McCarthy, hoping to confront Kennedy in front of rolling news cameras, and the McCarthy entourage started walking toward the bus. Larner sent three young female volunteers ahead, with instructions to block Kennedy's car in the event that he saw them and tried to drive away—which is precisely what happened. When Kennedy saw the McCarthy group approaching, he rushed toward his car and jumped in. His car sped away, nearly hitting the three McCarthy volunteers, his escape captured on camera for the evening news. McCarthy supporters shouting "coward!" and "chicken" at the retreating automobile. McCarthy, amused by the affair, boarded the Kennedy bus and visited with reporters. That, too, made the evening news.

"He just had this fixation in his mind that he could not give McCarthy any kind of basis for being on an equal footing with him, even though, you know, it was clear to the people of Oregon," said Peter Edelman. "So he saw McCarthy coming and he just, you know, clickety-clack in his mind, can't be seen with him, hop into the car and get out of there—probably afraid that McCarthy would say something snide, you know, in front of the camera or something, get some play."

Edelman and others in the Kennedy circle watched Kennedy weakening from the harsh demands of the campaign. He continued to work long hours, often sixteen hours a day, but his trademark energy was flagging; he looked exhausted and worn out. He was irritable. He pushed himself to extremes in the final days leading up to the primary. McCarthy was getting to him. He was especially sensitive to discussions about debating McCarthy. He could dismiss the idea with the argument that front-runners traditionally did not debate their opponents, but there was more than that to his rejection. Kennedy did not wish to discuss the Drew Pearson columns, and it was likely they would come up in a debate. Then there was the issue of McCarthy himself: Kennedy, by anyone's definition, was no intellectual lightweight, but McCarthy rightfully traded on his intelligence and would be a powerful opponent in a war of words, especially if Kennedy didn't have time to properly prepare.

Edelman witnessed a full manifestation of Kennedy's woes—the exhaustion, irritability, impatience with debate discussions, and the fear that he might lose the primary—in an especially ugly scene at the campaign hotel. Kennedy had been through a grueling round-robin discussion about his debating McCarthy—his advisers were divided on the issue—and after concluding yet again that he was not going to do it, he tried to take a brief nap before dinner. It didn't work. Ethel Kennedy, displeased about something, argued with him in the bedroom, and Larry O'Brien, on the fence on the debate issue but tending to favor a public sparring with McCarthy, dropped by for another word with the senator. As they talked, they could hear loud talking and laughter in the hall outside Kennedy's room. Kennedy, clad only in his boxer shorts, opened the door and encountered Adam Walinsky, Peter Edelman, and a couple of others standing in the hall. Kennedy took out his anger and frustration on the group, particularly Walinsky.

"This is a serious business and O'Brien and I are breaking our butts, and you're sitting around, having a good time, thinking this is a lark," he charged. "I don't see the productivity anyway. Why don't you get back to Washington, stay in the Washington office." At the very least, he went on, they could go out and ring some doorbells. Kennedy spiced his tirade with a low blow aimed at Walinsky and his guitar playing and singing on the campaign trail—a habit Kennedy didn't care for. The mortified men started to walk away—all but Walinsky, who hoped to explain himself to his boss. Kennedy slammed the door in his face. Once back inside his hotel room, Kennedy turned to O'Brien. "Those fellows need to recognize who's running this show," he said.

O'Brien found the incident "somewhat troubling." Edelman was less sympathetic in his assessment. "I was really mad," he would recall. "I thought that was very inconsiderate and very nasty to say to somebody who'd been so devoted, but I didn't say anything."

Kennedy was no different than other politicians when it came to evading—or at least delaying for as long as possible—discussion of topics he wished to avoid. One such topic was the U.S. relationship with Israel. Jewish leaders across the country were uncertain of Kennedy's position and demanded that he deliver a major speech on Israel, while Walinsky and Jeff Greenfield, as two of Kennedy's speechwriters, opposed it on grounds that Kennedy's views, while favorable to Israel, clashed with his Vietnam peace initiative. Kennedy's stance, they argued, was too hawkish.

But Kennedy also felt an ambivalence about the Arabs and Israelis that McCarthy and Humphrey didn't express. "He didn't feel, even though he was a senator from New York and representing a large Jewish constituency, that he could be pro-Israel to the exclusion of other countries in the Middle East," said Milton Gwirtzman, a member of Kennedy's campaign staff and, eventually, coauthor of a book about the campaign. "The Kennedy family had credit in the Middle East. John F. Kennedy had had relationships with all the Arab leaders. And Robert Kennedy had a sense about that. He didn't want to do things that would cause difficulty for him if he were elected president."

After the Indiana primary, Kennedy had delivered a brief position paper in New York, to be copied and circulated to Jewish leaders in the state. But the "small but significant Jewish community" in Oregon clamored for a speech of their own. Myer Feldman took the liberty of drafting a speech, which Walinsky and Greenfield—resigned to the likelihood of Kennedy's delivering the address, despite their protests—edited and partially rewrote. Feldman consulted with Kennedy and Jewish representatives and finally signed off on the speech.

Kennedy, wearing a yarmulke, delivered the speech at the Nevah Shalom Synagogue in Portland. Without naming Vietnam specifically, he made a point that Israel was "unlike so many other places in the world," that the United States' position was "clear and compelling": America was committed to fighting any efforts to destroy Israel. "We cannot and must not let that commitment waver."

In Pasadena, California, a twenty-four-year-old Jordanian American named Sirhan Bishara Sirhan watched the speech on television. Enraged, he decided that something had to be done to stop Robert Kennedy.

6 Oregon voted on May 28. Robert Kennedy had left the state by the time the votes had been tallied and a winner announced. Rather than hang around in Oregon for news that was all but certain to be bad, he opted to go to California for a day of campaigning. The week between the Oregon and California primaries would pass quickly, and he had a lot of ground to cover. The political topography in California was markedly different from what Kennedy had faced in Oregon. He was treated like a savior in Southern California, whereas he had to fight to receive any kind of notice in Oregon. "Sometimes I wish they'd booed me or kicked me or done something," he said on the day of the Oregon primary. "I just couldn't get much response."

As expected, Richard Nixon won the Republican vote, though his margin of victory was much higher than the numbers predicted by pundits expecting a much closer race. Nixon walloped Ronald Reagan, the second-place finisher, by fifty points, 73 percent to 23 percent, meaning he had swamped the competition in every primary he had entered. The Rockefeller write-in campaign had fizzled horribly, the New York governor managing a paltry 4 percent, far from the numbers he had enjoyed four years earlier.

Nixon was elated. It was time, he told reporters on election night, for people to jump on board the Nixon train before it left the station. "My chances of being derailed are pretty well eliminated," he said.

He now presented himself like a presumptive nominee rather than a favorite. A few days earlier, he had dropped his customary guard when a reporter asked him about possible vice-presidential candidates. The press might have anticipated Nixon's blowing off the question, which he usually did when he was called upon to speculate, but in this instance, he provided a short list of names.

Was this the new Nixon, as advertised by his publicity machine? The press had a right to be skeptical—after all, he was still stonewalling reporters when they asked him relevant questions about important issues—but even the most cynical of them had to wonder on the eve of the primary when Nixon offered a telethon that found him far removed from the man who detested television appearances. For two hours, in a program that featured highlights from his career, a very relaxed Nixon fielded questions called in by viewers across the country. Nixon's daughters, Julie and Tricia, were among those taking the calls, while Bud Wilkinson, the former football player and coach, acted as the interviewer, passing questions he had culled from those asked by callers. The telethon might have been orchestrated, like the rest of Nixon's campaign, but viewers were seeing the carefully constructed image of the new Nixon—a far cry from the man with the loser image.

But Nixon could find a way to drag gloom out of the brightest day, and it was the loser image that continued to haunt him. Despite the overwhelming results in the primaries, Reagan and Rockefeller might succeed in convincing the delegates at the Republican convention that they, and not Nixon, could defeat the Democratic nominee in November. After all, Nixon had been the Republican nominee in 1960 and had been beaten by a candidate with far less political experience and acumen. Nixon was irked that the press, who he had to admit had been fair to him otherwise, seemed willing to overlook the polls and his primary achievements and hold on to the faint possibility that he could still lose the nomination.

Ward Just, writing for the *Washington Post,* explored this angle in one of his campaign reports. Nixon, he wrote, "must be America's only major political figure who can win 70 percent of a state's vote and have the analysts talking about his opponent's 22 percent. Yet it happened in Nebraska with Gov. Reagan." If Kennedy or Humphrey had put together a similar string of lopsided victories, Just proposed, they wouldn't have been put through this type of treatment. "Why then are there so many doubts about Nixon?"

■ ■ ■ ■ ■

Eugene McCarthy won the Democratic vote, giving him a badly needed victory after two bitter defeats, and boosting his hopes for a successful effort in California. The final pre-primary polls had Kennedy leading by a tiny, almost negligible margin, but neither candidate took it seriously. McCarthy had been charging at the end, and with so many of the poll recipients undecided about how they were going to cast their votes, both the McCarthy and Kennedy camps speculated that these voters would probably be true to their Oregonian natures and vote for the cool, calm senator from Minnesota rather than the intense, hard-driving senator from New York. The final rallies, held the night before the primary, hinted at what lay ahead: a Kennedy rally, held at the Sheraton Motor Hotel in Portland, drew fifteen hundred people, while a McCarthy rally elsewhere in Portland attracted seven thousand. "That about summed it up," Larry O'Brien observed later. "It was McCarthy's state and he could draw five times the crowd."

The next day, in California, Kennedy was kept abreast of the primary developments, and the reports were not encouraging. Poll watchers indicated an early McCarthy lead—a lead he would never relinquish. CBS and NBC television showed McCarthy winning in the crucial precincts, and both networks projected McCarthy as the winner soon after the polls closed. Kennedy was boarding a plane headed back to Oregon at eight thirty in the evening when a reporter from the *Los Angeles Times* gave him the news. Bobby Kennedy became the first Kennedy to lose a primary or general election, a streak that extended through twenty-six elections.

He was strong and gracious in defeat. On the flight back to Oregon, knowing that he would soon be facing a throng of disappointed, depressed supporters, along with a curious press corps eager to get quotations for the next day's papers, Kennedy walked the aisle of the plane, visiting with those closest to him, trying to lift their spirits, exhorting them regarding the days ahead in California, even apologizing for letting them down. He had already discarded his earlier proclamation—that he wouldn't be a viable candidate if he lost a single primary—and he was preparing for what would be a grinding week in California.

Meanwhile, back in Oregon, his staff was contending with the unfamiliar detritus that followed defeat. Reporters wanted an immediate reaction from the Kennedy campaign, which Larry O'Brien handled in Kennedy's absence. There was also the matter of how—or if—to congratulate Eugene McCarthy on his victory. This led to a cantankerous discussion among Kennedy's lieutenants. McCarthy hadn't bothered with the gesture after losing to Kennedy in Indiana and Nebraska, a snub that bothered Kennedy and everyone around him, and this played into the discussion about whether to send a congratulatory note to McCarthy.

"There were two schools of thought," said Larry O'Brien, who was part of the argument. "The younger group, as I recall it, saw no reason to congratulate McCarthy. They reflected on what they considered an awfully bitter campaign, and Gene had said a lot of mean things. We, however, concluded that a telegram should be sent."

When he arrived at the hotel, Kennedy made an appearance at the ballroom for a final address in Oregon. He tried to lighten the mood by quipping that he was shoring up his campaign's organization by sending his dog home. He spoke of how he appreciated the state's natural beauty, and how he hoped to visit it again. He read the telegram that he had sent to McCarthy, in which he had mentioned that he and McCarthy could both "take some satisfaction in the overwhelming expression of the Oregon voters for a change."

■ ■ ■ ■ ■

Eugene McCarthy supporters celebrated well into the night. Nearly two months had passed since they had had occasion to toast a victory. Beating Kennedy, the interloper with a bankroll capable of outspending any candidate, was equally pleasing. When the last of the votes were counted, McCarthy had taken 44.7 percent of the vote to Kennedy's 38.8 percent—hardly a mandate but enough to restore the faith of those watching the McCarthy slide in recent weeks. Lyndon Johnson, on the ballot because he had announced his noncandidacy too late to have it removed, totaled 12.4 percent, while Hubert Humphrey, the write-in candidate, was named on a paltry 4 percent of the ballots.

When McCarthy eventually joined his victory party, he stepped into the blare of the usual assortment of sped-up renditions of campaign standards, played by a loud brass band, and the high-volume chanting of rhyming slogans ("Gene in '68! The rest will have to wait!"). McCarthy sponged up the atmosphere; this was his night. He opened his victory speech with the Oregon Trail metaphor he had been using since his final day in Nebraska.

"Every wagon train gets as far as the Missouri River," he said, "but the real test starts up the Oregon Trail." Nebraska, he announced, had been a place for determining weaknesses—in both his and Kennedy's campaigns. He came away satisfied with his assessment. "We knew who had the best horses and the best wagons and the best men and women, and I think we proved that in Oregon."

McCarthy was not about to step away from the microphone without getting in a dig at his skeptics, especially those in the press, the ones who believed that he was a stalking horse for Hubert Humphrey, or, more often, the ones who believed that his primary run was essentially a dumb show exercise that would ultimately end with McCarthy's turning over his delegate votes to Kennedy or Humphrey in Chicago. This, he promised, was not going to happen. The Oregon campaign had helped him define his constituency. "Our campaign here didn't bridge the generation gap," McCarthy continued. "It was solid all the way, and it will be solid all the way to Chicago."

The victory not only reestablished McCarthy's position as a contender, but it also reaffirmed him as a voice of the new politics. McCarthy thought of himself as conservative in comparison to his opponents, but Tom Wicker, in a *New York Times* column, called McCarthy's message "the most radical theme of any man in the race": "Far from being the 'one-issue candidate' he was considered when he began in New Hampshire, he now is challenging not just the war, not just American policy in the world, but the whole basis for that policy."

12 California
A Time to Be Born, a Time to Die

1 "I am not the candidate I was before Oregon, and I can't claim that I am."
Robert Kennedy meant every word of his confession. The Oregon primary marked the end of his grand march through the primaries, his invincibility no longer in question. His loss had jolted new life into the McCarthy campaign. Only a few weeks earlier, Kennedy believed that he could drive the Minnesota senator from the campaign; on election night, McCarthy was singing "California, here I come" in front of his cheering supporters. Analysts differed in their interpretations of the meaning of Kennedy's Oregon loss, but not all agreed that it had fatally damaged his campaign. Jack Newfield, for one, felt that the loss might have actually helped Kennedy in the way it altered his image.

"Once defeated, he looked less ruthless, more sympathetic, more human to the politicians and the press," Newfield wrote. "Defeat peeled off another layer of myth, and permitted a few more people to see Robert Kennedy."

"Oregon was the best thing that happened to him," Walter Sheridan, a campaign coordinator stated, "because all of a sudden for the first time in his life he was an underdog. . . . All the ruthless thing went out the window and from that point on, everything was uphill. Oregon was really the clincher as far as California went."

May 29, Kennedy's first day in Los Angeles following the Oregon primary, gave the Kennedy campaign a sampling of what it might face in California— or at least the large urban areas. After a press conference at the airport, during which Kennedy displayed a modest, almost somber side appropriate for his downfall in Oregon, he encountered a tumultuous midday reception in downtown Los Angeles. Kennedy backers poured out into the streets, running alongside the motorcade, reaching up for a handshake or any kind of contact with the man, clawing at his clothing, shouting their support, even jeopardizing their safety by running out in front of the car in an effort to slow it down. Kennedy, who had removed his suit jacket in the Southern California heat, was in fine form. He pressed flesh with as many people as possible, waved to those standing in the distance, and called out for their support at the voting booths. Scenes like this wore him down, but he loved it.

He also needed it. He had very little time to win over the voters in the nation's most populous and diverse state, and he knew, even as he was showered with confetti and ticker tape from the offices bordering the motorcade's route, that the days ahead would not always go this well. McCarthy did better in the suburbs, college towns, and upper-class enclaves; he was running stronger than Kennedy had anticipated, and while he didn't fear McCarthy, he accepted the fact that he had no margin of error in California. During his press conference at the airport, he again hinted strongly that he would drop out of the race if he lost the primary. He couldn't mask his disappointment over Hubert Humphrey's increasing delegate totals, which meant that the Democratic Party's two antiwar candidates were losing ground to the moribund status quo in the Vietnam War debate. The early polls had Kennedy leading McCarthy by a 40 percent to 25 percent margin, but the margin tightened every day.

Kennedy's strategy for California differed from his game plans in other states only in ambition. Already known for his energy and nonstop campaigning, Kennedy would be pushing himself even harder in California, making more public appearances, working longer days, flooding the newspapers and radio stations and television outlets with ads, outspending his opponent by a substantial margin, and, in his biggest concession to date, debating Eugene McCarthy. The best and most experienced of his campaign staff were spread out across California, with Jesse Unruh—speaker of the California Assembly and the most dynamic Democratic presence in the state, director of John Kennedy's California campaign in 1960—running the show. Kennedy was prepared. After the motorcade in downtown Los Angeles, Kennedy dramatically but joyfully declared, "If I died in Oregon, I hope Los Angeles is Resurrection City."

In Cesar Chavez, he had a strong ally to help him with one of the most significant voting blocs in the state. Mexican American voters made up 10 percent of California's population—the largest minority population in the state. Chavez, the charismatic forty-one-year-old founder of the National Farm Workers Association (later the United Farm Workers of America, after a merger with the AFL-CIO), had become a good friend of Kennedy's when the two had met in 1966, when RFK, as a member of the Senate Subcommittee on Migratory Labor, investigated the farmworkers' strike in California. The two had much in common, from their slight physical statures to their oversized dedication to human rights. On March 10, 1968, shortly before announcing his candidacy, Kennedy had flown out to California to be with Chavez when he ended a twenty-five-day hunger strike. Now, with Kennedy needing his help in the California campaign, Chavez was prepared to repay some favors. Using his influence as an individual and labor leader, Chavez pushed to bring out the Mexican American vote on primary day. One hundred volunteers canvassed the East Los Angeles neighborhoods alone.

After much discussion and argument, Kennedy and his brain trust chose to concentrate on his strengths during his limited stay in California. It would have been impossible for him to blanket the entire state—the return would have been minimal, in many cases, where the Republican vote was strongest—and rather than scrap for a vote here and there in McCarthy country, Kennedy decided to use his campaign ads to address those living outside such large ur-ban areas as Los Angeles, San Francisco, Oakland, and San Diego. He would campaign in densely populated areas. These were huge media centers, and the masses attending his appearances were certain to draw attention. These were also places where his campaign messages were likely to play best. Kennedy would make appearances in the suburbs, as well, in the effort to chip away at McCarthy's voter base.

Not that Kennedy received hero-worship treatment in every black neigh-borhood that he visited. In Oakland, after an exhaustive day of whistle-stop touring in the Central Valley that included stops in Fresno, Modesto, Sacra-mento, Lodi, and other towns, Kennedy met at midnight with a group of about one hundred Black Panthers and other militant blacks, none in any frame of mind to listen to a white politician patronizing them or offering promises that he would never deliver. On the way to the meeting at West Oakland's Taylor Memorial Methodist Church, Kennedy warned those in the car with him that the meeting could be rough. The African Americans in the group, he said, had "a lot of hostility and lots of reasons for it. When they get somebody like me, they're going to take it out on me."

Kennedy advised them to hold their tempers, no matter what was said—which turned into a challenge for black Olympic decathlete and Kennedy sup-porter Rafer Johnson, acting as one of RFK's bodyguards in California, who managed to keep his inner furies private while Kennedy was assailed as just another white politician. When, at one point, Johnson tried to apologize to Kennedy for the behavior of some of the black militants, he was scorned as an Uncle Tom. As rough as it was, Kennedy regarded the diatribes as an ef-fort to communicate. Kennedy listened to his antagonists and answered their questions. As it turned out, he was reaching some of them. Curtis Lee Baker, a man known by the locals as Black Jesus, held nothing in reserve during his confrontation with Kennedy. "What the goddamned hell are you going to do, boy?" he said. "You bastards haven't did nothing for us." Kennedy listened to him, and when he spoke, he did so directly, without any political double-talk or the kind of sugar-coated responses that blacks were accustomed to hearing from white politicians.

The morning after meeting with the black caucus, at a rally in West Oakland, Kennedy spotted Black Jesus in the crowd. Black Jesus, Kennedy learned, had been distributing leaflets asking attendees to treat him with "utmost respect."

"We thought this Black Jesus was going to be out working as hard as he could against Bob," Fred Dutton told interviewer Jean Stein.

The crowd was almost all black, and there was the Black Jesus. Only, instead of being in his flowing red robes, he was in black tight pants, black turtleneck sweater, African hat, and had a big long walking stick. He helped clear the way for us, and he was telling everyone who would listen what a great man Kennedy was. He turned out to be one of the best friends Bob had in the area.

2   Eugene McCarthy enjoyed some of the spoils of his Oregon victory when, the day after the primary, Kennedy agreed to a televised debate. To McCarthy, this was a major admission that Kennedy felt he was running behind, or at least too close for comfort, as they headed into a primary that might knock him out of the race. McCarthy liked his odds of beating Kennedy in a debate, and he believed that a strong showing would put him over the top in the California primary. He disagreed with the Kennedy camp's preferred format for the debate, however; that would have to be negotiated.

The polls, as usual, offered mixed signals. In a poll pitting Democratic candidates against the Republicans, released just before the Oregon primary, McCarthy was the only Democrat projected to beat Richard Nixon, Nelson Rockefeller, and Ronald Reagan. In that same poll, Robert Kennedy led only Reagan, while Hubert Humphrey tied Nixon and lost to Rockefeller. Another poll, conducted by Oliver Quayle for NBC News, had Kennedy beating McCarthy by 14 percent in California. What did it mean? Informed of the poll results, McCarthy responded in his typical offhanded way. He wouldn't predict a victory over Kennedy in California, though he said that he would consider the primary a disaster if he won only 20 percent of the vote. He declined to comment on his chances of winning his party's nomination, though he did manage to get in a dig at Kennedy when he said, "I think the Democratic choice is narrowing down to Vice President Hubert Humphrey and me."

The remark, a response to Kennedy's decision to ignore him and concentrate on Humphrey during the Oregon campaign, was just one example of McCarthy's antagonistic public stance on Kennedy, an obsession that had grown exponentially over the past month to six weeks. McCarthy had recognized the potential for personality conflicts when Kennedy entered the race, and his analysis had been on the mark. In an interview with *U.S. News and World Report,* published a short time after Kennedy announced his candidacy, McCarthy warned of the damage a contest between two similar candidates might cause to their wishes for peace:

> I'm of the opinion that our being in the same primary is not really a particularly helpful way to make the case. It would be divisive. The split that would have developed in the Johnson-McCarthy contest was on issues, and I think could pretty well have been healed. But in the case of the Kennedy-McCarthy contest, a division on personality may take place, which may cause people to leave us and not come back.

McCarthy's campaign strategy for California was similar to Kennedy's: hit your points of strength—in this case, Jews, students, suburbanites, the affluent—and secure their votes while spider-webbing out to other demographic groups. His organization was strong, closer to what he had enjoyed in the early days of New Hampshire and Wisconsin than what he had in Indiana and Nebraska. He had headquarters throughout the state—more than two hundred overall. The state was divided into two parts, Gerald Hill and G. W. Holzinger calling the plays in the north, Curtis Gans in the south. Television advertising and exposure were going to be critical, and while McCarthy couldn't dream of matching the Kennedy war chest for money assigned to television, his Oregon victory had led to a new flow of urgently needed contributions.

Further, Hubert Humphrey backers, with the blessing of the Humphrey campaign, contributed $50,000 to the McCarthy effort in a blatant attempt to oust Kennedy from the race. McCarthy was happy to accept the money, especially if no quid pro quo was involved. California was bound to be far more costly than any state in the campaign thus far, and McCarthy needed as much as he could scrounge up in his pursuit of the state's 174 delegate votes. As Arthur Herzog reported, fund-raising took a creative turn in a state known for its entertainment industry and quirky characters. "Only in California would a marijuana pusher contribute half his weekly take to the campaign," or would a daring young woman enter a topless competition, with proceeds earmarked for the McCarthy campaign. "It was a strange world," Herzog concluded.

McCarthy made a strong effort to court the black and Mexican American vote, with marginal success. The Mexican Americans, thanks to Cesar Chavez, were committed to Robert Kennedy, while African Americans, already divided among themselves, were split in their acceptance of McCarthy. McCarthy appeared in the Watts section of Los Angeles, in the Fillmore section of San Francisco, and in West Oakland; he met privately with black leaders. He fared better in the smaller meetings, where he could address ideas and concerns in a way that was more direct than he could achieve out on the street. Try as he might, McCarthy struggled to connect with those heavily influenced by the language and attitudes of the Black Power or Black Panther groups. His thoughts came across as so many words being bandied about by a white politician at a time when action was required. He lacked Kennedy's charisma. In Watts, a "rather small and inattentive crowd" of an estimated four hundred listened as McCarthy endorsed Black Power—with a noteworthy qualification. "The question becomes one of how you organize and what you do," he said, offering an obvious, generic condition that white Americans might embrace, but one which black America, tired of being asked for patience and more time, might disallow.

He would never escape the complications that his intellectualism presented. He believed as deeply as Kennedy in the importance of integration, fair employment practices, a major boost in education, fair and decent housing, badly needed health benefits, and racial equality in every social, economic, and political issue, and in the need for integration that broke the feeling of isolation that blacks experienced in the ghetto, but he had trouble articulating his thoughts in a way that didn't sound like they were being masticated and regurgitated by a university professor. Or, as Jeremy Larner observed, "He was light on detail, but his general approach cut to the roots of the problem."

Even so, McCarthy gained support in the black community, one black leader going so far as to record several radio spots for him. McCarthy fulfilled his expectations in the suburbs and on college campuses; he connected with the old Adlai Stevenson liberals. In a city like Los Angeles, where people spent much of their time in their cars, driving to and from work, radio ads, aside from being cheaper than television, reached a sizable number of voters.

"McCarthy was smarter, I thought, in some ways than we were," Walter Sheridan, a Kennedy coordinator in California, conceded. "He had a lot of ads on radio, on car radios. Every time you turned on the radio, it was McCarthy. You never heard a Kennedy ad. There were some things the McCarthy people did that I thought were very clever and very imaginative, and very, very helpful."

3 The eagerly awaited debate between Robert Kennedy and Eugene McCarthy commenced on Saturday, June 1—three days before the primary voting—on a special edition of ABC's *Issues and Answers*. Hubert Humphrey was invited to participate, but he declined. The hour-long showdown was set up for an ABC affiliate in San Francisco and was televised nationally.

Oddly enough, neither candidate seemed dedicated to preparing for the event. Fred Dutton, Jesse Unruh, Frank Mankiewicz, Ted Sorensen, and Peter Edelman arrived at Kennedy's hotel suite at nine thirty on the morning of the debate, armed with black loose-leaf binders holding briefing materials on the major issues likely to be addressed that evening. Included were McCarthy's past statements on each issue. Kennedy curled up on a couch, his attention ping-ponging between the task at hand and his suite's breathtaking view of San Francisco Bay. The weather was spectacular, and Kennedy wanted to be out in it. The briefing session lasted an hour and a half before Kennedy decided to head to Fisherman's Wharf for lunch, a bit of sight-seeing, and some impromptu campaigning.

The afternoon session was more productive, with Kennedy, as Arthur Schlesinger wrote in his journal, "in excellent form, funny, ironic, and very much on the ball." Surrounded by a roomful of staff and advisors, Kennedy went over talking points that ranged from his stronger subjects (the inner city, relations with minorities) to his weaker ones (the economy and, in a debate with McCarthy, Vietnam). Kennedy hoped to show that despite the age and experience differences between him and McCarthy, he was not the ruthless, spoiled rich kid, as depicted by his critics, but, instead, a knowledgeable candidate who, youthful age and appearance aside, was capable of handling the duties of the presidency.

McCarthy's handlers took a similar approach to preparing their candidate for the debate, with even more disappointing results. McCarthy was supremely confident in his ability to match wits with and defeat Kennedy in a debate, and he was still basking in the glow of his victory in Oregon. He had been to California several times prior to this latest jaunt, and the polls showed signs of his cutting into what had been a large Kennedy lead.

Thomas Finney, a politically savvy attorney brought in to oversee McCarthy's California campaign, worried about distractions: McCarthy was as likely to engage in a discussion about poetry with Robert Lowell as he was to concentrate on the finer details of what lay ahead in the final days leading to the June 4 vote. This, of course, was no different than what McCarthy's supporters had seen in other states, but California was too important for McCarthy to jeopardize with a blasé attitude toward campaigning. On the day of the debate, in an effort to eliminate the distractions, Finney secretly moved McCarthy from the Fairmont Hotel, where Kennedy was also staying, to San Francisco's Hilton Hotel, where he hoped to quiz McCarthy on debate topics. A group that included Paul Gorman, Jeremy Larner, Thomas Morgan, and Ben Stavis, with briefing materials of their own, grilled McCarthy and offered their ideas on how Kennedy might respond. Unfortunately for the group, the Hilton hideout was discovered, and in the late afternoon, newspaper columnist Mary McGrory, *Life* magazine reporter Shana Alexander, and Lowell invaded the Hilton and put an end to the preparations, which Lowell deemed to be beneath McCarthy's intelligence, in any event. McCarthy and his new visitors dumped the idea of preparing for the debate and spent the rest of the time leading to their departure for the television studio talking literature and reading poetry. On the drive to the studio, McCarthy and Lowell composed a new poem of their own.

The setup for the debate was a little outside the standard format. Moderator Frank Reynolds, joined by ABC reporters Robert Clark and William H. Lawrence, sat at a round table with the candidates and alternated in asking questions. A candidate would answer a question, and the other would have the opportunity to respond—a format, wrote Dennis Wainstock, author of a book on the election, that "was more like a joint press conference than a formal debate."

For all the hoopla leading up to it, the debate—the only time the two candidates would meet face-to-face during the campaign—proved to be a disappointment. With only an occasional spirited exchange, the back-and-forth was flat and uninspired, Kennedy and McCarthy displaying their similarities more than their differences. This was not an event likely to change minds.

The very first question, probably of no surprise to anyone, was about Vietnam: "If, in fact, you were President, what would you do at this time that President Johnson is not doing in order to bring peace in Vietnam?"

Both candidates favored a negotiated settlement, and both proposed a coalition government, but they differed on how the government should be set up. McCarthy, who answered first, suggested a coalition government in which the

National Liberation Front be included as a prerequisite to any negotiations on how this new coalition government would be formed. Kennedy, interpreting this as "forcing a coalition on the government of Saigon," strongly disagreed, stating, "I would make it quite clear that we are going to this negotiation table, not with the idea that we want the unconditional surrender, and that we expect that the National Liberation Front and the Vietcong will play some role in the future political programs of South Vietnam, but that should be determined by the negotiators, and particularly by the people of South Vietnam."

The disagreement illustrated the strong division between McCarthy and Kennedy on foreign policy, in general, and Vietnam, specifically. In recent weeks, McCarthy had been very critical of Kennedy and Humphrey, suggesting that both were part of the old politics of the United States policing the affairs of the world, a mind-set that led to Vietnam and other international disruptions. Kennedy, McCarthy felt, had watered down his opposition to the Vietnam War to the point where his views were converging with those espoused by Humphrey—and Johnson. This might not have been a fair assessment, but it was not totally incorrect either. Kennedy's long-standing dislike and distrust of Communism, dating back to his time working for Joe McCarthy, colored his judgment on solutions to global issues. But in portraying Kennedy this way, McCarthy, forceful in his criticism of Kennedy's taking an endorsement from Robert McNamara, conveniently overlooked the fact that Kennedy (and McNamara) changed positions on Vietnam when it became evident that it was an unwinnable, costly war being waged by military, rather than political, minds.

Kennedy was on safer, more familiar ground when he tangled with McCarthy over solutions to inner-city problems. McCarthy ventured down a slippery ideological path when he proposed solutions to inner-city problems that involved relocating ghetto residents to the suburbs, where, with the help of government money, they could afford better housing, a healthier environment. An incredulous Kennedy attacked McCarthy's ideas. "You say you are going to take 10,000 black people and move them into Orange County," he said, either disingenuously or sarcastically, since McCarthy had said no such thing. "If you are talking about 100 people, this is one thing," Kennedy went on. "But if you are talking about hitting the problem in a major way, to take these people out, put them in the suburbs, where they can't afford the house, where their children can't keep up with school, and where they don't have the skills for the jobs, it is just going to be catastrophic."

He preferred rebuilding the inner cities to relocating their residents. Kennedy suggested better housing, through the construction of new houses and apartment buildings, along with tax incentives to new businesses and industry in the inner cities, as components to a solution to the decaying ghettos. McCarthy, who had heard Kennedy's proposal before the debate, dismissed the idea as another form of apartheid. "The ghetto may have a few more factories and a few more jobs," he stated a few days prior to the debate, "but it will remain a colony."

The testiest exchange of the debate had nothing to do with issues and answers but, rather, with the escalating acrimony between the two candidates. The fact sheets about McCarthy's voting record distributed by Kennedy supporters continued to turn up in California, despite Kennedy's disavowals and promises to see that they would disappear, while Kennedy bitterly objected to a full-page McCarthy newspaper ad that tied him into decisions made while he was part of his brother's administration. Kennedy, sensitive to any criticism of his brother, was perturbed specifically by what he felt were distortions of his record. The similarity between the Kennedy and McCarthy complaints prompted a question in the debate.

"Senator McCarthy," began Robert Clark, "the McCarthy for President Committee, your McCarthy for President Committee, has been running full-page ads in California papers in recent days saying that Senator Kennedy must bear part of the responsibility for the decision to intervene in Vietnam, and the implication seems to be that even though he has been a war critic for the past three years, he should be ruled out as President because of his participation in that decision in the Kennedy Administration. Is that what you mean?"

"I don't think we said it should be ruled out at all, Bob," McCarthy responded. "He has said he would take some responsibility for it. The question is, how much responsibility? I was talking more about the process. I said this is one of the things we ought to talk about, is the process by which decisions were made with reference to this war, because one of our problems has been to find out who decides and who is responsible, and on what kind of evidence did we have this kind of escalation?"

"It also said that I intervened in the Dominican Republic," Kennedy interjected.

"That's right," said McCarthy.

"Now how did they get that?" Kennedy challenged.

"Well, I think they did. I had—"

"I wasn't even in the government at the time," Kennedy said.

"Well, you weren't out very long."

"But I—"

"I don't want to fault you on that," McCarthy admitted.

"And then it ran again today," Kennedy said of the ad.

"We stopped it—it may have run in two papers, but I don't think it ran twice."

"I saw it again this morning," Kennedy insisted. "I wasn't involved in the Dominican Republic. I wasn't even in the government and I criticize this."

McCarthy's attempts to counterpunch—by tying the Dominican Republican invasion to the Vietnam War—were weak. "What I said was that this was a process that was involved in our going into Cuba, involved in our going into the Dominican Republic, and also into Vietnam, and I wanted to talk about the process. In any case, I had not seen the ad. When I saw it, I said, 'Stop it,' and they stopped it as soon as they could."

Kennedy accepted the explanation, but McCarthy wasn't finished. He still had complaints about the fact sheet that he wanted to address.

"Would you like to respond to that?" Frank Reynolds asked Kennedy.

"I don't know to what he is referring," Kennedy answered.

"I have it in my pocket." McCarthy reached for the ad, but Reynolds cut him off. It was obvious that both men had legitimate gripes about the conduct of the other, and after determining that Kennedy and McCarthy were complaining about essentially the same thing, the conversation moved on to other issues.

Toward the end of the hour, each candidate was given time to summarize his position. Kennedy, unaware that he would have this opportunity, was caught flat-footed. His extemporaneous wrap-up paled in comparison to McCarthy's—at least in terms of content. McCarthy was smooth in his summation, but for viewers, his laconic style indicated a lack of the passion always present in a Robert Kennedy speech. The debate ended as civilly as it began. The two men stood, shook hands, and went their separate ways.

The debate received plenty of news coverage, but the media response was tepid, the consensus being that neither candidate had done much to strengthen his position in the race. Respondents to a *Los Angeles Times* poll, taken immediately after the debate, declared Kennedy the winner by a margin of two and a half to one. The hometown newspaper, the *San Francisco Chronicle,* might have given the most precise assessment when it stated that "neither candidate won a cleancut decision." The most emphatic—and negative—critique came from McCarthy's California campaign manager. "He flubbed it!" said a frustrated Thomas Finney, who believed that McCarthy might have blown his chances in California by allowing Kennedy to be the aggressor in the debate. McCarthy, Finney thought, wasn't in the position to take a low-key approach when he was running behind in the polls. "How can you get him elected?" he wondered.

Like two chess masters locked into a match in which neither has an advantage, Kennedy and McCarthy seemed to be satisfied to settle with a draw. McCarthy pulled out a boxing simile when talking to reporters after the debate, calling it "kind of a no-decision bout with three referees." Whatever Kennedy's feelings, he kept them to himself. "I thought it was fine," he shrugged.

But in this high-stakes game, "fine" was better than a "no-decision." It was probably enough to propel Kennedy to victory in a state he had to win.

4   By June 3, the day before the primary, the hyperkinetic days of campaigning were having a strong effect on Robert Kennedy. He was tired, and to those closest to him he seemed mentally exhausted, struggling to hold his thoughts together. His boyish appearance had failed; he now looked his age. His advisers encouraged him to slow down. His popularity had enjoyed a slight upturn in the aftermath of the debate—one poll had him leading McCarthy by nine points—so the onus was on McCarthy to close the distance over the final day leading to the vote.

Kennedy disagreed. That same poll had 31 percent of the voters stating that they were either uncommitted or undecided. This was too big a number for comfort. RFK reasoned that the uncommitted votes would swing to California attorney general Thomas Lynch, a favorite son running as a stand-in for Humphrey. The 18 percent claiming they were undecided concerned Kennedy. In the earlier primaries, the undecideds had tended to vote for McCarthy. Kennedy had a full schedule facing him on June 3, from San Francisco to San Diego, and he decided to keep it. The first events of the day—a motorcade through San Francisco's Chinatown and a luncheon at DiMaggio's restaurant on Fisherman's Wharf—were uneventful, other than an edginess caused by firecrackers set off in Chinatown. There had been a mounting concern for Kennedy's safety as the primary season progressed, and these concerns had reached a peak in California, where Kennedy seemed especially exposed in motorcades. The exploding fireworks terrified Ethel Kennedy, who had heard some of the talk about her husband's vulnerability.

His appearances in Southern California later in the day whittled down his strength even further. In Los Angeles, the motorcades were as lively as ever, finding Kennedy's bodyguards gripping him tightly to prevent him from being pulled out of the car. By now, he was accustomed to the physical toll his public appearances took on him. At the end of a day, he would be bruised and scratched from the grabbing and tugging during any given motorcade. His cuff links and tie clasps were ripped away; on one occasion he lost both of his shoes. The Los Angeles swing sapped him of his energy. By the end of the afternoon, he was weak and nauseated, and yet he still boarded a flight for a scheduled appearance in San Diego.

A huge crowd had gathered at the El Cortez Hotel, and to accommodate everyone, officials decided to divide Kennedy's San Diego appearance into two segments. Sick, dizzy, trembling, and "in a state well beyond fatigue," Kennedy rushed through his first speech, stumbling on his words and coming across as semicoherent. He cut the speech short, and on the verge of collapse, he sat down on the edge of the stage. He covered his face with his hands and tried to collect his thoughts. A half hour later, after being guided by his body-guards to a men's room, where he attempted to freshen up, he stood in front of a roomful of new supporters, his final day of campaigning in California merci-fully coming to a close.

■ ■ ■ ■ ■

The next day, he won the primary, as the polls predicted, though the vote was hardly a mandate. He won 46.4 percent of the vote to McCarthy's 41.8 percent, with Lynch taking 11.9 percent. When the voter demographics were broken down, there were no surprises. The blacks and Mexican Americans put Ken-nedy over the top. Cesar Chavez and his volunteer workers had come through for Kennedy in a big way: California's Mexican Americans had turned out in record numbers, and fourteen of fifteen had cast their votes for Kennedy.

Kennedy spent primary day with his family at filmmaker John Franken-heimer's estate, and, for a while, swimming in the ocean. The exit polls looked very promising, and for the first time since the beginning of his campaign in Oregon, he was able to relax. He had a long day ahead. Aside from the Cali-fornia primary, which would be commanding most of his attention, there was a primary in South Dakota, a state that might not have a large impact on the delegate vote total but that Kennedy wanted to rebuild his momentum. Shortly after six, Frankenheimer drove him from his Malibu estate to Kennedy's head-quarters in the Los Angeles Ambassador Hotel.

The mood in Kennedy's fifth-floor suite was festive. The South Dakota polls closed two hours earlier than California's, and when Senator George Mc-Govern called in with the results of the primary, Kennedy received a welcome surprise. He had exceeded expectations, taking nearly as many votes as John-son (on the ballot, rather than Humphrey, though it was widely advertised that a vote for Johnson was a vote for Humphrey) and McCarthy combined. The results were significant. Hubert Humphrey had been born in South Dakota, and both were senators from neighboring Minnesota; Kennedy was the outsider, a wealthy East Coast politician invading a conservative Republican state. Yet, as the *New York Times* reported, "Kennedy ran strongly with every segment of South Dakota's Democratic voters—urban dwellers, farmers, ranchers, miners, Indians and residents of college towns." To win by such a large margin, McGovern thought, was "remarkable." Kennedy, buoyed by adding a rural, white state to his list of primary victories, was especially pleased that South Dakota's largest minority, the Native American population, had voted overwhelmingly in his favor—and all this after only two days campaigning in the state and being outspent by Humphrey.

As the evening progressed and the California voting totals were announced, it became apparent that Kennedy was going to overcome an early McCarthy lead and win. The only question was by how much. The Kennedy group optimistically hoped for a majority vote, while Jesse Unruh, who knew the state better than anyone in the suite, didn't like the signs. Kennedy would win, he said, but the victory margin would be narrower than the Kennedy camp projected. McCarthy had promised to stay in the race, win or lose in California, so the men in the suite began plotting strategy before the final results were tabulated. Kennedy believed that it was now a two-man race between him and Humphrey—Kennedy delegate estimates projected Humphrey with 944 delegates, Kennedy with 524½ and McCarthy with 204, with 872 undecided—but McCarthy's presence in the race was going to make catching Humphrey that much more difficult. Kennedy would be devoting two weeks' time campaigning for the New York primary, while Humphrey continued to work in multiple states. "I'm going to chase Hubert's ass all over the country," Kennedy declared. "I'll go wherever he goes."

Kennedy huddled with Richard Goodwin for a discussion about the McCarthy situation. They were joined by Ted Sorensen, and the three mapped out their next move. There had to be a way to shake McCarthy. It was very unlikely that McCarthy would accept the proposition of joining forces at this late hour, but Kennedy felt he might reconsider if he were offered the position of secretary of state if he withdrew and Kennedy won in November.

"Even if McCarthy won't get out, his people must know after tonight that I'm the only candidate against the war that can beat Humphrey," Kennedy said, repeating a theme he had been using throughout his California campaign. "That's what they want to do, isn't it, to end the war?"

Kennedy knew that he had a difficult job ahead. Humphrey was much closer to the 1,312 delegate votes needed for the nomination than he was, and his only realistic chance was to gain enough delegate votes to block a first-ballot nomination at the convention and convince the Democratic movers and shakers that Humphrey, with his Vietnam War baggage, could not win.

The press, patient throughout the evening, now called out for interviews. Time was growing short for any hope of a one-on-one interview. Once he had left for his victory speech, in the ballroom, there would be scant chance for interviews. Kennedy would deliver his address, meet with reporters in a press conference, and move on to a private party at The Factory, a Los Angeles dance club. National television producers had placed personnel in areas where Kennedy was likely to pass when he left his suite, but Kennedy showed no signs of abandoning his privacy behind closed doors. When he could delay no longer, Kennedy agreed to two television interviews, both with interviewers with whom he was comfortable.

The first, with NBC's Sander Vanocur, could have been a rehearsal for what Kennedy intended to say in his victory speech. Kennedy jogged over the now-familiar terrain about the country's need for change; the unacceptability of the path being followed by the current administration, of which Hubert Humphrey was a part; and a deplorable disparity between the haves and have-nots in the United States. Perhaps most interesting, he spoke of the necessity of the Kennedy and McCarthy camps to combine forces in an effort to defeat Humphrey. The election results—a much closer margin than Kennedy could afford—were making this almost obligatory.

The second interview, with CBS correspondent Roger Mudd, turned out to be one of the finest Kennedy had given at any point in his campaign. A relaxed Kennedy seemed to be trying to dispel any vestige of his ruthless image; he displayed a humorous, even playful side—he was "liberated," as Jack Newfield described him. The old Robert Kennedy might have chafed at Mudd's pointed questions, but on this night, Kennedy, now experienced with the campaign interview, brushed off some of the questions and offered humorous asides or answers; he refused to take the bait when his interviewer tried to engage him in conjecture about his opponents.

"It appears, though, doesn't it, that you're not going to be able to shake Eugene McCarthy?" Mudd asked early in the interview, after Kennedy again suggested that he and McCarthy might work together "to accomplish what we all started out to accomplish, which was for a cause, not an individual."

Kennedy recognized the trap in the question, and he stepped around it without hesitation. "I think, really, it's up to him," he responded. Kennedy had suggested that his speechwriters include something positive about McCarthy in his acceptance speech; he certainly wasn't going to bash him in a nationally televised interview before he gave that speech. Instead, he chose to talk about how his primary victories, coming as they did from urban and rural states, indicated a national interest in a change from the status quo. When Mudd pounced on the transition and asked whether there was any way for Kennedy to draw Hubert Humphrey into a fight before the Democratic National Convention, Kennedy laughed. "Do I have to put it that way?" he asked Mudd. Instead, he took a firm but more conciliatory approach to the question. It was unfortunate, he said, that Humphrey had not been directly involved in the primaries, because he would have seen that the country was committed to a change in the current policies. Kennedy suggested that he and Humphrey come together for a serious discussion about Vietnam, the problems in the cities, and what could be done for the farmers. "I think it would be very important for the Democratic Party and for the people prior to the time we go to the convention in Chicago," he offered. "That's what I would like, and I would hope that he'd be willing to meet me."

After an unsuccessful attempt to draw Kennedy into criticizing the Democratic Party if it chose Humphrey as its candidate, Mudd returned to Kennedy's notion of his working with Humphrey, but not at the cost of compromising his principles.

"And you would not be willing to join with Mr. Humphrey in order to help the Democratic Party win if it comes to that?" he asked Kennedy.

"In what way?" Kennedy asked.

"As vice president."

Kennedy laughed. "In what order?"

Kennedy parried with Mudd throughout the interview, but his rebuttals were gentle and his declarations strong. He winced at the way his interviewer framed some of his questions, but he held fast to all his campaign's talking points, whether he was discussing his opposition, his party, his goals for obtaining delegate votes, or his immediate campaign strategy. This was Kennedy exorcising some of the demons of recent interviews, when the tension from the Oregon and California campaigns had him in less than optimal form. By the time the interview was ending and Mudd was promising to "work on my language for the next time," both men were in jovial spirits.

Kennedy submitted to two more interviews—one for ABC-TV's Robert Clark, the other for Metromedia News' Dan Blackburn—before returning to his suite. It was getting late, and the throng of supporters jamming into the hotel's ballroom were clamoring for a victory speech. Kennedy met with Fred Dutton and Frank Mankiewicz and discussed the focus points of his speech, and at 11:45 PST, he took a service elevator down to the ballroom.

■ ■ ■ ■ ■

The assassin, armed with a snub-nosed .22 caliber revolver, waited in a pantry leading to the ballroom's kitchen. His evening had been eventful. He had dropped by several election parties for other state candidates and had even wandered into a room where Kennedy's press corps was hard at work. Nothing about his physical appearance or demeanor suggested that he differed from any of the others happy to catch a glimpse of Kennedy—or, better yet, the chance to shake his hand.

He had been busy since the night he had seen Kennedy deliver his Oregon speech on Israel. Enraged, he had determined that Kennedy had to die. "My determination to eliminate RFK is becoming . . . more an unshakable obsession," he wrote in a notebook. "Robert F. Kennedy must be assassinated before 5 June 1968."

On June 5, 1967, the six-day Arab–Israel war had begun, with Israel launching preemptive strikes against Egyptian forces occupying the Sinai Peninsula and portions of the Gaza Strip. Fierce fighting also broke out between Israel and Jordan, and Israel and Syria. The Arab forces sustained heavy losses, and Israel claimed land in the Sinai Peninsula, the Gaza Strip, and the West Bank. The assassin, born in Jerusalem and raised in Jordan, although not known to be overly political, would later claim that his actions had been on behalf of his country.

He would have preferred to use a .357 Magnum, but he settled on the .22 when he visited a gun shop that didn't have any ammunition for the much more powerful weapon. He took the handgun to a target range and fired off countless rounds, perfecting his aim and learning how to fire as quickly as the gun permitted. He left his parents' Pasadena home, where he lived, in plenty of time to situate himself in a spot where he could shoot at Kennedy at close range. Others would say that they saw him in a number of places, including an area near the back through the kitchen when RFK walked from the service elevator to the ballroom.

■ ■ ■ ■ ■

The ballroom erupted in cheers and applause when Robert Kennedy finally stepped onto the overcrowded stage. He slowly worked his way to the podium, pausing to shake hands or say a few words to those assembled on the stage. His speech, watched and listened to on countless occasions in years to come, was standard fare, memorable only for its place in history.

He began by congratulating the Los Angeles Dodgers' future Hall of Fame pitcher Don Drysdale, who had pitched his sixth consecutive shutout, a National League record, earlier that evening. "I hope we have the same good fortune in our campaign," he remarked. From there, he was off to the obligatory expressions of gratitude, beginning with brother-in-law Steve Smith, who, Kennedy quipped, was "ruthless" in the way he worked on his California campaign. He thanked Cesar Chavez, Jesse Unruh, Paul Schrade, Rafer Johnson, and Roosevelt Grier. Playing the audience for laughs, he thanked Freckles, his dog. "I'm not doing this in order of importance," he said before adding, "I also want to thank my wife, Ethel."

This was the moment of relief, an exhaling from the past two weeks of seemingly endless campaigning. Kennedy needed no one to remind him of his uneven temperament during this period. His California numbers didn't match his expectations, but his candidacy still had a pulse.

Kennedy outlined his current position and the work ahead in the main body of his speech, which was largely a reprise of what he had said in his interviews earlier in the evening. New or not, his ideas were embraced by supporters inclined to cheer anything he had to say. It was a night for hope. Kennedy, once afraid of fracturing the Democratic Party by entering the race—and he had done just that—now pleaded for unity at a time when the country seemed to be unraveling in domestic and foreign affairs.

"I think we can end the divisions within the United States," he said. "What I think is quite clear is that we can work together in the last analysis. And despite what has been going on with the United States over the period of the last three years—the divisions, the violence, the disenchantment with our society, the division, whether it's between age groups, or over the war in Vietnam—we can start to work together again. We are a good country, an unselfish country, and a compassionate country."

Kennedy concluded by thanking all of the unnamed, unrecognized, and underappreciated supporters who had labored behind the scenes, working to keep his name in front of the voters, encouraging people to get out to vote, volunteering to do the thankless jobs.

"I was a campaign manager eight years ago and I know what a difference that kind of effort and that kind of commitment can make. So, my thanks to all of you, and it's on to Chicago, and let's win there."

He punctuated the end of his speech with a wave to the hall full of people, followed by his flashing two fingers in a victory or peace salute. Kennedy, offering a toothy smile, leaned over the edge of the stage or touched hands reaching up to him. His backers shouted, "We want Kennedy! We want Kennedy! . . ."

He drank it all in for a few moments, then turned to go. He still had more evening ahead. During his speech, he had joked about Los Angeles mayor Sam Yorty, no friend to the Kennedys, wanting him to wrap things up. It was time.

5   When Robert Kennedy stepped away from the lectern at the completion of his speech, he made a decision based on time and convenience. He was scheduled to meet, first, with an overflow of supporters who had watched his victory speech on closed-circuit television, and, second, with the press in another room at the hotel. Kennedy decided to skip the gathering of supporters. Time was an important factor: it was already after 3:00 a.m. on the East Coast, and to reporters struggling to meet deadlines on a story as important as Kennedy's California victory, every minute was crucial. Under the usual circumstances, Kennedy would have left after the rally the way he came in, by making his way through a mass of supporters; this would have taken a substantial period of time. Rather than make reporters wait an inordinate amount of time for his arrival, Kennedy and some of his aides decided to leave through the kitchen attached to the ballroom. Kennedy would still be encountering people, but nowhere near the numbers he would have to go through if he left in his customary way. Nor was this the first time he had left this way; he had gone through a kitchen as recently as a rally in Oregon.

The noise and bedlam contributed to all that followed. The crowd, seeing Kennedy leaving, surged forward, and some of Kennedy's aides were caught up in the crush. Bill Barry and Rosey Grier, always at Kennedy's side as security in rallies such as this, assisted Kennedy's pregnant wife from a three-foot riser to the stage and were temporarily separated from the candidate, who was moving toward the kitchen at a brisk pace. Karl Uecker, the Ambassador Hotel's assistant manager, guided Kennedy while Kennedy answered Mutual Radio reporter Andrew West's questions as they walked. In the pantry leading to the kitchen, a group of well-wishers shouted greetings or held out hands for contact with Kennedy. For as wild as it seemed, the scene was not that different from what Kennedy had been experiencing throughout his campaign in California.

Not that there wasn't constant concern about the senator's safety. Bobby was always at loggerheads with those trying to protect him. As a champion of the minorities, the poor, the neglected, and society's underdogs, he was keenly aware of the effect a strong police presence had on this constituency, and he turned down police protection as a matter of personal policy. Nor was he happy with those who attempted to create distance between him and his supporters. He wanted the physical contact. He knew as well as anyone of the risks he was taking. He spoke often to those closest to him about his fear of being assassinated like his brother, but he refused to compromise his campaign style to accommodate those fears. "If anyone wants to kill me, it won't be difficult," he insisted.

Kennedy continued his interview with Andrew West as they walked through the pantry. He had just begun to answer a question about his strategy for countering Humphrey's growing delegate count when a young man, later identified as Sirhan Sirhan, rushed forward and fired a series of shots from a .22 caliber Iver Johnson Cadet revolver. One shot, fired at Kennedy from a distance of no more than a few feet, tore into Kennedy's skull and became lodged in his brain. Kennedy collapsed to the floor, although he remained conscious. The pop-pop-pop-pop-popping of the handgun reminded many in the room of the sound of firecrackers, bursting balloons, or even the sound of caps used in toy guns. Bill Barry, Rosey Grier, Rafer Johnson, author/editor George Plimpton, and others fought to subdue Sirhan and wrestle him to the floor, while Ethel Kennedy worked her way to her husband's side. Horrified and angry witnesses attempted to reach Sirhan, but their efforts were thwarted by others fearful of a repeat of Jack Ruby's killing of Lee Harvey Oswald two days after John Kennedy's assassination. News photographers jockeyed for positions to take pictures of the mortally wounded presidential candidate, the most enduring photo depicting Kennedy on the floor, his head propped up by Juan Romero, a young kitchen worker who offered him a rosary. Sirhan Sirhan had used up all eight bullets in his gun's chambers; besides Kennedy, five others had been hit, though none of their injuries were life threatening.

Kennedy remained conscious for most of the ten minutes it took for an ambulance to arrive. He said very little, although he did inquire about whether everyone else was all right. Ethel stayed with him, stroking his forehead and asking gawkers and photographers to stand back and give him room to breathe. Outside in the ballroom, word spread quickly of the shootings that had occurred. Most of Kennedy's supporters had hung around to celebrate his victory; they now shuffled about in disbelief. They knew that Kennedy was still alive—there was a constant call for any doctor in the house—but it was hard to comprehend that a second Kennedy in five years had been gunned down in public. They reluctantly left the hall when Kennedy aides asked them to leave, but many were still around when an ambulance finally arrived.

Two hospital attendants placed Kennedy on a gurney. "Gently, gently," Ethel pleaded. "Don't lift me, don't lift me. Oh, no, no," Kennedy whispered, "don't." He lost consciousness when he was being taken out and loaded into the ambulance. He would never regain it.

6 Eugene McCarthy, watching the returns in his ninth-floor suite in the Beverly Hilton Hotel, found it odd that Robert Kennedy would be giving his victory speech before the California primary totals were final. He was enough of a realist to accept the likelihood of a Kennedy win—he and members of his staff had begun composing a congratulatory telegram about the time Kennedy gave his speech—but it was still mathematically possible, as unlikely as it seemed, that he could rally and squeak by.

California had been a rough, exhausting campaign, but McCarthy was unbowed, even in defeat. The Kennedy camp had made it known that Robert Kennedy was still interested in joining forces with McCarthy in an effort to derail Hubert Humphrey, but McCarthy wouldn't consider it. After all, *he* had been the one to challenge not only a powerful sitting president but also the system that got him elected. *He* had defied the cynics by staging a grassroots campaign unlike any in American history—a campaign that successfully drove an unpopular president out of office. Kennedy had done none of this, yet here he was, as much a product of the established order of business as Johnson or Humphrey, on the cusp of his most impressive victory to date, sweeping McCarthy to the limits of relevance. This was a bitter defeat, but McCarthy vowed to stay in the race.

Then, in a way he had not foreseen, it ended. CBS reporter David Schoumacher interrupted McCarthy's composition of his congratulatory telegram with the news of the shooting. He had almost nothing in terms of details, but he assured McCarthy that he would keep him informed.

McCarthy, joined by his wife and two of his daughters, took a seat in the corner of the room. Violence was always shocking, but in this instance it had stunned him into further contemplation about the process of electing the individual holding the highest office in the country. "Maybe we should do it in a different way," he thought out loud. "Maybe we should have the English system of having the Cabinet choose the president. There must be some other way."

The next morning, upon hearing that Kennedy's condition had deteriorated to such depths that he was not expected to live, McCarthy decided to visit Ted and Ethel Kennedy at the hospital before catching a flight back to Washington, D.C. Remaining in Los Angeles, with its deeply depressing environment and the outside possibility that there might be an attempt on the lives of others, was out of the question. The police escorted his car to the hospital, but Robert Kennedy's wife and brother were both napping. McCarthy left for the airport without seeing them.

■ ■ ■ ■ ■

Hubert Humphrey was sleeping in the officers' quarters at the Air Force Academy in Colorado Springs when one of his aides, D. J. Leary, awakened him with the news that Robert Kennedy had been shot. Humphrey was in Colorado to deliver a commencement address at the academy the next day. He had kept close watch on the California returns, knowing that the results would impact his campaign. On the ride in from the airport, Humphrey had talked with an aide, Ted Van Dyk, about what he hoped to see happen in the California primary. It would be best, Humphrey speculated, if Kennedy won convincingly. As Humphrey saw it, Kennedy had alienated too many of his party's leaders for any chance of a nomination at the convention; he would lose, and being a good party man, he would support Humphrey, if for no other reason than to show party loyalty. Humphrey would need the minority vote to defeat Nixon, and Kennedy could deliver it. McCarthy, on the other hand, was not nearly as predictable, regardless of his and Humphrey's twenty-year personal and political friendship. "If he wins tonight, he'll plague Bobby and me all the way to the convention," Humphrey predicted.

The primary results had not been announced when Humphrey decided to turn in for the night. A half hour later, Leary burst into the room and shook him awake. "Mr. Vice President, Mr. Vice President, they hit Bobby, they hit Bobby," a trembling Leary said. "They shot Senator Kennedy."

Humphrey, still in a sleepy haze, initially thought Leary was joking, but when he walked into the parlor, switched on the television, saw the reports, and watched Secret Service agents and his aides drift into the room, he realized that Kennedy had, indeed, been shot. He was told that Kennedy had been rushed to a hospital and that his would-be assassin was in police custody. With television news reports sketchy on the specifics of the shooting, Humphrey hoped that the senator hadn't been seriously injured. A call to Pierre Salinger informed him otherwise. Salinger, sobbing as he spoke, told Humphrey that Kennedy had been shot in the head and was in very grave condition.

Humphrey was joined by his personal physician, Edgar Berman, who had traveled with him to Colorado. Berman talked to a neurosurgeon at the hospital and learned about the extent of the injuries to Kennedy's brain. In the unlikely event that he survived, Kennedy would suffer permanent disability, physically and mentally. During Berman's conversation with the surgeon, Humphrey called Ted Kennedy, who asked if there was any way Humphrey could arrange to fly in James Poppen, a neurosurgeon and Kennedy family friend in Boston. Humphrey advised the youngest Kennedy brother—and quite likely the last surviving one, given Bobby's worsening condition—that he would see that it was done. He called the operations officer at the Air Force Academy and requested a plane to be dispatched to Boston. The officer, following protocol, asked who had authorized the order. "I am Vice-Commander-in-Chief," Humphrey shouted angrily, creating a nonexistent position on the spot, and the officer, rather than challenge him further, agreed to send the plane.

Humphrey pressed on. He ordered a plane to pick up several of Kennedy's children and bring them to Los Angeles. If the president had any problem with the orders, Humphrey would deal with it later. All that mattered now was immediate action. It was a depressing position to be in. Only a few hours earlier, he and Kennedy had been adversaries, perhaps bitter ones, but all he could think of now were the needs of a friend and former colleague, fighting for his life, and the needs of the people he loved. He would grapple with politics on another day, under other circumstances.

Aside from the Kennedy concerns, Humphrey had a personal matter to address: in hours, he was scheduled to address graduates of the Air Force Academy. He couldn't imagine delivering a speech under these circumstances. It might seem disrespectful, especially if Kennedy died before he gave the address, and it was likely that his appearance would be judged as a political maneuver. Humphrey placed a late-night call to the academy and canceled his appearance.

But it wasn't over. A few hours later, Humphrey was visited by Air Force Secretary Harold Brown, Chief of Staff John McConnell, and other air force brass. Humphrey was in the bathroom, half-dressed and standing at the sink, shaving, when his visitors arrived. The men asked Humphrey to reconsider his decision. "It's the manly thing to do," they told him. "Stand up at a moment of adversity. These are our future officers preparing to go off to battle. They deserve to have a commitment honored."

"Brown emphasized the importance of it to the academy [and] the morale of the Air Force," said Edgar Berman, who was present during the meeting. "I saw Humphrey's gorge rising by the chill in his eyes."

Humphrey could barely keep his composure when McConnell brought up the angry, critical letters he received about Vietnam. "General," he responded, "I get those letters, too. I get one hell of a lot of letters."

The meeting was over. Humphrey repeated emphatically that he would not be giving the commencement address. Then he invited them to leave—the sooner, the better.

■ ■ ■ ■ ■

At 7:25 on the morning of June 5, Frank Mankiewicz stood before reporters in a makeshift press room at the Good Samaritan Hospital. His grim expression left no doubt about the severity of his message. He had addressed the press at 4:45 a.m., delivering the message that a team of surgeons was working on Robert Kennedy's brain. Kennedy's vital signs—heartbeat, blood pressure, and respiration—had stabilized, and surgeons were working on removing bone and bullet fragments from his brain. What he did not say, either because he didn't know or because it wasn't time to inform the public, was that Kennedy had been in "extremely critical" condition when he was transferred to Good Samaritan from Central Receiving Hospital. He had lost a large volume of blood between the time he was shot and his arrival at Central, his pulse was very weak, his breathing shallow, and his blood pressure so low that hospital personnel struggled to get any reading. He had been shot in two places. The lesser of the wounds had entered his right armpit and worked its way upward, finally lodging in his neck. The other bullet had entered his head from behind his right ear. The efforts of the Central Receiving staff had brought enough stability to permit his transfer to surgery at Good Samaritan, though the prognosis for his survival was very low, and the chances for a complete recovery were zero.

Still, after three hours and forty minutes of surgery, Dr. Henry Cuneo, a neurosurgeon from the University of Southern California School of Medicine overseeing the operation, was optimistic enough to say that Kennedy had "stabilized pretty well"—which was essentially the message that Mankiewicz delivered to the press when the surgery was completed. Mankiewicz, however, was cautious in describing Kennedy's condition. On a positive note, Kennedy was breathing on his own; on the other hand, his brain had been denied the blood supply necessary to govern physical processes, and there was no telling how his vital signs would be affected. The next twelve to thirty-six hours were crucial to the senator's survival.

▪ ▪ ▪ ▪ ▪

Los Angeles mayor Sam Yorty, whose love of publicity was legend among the news media, held a supposedly impromptu press briefing in the early afternoon. Since there was nothing new to report on Robert Kennedy's condition, the press was starving for any available information on the man who shot him. The suspect, identified as Sirhan Bishara Sirhan, had been in police custody, under heavy guard, since his arrest at the Ambassador Hotel. Attempts at interrogating him were coming up empty; he answered an innocuous question here and there, but he remained silent on his motives for shooting Kennedy and on details of the time leading up to the shooting. The police located his residence and talked to members of his family. No one else seemed to be involved, and the family cooperated to the best of their ability. Police searched Sirhan's room and came up with the mother lode of evidence: journals outlining Sirhan's intentions of murdering Robert Kennedy.

A police inspector fed the media selected details about the law enforcement efforts, but he was cautious about providing information that might hinder further police investigations and about making statements that might blow the case up in court. He spoke of Sirhan's two brothers, who had voluntarily visited the police station, and said that Munir Sirhan spoke of his brother's purchasing the weapon he had used to shoot Kennedy, that Sirhan Sirhan attended Pasadena City College, worked as an exercise boy at Hollywood Park, and spoke other languages, including Russian. Whenever asked about Sirhan's motives for shooting Kennedy, the police inspector admitted that he had spoken to Munir Sirhan about possible political motives, but he, the inspector, had no wish to say more about it.

As if on cue, Mayor Yorty walked into the briefing room, and the real interrogation began. The press, aware of Yorty's proclivity for self-aggrandizement, posed questions that no one investigating the shooting was likely to address.

"It appears that Sirhan Sirhan was a sort of loner who harbored Communist inclinations, favored Communists of all types," Yorty stated. "He said the U.S. must fall. Indicated that RFK must be assassinated before June 5, 1968. It was a May 18 notation in a ringed notebook. When he was arrested, he had a column by David Lawrence about Robert Kennedy wanting the United States to supply arms to Israel."

This was just the type of juicy information the press was looking for—hot type that, by its very nature, couldn't be verified or corroborated, offered by an authority whose position guaranteed the story a slot on page one. The attending press represented some of the most highly regarded news outlets in the country. Any inaccuracies from Yorty would be worked out in the days ahead.

Robert Blair Kaiser, who would eventually write a book about the Kennedy assassination and the investigation of Sirhan Sirhan, was present at the news briefing as a stringer for *Life* magazine, and he saw a different—and possibly damaging—angle in what he was hearing. The man being detained by police would eventually stand trial for his actions, and Yorty's words, given weight by his position, might have a bearing on the accused's right to a fair trial.

"The mayor spilled as much prejudicial information as any public official could," Kaiser concluded.

■ ■ ■ ■ ■

Kennedy's condition steadily worsened throughout the day, and when Frank Mankiewicz spoke again to the press at 5:30 p.m., he offered very little to anyone still clinging to the hope of Kennedy's recovery. "The team of physicians attending Senator Robert Kennedy is concerned over his continuing failure to show improvement during the post-operative period," he announced. "Now, as of 5 p.m., Senator Kennedy's condition is still described as extremely critical as to life." Mankiewicz concluded his brief statement by saying that there would be no further regular bulletins until early the next morning.

The vigil in Kennedy's room went on, with Ethel Kennedy, Bobby's sisters (Jean Smith and Patricia Lawford), brother Ted, and several of Bobby's children at his bedside. Early in the evening, Jacqueline Kennedy arrived, prepared to comfort Bobby's family the way he had helped her after Jack's death. People whispered to Bobby, held his hand, and braced themselves for the inevitable. A flat line appeared on the screen monitoring his brain's activity. Only a ventilator kept his heart and lungs functioning. A doctor conferred with the Kennedy family at roughly 1:15 a.m. on June 6, slightly more than twenty-five hours after the shooting at the Ambassador Hotel. Ethel Kennedy asked if there was any chance at all of her husband recovering, and after learning that there was none, she asked the doctor to turn off the ventilator. Kennedy quit breathing a short time later.

A grief-stricken Frank Mankiewicz made his final report to the press at 2:00 a.m. "Senator Robert Francis Kennedy died at 1:44 a.m. today, June 6, 1968," he announced, noting that Kennedy had been forty-two years old. He listed the names of those in the room with Kennedy at the time of his death and stated that Kennedy's death had been caused by the gunshot wound to his head.

Lyndon Johnson offered a brief statement at the White House before ordering all flags on public buildings to be lowered to half-mast. He designated Sunday, June 9, to be a day of national mourning.

7 A torrent of newspaper and magazine articles, news reports, editorials, tributes, obituaries, memoirs, and public response pieces, addressing every topic imaginable, including reconsiderations about the way candidates were protected, gun violence in America, and the Kennedy family tragedies, followed the announcement of Robert Kennedy's death. Lyndon Johnson, ordering Secret Service protection for all presidential candidates, appointed a Commission on the Causes and Prevention of Violence, chaired by Milton Eisenhower, the former president's brother; skeptics argued that Nebraska's senator Roman Hruska, one of the gun lobby's friends, all but guaranteed that nothing of substance would come out of the commission's study.

All presidential candidates suspended their campaigns indefinitely. Both parties shut down their headquarters in New York, where candidates were scheduled to campaign next, and New York officials called for public restraint, lest the city have the kind of blowback that happened in the wake of the Martin Luther King assassination.

"People in Harlem identify with Kennedy more than any other white man," said Percy Sutton, the president of the Manhattan borough. "They wanted to know if this meant that anyone who stood up for us was going to be shot down. I thought, 'My God, are we going to have repetition of the trouble after Martin Luther King was killed.'" "I hope there is no reaction this time, except one of deepest sorrow," added New York City mayor John Lindsay. "We've had enough violence in the streets, on the campuses and in Vietnam."

Fortunately, as if in silent appreciation of Kennedy's message, the streets in New York and elsewhere were subdued.

Eugene McCarthy offered a sober, eloquent analysis about what Kennedy's assassination said about violence in America and throughout the world. "It is not enough, in my judgment, to say that this is the act of one deranged man, if that is the case," he stated. "The nation, I think, bears too great a burden of guilt, really, for the kind of neglect which has allowed disposition of violence to grow here in our land." This violent disposition, he cautioned, was "a reflection of violence we have visited upon the rest of the world, or at least in a part of the world."

Robert Kennedy's body was flown to New York and taken to St. Patrick's Cathedral. On Friday, June 7, an estimated fifteen thousand mourners, hundreds gathering at the cathedral before dawn, filed past Kennedy's flag-draped mahogany casket. The line of those awaiting entry into the cathedral stretched out for more than a mile, as mourners waited for up to seven hours for their opportunity to pay their respects. The visitation lasted from 5:30 a.m. on June 7 until 5:00 a.m. the following day.

Richard Cardinal Cushing read a solemn high mass on Saturday morning, with Lyndon Johnson, Hubert Humphrey, Richard Nixon, Eugene McCarthy, Nelson Rockefeller, Coretta Scott King, and Ralph Abernathy among the two thousand in attendance. The hour-and-forty-minute service offered a number of poignant moments, including a procession of Robert Kennedy's children, walking in pairs up the aisle and delivering the hosts and wine for Communion; thirty members of the New York Philharmonic, conducted by Leonard Bernstein, playing a movement from Gustav Mahler's Fifth Symphony; and Andy Williams singing "The Battle Hymn of the Republic." The service's most moving moments came when Ted Kennedy delivered his eulogy to his fallen brother.

"My brother," he said at the at the end of the eulogy, "need not be idealized or enlarged in death beyond what he was in life, to be remembered simply as a good, decent man, who saw wrong and tried to right it, saw suffering and tried to heal it, saw war and tried to stop it. Those of us who loved him and who take him to his rest today pray that what he was to us and what he wished for others will someday come to pass for all the world. As he said many times, in many parts of this nation, to those he touched and who sought to touch him: 'Some men see things as they are and say, Why? I dream things that never were and say, Why not?' "

At the conclusion of the funeral mass, Kennedy's casket was taken by hearse to the Pennsylvania Station, where it was placed in the last car of a twenty-one-car train bound for Washington, D.C., and Kennedy's burial at Arlington National Cemetery. The train's cars were filled with Kennedy's family and friends, politicians and other dignitaries, entertainment celebrities, athletes, and members of the press. The train left the station at 1:00 p.m. and did not arrive in the nation's capital until after nightfall. An incredible throng of people—one estimate placed the number at a million—lined the tracks between New York and Washington, many holding hand-lettered signs bidding Kennedy farewell, others standing silently under the oppressive sun, or waving and saluting, as the slow-moving train passed them. They gathered as they were compelled to gather, the factory workers in stained shirts and with grime beneath their fingernails, the newlyweds wagering hope in their futures, the children unburdened by the cynicism of politics, the minorities standing on their porches and watching for the last car on the train for a glimpse of the casket of a hero lost to eternity, the shopkeepers and schoolteachers, those struggling to pay their rents or mortgages, people in homemade dresses and their Sunday best, retail clerks and waitresses, a small group of nuns in a pickup truck—Robert Kennedy's people. Boats grouped on the waters, their captains ordering a respectful blast of their vessels' whistles when the train passed on a bridge overhead. There were tears, not only for the loss of the man but for the loss of what he represented. For eight and a half hours, the train moved ahead, its progress painfully slow, the people inside speaking in respectfully low tones, Ethel Kennedy roaming the aisles for a word with her guests.

The private gravesite ceremony was brief and modest. The burial was the cemetery's first to be held after nightfall, and there was some confusion in the darkness lit only by mourners' candles. New Orleans Archbishop Philip M. Hannan officiated the fifteen-minute service, offering a few words, prayers, and a blessing in a service that was strictly religious. Ethel Kennedy had requested that there be no military displays, including the customary twenty-one-gun salute and the blowing of Taps, although John Glenn did present the family with the folded flag that had draped the coffin. The Harvard band played "America the Beautiful." Then Robert Kennedy was lowered into the earth, only sixty feet downhill from where his brother was laid to rest.

13   Summer Doldrums

1 The death of Robert Kennedy, coming so soon after the assassination of Martin Luther King, left the country spiritually deflated, the depressing violence of the times overwhelming the hopes for change that accompanied the election of a new president. Violence dominated worldwide events in 1968, but the United States seemed to be at the epicenter of it, whether it was a collective effort, such as the war or campus unrest, mass rioting in the nation's inner cities, or the flashpoint of a single assassin's bullet. And rightly or otherwise, a great weight of the blame lay on the back of the Democratic Party, the party in power.

"I think the whole Democratic Party lost momentum," Hubert Humphrey reflected. "I think that the people really then turned against us. I think they thought that all this violence and everything else was a kind of byproduct of the way that the country had been operated, the way it had been managed, the way it had been governed. And I was caught up in that."

Muriel Humphrey was more blunt in her assessment of how the Kennedy assassination affected her husband's candidacy. "The bullet that killed Bobby Kennedy also wounded Hubert," she said.

Humphrey's cash flow took a hit immediately after Kennedy's death. A sizable percentage of his campaign funds had come from anti-Kennedy factions, from contributors opposed to Kennedy's liberalism or to the Kennedy family in general. With Kennedy gone, there was no longer a need to support Humphrey as a means of opposing Kennedy. The more moderate or conservative contributors defected to Nixon.

Time would show how deeply Kennedy's assassination affected the election, but the two remaining Democrats in the race felt it immediately. "Everything in politics for me on that night soured," Hubert Humphrey would remember.

It had already started earlier with the Tet Offensive, with Gene McCarthy telling me in December 1967 that he was going to run and why. . . . The troubles and tribulations the administration went through in those months of January, February, up to March, with Doctor Martin Luther King's assassination in April, and the President's pulling out of the race March thirty-first, and then with Bobby Kennedy getting shot, it just seemed like it was too much. I think that my reactions were just like the country's. It was just more than a guy could take.

Eugene McCarthy felt similarly. On their flight back to Washington, D.C., the day after Kennedy was shot, Tom Finney asked McCarthy about his plans, immediate and in the months leading to the Democratic convention. "It's not going to make any difference," McCarthy replied. "What we have to do now is cut down and just see what influence we can bring to bear on the situation between now and August. It's all over."

In the days following Kennedy's death, McCarthy fell into a psychological tailspin that found him reassessing his candidacy. He had entered the race to effect change, end the war, search for solutions to his country's problems, and alter the way presidents were elected; the presidency was a means, not an obsession. The murder of Robert Kennedy, although perhaps not surprising but stunning nonetheless, upset his intellectual equilibrium and forced him into the uncomfortable position of considering the value of what he was pursuing. As his wife remembered, he was uncharacteristically distracted. "In the days after the funeral, Gene seemed deeply depressed and almost unreachable," she wrote in her autobiography. "Night after night he lay beside me sleepless, staring at the ceiling."

McCarthy's resignation, while understandable given the circumstances, was dismaying if viewed as just a fragment in the mosaic of American violence. As noted by the *New York Times*, violence was part of American heritage. When attempting to answer the question, "What kind of nation is it in which Robert Francis Kennedy was murdered last week?" the *Times* answered its own query with a series of questions, concluding with, "Is it, finally, a nation whose frontier heritage is so close in time and so romantic in aspect that it perpetrates violence, enjoys it on its television screens and tolerates it in its streets, as if violence were—in H. Rap Brown's phrase—'as American as cherry pie'?"

There was no definitive answer, any more than there was meaningful discourse on the issue of gun control, a topic springing to the forefront of the news every time there was an assassination or attempted murder of any prominent

American. The topic of violence in America gained some heft in the law-and-order discourses of George Wallace and Richard Nixon, both seeking stronger measures to counter the increasing violence in the American streets.

2 On the night of Robert Kennedy's California victory, there had been discussion among the Kennedy brain trust about how to approach the next big contest: the June 18 primary in New York. Kennedy had little enthusiasm for this race. He was one of the state's two senators and should have been a favorite, but New York also had a strong pro-McCarthy, anti-Kennedy faction that figured to siphon off support Kennedy might have received from voters unhappy with the Johnson administration. Hubert Humphrey, with the backing of unions, offered significant opposition as well. Kennedy would have preferred to take a page from the Humphrey book and work for delegates in the nonprimary states, but the narrow voting projection in New York demanded his attention, energy, time, and money in that state.

His assassination changed the primary's dynamics. Humphrey and McCarthy had already campaigned lightly in New York, but their self-imposed moratorium on campaigning after Kennedy's death ended their personal involvement in the primary. Humphrey felt it the most, mainly in terms of an interruption of momentum; his overall lead over McCarthy was almost insurmountable. McCarthy's corps of young volunteers covered the state as well as possible, knocking on doors and passing out literature, keeping the McCarthy brand in front of the public in his absence.

Their efforts paid off. McCarthy, expected to finish behind Humphrey and Kennedy, was the surprise victor, capturing 63 of the state's 123 available delegate votes, with Kennedy taking 30, and Humphrey a disappointing 11. The numbers corroborated McCarthy's claim that in backing the old system, Humphrey was engaged in a Sisyphusian task: he would score heavily with the Democratic bosses and establishment, all but assuring himself of a victory in Chicago, while McCarthy could take his case directly to the voters and win their support. He would win a moral victory but lose the trophy.

He would call New York his most satisfying primary victory—an irony even he had to recognize, given how he had toiled to win in Oregon and how little he had worked to win in New York. Mired in the doldrums, he had canceled appearances, including an event for the Poor People's March, some of the cancellations coming at the behest of the Secret Service—now attached to his campaign per presidential order in the wake of the Kennedy assassination—who deemed some of his ghetto stops to be too potentially dangerous to risk;

other decisions arose from McCarthy's malaise and discontent. When asked to appear at a rally featuring other Democrats running for office in New York, he flatly refused. He alarmed his staff by making himself unavailable, including to higher-ups with urgent needs to see him. His statements to the press were reduced to a trickle, and when he did meet with reporters, his responses to questions were confusing or downright cryptic. Asked why undecided delegates should support him, rather than Humphrey, he shrugged off the question by stating that he simply wanted them to be "responsible delegates" who examined the issues, questioned who was likely to bring the issues to the country, and voted accordingly. "I just ask them for a reserved judgment," he said. Perhaps most mystifying—and, to his staff, astounding—was his announcement to the press that he was now going to run "a limited campaign."

It was probably his only option. By the end of the primary season, capped by the New York vote, the Republican and Democratic nominees were all but set. Richard Nixon, shedding his loser's image within his party, had convincingly vanquished his opposition. Ronald Reagan had placed his footprint on the national landscape, but he was a man of a more conservative future—no earlier than 1976, if Nixon won the presidency now. The best he could hope for was to be drafted at a deadlocked convention. It was the same for Nelson Rockefeller. By virtue of his indecision over entering the race, Rockefeller was less positioned than Reagan for a future run. Nixon had invited him to the ring, and then he had schooled him, first in Oregon and then in his own backyard in New York. Once the moratorium on campaigning had ended, Rockefeller had relentlessly pursued a win in New York, spending heavily on advertising, hitting the streets for personal appearances. It ultimately failed. He couldn't carry his home state.

For Nixon, the Republican convention wouldn't be arriving soon enough. In the summer weeks ahead, all he had to do was maintain the illusion that he was available, when, in fact, he was avoiding making a fatal mistake by staying away from the press and the public as much as possible. Current events had placed him in a commanding position on the election's two biggest issues—Vietnam and law and order—and all he really had to do was stand back and let the Democrats self-destruct.

3 Hubert Humphrey resumed his campaign on June 20 with a major address at the National Press Club in Washington, D.C. Designed as a statement on the important issues facing him on the road to the Chicago convention, the speech was also a tightrope walk in which Humphrey offered support of the president while cautiously moving toward establishing his independence of unpopular policy. The press was waiting for this. Four days earlier, during a radio interview, Bill Moyers, Johnson's former press secretary, who had split with Johnson over the war, had praised Humphrey as "a man of unlimited compassion" suffering from "believing that everyone else is as good and decent as he is." Moyers had intimated that in days to come Humphrey might be breaking from the president's position on Vietnam. In his Press Club speech, Humphrey dismissed Moyers's comments as a misunderstanding—he still backed Johnson on the war—and he also made it clear that when establishing his own voice and position on an issue, he was not rejecting his boss. "One does not repudiate his family in order to establish his own identity," he stated.

"Humphrey as vice president is a member of a team," he pointed out. "Humphrey as president is captain of the team."

While supporting Johnson on the delicate issue of the best means of resolving the Vietnam conflict, Humphrey put more distance between himself and the president on the law-and-order issue. Like Johnson, he initially had been a critic of the Kerner Report, but he was now modifying his stance. He believed that the report's recommendations were correct but cautioned against condoning the violent behavior rising out of frustration and anger over poor living conditions. "This relationship between 'law and order' on the one hand and 'social justice' on the other hand should be made plain to every American," he advised.

This, to Humphrey, was a crucial distinction, and one that had to be made in the violent climate saturating the country during the first months of 1968. It was also a point that Johnson would not debate. Humphrey had had a long sitdown with the president during his hiatus from campaigning, and they had discussed a spectrum of topics important to Humphrey's campaign. Johnson told Humphrey that he was still backing his candidacy, even if behind the scenes he criticized Humphrey as being weak, too talkative, and not the best fit for the office. Johnson counseled Humphrey to say nothing about his preference for a running mate. Better to remain secretive and build the drama during the convention week. Humphrey, of course, was all too familiar with the strategy.

The idea factored into Humphrey's speech at the Press Club. Rumors were circulating that Humphrey was considering Ted Kennedy as a running mate, but Humphrey denied any such plan. "There have been no commitments on the Vice Presidency," he insisted, "no talks with Senator Kennedy, no conversations with anyone about the office." Columnist Mary McGrory, a McCarthy backer, was skeptical. "The great hope," she wrote, "is that Sen. Edward Kennedy, D-Mass, can be persuaded to go on the ticket with the vice president, which would save the day and presumably bring back the disenchanted and alienated McCarthy supporters to the fold."

McGrory wasn't the only journalist skeptical of Humphrey's weak attempts to create some distance between himself and Johnson. The consensus among press members was that Humphrey's loyalty to Johnson could be rewarded only by success at the Paris peace talks. As it now stood, Humphrey was viewed as a surrogate for LBJ's failures in Vietnam. His campaign stops were marked by antiwar demonstrations, often by young people sporting McCarthy campaign buttons.

Humphrey liked to present himself as a man of the future, but that simply was not the case. If anything, he was more chained to tradition than either Eugene McCarthy or Richard Nixon. He favored the old way of doing business, which meant that he dealt heavily with the political bosses and party movers and shakers. He was viewed—correctly—as a populist, but in this particular race, in which he did not take part in the primaries, he was devoting most of his time to state caucuses and conventions. He would have to win the nomination before he took the bulk of his case to the voters.

Johnson would be a problem, and not just because Humphrey, as his vice president, had promised his loyalty. Johnson had viewed Robert Kennedy as the man Humphrey had to beat—he waved off Eugene McCarthy as inconsequential—but with his old rival and enemy no longer involved in the race, he could take a more aggressive stand in defending his policies on Vietnam and the urban and racial crises. This placed Humphrey in the uncomfortable position of defending unpopular policy at a time when he was trying to extricate himself from Johnson's clutches. The rumor mill was rife with speculation that Humphrey was about to deliver a speech indicating a significant split with LBJ over Vietnam, but rather than offer such a statement, Humphrey allowed the president to preview his remarks, which he had titled "Vietnam: Toward a Political Settlement and Peace in Southeast Asia." Johnson was not pleased. Aside from his disagreement whenever Humphrey veered away from his official policies in Vietnam, Johnson told Humphrey that the speech might jeopardize the Paris peace talk negotiations; finally, Johnson considered Humphrey's speech to be an insult to his two sons-in-law serving in Vietnam. To put an exclamation mark on his reaction, Johnson made sure that Humphrey understood that he would destroy him if Humphrey delivered his remarks. After Johnson's critical vetting, Humphrey set his speechwriters back to work and publicly announced that he was maintaining his position on the war.

This vacillating cost him dearly. In what the *Christian Science Monitor* called "an enthusiasm gap," the public showed only lukewarm interest in Humphrey's campaign appearances throughout the summer. An early July visit to Cleveland brought his predicament into sharp definition: his appearances were disappointments in terms of attendance and were disrupted by the usual noisy antiwar demonstrations and DUMP THE HUMP signs, yet at the same time he convinced 90 of Ohio's 115 convention delegates to vote for him in August. "He may have to keep two sets of books—one counting the votes he ought to get, the other counting the votes that will not be cast," the *Monitor* observed.

It went poorly elsewhere as well. A trip to California, rescheduled when Humphrey fell ill with "a grippy condition" and had to cancel his appearances in the state, found Humphrey in front of demonstrators who jeered him, who commandeered a cable car he was riding in San Francisco, shouting for him to wipe the blood off his hands, and who poured blood in his hotel's fountain in Los Angeles. It was bad enough that he had to bite his lip when he was lampooned by conservative columnist William F. Buckley, who ridiculed him as "a fresh symbol for Soviet-American relations" when he refused to endorse sanctions "against a country which tolerates no labor unions, no political liberty, no freedom of speech, no freedom of assembly, no freedom of religion, no freedom of emigration, [and] no freedom of economic movement." "If only we could contrive to elect him president of the Soviet Union," Buckley concluded, "he might be in a position to prove that his times will change to harmonize with the requirements of the politics of joy."

Humphrey expected that sort of treatment from an old political adversary. But he cringed when, facing shouts of derision while visiting the Watts section of Los Angeles, he was forced from the stage by protesters after only fifteen minutes; later, he was booed as he spoke in a vacant lot, with soul singer James Brown at his side. The events left him confused and bitter: he had repeatedly risked his political future by advocating for the blacks, yet here he was, in one of the country's largest ghettos, under attack as if he were the enemy.

Two recently published biographies, one by a liberal and one by a conservative, timed to cash in on Humphrey's candidacy, slashed away at him further. A reviewer for the *New York Times,* in a negative review published on the front page of the newspaper's book review section, ripped the biographers' lack of objectivity—"both are out to prove that Hubert Humphrey is the devil incarnate"—and concluded that "[t]hey succeed in documenting that Humphrey is a shrewd, glib, compromising, fancy-stepping pragmatist—in short, the sort of fellow we usually choose to be our President." Despite the tone of the review, its inclusion and conspicuous placement in the nation's most highly regarded newspaper book review section did Humphrey no favors.

The polls reflected Humphrey's conundrum. In one Gallup Poll, Humphrey and McCarthy both trailed Nixon in head-to-head competition. In another, published in early August, just prior to the Republican National Convention, Humphrey led McCarthy, 53 percent to 39 percent, among those likely to vote Democratic, though McCarthy led among young, college-educated voters. McCarthy led significantly (57 percent to 32 percent) among voters dissatisfied with Lyndon Johnson's performance.

The *Wall Street Journal,* in a lengthy piece, attempted to analyze Humphrey's weaknesses as a candidate. Too many voters, the *Journal* said, viewed Humphrey as "Lyndon Johnson's boy," despite Humphrey's efforts to prove otherwise. His inability to connect with African American voters was also a concern, especially in light of his problems in California. "The trip, designed to boost his standing in the public opinion polls, also served to illustrate some of the persisting problems that face him in in his drive for the Presidency," the *Journal* concluded.

Every salvo hit Humphrey, but his extensive experiences in confronting adversity had taught him that, for him, the best practice was to work through the difficult times. He compiled a list of thirty essential issues that needed to be addressed during his campaigning, and assigned groups to research them. Vietnam was his main priority. He spoke of the need for an open presidency, which would involve the participation of as many Americans as possible. He went on a delegate hunt in a four-state sweep and obtained more than enough delegate support to win on the first ballot in Chicago.

4   Richard Nixon was not one to leave anything to chance. By the time summer 1968 had rolled around, his campaign might have seemed to be a template for future pursuits of a party's presidential nomination. Although he had yet to secure the votes necessary for a first-ballot victory at the convention, Nixon had put enough distance between him and Nelson Rockefeller and Ronald Reagan to convince even the greatest of skeptics that he was the man best suited to take on the Democratic challenger in the general election. The Oregon primary, in which he had steamrolled Rockefeller and Reagan, proved as much. While Rockefeller and Reagan had stayed away, Nixon had campaigned in the state as if he expected a close vote. His resounding victory led him to a rare moment of jubilation.

"We got rid of three things by going down the primary road," he said. "We got rid of the idea that Nixon is bad on television, and the idea that Nixon can't get along with the press. And I hope to God we laid to rest the notion that Nixon is a loser." In looking ahead, he had ignored McCarthy as a possible opponent in November. Bobby Kennedy was still alive at that time, and Nixon, insisting that he and Kennedy were similar in their policies, saw a head-to-head battle with Kennedy as "a contest between men." Against Humphrey, he continued, it would be a "contest between politics." In that battle, Nixon had every intention of attacking Humphrey's close attachment to Lyndon Johnson.

But Nixon was realistic enough to avoid the pitfall of overconfidence. It was true that he was looking ahead to the general election, but the convention was never far from his mind. With the primary season concluded, he trained his eye on the nonprimary states and their delegate votes. Rockefeller, with his Nixon-can't-win message, was still hanging around like an unwanted guest, and Nixon wanted to shoo him out while he was still the heavy favorite over the New Yorker. He had what appeared to be a new ally in Spiro Agnew, who seemed poised to abandon his favorite son status and throw his support to Nixon. Agnew, goaded by the violence in the inner cities and on college campuses, had moved much further to the right than he had been during his days of supporting Rockefeller. His outspoken opposition to protesters of any stripe elevated his position in the GOP. Nixon was happy to welcome him to the fold.

More an irritant than a serious threat to Nixon, Nelson Rockefeller persisted, citing polls placing him ahead of Nixon in face-offs against Humphrey, promising to unify the badly divided country, and assailing Nixon's law-and-order statements as being off target. "I do not believe, as my opponent for the Republican Presidential nomination has stated, that the Supreme Court has given the 'green light' to crime," he argued. "And I do not believe, as he has also stated, that poverty had been 'grossly exaggerated' as a source of crime in America."

In what might have been interpreted as more desperation than definition, Rockefeller took the risky move of openly comparing his goals to those of Robert Kennedy. With a nation still in mourning, Rockefeller, extolling Kennedy as "a man who cared," vowed to appoint as Kennedy's successor as Senator a man who shared Kennedy's ideals and unfulfilled dreams. He, Nelson Rockefeller, was friend to minorities and working stiffs, just as Kennedy had been friend to these groups. Indeed, as a governor, Rockefeller had a track record to stand by his claims; he just didn't get much traction at this stage of the race.

Rockefeller spent heavily on his campaign, especially on advertising, and he worked overtime in efforts to appease the public and Republican leadership. He solicited endorsements at the Republican governors' conference in Tulsa—or at least a promise from favorite son governors to hold their votes until the convention—but he left the convention with no such promises and only one endorsement. It was brutal. Rockefeller had a winning personality, a strong television presence, and a thoughtful list of campaign issues and promises—all traits that Nixon lacked—but he could make no headway. Maybe his late entry into the race had given rise to the belief that he was not as serious a candidate as Nixon, or there might have been a hangover from his refusal to back his party's candidate in 1964, or, very likely, it could have been that Richard Nixon appeared to be the strongest candidate the Republicans had. Whatever the reasons, Rockefeller spent the weeks leading to the convention running in place, unsuccessfully trying to sell his message that Nixon was still a loser, failing to convince conservatives that his moderate policies would work, toiling in high-visibility markets but gaining no ground on the front-runner. Wisconsin GOP congressman Melvin Laird, a Nixon supporter and chairman of the House Republican Conference, might have summed up the situation better than anyone when in early June he urged Rockefeller to drop out of the race. "The only chance he has to be nominated is not to be divisive," he said of Rockefeller, "and the only way he can win without being divisive is for Nixon to stub his toe. And I don't think Nixon is going to stub his toe."

Nixon's campaign plan was designed to prevent that from happening. He was a master of assigning his lieutenants the tasks of speaking in his place or attending events that gave him a presence while he pursued other options. He declined to engage in debate, formal or otherwise, when Rockefeller tried to back him into corners. When, for instance, Rockefeller criticized him for having no firm plan for Vietnam, Nixon responded by dredging up an old standby statement: he would say nothing about his plans for fear of jeopardizing the Paris peace initiative.

Rockefeller did succeed in forcing Nixon to modify his law-and-order position. In the weeks following Robert Kennedy's assassination, there had been strong efforts to pass gun control legislation on Capitol Hill. Nixon's position on gun control had been namby-pamby. It had not been included in his recent white paper on crime, and when an Oregonian caller had questioned him about gun control during his telethon prior to the Oregon primary, Nixon answered that he thought the federal government should require a perspective mail-order gun purchaser to sign an affidavit "indicat[ing] that he has complied with state law"—as if a potential assassin or terrorist would do such a thing. If one wanted to hinder the growing number of guns in private hands, Nixon told the caller, one had to address the issue of crime, "because that's the reason a lot of people are purchasing firearms."

Pat Buchanan had suggested that Nixon take the initiative on gun control, and Nixon approved the idea. However, Nelson Rockefeller struck first, in a full-page newspaper ad appearing in forty-five papers across the country. Cities, Rockefeller said, could not be saved by politicians making proclamations about law and order without so much as a mention about gun control. Buchanan urged Nixon to avoid a debate with Rockefeller on the issue; silence was best. As it was, the issue was a minefield: nearly 85 percent of Americans polled felt that new gun control laws were necessary, but the National Rifle Association was a powerful lobbyist in Washington, D.C., and the pushback on new legislation would be substantial. In addition, a new crime bill, with gun control provisions, awaited Johnson's signature. Nixon moved hastily but judiciously. He urged Johnson to sign the existing bill and work on a follow-up bill that included provisions not included in the first. Nixon addressed the press on these issues, trying to look proactive on gun control when, in fact, he was actually stalling on backing a crucial point in the debate—gun licensing and registration. Nixon argued that gun licensing and registration should be left up to the individual states, rather than the federal government; it was a move that took the teeth out of national measures of gun control and, no doubt, held the National Rifle Association at bay. Then, lest he seem soft on the issue, Nixon proposed another measure that encouraged the states to pass laws that carried "a jail sentence for any unlicensed person carrying a weapon—and a mandatory prison sentence for anyone using a gun in the commission of a crime." Nixon wasn't blazing any trails in any of this, but he looked sincere in adding muscle to his law-and-order posture.

Nixon glided effortlessly through June and July, his confidence in gaining the nomination reaching the point of certainty. He received a huge but expected endorsement from Eisenhower, his old boss and future father-in-law to his daughter Julie; Eisenhower had been expected to offer his endorsement at the Republican National Convention, but a recent heart attack made his attendance in Miami unlikely. Nixon let three hundred top Republicans know just how certain he was of his pending nomination when he sent them a letter asking for their suggestions for a running mate. He had been in this position eight years earlier, when, as the vice president for a popular president, he had accepted his party's nomination at the Amphitheatre in Chicago. Now, barring a major turn of events, he would be facing a vice president for an unpopular president, a Democratic candidate about to be nominated in the same city, in the same venue, under what, if one could believe the rumors, were likely to be very different circumstances.

5 George Wallace's mourning period for his wife was brief but intense. He removed himself from the public eye, and to those friends and associates who saw him, he seemed shattered. When Albert Brewer, Wallace's replacement as governor, attempted to offer his condolences and cheer Wallace with a reference to his political future in Alabama, Wallace rejected him with "The only Wallace candidate who will be running for governor in 1970 will be you." Out of the governor's mansion, where politics had constantly swirled around him, even in privacy, Wallace now sat quietly at home, alone with his thoughts, a visit to Lurleen's grave part of his daily routine. Those closest to him were unsure of what to make of it. Starting back on the campaign trail might have seemed inappropriate; staying away from it, uncharacteristic of a man whose existence depended on his being in the eye of the hurricane.

But Wallace knew better than to delay for too long. If he was serious about his candidacy—and he was—he had to raise money and place himself back in front of the voters. As a presidential hopeful, he was on his own. His decision to run as a third-party candidate had been a wise one: he had not been shackled to primary dates and campaign schedules, or to contests where he could be thrashed and pushed out of the race. He could siphon off votes from other candidates, most likely from conservatives otherwise leaning toward Nixon. He could be a distinct voice, unencumbered by party politics. That was the upside. On the downside, he was receiving no assistance, most notably money, from the two parties and their major contributors. If he intended to compete, he needed to do some fund-raising.

He was back on the road on June 12, with an itinerary that included stops in Tennessee, Virginia, North Carolina, South Carolina, Florida, Louisiana, Mississippi, and Texas. Armed with his old message that included more criticism of his perceived enemies of the American way than solutions to the problems facing the nation, Wallace stormed through the South, preaching to the choir, feeding off the energy of the thousands packing auditoriums and stadiums, absorbed in a pageantry only he could create. Assailing the Republican and Democratic Parties as inept and indistinguishable, Wallace presented the need for change with a manner that was part fire and brimstone, part disdain. His audiences responded with high-volume appreciation.

And money. Contributions poured in, usually in five- and ten- and twenty-dollar installments, the bills stuffed in plastic buckets carried down the aisles during his speeches. As Dan T. Carter noted in *The Politics of Rage,* his biography of Wallace, a dozen or so high rollers would pay a thousand dollars to sit at a table with Wallace for lunch, while the less wealthy plopped down twenty-five dollars to eat mediocre food at one of his fund-raising paper-plate dinners.

Wallace was back to being his old self in no time. "His handlers had only to point Wallace in the direction of a set of microphones or a speaker's platform and stand out of the way," Carter wrote.

His war chest grew. He had entered this portion of his campaign in the red, owing an estimated half million dollars to advertisers, to companies printing flyers and campaign buttons, and for other expenses, but the debt evaporated, and his bank accounts bulged to such an extent that rumors had him being bankrolled by such luminaries as Texas oilman H. L. Hunt and actor John Wayne, the latter, starring in the summer's propaganda film *The Green Berets,* supposedly contributing three hefty checks to the Wallace cause.

Wallace manipulated his followers by playing into their fears. His speeches rarely varied. Big federal government was stomping all over states' rights, he charged. Egghead and pseudointellectual college professors, along with their Communist-sympathizing students, traitors if not downright treasonous enemies of the state, insulted the bravery of young men risking their lives on the battlefields and in rice paddies in Vietnam. Blue-collar workers, the backbone of the country, were bullied by briefcase-carrying politicians, lawyers, and bankers. Wallace, as shrewd as they get when it came to lathering up his followers, was as much an entertainer as a politician; his insults elicited as much laughter as his message drew applause. If he was going to win the presidency, he told his supporters, it would be as a result of the voices of decent, hardworking Americans demanding a change.

There was no disputing Wallace's large following of working-class citizens struggling to get from week to week on small wages and with little hope for advancement, but the most visible (and vocal) of his backers were the open bigots, the Klansmen and Birchers, the white supremacist pamphleteers who churned out hateful screeds on small press and mimeograph machines, the politicians who won their positions by espousing segregationist politics, the National Socialists in the design of George Lincoln Rockwell, and the political ideologues so unstable that even their friends called them crazy. Wallace needed their money and votes, too, and he wasn't beneath rubbing shoulders with them, though he made a point of seeing that the press understood that he did not belong to any of these groups and that he used them for political expediency. Randy Newman would characterize these people in his classic 1974 recording about the South, *Good Old Boys.*

The press, once content to ignore Wallace as just another crackpot, were now forced to take his candidacy seriously. His numbers in the polls were slowly creeping upward, enough so that pundits had to concede that while he still trailed the other candidates in both parties, he just might have enough support to prevent either of the two other candidates from having the needed number of Electoral College votes to win, which would throw the election into the House of Representatives. If that happened, Wallace's power could be substantial. It was hard to predict what concessions either party might have to make to procure his Electoral College votes. During a June 30 interview on *Meet the Press,* Wallace, after addressing a host of questions about race, spoke about what he considered to be the important issues in the eventuality that the election was brought to the House of Representatives. At the top of the list was a demand that the federal government relinquish some of its control over the states, placing authority back where it belonged. Wallace also demanded that the United States quit giving aid to its enemies and that the government find some way of silencing Communist sympathizers, especially those critical of the American efforts in Vietnam. Finally, he required a guarantee of the placement of more conservative judges on the Supreme Court—appointments would assure the legal backing of his other demands. But as far as Wallace was concerned, Congress deciding the winner of the election wasn't an issue. He told panel moderator Edwin Newman that he intended to win the election outright; the House of Representatives wouldn't be needed.

Wallace's *Meet the Press* appearance offered evidence of what liberals found so vexing about the candidate: he was calm, well spoken (even when he was contradicting himself), surprisingly intelligent, and focused; he presented himself as reasonable, even if he wasn't. As the panel bore in on the race issue, Wallace came across as hunted, not haunted, by his past statements. The press was not going to let Wallace escape with his simplistic or convoluted definitions of racism ("A racist, I suppose, is someone who dislikes people because of color—that's the common definition—and I do not dislike any of the handiwork of God," he told interviewer John J. Synon in another interview), not when the polls were indicating a bump in his popularity. From this point forward, George Wallace's every move would be scrutinized.

6 Much to Lyndon Johnson's frustration, the Paris peace talks were at an impasse. His initial optimism disappeared soon after the North Vietnamese indicated they were open to meetings negotiating a settlement to the war. In a no-win war, all sides were seeking a way to disengage with honor. The North Vietnamese, losers in the Tet Offensive, bombed mercilessly and seeing no end to it, and suffering heavy casualties daily, were anxious to end the war but not at the cost of caving in to an opponent it had fought with such determination. Hanoi was also aware of the antiwar movement tearing America apart, and

recognized the leverage this could bring them at the negotiating table, depending on how badly the United States wanted to withdraw from the country. The South Vietnamese had the most to lose from an American withdrawal. The country's troops were no match for the enemy, and unless terms were carefully negotiated, Saigon was almost certain to be overrun as soon as the United States withdrew. The ideal scenario would be to stall negotiations until the election in the United States. The new president—Nixon?—might be hawkish enough to insist on military protection of South Vietnam.

The United States was a mass of contradictions. The war had cost the president his job, and his Democratic successor, if elected in November, appeared to be ready to continue Johnson's policies in Vietnam. Johnson, famously stubborn, was torn on the appropriate actions to take. He wanted to find a peaceful way to end the war but not at the cost of America's losing face at North Vietnam's installing a Communist government after overrunning the country. Johnson understood South Vietnam's concerns. "They're frightened to death," he said, "that if this ball bounced the wrong way that they—all of them—would be assassinated and they would be run over, they would be locked up and they would be in concentration camps and they'd be slaves—if the Communists take over."

Johnson's own advisors were deeply divided on the measures to take. Clark Clifford and Averell Harriman favored withdrawal, regardless of Saigon's wishes. According to David Halberstam in his book *The Best and the Brightest,* Clifford and Harriman "were pushing very hard for the kind of political decisions which would see diminishing importance placed on the wishes of the Saigon government, with the United States, if need be, ready to by-pass Saigon."

As Clifford saw it, "The goal of the Saigon government had become utterly antithetical to the goal of the United States." Clifford was certain that Saigon was in no hurry for the war to end, and they certainly didn't want the Americans to leave the country. Vietnam was safer with more than a half million American troops protecting them, and President Nguyen Van Thieu believed that the Americans and South Vietnamese troops could outlast the North. Finally, there was the issue of money. South Vietnam (and its corrupt government) stood to benefit enormously from American money spent in the country. Clifford recommended that the United States leave Vietnam as soon as possible.

Johnson, backed by Ambassador Ellsworth Bunker, could not accept this position. South Vietnam, they countered, was just too vulnerable to abandon entirely at this point.

This was just some of the baggage carried by the different interests as the peace negotiations were being hammered out. From the onset, when the location of the negotiations was being suggested and rejected repeatedly, it was obvious that the talks would be difficult. It took three weeks for the sides to agree on Paris (out of fifteen suggested cities and, incredibly, a ship anchored in Indonesia) as the site for the talks. Then there was a protracted debate on the size and shape of the negotiating table. Meanwhile, some of the heaviest fighting in the war's history, with alarming casualty numbers, was taking place in Vietnam. When the formal talks eventually commenced, there was very little movement. All sides held firmly to their positions. "It became clear to most of the world that Hanoi was merely using the sessions for propaganda purposes," Johnson would recall in his memoirs.

Johnson's hopes were elevated, albeit only slightly, when he received an unexpected letter from Aleksei Kosygin, in which the Soviet chairman suggested that North Vietnam might be willing to negotiate a peaceful settlement if the United States ceased its bombing of enemy territory. Johnson and his advisors deemed Kosygin's proposal "significant," although they were uncertain of using heavy bombing as a means of buckling the enemy's resolve. A cease-fire had not worked in 1965, when the Soviet Union had made a similar proposal and the United States had quit bombing for thirty-seven days, and the relentless bombing had not worked either. Johnson met with his advisors, and they tried to read between the lines of Kosygin's letter. What did it mean? How would the Soviet Union be involved in all this? Johnson replied to Kosygin with a letter asking what he felt were appropriate questions and stating that the United States was open to a bombing halt if the Soviet Union could assure that such an action wouldn't place American troops in jeopardy. Unfortunately, nothing ever came of the suggestions in Kosygin's letter.

Johnson had expected a tough go of it in negotiating a peace settlement, but as a veteran of hard-line negotiating during his time in the Senate and his experience in the White House, he had a history of winning even the most contentious battles. This was not happening in Vietnam. The United States seemed to be at odds with all sides in the war and peace process. One might have reasoned that South Vietnam, defended by United States troops for years, would have been receptive to efforts to end the fighting and establish a political order between the two warring governments, but this was not the case. In fact, South Vietnam had lost much of its trust in the United States. South Vietnamese president Thieu, suspicious of American motives and plans to such an extent that he wondered, earlier in the year, if the United States had supported the Vietcong during the Tet Offensive as part of a plan to overthrow the South

Vietnamese government, fought bitterly against including certain North Vietnamese groups in the negotiations in Paris. A coalition government was the last thing he wanted.

Johnson also had to deal with presidential candidates facing increasing pressure to deliver plans for bringing an end to the war. The president had given up on influencing Eugene McCarthy a long time ago—their adversarial relationship had begun as a result of McCarthy's entering the race as an antiwar candidate—and nothing he could say or do now, outside of pulling out America's troops, was going to appease the senator. Johnson did, however, approach the other major candidates and ask that they refrain from commentary while the sensitive Paris talks continued. It was really an unnecessary exercise: neither Nixon nor Wallace had anything to offer on the topic of Vietnam, and Humphrey, as vice president, had to stand by the administration's position. Johnson sweetened the deal for Humphrey by assuring him the presidency if the war ended prior to the election.

On July 18, Johnson and General Creighton Abrams, a recent replacement for William Westmoreland as commander of Vietnam operations, and others flew to Honolulu to meet with President Thieu and other South Vietnamese representatives. Clark Clifford, fresh off a fact-finding mission to Vietnam, joined them there. Clifford briefed Johnson, Dean Rusk, and Walt Rostow on his findings prior to the conference. Clifford was convinced, more than ever, that the United States could not win the war, and that South Vietnam, as long as it received protection by American troops, did not want the war to end. He pointed out that South Vietnam's demands for matériel—"between 300 and 400 helicopters, T-39 trainer jets to be used as private aircraft for senior officials, and so on"—were outrageous. The South Vietnamese, Clifford suggested, should be told that the United States intended to withdraw from Vietnam within six months and that the new president-elect might take a tougher position on the war.

Rusk, in particular, disagreed with Clifford's assessment, as did Rostow and, once briefed on the meeting, Ellsworth Bunker. "I recommended against [withdrawal], because I didn't think the Vietnamese were ready for it," Bunker said. "I didn't think that they had enough confidence in themselves at that point, that we should wait a little bit longer and continue the training a little more intensively for a longer period."

Rusk strongly objected to the recommendation of withdrawal. "Our position never included withdrawal from South Vietnam regardless of the consequences," Rusk argued. "We didn't want a repeat of the Laos accords of 1962, where we got a good agreement on paper but no performance by North Vietnam. We weren't willing in 1968 to accept any formula in which the Americans withdrew from South Vietnam yet allowed North Vietnamese troops to remain; that was tantamount to surrender."

Over the course of the following two days, the United States and South Vietnam exchanged ideas and opinions about every facet of the war, including military and political solutions, and the possibilities of a U.S. withdrawal from the war. Despite their weak bargaining position, the South Vietnamese refused to back down on their refusal to participate in the Paris talks. There was no way that would happen, they said, as long as representatives of the National Liberation Front were seated at the table. Thieu asked that American bombing of the North continue as long as North Vietnamese troops were in South Vietnam, and he sought assurance of the United States' commitment to the war effort. Although unhappy about it, and conceding that he couldn't make a significant move with his staff so badly divided, Johnson agreed, leading Clifford to conclude that the meeting in Honolulu was "a misguided venture that set back our negotiating efforts in Paris without advancing our military objectives in Vietnam."

The Honolulu gathering received very little media coverage, but it had a debilitating effect on the Hubert Humphrey campaign. The lack of progress in the Paris talks, along with the stifling lack of any notable improvement stemming from the Johnson administration, led to a regression of the public's perception of Humphrey the candidate. Vilified at almost every public appearance, branded a Johnson stooge, labeled a hawk by the McCarthyites, and criticized as being just another cog in the machinery of a large political problem, Humphrey was a stagnant presence in an electoral process now tilting toward the Republicans. And the upcoming convention in Chicago was shaping up to be a battle of unimaginable proportion.

7 Richard Nixon held a secret with the explosive potential of not only changing the game in the presidential election but of influencing the events in Southeast Asia. The secret centered on his friendship with Anna Chennault, a Chinese-born American, widow of World War II Flying Tigers legend General Claire Chennault and a well-connected Republican, anti-Communist mover and shaker with a keen interest in events transpiring in Southeast Asia.

Born in 1925 in Peking and educated in Hong Kong, Anna Chennault spent her early working years as a journalist, first as a war correspondent for the Central News Agency, then as a reporter for *Hsin Ming Daily News* in Shanghai. She and her husband were married in 1947, and she bore him two daughters.

Thirty years her senior, General Chennault died of cancer in New Orleans in 1958. She worked as a publicist before turning her interest to politics. She was a Republican, she would say, because that party had asked first. She was only marginally knowledgeable about the American political system, but she was a fast learner. She worked as a volunteer on Nixon's campaign in 1960 and served the Kennedy administration as director of Chinese Refugee Relief. She loved the quick pace, the gossip, the exchange of ideas, and the power in Washington, and by the time Nixon came calling, she was ready.

She had met Nixon previously, and if one could believe the boasts in her autobiography, she knew John Mitchell well enough to have his private telephone number. She and Nixon had crossed paths on several occasions dating back to his vice presidency, but never for any notable length of time. This changed in 1967 when after deciding to run for the presidency, Nixon contacted her and requested a meeting. Nixon had seen her in action and had heard enough about her to know that she was intelligent, gracious, comfortable with the powerful, and, perhaps most important of all, faithful to her convictions. He had called her with a specific purpose: he believed that the Vietnam War would be a crucial issue in the 1968 race, and he needed solid, trustworthy inside information on everything going on in Southeast Asia—information that he could not obtain from the State Department or even his close associates in the government. Nixon hoped that Chennault, who knew people in high places in Vietnam, would keep him informed of all important new developments in the country. Chennault, "flattered by the request," agreed. As the campaign picked up steam, Chennault, by her own account, was in daily contact with John Mitchell or his assistants.

She met Nixon at his Manhattan apartment on July 12, 1968, one week to the day before Lyndon Johnson conferred with the South Vietnamese leaders in Honolulu. The timing of the Nixon–Chennault meeting was coincidental, but the results were as vital to the Paris peace talks and the South Vietnamese involvement in them as any conclusions coming out of Hawaii. Chennault recognized the benefits that might rise out of an alliance with the front-runner in the presidential campaign, and she proposed, through John Mitchell, a meeting that also involved Chennault's friend Bui Diem, South Vietnamese ambassador to the United States. Like the South Vietnamese leaders, Chennault feared what might come of the North Vietnamese involvement in the peace talks or the United States withdrawal from the war. Her intentions for a meeting with Nixon: find a way to keep either of these events from happening. She could use her connections, along with her impressive abilities in Republican fundraising, as bargaining chips in establishing an association with Nixon.

The July 12 meeting had not been unexpected. The Paris talks had raised the stakes on the information Nixon needed for his campaign, and Bui Diem anticipated his call. Diem had been hearing from representatives from Republicans and Democrats alike, and he was unhappy about the pressure. He was certain that his phone was tapped and that his messages to Saigon were being intercepted and read. A meeting with Nixon might be helpful.

During the meeting, Nixon tried to drive home two points: first, if elected, he would be sending a team to study the war—which he still vowed to win—and he would set up a personal meeting with Thieu; second, all communications between South Vietnam and Nixon should be channeled through Anna Chennault, and he would be using her as a conduit for all his messages to Saigon. "Anna is a very dear friend," Nixon told Diem. "We count on her for information on Asia. She brings me up to date."

All this, of course, had to be kept secret.

Nixon knew the hazards of becoming involved in this type of arrangement. Law specifically prohibited private citizens from hindering government business through associations of this nature. If caught, he could be subject to prosecution; at the very least, it could be career threatening.

He decided it was worth the risk.

Book Three
THE CONVENTIONS

14 Miami
"Let's Win This One for Ike"

1 If the Republican National Convention was "a coronation" for Richard Nixon, as journalist Jules Witcover deemed it, Miami Beach was the place in which to stage it. New York City might have been an excellent location for the sheer energy and self-congratulatory explosion of sign-waving, straw-boater-wearing, button-brandishing, hootin' and hollerin' minions, driven to crescendos of slogan shouting by bands playing all the predictable songs. New York, after all, was the capital of loud. Chicago, the nation's second-largest city, already had a convention on the docket. Los Angeles, with its high focus on entertainment, had the glitz and glamour, but it was not a GOP stronghold, even with a Republican governor in the statehouse. The big Texas cities, Dallas–Fort Worth and Houston, were out, victims of the long shadow cast by the Democratic president, as were such convention-friendly cities as San Francisco and Las Vegas, the latter crushed by a gross artificiality that even the Republicans, with their upper-middle-class, white constituency, couldn't bear.

No, Miami Beach was the ideal location, a finger of land, once swamp, developed into a vacationers' paradise over the course of the twentieth century, separated from the mainland by a narrow slash of water, which might have been imagined by developers if it hadn't already existed. The 1968 Republican Convention was the first political convention of its kind to be staged in Miami Beach, and the organizers planned it to be the perfect mirage within a mirage. In this city of hotels, fine food, beautiful young women, well-maintained beaches, high-class entertainment, and happy, temporarily displaced visitors, a five-day superevent, televised from coast to coast, would be dangled in front of those not fortunate to be present for the festivities. For those who were there, it would be a time to remember.

Miami and its environs were Richard Nixon territory. The former vice president regularly sought refuge in Florida, with its year-round warmth, coastal ocean and gulf, and a population a tad more sedate than one found elsewhere.

But make no mistake about it: Miami knew how to party. Of course, when Miami was awarded the convention site late in 1967, at record price, soon to be topped, of $850,000, no one knew that Nixon would be the presumptive nominee, but that eventually might have made the location all the more special.

Two other candidates—Nelson Rockefeller and Ronald Reagan—harbored hopes for the Miami convention, although their hopes, in light of the Nixon stampede, bordered on the delusional. Both banked on brokering a victory at the convention, their only chance hinging on the argument—and a weak one, at that—that they, and they alone, could defeat Hubert Humphrey in the general election. Nixon, they would try to convince the power brokers, was still a loser, just as he had been in 1960, when as an eight-year vice president, he had been unable to defeat an upstart young senator from Massachusetts.

The most creative minds in sales and advertising could not have imagined it better. Nixon had been a diagnostician with no stated plan for treatment. He had seen the cancer afflicting the nation, pointed it out to the American people, and offered to make it go away, without so much as a hint about how he intended to treat it; somehow, voters in all parts of the country trusted him. Only a major gaffe would prevent his nomination, and he was smart enough to avoid the public eye and the possibility of ruining his candidacy. He would be the prohibitive favorite in a town of high rollers.

Reagan and Rockefeller had precedent to inflate their hopes of stalling the leader's momentum and winning on a later ballot. In 1940, Thomas E. Dewey of New York had been the favorite at the opening of the Republican National Convention in Philadelphia. The former governor, hoping to oppose President Franklin D. Roosevelt in the general election, was challenged by Robert A. Taft of Ohio and Wendell L. Willkie of Indiana, and he was unable to secure the needed delegate votes on the first five ballots. Willkie wound up winning the nomination on the sixth ballot.

Twenty-eight years later, the two Republican challengers formed an un-likely alliance as they entered the convention, Ronald Reagan representing the Far Right, Nelson Rockefeller the liberal side of the party. The strategy: join forces, deny Nixon a first-ballot victory, and hope to gain votes as del-egates switched allegiances. Neither had a realistic chance of beating Nixon or denying him a first-ballot win, but by working as a team, they might make it work. If they gained delegate votes in the regions where they were strongest—Reagan in the West and South, Rockefeller in the Northeast—and added their totals to the large sum they already had from the states they governed, they might prevent Nixon from tallying the 667 votes required for the nomination.

Reagan's candidate status was turning out to be a prickly issue. When he arrived in Miami Beach on August 4, he was still playing cagey, insisting that he was a favorite son and not a candidate. No one was accepting this, even in a year when reluctance seemed to be a qualification for serious candidacy. In addition, Reagan's name was being tossed around as a vice-presidential possibility on a Nixon ticket. Both Reagan and Nixon squelched that rumor, but once again it placed the California governor in an awkward position. What, really, was he going to do? Reagan had tested his popularity in the South during his visits to some of the region's states, but he learned that he would be supported only if he formally declared his candidacy. His own state was growing restless. The day after Reagan's arrival, a caucus of California delegates convened and pushed Reagan forward by passing a resolution stating that Reagan was "a leading and bona fide candidate for president." Reagan, in his best "aw, shucks" manner, confirmed to the press that he was indeed a candidate. After all, the resolution said as much.

The Reagan and Rockefeller camps pushed to determine their level of support from other favorite son candidates. Rockefeller struck out when he approached Spiro Agnew. Only a few months earlier, Agnew had begun leading the charge for Rockefeller; now, after being humiliated by Rockefeller's initial refusal to enter the race, Agnew was backing Nixon.

Reagan had problems of his own. He couldn't afford to split any state's delegate votes with the other Republicans; he needed unit votes, in which a state delivered all of its delegates to a single candidate. That wasn't going to occur. In Florida, for instance, Reagan thought he could count on just under half of the delegates. Nixon would be the beneficiary of the others. Reagan tried to cajole more votes out of the state, but the delegates stood firm in their commitments. It went this way elsewhere, as well. According to the calculations of F. Clifton White, who had led the Goldwater effort in 1964 and now worked as a chief advisor and vote counter for Reagan, Reagan stood no chance of achieving his goal without the delegate votes of Florida, Georgia, Mississippi, and Louisiana. When the votes were eventually cast, Reagan won seven of Louisiana's twenty-six votes, one of Florida's thirty-four, seven of Georgia's thirty, and none of Mississippi's twenty. Reagan not only failed to erode Nixon's support in the South, but he also he learned that he was nowhere near as popular as he had thought.

Everyone seemed to have a different vote count. The press, fighting off boredom in what looked to be an oppressively dull convention, devoted much of their efforts to prognosticating about Nixon's possible running mate, trying to find angles for news stories and profiles, and drawing up their own tallies on delegate votes. Reporters kept an eye on the Reagan and Rockefeller efforts, but it was hardly scintillating stuff. If anything, they felt sympathy for the two candidates as they stretched grimaces into smiles while they denied the awful truth and marched ahead. Rockefeller and his polls symbolized the futility. Rockefeller had arrived in Miami Beach with an encouraging poll, which he commissioned himself, indicating that he could beat Hubert Humphrey in a general election, and a Harris Poll indicated the same. The results of the polls meant nothing to those who had been covering Rockefeller for any period of time. He was always popular with voters; his biggest obstacle was his own party, which backed the less popular, less telegenic, less financially well-heeled Richard Nixon. Nothing Rockefeller could say or do would alter that.

2 The Republican platform, introduced to the convention on Monday, August 5, found the party moving closer to the center than it had been four years earlier. This was not good news for Ronald Reagan and his ultraconservative agenda, though Reagan would not have objected too strenuously to the wording to some of the platform's main points—law and order, and the urban crisis, to mention two. In its call for a "Republican Resurgence" and a change in direction from eight years of Democratic control of the presidency, the platform document described Americans as "uncertain about the future and frustrated about the recent past"—a country in urgent need of significant change. In its call for change, the platform named two Republican presidents of the past—Abraham Lincoln and Dwight Eisenhower—as examples of the type of leadership required in times of "turmoil." Lincoln had challenged Congress 106 years earlier, and the platform quoted him early in its proposal for change:

> The dogmas of the quiet past are inadequate to the stormy present. The occasion is piled high with difficulty and we must rise with the occasion. As our case is new, so we must think anew and act anew. We must disenthrall ourselves and then we shall save our country.

The Republicans' move to the center, which Tom Wicker described as more of an "urge to unity than of any deep-going changes in the Republican psyche," indicated a compromise, a will to adapt if it led to victory. Richard Nixon had become a symbol of this spirit. Two years earlier, while campaigning for Republican candidates across the country in the off-year election, Nixon had been a hawk in support of American efforts in Vietnam, although in private he predicted the war would be the defining issue of the 1968 presidential election. If Johnson hadn't ended the war or taken steps in that direction, he said, it would be his undoing. He was accurate in his prediction, though there was an irony to it: Nixon had to forsake his hawkish tendencies if he hoped to win the election. "The war must be ended," he said to the platform committee, days before the opening of the convention. "We must seek a negotiated settlement."

This came as a noteworthy reversal of position for a man who had earned part of his reputation by speaking out as a dedicated opponent of Communism. In his younger days, he would have consumed hemlock before giving the Communists even the partial victory they would gain in a negotiated settlement. But that was now the reality he faced, and the Republican Party's position, buried deep in the platform document, might have been written, with only a few amendments, by either McCarthy or Kennedy. After going on at length about the Johnson administration's failures in Vietnam and the reasons for those failures, the Republicans proposed a change of course that included a negotiated settlement "based on the principle of self-determination, our national interests and the course of long-range world peace." Nixon could live with this. The platform, like his campaign speeches, was bereft of specifics about how a new Republican administration would achieve these goals. The party's plans for the military draft, a focal point in demonstrations throughout the country, was surprisingly detailed: "We will further revise Selective Service policies and reduce the number of years during which a young man can be considered for the draft, thereby providing some certainty to those liable for military service. When military manpower needs can be appreciably reduced, we will place the selective Service System on standby and substitute a voluntary force obtained through adequate pay and career incentive."

Nixon's consent on the platform language settled what had been a contentious debate over the party's position on Vietnam. The Reaganite conservatives and the Southern states, still pressing for a military victory in the Southeast Asian country, battled with moderates like Nelson Rockefeller and Jacob Javits, who lobbied for a negotiated settlement that permitted America to leave Vietnam in a dignified way. Rockefeller was particularly unyielding: he was prepared to abandon the party and campaign for a Democratic candidate if the Republicans refused to include language calling for a peaceful settlement of the war.

The party had much less difficulty with the law-and-order provisions in the platform. There was no disagreement over the plight of impoverished urban centers, or about the crime and violence that rose out of the hopelessness from the realization that, as it now stood, there was little or no chance of escaping ghettos, which deteriorated every year. "Millions of our people are suffering cruelly from expanding metropolitan blight—congestion, crime, polluted air and water, poor housing, inadequate educational, economic and recreational opportunities," the platform committee wrote. "The continuing decay of urban centers—the deepening misery and limited opportunities of citizens living there—is intolerable in America. We promise effective, sustainable actions enlisting new energies by the private sector and by government at all levels."

The platform committee avoided proposing detailed solutions. Indicting Johnson's Great Society programs, meticulously designed to address urban problems, would have been risky, and the less said about the conditions of the inner cities, the stronger the platform's statements about law and order would be. There could be no acceptable excuses for the country's recent inner-city disruptions.

The platform went on to say as much: "America has adequate peaceful and lawful means for achieving even fundamental social change if the people wish it. We will not tolerate violence."

This attitude, written by white, middle- to upper-class Republicans, was dismissed by the party's progressive leaders. Rockefeller, with extensive experience in dealing with the problems in New York City, felt that this attitude was unrealistic. Senator Jacob Javits, also from New York, was even more vocal in his feelings about the way the party, specifically the Nixon supporters, reduced complex issues to fresh simplicity. "All these people here who support Nixon are as nice as they could be," he stated, "but they don't begin to understand the problems of the cities, the urgency of the ghettos, the heat of the subways."

But for all its lip service to the dwellers of big cities and their inner-city struggles, this was not a platform designed to change the minds of the large percentage of Democrats—or moderate Republicans—concerned with pressing urban issues. The targeted audience was the Silent Majority, the people who lived in muted fear of scenarios they were unlikely to face, the people enraged by demonstrations that seemed unpatriotic, those believing that America had taken a turn for the worst, those seeking change, in whatever form, because Johnson and the Democratic Party had failed them—people who fancied themselves to be good, traditional citizens, those seeking to return to the Eisenhower years, when all was quiet and America was growing in size and mobility. The platform's mission was to fan the flames and promise to put out the fire.

A decision had been reached. This would be an election about restoring law and order and reestablishing faith in the country's system:

> Republicans believe that respect for the law is the cornerstone of a free and well-ordered society. We pledge vigorous and even-handed administration of justice and enforcement of the law. We must re-establish the

principle that men are accountable for what they do, that criminals are responsible for their crimes, that while the youth's environment may help to explain the man's crime, it does not excuse that crime.

The Johnson administration, the platform purported, had ignored the recommendations of its own crime commission, opposed legislation aimed at assisting law enforcement officials in doing their jobs, and fought against taking an aggressive stand against "identified subversives." The administration "ignored the danger signals of our rising crime rates until very recently and even now has proposed only narrow measures hopelessly inadequate to the need." The Republicans proposed an "all-out, federal-state-local crusade against crime" that included a war against drugs, organized crime, juvenile delinquency, and repeat offenders.

The plank addressed many other issues, of course, but the committee devoted the most time to the two issues—law and order and Vietnam—that had come to define the election. The Democrats would be focusing on almost all of these issues when they gathered for their convention a couple of weeks later, but in delivering their platform first, the Republicans enjoyed the advantages of the preemptive strike. The Democrats would be on the defensive.

3   Richard Nixon sat near a television in his hotel suite and waited for the delegate voting to begin. Although he had been assured by his staff that he had the votes necessary for a first-ballot victory, he was a chronic worrier. What if Rockefeller or Reagan found a way to make their stop-Nixon campaign work? Were the Southern states really committed to voting for him? A lot of favorite son candidates had yet to commit; would they swing their votes to him? His vote counters urged him not to worry, and he tried to heed their advice. But still, he was a time-tested candidate of tough election nights. This time around, things had been going almost too smoothly.

That certainly had been the case from the moment his plane touched down in Miami. He had spent the week prior to the convention at Montauk Point on Long Island, New York, tucked away from the press and the public, consulting with the Republican platform panel and shaping the peroration of his acceptance speech. At the Miami airport and upon his arrival at the swank new Hilton Palace hotel, in which he had established a two-hundred-room command post, he was greeted like a returning hero, home at last, ready to fulfill his ultimate goal of national leadership. NIXON'S THE ONE, his campaign buttons declared, and those greeting him believed it.

He needed the South, and he had immediately set about wooing the states' delegates. He and Strom Thurmond had established a kind of détente before Nixon's arrival in Miami, Thurmond knowing full well that the Southern states were not enamored with Nixon and preferred Reagan, and Nixon conceding that in the general election George Wallace's independent candidacy, along with the old Dixiecrats, would probably sink the Republicans. However, Nixon and Thurmond shared one important belief: the Democrats were vulnerable, and it was time to pit the best GOP candidate—Nixon—against them. "Our country needs him, and he needs our support in Miami," Thurmond stated in a telegram to delegates before the convention. Nixon, he asserted, employing a pragmatism that overruled personal feeling, was the best choice for party unity and a November victory for conservatives.

In exchange for Thurmond's support, Nixon had to find a way to appease the South without compromising his support elsewhere. His party, he said, would remain united, and with that in mind, he promised to choose a vice-presidential candidate that would appeal to everyone—in short, no liberals. Then there were the civil rights issues: the platform promised its backing of civil rights legislation. Nixon responded by inching closer to George Wallace's states' rights position. Slipping into his chameleonlike political skin, Nixon assured Thurmond and the Southern delegates that his administration would not be browbeating states on issues that state and local governments were well equipped to handle, and he saw that this was worked into the plank. By the time the delegate ballots were cast, he had won the South.

Nixon was at the convention center, still wandering the floor, when Gerald Ford sounded the gavel to begin what looked to be a long, torturous process of nominating the presidential candidate. Aside from Nixon, Rockefeller, and Reagan, eight favorite son candidates stood in line to hear their names entered as candidates, meaning a series of mind-numbing nominating and seconding speeches to be delivered before the casting of the first ballot. Rockefeller was nowhere to be found, Nixon retreated to his hotel suite, and Reagan, still hoping for a miracle, held eleventh-hour meetings with delegates he hoped to win over. The biggest surprise of the evening was the number of favorite sons— especially James Rhodes of Ohio and George Romney of Michigan—who declined to release their delegates prior to the first-ballot vote. The nominating speeches, with the exception of those delivered by Maryland governor Spiro Agnew and former secretary of the treasury Ivy Baker Priest Stevens, were standard fare, followed by the obligatory demonstrations and band music expected to elevate whatever excitement the speeches might have engendered. Agnew's speech nominating Nixon was a workmanlike effort, notable mainly because Agnew, known only slightly, was an interesting choice to deliver it. Stevens's speech for Reagan presented a candidate removed from the party platform and the other candidates, a no-holds-barred conservative prepared to confront the law-and-order and Vietnam issues on terms much tougher than his more progressive-thinking Republican counterparts. Reagan, she told the hall, was "a man who will confront the radicals on our campuses and the looters in our streets and see the laws will be obeyed." As for Vietnam, Reagan was a candidate who believed "if we must fight for our freedom, we will fight to win." Negotiations, apparently, were not part of Reagan's style.

The speeches and celebratory demonstrations droned on until 1:20 a.m., when the voting finally began. Nixon, seated on a circular couch in his hotel suite, surrounded by friends, family, and a television crew awaiting his reactions to the votes, kept track of the voting on a legal pad. Elsewhere, Rockefeller, his wife seated next to him, and a smattering of guests, including three of his brothers, watched from his Americana Hotel room. Reagan took it in at the convention center.

Any thoughts of a significant upset ended early, when it became evident that Ronald Reagan had not made the kind of inroads he had hoped for in the South. Alabama allotted 14 votes to Nixon and 12 to Reagan; Arkansas reserved its 18 votes for its favorite son, Winthrop Rockefeller. Any suspense evaporated when Florida, one of Reagan's essential states, gave 32 votes to Nixon and only 1 to Reagan and Rockefeller. Rockefeller would say later that he knew the stop-Nixon effort was doomed at that point. Georgia quickly followed by giving 21 of its 30 votes to Nixon. It was over. The only question left was whether Nixon would win on the first ballot. With Reagan claiming all the votes from California, and Rockefeller taking all of the votes from New York, it was going to be close. Wisconsin, the second to last state to vote, put Nixon in the winner's circle. The final first-ballot vote tallies: Nixon, 692; Rockefeller, 272; and Reagan, 182; with the remainder of the votes split among the dark-horse candidates.

Nixon accepted a gracious congratulatory call from Rockefeller before ignoring the wee hours of the morning and going back to work. He had a vice president to select and no time in which to do it.

■ ■ ■ ■ ■

While Republicans were busy celebrating and going about the task of selecting a nominee in the insulation of the convention hall, a large, violent melee was taking place six miles away, in a run-down stretch of Biscayne Bay called, amazingly, Liberty City. The origins of the outburst were never totally known, but before order was restored by the National Guard, 3 African Americans lay dead, 5 more were critically wounded, 150 were arrested, and vandals and looters had laid waste to businesses throughout the area. Snipers targeted police trying to quell the rioting, and police returned fire, leading one lieutenant to remark that the bedlam reminded him of a firefight in Vietnam. Asked how he intended to put an end to the rioting, Governor Claude Kirk replied that he would employ "whatever force is necessary" to take back the streets. This was the first riot of its kind in Miami's history. A curfew was enforced, and one hundred blocks of the area were occupied by the National Guard.

If nothing else, the rioting framed the disparity between the high-rolling partiers in the convention hall and reality only a few miles away. African Americans were not—and would not be—enveloped into the Republican Party, which had a demographic far removed from absentee landlords, second-hand shops, decaying buildings, and street crime. According to a study of more than half of the convention's delegates, "the average delegate to the Republican National Convention [was] most likely a college graduate, a businessman, a Protestant, white, a veteran and a convention participant for the first time." Only a small minority were women. These folks were not likely to be sympathetic to those staging violent street demonstrations.

Nor were they likely to take much notice in Ralph Abernathy's Poor People's Campaign, complete with covered wagons positioned strategically outside the convention hall. Abernathy, the most visible and vocal of Martin Luther King's disciples, had met reporters in the Fontainebleau hotel. He offered a statement in keeping with the solemnity of his purpose meeting head-on with a loud political convention—"If the Republican Party can afford this lavish convention, and the Administration can spend billions of dollars in a disastrous war, and America can subsidize unproductive farms and prosperous industries, surely we can meet the modest demands of the Poor People's Campaign"—followed by a question-and-answer session with the press. For a man knowing in his heart that the attention paid him, by the press and by the Republicans, was more a matter of politesse than keen interest, Abernathy was remarkably patient in addressing the inquiries, many of which he had heard on countless occasions in the past. The Poor People's Campaign, he said, suffered from problems of perception: if the press continued to portray the movement as a failure, people would see it that way, when, in fact, the campaign had raised millions of dollars in support. "Poor people," he said, "no longer will be unseen, unheard, and unrepresented. We are here to dramatize the *plight* of poor people." And thus the covered wagons: "Part of our Mule Train will be here in Miami Beach to dramatize *poverty* in this beautiful city of luxury."

He had spoken these words prior to the rioting in Liberty City. Now, with more death and destruction, his words highlighted the chasm between the haves and have-nots, the masses of privilege and the denizens of poverty, a division that poisoned the soul of a country that ordained itself united.

4 When Nixon arrived in Florida for the convention, he already had a preference for a running mate, though he was careful not to reveal his name. He had sent letters to three hundred friends and political associates, soliciting suggestions for a VP candidate, and he had gone over the responses. Two weeks before the convention, he and John Mitchell had discussed the necessary qualifications of the ideal candidate, as well as traits that might disqualify a candidate. As a practical matter, Nixon wanted someone who might strengthen his standing in the southern border states—or "rimland states," as he liked to call them. He had no delusions about defeating George Wallace in the South; the best he could hope to accomplish would be to corral Wallace into the obvious states—Alabama, Mississippi, Louisiana, and maybe a couple more—without Wallace's popularity bleeding into such border states as Virginia, Kentucky, and Maryland.

Nixon, ever the centrist, also felt strongly about selecting a vice-presidential candidate who didn't stray too far in either direction from the middle. That all but eliminated Senators Mark Hatfield and Charles Percy, Mayor John Lindsay, and Governor Ronald Reagan from contention. Since he believed his greatest strength was in foreign policy, Nixon hoped to find someone with a strong background in domestic affairs, preferably a governor, to balance the ticket. That person would have to share his hard-nosed ideas about law and order and have a fair but firm stance on civil rights.

Personality traits also factored into Nixon's decision. He knew, from his own experiences as Eisenhower's vice president, what characteristics he preferred. First, he didn't want to be overshadowed, as a candidate or president, by a stronger, more charismatic figure. Conversely, he wasn't interested in hitching up with a passive bystander. That had been a problem when he selected United Nations Ambassador Henry Cabot Lodge as his running mate in 1960. Lodge was well known and experienced, but he was soft on the campaign trail and certainly no match for Lyndon Johnson on the Democratic ticket. It was an uneasy balance, but Nixon needed someone strong enough to stand out on the campaign trail but not someone who would overwhelm his own presence. Finally, should Nixon win in November, the candidate had to be someone willing to step back and be second-in-command—not a sycophant but someone who wouldn't get in the way.

Nixon and Mitchell were aware of the names being tossed around among

Republicans and in the media. Rockefeller and Reagan, two favorites, were quickly discarded; both had been opponents, and Nixon was well versed in their strengths and weaknesses. Others, including suggestions from Nixon's advisors, were debated, some names easily eliminated, others held for future advisement at the convention. After all their discussion, one name remained as the best candidate in Nixon's and Mitchell's minds: Maryland governor Spiro T. Agnew.

Both men conceded that their choice was guaranteed to draw criticism, largely because he was a virtual unknown to the public and to most politicians outside his home state. Nor was he a top priority to party leaders. Twelve months earlier, he hadn't been on Nixon's radar. Nixon became aware of him when he spearheaded early efforts to induce Rockefeller to run, and they had met, thanks to Mitchell, soon after Agnew had invited the press to his office to witness Rockefeller's press conference announcing his candidacy, only to be humiliated when Rockefeller did an about-face and told everyone listening that he wasn't going to run after all. Nixon knew something about humiliation, and over the months of 1968, he learned that he had much in common with the governor. They were both self-made men, the products of tough backgrounds; they were iron willed by nature, ready to fight for their principles. For all his bluster, Agnew could be a modest man, as Nixon discovered when he asked Agnew what he might want, should he be elected. Agnew replied that a cabinet post would be nice, but he would be satisfied with a federal judge position.

But Nixon was not about to spring his preferred candidate on his party, if for no other reason than he didn't want to divide Republicans. Besides, it wasn't his style. He would make everyone feel part of the selection process— and who knew? Maybe someone would make a convincing case for someone else. He himself had two other possibilities in mind, friends he wanted to consult before he made a final decision on Agnew. Neither, it turned out, would take the job. California lieutenant governor Robert Finch, described by Nixon as "my closest friend in politics," turned him down flat, arguing that he was unqualified for the job, that the step up from his current position to the vice presidency was too great. A split with his boss, Ronald Reagan, who had presidential aspirations, might be problematic, dividing California voters. It was the same with Maryland congressman Rogers Morton. Nixon had approached him under the auspices of gathering information about Agnew, but when Morton's report was less than stellar—Agnew, he said, could be lazy, and it was best to keep him busy—Nixon changed direction. "Maybe you would be the better choice for me," he suggested. Morton countered that he wasn't qualified and would be perceived as a poor candidate by the Republican Party. "If you want to know the truth," he told Nixon, "if it's between me and Ted Agnew, Ted would make the stronger candidate."

By the time he was turned down by Morton, Nixon had hosted three meetings with advisors and Republican notables, each meeting with a different cast of consultants, the first commencing within an hour of Nixon's receiving the nomination. This initial meeting brought together a group of Nixon's core advisors and staff (including John Mitchell, H. R. Haldeman, John Sears, Robert Ellsworth, Maurice Stans, Patrick Buchanan, Leonard Garment, and Frank Shakespeare) and a handful of other trusted politicians and friends—twenty-four members in all. Nixon said little while the assembly mulled over the merits and demerits of a list of vice-presidential candidates. The names on the list were predictable, and the discussion similar to the one between Nixon and Mitchell two weeks earlier. Agnew's name never came up until Nixon asked what people thought of him. The response was tepid. Most knew very little about him. The meeting ended without consensus, other than the recommendation that Nixon's choice be a centrist.

Twenty-two men, including Senators Strom Thurmond and Barry Goldwater, Congressmen Donald Rumsfeld and John Rhodes, and Governors Louie Nunn and Jim Rhodes, attended the second meeting. The names of many proposed running mates matched those suggested in the first meeting, though Thurmond listed Agnew on his list as being acceptable. Thurmond and Goldwater openly opposed any liberal candidate. Howard Baker, the young senator from Tennessee, was brought up to some enthusiastic response. As before, Nixon listened intently, and as in the earlier meeting, he praised Agnew's nominating speech the previous evening. The meeting wrapped up, and as he led Goldwater to the door, Nixon showed as much of his hand as he would before announcing his nomination. "Could you live with Agnew?" he asked the former Republican nominee. "Hell, yes," Goldwater answered, "he's the best man you could have. He's been firm, and so what if he's not known. No vice-presidential candidate ever is."

How Nixon, a former VP nominee, felt about Goldwater's statement is unknown, but he walked away from the meetings discontent, still bothered by the general lack of interest in his candidate. He had worked through the night, but the first two meetings brought him no closer to Agnew than he had been before he began.

The third—and supposedly final—meeting took place about nine-thirty the following morning. It was the smallest group yet, less than half in numbers to the previous gatherings, but their credentials were impeccable: Senate Minority Leader Everett Dirksen, House Minority Leader Gerald Ford, national party chairman Ray Bliss, Texas senator (and Nixon friend) John Tower, Robert Finch, Rogers Morton, and three others. In a way, the meeting was a formality, a chance for Nixon to see that no important party members were excluded from the discussion process. He maintained his outward neutrality. Another name, Massachusetts governor John Volpe, was added to the short list of candidates, but by now, Nixon had grown tired of all the talk, and those around him accepted that he had already decided his pick. Throughout what had turned into an arduous process, Nixon was aware that the polls had already supported one of his old beliefs: Nixon felt that a vice-presidential candidate could hurt, but not help, a presidential candidate, and one of his polls had him polling a better percentage of votes on his own than when he was paired with potentials VPs. It was time to make his decision. He asked Rogers Morton to contact Agnew.

Agnew would say that he didn't expect to be picked by Nixon, but he gave no indication of that when Nixon took the phone from Morton and asked Agnew to be his running mate. The call was extremely brief, with Nixon offering the position, and Agnew answering that he would be honored.

An exhausted Richard Nixon met the press at twelve thirty and made his formal announcement. *Spiro who?* became the reaction of the moment, as dumbfounded reporters scrambled to learn anything they could about the man Nixon chose to be qualified for the top job, should anything happen to him. Agnew's giving Nixon's nominating speech had been somewhat surprising, but given all the possibilities, the VP selection was nothing less than stunning.

John A. Farrell, Nixon's biographer, deemed Nixon's choice an unqualified failure. "The selection of Spiro Agnew," he wrote, "revealed Nixon at his worst. It was a cynical nod, a race-baiting wink—and a catastrophic blunder. It was Nixon's first 'presidential' decision—the choosing of a running mate—and a disaster."

Nixon might have known that his selection would meet some resistance within his own party. The Democrats had occupied the White House for the past eight years, and while the election of a Republican in 1968 looked promising, the party needed as strong a ticket as possible to achieve that goal. Moderate and liberal Republicans, in particular, objected to the Agnew selection, which they felt was a not-so-subtle extension of an uplifted middle finger to Nelson Rockefeller, who had treated Agnew so poorly that he fled to the Nixon camp. Thus, Rocky's loss was Nixon's gain. Further, the liberal Republicans were attempting to regain the black vote lost in 1964; Agnew's edgy relationship with African Americans, brought to light during the looting and arson in Baltimore following Martin Luther King's assassination, would hinder efforts to regain lost votes.

A revolt was dicey, at the very least, but that didn't stop a small group of moderates from attempting a challenge of Nixon's choice. Finding a suitable candidate in such limited time proved to be daunting. John Lindsay, the group's first choice—and a name supported by three out of four Republicans polled in the House of Representatives prior to the convention—turned them down. He was backing Agnew and would be seconding his nomination at the convention later that evening. George Romney, the second choice, agreed, but his heart wasn't in it. Nixon lost his temper when he heard about the maneuver. "If the sore losers get away with something like this now," he groused, "they'll do the same damn thing during my presidency."

He shouldn't have been concerned. When the roll call vote was taken that evening, Agnew tallied 1,119 votes to Romney's 116, with Lindsay receiving 10 from the diehards. The rebels, including Rockefeller backers, fell in step with the party after this final challenge to Republican unity fell by the wayside.

Agnew was gracious when he met with reporters shortly after Nixon's press conference. He admitted that he was surprised by Nixon's selecting him, and he was grateful for the opportunity. "I can't analyze any strengths I bring," he allowed, "and I agree with you that the name of Spiro Agnew is not a household name. I certainly hope that it will become one within the next couple of months."

The surprise selection had the convention hall, from delegates to the press, speculating about Nixon's motivations. Was this Nixon's attempt to mollify the South? Was his centrist choice a way of trying to unite the party? Or was this a preemptive strike against George Wallace, who, oddly enough, tried to take credit for influencing Nixon's choice. Agnew's tough law-and-order stance, Wallace said, was similar to his, and Nixon's selection was a concession to Wallace's success. "They're talking like we do," he crowed, when asked about the vice-presidential candidate while he was on the campaign trail. "It's too late, but at least it's progress."

■ ■ ■ ■ ■

Spiro Agnew's biography was a brief but impressive textbook reading of the American Dream realized. It was also a study in how a malleable politician could be shaped by events. Agnew's father, Spiros Theodore Anagnostopoulos, a Greek immigrant, arrived in the United States in 1897 and changed the family name to Agnew. He married Margaret Pollard, a widow from Virginia.

Spiro Theodore Agnew, who preferred to be called Ted, was born in Baltimore on November 9, 1918. He was a bright but unexceptional student. After graduating from high school, he kicked around at several different schools, first at Johns Hopkins University, where he studied chemistry before leaving for the University of Baltimore Law School. He met and married Elinor Judefind, but his domestic and academic lives were interrupted by World War II and, in 1951, the Korean War. In Europe during World War II, Agnew acted as a company commander of the Tenth Armored Division and earned a Bronze Star for his service. Upon returning home he completed his degree and practiced law for a few Baltimore law firms.

Agnew's rapid ascent in politics began in disaster when, in 1960, he finished last in a five-candidate field for judge in Baltimore County. Two years later, he was back at it, competing in a race for county executive of Baltimore County. He had the good fortune of running at a time when Baltimore's Democratic Party was badly divided, and despite the GOP's usual status of landing on the losing end in the county's elections, Agnew (and his moderate positions) won. He reached his apex in 1966, when he ran for governor and won by the largest margin in his brief political career. Good fortune had blessed him again: his Democratic opponent, George P. Mahoney, ran a campaign based on racism and fear. His campaign slogan ("Your Home Is Your Castle—Protect It") rubbed too many people in the wrong way, coming, as it did, at a time when the people of Maryland felt safe.

As governor, Agnew served up a socially progressive menu. He ushered in a tough, antipollution law, but even more important, he pushed a civil rights agenda that included the state's first fair-housing legislation. He brought blacks into his administration and established strong lines of communication with black community leaders. He felt betrayed by the April 1968 rioting that left Baltimore badly damaged, and in a meeting with about one hundred black community leaders, he unloaded his anger and complaints, lecturing them so harshly that most walked out on him. Agnew's feelings about African Americans might not have changed on that day, but his attitudes toward law and order surely did. Like Mayor Richard Daley in Chicago, he spoke publicly and forcefully about the methods that might be used to combat urban violence. He rejected the Kerner Commission report as being too soft on violent perpetrators. He made it very clear that he blamed black leadership for failing to control their black community.

During his initial press conference following Nixon's announcement that he was his choice of running mate, Agnew addressed pointed questions about his apparent change in attitude about African Americans. Nonplussed, Agnew explained that he was still a civil rights advocate, that he intended to talk to black leaders and visit inner-city neighborhoods while campaigning for Nixon; he believed in equal opportunity. He did not, however, condone the kind of violent civil disobedience he had confronted during the disturbances in Baltimore.

5 Richard Nixon stood at the podium in the convention hall, soaking up the ovation that was nothing less than a deafening validation of a comeback so unlikely that the press was referring to it as a resurrection. Nixon, worried about his candidacy until the final delegate numbers were recorded and announced, could finally exhale. As he would say later, the only moment that could top this one would be the moment before he began his acceptance speech after winning the presidency. And he could feel that eventuality within his reach.

It had been the grandest of days. Earlier in the evening, Spiro Agnew had faced this same packed hall of Republicans. A large number of delegates were displeased with Nixon's choice, but they would not show it on this night, not in front of the national television coverage of the convention, not when the party, splintered four years earlier, needed a display of unity and support for a ticket suddenly competitive against a vulnerable Democratic Party, not when the sweet smell of a national conservative agenda graced the air. Agnew had their attention, and when he spoke of the next administration's actions being more important than anything he could say on the campaign trail, he had their hopes.

Nixon might have identified with Agnew's admission of the "improbability" of his successful candidacy, and near the end of his acceptance speech, he remarked on the long road he had traveled to reach this point, contrasting his personal victory with the losses suffered by those who never realized their dreams:

> Tonight I see the face of a child. He lives in a great city. He is black. Or he is white. He is Mexican, Italian, Polish. None of that matters. What matters, he's an American child.
>
> That child in that great city is more important than any politician's promise. He is America. He is a poet. He is a scientist, he is a great teacher, he is a proud craftsman. He is everything we ever hoped to be and everything we dare to dream to be.
>
> He sleeps the sleep of childhood and he dreams the dreams of a child.
>
> And when he awakens, he awakens to a living nightmare of poverty, neglect and despair. He fails in school. He ends up on welfare. For him the American system is one that feeds his stomach and starves his soul. It breaks his heart. And in the end it may take his life on some distant battlefield.
>
> To millions of children in this rich land, this is their prospect of the future.
>
> But this is only part of what I see in America.

I see another child tonight. He hears the train go by at night and he dreams of faraway places where he'd like to go. It seems like an impossible dream.

But he is helped on his journey through life. A father who had to go to work before he finished the sixth grade, sacrificed everything he had so that his son could go to college. A gentle, Quaker mother, with a passionate concern for peace, quietly wept when he went to war but she understood why he had to go. A great teacher, a remarkable football coach, an inspirational minister encouraged him on his way. A courageous wife and loyal children stood by him in victory and also defeat.

And in his chosen profession of politics, first there were scores, then hundreds, then thousands, and finally millions worked for his success.

And tonight he stands before you—nominated for President of the United States of America.

You can see why I believe so deeply in the American Dream.

He addressed his past early in his speech. After acknowledging his debt to Eisenhower, who, he reminded his listeners, had been "one of the greatest Americans of our time—or of any time," he spoke of the honor he had felt eight years earlier, when he had stood on a similar stage and accepted the nomination for the presidency. "But I have news for you," he continued. "This time there is a difference. This time we are going to win."

This was Nixon at his predictable best: his acceptance speech, essentially the very same speech he had been giving for months while stumping on the campaign trail, condemned the Johnson administration as a failure, domestically and abroad, while, invoking Eisenhower and his presidency on several occasions, it sought to appeal to a nostalgia for better times, when there were no Vietnams, no violent disruptions in the cities, no demonstrations and disruptions on college campuses. Nixon's America stood in stark contrast to the country to which citizens stood and pledged allegiance:

As we look at America, we see cities enveloped in smoke and flame. We hear sirens in the night. We see Americans dying on distant battlefields abroad. We see Americans hating each other, fighting each other, killing each other at home. And as we see and hear these things, millions of Americans cry out in anguish. Did we come all this way for this?

This was going to be a law-and-order speech, above anything else, but before he further darkened his picture of America or assailed the current administration for its inability to make Americans feel safe in their own homes, Nixon wisely chose to depict the victims of this mayhem. Not surprisingly, these were the voters he hoped would be supporting him in November, a Silent Majority, as they would be called, the powerless millions so disenfranchised that, as the Rolling Stones sang in their 1968 song "Salt of the Earth," they were trapped into "a choice of cancer or polio."

"It is the quiet voice in the tumult and the shouting," Nixon said.

It is the voice of the great majority of Americans, the forgotten Americans—the non-shouters, the non-demonstrators. They are not racists or sick; they are not guilty of the crime that plagues the land. They are black and they are white—they're native born and foreign born—they're young and they're old.

They work in America's factories. They run America's businesses. They serve in government. They provide most of the soldiers who died to keep us free. They give drive to the spirit of America. They give life to the American Dream. They give steel to the backbone of America. They are good people, they are decent people, they work, and they save, and they pay their taxes. And they care. Like Theodore Roosevelt, they know that this country will not be a good place for any of us to live in unless it is a good place for all of us to live in.

This I say to you tonight is the real voice of America. In this year 1968, this is the message it will broadcast to America and to the world. Let's never forget that despite her faults, America is a great nation.

And America is great because her people are great.

These words drew a joyously frenzied response from the convention hall. Nixon had crafted his speech to elicit such response, and it didn't matter that it was sticky-sweet patriotism at its most obvious: the assembly, entrapped in a week's worth of dull activities capable of boring all but the most dedicated political creatures, needed something, even if predictable and shopworn, to massage their hearts. Dick Nixon had accomplished this with straight talk. He had obeyed the first commandment of electoral politics: give the voters what they want to hear.

This was a speech high on emotion and bereft of solution. Nixon addressed all the major issues—Vietnam, the Cold War, law and order, poverty, the sputtering economy, crime, racial division—but he offered no concrete solutions or courses of action. He suggested that the United States, as powerful as the country had been throughout its history, was at a low point. "America is in trouble today," he stated, "not because her people have failed but because her leaders have failed. And what America needs are leaders to match the greatness of her people."

These words were the keel upon which Nixon had constructed his campaign. The country had failed miserably over the past five years—he was careful to avoid any hint that John Kennedy had been party to this failure—and it was time for a change, a revolutionary one. There had been talk of revolution throughout the year, almost always coming from the young, the disenfranchised, those who would spit on or burn the flag, those who distrusted the country and its leaders; one of the most popular songs of the year had been the Beatles' "Revolution." Nixon brought up another revolution—the American Revolution—on a few occasions during his speech, and he made certain that his listeners knew that the revolution was an ongoing process that would extend into the bicentennial and into the next millennium. It was time to make America great again in the eyes of the world.

Nixon spoke for more than a half hour, his speech repeatedly interrupted, as speeches of this nature always were, by deafening cheers and ovations. As an orator, Nixon would never be compared to Martin Luther King, but on this night, while trying to rally a party that had been shattered during the last presidential election, Nixon was a hope-peddling winner.

"My fellow Americans, the long dark night for America is about to end," he promised at the conclusion of his address. "The time has come for us to leave the valley of despair and climb the mountain so that we may see the glory of the dawn—a new day for America, and a new dawn for people and freedom in the world."

15 Resistance

1 They were coming to Chicago—the not-so-loyal opposition, the patriot reb-
els, the rabble-rousers and Enemies of the State, those dedicated to change,
the curious, the dark partiers, the ununiformed troops spoiling for battle, the
Yippies, the peacemakers, the political junkies, the battalions of sex-drugs-
and-rock-and-rollers. The names of some of their leaders and organizations—
Tom Hayden (Students for a Democratic Society), David Dellinger (Mobe),
Bobby Seale (Black Panthers), and Jerry Rubin and Abbie Hoffman (Youth
International Party)—were nationally recognized, and the FBI, declaring them
to be dangers to the public safety, had devoted countless man-hours to observing them and reporting what they had learned. The demonizing of what came
to be called the counterculture was unrelenting. To hear J. Edgar Hoover's side
of the story, the counterculture, if left unchecked, would create a havoc capable
of destroying the American way. The rebels, although nowhere as anarchistic
and violent as portrayed, loved playing along with their reputation. Their goal,
after all, was to disrupt the American way as it currently existed. They encouraged revolution.

Their numbers, according to doomsday reports, had been swelling for more
than six months, to the extent where an originally expected few thousand had
grown to a possible million, all gathering in the city, disrupting the convention,
sleeping (or worse) in the parks, openly using drugs, and vandalizing property. A violent confrontation between their forces and Chicago mayor Richard
Daley's guardians of order appeared to be inevitable. Or so the media believed.
If Abbie Hoffman and Jerry Rubin and others possessed genius, it was in their
understanding of media manipulation. In their quest to report the next big
story—and be the first to do so—press members fell over themselves in the
rush. They believed anything, no matter how outrageous or unlikely, regardless
of whether it was whispered by a waif in an alleyway or shouted by a monster

perched on a dung heap. The facts would sort themselves eventually. Rubin, a former reporter, and Hoffman believed this, and their encounters with the press proved it. Once something was reported in the papers or on television, it spread through dry imagination like wildfire.

A case in point: Jack Mabley, a reporter and columnist whose style represented that of the town crying of Chicken Little, repeated the rumor that the Yippies were going to spike the city's water with LSD. Rebellious youths had spiked the water supply in the movie *Wild in the Streets,* leading to the overthrow of the government. It didn't matter to Chicago authorities or the media that such an act of urban terrorism was essentially impossible to pull off; it made good copy. The verbal jousting between the Yippies and the press and civic leaders, in the opinion of Paul Krassner, one of the founders of the Youth International Party and an unofficial spokesperson for the Yippies, was "a clash between *our* mythology and *their* mythology," with the press willing to publish almost anything anybody said. "If you gave a good quote," Krassner noted, "they would give you free publicity."

Not all reporters were ensnared in this, of course, but enough contributed to the rumor mill to make the Chicago convention a top news item. Mabley alone acted as a one-man warehouse regarding Yippie plots against the city and convention. Writing for the *Chicago American,* Mabley warned readers of dangers beyond the spiking of the city's water supply. Militants, he cautioned, had threatened to block the freeways with old cars, drug or poison food in restaurants, put gas in the air-conditioning system of the Amphitheatre, pose as prostitutes in an effort to seduce delegates and lace their drinks with LSD, and fire mortar shells at the convention center. "How many other sophisticated schemes of sabotage exist may only be imagined," he wrote.

Like Krassner, Abbie Hoffman found the press coverage to be amusing but valuable publicity. "True, there would be monkey-warfare highjinks, but our strategy did not include plans for organized violence or riot although fanciful literature carried our dope-induced hallucinations," he wrote in his autobiography.

We revealed that the Potheads' Benevolent Organization had been busy all spring strewing seeds in the vacant lots of Chicago, anticipating the ideal growing weather of the predicted Long Hot Summer. We spread the rumor that battalions of super-potent yippie males were getting in shape to seduce female convention-goers and that yippie agents were posing as hookers. There was no end to our nefarious plans. We would dress up people like Viet Cong and send them into the streets to shake hands like ordinary American politicians. We would paint cars taxi-yellow, pick up delegates and drop them in Wisconsin. Planning to hijack the Chicago office of the National Biscuit Company and distributing bread and cookies to the masses might have sounded a little incendiary, had there been a Chicago office of Nabisco. There wasn't. Later HUAC took all this dead seriously, even suggesting we had planned to blow up a baseball diamond in Lincoln Park.

The FBI needed no persuading to fear the worst, if one could judge from the memos circulating in the Bureau.

Hoffman scoffed at all the discussion about the Yippies' carefully organized plans. "Conspiracy?" he laughed. "We can't even agree on lunch."

2 The Youth International Party began as a whim born from serious discussion. In time, the origins of Yippie!, as the loosely structured organization liked to be known, developed its legend, with all the conflicting stories one might expect, but there was no disputing that the party began when serendipity merged with serious political commitment, and the founding members, steeped in political activism, attempted to find a way to marry their political vision to the masses of people migrating to the Democratic National Convention in Chicago.

The seed of the idea germinated in December 1967. Abbie and Anita Hoffman, along with Paul Krassner, publisher of *The Realist* and antiwar activist, were vacationing in a rented cottage on Ramrod Key in the Florida Keys. They smoked pot, dropped acid, went swimming with dolphins, and spent hours arguing about politics. One evening just before Christmas, after attending Dino De Laurentiis's film *The Bible,* Hoffman and Krassner returned to a favorite topic—revolution—using the movie as a focal point in their argument. They discussed the story about God's ordering Abraham to kill his son. Krassner, a pacifist by nature, disliked Abraham's blind, unquestioning obedience, while Hoffman felt it was a symbol of "revolutionary trust." Krassner had been to Cuba, and he could understand how in such extraordinary circumstances as the Cuban Revolution, violence might be necessary for change. Hoffman, who was actually no more violent than Krassner, strongly believed in *action,* and if violence was an ingredient in a revolt against an intolerable status quo . . . so be it. Both men wanted to attend the Democratic National Convention, and, as Krassner remembered, it was almost a given that violent confrontation with law enforcement personnel would occur. Further discussion led them to believe that a festive environment in the aftermath of the Summer of Love—a

Festival of Life, complete with music and peaceful demonstrations—might be a way to ward off violent conflict. The idea appealed to them to such an extent that they cut short their vacation and returned to New York for further planning. "The conspiracy," Krassner would remember, "was beginning."

Krassner would say that the Florida discussions constituted the conception of the Youth International Party; its birth, he continued, would occur on the afternoon of December 31, 1967, when he, Jerry Rubin, poet/musician/activist Ed Sanders, and a few others gathered at Abbie and Anita Hoffman's New York apartment to ring in the new year. According to Krassner, a lot of Colombian pot had been smoked by the time the discussion turned to their plans for the Chicago convention. The Florida conversations had led to initial plans for a Festival of Life—a stark contrast, they felt, to the Festival of Death that the convention represented. A Festival of Life would be modeled on the successful "be-ins" of the past year, including the huge gatherings at Golden Gate Park in San Francisco and the Monterey Pop Festival. Rock bands would play, there would be singing and dancing, and workshops addressing everything from spirituality to alternate forms of government would be held. Everything would be free. All you had to do was show up. Hoffman said, "This would go along with our philosophy that people were basically good, they had innate potential for creativity and for life if we just created the kind of conditions in which these potentials could come to the fore."

There was a built-in naïveté to such idealism: this anarchistic, do-your-own-thing line of thinking had all sorts of pitfalls. For one, you were not about to *lead* a large group of anarchists into any organized activity; people would behave as they pleased. Logistical concerns also clouded the picture. Permits would be required for live music, assembly and sleeping in the parks, and any sort of mass demonstration, and given Mayor Daley's response to the rioting in Chicago after the assassination of Martin Luther King, obtaining these permits was going to be difficult. The potential for violence overshadowed everything: what would happen if (or, most likely, *when*) plans broke down and people traveling in from all over the country found themselves with nowhere to stay and nowhere to gather? Clashes with police were likely.

Rubin and Hoffman disagreed, as they often did, on the specter of violence. Both agreed that violence was standard in any revolution, but Hoffman, a provocateur by nature, felt nevertheless that it shouldn't be invited; years of activism, with all the attendant beatings and arrests, had taught him as much. Hoffman, a trickster, believed in guerilla theater. Ridicule and black humor unnerved the power brokers—or at least it weakened them in the public eye. He viewed his role as that of the catalyst. Rubin, on the other hand, took himself and his role as a revolutionary much more seriously. Bloodshed, he insisted, was an inevitable part of the overthrow of the system. Like Hoffman, he was a confrontationist, but he did not believe he would walk away unscathed. Violence, he felt, was "an effective form of communication, the best means for the movement to get public attention."

But these concerns were not at the core of discussion on that New Year's Eve. In tossing around their ideas, the group was looking for a loose structure. For openers, they needed a name for their following, and Krassner came up with Youth International Party by going backward on the handle. *Party* was easy because the group had talked about running a pig for president as a bit of political theater, and the pig would have to be affiliated with a political party. *Party* also included other implications, from the sober notion that the members would be part of something, however loosely structured, to the idea that this group could be having fun while it assembled for a serious cause. *International* grew out of the simple idea that anyone, regardless of nationality, could be a member. With the *I* and *P* in place, Krassner began fumbling around with letters to make a memorable acronym. He had been considering the word *youth* in other possibilities, and including it now made sense. Yip could stand for Youth International Party, but its members—Yippies—maintained the playfulness that would be a strong part of the group's politics. Yippie, after all, was a shout of joy. The others in the apartment endorsed the name. The Youth International Party would be the sponsor of the Festival of Life.

It took little time for the rest to fall into place. A press release announcing the party's formation and the forthcoming Festival of Life also served as a manifesto:

> The life of the American Spirit is being torn asunder by the forces of violence, decay, and the napalm cancer fiend. We demand the politics of ecstasy. We are the delicate spoors of the new fierceness that will change America. We will create our new reality. And we will not accept the false theater of the Death Convention. We will be in Chicago. Begin preparations now! Chicago is yours! Do it!

Such behavior would be branded radical by the so-called Establishment, but Krassner dismissed the characterization. The Yippies, he said, were furthering a long-standing pattern of behavior. "The Yippies were part of an age-old tradition of tricksters, and that spirit lives on in those who taunt sitting politicians. We borrowed a trick from the CIA: you don't have to manipulate the media if you can manipulate the events the media cover. The Yippies did guerrilla theater."

The Yippies formally announced their existence and plans for the Festival of Life at a press conference at Manhattan's Hotel Americana on March 17, with Jerry Rubin, Abbie Hoffman, Phil Ochs, Allen Ginsberg, Arlo Guthrie, and others in attendance. The festival, Ginsberg told the gathering, was to be a peaceful affirmation of and commitment to the future of the planet. The first large Yippie event—a "Yip-in" intended to celebrate the end of winter and the arrival of spring—was scheduled to take place at the Grand Central railroad station on March 21–22. This was to be a celebration, a dry run, on a much smaller scale, of what Hoffman and Rubin hoped to see in Chicago. According to the plan, the Yippies would hold a rally at midnight at the railroad station and then head to Central Park, where they would watch the sunrise. The Yippies played by the book in setting up the gathering: they met with Mayor John Lindsay, proposed their plans, and received his blessing; they filled out the required permit paperwork and publicized the event on the radio. There was talk of offering flowers and popcorn to the commuters, and a Yippie flyer advertising the event encouraged attendees to "bring bells, flowers, beads, music, FM, radios (to WBAI), pillows, eats, love and peace." This was the place to meet other Yippies and exchange ideas for the Festival of Life in Chicago.

As one might have expected, there were concerns about crowd control. On any given day, the Grand Central Terminal was roiling with travelers leaving and arriving in New York. The sudden influx of a mass of Yippies was bound to affect movement to and from the trains. There was no predicting the behavior of the Yippies, whether they were demonstrating or interacting with irate passengers or the police. After much discussion, the police chief ordered a much larger detail of police for the terminal, though the great majority were sequestered in rooms out of sight of the general public.

The evening began without incident. Yippies began arriving earlier and in greater numbers than anticipated, and by late evening, a crowd of an estimated two thousand to three thousand, swelling to an estimated five thousand by midnight, had spread out throughout the terminal. Rubin was there, though he preferred to stay removed from attention. Hoffman arrived, decked out in an American Indian costume; he was clearly enjoying the show. Others wore costumes, as well. A banner reading "Liberty, Equality, Fraternity" was unfurled. The police patrolling the terminal, as one report had it, were also enjoying the spectacle.

But as Hoffman, Rubin, and others would see a few months later in Chicago, it took very little to change the mood of those attending an event. A group of East Village radicals calling themselves the Up Against the Wall Motherfuckers, known for their unpredictable behavior, arrived and staged their own series of protests. Most of their actions were harmless, including several members' climbing onto the main terminal clock and shouting slogans about the unimportance of time. The problems began when they tried to remove the hands from the clock, and some of the Yippies began setting off firecrackers and cherry bombs. Police, including those kept from public view, flooded the area at 12:50 a.m., and when they were unsuccessful in removing the Motherfuckers from the clock, they attempted to clear the Yippies from the building. "Some of the police were visibly angry," the *New York Times* reported.

Pandemonium ensued. The angry confrontations escalated into violence, the police using their batons on anyone, including train passengers, in their paths. *Village Voice* reporter Don McNeill was pushed through a glass door. Abbie Hoffman was beaten ruthlessly and wound up at Bellevue Hospital. Young Yippies, forced out one door, returned through another. A New York civil liberties attorney, on hand as a Yippie legal adviser, called the police behavior "the worst example of police brutality I've ever seen outside of Mississippi." The disturbance lasted for hours, until the Yippies left and headed to Central Park for the daybreak festivities. In all, fifty-seven people were arrested, and twenty wound up in the hospital for treatment.

The Yip-in received full press treatment, with the police bearing the brunt of the criticism. The Youth International Party had won the publicity the party founders sought. It also was served a sneak preview of what lay ahead in days to come.

3 Abbie Hoffman and Jerry Rubin were perceived to be radicals with little agenda other than to cause trouble, but a close examination of their backgrounds reveals a sense of commitment exceeding that of all but a tiny percentage of dissidents. Both had come from middle-class backgrounds, but they had taken different paths in their activism. Both were considerably older than the youths that they led.

Abbot Howard Hoffman was born in Worcester, Massachusetts, on November 30, 1936, the first son of middle-class Jewish parents. His father, John Hoffman, a pharmacist, would struggle his entire life to reconcile his son's intelligence with a rebellious streak that repeatedly landed him in trouble. Abbie, who would fondly remember his childhood, clashed with figures of authority at an early age, and while he was not large or powerfully built, he was streetsmart, tough, and athletic enough to hold his own in schoolyard fights. During his sophomore year of high school, he was expelled from school for turning in a twenty-page paper arguing against the idea of God, who, he claimed, would never have allowed suffering on Earth if he existed; he and his teacher were involved in a physical altercation when the teacher tore up the paper. "Not exactly prime Spinoza," Hoffman said of the paper, "it was written nonetheless from the heart and head." The expulsion, he claimed, was the first time a Jew had been thrown out of the school. "Mama made a lot of trips to intercede," he recalled, "but I was sixteen now, and legally the state could absolve itself of all responsibility for my education."

Hoffman's education, he would have argued, was more likely to take place in a pool hall than within the walls of a schoolhouse. By the time he graduated from high school, he was wandering freely down the halls of rebellious thinking. His choice of colleges—Brandeis University—defied his parents' expectations, but he found the environment liberating. The university had opened its doors in 1948, and its faculty included Marxist Herbert Marcuse and psychologist Abraham Maslow; both powerfully influenced Hoffman's interest in breaking away from the American status quo. Not that he began at Brandeis as a full-blown revolutionary. In looking back, he would describe his early college years as being fairly typical, from his study habits to his place on the tennis team, which was coached by Bud Collins.

Hoffman's father would complain that the university had corrupted his son, changing him into the radical he became, but Abbie disagreed, at least in part. "I think I've been totally shaped by my environment as I went along," he told an interviewer in 1981. "I'm the product of the sum total of my environmental experience and obviously Brandeis, this first encounter with intellectual ideas, was important."

Hoffman married his first wife, Sheila Karklin, in 1960 in a traditional Jewish wedding in Rhode Island. She was pregnant when they married, and she would have two children with him during their six-year marriage. At first, Hoffman seemed resigned to a life with a wife, kids, a house, and job tucked away in suburban living. He was changing, however, with each passing month. He was eager to pursue an against-the-grain agenda that put him on the street rather than at a desk. He was not a man inclined to spend all of his hours in coffeehouse banter; he thrived on the energy and camaraderie found in demonstrations and political activism. As a protester, he attended two significant, influential demonstrations in 1960. As he would write, these were two "generation-shaking events" that would "mold my consciousness forever."

The first occurred on May 1 at the San Quentin prison, where several hundred protesters, including actors Marlon Brando and Shirley MacLaine, had gathered to bring attention to the execution of Caryl Chessman, a man convicted of multiple rapes and symbol of a mounting opposition to capital punishment. Chessman, convicted solely on circumstantial evidence, had managed to buy twelve years of life after his 1948 conviction by exhausting every legal avenue open to him; his final hope, a stay of execution from California governor Pat Brown, did not materialize, even though Brown confessed that he opposed capital punishment. The warden, offering coffee and doughnuts to the protesters, allowed that he was also against it. The incongruity of it offended Hoffman's sensibilities: if such powerful figures, as well as other individuals and a large percentage of the public, opposed capital punishment, why was he executed? How was this democracy at work?

The second event took place ten days later in San Francisco. The House Un-American Activities Committee (HUAC) was holding meetings, supposedly open to the public, in the city's Federal Building, but when a large group of would-be attendees arrived and discovered that the seats were going mainly to people associated with the government, an impromptu demonstration commenced. The police, batons swinging, tore into the crowd and ruthlessly clubbed the demonstrators and public alike. Water-hose teams opened up on those trying to flee the scene. Hoffman escaped unharmed, but he was surprised to see that only a few blocks away from the brutality no one on the street seemed to be aware of what was going on. America, he wrote in his autobiography, was being introduced to the 1960s.

Over the next seven years, Hoffman took what was eventually a crash course in free-form activism. He discovered that, unlike Sheila, who was socially and politically astute but organized, he could use the sheer power of personality as fuel for getting people to respond to a call to action, but the realization did not simply hit him like a satori. It was an evolutionary process, with every new year and each new experience serving as a building block in the development. In the beginning, while he was still maintaining a household and using his degree in his job at the psychiatric department of Worcester State Hospital, he was learning his first lessons in public speaking and persuasion, whether he was lecturing on behalf of the American Civil Liberties Union at screenings of the controversial film *Operation Abolition,* or canvassing the state on behalf of an independent party senate candidate with strong antimilitary opinions. He was shouted down by right-wing audiences, called a pinko-agitator (and worse), and had doors slammed in his face. Rather than feel discouraged, he wrote it off as a learning experience. "It was exhilarating," he claimed. "There is no better way to learn the skills of organizing than canvassing door to door. If you stick to it, you can't help but develop into a good organizer. The people force you into becoming convincing—and the more varied the people you meet, the better you get."

He was able to apply some of these newfound skills in his work in the civil rights movement. He volunteered at the local Worcester chapter of the NAACP and, finding it staid and ineffective, all but took over the group's leadership. From there, he moved on to the Student Nonviolent Coordinating Committee, gaining invaluable field experience in the summers of 1964 and 1965, when he traveled to Mississippi and ran into nasty confrontations with white citizens and law enforcement officials unhappy about Northerners invading their state and stirring up trouble by insisting that segregationist communities abide by the Civil Rights Act. The townsfolk were content to see blacks in squalid, impoverished conditions, where justice was just a word, if it was recognized at all. During his visits to the South, Hoffman became acquainted with jail cells. "Throughout all this, I had the feeling I was learning American civics for the first time," he would remember.

In 1966, his marriage, never stable to begin with, had ground down to an ending, and his job as a salesman for Westwood Pharmaceuticals, which he had held for three years and actually excelled at, concluded with his getting fired for not working enough. Massachusetts, he decided, was a dead end, and he moved to New York. As an activist, he was growing more radical but was still closer in deportment to the straitlaced organizers than to the anything-goes persona for which he became known. He had lost most of his faith in the system, but he knew of no effective way to operate than from within it.

Before departing Massachusetts, Hoffman discovered drugs, mostly marijuana and LSD, and he enjoyed their effects on him. His wife would have nothing to do with them, so he found himself smoking pot or dropping acid with friends at their homes—his new obsession doing little to repair the shambles of his marriage. After moving to New York, he plugged into the East Village scene, with its unorthodox behavior and sex, drugs, and rock-and-roll environment. He fit in. By day, he ran Liberty House, a cooperative that sold Southern-produced crafts in the North to benefit the Southern poor; at night, he was organizing in the street and sharing a ramshackle apartment with a medical student.

Hoffman recalled this as a fertile time in his development as an activist, and he had fond memories of his work at Liberty House. "It was kind of an alternative economy and protest," he said. "I thought this was a valuable contribution, in terms of the civil rights movement and the role that white people could play in it."

While at Liberty House, Hoffman met Anita Kushner, a Liberty House volunteer and civil rights activist, who Hoffman would say was his female counterpart. Possessing a formidable intellect and a master's degree in psychology from Yeshiva University, she, like Hoffman, had extensive experience in civil rights and antiwar demonstrations and was hoping to organize a strong antiwar protest movement in New York. She and Hoffman became inseparable. They moved in together in a Greenwich Village apartment and married on June 8, 1967, in a public ceremony in Central Park.

The final piece of Abbie Hoffman's development fell into place when he met the Diggers, a radical offshoot of the San Francisco Mime Troupe. The Diggers, who believed that life and art were the one and the same, were a dynamic presence in the Bay Area. Their street theater, usually resulting in a message as part of the act, fit perfectly in the Haight-Ashbury section of San Francisco during the Summer of Love. Their actions, often presented as skits, complete with props and costumes, spoke louder than slogans or speeches. In the Diggers' world, life was as free as the soup they distributed to the poor out of twenty-five-gallon milk cans. They even had a free store, where customers could enter and take what they needed. The Grateful Dead and other area bands provided a soundtrack to it all.

The first time Abbie Hoffman met Emmett Grogan, Peter Berg, Peter Coyote, and other members of the Diggers, he instinctively understood that they represented the way he could deliver his message as an activist, the more humorous and unorthodox the better. ("I'm only interested in humor as a weapon," he would say, "a revolutionary weapon.") The Diggers could be funny, subtle, maddening, on target, out of line, cruel, kind, compelling, obnoxious— but never boring—and there was never a shortage of material to address or lampoon. Hoffman and his friends began practicing their own versions of street theater, which included organizing be-in type gatherings and distributing leaflets on such topics as drugs and venereal disease. On one occasion, they joined a patriotic, right-wing "Support Our Boys in Vietnam" parade. On another, they mailed joints to names pulled randomly from the phone book, and to television news personalities. Hoffman loved the manic pace.

He pulled off his most memorable prank at the New York Stock Exchange, two days after he and Jerry Rubin met for the first time. Hoffman was looking for a new angle to protest the Vietnam War, and a friend and fellow activist, Jim Fouratt, suggested an event at the stock exchange. After all, American soldiers were dying in huge numbers while investors were hauling in money without any risk to their welfare. "We decided to focus on who really ran the war and who the war really affects," Fouratt explained.

Hoffman set the plan in motion by using a fake name and credentials to gain entry to the stock exchange. He then called a select group of reporters and saw that there would be plenty of media coverage. At the appointed time, Hoffman and about fourteen others, including Rubin, each armed with a roll of one-dollar bills, gathered at the stock exchange and entered the gallery set high over the floor. At Hoffman's signal, the group began tossing the bills over the rail. Action on the floor froze, as investors watched the bills fluttering through the air. Many did not react, but, as Hoffman expected, many crawled around on the floor, trying to capture as many of the bills as possible. Hoffman's group was escorted from the premises, but not before the pandemonium had proven his point. Outside, Hoffman and the others met with the media, assuring that the prank would gain television and newspaper coverage. With cameras rolling, Hoffman and Rubin burned five-dollar bills and explained their protest.

Hoffman and Rubin became fast friends. Rubin, an energetic organizer, nationally known for his organization of antiwar demonstrations, had never met anyone like Hoffman, who seemed to be connected to everyone in New York and willing to do just about anything as a form of protest. In Rubin, Hoffman found someone with the personality and commitment to complement his own. Both possessed enormous egos, and they would disagree often and heatedly, but they shared the dream of wanting to tear down society and rebuild it.

"We were two people who sensed the opportunity of blending the political and cultural revolutions," Hoffman observed.

> Jerry's forte was political timing, mine dramatic. I trusted his political judgment more than anyone's in the country. We were anarchists, but even among anarchists there are not that many who can map out a strategy and lead. Some anarchists are just more equal than others in that ability. Stubborn, attentive to the ways of power and the universe, Jerry had the drive and the political instincts to ride the movement waves.

4 Jerry Rubin, it so happened, had his own plans for an ambitious event. Rubin and David Dellinger, leader of the Mobilization to End the War in Vietnam (Mobe), were piecing together a massive march and rally at the Pentagon in the biggest antiwar demonstration to date. The Mobe was far less frenetic than the kind of happenings organized by Rubin on the West Coast, and Rubin was brought in to add energy to the event.

Very little about Rubin's early years offers an indication of his eventual status in the counterculture. Born in Cincinnati on July 14, 1938, Jerry Clyde Rubin lived a comfortable middle-class youth and, by all indications, seemed destined to a similar life as an adult. His father, Bob Rubin, a high school dropout, drove a bread truck, volunteered as a Cub Scout leader, and, with a boost from Jimmy Hoffa, served as secretary-treasurer in the bakery drivers' chapter of his local Teamsters. Jerry's college-educated mother, the former Esther Katz, came from an upper-middle-class background, and her family, in Jerry's eyes, looked down on his family, particularly on his father.

"My whole life has been a battle of the Rubins against the Katzes," Rubin said.

The Katzes were snobs. From their suit-and-tie, middle-class, salesman point of view my father was always a schlepper. But he didn't look at things that way. Even when he was a union official he was always very very egalitarian. I got some of that from him. I'm a lot like my father.

Jerry idolized his father, and in spite of being someone who could be very intolerant of others, he defended him even when the elder Rubin tried to counsel his two sons to follow the type of middle-of-the-road to conservative Cincinnati life that Jerry despised. "He tried to teach his kids," Rubin wrote of his father. "He told us not to do anything that would lead us from the path of Success."

Jerry's teen years reflected his passionate concerns but, when analyzed, weren't all that different from those of youths of the time. He collected baseball cards, passionately followed the Cincinnati Reds baseball team, and aspired to be a sportswriter. Photographs from his high school period depict a well-groomed, short-haired, jacket-and-bow-tie young man with a winning smile—a typical teenaged boy during the Eisenhower years. His liberal politics, such as they were, were manifest by his volunteer work on Adlai Stevenson's two presidential runs. He coedited the *Chatterbox*, his Walnut Hills High School newspaper, and while still in high school, he contributed to the *Cincinnati Post* and eventually became a news feature writer and editor there. After graduating from high school, he unhappily attended Oberlin College for a year but dismissed it as "a lot of academic bullshit."

His life changed dramatically when he lost both of his parents within ten months of each other—his father from a heart attack and his mother from cancer—and he was pressed into raising his thirteen-year-old brother, Gil. He considered taking Gil to India, where Jerry had won a scholarship to study, but his mother's family threatened to sue for custody if he did; instead, he traveled to Israel, to which his Jewish relatives offered no objection. He settled in Tel Aviv, lived on a kibbutz, and studied sociology at the university. He stayed in Israel for a year and a half, the experience both unsettling and educational. His political views were swinging much further to the left, bordering on Marxism, and he struggled with what he witnessed in Israel. The country, he felt, was not much different from the United States, with citizens pursuing money and status, with similar class distinctions. He grew increasingly dissatisfied with Israel's attitudes and policies, especially toward Palestinians. ("So here I came for idealism, and I got—America," he would say.) He returned to the States in 1964, traveling to Italy, Germany, and England on his way home, and registered to study sociology in the PhD program at the University of California at Berkeley.

His timing was exquisite. Berkeley was percolating from the scenes of the day (mainly the civil rights movement), the changing consciousness of students encouraged by liberal teachers to think on their own and respond accordingly, growing tensions between two generations at loggerheads over the best ways to solve festering political arguments, growing media coverage of campus activities, and an awakening of organized opposition to the Vietnam War. Students distributed pamphlets on civil rights; meetings were held. The Berkeley campus was turning into a hot spot for debate, and Rubin was quickly immersed in it.

That summer, Rubin joined eighty-three others on a trip to Cuba. The Cold War was at its peak, and travel between the United States and Cuba was prohibited. Rubin, with a revolutionary's zeal of defying the authorities, took a plane to Czechoslovakia, the nearest Soviet bloc country, and from there he caught a flight to Cuba. He and the others hoped to learn about the revolution by speaking to those who fought in it. They met for four hours with Che Guevara, who, in full uniform, a pistol at his side, explained that he was envious of the Americans. They were in the center of a revolution to come.

Back in Berkeley, during the fall semester of classes, Rubin, who had dropped out of school and was living on his inheritance, became involved in the Free Speech movement, an ongoing battle between the school's administration and students that was gaining national attention. This was the first extended mass demonstration on a college campus in U.S. history, and it set the precedent for all that would follow. University officials decided to enforce long-standing regulations prohibiting or limiting political activities on campus property. These restrictions included the dissemination of pamphlets and literature, distributed by hand at tables set up outside; recruitment for membership in political organizations; fund-raising; the invitation of guest speakers not approved by the university beforehand; and unendorsed assemblies.

On October 1, Jack Weinberg, a former graduate student and civil rights advocate, was arrested after refusing to produce his identification for campus police, touching off a spontaneous demonstration when angry students encircled a police car, sat down, and refused to move; the standoff lasted for thirty-two hours, with Weinberg and police trapped inside the car, surrounded by thousands of students. It ended when the charges against Weinberg were dropped. Over the ensuing weeks, student leaders and school officials attempted to forge an agreement over the campus rules, but negotiations stalled.

Mario Savio, a twenty-two-year-old from Queens, New York, and a junior at the university, rose to a position of student leader and spokesperson for the growing movement. An exceptional orator, Savio would remember the movement as a large-scale demonstration against censorship—hence, the Free Speech moniker tagged to it.

"At first we didn't understand what the issues were," he told *Life* magazine. "But as discussion went on, they became clear. The university wanted to regulate the content of our speech. The issue of the multiversity and the issue of free speech can't be separated. There was and is a need for the students to express their resentment without having to submit to the administration's arbitrary exercise of power."

On December 2, two thousand attended a mass rally. Folk singer and activist Joan Baez performed, and students occupied the administration building. The clash between the students and police saw 773 arrests. A student strike was called, classes were canceled. Faculty and department heads, now in the students' corner, helped raise bond for those held in jail, and over the next few days, negotiations between administration and faculty, and administration and students, were held. An agreement was eventually reached, but not before a new balance of power had been established.

These were precisely the types of issues and actions that appealed to Rubin's growing radical sense of a need for disruption to counter unacceptable laws and behavior. The old ways weren't working. Rubin became a familiar face at campus protests; by his own admission, he couldn't pass up a sit-in without participating. One specific issue—the Vietnam War—captured his undivided attention, and by the spring 1965 semester, he was cofounding the Vietnam Day Committee (VDC), an organization devoted to teach-ins, sit-ins, mass demonstrations, occupations, draft-card burnings, and anything else they could come up with to oppose the war. The United States had yet to fully escalate the troop involvement in the war—that would come later in the year—but Rubin and the VDC felt an obligation to inform the country that an undeclared war being fought halfway around the world was not in America's best interests.

The workload was prodigious. "We were putting out a weekly newspaper, organizing door-to-door discussions about Vietnam in the black ghetto in Oakland, sending out speakers everywhere, leafleting soldiers at airports [and] telling them to desert, advising young kids how to beat the draft, and coordinating research, petition drives, massive and mini-demonstrations," Rubin wrote.

The VDC's early protests met with mixed success. They tried to stop trucks carrying napalm. They attempted to block transport trains from delivering troops to the Oakland Army Terminal; in what turned into a cat-and-mouse game, protesters gathered on the tracks, confronted police assembled to keep them away, and faced death when they learned that the train conductor had no intention of stopping. They eventually succeeded in getting the train, first, to slow down and, eventually, stop.

These day-to-day activities were small in comparison to the VDC's big plans for the fall semester: a large-scale series of events that included teach-ins, demonstrations, and a march through the streets of Oakland. Rumors, aided by the VDC, circulated that there would be an attempted takeover of the army base. In a world of hyperbole, who could one believe? Rubin, feeling that outrageous actions and speech attracted more participants and press coverage, reveled in the confusion, while behind the scenes, he and others attempted, unsuccessfully, to secure the permits needed to keep the activities legal. Rubin boasted that this was going to be the biggest antiwar conglomeration of activities in history—and if one could believe the hype, he was speaking the truth. But with such pronouncements came the pushback. The police presence would be enormous. The Hell's Angels motorcycle club, society's outcasts but politically conservative by nature, threatened to band together and beat up any demonstrators in their path.

The VDC pulled off the event but not without a hitch. The originally scheduled march was cut short when organizers decided, mid-march, that it would probably end in a bloodbath; a new march would be scheduled. Rubin, on the losing side of the vote, was enraged: "A movement that isn't willing to risk injuries, even death, isn't for shit." The teach-ins, not active enough for Rubin's tastes, were a success. Plans for a new march began. Poet Allen Ginsberg and novelist Ken Kesey met members of the Hell's Angels at Kesey's ranch, dropped acid, listened to music, and discussed the march, the Angels leaving the meeting with a vow of not injuring any demonstrators. A judge ruled that the marchers could not shut down the Oakland Army Terminal, but they could walk in the streets. Thousands of people—twenty thousand, by Rubin's estimation—amassed for the march, which went off with little incident. Rubin, put off when Oakland's mayor praised the march for its orderliness, was disappointed: revolutions weren't supposed to be so tidy.

His name, however, was now known from coast to coast. He was part of Oakland's political lexicon. The VDC disbanded, but he remained active. Lyndon Johnson had escalated U.S. involvement in Vietnam with a large influx of ground troops in the country (and the inevitable rise in casualties). A nationwide antiwar movement, spurred on by the protests in Berkeley, seemed to spring up overnight. Rubin's role in the movement received further legitimization when he was subpoenaed to appear before the House Un-American Activities Committee. After speaking to Rennie Davis, a member of the San Francisco Mime Troupe and a future organizer of the protests at the Chicago National Convention, Rubin decided to make his HUAC appearance a theatrical event; he turned up wearing a rented Revolutionary War uniform, complete with a tricornered hat.

Rubin changed suits, trading the revolutionary's garb for a jacket, white shirt, and tie, when he decided to run for mayor of Berkeley. In the beginning, Rubin perceived the campaign as another piece of political theater, a means of ridiculing the process of electing officials. The effort changed somewhere along the way when he determined, or at least talked himself into believing, that he might stand a chance of winning the election. He created fliers, campaigned in front of supermarkets, spoke before church groups and business organizations. The sitting mayor was popular, but Rubin felt he might be vulnerable among students, young adults, blacks, and comfortable liberals. He was surprised, as he campaigned, to see the voter apathy; many voters couldn't even identify the mayor by name. He worked harder, alienating friends who believed he had sold out to the society that only a few months earlier he was trying to replace. When the final votes were counted on election night, he had taken 7,385 votes—or 22 percent of the total vote. He had won the four precincts nearest to the Berkeley campus, but that was all. Embittered, he swore he would never run for office again. "I learned the hard way that you can't build a new society while scrounging for votes in elections," he complained, admitting that he had abandoned his past while campaigning for office. Disgusted by what he felt was a lack of intellectual life on the West Coast, he agreed to work as a roving correspondent for the *Berkeley Barb,* an alternative newspaper with a considerable following; he would be writing about events in Europe, the Middle East, and Africa. The *Barb* formally announced the move in its July 6 issue.

Rubin had yet to leave before he heard from David Dellinger, leader of the National Mobilization to End the War in Vietnam, who asked if Rubin would be willing to act as the project director for a mass march on the Pentagon in the fall. Rubin flew to New York to meet Dellinger. As an unexpected bonus, he was introduced to Abbie Hoffman. Rubin's time on the West Coast had ended.

5 David Dellinger would always pinpoint the precise moment when he turned his back on violence as a resolution to a dispute. The incident occurred when he was a student at Yale. He had attended a football game between Yale and Georgia, and afterward a fight broke out between Yale students and New Haven "townies." Dellinger found himself squaring off against a young townie combatant. Dellinger had been in a number of fights in his youth, and while he was tall and athletic and could handle himself in a fight, he had no stomach for it. In this case, he was angry: the young man, he believed, had taken a cheap shot at him and run. Dellinger caught him. The two exchanged a few harmless punches before Dellinger connected with a haymaker to his opponent's chin. The young man collapsed, unconscious.

"I shall never forget the horror I felt the instant my fist struck solid flesh," Dellinger wrote in his autobiography, *From Yale to Jail.* "It was the exact opposite from what Robert Frost speaks of as hearing 'the clean sound of the axe striking good wood.'"

Dellinger dropped to the ground, cradled the young man's head and upper body until he regained consciousness, and accompanied him home, in the event that he might need assistance. His feelings, he would recall, were of "sadness, shame and love." "The lesson I learned," he wrote, "was as simple, direct and unarguable as the lesson a child learns the first time it puts its hand on a red-hot stove: *Don't ever do it again!* But the pain I felt was a spiritual pain, as if I had suddenly emerged from a fit of anger and realized that I had pressed a child's hand onto the stove. I knew that I would never be able to strike another human being again."

The dedication to nonviolence would be tested throughout his life, especially when he was called for active duty during World War II, but he held firm, his pacifism emboldening him to take active stands against wars and conflicts. But it would be his opposition to Vietnam that would bring him to national attention. Paul Berman, author of *Tale of Two Utopias,* a study of radicalization during the 1960s, called Dellinger "the single most important leader of the national antiwar movement, at its height, from 1967 through the early 1970's."

Born in Wakefield, Massachusetts, on August 22, 1915, Dellinger could trace his New England roots back to the days of the Revolutionary War. Raymond Dellinger, David's father, was a successful attorney, a Yale alumnus, the chairman of Wakefield's Republican Party, and a close enough friend of Calvin Coolidge to take his son to a private luncheon with Coolidge at the White House. An outstanding student, David also played a good game of golf and lettered, first in high school and eventually at Yale, in cross-country. He attended the university with the intention of becoming a lawyer like his father.

ABOVE Hubert Humphrey's impassioned civil rights speech at the 1948 Democratic National Convention established him as an up-and-coming national presence.

Copyright Bettmann Archive/Getty Images.

RIGHT Eugene McCarthy, a poet and former college professor, appealed to intellectuals in the Democratic Party, though he could occasionally be too esoteric for his own good.

Photograph by Ray Lustig. University of Minnesota Libraries, Special Collections and Rare Books.

Richard Nixon and John F. Kennedy, opponents during the 1960 presidential election, seen here shortly after JFK's victory in November. As presidential candidates, they staged the first televised debates, and Kennedy's strong performance probably made the difference in an extremely close election. Courtesy of the U.S. National Archives.

Robert Kennedy, attorney general during his brother's and Lyndon Johnson's presidencies, in 1964. He actively sought to enforce civil rights laws long overlooked in the South, and his hard-nosed persistence helped pave the way to national legislation in 1964 and 1965.

Photograph by Yoichi Okamoto. LBJ Presidential Library.

George Wallace's pugnacious personality and willingness to stand up to the federal government made him one of the strongest figures from the South in the 1960s.

Copyright Associated Press/AP Images.

ABOVE Segregationist George Wallace, running as a third-party candidate in 1968, earned his national reputation on June 11, 1963, when, as governor of Alabama, he blocked the entrance of the University of Alabama when two African American students attempted to enroll at the school. In his first inaugural address as governor he vowed, "Segregation now! Segregation tomorrow! Segregation forever!" Photograph by Warren K. Leffler. Library of Congress..

BELOW Lyndon Johnson and Hubert Humphrey at the LBJ ranch in Texas, November 1964. They had a volatile working relationship after Humphrey became Johnson's vice president. Photograph by Cecil Stoughton. LBJ Presidential Library.

ABOVE With Martin Luther King Jr. standing behind him, President Lyndon Johnson signs the 1964 Civil Rights Act into law on July 2, 1964. The law became the centerpiece of LBJ's presidency.

Photograph by Cecil Stoughton. LBJ Presidential Library.

LEFT The Berkeley Free Speech movement in fall 1964, led by charismatic speaker Mario Savio, became a template for the national campus protests that followed.

Photograph by Steven Marcus. Bancroft Library, University of California–Berkeley.

ABOVE Most Americans received their news of Vietnam in their living rooms, via television. Antiwar demonstrations and protests increased exponentially as Americans recognized the gulf between what they were told by government and military officials and what they were seeing on television. Walter Cronkite's special report on Vietnam as he visited the country greatly changed Americans' thinking.
Photograph by Warren K. Leffler. Library of Congress.

BELOW Defense Secretary Robert McNamara, the architect of the escalation of the Vietnam War, on April 25, 1965. McNamara would regret some of his decisions and would be fired by President Johnson in late 1967, but by then it was too late to stop a war that seemed rolling out of control. Photograph by Marion S. Trikosko. Library of Congress.

RIGHT As president, Lyndon Johnson oversaw the passage of two of the most significant federal civil rights laws in history, but his relationship with Martin Luther King Jr. could be strained when King sought quicker progress while Johnson pursued his Great Society legislation.
Photograph by Yoichi Okamoto.
LBJ Presidential Library.

BELOW "We Shall Overcome." The first attempt to march from Selma to Montgomery, Alabama, ended in one of the bloodiest confrontations in civil rights history. Civil rights icon John Lewis (*center, on ground*) suffered a fractured skull when uniformed thugs beat unarmed men, women, and children.
Copyright Associated Press/AP Images.

Robert Kennedy in Mississippi, 1967.

ABOVE

More than one hundred
thousand demonstrators
faced off with the
U.S. Army at a massive
protest at the Pentagon
in Washington,
October 1967.

Courtesy of the U.S.
National Archives and
Records Administration.

LEFT

The ruins of Cholon,
a suburb of Saigon,
after the Tet Offensive.

Courtesy of the U.S.
National Archives and
Records Administration.

ABOVE By early 1968 and after the Tet Offensive, the Vietnam War had deeply divided the United States. Neither Hubert Humphrey nor Lyndon Johnson, conferring here with General Creighton Abrams and General Earle Wheeler (*partially obscured*), could find a peaceful solution. Photograph by Yoichi Okamoto. LBJ Presidential Library.

BELOW March 31, 1968: Lyndon Johnson, encumbered by sinking approval ratings brought on by his inability to end the Vietnam War, stunned the nation by announcing in a nationally televised address that he would not seek or accept the nomination for another term as president. Photograph by Yoichi Okamoto. LBJ Presidential Library.

ABOVE Vietnam, May 1968. Women and children pass the bodies of three Vietcong soldiers.

Courtesy of the U.S. National Archives and Records Administration.

LEFT "Hey, hey, LBJ, how many kids did you kill today?" The Vietnam War exacted a tremendous toll on Lyndon Johnson. Here he listens to a tape sent to him from Vietnam by his son-in-law Charles Robb in July 1968. He hoped that peace talks in Paris might resolve the fighting, but it was not forthcoming during his presidency.

Photograph by Jack Kightlinger. LBJ Presidential Library.

ABOVE Robert Kennedy delivers news of Martin Luther King Jr.'s assassination at an inner-city campaign appearance in Indianapolis. Kennedy appealed for restraint in the aftermath of King's death and for the first time in public spoke of his brother's assassination nearly five years earlier.

Courtesy of the Indianapolis Recorder Collection, Indiana Historical Society.

FACING ABOVE On April 23, 1968, the campus of Columbia University was shut down during a tense standoff between students and university administrators. New York SDS leader Mark Rudd led the takeover that eventually ended in violence and acted as a rallying point for law-and-order debate. Copyright Associated Press/AP Images.

FACING BELOW Rioting in major U.S. cities in the aftermath of the assassination of Martin Luther King Jr. left inner cities in shambles (including Washington, D.C., seen here). The violence largely changed the focus of presidential campaigns from Vietnam to law and order. Photograph by Warren K. Leffler. Library of Congress.

ABOVE Robert Kennedy was treated more like a rock star than a presidential candidate by the throngs of supporters at his rallies. He would return from a day of campaigning with scratched hands, cufflinks missing and dress shirt torn, and his body bruised. Someone even stole a pair of his shoes. Despite his vulnerability, he insisted on campaigning close to the voters.
Copyright Associated Press/AP Images.

LEFT Eugene McCarthy and Robert F. Kennedy in a rare debate during the 1968 campaign.
Courtesy of University of Minnesota Libraries, Special Collections and Rare Books.

Pundits generally conceded the youth, intellectual, and suburban vote to Eugene McCarthy, but his popularity extended well beyond that. A grassroots candidate running in open opposition to the Vietnam War, he appealed to voters who were seeking an alternative to the old ways of government.

Courtesy of University of Minnesota Libraries, Special Collections and Rare Books.

Eugene McCarthy's victory in the Oregon primary placed him back in contention for the Democratic nomination—but his loss to Robert Kennedy in California and RFK's assassination in Los Angeles all but ended his hopes.

Courtesy of the Minnesota Historical Society.

A powerful speaker, Hubert Humphrey combined dramatic messages
with a homespun delivery that contributed a human touch to his speeches.

Hubert Humphrey made
a good selection when
he named Maine senator
Edmund Muskie his
running mate. Muskie's
wit, calm demeanor, and
precision were welcome
in a campaign desperate
for a change in direction.

ABOVE Former Alabama governor George Wallace reaches out to his supporters at the Texas state convention of his American Party in Dallas, September 17, 1968. Copyright PhotoQuest/Getty Images.

BELOW Curtis LeMay and George Wallace at Madison Square Garden in New York on October 25, 1968. The opinion polls indicated that Wallace's popularity was slipping badly as Election Day approached, but the New York appearance was an enormous success. Copyright Bernard Gotfryd/Getty Images.

In the lead-up to the election, Richard Nixon's rigorously constructed campaign helped him erase his loser image among voters.

Courtesy of the U.S. National Archives and Records Administration.

Richard Nixon and Lyndon Johnson at a meeting in the Cabinet Room in the White House on July 26, 1968. Johnson secretly felt that Nixon would make a better president than Hubert Humphrey, but he had no idea that Nixon was attempting to torpedo the Paris peace talks through illegal negotiations with South Vietnam.

Photograph by Yoichi Okamoto. LBJ Presidential Library.

ABOVE Governors Nelson Rockefeller (New York), George Romney (Michigan), and Ronald Reagan (California) attend the National Governors' Conference onboard the S.S. *Independence*, cruising the Virgin Islands. All three had designs on the Republican presidential nomination, but none was able to displace Richard Nixon as the party favorite. Copyright Bettmann Archive/Getty Images.

FACING ABOVE Spiro Agnew with Governor Claude Kirk of Florida at the Republican National Convention in Miami Beach. Agnew was a surprise choice for Nixon's running mate. His controversial comments damaged Nixon's campaign but never sank it. Courtesy of the State Library and Archives of Florida.

FACING BELOW Eugene McCarthy, Hubert Humphrey, and George McGovern debated in Chicago during convention week. Senator McGovern, the Democratic Party nominee in 1972, won the debate but had entered the race far too late to compete for the 1968 nomination. Photograph by Sheldon Ramsdell, University of Minnesota Libraries, Special Collections and Rare Books.

ABOVE An enraged Mayor Richard Daley, surrounded by the Illinois delegation, reacts to Senator Abraham Ribicoff's critical remarks on August 28, 1968, at the Democratic National Convention in Chicago. The violence in Chicago's streets and parks ruined Daley's plans to make the convention a showcase for his city and his rule over it. Photograph by Warren K. Leffler. Library of Congress.

BELOW In the wake of violence at the Democratic National Convention, eight activists (including Jerry Rubin, David Dellinger, and Abbie Hoffman, shown here) were indicted on charges of conspiracy to incite a riot. All were eventually acquitted, but not before a toxic trial further exposed the divide between the counterculture and the establishment. Photograph by Robert Kradin.
Copyright Associated Press/AP Images.

Hubert Humphrey staged a furious charge in the final weeks of the campaign, resulting in one of the closest presidential elections in U.S. history, but Richard Nixon emerged victorious. Copyright Hulton Archive/Getty Images.

Life altered his plans. One of his closest friends, Walt W. Rostow, an adversary later in life when Rostow served as a Vietnam advisor to Presidents Kennedy and Johnson, was studying economics, and Dellinger switched to that discipline. He was distraught by some of what he learned, especially of the ways capitalism divided the haves and have-nots, He was arrested for the first time while picketing to unionize Yale workers. He spent a summer hopping freight trains and traveling with hoboes, another as a laborer in a factory in Maine.

He graduated magna cum laude with an economics degree and won a fellowship to Oxford. Once again, his education was supplemented by what he witnessed. He saw the rise of Hitler in Germany and drove an ambulance in Spain during the country's civil war. Appalled by what he saw, he changed plans and decided to enter the ministry when he returned to the United States.

The outbreak of World War II and the creation of the draft tested his commitment to nonviolence. As a student in the seminary, he would not have been drafted, but he refused to register, even with this exemption. He was convicted of draft evasion, a felony, with other seminarians and sentenced to one year and a day in Danbury prison. Upon his release, he was notified to report for a physical, and he refused. This time, he was handed a two-year sentence to be served in Lewisburg, a maximum security facility.

His two stints in prison forged his commitment to nonviolent activism. Officials of both facilities regarded him as a troublemaker—and with good reason. He would not kowtow to authorities and what he felt were racist or profoundly ridiculous regulations, and he was willing to act as an organizer of prisoner protests, most notably hunger strikes. He paid the price with visits to solitary confinement and, worse, a concrete room called the Hole, so nicknamed for the hole in the floor into which prisoners were to relieve themselves. Rather than breaking his spirit, which prison officials were hoping for, Dellinger's incarceration fortified his convictions and showed him, one example after another, that he could thrive under the harshest circumstances.

He learned this during his first night in the Hole. He had heard enough from other prisoners to fear the effects this form of solitary confinement might have on him, but after a brief, fearful time, a powerful feeling overcame him. "For no reason I can explain, I began to discover how little it mattered where you are or what anyone does to you," he reflected later. "I was sure that what I had done to get there was right and somehow the longer I was there the better I felt."

When recalling his time in prison, Dellinger characterized it as a learning experience. "I went from Yale to jail and got a good education in both places," he said.

His was not to be a quiet, sedate life; jail cells would become so familiar that he would lose count of how many times he had been arrested. During the period between his draft-related prison terms, he met and, after a brief courtship, married Elizabeth Peterson, his companion for life. A native of Oregon, she was as devoted an activist as he, though motherhood and the duties of parenthood kept her from the political barricades more than she would have preferred. She and Dellinger met after he delivered an antiwar lecture, when, as a reporter, she requested an interview. Their life together constituted answers to countless questions.

Although his life would be largely remembered as that of a protester—or, as he preferred, a moral dissenter—his calendar pages were filled with the dates of demonstrations, marches, travel, lectures, jail time, and, when necessary, recovery, his mind brimming with the words of such nonviolent practitioners as Gandhi and King. He was a political and social renaissance man, a dervish of exhaustive activity. He ran a printing press and edited or published a handful of magazines (*Liberation* being the most memorable); he met and worked with such like-minded peace activists as Daniel and Philip Berrigan, two brothers and Roman Catholic priests devoted to bringing an end to the war. His travels to North and South Vietnam were not only fact-finding missions in which he gathered firsthand information on an ever-growing conflict dividing the United States; he became trusted by both sides in ways that defied the dualistic thinking necessary to wage war. He became an integral part of prisoner-of-war releases. The huge antiwar demonstrations defined him. For inspiration, he looked to Martin Luther King.

Much of Dellinger's work was accomplished under the aegis of the National Mobilization Committee to End the War in Vietnam. Dellinger, among many others, had watched the antiwar movement gain exponential impetus after Johnson's escalation of troops in Vietnam. Groups opposing the war sprouted in every state in the country, each group following its own objectives and set of prioritized activities, with friction developing between groups sharing the ultimate goal of ending the war but disagreeing on the methods to adopt to do so. In the months following the initial Berkeley teach-ins and demonstrations, a change in tone, slight at first but growing more evident by the month, had further guided the groups' thinking. In the early days, the groups opposing the war had focused on *dissent;* with the increasing numbers of groups and the media attention they were getting, the focus shifted to that of *resistance.* A group calling itself the Inter-University Committee for Debate on Foreign Policy, comprised largely of organizers of campus demonstrations and teach-ins, called for a national conference in Cleveland on September 10–11, 1966, with a goal of finding ways to use the antiwar movement to influence the November elections.

The organization changed its name to the Spring Mobilization Committee to End the War in Vietnam (known as later the Mobe) after the elections. It began preparing for an ambitious event: April 15, 1967, rallies in New York City and San Francisco. As a result of his leadership role in an October 1965 demonstration in New York—the first of its kind in the state—Dellinger knew of the complex logistics in setting up a legal event of this magnitude in the nation's biggest city. Aside from obtaining the necessary permits and clearances from the city and making the obligatory arrangements with the guest speakers, Dellinger had to contend with the demands of the various organizations participating in the demonstration. For instance, a disagreement broke out within the Mobe when one of its groups wanted to stage a draft-card burning during the event and other members opposed it. Further complicating the disagreement was the knowledge that Martin Luther King, appearing in his first major event opposing the war, found the action of draft-card burning offensive, similar to burning the flag. After a vote among the leadership of the groups within the Mobe, the card burning was rejected as part of the official Mobe activities in the New York event. Dellinger was not opposed to draft-card burning, or any kind of nonviolent draft resistance for that matter—he had attended other such events—although the argument, in his view, was illustrative of the disparity between the old dissent factions and the newer resistance ones. It could be a very fine line between the two types of protesters, but it was very real.

Dellinger hoped to find a way to unite all of the differing factions, but his ideal scenario was rooted in much simpler times and actions. "I wanted the demonstrations to become more like some of the meetings I had attended in Black churches in the South," he wrote.

> They had been marvelous examples of both individual and communal self-expression. The singing, praying, talking and enthusiastic shouts of "Amen," Tell it Brother," "Teach Sister" were even more inspiring for me than our best antiwar rallies. But when the meetings climaxed, no one said, "That was wonderful, when do we do it again?" The words one heard were, "Let's go!" and they opened the doors and marched into the streets to face the clubs, police dogs and jailings that stood between them and their goal of racial justice. And the impact of what they did was heightened by the nonviolent spirit and practice with which

they did it. In my mind, we had reached—or should reach—the stage in which our antiwar marches and rallies should climax in similar fashion. And that was what I and others proposed.

The New York rally, attended by an estimated 100,000 to 125,000 demonstrators, found the masses assembling in Central Park before marching to the United Nations building. Dellinger couldn't have imaged it better. Aside from an occasional scuffle between marchers and Vietnam supporters, and the dropping of eggs and red paint on the demonstrators from buildings towering over the demonstrators, the event transpired with very little problem. Draft cards were burned, marchers chanted anti-Vietnam slogans in an orderly fashion. Martin Luther King, Benjamin Spock, Pete Seeger, Harry Belafonte, and Stokely Carmichael spoke or sang, and King told the media that the march and assembly was "just a beginning of a massive outpouring of concern and protest activity against this illegal and unjust war."

■ ■ ■ ■ ■

Neither Jerry Rubin nor Abbie Hoffman felt strongly about the agenda planned for Washington, D.C. The demonstrations, speeches, and acts of civil disobedience were growing stale. These events, to which Rubin and Hoffman had no objection, needed something memorable to add color and depth to the customary antiwar displays, something to draw attention to what threatened to become ordinary. Americans saw footage of demonstrations on their televisions; newspapers featured now-familiar photographs of these large gatherings, the protesters usually contained by uniformed police and their billy clubs. Hoffman and Rubin wanted *action* along the line of the Wall Street protest—street theater that drew attention to the antiwar statement while offering a dash of the humorous or outrageous as a spice. The more Rubin absented himself from Mobe activities and planning, the more disgruntled the Mobe members became with his lack of leadership.

When David Dellinger investigated the complaints, he found Hoffman and Rubin engaged in developing the most over-the-top antiwar activity to date: a levitation of the Pentagon, which, they gleefully insisted, would rid America's big war symbol of its power and open the doors to peace in Vietnam. The goal was to announce that they hoped to lift the Pentagon three hundred feet off the ground, the gigantic complex would glow orange, and the demonic war presence would be expelled. This would be accomplished by twelve thousand demonstrators encircling the Pentagon and engaging in a combination of prayers, chanting, music, drumbeats, and a special incantation written by Allen

Ginsberg, who had recently performed an exorcism in Appleton, Wisconsin, where he, Ed Sanders, and a group of students and citizens had gathered at the grave site of Senator Joseph McCarthy to drive all the evil demons from his spirit. That controversial event had drawn a lot of press coverage. One could only imagine what might transpire during a mass effort to dismantle Lyndon Johnson's war apparatus. The theme of the march was "Confront the War Machine."

The Pentagon confrontation took on different meanings to those participating, though none was unexpected. Robert McNamara, in his last months as secretary of defense, hoped to avoid the violence that had accompanied most demonstrations elsewhere, just as he wanted to protect the Pentagon from invasion or vandalism. His protective measures included stationing 2,400 troops near the Pentagon, flying in a brigade from the Eighty-Second Airborne stationed at Fort Bragg, and having an additional 12,000 soldiers, National Guardsmen, and police on stand-by. McNamara specifically ordered the troops at the Pentagon, the overwhelming majority kept hidden from public view inside the Pentagon, to stand down unless they received orders to engage with the demonstrators. "It was a concern that events would get out of hand and there would be violence on one side or other that would lead to continued violence," he explained later.

The opening of the day's activities—an assembly at the Lincoln Memorial —was low-key, almost festive. The gathering included almost every type of antiwar demonstrator possible, from well-groomed and well-dressed college students to hippies, from hard-core radicals to the politically curious, from slogan-chanting youths to quietly reserved seniors, from registered Democrats to anarchists carrying Vietcong flags, from the jubilant to the angry, pressed shoulder to shoulder with one common focus. Parents brought their children. David Dellinger and Dr. Benjamin Spock gave speeches; Peter, Paul, and Mary performed a combination of folk and protest music; and agit-prop singer-songwriter Phil Ochs sang "The War Is Over," a new song declaring an end to Vietnam. Norman Mailer, whose *The Armies of the Night,* a book-length account of the day's events, would win the Pulitzer Prize and National Book Award, expected to be arrested for being a participatory journalist; he quipped that the early goings were so mild in tone that he anticipated being arrested, posting bail, and being home in time for dinner that evening.

He needn't have been so confident. Order broke down. When the events at the Lincoln Memorial concluded, the march to the Pentagon began. A small faction, perhaps no more than a few hundred, intended to take on the official police and military guard at the Pentagon. When they saw the opposition standing in line between them and the Pentagon, they broke rank with the marchers, charged ahead, and were met by those stationed outside the world's largest office building. Other demonstrators splintered away from the main crowd and made their way to the meeting place for the exorcism. An attempt to surround the Pentagon commenced; the Fugs played music and encouraged their audience to begin the exorcism chant. In the ensuing chaos, fighting continued between demonstrators storming the Pentagon and those assigned to protect it. Many of those closest to the Pentagon entry surged into the building, only to be beaten and driven back by the troops, armed with rifles and bayonets, inside. A large number of demonstrators, seeing the truth and wanting to avoid a beating or arrest, left for home. McNamara, seeing the carnage and arrests, decided to let nature take its course: after nightfall, the demonstrators would grow cold and hungry, and that, along with boredom, would eventually clear the grounds. The next day, a Sunday, would give them all the time they needed to clean up. It worked, at least to an extent. The artificial lighting outside the Pentagon cast a white glow over demonstrators reduced to silhouettes. There were pockets of fighting, and before daylight, the demonstrators were ordered to leave. When they didn't, the police moved in and hundreds were arrested. By final count, 683 people were arrested, and scores injured badly enough to require treatment.

The Mobe declared victory in the confrontation, which the *Washington Post* dubbed "a cultural touchstone of the decade." The protest had been staged in the nation's capital, in front of a national audience, and it was growing more and more evident, to those participating and those analyzing, that the government was losing its grip on the war debate.

A photograph, soon to become iconic, illustrated the new lines of division: a young hippie, facing a line of soldiers, placed a flower in the barrel of a trooper's rifle.

6 Of all the speeches, essays, documents, and manifestos addressing alternative political thought in the 1960s, few compared to *The Port Huron Statement,* a call for participatory democracy, written by Tom Hayden, a University of Michigan graduate and cofounder of the Students for a Democratic Society. A call to intellectual arms and physical movement and written under the heavy influence of C. Wright Mills and University of Michigan philosophy professor Arnold Kaufman, who coined the term *participatory democracy, The Port Huron Statement* exhibited the differing SDS points of view, tugging them in all directions, its center holding because Hayden was capable of shepherd-

ing diverse ideas under a single umbrella. The goal: to eliminate the feeling of powerlessness that individuals felt in their daily lives, and to eliminate the disenfranchisement they felt due to the forces that kept these individuals believing they had no say in their lives. In *The Power Elite,* C. Wright Mills had written about the powerless masses bearing the yolk of difficult lives they could not control or change; in providing guidelines by which individuals, gathered into groups, could influence the direction of their lives, *The Port Huron Statement* was ultimately a field guide to hope.

For a manifesto deemed radical in its time, *The Port Huron Statement* started out modestly, with a concession that all that would follow was written by comfortable youth:

> We are people of this generation, bred in at least modest comfort, housed now in universities, looking uncomfortably to the world we inherit.
>
> When we were kids the United States was the wealthiest and strongest country in the world; the only one with the atom bomb, the least scarred by modern war, an initiator of the United Nations that we thought would distribute Western influence throughout the world. Freedom and equality for each individual, government of, by, and for the people—these American values we found good, principles by which we could live as men. Many of us began maturing in complacency.

The "we" in the opening not only referred to Hayden's generation but also referenced those contributing to the document's ideas and priorities.

The Port Huron Statement represented a dramatic departure from Hayden's youthful goal of attending the University of Michigan, earning a journalism degree, and spending his life as a foreign correspondent, right down to the jacket, tie, and trench coat. His middle-class, Catholic upbringing instilled in him a conformism totally different from the spirit of the man he was to become. Born in Royal Oaks, Michigan, on December 11, 1939, to Irish Catholic parents John Hayden, an accountant at Chrysler, and the former Genevieve Garity, a film librarian, Thomas Emmett Hayden grew up at a time when post-Depression, New Deal politics, World War II patriotism, and the Eisenhower years stamped on America a comfortable form of nationalism that made McCarthyism, the HUAC hearings, and the Cold War palatable to a public suspicious of anything disruptive of its ease of living. The threat of nuclear annihilation, as Hayden would remember, hung over everyone's consciousness, and fear, even if not recognized or identified as such by individuals, lurked as a dark motivator. People leaned on their leaders for assurance and guidance, the way they had depended on Franklin D. Roosevelt in the days of the Depression and World War II.

This was Hayden's youthful world. His parents' marriage was an unhappy (and occasionally violent) one, and they divorced when Tom was ten. An only child, he was raised by his mother and educated by the authoritative teachers and environment of parochial schools. The pastor of his parish, Father Charles Coughlin, an anti-Semite right-winger who had had his own radio show during the Depression years and thereafter, awakened Hayden's early rebellion against authority but not in any way that hindered his student life. He was through with Catholicism, though. A bright student, he wrote for, and eventually edited, the *Daily Smirker,* his high school newspaper, and in his final editorial, about overcrowding in the schools, he left an indelible impression on his readers and school officials: each paragraph began with an enlarged, bold-faced letter of the first letter of the paragraph's first word, and when you read down the page, the letters spelled out *Go to Hell.* He was not allowed to attend his graduation.

This mischief was more of a high school prank than a rebellious statement. He admired the Beat generation writers and such Hollywood rebels as Marlon Brando and James Dean, but as he would later attest, he knew nothing about politics when he enrolled at the University of Michigan in 1957. That changed quickly, thanks to his friendships with teachers and students who were older, vastly more educated and knowledgeable, and politically active on the grassroots level. His work on the *Michigan Daily,* the campus paper that introduced him to college life, rules, officials, and practices, making him aware of a growing activism on campuses across the country, educated him on matters he hadn't considered prior to his going away to school. His natural curiosity and learned ability to follow up on news that needed further researching, given depth through his interviews for news stories, caught the attention of school officials and student organizers alike, the officials wanting to avoid any grain of controversy while the organizers sought anyone with his kind of mind and writing talent.

Robert Haber, in particular, took notice of Hayden. Haber lived in a small, book-lined apartment near the *Daily* offices, and he, his girlfriend Sharon Jeffrey, and their friend Bob Ross, who had grown up in the Bronx, were hoping to take over the Student League for Industrial Democracy, a group based in New York and peopled, as Hayden would remember, by "students who were from Jewish, immigrant, New York backgrounds"—a group chained to its ideology but ineffective in action. Haber wanted to retool the group, make it a national organization, and call it Students for a Democratic Society. Haber,

Hayden discovered, could be very persuasive but not enough to lure him away from his position on the *Daily*. His career, he continued to believe, was still in journalism.

That career choice, however, was endangered by his rapid, continuously growing interest in social issues, the budding civil rights movement topping his list. Hayden watched, as a journalist and supporter, when Haber, Jeffrey, and Ross joined others in picketing an Ann Arbor Kresge's following the arrests of four young African American men who staged a sit-in at a lunch counter in Greensboro, North Carolina, on February 1, 1960; he wrote about this and other civil rights stories involving student groups for the *Daily*. He was now placing his plans in jeopardy, even as a nonmember of any campus group: he had designs on the *Daily*'s editor-in-chief position, but his liberal writings were not ingratiating him to the faculty making the decision on the position.

Hayden won the editorship and set off to spend the summer of 1960—the months between his junior and senior years at Michigan—on the road, first on the West Coast, where he intended to visit Berkeley and San Francisco, and to witness its student action firsthand before heading to Los Angeles, where he would be covering the Democratic National Convention for the *Daily;* after that, he would venture to Minneapolis and attend the National Student Association congress. He would be doing his best Jack Kerouac impression—traveling via hitchhiking—which meant he would be seeing a lot of the United States along the way. He would later refer to this period as his "summer of transformation."

He judged the Bay Area to be the hub of "utopian spirit." In San Francisco, students and local residents protested the HUAC hearings, and the police used fire hoses to knock protesters off their feet and down concrete steps. In Berkeley, he stayed with a group of student activists, who, on learning of his work with the *Daily,* took it upon themselves to brief him on social issues being addressed by student groups. Herb Mills, one of the activists, gave him an eye-opening guided tour, first to Livermore National Laboratory, where hydrogen bombs were built, and then to a nearby farm for a look at the conditions in which Latino workers labored for next-to-nothing wages. At Livermore, Hayden interviewed Dr. Edward Teller, the model for a character in Stanley Kubrick's film *Dr. Strangelove,* who tried to convince Hayden that the planet could withstand nuclear explosions—or, if not, it was "better to be dead than red." The farms turned Hayden's gaze in another direction: the workers, whom Mills and others were trying to organize, labored for long hours in deplorable conditions that white workers never would have accepted.

In Los Angeles, Hayden met Robert Kennedy and attended a speech given by his candidate brother, whom he felt offered refreshing idealism absent in 1950s politics. He met Martin Luther King at a civil rights picketing, and the civil rights leader offered him what turned out to be valuable advice: "Ultimately, you have to take a stand with your life."

"As I left Los Angeles," Hayden recalled, "I asked myself why I should be only observing and chronicling this movement instead of participating in it. King was saying that each of us had to be more than neutral and objective, that we had to make a difference. That was something I realized I always wanted to do."

"The divisions in me had grown further," he noted in a 1973 interview. "I was writing articles back to the *Michigan Daily* proclaiming the birth of an American student movement, given what I had seen in California, and the university officials were quite upset in Ann Arbor, because apparently they sensed the danger in this, even though I had no idea of it, and they immediately began a campaign to control me as editor of the newspaper."

Hayden further witnessed the type of division between the old and new when he attended the National Student Association gathering in Minneapolis. One thousand young activists attended the congress, including a delegation from the Student Nonviolent Coordinating Committee (SNCC). The group, impassioned in its speech and experienced enough to have felt the painful and often bloody effects of standing up for civil rights in the South, seemed to embody King's earlier message to Hayden, and by the time he returned to Ann Arbor for the fall semester of his final year at the University of Michigan, he was, as he would later say, a new devotee to the idea that progress had to rise from a democratic, grassroots commitment. Hayden didn't abandon journalism or his position as editor of the *Daily;* he simply believed that objective reporting, even when it was good, was no longer fulfilling enough for him. He wanted to be part of a growing movement.

Hayden's zeal for personal involvement in social issues, bolstered by his readings and new friendships, grew throughout his senior year. His writings encouraged greater student involvement in university affairs, and he wrote numerous articles on civil rights issues. He packed his class schedule with political science and philosophy classes. In October, he attended a weekend SNCC conference in Atlanta, which made him yearn for a role in a movement both dangerous and compelling. The Freedom Riders movement was just starting up, and the reports coming out of the South were devastating, forcing Hayden to reassess his commitments. His earlier involvement with protesting and sitting in had been almost reluctant. He had known no one from the South and few black students at Michigan. He had believed in student involvement and paid lip service to it in his writings and occasional speeches, but he had also avoided membership in the SDS at Michigan. The Atlanta conference affected him powerfully: "It wasn't until then that I was really moved by them, by the concept of direct action, by the concept of being able personally to make a difference."

He engaged in his first true field experience in February 1961, when he learned about a large group of African American sharecroppers evicted from their homes for attempting to register to vote, living in tents in Fayette County, Tennessee. Hayden and a few friends loaded a station wagon with canned food and warm clothing and set off to help people who, as he noted in his memoirs, hadn't been allowed to register to vote since the Reconstruction. Hayden and his friends were quickly introduced to local residents unhappy about their presence. Hayden convinced two sheriffs confronting him at the tent city that he was a reporter working on a story for the *Daily,* and when his group drove to the local newspaper offices to file the story, they were confronted by a mob waiting for them outside. The sheriffs intervened on their behalf, and Hayden and his friends piled into their car and sped away, the white mob pursuing them until they reached the county line.

By the time his graduation day rolled around, Hayden had reached a personal crossroads. He had a girlfriend (who would soon become his wife) and a job offer to work for the *Detroit News* in Washington, D.C., but he was no longer interested in the type of life pursued by the average college graduate. The SDS was pressuring him to join, and he was leaning toward it, but he also wanted to move south and become directly active in the civil rights movement. It was a classic case of having to choose between the head and the heart. To his parents' great disapproval, Hayden chose the latter.

The SDS made him an offer he was happy to accept. Hayden became an SDS field secretary in Atlanta. He was expected to travel north from time to time, to give a speech or attend a conference, but the bulk of his time would be devoted to civil rights activities in the South, an endeavor that could be alternately exhilarating and deadly, especially in Alabama and Mississippi, where white resistance to voter registrations and segregation was manifest in beatings, harassment, Ku Klux Klan intimidation, and, often enough to keep fear at a high level, lynchings. Court hearings in front of white judges and all-white juries brought predictable results. Hayden admired the courage of the SNCC, whose members risked everything in their pursuit of progress in areas largely unchanged since the Civil War.

It didn't take long for Hayden to conclude that change was going to be possible only if the SNCC was successful in coaxing people to get out and vote—

and that was going to be an almost impossible task. Three targeted counties in Mississippi—Pike, Amite, and Walthall—were proof of the challenge:

> In Pike, where blacks totaled 38 percent of the twenty thousand residents of voting age, only 200 cast ballots in 1960. In Amite, with blacks 47 percent of the eligible, only one individual voted. In Walthall, not a single one of the eligible blacks voted. No one could recall civil rights organizers in these three rural counties, except briefly in the fifties. According to reliable legend, the first of them was shot and killed in 1952, and a second shot and run out of state shortly after.

Hayden escaped this fate during his visit to Mississippi—but just barely. One day in the town of McComb, a city of twelve thousand in the Mississippi delta, while observing a civil rights march by black high school students, Hayden and Paul Potter, a young NSA official traveling with him, were dragged from their car and mercilessly stomped, only to be arrested, supposedly for vagrancy. They were offered a choice of leaving town or facing the consequences of staying. They left. The beating demonstrated to Hayden the gulf between idealism and naïveté and reality in lawless communities. Blacks had been beaten, murdered, imprisoned, and fired from their jobs when they attempted to vote or register to vote. They lived desperate lives away from white society, in tarpaper shacks with no running water. The SNCC could convince them that only voting could improve their lives, but they could not exorcise their fears.

Nor, it appeared, could the federal government. After the beating, Hayden flew to Washington, D.C., and met with Burke Marshall, a sympathetic assistant attorney general assigned to civil rights cases. Marshall listened to Hayden's account and responded in a way Hayden hadn't anticipated: was there any way that Hayden could help him convince Bob Moses and the SNCC workers to leave the area? If they didn't, they were likely to be killed. The thought, coming from a man Hayden respected—a man Hayden conceded was just trying to do his job and avoid further trouble—infuriated him. He had hoped for a better response from the new Kennedy administration.

"In other words, this Justice Department official, this top law enforcement officer of the United States, was encouraging us not to register people to vote because we would be getting into trouble of the kind he could do nothing about," Hayden complained.

He returned South in time to become a statistic in Albany, Mississippi, where a record number of civil rights–related arrests were taking place. Hayden and his new wife, Casey, were taken into custody after they rode with blacks in a segregated train car. Hayden was shocked. This was the most openly racist environment he had ever seen. The police chief hated blacks and reveled in making their lives miserable. Anyone stirring up trouble or participating in it—or even being around to witness it—was hauled off to jail, often after taking a beating. Hayden spent two nights in jail, one on his twenty-second birthday, before he was bailed out. The sheer number of arrests was jaw-dropping: 267 were arrested on one day, another 200 the next. The Albany arrest completed the transformation of Tom Hayden. He questioned King's nonviolent approach to change and wondered what he, Tom Hayden, was accomplishing in his SDS-sponsored position in the South. What, precisely, was he accomplishing by being arrested and beaten? Perhaps it was time to devote his energy to creating a larger, nationally inclusive SDS. While stewing in jail, he composed a long letter to the SDS leadership, in which he outlined his hopes for the organization. The letter, which challenged readers to commit to the organization, became the genesis of *The Port Huron Statement.*

The document, assigned to Hayden by Robert Haber, begun while Hayden was living in New York after moving away from his Atlanta-based SDS position, was intended to be, in Hayden's words, an "agenda for a generation," which decades later he would describe as a "grass-roots democracy." Hayden would admit that there was a youthful naïveté saturating the idea of writing a revolutionary manifesto, but it was necessary to inspire activists to become involved in the civil rights and, later, antiwar movements. "I don't know if people understand how important a certain naïveté is when you're about to risk your life," he would say.

The manifesto had been an ambitious undertaking from the onset, combining elements of political science and philosophy with the SDS's basic mission statement, but it grew into something much larger than Hayden envisioned. Part of this extended length was the result of discussions Hayden had with Robert Haber, and part came about after Hayden received input from SDS members at a June 11–15, 1962, convention in Port Huron, Michigan. (The document received its title from the convention.) Squabbles broke out over the wording in *The Port Huron Statement* and the direction the SDS was taking—arguments that would splinter the organization in years to come. The most serious of the confrontations were generational, between the older League for Industrial Democracy members and the younger members of the SDS, between the anti-Communist factions and the Marxist sympathizers, between those caught up in philosophy and those dedicated to action, and, ultimately, between those who wanted the SDS to be campus oriented and those who wanted it to fan out into community action. With Hayden at the helm, the document was revised, expanded, and adopted.

"In the beginning we had offended some allies; in the end it didn't seem to matter," Hayden recalled. "We were fused by the power of imagination, transformed into seeing ourselves as some sort of wandering tribe that had found its lost identity and spoken its first authentic words to a wider world."

Hayden and Haber drove to Washington, D.C., and hand-delivered a copy of *The Port Huron Statement* to the White House. Twenty-thousand copies were printed and sold for thirty-five cents each. Hayden was rewarded by being elected the SDS's first president.

The euphoria was short-lived. John Kennedy's assassination ended America's utopian spirit. Infighting among SDS members split the group into factions. Hayden, who had hoped to find ways to work cooperatively with the Democratic Party and organized labor, was shocked when Hubert Humphrey, working at Lyndon Johnson's behest and poised to be named LBJ's running mate at the 1964 Democratic National Convention, refused to seat the black Mississippi delegation on the convention floor. He soured further on the Democrats when Johnson, once reelected, escalated the war in Vietnam after saying he would do no such thing at the convention.

Hayden's interests were now divided between civil rights and the war. Between 1964 and 1967, he lived in a slum in Newark, New Jersey, trying to apply his goal of making community work an outreach of the SDS. He educated himself on Vietnam and found, not surprisingly, that he vehemently disagreed with the U.S. intervention in the country's internal battles. He was enraged when the United States began its heavy bombing of North Vietnam. He traveled, against State Department wishes, to North Vietnam, for a firsthand look at the country, the war, and the death and destruction. Hanoi, in what was determined as a gesture of solidarity with the SDS, released three prisoners of war into Hayden's custody, setting off a firestorm of criticism in the United States. The antiwar movement, gaining momentum that reached its peak with the 1967 march on the Pentagon, had a new hero. As Hayden would learn later, he had also earned the attention of the FBI.

His community work in Newark frustrated him. He had made many friends and had seen small victories in his efforts to organize citizens into active groups, but progress was slow. The summer of 1967 riots, of which he was an eyewitness, had dealt a fatal blow to any organizing in the riots' aftermath. Blacks, angry and depressed by the violence, police brutality, and apparent government apathy, were interested in lashing out, not building up. "Americans have to turn their attention from the lawbreaking violence of the rioters to the original and greater violence of racism," he concluded.

Back in New York, Hayden stepped up his antiwar activities. He thought ahead to the following summer's Chicago convention and felt that the SDS might join forces with the Mobe in mass antiwar rallies during convention week. The events of early 1968—the Tet Offensive, Johnson's announcement that he would not run, the Paris peace talk potential, and Robert Kennedy's entering the presidential race—flashed by in what seemed to Hayden to be incredible speed, his involvement in the war changing almost as quickly. He and Kennedy had differed on the war, but their opinions were coming together. In trying to decide how to address the war, Kennedy had initially supported the domino theory; he had been in the awkward position of addressing his brother's decisions on Vietnam. By the end of 1967, he was still supporting Lyndon Johnson's position, but he had lost faith in America's ability to achieve a military victory. By early 1968, he and Hayden were essentially in agreement.

Hayden and Kennedy met on several occasions. They discussed the war and their ideas about how the United States might disengage from it. Hayden sensed that Kennedy had grown more serious about running against Johnson, and Kennedy's public break from Johnson convinced him of it. The game changed yet again when, shortly after Kennedy announced his candidacy, Johnson withdrew from the race and subsequently announced plans for peace talks. What, Hayden wondered, should the SDS do? Should the members continue to plan on a mass demonstration in Chicago? Should they stand by and see how the peace talks progressed? Hayden met with Averell Harriman, whose name was closely connected to the peace talks. Hayden had met Harriman in November 1967, when Harriman was an ambassador-at-large and Hayden had just returned from North Vietnam with the three released American POWs. The meeting had gone well, and Harriman had been instrumental in Hayden's avoiding trouble with the State Department over his unauthorized trip to Hanoi. Hayden visited Harriman in Washington, D.C., several days after the assassination of Martin Luther King. As they talked, Hayden looked out the window and saw the nation's capital burning. Harriman was due to leave for Paris and the planning of the peace talks. Hayden briefed him on all he knew about North Vietnam and offered ideas on how to negotiate with the country's representatives. Harriman was also hopeful that more POWs might be released.

The Columbia University student takeover involved Hayden much closer to home. After the students took over the university, Hayden contacted Mark Rudd and volunteered his services in on-campus activities or in negotiations with school officials. Hayden, nine years older than Rudd, offered a wealth of experience, even though Rudd disagreed with the SDS on their tactics. Hayden's reputation as a radical organizer leant credibility to the takeover— *Life* made a point of photographing Hayden for the magazine's extensive coverage of the events taking place—but his influence was marginal. Hayden came away impressed.

His questions about his involvement in the Chicago convention ended abruptly on June 6 with Robert Kennedy's death by an assassin's bullet. He had spoken briefly with Kennedy in California after RFK's debate with Eugene McCarthy; he had felt hopeful about Kennedy's chances for the nomination, especially if he won the New York primary. Now, for the second time in two months, Hayden found himself staring at his television and wandering aimlessly for days after the assassination. What now? he wondered.

He and fellow SDS leader Rennie Davis would be joining the Mobe in Chicago.

7 The Yippies, Mobe, and SDS faced great uncertainty as they made their ways to the scenic western shore of Lake Michigan for the Democratic National Convention. The city of Chicago continued to stall or refuse permits for assembly and sleeping in the parks, leaving the groups' leadership in a shaky position: where would the members gather and sleep? The press, goaded on by Abbie Hoffman, Jerry Rubin, and others, had succeeded in frightening the public into believing that anything was possible during convention week, and Mayor Richard Daley, who hated the protesters in any event, wasn't taking any chances. There would be a huge police and military presence to welcome the dissidents, and the potential for violent clashes between the two groups was very high. David Dellinger, for one, worried about the possibility of bloodshed; active dissent was one issue, getting heads cracked, another. Allen Ginsberg, who had been delighted about the prospects for a "Festival of Life" similar to the Human Be-In in San Francisco a year earlier, now worried about a trap awaiting those traveling to the Windy City; he wanted to avoid the convention but decided that, as one responsible for promoting the huge gathering, he had an obligation to go to Chicago and to help calm the gathering.

Thunderheads darkened the skies over the Midwest.

16 Chicago
Preserving Disorder

1 Chicago and Mayor Richard J. Daley: the two seemed synonymous. Daley, the city's mayor since April 20, 1955, lorded over Sandburg's City of Big Shoulders as if the nation's second-largest city was his personal fiefdom. His system of patronage, chock full of the best and worst politicians that money could buy, moved the city along like silent, invisible gears. The city worked— and for those who braved the frigid winds blowing in off Lake Michigan, the mountains of snow that piled up in front yards during the winter, the blast-furnace heat of the summer, the masses of people who commuted to the city for day jobs, the parking snafus one expected in big cities, the crime rate that seemed barely under control, the poverty on the city's South Side and wealth on its Gold Coast, the magnificent skyline that seemed to fade into squalid housing projects, the ballparks that housed the Cubs and White Sox, the strong and the weak . . . Chicago, like its mayor, was larger than life. Pulitzer Prize–winning newspaper columnist Mike Royko, who dedicated his career to standing up for the little guys while lambasting the authorities who kept their faces ground in the dirt, relished his role as Daley's nemesis and seized every opportunity he could find to puncture the mayor's ego. In his best-selling book *Boss,* a scathing portrait of Daley, Royko began with a memorable description of his subject's ego:

> They give soldiers pensions after twenty years, and some companies give wristwatches. He'll settle for something simple, like maybe another jet airport built on a man-made island in the lake, and named after him, and maybe a statue outside the Civic Center, with a simple inscription, "The greatest mayor in the history of the world." And they might seal off his office as a shrine.

The statement was amusing, served with Royko's trademark smirk, but in terms of describing Daley's power and standing with his constituents, it was true. He was, in every way, the master of his midwestern city. He didn't tolerate any kind of obstruction, and he didn't take criticism well. You didn't cross Daley if you intended to enjoy a long career in Chicago politics. Signs scattered throughout the Loop and the Amphitheatre environs during convention week welcomed visitors to "Mayor Daley's Chicago."

This was the way he wanted it. He had only occupied the mayor's office for a year when Chicago hosted its most recent Democratic convention, and that one had been an homage to Adlai Stevenson, the Illinois senator running for the presidency. Daley had not dominated the planning for that convention the way he had overseen this one. He was now one of the last big-time political bosses, a political dinosaur, the personification of the word *clout*. He ran his party the way he ran his city. People still talked about his role—or rumored role—in the 1960 presidential election, when he delivered the Cook County vote to John F. Kennedy, a vote that put Kennedy over the top in Illinois and, ultimately, the nation. More than a few analysts grumbled that Daley had sent his minions on a mission of finding votes, living or dead, to accomplish this, and that the election had been one of the most crooked in history. Daley, of course, denied it, but he wasn't inclined to care much what anyone thought, in any event.

He had pushed hard for Chicago to win the 1968 convention over such competition as Philadelphia, Houston, and Miami, with his friend Lyndon Johnson backing him all the way. Johnson's dropping out of the race had only slightly hindered him. He intended to showcase his city, his party, and himself—and not necessarily in that order. This would be the biggest bash in the history of Chicago. The money pouring into the city during trying financial times wouldn't hurt either.

He faced considerable obstacles. Recent years had signaled changes that he could barely tolerate. The people he had easily controlled in the past were now making trouble; they had turned into confrontationists. Blacks, angry about being confined to areas in which whites were afraid to drive, let alone live, had rioted the past two years, burning and looting, breaking glass and discharging weapons, fighting with police, packing overworked courtrooms and taxing the already overcrowded Cook County penal system. Daley's shoot-to-kill directive during the disturbances earlier in the year had been assailed, and to make matters worse in Daley's eyes, the scholars were treating perpetrators like victims. Daley agreed in general with the Kerner Report, but he drew the line when the police were portrayed as villains and the perpetrators as victims.

The antiwar groups, although not as violent, bothered him almost as much.

He had read the reports about their plans for convention week; if they brought in the huge numbers they were projecting, the convention could be seriously disrupted. Although an opponent of the war himself, Daley hated civil disobedience and the disrespect for order that it engendered. These dissenters, or people like them, had been responsible for driving Lyndon Johnson from office. Groups like the Mobe and SDS were organized and had large memberships, and Daley was at least marginally informed of their plans. Some of his operatives, including 850 members of the Red Squad, the security section of the police department's Intelligence Division, had infiltrated different groups, sat in on their meetings, and briefed Daley on what they had learned. Daley justified such covert surveillance by reasoning that he approved it for the safety of Chicago.

He was not alone in infiltrating the dissident groups. J. Edgar Hoover, already on record as describing the hippies as dangerous to the public welfare, oversaw a massive FBI effort to discredit the antiwar groups in any way possible, from using plainclothes agent provocateurs to disrupt activities and demonstrations, to infiltrating the various groups and using information obtained to plan against them. In a May 9, 1968, FBI memorandum, C. D. Brennan called for a "new Counterintelligence Program [to] be designed to neutralize the New Left and the Key Activists. . . . The purpose of this program is to expose, disrupt and otherwise neutralize the activities of this group and persons connected with it." On May 27, another memo, originating from a special agent in Newark, New Jersey, attempted to clarify the earlier memo:

It is believed that in attempting to expose, disrupt, and otherwise neutralize the activities of the "new left" by counterintelligence methods, the Bureau is faced with a rather unique task. Because, first, the "new left" is difficult to define; and, second, of the complete disregard by "new left" members for moral and social laws and social amenities.

It is believed that the nonconformism in dress and speech, neglect of personal cleanliness, use of obscenities (printed and uttered), publicized sexual promiscuity, experimenting with and the use of drugs, filthy clothes, shaggy hair, wearing of sandals, beads, and unusual jewelry tend to negate any attempt to hold these people up to ridicule. The American press has been doing this with no apparent effect of curtailment of "new left" activities. These individuals are apparently getting strength and [becoming] more brazen in their attempts to destroy American society, as noted in the takeover recently at Columbia University, New York City, and other universities in the U.S.

It is believed, therefore, that they must be destroyed or neutralized from the inside. Neutralize them in the same manner they are trying to destroy and neutralize the U.S.

While the FBI went about its business of neutralizing and discrediting the antiwar groups, Daley proceeded with his own program, working secretively and internally through his city's law enforcement departments to find ways to prevent disruption of the convention. The logistics of the protective measures were complicated by the locations of the convention and the hotels housing the candidates and delegates. The convention was going to be held at the International Amphitheatre near the stockyards on the city's South Side, while the hotels were located five miles northeast, near Chicago's downtown, the Loop. Two large parks—Lincoln Park and Grant Park—were situated within walking distance of the hotels. Security was needed at all of these locations, as well as traffic control on the roads and sidewalks connecting them. Lake Shore Drive, the highway leading into and out of the Loop, had to be watched as well.

Daley prepared his city for an onslaught of antiwar demonstrators by creating an army to drive then back. No measure or detail was too miniscule. Twelve thousand members of the police department, still temperamental after the rioting following the assassination of Martin Luther King, would be mobilized to the maximum. No one was allowed to take time off during convention week, and the daily work shift increased to twelve hours. More than 7,500 army troops were brought in from Oklahoma, Colorado, and Texas. The Illinois National Guard would be on standby, with five Chicago schools designated as quarters to accommodate 7,500 troops. Vehicles had been customized to stave off violence. Garbage trucks had been outfitted with reservoirs of tear gas and hoses for use on stubborn demonstrators; the grills of jeeps had been fitted with barbed wire. Squad cars and paddy wagons were not sufficient for the anticipated arrests; buses would be the answer for the mass transport of detainees. Command centers were spaced throughout the city's lakeside. Police were to guard the water stations in the event that the Yippies tried to make good their promise to drop LSD in the water supplies.

The International Amphitheatre had been converted into a fortress virtually impenetrable to anyone not specifically authorized to be there. Security strung 2,136 feet of chain-link fence, topped with barbed wire, around the building's perimeter. Manhole covers were sealed to prevent anyone from moving about underground. The street at the front of the building was blocked off for a mile. All entrances but one were locked, and everyone entering the hall would be subjected to a battery of checkpoints to reach their seats. Inside, a catwalk extending the entire length of the building and hanging ninety-five feet over the floor would be manned by security officials armed with rifles and walkie-talkies.

Work stoppages, timed to coincide with the convention, had to be handled. The International Brotherhood of Electrical Workers, striking against Illinois Bell, threatened the wiring and communications systems at the Amphitheatre. Daley, through delicate negotiations, convinced the workers to set aside their strike and install 3,200 telephones and 200 teletypes at the hall before the opening of the convention. He wasn't as fortunate in his efforts with striking taxi drivers, badly needed to move delegates from their hotels to the hall. Daley pleaded but they wouldn't budge. He finally found a limited solution to the problem by renting buses to shuttle the delegates. Auto manufacturers donated an additional three hundred cars to transport convention VIPs.

As the time for the convention neared, Daley and his city officials made it clear that no permits allowing sleeping in the park, peaceful assembly, or any other kind of demonstration would be issued. Chicago would not be a staging ground for anything other than a convention. Daley was prepared to meet unwelcome guests head-on, forcefully, if necessary.

A confrontation was now inevitable.

2   The Yippies' first stunt for the Democratic convention—nominating a pig as the Youth International Party's candidate for the presidency—had been in the works since the earliest planning days of the Festival of Life. The Yippies had labeled the Democratic National Convention the "Festival of Death," and, as one might have expected, they refused to even consider endorsing one of the Democratic candidates, particularly Hubert Humphrey, who impressed them as the darkest of all choices. The Festival of Life was the Yippies' own hand-fashioned counterpart to the convention, and what better candidate than a pig, which provided both a savage and hilarious edge to whatever candidate the Democrats chose to nominate. A pig, Jerry Rubin quipped, wouldn't let the voters down. If it did, it would be eaten. His campaign slogan would be: "Why take half a hog when you can have the whole hog?" There were jokes about campaign buttons, bumper stickers, even official campaign headquarters spread throughout the United States.

The Yippie hierarchy, such as it was, enthusiastically supported the idea as political theater, but by the week before the convention, Abbie Hoffman and Jerry Rubin were hardly speaking to one another. The rift, brought on by two substantial egos stretching for the spotlight, was the result of a disagreement over Pigasus (the candidate's name, even before they procured the pig) and the underpinnings of his candidacy. Rubin felt that Hoffman, who suffered from bipolar disorder, then called manic depression, had been driven by the upcoming convention into a highly manic state—and there was evidence to support that assertion—and, consequently, thought of the prank as one big joke. Hoffman countered that Rubin was treating the Pigasus nomination as a serious revolutionary act, which, of course, it was not. As offbeat and strange as it seemed, the fight was serious. "It looked like the Yippies were gonna split up," one observer recalled. "Abbie was the flower, Jerry was the clenched fist."

Hoffman, Rubin, Paul Krassner, Stew Albert, and other Yippies arrived in Chicago during the week before the convention. Abbie and Anita Hoffman, budgeted twenty dollars from funds raised from the sale of Yippie posters and campaign buttons, attended a farm auction, where they purchased a small, pink pig. Rubin rejected the pig as soon as he saw it. The pig, he argued, had to be larger, uglier, and smellier—something consistent with a two-legged candidate. He, Stew Albert, and Phil Ochs piled into a borrowed jeep and drove around rural Illinois, looking for a replacement. They found a six-month-old, two-hundred-pounder at the second farm they visited—they told the farmer they needed it for a school play—and drove it back into the city, the pig squealing in complaint the entire way.

On Friday, August 23, two days before the opening of the convention, the Yippies called a 10:00 a.m. press conference, held in an alleyway near the Civic Center. The press and an estimated two hundred observers turned out and listened while Rubin spoke of the Youth International Party's "Garbage Platform" and placed Pigasus in competition as an official candidate for the presidency. The police arrived while Rubin was delivering Pigasus's acceptance speech. The Yippies had no permit for the assembly; worse, they had brought livestock into the city. Rubin, Hoffman, Krassner, Ochs, Albert, and two others were arrested and, along with the pig, placed in the back of a paddy wagon.

They were quickly booked and released, but not before one final humorous event placed an appropriate punctuation mark on the episode. A police officer approached them while they waited in a large holding cell. "Boys," he said, "I have some bad news for you. The pig squealed."

The week—and the tempers of the Chicago police—would take a dramatic turn for the worse in days to come, but even Hoffman and Rubin had to agree that their kickoff event had been a huge success. Aside from gaining them the attention they craved, the Pigasus event had the unanticipated effect of elevating the Yippies' status with the press and public. "From that point on," noted Hoffman biographer Marty Jezer, "the media tended to describe all demonstrators as Yippies, while casting the Yippies as pranksters and the police as humorless heavies."

The rest of the weekend before the convention remained peaceful during the daylight hours. In Lincoln Park, the sounds of guitars, bongo drums, flutes, and other musical instruments filled the air. Uniformed police, moving throughout the 11,085-acre park in groups of three or four, mingled with the growing number of youths under warm, sunny skies. Very little indicated the adversarial positions they would be taking in the future. According to the *Walker Report,* the official report detailing the events of the week, "The scene seemed cordial, with police often chatting with the crowd." Tables distributing leaflets and free food and clothing were set up. The Yippies held classes in karate, self-defense, wasshoi, and snake dancing. David Dellinger and Mobe organizers conferred for a planning session for a scheduled Sunday march to the Hilton, the hotel housing the candidates, their staffs, and many delegates. Women Strike for Peace picketed the Hilton without incident.

Allen Ginsberg, who had arrived in Chicago earlier in the day, surveyed the park and met with William Burroughs, Abbie Hoffman, Jerry Rubin, Paul Krassner, Ed Sanders, and others to plot strategy. The police weren't allowing a flatbed truck, needed to stage the musical acts in the park; the group decided to plug into the electricity from a concession stand on Sunday. More disconcerting were the prospects for what might happen at curfew time that evening. The city had refused to issue permits allowing the visitors to sleep in the park, and no one doubted that the police would be called in to remove everyone at eleven o'clock. Ginsberg feared a bloody confrontation, but Rubin doubted that it would come to that. Hoffman didn't think the park was worth the fight. Ginsberg, Hoffman, Rubin, Sanders, and Krassner wrote brief, individual messages to those in the park, urging them to comply with the curfew. The Mobe was working to find places where groups of people could stay. Violent confrontations would only undo any good the Festival of Life was accomplishing during the day hours. ("Sleeping in Lincoln Park isn't as important as living the revolution there the rest of the day," Krassner wrote.) The statements were typed, mimeographed, and posted throughout the park.

After nightfall, bonfires were built in garbage cans, and groups gathered around them. At ten thirty, a half hour before curfew, police swept through the park and ordered everyone to leave. Ginsberg, seeing a tense situation developing and worried about violence breaking out, began to chant "OM." He and Sanders began walking toward the park exit. They led a large number of young people, who joined in the chanting and escaped the park without a problem. The police emptied the park with little resistance. Three people were arrested, but it could have been much worse.

The serious trouble began on Sunday evening, following another quiet day in Lincoln Park, when police again tried to clear the park at curfew. This time, however, the police were using their nightsticks and tear gas. Anyone confronting them—and there were many—faced being beaten or arrested. Kids hurled rocks and bricks at the police; they cursed and chanted slogans. The police chased them out of the park, into the streets, and into the Old Town section of Chicago; they clubbed reporters, news photographers, and innocent civilians. The confrontations, though far from the worst in upcoming days, marked the beginning of what would be a very ugly week.

3 Eugene McCarthy arrived in Chicago on Sunday, with virtually no hope of winning the nomination. Over the five months passing between his surprising showing in the New Hampshire primary and the convention, he had seen his optimism slide down a slope toward cynicism; he could be bitter if he allowed himself to be, because, despite all of his efforts and those of the thousands who worked for him as staff and volunteers, he had been flanked by Hubert Humphrey, the Democratic National Committee, and the old politics. Humphrey had collected his delegate votes—legitimately, by the ways of the old system—but could he say, at a time when the sitting president had been rejected by a majority of Americans, that he, the vice president and open supporter of Lyndon Johnson, had won over the public? The DNC, McCarthy suspected, had little faith in his ability to defeat Richard Nixon in the general election; Humphrey, on the other hand, might give him a very strong running. And Nixon's nomination and strong party support after two significant defeats in the past seemed to indicate a general concession to the old ways, in light of the importance of the prize.

Not that McCarthy had given his best efforts in the time leading to the convention. He had campaigned in the weeks leading to the convention. But aside from his prodding Humphrey on his Vietnam policies, and an occasional broadside aimed at the old politics and the way the Democrats practiced them, McCarthy showed very little fire for his campaign. Analysts criticized his "reliance on issues instead of personality," and he showed no inclination to change at the convention. He was hesitant to discuss issues that, he claimed, he had been talking about for months, and rather than mingle with delegates at the convention, he holed up in his hotel suite, coming out only on occasion. If his staff and volunteers wondered about his candidacy, he set them straight early in the week when he told an interviewer from the Knight newspapers that he thought Humphrey had the nomination sewn up. When his advisors pleaded with him to talk to party officials and state delegates gathered in the Amphitheatre, if for no other reason than to argue his peace platform, McCarthy, citing convention tradition, concluded that it would be bad form to do so before his name was formally entered into the nominating process. "In exercising his utter independence," observed Jeremy Larner, "McCarthy had locked himself into a kind of prison."

McCarthy's apparent disregard for his candidacy had pushed South Dakota senator George McGovern into an August 10 announcement of his candidacy for the Democratic nomination. For all the talk about McGovern's chances, he was entering the race far too late to expect anything but a small minority of the delegate votes. He was not, however, without power. He was close to the Kennedy family, and he might be expected to attract some of Robert Kennedy's delegates, if rumors of Ted Kennedy's eleventh-hour running didn't pan out. Further, McGovern, a vocal opponent of the Vietnam War, would have influence on the writing of the Democratic platform. A battle was brewing, and the doves needed backing on what was expected to be a fight with Lyndon Johnson, platform committee chair House Majority Whip Hale Boggs, and others. McGovern would be a formidable ally.

McCarthy was not pleased by the way the McGovern entry muddied the waters around his own candidacy, but the party platform weighed significantly on his decision to travel to Chicago. "We hoped to do three things at the convention," he said—the three underscoring his original reasons for joining the campaign:

- To make clear the need for reform of processes within the Democratic Party, both along the way to a convention and at conventions themselves, and prepare the way for reform;
- To obtain the strongest possible platform plank seeking a change, in Vietnam policy; [and]
- To make the best possible challenge for the nomination.

The preliminary skirmishes over the platform had run their courses before the convention opening. Three basic paths for the immediate future in Vietnam—all open to discussion and amendment, and all representing the positions of Hubert Humphrey, Eugene McCarthy, and George McGovern— emerged from the initial platform meetings. The McCarthy plank called for an unconditional bombing halt and a coalition Vietnamese government that included contributions by the National Liberation Front. Humphrey also called for a bombing halt, but he was not favorable to NLF participation in the new coalition government. A third proposal, drawn up by Kennedy and McGovern advisors, along with a few McCarthy aides, demanded a cease-fire, American withdrawal from Vietnam, and negotiations between North and South Vietnamese representatives. The three plank proposals were submitted between August 17 and August 20, giving Boggs and his committee a week to examine the wording of the suggestions, propose revisions, and have a plank ready to offer during convention week.

Lyndon Johnson opposed all three platform suggestions, and Secretary of State Dean Rusk met with the committee to express the administration's position. Johnson's biggest objection was to the bombing halt. This, Johnson declared, would give the enemy no incentive to bargain and would only encourage the North Vietnamese to build up troops and supplies near the DMZ, which would endanger American troops. This was the position of Johnson's military advisors, and the president was inflexible on it. "We are willing to take chances for peace," he told a packed house at the Veterans of Foreign Wars convention in Detroit, "but we cannot make foolhardy gestures for which our fighting men will pay the price by giving their lives."

The debate was temporarily interrupted on August 20, when the Soviet Union invaded Czechoslovakia, effectively ending Johnson's plans for an East–West summit conference later in the year. When asked about the invasion, McCarthy offered what reporters and commentators judged to be a flippant response, when he said the invasion was not a major crisis. The comment, offered when televised news reports contained footage of Soviet tanks moving down the streets of Czechoslovakia, received harsh criticism, with the *Los Angeles Times* concluding that "[h]e has pretty well forfeited any right to serious consideration for his candidacy." McCarthy argued that there was nothing the United States could do about the invasion, that it was a matter between the Soviet Union and Czechoslovakia, and he later accused Johnson of "using the Communist scare and the atmosphere of crisis to try to influence the convention to support his position on the war in Vietnam." His analysis proved to be remarkably astute.

On the night of McCarthy's arrival in Chicago, Boggs and two platform committee members met to hammer out the wording of the Vietnam portion of the Democratic plank. Boggs had flown to Washington, D.C., to confer with the president, supposedly about Czechoslovakia. Johnson wanted to talk about Vietnam. According to Johnson, the North Vietnamese capabilities would increase 500 percent if the bombing stopped; American troops would be in grave danger. Johnson reiterated his position that he would oppose any platform offering an unqualified bombing halt. Boggs returned to Chicago with the determination that he would not support a plank that the president rejected, and that he would leave his position as committee chairman if the others disagreed.

So, the wording was set to meet Johnson's approval; the bombing halt was watered down by conditions unacceptable to McCarthy. The best he could hope for now was a strongly worded minority platform capable of swaying delegate approval, and that, he knew, faced long odds. Still, in an election where the war was the number one issue, when a president had been unseated due to public disapproval of his handling of that war, to allow that president to dictate the terms of the platform was unacceptable.

McCarthy did better in his efforts to reform the nominating process. The process of selecting a candidate, beginning with the primaries and running through to the convention itself, was not truly democratic, McCarthy insisted. The unit rule, still in effect in nine states, needed to be abolished. There had been very strong agreement on this in the past, but the party had never acted on it. There was also the issue of when delegates were selected; in 1968, six hundred delegates had been selected in 1966, which was too far in the past for McCarthy's liking. Finally, McCarthy wanted to see minority delegates chosen in proportion to the population in their respective states. None of these issues was hotly contested by the Rules Committee, with the exception of the date of the abolition of the unit vote. McCarthy proposed that it happen immediately; it was ultimately pushed back to 1972. For 1968, a special provision freed delegates to vote their consciences. McCarthy was satisfied. The old system, which allowed the party's bosses to run the show, was out; the new changes opened the convention more than ever.

As for his candidacy, McCarthy didn't know what to expect. The rumor mill had never been so busy. A draft-Johnson movement was in the works, McCarthy was told; Ted Kennedy, informed that none of the existing candidates stood a chance in November, was being pushed into considering his options. McCarthy knew that he would never receive Johnson's or Daley's endorsements. On paper, Humphrey had enough delegates to win the nomination, but a persistent rumor insisted that the Southern Democrats, angry at Humphrey's waffling on his unit rule position, were considering pulling their backing. McCarthy braced himself for a volatile convention ahead.

4   Hubert Humphrey brimmed with self-confidence when he boarded his plane to Chicago late Sunday afternoon. Earlier in the day, he had appeared on *Meet the Press* and held his own when answering the news program's six-man panel. With the convention looming in the days ahead, the panel sought Humphrey's position on the major issues of the day, particularly Vietnam. Humphrey had no trouble with the questions concerning domestic issues; he had been facing these types of panels for so long he could sleepwalk

through their queries. The questions about Vietnam and Humphrey's willingness to split with Johnson over the war brought out a bit of the combativeness in the Happy Warrior. He was his own man, but the way things were going, he had no second thoughts about supporting the president. "I think the policies the President has pursued are basically sound," he said.

He might have found this difficult to say on other occasions. His loyalty to Johnson had earned him criticism wherever he went, and analysts were predicting that it might cost him the election. A few advisors had floated the idea of his resigning the vice presidency, and in his darker moments, he had considered it, only to reject the thought. He owed much of his career to Johnson. He now had reason to believe that Johnson might be softening his position on the war. Humphrey, as instructed by Johnson, had run his Vietnam platform proposal past Dean Rusk and Walt Rostow, and they had voiced their approval. Humphrey assumed that Johnson would approve it as well. So he had no misgivings about backing the president at this point.

His buoyant mood was punctured when his plane touched down in Chicago. The crowd awaiting his arrival was sparse, and Mayor Daley, supposedly Johnson's good friend, was nowhere to be seen, nor were any other of the city's top officials. The sounds of a bagpipe band, sent to the airport by Daley, added a funereal background to what was developing into a gloomy mood. His day grew darker. Rather than immediately check into his hotel, Humphrey went to the Sherman Hotel, where the Illinois delegation was caucusing. Daley was there. But instead of receiving the backing he expected, Humphrey, after talking to Daley, received bad news: Daley wanted to hold back on the Illinois delegates. Humphrey faced his day's final insult when he checked into the Hilton and encountered a lobby filled with young, jeering McCarthyites. Luckily, he had booked Muriel and his family in another hotel.

"He entered more a pariah than a political potentate," Edgar Berman wrote of Humphrey's ignominious introduction to Chicago. "We came in like thieves in the night, hustled through a bustling hotel lobby to our rooms, with sighs of relief all around when we made it."

There would be little relief for Humphrey. He expected and even welcomed some of the forthcoming battles with his opponents and their supporters, but two of the top Democrats he thought he had working in his favor, Lyndon Johnson and Richard Daley, were behaving in ways that jeopardized his candidacy. Daley, unbeknownst to Humphrey, was working behind the scenes against him. At a preconvention breakfast with California kingmaker Jesse Unruh, Daley came right out and called Humphrey a "lousy candidate." Unruh agreed. Daley suggested a draft-Johnson boomlet, but Unruh, as head of the

California delegation, countered that there was no chance that his state, so pro-Robert Kennedy, would back Kennedy's old nemesis. Well, then, why not draft a Kennedy? Sentiments ran high in support of a Ted Kennedy candidacy, and while the senator had rebuffed previous entreaties that he run, he might change his mind if there was a big enough call for it. Kennedy turned down the idea when Daley called him about it, but when Daley persisted, Kennedy advised him to talk to his brother-in-law Stephen Smith if he wanted to contact him further.

Humphrey hadn't heard the backstory, but he had heard the Kennedy rumors on Monday, the official opening of the convention. He was aware of Kennedy's earlier rejections, but he had tussled with Kennedys enough in his past to know better than to overlook the potential of their standing in his path to the White House. He felt confident that he could defeat Kennedy, should he enter this late in the process, but he also recognized the shot his candidacy would take if he lost the delegates from California, where Kennedys were revered, and Illinois, which had supported John Kennedy in 1960. The fresh rumors on Monday, along with the news that a Kennedy for President headquarters had been established in the Sherman House Hotel, unsettled him.

Humphrey might have been more concerned if he hadn't found himself in another bitter disagreement with the president. His conversations with Dean Rusk and Walt Rostow had led him to believe that Johnson would stamp his approval on his Vietnam platform. "It isn't all we'd like," Rusk had told him, "but under the circumstances, it will do. It's a constructive, sensible plank. We can live with this, Hubert."

Humphrey learned otherwise on Monday. Johnson, sitting out the convention and staying at his Texas ranch, had seen the Humphrey plank. He placed an angry call to David Ginsburg, a Washington attorney working on the plank's wording. He shouted his objections at a surprised Ginsburg, making clear that he would not approve the plank as written. Humphrey, informed of the call, was angry and shocked. Johnson's objections seemed to be over the wording more than the content, and Humphrey felt he might be able to convince the president to go along with it. He had an extremely busy day ahead—meetings with delegates, three television interviews, a long list of calls to Southern senators, and the opening of the convention. He would call Johnson on Tuesday.

In the meantime, his approach—his *tone*—shifted, by design or otherwise. He presented himself as an underdog, embattled in difficult times, a man confronting a powerful foe in a very important election. Alluding to, but not specifically mentioning, the polls, he conceded that he was not the favorite in the minds of the pundits and reporters. While talking to the Missouri delegates, he compared himself to Harry Truman, a Missourian predicted to lose in 1948, the same year he, Humphrey, running for the Senate, was expected to lose in Minnesota. "I've been a Truman man, and I guess I'm kind of a Truman character myself," he said. "I get into a certain amount of trouble on occasion and try to work my way out of it. I've had to fight uphill battles many times."

Later in the day, while speaking to the Labor Committee for Humphrey, he lauded Nixon as a tough opponent not to be underestimated. "Any man that can give John Kennedy the close race that Mr. Nixon gave him in 1960 is no soft touch."

■ ■ ■ ■ ■

The scenes in the parks and streets became more hostile on Monday, as the police and young people ratcheted up the tension between them. Word circulated that the police intended to attack the press, most notably anyone attempting to film or take photographs of their actions. Members of the clergy gathered at St. Paul's Church and discussed how they might quell the violence by acting as intermediaries between the two sides. For the first time, Grant Park, located near the Hilton, became a focus of activity.

In Lincoln Park, the mood was one of guarded triumph. Daily newsletters such as the SDS's *Handwriting on the Wall* and *Ramparts Wall Poster* crowed about the previous evening's events. The police had driven the demonstrators from the park, but that had left the Loop open for conquer, as freelancing groups walked down Michigan Avenue in the Loop and Wells Street in Old Town. The police chased them with little effect, other than an occasional arrest or beating. "Great surging feeling," noted one writer in *Handwriting*. "100% victory in propaganda," wrote Tom Hayden in *Wall Poster*. At an 11:00 a.m. Yippie press conference, Jerry Rubin announced that the Yippies had sent a telegram to United Nations Secretary-General U Thant, requesting that an impartial observer be sent to Chicago to witness the police chaos and brutality.

The Mobe and Yippie leadership—Jerry Rubin, Abbie Hoffman, Tom Hayden, Rennie Davis, and David Dellinger, among others—were under twenty-four-hour surveillance. Undercover police had been assigned the job of following them wherever they went. With the exception of Rubin's tail, who looked like a motorcycle biker, the undercover cops looked like undercover cops, and the Yippies and Mobe came to know them by name. The FBI also attached agents to these leaders, who made a sport of losing them in the park or on the street. Hayden, who occasionally donned disguises, eluded the agents constantly. On Sunday night, he and Wolfe Lowenthal spotted Hayden's tail's car in the park, and in an effort to slow down his pursuit, Lowenthal let the air out of one of his tires. He was caught in the act. Both might have been arrested, had it not been for a group of young people who surrounded the police and menaced them enough for them to release Hayden and Lowenthal.

They were not as lucky the next day. Police saw the two in Lincoln Park, in a meeting with other Mobe members, working out the details for a march from the park to the Hilton. They were arrested, taken to the police station, and booked on charges of resisting arrest (leaving the scene after the aborted arrest the previous evening), obstructing the police (leading their assigned tails on wild chases), and disorderly conduct (letting the air out of the police car tire). In Lincoln Park, Rennie Davis assembled four to five hundred people for an impromptu march to police headquarters. The march was orderly. Marchers obeyed traffic lights and moved along in a file taking up half a sidewalk, careful to avoid any problems with the police accompanying them. Exchanges between the police and marchers were held to a minimum, and only three demonstrators were arrested during the entire protest. When they arrived at the station, they encountered a battery of police surrounding the station. They chanted loud enough for Hayden and Lowenthal to hear them in their cell. After a short time, Davis and others decided to march to Grant Park. They hoped to assemble in the part of the park facing the Hilton.

They reached the park without incident. Once there, however, several hundred left the main group and ran across the park toward a large statue of Civil War General John Logan. They surrounded the statue and a few climbed onto it. More protesters joined, until the total was an estimated one thousand. Dozens of police, clubs out, charged into the mass of youths. They cleared the park, but not before youths had been arrested and beaten. One teenaged boy's arm was broken when he refused to climb down from the statue.

At curfew time, it was clear to anyone in the park that a large confrontation would be taking place. Battle lines had been drawn. Uniformed police, armed with rifles, tear gas canisters, and nightsticks, assembled in formation and faced kids assembled behind a barrier roughly thirty yards long and constructed out of picnic tables, branches, trash receptacles, and anything else the builders could find to pile on. Fires burned in trash barrels. The kids shouted at the cops, calling them pigs and yelling obscenities. Five blocks away, three buses packed with police parked and waited. The police stood by for orders. They had removed their badges and taped over or removed their name patches.

For all his hyperactivity and talk of revolution, Abbie Hoffman feared what might happen next. Whatever their station, whether they had come to Lincoln Park with revolution on their minds or were merely curious, the young people around him were not, as they might have thought, protected by the law; they were at risk of being badly beaten by it. "After the curfew," Hoffman noted, "a hippie walking down the streets was about as safe as a Jew in Hitler's Berlin."

Hoffman tucked his hair under his hat and tried to disguise himself as well as possible. He moved from group to group, advising them that the park was not worth the battle ahead. "We're not here to fight anybody," he said. "If we are told to leave, then leave."

Very few listened.

The standoff lasted until after midnight. The police, hesitant to spark what was certain to be a riot, listened as kids behind the barricade threw rocks, bottles, and pieces of tile at them. "Kill the pigs!" some shouted. "Fuck the pigs!" The violence broke out after a squad car approached the barricade. The kids, thinking they were under attack, threw bottles and rocks, breaking the windshield of the squad car; the police, seeing two fellow officers in distress, disregarded their commanding officer's orders to stand down and charged the barricade.

What followed—the culmination of three days of rage and frustration on both sides—was by far the greatest concentration of unfettered violence to that point during the convention week. The police, cursing their victims, beat anyone within club-swinging distance. Young demonstrators, after absorbing a beating, were thrown into a lagoon. Many of the cops focused on reporters and photographers; cameras were destroyed, and the media ruthlessly attacked. Any pretense of police procedure disappeared. Two young seminarians, part of the ministry in the park, trying to calm the panicked youths, were soundly beaten, one struck on the head by a rifle butt and kicked when he fell to the ground; he was taken to the hospital, his skull fractured. Some of the kids fought back; they threw anything they could find at the police, the boldest engaging in hand-to-hand combat with their attackers. Demonstrators, choking and blinded by tear gas, no longer had the option of leaving the park in an orderly fashion: they were beaten until they reached the street, where they were met by other cops, who beat them further. Innocent bystanders, simply out for an evening walk, were beaten. In residential neighborhoods, peoples sitting on their porches were dragged down their front steps and assaulted. The police, screaming obscenities, slashed the tires of cars parked on the street. While convention delegates celebrated the opening of the festivities at the International Amphitheatre, the Chicago police were taking back the city's streets.

The media recorded the rioting but not without paying a steep price. Police Superintendent James B. Conlisk had issued a directive ordering the police to leave the press alone and allow reporters and photographers to do their jobs, but his orders, according to the official report on the violence, were ignored:

Monday, August 26, was to be one of the most hazardous days for news-men. On Monday afternoon, a TV reporter was warned by two police detectives, separately, that "the word is being passed to get newsmen" and "be careful—the word is out to get newsmen."

Norman Mailer, on hand to cover the convention for *Harper's,* wrote of the violence: "The counterrevolution had begun." In taking out the media, the po-lice had signaled a powerful shift in the street dynamics for the week. "It was as if the police had declared that the newspapers no longer represented the true feelings of the people. The true feelings of the people, said the policemen's clubs, were with the police."

5 The Democrats, although largely insulated from the violence erupting around them, fought their own chaos. Was Ted Kennedy going to an-nounce his candidacy? Would Hubert Humphrey come to his senses and break with the president? Could George McGovern stage any kind of meaningful charge? Had Eugene McCarthy taken himself out of the race? The questions gave reporters plenty to write about, even if their published pieces failed to of-fer a shred of an answer. Tom Wicker of the *New York Times,* in a column about Ted Kennedy's possible entry into the race, brought the confusion into sharp relief. As the column pointed out, in its title ("The Man Who Isn't Here") and on two occasions in the body of its text, Kennedy, at home in Hyannis Port, was a conspicuous absence from the convention, and no one seemed to know who was behind a movement that was serious enough to be printing "Draft Ted" stickers. On Monday, McCarthy had stated that he would be willing to back Kennedy if he decided to run, which, Wicker wrote, "added smoke, if not fuel, to the fire." As a final item to his speculative piece, Wicker noted the likelihood of "enormous pressure on Ted Kennedy as the Vice Presidential candidate." At no point, however, did Wicker note that Kennedy had already rebuffed a movement to draft him. This made good reading but only went to illustrate how confused the Democrats were at a time when they were expected to be united behind a single candidate.

The process of selecting the candidate was now looking to be one of at-trition, leaving the last man standing—Hubert Humphrey, it appeared—an unsettling choice. The first big event of the day—a debate between Hum-phrey, McCarthy, and McGovern before the California delegation and telecast nationally—left little doubt of this. This was to be McCarthy's last stand be-fore the convention balloting, and it would be a battle against very long odds.

He had already lost the California primary to Kennedy. McGovern more than McCarthy was the favorite to gain most of Robert Kennedy's delegate votes; they certainly wouldn't be going to Humphrey. For McCarthy, the task ahead was to put on the performance of his career during the debate. He might be able to pick up some California scraps and . . . who knew? Maybe he could turn heads in other states.

McCarthy used this occasion to deliver his worst showing of his campaign, an appearance so horrid that second-guessers wondered if he was actually trying to sabotage his campaign. For someone who had spent months campaigning with an antiwar message and who had deep feeling about the Vietnam platform being debated as he spoke, McCarthy acted as if a statement on or questions about the war were impositions unworthy of response. "I do not intend to restate my case," he said at the opening of his allotted time to speak, "but I must say I am somewhat surprised to find that a lot of people who I have hoped followed this campaign for at least six months have suggested that I had in mind to impose a government on South Vietnam."

A puzzling way to solicit support: Was he saying that restating his position was a waste of his time? That his audiences weren't bright enough to understand what he was saying? That he was incapable of stating his case in an easily digestible manner? Whatever his intentions, it was a poor way to open a speech.

Rather than vigorously presenting his views on Vietnam or addressing the law-and-order issue that had gained so much momentum as a talking point, McCarthy devoted an inordinate amount of time to verbally jousting with George McGovern, who, the day before, had worried that McCarthy was too "passive and inactive" to address the difficult times "that will require an active and compassionate president."

"I think a little passivity in that office is all right—a kind of balance, I think," McCarthy argued.

McCarthy had his moments during the debate—his summation of the Supreme Court was outstanding, as was his closing three-minute summation—but these moments were negated by his stubbornness, such as his scolding one questioner for asking him a question he considered unmeritorious, or his complaining of having to "explain nine months in three minutes." He held firm in his position that he would not support a candidate whose Vietnam policies conflicted with his and supported the president's.

After the sour tone of McCarthy's statement, the gathering of roughly one thousand, packed into the ornate, nineteenth-floor ballroom of the LaSalle Hotel, was primed for a rousing speech and something to cheer about, and

McGovern delivered. The format permitted each candidate to use up to ten minutes in an opening statement, with questions from the audience to follow. McGovern began his portion by praising his opponents and promised to back either if he was nominated. After stating what everyone knew—that he was a late entry into the race—he joked that coming on at the last minute, after the big buildup in the primaries, had saved him a lot of money and spared him the danger of peaking too early. Then he got down to business:

> I seek this nomination because I believe very strongly in the purposes and the mission of the Democratic party, and because for five years I have been expressing that concern on the floor of the United States Senate about young men dying 10,000 miles away from our shores, trying in a desperate effort to save a regime in Southeast Asia that cannot or will not command the respect and the confidence of its own people.

The audience erupted in an enormous ovation. McCarthy, the original peace candidate, had offered a laconic lecture; this man was speaking from the heart! He was on the offensive, his words aimed at the failed policies of war, as practiced by the current commander in chief. One could only speculate on what was passing through Hubert Humphrey's mind at this moment. He would not only have to follow this act; in supporting the president's position, he would be asking his listeners to step back, draw a fresh breath, and reconsider a message they didn't want to hear.

McGovern didn't dwell on the war. There were bound to be questions about it from the audience. Instead, he moved on to law and order. Unlike McCarthy, who chose to pass over the two biggest issues of the campaign, perhaps in anticipation of the audience's questions, McGovern brought them into the open. He took a safe, liberal's approach: of course there was a need to address the problems prevalent in the urban areas, problems that threatened the safety of the American people, but "while law and order are aspirations and objectives of the highest importance, and of the greatest concern to all of us who want to live in a country of law and in a country of order . . . we must also add to the concept of law and order the concept of compassion, of justice, of concern for those who are neglected in the internal city, and in the ghettos, on the farms, in the various areas of the country where we have divisions to be healed and problems long neglected to be taken care of."

This was the message that Robert Kennedy had brought to California, a message he had delivered, in victory, on the last night of his life, a message that might reverberate in the Democratic Party, despite the strides made by Johnson and the Great Society in recent years. The California delegation rewarded Mc-Govern with another ovation.

Humphrey's message, in comparison, sounded shopworn. He spoke of the "politics of hope." He leaned on his past. He spoke of his days as mayor of Minneapolis, of his time in the Senate. He considered peace and its cost, arguing that no one candidate could claim to be *the* peace candidate. He disagreed with McGovern: "We are not defending a regime. We are trying to defend a people." Those waiting for Humphrey to split from Johnson were going to have to wait longer. He made that apparent when, during the question-and-answer portion of the debate, he was asked how, if at all, he disagreed with Johnson's position on Vietnam.

"The President of the United States is not a candidate," Humphrey replied, "and I did not come here to repudiate the President of the United States. I want that made quite clear." Humphrey went on to give a brief history of American involvement and objectives in a war that quickly grew out of hand—or, as Humphrey stated clumsily, "wars have built-in escalations." If Humphrey believed that he was going to win over the California delegates, or any of those voters watching the debate on television, by defending the current policies in Vietnam, he was mistaken. After the debate, there would be private discussion about whether Humphrey had defended Johnson because as vice president he was obliged to do so, or if he truly believed in everything he was saying. McCarthy, for one, maintained that Humphrey was speaking for himself.

So, the debate, the only time the three candidates would square off during the campaign, ended with a thud. Analysts favored McGovern as the winner. "The meeting plainly was captured by Senator McGovern," wrote the *New York Times,* "while the least warm reception went to Vice President Humphrey."

The Humphrey–Johnson connection was noted again when the Democrats presented their Vietnam platform, which stood as an affront to McCarthy, McGovern, and the antiwar factions in and out of the convention hall. Humphrey had tried without success to change Johnson's mind on his opposition to the wording of his favored platform. During Humphrey's call to the Johnson ranch, Johnson disregarded Humphrey's assertion that he had run the platform past Dean Rusk and Walt Rostow, as instructed; their approval was of no consequence, Johnson argued, and in a cruel slash at Humphrey's loyalty, Johnson reminded his vice president that the war policy was part of Humphrey's doing too. There would be no compromises, no unconditional bombing halt, Johnson declared. His preferred wording laid down the conditions: "Stop all bombing of North Vietnam when this action would not endanger the lives of our troops in the field; this action should take into account the response from Hanoi"—wording eventually adopted by the platform committee.

If this was a test of Humphrey's loyalty, Johnson won, as he always did. There would be a floor fight on Wednesday—a tussle is more accurate—a minority plank would be entered, and Johnson would prevail, as he always did. The final vote: 1,567¾ to 1,048¼. Delegates from six states—New York, California, New Hampshire, Wisconsin, Oregon, and Colorado—staged a spontaneous demonstration against the majority vote, the protesters wearing black armbands, praying, and singing "We Shall Overcome" to no effect, other than to further illustrate the division within the party.

Humphrey, bitter in defeat, would second-guess his decision to support Johnson for the rest of his life. Johnson could have made his nomination difficult if Humphrey had defied him, but Humphrey turned out to be his own worst critic when judgment was meted out on his support of the plank. "I should not have yielded," he wrote in his autobiography. "Now I know, in retrospect, that I should have stood my ground. I told our people I was still for the [earlier] plank, but I didn't put up a good fight. That was a mistake."

Elsewhere, another crucial decision was at hand. Throughout the day on Tuesday, phone lines buzzed with talk of the Draft Ted Kennedy movement. Kennedy had been explicit in stating back in July that he was not interested in the vice presidency, and within the past twenty-four hours that he would not run as a candidate for the presidency. On July 26, he had issued a brief statement saying that due to personal reasons, it would be impossible for him to run in 1968; he had hoped at that time that he had put the discussion to rest. But those pushing him as a candidate refused to believe it. Kennedy, they felt, would accept a draft if the bidding was strong enough.

The idea had gained better footing on Monday, when McCarthy, of all people, had become involved. McCarthy had heard the mounting rumors about Kennedy, and after a morning staff meeting on Monday, he had approached Richard Goodwin. "What about this 'Teddy thing?'" he asked. Goodwin doubted that Kennedy would run; it was too soon after his brother's death. McCarthy surprised Goodwin by countering, "Well, we might do it together. After all, experience isn't important in a president as long as he has the right advisers. Character and judgment are the real thing." As for Kennedy's youth, McCarthy pointed out that the men who had fought in the Revolution, patriots such as Jefferson and Hamilton, had been young. Goodwin called Steve Smith and suggested that he meet McCarthy and listen to what he had to say.

The meeting took place on Tuesday afternoon, and lasted about ten minutes. It opened with a brief discussion about the Vietnam plank. Smith was active in drawing up a platform proposal, and McCarthy used that discussion about the plank as a smoke screen to hide from the press the true reason for the meeting. It didn't take long for them to settle on the topic of Kennedy's candidacy. Smith was adamant: Ted Kennedy still had no intention of running for the presidency. He wasn't being coy and secretly promoting a presidential run for his brother-in-law, nor was he seeking McCarthy's support. McCarthy, who had all but thrown in the towel after his disastrous debate earlier in the day, stated outright that he had no chance of getting the nomination, but that he and Kennedy, working together, might defeat Humphrey. A joint effort made sense, since McCarthy and Kennedy shared similar views. McCarthy was willing to release his delegates to Kennedy, though he hoped that he could enter his name on the first ballot, as a way of acknowledging those who had worked so hard for him over the past months; if this wasn't feasible, he would release them immediately. Smith listened but made no commitment. Just before the meeting broke up, McCarthy made a remark for which he would not be forgiven: "While I'm doing this for Teddy, I never could have done it for Bobby."

The comment infuriated Smith, though he hid his emotions and told McCarthy that he would deliver the message to Kennedy. The remark ended any remote chance of Kennedy's entering the race, and in his inability to walk away from the contentious campaign he had waged against Robert Kennedy, McCarthy ended any outside chance that he had of going anywhere but home after convention week.

■ ■ ■ ■ ■

Tom Hayden's Tuesday began in a jail cell, after he had been arrested for the second time in less than twenty-four hours. He had been standing outside the Hilton talking to Jack Newfield and a couple of others, when one of the undercover police assigned to follow him attacked him from behind, dragged him through the street, where he was beaten senseless by other police and thrown into the back of a squad car. It was around midnight, and the streets were still seething from the violence in Lincoln Park. Hayden was tossed into a holding cell, where he recognized other SDS members, beaten and bloody, on the floor. Frightened and angry, he decided he would have to take a different approach to leadership if he expected to survive the week.

Any pretense of idealism had evaporated. Like so many in the park—recipients of unimaginable police brutality—his position had hardened into that of a revolutionary. He had seen the conversion in the civil rights movement, which had begun with Martin Luther King and nonviolent protest, with the SNCC and Freedom Riders; organizers had hoped to lead by example, to educate white America about the need for change. There had been great resistance and violence, and such leaders as Malcolm X calling for measures to aggressively counter the violence had led to the formation of the Black Panthers.

The beatings and murders executed by the Ku Klux Klan and open racists were now being waged between blacks and the cops in the name of law and order. Hayden had witnessed this as a participant in the civil rights struggle, and now as he roamed through Lincoln Park, wearing a disguise fashioned for him at a stagecraft store, he reconsidered the similarities between the civil rights and antiwar movements.

These thoughts coalesced in Hayden's mind when Bobby Seale, cofounder of the Black Panthers and current leader of the Oakland chapter, spoke to the masses gathered in Lincoln Park. Seale initially discouraged blacks from traveling to Chicago and participating in the antiwar demonstrations, even though the Vietnam War was being fought by a disproportionate percentage of African Americans. The street battles between the police and Chicago residents after Martin Luther King's murder had convinced him the convention would be a trap, and Seale judged the white, middle-class, largely student demonstrators to be buffoonish, or at least amateur, in their efforts at demonstration. He eventually accepted Hayden's invitation to speak, and he was introduced to the crowd in the park by Jerry Rubin, a familiar face from Rubin's previous days in Oakland.

Hayden: "It must have been a truly disorienting sight for the undercover agents: a stern Black Panther in beret and black leather jacket boasting of the necessity of 'picking up the gun,' together with a hairy Yippie dressed, I recall, in love beads and plastic bandolier." The Black Panther's revolutionary message, said Hayden, included "the acceptance of violence [as] a purifying step toward self-respect."

Seale brought his incendiary message to a receptive audience.

"If a pig comes up and starts swinging a club, then put it over his head and lay him out on the ground," he advised. The Black Panthers, he stated, were revolutionaries waging a war "as human beings, to remove the pigs and hogs that are terrorizing people here and throughout the world." Seale urged blacks to arm themselves for the battle ahead. The mostly white crowd in the park, he said, could learn from the oppression of blacks. "Black people know what police brutality is," he continued, "and you white people who have been asking whether it's real found out last night."

Despite the large police presence in the park, no violence followed Seale's speech. Those in the park, however, faced a different kind of confrontation at curfew time.

Tuesday was Lyndon Johnson's sixtieth birthday, and both sides had planned events to commemorate the occasion, Daley an over-the-top birthday party to be staged in Soldier Field, the Yippies an un-birthday party, complete with music, speeches, and marches, all part of the Festival of Life. Plans changed when Johnson announced that he would not be attending the convention, his decision based on advice from Secret Service claims that his safety would be at risk in Chicago, and by the likelihood of a negative reception from those in the convention hall. Instead, Johnson cast an enormous shadow over the convention from his ranch, where he could manipulate events by telephone. The mayor's plans for a huge party were moved indoors.

The Yippie party went off as scheduled, with six thousand Yippies and members of the Mobe gathering at the Coliseum for what became the largest nonviolent assembly of the week. Comedian Dick Gregory gave a speech, as did William Burroughs, Abbie Hoffman, David Dellinger, and French writer Jean Genet; Allen Ginsberg, scheduled to speak but too hoarse from days of chanting in Lincoln Park, asked Ed Sanders to read his prepared statement. Phil Ochs provided the highlight of the evening when he took the stage and sang "I Ain't Marching Anymore," his signature song protesting America's long, bloody history of warfare:

> It's always the old to lead us to the war,
> Always the young to fall,
> Now look at all we won with a saber and a gun,
> Tell me, was it worth it all?

As his sang and strummed his guitar, he looked out over the mass of people in the Coliseum. Suddenly, without prompting, a young man rose and set fire to his draft card. He was followed by another, and then another, and many more, until the hall was dotted by hundreds of draft cards burning in protest. Ochs had performed the song at antiwar rallies in concert on more occasions than he could recall, but never to this effect. When he finished, he left the stage and was embraced by Paul Krassner. "This is the highlight of my career," he told Krassner.

Any exuberance the crowd at the Coliseum felt was tempered by another rough night in Lincoln Park. In an effort to curtail the violence, a multidenominational group of ministers, priests, and rabbis gathered at the Church of the Three Crosses and, carrying a ten-foot wooden cross, walked to Lincoln Park. They anchored the cross and held a prayer vigil, leading those gathering around them in singing hymns and folk songs. Fifteen hundred kids formed a semicircle around them. At curfew time, police stood in formation about one hundred yards away. Arguments broke out between those demonstrators wanting to fight the police and the much larger number preferring a nonviolent protest. A contingency of clergymen approached the police and after locating the commander, inquired about the police intentions. The commander answered that the police would be clearing the park "but with restraint." The clergymen advised the crowd to either leave the park or sit, arms locked, and wait for the police action.

A standoff similar to those of the previous nights stretched out until after midnight. Firetrucks shined their lights on the scene; city trucks equipped with tear gas nozzles arrived. The clergymen, carrying the cross, approached the line of police and positioned themselves between the police and protesters.

A Chicago attorney, dressed in a suit and, by his own description, looking like he might be a city official, had mingled with the police for roughly an hour and a half. As he would later testify,

> There seemed to be, almost without exception, an attitude or mentality of impatience about "getting started" and it was a normal thing for policemen to talk about how anxious they were to crack some heads. As I wandered from group to group, those who were saying anything seemed obsessed with getting a "Commie" or "Hippies" and what they would do to them. I am sure that there were many policemen who did not think this way, but they were not talking or protesting what the other officers were saying. What I am trying to say is that there was almost a circus air about the hoped-for opportunities to show the protestors what they thought of them.

The confrontation broke out when police hurled tear gas canisters at the cross. The sight of the gas enveloping the cross, with the clergymen choking and retreating, enraged the kids. They shouted obscenities at the police and hurled everything they could find at them. The cops countered with more tear gas. Kids rushed toward the entrance of the park, but they were sandwiched between the advancing police and trucks armed with tear gas. Some of the kids fought back but most streamed out of the park as quickly as they could find a way.

The riot relocated to Grant Park, where a planned march to the Hilton was under way, the police in determined pursuit. Convention delegates, aware of the ongoing skirmishes between the police and protesters, watched the melee, most from the safety of their hotel windows, the braver or curious from the sidewalks outside the Hilton. One of the ministers shouted at the figures in the windows, "If you are with us, blink your lights." Lights blinked from about twenty windows.

The police continued to use tear gas on the kids, until the entire area around the Hilton was clouded; gas worked its way into the air-conditioning ducts and eventually into the delegates' rooms. The police had warned the media to stay away; those reporters and photographers who remained in the park or on the street were beaten and had their cameras destroyed. Kids screamed obscenities, without letup, at the police. National Guard reinforcements arrived and relieved the cops, and by dawn the area was secure and quiet.

Tom Hayden was the last of the radical leadership to speak to those assembled outside the Hilton. It was just after four in the morning when Hayden, peeking out from beneath a porkpie hat that was part of his disguise, took a small microphone and tried to summarize what had happened over the past few hours. He had "gone underground," he said, "to get the pig off my back." The police, he continued, were now on the collective back, and it seemed like everyone would have to go underground. "We have found," he said, "that our primary struggle has not been to expose the bankruptcy of the Democratic Party; they have done that for themselves—but our primary struggle is a struggle for our survival as a movement."

Hayden advised his audience to travel in groups, find a place to sleep, and prepare for the following day. There was a big march to the Amphitheatre planned, and they would find their way there "by any force necessary."

6 Hubert Humphrey opened what promised to be an eventful day on a positive note. He and Mayor Daley had breakfast together, and Humphrey was relieved to find that after keeping him on the hook for several days while waiting to see if Ted Kennedy would back down on his refusal to run, Daley was finally throwing his state's support to him. Not that there was a lot of conviction in Daley's support: the mayor still had reservations about Humphrey's chances of defeating Nixon, but he stood a much better chance than McCarthy. Humphrey, who had learned how to count votes from his boss, gladly accepted the Illinois support, which, barring an unforeseen turn of events, would put him over the minimum votes required for the nomination.

Nothing about the convention had gone the way he might have imagined. The violence in the streets sickened him. The fight over the Vietnam platform had left him irritable and exhausted. The uncertainties—the Kennedy rumors, the lack of support from Richard Daley and Lyndon Johnson, the disposition of the Southern delegation—had removed the joy from his politics and left him so morose that he had to force a smile when television cameras were on him. The city was an armed camp. The convention hall, usually a place of hope and some celebration, was about as free as a maximum security prison. The security was so tight that his son-in-law, Bruce Solomonson, was subjected to long lines every day when he tried to obtain extra tickets for the Humphrey family. The previous evening, Dan Rather, one of the most highly respected television news reporters covering the convention, had been punched and assaulted by a security agent, prompting an angry Walter Cronkite, already well versed on what was happening on the Chicago streets, to state that the convention appeared to be under the control of "thugs." CBS reporter Mike Wallace was similarly attacked during the week, punched in the jaw by a security official. NBC coanchor Chet Huntley, noting the beatings and equipment destruction perpetrated by the police in the parks, noted on air that "the news profession in this city is now under assault by the Chicago police."

Humphrey, last of the old-school candidates standing, knew where to place the blame for any thuggery taking place at the convention: if the past few years had proven anything, it was the probability of a violent blowback to any group physically opposing figures of authority. The demonstrators, Humphrey reasoned, invited trouble simply by being in the wrong places; most of the protesters, he allowed, were exercising constitutionally protected rights, but the troublemakers, the groups advocating violence and the individuals engaged in obscenity-laced diatribes against law enforcement officers—that was a different story. Humphrey inevitably took this approach when answering questions about the violence posed by the press. His own staff cringed at his answers and at the response they would elicit from the press.

Humphrey's Wednesday, destined to be one of the most bittersweet days of his life, continued favorably when he received a call from Ted Kennedy and learned that the Kennedy boom had come to a close. Stephen Smith had delivered Eugene McCarthy's message, as promised, and Kennedy had reacted as one might have predicted: he had not wanted to run in the first place, and he was damned if he was going to be obligated in any way to someone who insulted his slain brother. A pragmatist, Kennedy certainly wasn't going to jeopardize his future as a presidential candidate by stepping now into a fray that might drive voters to Nixon. No, he would not be running, and he would not consider a vice-presidential bid, and that was the end of the discussion. The announcement not only ended all optimistic speculation but also had the effect of confirming Humphrey as the Democratic nominee. McCarthy and McGovern did not have Kennedy's charisma, and the Kennedy name was about all that had stood between Humphrey and a first-ballot victory.

Humphrey stayed in his hotel suite for most of the day, conferring with his speechwriters over his acceptance speech, greeting a steady stream of guests, lunching with Jackie Robinson and basketball star Elgin Baylor, and watching the floor debates on the Vietnam platform, which, predictably, went the president's way. The contentious debate, eventually settled by vote, bothered him. The issue would hound him for the rest of the campaign, and in backing Johnson, Humphrey was going to lose a lot of votes. He hoped that McCarthy would endorse him, if for no other reason than to keep Nixon out of the White House, but he couldn't depend on it. The campaign had fractured their long-standing friendship.

He was aware of the clash between the police and demonstrators taking place on the street twenty-five floors below him, but he was too busy to investigate it. He could hear the "Dump the Hump" chants amid the great din from the fighting, and tear gas eventually wafted into the rooms via the air-conditioning ducts, giving him a sampling of what was taking place outside. His eyes stung and his throat burned. He retreated to the shower to wash it off. Anger welled within him. The violence marred the day—*his* day. Didn't these young people realize that he wanted an ending to the war as much as they did?

Max Kampelman, a Humphrey friend, confidant, and political ally, sympathized with Humphrey's struggles: "Humphrey, who wanted to be loved and who was filled with love, who was a conciliator and a compassionate public servant, found his moment of triumph tainted by the bitterness and divisiveness of the convention. He left Chicago with a greater sense of sadness than euphoria."

During the day, Humphrey had been given a radical alternative to his acceptance speech—and, more significantly, his plans for the immediate future. A group of Humphrey backers, all friends of the vice president, had put together a proposal and alternate acceptance speech guaranteed to be a game changer: during his acceptance speech, Humphrey would disassociate himself from Lyndon Johnson by resigning his vice presidency. The timing of the announcement was so important that the group had drawn up a timeline for it. Humphrey would seal copies of the speech in envelopes and give them to the press, with explicit instructions that they not be opened until he began his speech. (Why they believed that the press wouldn't open the envelopes ahead of time and leak the information to the public is anyone's guess.) After distributing the speech, Humphrey would fly to Washington, D.C., and hand deliver a copy of the speech to the president; Humphrey would tell Johnson that the press already had a copy of the address, that his decision, like Johnson's months earlier, was final and irreversible. The speech itself would be respectful but firm. Humphrey would openly praise Johnson's sacrifice of a long, outstanding career in exchange of the hope for a peace settlement in Vietnam.

Humphrey, in essence, would be doing the same thing: he would be giving up the vice presidency so he could speak freely as a candidate, without the worry of wondering if people thought he was speaking on behalf of LBJ.

The group waited until Wednesday, August 28, when Humphrey could feel confident that his nomination was assured, before presenting the proposal. They took it to Lawrence O'Brien and asked that he deliver it to Humphrey. O'Brien, already on record as backing a Humphrey break with Johnson on Vietnam, read the proposal and found it meritorious. He took the proposal to Humphrey, but without the speech. Humphrey, only hours from accepting the nomination, carefully considered the proposal but rejected it. Resigning the vice presidency, he told O'Brien, would look like political grandstanding. It would also infuriate the president, who was capable, even at this late hour, of causing great damage to his candidacy.

Humphrey and McCarthy, closeted in their hotel suites, watched the chaotic nominating process on their hotel television screens. Cutting into the programming were scenes from the street, gut-wrenching footage of police savagely beating everyone in their paths. Humphrey felt a flush of anger; McCarthy, sadness and resignation. Humphrey resolved that if elected president, he would look into how this kind of confrontation might be prevented in the future; McCarthy, who had stood at his window and witnessed the brutality outside the Hilton, wondered if there was anything he could do now to bring peace to the streets.

Those in the convention, although aware of the violence in Chicago during the week, had been spared, due to the electrical strike, the live footage they might otherwise have seen on the hall's monitors. They, too, were divided on whom to blame for the bedlam. The division grew even deeper when filmed footage was eventually brought to the Amphitheatre and shown in the hall. The law-and-order issue had a fresh face—or thousands of new faces—on it.

The nominating and seconding speeches might have been written off as formulaic had it not been for Senator Abraham Ribicoff's nomination of McGovern. In nominating McCarthy, Governor Harold Hughes pressed on about McCarthy's exemplifying the country's need for change, for a candidate of the people and for the people. "We Democrats cannot claim to have found him," Hughes said. "The people found Gene McCarthy for us. They found him; they have urged him on us. He is more accurately the people's candidate than any other man in recent history." John Kenneth Galbraith, in a seconding speech, drove home the point that only McCarthy and Kennedy brought their cases directly to the people in the primaries, and that "when the people had selected the delegates, the delegates [were] for McCarthy."

Humphrey had chosen Joseph Alioto to deliver his nominating speech, and the San Francisco mayor focused on Humphrey's record and how it recommended him for the job. Cleveland's Carl Stokes, one of the few black mayors of a major city, cited Humphrey's dedication to civil rights, but, in what must have seemed like the final insult of a very trying day, NBC cut away from his speech and televised footage of the violence in the streets. Humphrey's anger over the fighting boiled over during a ten o'clock press conference in his hotel suite. "They don't represent the people of Chicago," he said of the young people, although accounts published later estimated that half of those gathering in the parks were from the Chicago area, that the huge, out-of-state crowds had never materialized. "We knew this was going to happen. It was all programmed."

But the night belonged to Connecticut Senator Abe Ribicoff, who placed George McGovern's name in nomination. Ribicoff held a prepared speech but told the hall that he was going to speak from the heart. "With George McGovern as President," he said, "we would not have such Gestapo tactics in the streets of Chicago."

Mayor Daley, seated in the front row near the podium, exploded. He jumped to his feet and, his face purple with rage, bellowed at the senator. "Fuck you, you Jew son of a bitch!" he screamed at Ribicoff. "You lousy motherfucker! Go home!"

"How hard it is to accept the truth," Ribicoff, looking down at Daley, responded. "How hard."

To this point, Daley had been an exemplar of control; he had drawn up the rules, and he had seen that they were enforced—inside and outside the Amphitheatre. Ribicoff's words acknowledged *and* punctured that fact. Daley had been brilliant in choreographing the events in the hall. He had been speedy with the spontaneous order. At the first sign of a dissenting opinion, he had seen that the power to a speaker's microphone was cut; when delegates sang folk songs critical of the system, he had struck up the house band and overpowered them with "Happy Days Are Here Again." His supervisors had seen that "WE LOVE MAYOR DALEY" signs peppered the hall. But now, in an unguarded and unforeseen moment—on national television, no less—he had been humiliated by a senator from a small East Coast state. Daley would later argue that he hadn't shouted those exact words—one claim had him using the word *fake* rather than the famous obscenity—but those who had witnessed him weren't buying it.

Cheers and boos filled the hall. Ribicoff's rebuke would receive national attention, and for all he accomplished in his political life, Ribicoff would be remembered for this statement more than anything. Twenty-eight years later, when Chicago was preparing to host another Democratic convention, Ribicoff stood by his controversial remark. "It was something that had to be said, and it was something that was important to be said," he told the *New York Times*. "And, I would do it all over again because I thought that what was going on was absolutely the wrong thing to happen."

The vote was anticlimactic, a formality, further evidence of division, the bitterness, exhaustion, and, to some measure, the hope that somehow when the convention ended and the final two months of the campaigning commenced, the party would come together for a victory in November. The Wisconsin delegation requested that in light of the violence taking place in the street, even as votes were being cast, the voting be postponed and taken up in another location; the motion was shot down. The process lumbered on, with the states voting in alphabetical order, as they always did, and it became apparent to poll watchers that there would be no surprises on this night.

McCarthy watched his television out of sheer sense of obligation. A realist, he knew how it would end. Humphrey jumped out to an early lead and never relinquished it. At one point, early in the voting, McCarthy called his people in the hall and wondered if he should just have his name removed from consideration; it might, he proposed, offer some relief in the streets, where there was such division between his supporters and those supporting the vice president. Humphrey beat him badly—38½ to 13½—in their home state of Minnesota, a vote he might have predicted but a bitter pill nonetheless. He felt a sadness for all the young people who had worked so diligently for him and believed a change was possible, when, in fact, the convention belonged to the old. He could take heart in knowing that his candidacy had effected some change, just not enough. He felt like the leader of "the government of the people in exile."

Humphrey, on the other hand, had different thoughts. He sat in front of his television, recording the vote tally on a vice-presidential pad, his excitement growing with every vote in his favor. At 11:47 p.m., Pennsylvania awarded him 103¾ votes, placing him beyond the minimum needed for the nomination. Humphrey jumped—literally—into the air and celebrated a victory he could not have predicted nine months earlier. When the television screen showed a beaming Muriel Humphrey on the convention hall floor, Humphrey rushed to his TV set. "There she is," he gushed. "I wish Momma was really here. See how pretty she looks." With that, he leaned down and kissed the television screen. The week, which had begun so poorly and tested him throughout, had ended with a dream realized. A short time later, he received congratulatory calls, first, from Lyndon Johnson and, then, from Richard Nixon.

Humphrey, though, had little time to party. He had to choose a running mate.

■ ■ ■ ■ ■

The news footage broadcast on the screens and seen by those in the Amphitheatre represented but a fragment of the events of the bloodiest day in political convention history.

The day began ominously, shortly after eight in the morning, when police arrested Abbie Hoffman while he was eating breakfast with his wife and Paul Krassner in a restaurant near Lincoln Park. Hoffman had printed the word FUCK on his forehead in lipstick. The gesture, he explained, was not intended to be willfully provocative; he had covered it with a cowboy hat and had left it on while he was eating. He had applied the objectionable word to his forehead because he knew that he would be arrested during his participation in the day's events, and he was in no mood to be caught on film by news cameras and photographers. The word would guarantee as much. The police catching up to him in the restaurant had no interest in his explanations. They demanded that he remove his hat, and when he did, he was dragged out to a paddy wagon waiting outside. To the police, he was a prize catch. He had voluntarily set himself up for a bust—a fortuitous one, in this instance. The police now had reason to hold him long enough to keep him from participating in the mass rally and march planned for that afternoon. All they had to do was keep him on the move and away from bail money.

"The police moved me from precinct to precinct, cell to cell, for thirteen hours, without food, phone calls, or lawyers, while the cops beat the shit out of me," he would remember, saying that he was so amped up from the tension and lack of sleep that he laughed through the beatings. "One of the cops shoved a bullet in my face and said, 'See this? It's got your name on it. I'm gonna get you tonight.'"

The rally, set for Grant Park, and the march from Grant Park to the Amphitheatre, planned to coincide with the day of voting for the Democratic nominee, was the Mobe's big event of the week. It had been well publicized, and David Dellinger expected massive participation. Dellinger was concerned about the general temperament of the anticipated crowd, as well as that of Tom Hayden, Rennie Davis, and the SDS organizers. They had all worked together to plan the event as a nonviolent demonstration, but that had been months ago, long before the police had roughed up demonstrators in previous days. Dellinger had become "especially nervous" about Hayden, who, Dellinger feared, seemed to have abandoned his nonviolent stance in the wake of the brutality. "Tom had walked a thin line for several days," Dellinger wrote later. "[N]ow he had crossed over to the other side."

Even without this concern, Dellinger worried that he might be leading thousands of marchers into a trap. His last-minute requests for a permit had been denied, and the police had printed and were distributing throughout Grant Park a flyer advising potential marchers that any march was unlawful and that all marchers would be arrested. This would not deter Dellinger's plans; he doubted that the police would engage in mass arrests on the day the Democrats were announcing their presidential nominee. Security in the area was heavy. Six hundred officers were dispatched to the area around the park's bandshell, where the speakers were positioned, and poorly disguised plainclothes cops walked around the park in small groups. The National Guard had the detail near the Hilton, and the Second Battalion of the 129th Infantry stood by on the roof and parking lot of the Field Museum near the park.

Dellinger, Hayden, Davis, and others met to discuss the march. Hayden proved Dellinger's suspicions to be accurate: Hayden wanted to take a tough, assertive approach to the march, and he pushed for the adoption of an alternate march in the event that the police sealed off the approaches to the Amphitheatre. After considerable discussion, the three leaders agreed to offer rally attendees three options for action after the rally. They could join Dellinger and march in an orderly fashion to the Amphitheatre, or they could just head out on their own and meet at the convention hall; finally, they could return home and avoid confrontation with the police.

The crowd swelled, but aside from an isolated altercation, there were few confrontations between the police and those in the park. The crowd consisted of every type of demonstrator imaginable, from hippies and Yippies to elderly protesters dressed in much more conservative attire, from anarchists waving Vietnamese flags to McCarthy kids, from those armed with rocks and bottles to those out mainly to witness the goings-on. By three o'clock in the afternoon, an estimated ten thousand to fifteen thousand had squeezed into the park.

The speakers began. Jerry Rubin compared those in the park to the Black Panthers and urged his audience to take back the streets after the march. Phil Ochs sang "I Ain't Marching Anymore." William Burroughs praised the demonstrators' efforts, telling them, "You are doing something workable about an unworkable system."

Sometime between three-thirty and four in the afternoon, a shirtless young hippie scaled a flagpole and attempted to bring down the flag. A blur of activity followed. The crowd encouraged him to remove the flag or lower it to half-mast. Police rushed to the flagpole and tried to pull him down. When they succeeded, they clubbed him with their nightsticks or beat him with their fists. (The police would deny this.) Young people nearby threw "heavy chunks of concrete, sticks, cans [and] bags of what looked like paint" at the police. Badly outnumbered, the police fought back. Davis, trying to calm demonstrators, was attacked from behind; a police baton opened a large cut on his head and rendered him unconscious.

From his vantage point on the bandstand platform, Dellinger tried to calm the mass of hysterical people. He urged them to sit down peacefully and let the world see who the assailants were. Hayden, agitated by what he had seen the police do to Davis, joined Dellinger on the platform and told Dellinger that he was taking over the proceedings. Dellinger refused to yield the microphone until he had advised the masses of the three alternatives the Mobe and SDS had discussed earlier. Dellinger asked Allen Ginsberg, Jean Genet, and Robert Lowell to say a few calming words. After they had spoken, he turned the microphone over to Hayden.

The SDS leader was not searching for a quiet resolution to the violence:

> Rennie Davis is in the hospital with a split head. He's going to be all right, but he would want you to do for him what he is unable to do . . . and that is to make sure that if blood is going to flow, it will flow all over the city. . . . If we are going to be disrupted and violated, let this whole stinking city be disrupted and violated. . . . Don't get trapped in some kind of large organized march which can be surrounded. Begin to find your way out of here. I'll see you in the streets.

Fortuitously, the eruption of hostilities was dying down, the battleground near the flagpole littered with bleeding victims, demonstrators, and police alike. The time for the march was approaching, and Dellinger spent the next hour in one last failed attempt to negotiate with officials on the scene. It was going to be a nonviolent march, he said, arguing that this kind of march was guaranteed by the Constitution. Deputy Superintendent of Police James Rochford and city corporation counsel Richard Elrod offered a compromise that would have allowed the marchers to assemble somewhere other than the Amphitheatre, but Dellinger rejected their offer. Marchers pushed their way forward toward the front, creating a massive logjam of increasingly impatient humanity. The police repeated their warning that marchers would be arrested.

The march was out of Dellinger's control. Hayden and a group following him broke away and ran toward the Loop. Some of Dellinger's followers sat on the sidewalk and sang; others tried to break through the policed lines and head toward the Amphitheatre. The National Guard and police blocked the bridges and streets in an effort to contain the demonstrators and keep them away from the Loop. At the Hilton, another skirmish broke out, as an estimated two thousand people, including guests of the hotel and people from the neighborhoods, confronted police struggling to maintain order. People inside the Hilton dumped rolls of toilet paper on the police below; at least one officer was hit with a bag of urine. The assembled youths shouted slogans and obscenities.

Dellinger had been correct in worrying about a trap. With thousands of people trying to leave the park or run across bridges, clogging the streets, shouting at police, chanting or coughing from tear gas, blocking traffic, or walking slowly away from the chaos, general confusion led to inexcusable actions. A car with two elderly women stopped long enough for two badly gassed kids to jump in back; National Guardsmen, seeing the car approaching a bridge, stopped the driver, dropped tear gas canisters outside it, and threatened to cut the car's tires with their bayonets. Police bludgeoned a man wearing a white lab coat and red-and-white medic's armband until he needed medical attention himself. Police used Mace on countless people and beat them when they were blinded. Thousands fleeing the police out of Grant Park ran into Ralph Abernathy's three-wagon Poor People's March, permitted by the city, and fell in with them as they made their way down Michigan Avenue toward the Loop; Deputy Superintendent Rochford ordered reinforcements to separate the march from the masses following it. The police and Guardsmen closed in on all sides, compressing people until they had nowhere to go. People were trampled when they stumbled, others were crushed against buildings and storefronts. A young man had an artery in his leg severed when police pushed him and others through a plate-glass window at the Haymarket Inn, the Hilton's restaurant.

Hayden was one of those pushed through the window:

We fell through the shattered street-level opening to the Hilton's Haymarket Lounge (named, strangely enough, in memory of Chicago police killed by an anarchist's bomb during a violent confrontation between police and protesters in 1886). The police leaped through the windows, going right by me, turning over tables in the swank lounge, scattering the drinkers, breaking glasses and tables.

"They attacked like a chainsaw cutting into wood, the teeth of the saw the edge of their clubs," wrote Norman Mailer, who watched the scene from his hotel window. "They attacked like a scythe through grass, lines of twenty or thirty policemen striking out in an arc, their clubs beating, demonstrators fleeing."

The soundtrack to the madness—the youths shouting, the police screaming "Kill, kill, kill," and the angry demonstrators chanting "Fuck the pigs!"—was soon overwhelmed by another chant: "The whole world is watching! The whole world is watching!" And indeed it was. News cameras recorded the violence, photographers took stills of police holding their batons high over their heads, prepared to bring down unarmed and often already wounded protesters. Faces from both sides, contorted from rage, were seen on the late-evening news and the pages of the next morning's newspapers. Television, so successful in bringing the Vietnam War into the nation's homes, now presented another war, where, as in all wars, the brutality of the moment could only hope for history's mercy.

7 Hubert Humphrey vacillated over his choice for a running mate—so much so that he kept postponing and backing up the starting time for the Thursday press conference in which he was to announce his choice. He had been considering candidates for months, dating back to a time when he finally dared to believe that the nomination was his. In recent weeks, he had narrowed down the candidates to two personal favorites—Maine senator Edmund Muskie and Oklahoma senator Fred Harris—but in the early morning hours of Thursday, exhausted by the week's events, he had yet to settle on his finalist. He had listened to so many suggestions, placed them on lists and crossed then out, conferred with party leaders, and considered and reconsidered putative candidates' track records that he might have been forgiven for having a blurry mind. The most important qualification, as far as Humphrey was concerned, was a vice president's readiness to assume the presidency at a moment's notice. Such candidates were not difficult to find.

Humphrey might have been describing himself when he spoke of the qualities he required of his vice-presidential candidate. Loyalty placed high on his priorities. When asked about his expectations of the vice president in the event of a disagreement, Humphrey responded in a way that detailed his relationship with Lyndon Johnson during their uncomfortable disagreement on Vietnam.

"I feel that the first thing that a Vice-President owes to the President is his loyalty," he said, "and I believe that before he ever has any disagreement with the President publicly, if he were to have one, he has a solemn obligation to try to work it out privately." This, of course, was exactly what LBJ demanded of him, a promise Humphrey had to make before Johnson named him his running mate in 1964; it defined his silence on his disagreement with Johnson about the heavy bombing of North Vietnam. Pressed about what he would do if a disagreement were over an issue that was a matter of conscience—"of deep spiritual involvement"—Humphrey offered that the vice president had a choice: "either keep his own counsel and bide his time, or he can speak out on the basis that it is more than he can take or endure." He made a point of stating that he had not experienced that moment of decision with Johnson.

From the very beginning, his primary choice for running mate had been Ted Kennedy. The Massachusetts senator possessed every quality that Humphrey could ask for. He had brought up the idea on several occasions, but Kennedy, still mourning the loss of his brother and, in all probability, at odds with Humphrey over his support of Johnson on the Vietnam War, rejected him every time. Sargent Shriver's name came up—he was, after all, a Kennedy, even if by marriage, and he was well respected—but Ted Kennedy opposed it, and Humphrey was only lukewarm on it in any event. Perhaps most unusual of all: an alignment ticket with Nelson Rockefeller, which would deliver the New York vote, along with those of Republican moderates throughout the nation, but Rockefeller refused to run as a Democrat.

Other names considered included Governor Terry Sanford of North Carolina, Governor Carl Sanders of Georgia, Governor Richard Hughes of New Jersey, and former Deputy Secretary of Defense Cyrus Vance, now working with the North Vietnamese on the Paris peace talks. Lyndon Johnson advised Humphrey to choose a Southerner, but Humphrey bristled at the suggestion of choosing someone based primarily on region, even if it had worked favorably for Johnson as John Kennedy's selection. He had dismissed a suggestion of San Francisco Mayor Joe Alioto for the same reason. Humphrey seriously considered Hughes, a textbook liberal and personal friend, but he eventually eliminated his name from the list.

In the final hours, the decision was a choice between Muskie and Harris. After he returned from the convention on his nominating night, Humphrey met with a group of Southern governors and then closed out his day by hosting a gathering of his closest aides and advisers. Lawrence O'Brien, present at the meeting, felt that Humphrey might have already decided to go with Muskie. Humphrey liked Fred Harris, a friend and ally of Robert Kennedy, and a possibility as a vice-presidential choice for Kennedy had he lived and been nominated, and as a Southerner, Harris would have strengthened the Democratic ticket, but he, like Muskie, lacked national recognition, and while his status was growing in the Senate, he lacked Muskie's overall experience.

O'Brien favored Muskie, and he felt that Humphrey might be "intrigued by what Muskie might bring to the ticket." "I thought Muskie had a recognition factor that was very favorable," O'Brien stated. "He was ethnic, which could be helpful. He was from the northeast, which could be helpful. Ed Muskie had a presence that could add a significant dimension to the ticket."

Harris and Muskie had very different personal styles. Muskie avoided the fray. Harris was vocal and aggressive; Muskie, although fiery when provoked, was a quiet, reserved man—a notable difference from Humphrey's demeanor. "I know I talk too much," Humphrey admitted. "I wanted someone who makes for a contrast in styles."

Muskie would also provide a significant contrast to Spiro Agnew, who since the Republican convention, had established himself as a brash, vocal, controversial candidate.

One could understand Humphrey's enthusiasm for Muskie, who bore a striking physical resemblance to a young Abraham Lincoln. Born to Polish parents on March 28, 1914, Edmund Sixtus Muskie grew up near the shores of the Androscoggin River in East Rumford, Maine. This was Republican country—and heavily so—but Muskie's father was a progressive, and Muskie followed suit. A quiet child who preferred to read or go fishing, he was nevertheless popular with his classmates in elementary school and high school, where he stood at the top of his classes in scholarship and in his late teens excelled as a debater. He received a law degree at Cornell and set up a private practice, cut short by the outbreak of World War II. He served in the navy in both the Atlantic and Pacific theaters, advancing to the rank of lieutenant, returning home in 1946 and resuming his career as an attorney. He preferred politics, however, to the courtroom. He was active in the Democratic Party and eked out a victory in a state legislative race in 1946. He rose steadily up the political ladder, largely because of his ability to work with both parties. He served two terms in the Maine House of Representatives and in 1954 ran for governor and became the first Catholic governor in the state's history and the first Democratic governor in two decades. He was reelected in 1956, and two years later he moved on to the U.S. Senate.

Humphrey had been in the Senate for ten years when Muskie took his seat, and Humphrey could see that this new senator was a rising star. Muskie had a fastidious work ethic, and he could be demanding of those around him; he would flash his volatile temper from time to time, but he cooled off quickly. Humphrey could think of no enemies that he might have accumulated. If the two were to have compatibility problems, they might have arisen over the war, but as Muskie related later, that wasn't the case. "He apparently had followed my career in the Senate long enough to understand that we were basically compatible philosophically," Muskie said, "that we shared the same general goals of the country, and I assumed that he took no exception to my softer Vietnam stands publicly. As a matter of fact, he seemed to welcome it."

No final decision was reached during the late-night session between Humphrey and his advisors, though Humphrey made it clear that he was leaning heavily toward Muskie. At three o'clock in the morning, after everyone had left but Bill Connell and Ted Van Dyk, Humphrey went over his list with them one more time, but he didn't offer his two closest aides his final decision.

He was prepared the following morning: it was going to be Muskie. He asked Van Dyk to go to Muskie's room and get him, and while he was away, he made a few calls for last-minute input. Johnson still contended that Muskie was a weak choice. Daley was merely lukewarm, but he had other things on his mind. Humphrey had one more bit of unpleasant business: the same vetting of Muskie's background as he, Hubert Humphrey, had been subjected to four years earlier. He brought in James Rowe to ask the questions. Muskie had a pregnant, unmarried daughter, but other than that minor stumbling block, Muskie gave no reason for pause.

Humphrey found it exceedingly difficult to talk to Fred Harris about his decision. "In an equal way you are just as good a man," he told Harris. "I could just as easily have taken you but for a few fine differences." Muskie had been stationed in another bedroom in the Humphrey suite for hours, talking to Humphrey, addressing Rowe's questions about his background, waiting for Humphrey to talk to Harris, before he heard from Humphrey of his decision. When he did, he had very little time in which to prepare his acceptance speech for that evening.

(The press was reserved in its reaction to the Muskie selection. At a time when the nation was divided, Humphrey might have gone after a bigger name. But the press had nothing negative to say about Muskie, either. The *New York Times* might have summed up the overall mood in an editorial rife with backhanded praise: "His selection is not a concession to any particular faction, and it arouses no marked admission among his fellow Democrats, neither does it dismay or outrage.")

Humphrey's acceptance speech, nearly three times as long as Muskie's, was bloated and, at times, touched down on the jingoistic and banal. For such a usually effective orator, Humphrey picked the highest point of his public career to deliver what sounded like a canned speech. He opened his address with a mention of "the troubles and the violence which have erupted, regrettably and tragically, in the streets of this great city," yet he did not mention or show any notable understanding of the causes of one of the most shameful episodes in American electoral history. Instead, he offered what sounded like a cliché ("violence breeds counterviolence, and it cannot he condoned, whatever the source") and concluded by reciting a brief passage from the famed prayer of St. Francis of Assisi, which he had read for emphasis on another occasion. Delegates had been watching the brutality on the streets for days, including on monitors in the convention hall, and the previous evening they had heard several nominating speeches, most notably Abraham Ribicoff's, that minced no words in addressing that violence, yet here was their presidential candidate in a moment that called for a few words of leadership sounding like an aldermanic candidate in a midsized city in the Bible Belt.

Humphrey was more successful in his efforts to unify the party. He dropped the names of some of the party's most powerful figures of the recent past (Franklin D. Roosevelt, Harry Truman, John F. Kennedy) but risked any goodwill he might have gained by lingering too long in his praise of Lyndon Johnson. He devoted more time to praising Johnson's achievements after taking over for Kennedy than he spent on any of the others, only to end in the type of gushing for which he was often criticized: "And tonight to you, Mr. President, I say thank you. Thank you, Mr. President." His efforts to reach out to Eugene McCarthy and George McGovern were awkward.

He acknowledged the "bitter debate" between candidates and Democrats in general. He pointed to three issues—Vietnam, law and order and the urban crisis, and nationwide unity—and addressed each in substantial segments of his speech. Anyone expecting anything but status quo on the Vietnam War were going to be disappointed, but he did score heavily when he spoke about international affairs, including the recent problems in Czechoslovakia and nuclear disarmament. Acceptance speeches were not occasions for in-depth proposals for solutions, but given the division within the party on the Vietnam and law-and-order issues, the speech merited less wind and more concrete than it received.

Substance was not the issue to those listening to a speech filled, as it was, with crowd-pleasing catchphrases. Humphrey's forceful delivery, the carefully constructed phrases (revised by Humphrey himself, from his speechwriters' words), the need to cheer after a week of chaos—Humphrey's audience was ready to cheer, and cheer they did, after almost every sentence, the lone exception being the lusty boos that greeted Humphrey when he spoke favorably of Johnson. Humphrey spoke of unity, and his party was prepared to demonstrate it.

Muskie fared better with his address, given just before Humphrey's. Known for his homespun, anecdotal style, Muskie kept his speech brief and at times entertaining. He spoke of how he hadn't learned of his selection until late, at almost four o'clock that afternoon, ·which was too late to fly his family to Chicago to celebrate the occasion. His family in Maine, he said, had been overrun by the press, and when one reporter supposedly asked his mother if she intended to vote for him, she responded, "If no one offers anyone better, I suppose I will."

Muskie's modesty—after his joke, he conceded that it was unusual to find a Maine Democrat even dreaming to rise to such a high position—was just one of the attributes that made him a wise choice for Humphrey. His speech struck a conciliatory tone, a reaching out to include the country's youth in deciding the direction the United States would take in the future, a depth of understanding of their concerns at a time when the welfare of youths was being sacrificed on the streets of Chicago. Muskie joined Humphrey in deploring the actions and attitudes of those devoted to destruction, but unlike Humphrey, who stated and restated his will to lead but offered little indication of his grasp of the ways to fill the chasm between the groups, Muskie emphasized a need for inclusion. "We must inspire their confidence that their efforts will achieve the dignity, the opportunity and the equality which they seek," he said.

Humphrey's anger was the key to the separation between his and Muskie's approach. Humphrey blamed the young people for the violence in Chicago. They had provoked, and the police had responded. He had heard—or worse yet, in his mind, Muriel had been subjected to—the derision, the taunts, the obscenities, the lack of any respect toward him or the process he revered; they had destroyed his big moment, his reward for a lifetime of work and planning. He was not about to forgive the demonstrators and other young people who had done damage to the convention, the Democratic Party, and, yes, to himself. "I think the blame ought to be put where it belongs," he told Roger Mudd of CBS television. "I think we ought to quit pretending that Mayor Daley did anything wrong. He didn't. . . ."

Daley and the general public supported Humphrey's assertions. Immediately following the closing of the convention, Daley sent a message to Police Commissioner James Conlisk, expressing his and the DNC's gratitude to the police department for "devotion to duty and a job well done." Daley, defiant in public, insisted that despite the outrage expressed in press coverage, his office had been inundated with calls and mail approving of the police actions, at a ratio of sixty thousand supporting the police to four thousand disapproving. The jeweled center of his triumph was the fact that no one had been killed during convention week. (A seventeen-year-old South Dakota runaway, in Chicago for the convention festivities, was shot by and killed police on Wednesday,

August 22, when, stopped on a routine curfew violation, he drew a gun and tried to use it on the police.) On September 9, Daley would issue a statement that became one of the most memorable utterances to rise out of the Chicago convention and its aftermath: "The policeman isn't there to create disorder; the policeman is there to preserve disorder."

The media's judgment of the violence was harsh and strong. Tom Wicker, writing for the *New York Times,* wrote a scathing indictment of Humphrey, Daley, and the Chicago police in which he called Daley "insensitive," Humphrey "inadequate," and the police "arrogant." "[The marchers] did not threaten law and order in Chicago, not if ordinary police prudence, common sense and legal procedure had been exercised," Wicker wrote. "The truth is that these were our children in the streets, and the Chicago police beat them up,"

"The cops had one thing on their mind," wrote New York newspaper columnist Jimmy Breslin. "Club and then gas, club and then gas, club and then gas." Breslin blamed the police and Daley for the violence, but he saved his most pointed accusations for the man who won the nomination. Humphrey, he said, displayed no authority, no ability to do what needed to be done to put an end to the violence. "If he could not find it in him to stand up to Richard J. Daley," Breslin continued, "then you must wonder what Hubert Humphrey will be able to do with generals in the Pentagon."

Another verdict would be entered at the end of the year, when Daniel Walker, director of the Chicago Study Team of the National Commission on the Causes and Prevention of Violence, after an extensive examination of the events taking place during convention week, called the police actions a "riot of the police."

By the time that report was published, Humphrey's fate in the election had been decided.

8 Eugene McCarthy intended to fly out of Chicago, on a charter jet destined for Washington, D.C., on Friday morning, August 30. The convention, he concluded, had been an unqualified disaster, from goings-on in the convention hall to the violence on the street. The Democratic Party, as he had seen in its representatives on the Amphitheatre floor, was not his party. On Thursday evening, he had refused to join Humphrey, Muskie, and McGovern on the convention stage for the traditional show of party unity; doing so, he reasoned, would have been an affront to all those who had worked so hard to help him reach an unattainable goal. The new politics he had hoped for, the

changes he had striven for, his plan to influence Humphrey's position on the Vietnam War—all had been defeated by the forces of the old. The Vietnam plank, a compromise that promised no immediate, acceptable resolution to the war, had been a sham. The bloodshed on the streets could only have led one to wonder if America was, in fact, becoming the police state that so many dissenters claimed it was. Faith had been broken—he wouldn't contest that—and as a spiritual man, a practicing Catholic, a poet, and a public servant, all requiring large measures of faith, he felt disassociated from the familiar.

He slept poorly on Thursday night and rose before five o'clock on Friday morning. Day was breaking, and as he looked out his hotel window to the street below, he could see young demonstrators gathered across the street. He decided to visit them. On his way out, he walked by the command post near the elevator on his floor. George Yumich, one of his staff members, his head bandaged and bleeding, sat at the desk. He had just been beaten by police. There was a melee taking place on the fifteenth floor, he told McCarthy.

McCarthy's young workers were staying on that floor. A makeshift hospital, serving the McCarthy camp's walking wounded, had been thrown together in one of the rooms there as well. McCarthy took the elevator down to that floor. When he stepped off and walked into a lobby area nearby, he was greeted by the sight of his workers, some bleeding profusely from head wounds, herded into a group and watched over by a group of police. Some of the young people were sobbing hysterically. The police, McCarthy learned, had arrived on the floor with hotel personnel, with orders to clear out anyone not registered for a room on the floor. Kids had been sleeping on the floor in rooms and in the hall, most of them partied out from the previous evening; many of those still awake were playing bridge. The police ordered them to disperse, some shoving the kids toward the lobby by the elevator. When McCarthy asked the police why the kids were being evicted, the police told him that they had been dumping beer cans, ashtrays, garbage, and worse out the hotel windows onto the police below. Police surveillance, in the form of binoculars or rifle scopes, had indicated that the offenders were in room 1506-A, on the fifteenth floor. With the exception of one young man, who admitted to tossing a smoked fish out a window, the McCarthyites and other witnesses disputed the allegation. The two sides would also disagree on what triggered the violence. Both admitted that one male, after being pushed around by the police, reached for a small table as if to use it as a weapon. The McCarthyites said he thought better of it and did nothing; the police countered that he struck an officer with it. One enraged cop shattered his nightstick on the young man, rendering him unconscious and setting off a brutal scene in which the police used their clubs on anyone within reach.

By the time McCarthy arrived, the police were already escorting young people to the first-floor hotel lobby; there was additional bedlam down there, McCarthy was told. An angry McCarthy set out to investigate. What he found was a scene similar to what he had left on the fifteenth floor: "The young people were still under orders, huddled on the floor by a ring of helmeted police; some of them bloodied by the beatings they had received from the police, and some of the girls were near hysteria."

McCarthy demanded to speak to the officer in charge. No one stepped forward. Assuming control, McCarthy instructed his battered followers to return to the fifteenth floor and head back to their rooms.

McCarthy couldn't understand or justify the police actions at the hotel. The police, he felt, had no business conducting the early-morning raid, which he branded "a massive invasion of privacy—action without precedent in the history of American politics," and he was alarmed to learn that attempted calls to his room had been blocked by the hotel's switchboard. The entire floor had been sealed off in what appeared to be a premeditated attack. Rather than leave Chicago on his previously scheduled flight, McCarthy remained at the Hilton until he was assured that all his supporters and workers had safely departed the hotel.

He eventually flew out of Midway Airport late in the afternoon. As the plane left the runway and lifted skyward, the pilot addressed his passengers in a way that McCarthy would never forget.

"We are leaving Prague," the pilot said.

Book Four

THE ELECTION

17 The Final Lap

1 If the Republican National Convention had been a matter of awarding Richard Nixon his crown, the Democratic convention had been the presentation of a certificate of participation to Hubert Humphrey. Humphrey's capitulation in Chicago, along with his grotesque switching of positions in reaction to the rioting in the streets, had won him a nomination but, unless things changed drastically, lost him an election. Candidates customarily enjoy a bump in popularity following a convention; this was not the case with Humphrey. The public opinion polls indicated a precipitous drop in Humphrey's popularity among survey respondents. When he arrived in Chicago, he and Nixon were in a dead heat for the presidential vote; when he left, he was trailing—by as many as double digits in some of the polls.

More disheartening, as far as the Democrats were concerned, was Humphrey's stubborn refusal to modify his positions on the war and law and order. He would argue that his public pronouncements represented his true feelings, but those feelings were not endorsed by likely Democratic voters. As a result, Humphrey entered the final stages of his campaign as an underdog—an inconceivable position a year earlier, when the Democrats were confident that the party would control the White House another four years.

Worse yet, Humphrey had no set plans for the last two months of the campaign or for reaching the voters whom he wanted to attract. The young voters were probably lost, a notable percentage now lining up behind the idea that it was better to sit out this election than vote for any of the three available candidates. If one could believe the polls, Nixon attracted the older, moderate voters; he fared better on the war and law-and-order issues.

The Humphrey campaign was beginning to look like the horribly failed Goldwater campaign of four years earlier, when the Republican Party had been badly divided and the public showed little interest in Goldwater's conservative agenda. In the 1964 general election, Goldwater had taken his home state of

Arizona, along with four Southern states (Mississippi, Georgia, Louisiana, and South Carolina). For Humphrey, the September polls showed a similarly devastating trend. A *Newsweek* poll had Nixon winning thirty-one states; Wallace, nine; and Humphrey, seven. A September 24 CBS News poll also projected Humphrey coming in third.

As usual, Humphrey's campaign organization was a disaster. Throughout his career, Humphrey enlisted the help of talented associates for his campaign teams, but he failed at delegating responsibility. He preferred to let the organization operate without ironclad guidance—a sure recipe for disaster. Gifted, creative minds were wasted as they dealt with uncertainty about where they were needed, or, worse, they became mired in infighting and power struggles among those confused about their station. When Lawrence O'Brien joined Humphrey on July 27, Humphrey's lifelong friend and political ally Secretary of Agriculture Orville Freeman felt threatened. He thought he was managing Humphrey's campaign, and when Humphrey corrected him on that score, he nearly quit. He stayed on only when Humphrey placed him in charge of issues and scheduling. This sort of disagreement existed on every level of Humphrey's organization, and as a result, tasks could be left undone or duplicated.

For Democrats, the unofficial beginning of the fall campaign traditionally began in Detroit on Labor Day, but for this election, Humphrey chose to march in Manhattan. It was a bust, with plenty of participants but negligible observers. Humphrey struggled to make headway, but he wasn't helped by President Johnson, who continued to treat his vice president like a disobedient child. When Humphrey told a University of Pennsylvania audience that he envisioned the beginning of American troop withdrawal from Vietnam as early as late 1968 or early 1969, Johnson corrected him in public the next day when, during a speech to the American Legion in New Orleans, he pointedly announced that there was no way of making that determination. Humphrey stewed, but he remained silent.

Every campaign stop became a confrontation between Humphrey and hecklers, even in usually friendly cities. In downtown Boston, in an appearance that should have been a boost to his campaign, Humphrey was joined by Ted Kennedy, who had made very limited public appearances since his brother's assassination. Facing a crowd of more than ten thousand, the two men were booed and shouted down when they attempted to give their speeches. Protesters chanted "Dump the Hump" and "We want Gene." Kennedy, who had never been booed on a campaign stop in his career, was shocked; Humphrey was mortified and angry.

Humphrey carried on, taking the beating of his life and moving on to the next one. With little to encourage him, he seemed destined to bear up under the ordeal until the election, when it would all be brought to a merciful end.

2 Richard Nixon entered the homestretch of his campaign well positioned to win the November election. He was well rested, well financed, and, as important as ever, well ahead in the polls. He had worked out his plans for the next two months with his staff in such detail that *Time* referred to his campaign as "smooth as a space satellite, precise as a computer." Much of the precision would be accredited to lessons learned in his 1960 campaign against Kennedy, and much was owed to a staff dedicated to seeing that the New Nixon image remained front and center in the public consciousness. And Nixon, micromanaging his campaign, was with them every step of the way.

The final two months of the race were going to be a sprint, and Nixon was prepared for it. Unlike during the fiasco against Kennedy, which had found him exhausted when he needed the energy the most, Nixon had paced himself throughout his current run. He had taken time away from campaigning on a regular basis; he had relaxed during the week of the Democratic convention, resting comfortably in Florida, avoiding the press, watching the Democrats implode in Chicago. There would be no repeats of his exhaustive schedule in 1960, when he had insisted on visiting all fifty states and pushed for every possible vote. He had worn himself ragged in pursuit of Electoral College votes of negligible consequence. He was eight years younger then. This time, he would focus on seven states—New York, California, Texas, Illinois, Pennsylvania, Ohio, and Michigan—whose combined total of 210 Electoral College votes were nearly enough to win the election. He had won California and Ohio in his race against Kennedy. He figured that if he took those two states again in 1968, he would have to cover at least two of the remaining five to win the election. Doing so would require every bit of energy that he had left.

The final stage of the presidential campaign always required vast sums of money—more than the candidates invested in all the primaries combined. The costs of travel, lodging, meals, entertainment, and advertising had risen substantially since Nixon's first presidential race. Maurice Stans, who handled Nixon's campaign finances, estimated that the Nixon campaign had run through $9 million to win the nomination; the final push, he told Nixon, would probably cost an additional $24 million, a record amount at that time. Stans collected money from the usual donation sources, but he scooped up the enormous stash of revenue through $1,000-a-plate dinners (which found Nixon speaking to each dinner by closed-circuit television) and $1,000 donations from wealthy Republicans. The money poured in. People loved backing a winner.

During the primary season, Nixon had been able to avoid backing himself into corners with a lot of policy statements. He would have to be more forthcoming in the final leg of his campaign. He would be appearing in public more frequently than ever, and he would be facing questions from the hated press corps at every stop. Nixon had strong feelings about the image he wanted to project, and he conferred with Bob Haldeman on the best ways to reach the public. In a September 5 memo to William Safire, Haldeman passed along six major points and themes that Nixon wished to emphasize throughout the home stretch of his campaign:

1. The Come-Back Theme
2. The Caliber of the Nixon Team
3. The Youth of the RN Organization
4. The Immense Effect of the RN Acceptance Speech
5. RN as Party Unifier
6. RN, "The Man for the Times"

These points would help create a better, more positive mood than voters were accustomed to seeing from the Nixon of the past. The voters demanded change, and the new Nixon was going to give it to them. He had changed since 1960. He had strength, confidence, and the answers to the country's ills. In his memo, Haldeman specified how he wanted Nixon to come across in his stump speeches and major addresses:

Of vital importance is the point that we must play the confident line from now until November, regardless of what developments occur. We are on the offensive and we must stay on the offensive. The Democrats are demoralized, and we must keep them demoralized. We must exude confidence, not cockiness, indicating that we're going to run an all-out campaign and pour it on, but that we do so knowing that we are ahead and plan to stay ahead and extend our lead so that we can elect a Republican House and a lot of Republican Senators as well. It is important that all of our major speakers take this line, and particularly important, that those who are on the plane and talking with the press, and the local politicos exude it. It is also important that those who have contact with RN take this line and not come in with long faces any time something goes wrong.

The key to the Nixon campaign was *control*. Haldeman's memo emphasized it, and in following his directives, Nixon's campaign staff and volunteers saw that, with only an occasional speed bump, the road to the election was smooth, easygoing, and so efficient as to be downright boring. This was the way Nixon wanted it; any style points he earned were purely coincidental. The typical Nixon day found him flying into a city, doing a motorcade between the airport and the city's downtown, maybe meeting with local journalists (or, better yet, going to a television station and taping an interview), and appearing at one headline event, always timed so its coverage would be on the evening or late-night news. By then, Nixon had already left town or was ensconced in his hotel room for the night.

Little changed from day to day. His speech—now referred to as "the speech" by his staff—was the same talk he had been giving for months. He had fine-tuned it as he went along, and while he might address specific issues at specific luncheons or dinners, the speech was always about the same issues. (Nixon was too shrewd to be trapped into talking about Vietnam in detail, and with an exception here and there, the same could be said about the topic of law and order.) His public appearances were well screened, with only an occasional protester or heckler getting through, and no unfriendly signs or banners found their way to hungry television cameras. Things could go poorly for those who managed to make it through security and disrupt a Nixon speech: the Secret Service had refused Nixon's request that they rough up the protestors, but off-duty police could be open to the idea.

Not surprisingly, Nixon turned down all of Hubert Humphrey's challenges to debate, the official explanation arguing that he would have to include George Wallace in such a debate, the press-recognized reason being that he had much to lose and very little to gain by matching wits with his Democratic opponent. Humphrey ridiculed him as "Richard the Chicken-Hearted" or "Richard the Careful," but to no effect.

As Nixon recalled it, George Wallace posed just enough concern to add a wrinkle or two to the campaign. Nixon estimated that he would have enjoyed a landslide victory if Wallace had not been part of the vote. Wallace—and his law-and-order stance, in particular—eroded Nixon's support in the South. Nixon enlisted Senator Strom Thurmond's help as part of his Southern strategy, but the powerful leader was only partially successful in drawing Wallace votes to Nixon. Nixon's desire to stay away from debates was largely based on Nixon's concern over the effect that free publicity might have on the Wallace campaign. "Wallace's campaign was depriving us of a substantial number of votes," Nixon suggested, "and anything I did to elevate Wallace would be self-destructive. It was not fear but self-interest that determined my decision on the debates."

Nixon's biggest fear—and one that clouded his self-confidence and released his darker, paranoid impulses—involved Lyndon Johnson and the Vietnam War. Nixon was safe as long as there were no new, dramatic developments in the war and the peace talks continued to stall; the Democrats would be blamed for the failure to end the war. But Nixon did not trust Johnson, despite their ongoing conversations about the war. The more Nixon prodded the president about the war, and the more Johnson assured him that nothing new was happening, the more Nixon became convinced that LBJ would be pulling off a last-minute move to benefit Humphrey. An end to the war, or a strong move in that direction, would have sunk the Nixon campaign, and an end to the U.S. bombing of North Vietnam might have had the same effect. Nixon had heard enough rumors of a bombing halt—which Johnson denied—that he had gone so far as to ask Henry Kissinger, Nelson Rockefeller's foreign policy advisor, to look into it. Kissinger, a future secretary of state and Nixon confidant, flew to Paris, investigated the rumors, and returned to the States with the information that *something* was afoot, though he wouldn't or couldn't say what. He advised Nixon to be very cautious about saying anything about Vietnam until something happened.

Nixon became obsessed with Vietnam. He continued to explore traditional White House and State Department channels for updates on plans. When he learned nothing and nothing happened overseas, his suspicions rose. It was time, he decided, to play his ace in the hole, a direct, though highly questionable, connection to the South Vietnamese government. He would do whatever was necessary to win the election.

3   As September drew to a close, Hubert Humphrey, beaten and depressed, concluded that he had to make a dramatic change. His campaign had become a cancer that diminished him, eating away at his resolve and energy. He considered scaling back his campaign and limiting his appearance schedule to a couple of days a week; he didn't have the money to do much more in any event. Fewer appearances meant fewer spiritual floggings at the hands of demonstrators turning up every time he accepted the dare of delivering a speech. But surrender was a mockery of the fighter in him. He would battle to the end.

How was he going to do this, given his lack of financial resources and support from his own party? He couldn't afford television spots, and he had sunk so low in the Democratic Party's eyes that he was asking candidates running on the state and local levels to mention his name when they were campaigning. He was still receiving coverage from the media, but far too often he was being portrayed as a sort of sad-sack victim of his own political foibles. He was suffering the same fate that Lyndon Johnson had endured before he bowed out of the race.

He found a lifeline in an unexpected place. George Ball, the former undersecretary of state, LBJ's nemesis on the Vietnam War, and current ambassador to the United Nations, had been watching Humphrey's fall, and aside from his concerns about the fate of the Vietnam War in Nixon's hands, Ball was considering a much larger picture disturbing enough that he suddenly resigned his position at the UN and joined the Humphrey campaign.

"I thought it was catastrophic for the Democratic Party that Humphrey should be beaten as badly as it appeared he was going to be," he explained. "I didn't have the faintest hope that he could win, but I was concerned that he make a fair showing because I thought the consequences for the party and for the political future of the United States would be seriously impaired otherwise."

By the time he and Humphrey spoke about his joining the campaign, Humphrey had reached a critical decision: after all the months of ceaseless public support of the Johnson war policies, Humphrey decided to break from the president's position on national television. Lawrence O'Brien had somehow found a way to pony up $100,000 for a half hour of television time. The address would be taped when Humphrey was in Salt Lake City on Monday, September 30.

Anger had been a motivating factor in Humphrey's resolve. He had flown to the Pacific Northwest for speeches in Oregon and Washington. The appearances ranked among the worst experiences of his campaign. At Reed College in Portland, he was greeted by an audience that included hundreds of demonstrators who walked out of his speech in unison, chanting the usual "Stop the War" and "Dump the Hump" slogans, as well as cries calling him a fascist, racist, and murderer. That evening, protesters gathered outside his hotel and relentlessly chanted "Stop the war! Stop the war!"

There was additional bad news awaiting him on that same day, when Humphrey received a copy of a forthcoming Gallup Poll. He had dropped three percentage points since the previous poll. Nixon, holding 43 percent of the respondents, led Humphrey by a discouraging 15 percent. Almost as alarming, Humphrey led Wallace by a mere 7 percent.

His appearance at the Seattle Center Arena the next night was even worse. A bloc of roughly two hundred students, arriving early and taking seats together in the balcony, booed and shouted catcalls at Senator Warren Magnuson when he attempted to introduce Humphrey. One of their members had a bull-horn, and Humphrey was shouted down every time he attempted to speak. Humphrey tried to quiet his tormentor, to no avail. Rather than shout over the young man with the bullhorn, Humphrey invited him to speak.

In response, the young man offered one of the most lacerating indictments Humphrey had ever had directed at him. "In Vietnam, there is a scream that does not end," the man began.

> There is a wound that does not cease its bleeding. I'm talking about the scream of death and the wound of war. Why is the scream being heard in Vietnam by our soldiers and innocent Vietnamese people? Why is there this wound because of war—not for democracy but a war which supports a puppet government, a government where the new number-two man said his hero is Adolf Hitler? You have supported this man. You have supported Johnson. You have supported this war, this needless waste, this murder. We have not come to talk with you, Mr. Humphrey; we have come to arrest you.

And so it went, the indictment of Humphrey as a war criminal, the charges that Humphrey was involved in the deaths of "thousands of Americans and hundreds of thousands of Vietnamese." Humphrey did not respond, did not say a word, though it must have been tempting, about the speech he had already begun composing that he hoped would help hasten the end of the war. Describing the group as "the loudest, rudest demonstrators reporters have yet seen on the campaign trail," an attending journalist portrayed Humphrey as "a desperate and angry figure."

Humphrey's anger was apparent when the demonstrators refused to yield to him after their leader had gone on until he admitted that he was finished. "I shall not be driven from this podium by a handful of people who believe in nothing!" Humphrey shouted. The confrontation lasted for half an hour, until the group was ejected by security guards. Humphrey delivered his planned speech, knowing that the disruption would be the lead in the next day's newspaper reports. "I went back to my room," he recalled, "disappointed, angry, depressed."

Humphrey would call the evening the turning point in his campaign. The television address in Salt Lake City, already the focus of bickering among his advisors and speechwriters, was being designed to free him from Johnson, but the Seattle experience had fired up his resolve. "I'm probably going to lose this election," he told his staff gathered in his suite late that evening. "But win or lose, I'm going to speak my mind, and I'm going to fight. I'm not going to be denied the right to be heard and I'm going to say what I feel."

The Salt Lake City speech challenged Humphrey and his advisors in its content, emphasis, and wording. Each word seemed to invite a debate among the staff. An early draft, not much more than an outline, duplicated the main points of Humphrey's rejected convention platform. George Ball had read— and rejected—this draft while he was flying from Washington, D.C., to Seattle; he had drawn up his own speech before his plane had landed. By then, another, more fleshed-out draft had been drawn up by the Humphrey group. Lawrence O'Brien hated it and told Humphrey over the phone that he was wasting his $100,000 if he went on television with it.

Humphrey's camp was bitterly divided, hawks versus doves. William Connell and James Rowe argued that as part of the Johnson administration, Humphrey had to remain loyal to the president or face his wrath; opposition to LBJ should be avoided. The speech itself could be suicidal. The doves—O'Brien, Ted Van Dyk, Fred Harris, and George Ball—believed that Humphrey had no choice but to break with the president.

The two sides quarreled throughout the discussions about the speech, the biggest bone of contention being the conditions for a bombing halt in North Vietnam. The hawks favored a continuation of the bombing until the North Vietnamese met certain conditions, such as the reestablishment of the demilitarized zone. The doves supported a bombing halt similar to the one proposed by Eugene McCarthy: an immediate end to the bombing with the condition that it could be resumed if the North Vietnamese failed to show good faith in the peacemaking process. Johnson, still holding fast to his generals' position, favored the hawks' argument; Humphrey tended to go along with the doves.

Humphrey listened to the heated disagreements until the early morning hours of the day he was to fly to Salt Lake City. Physically drained and irritable from all the hours of discussion, and impatient with all the accusations he had heard over the months that he wasn't his own man, Humphrey threw everyone out of his hotel room. "I don't care who it pleases," he told them. "I'm going to write the speech the way I want it, and if people don't like the speech, that's the way it's going to be."

Of all the concerns over the speech, Humphrey fretted most over how, if at all, it might affect ongoing negotiations in Paris. Johnson maintained his position that a bombing halt might discourage South Vietnam from entering the peace talks; Humphrey didn't know what to think. When he had finally dictated his speech to secretaries, he asked George Ball to contact Averell Harriman in Paris and read him the speech. Ball, a friend of Harriman's, had recently discussed the Vietnam negotiations over dinner with him in Washington, D.C. Ball called Harriman, and the peace talks negotiator voiced no objection.

Humphrey had one difficult task remaining: call the president and inform him of the televised speech. Humphrey had the well-earned reputation of being tardy for his appointments, and he arrived for the taping later than he anticipated. By the time he was prepared to go on camera, he had only fifteen minutes to talk to Johnson. The president had been expecting this turn of events for some time, and he wasn't surprised by Humphrey's message, but he wasn't pleased by what Humphrey intended to say.

"Hubert," he said, "you give that speech and you'll be screwed."

For once, Humphrey would not buckle to Johnson's demands. He was going to give the speech. "I don't think this is going to impair your hand," he told Johnson.

"I gather you're not asking my advice," Johnson said. He promised Humphrey that he would watch the speech and ended the call.

Humphrey made one other important decision—a symbolic one involving the staging of his speech. The props for his customary address included an American flag and the vice-presidential seal; he was always introduced as the vice president of the United States. On this occasion—and on all similar occasions until the election—the seal was missing, and he was introduced as the Democratic candidate for the presidency. His split with Johnson was final.

This was Humphrey's first nationwide address since the Democratic convention, but if that, along with the contents of the speech, made him at all nervous, he didn't show it. His voice was firm, but he looked relaxed. It had been twenty years since his historic integration speech at the 1948 Democratic convention, and this one demonstrated the same sense of purpose and courage. The meat of the discourse consisted of the three main points hotly disputed by those working on the speech:

> As President, I would stop the bombing of the North as an acceptable risk for peace because I believe it could lead to success in the negotiations and a shorter war. This would be the best protection for our troops.

This simple statement was the result of hours of arguing and a last-minute Humphrey change of wording. In the original, Humphrey stated that he "would be willing to stop the bombing," which Humphrey deemed to be too wishy-washy in comparison to the final "I would stop the bombing." In the latter, there was no doubting his break with Johnson.

There were, however, some conditions to the continuation of the bombing halt:

> In weighing that risk, and before taking action, I would place key importance on evidence, direct or indirect, by deed or word, of Communist willingness to restore the demilitarized zone between North and South Vietnam.

> If the government of North Vietnam were to show bad faith, I would reserve the right to resume the bombing.

In retrospect, Humphrey's departure from Johnson was significant more in its implications and nuance. Johnson was not that far removed from Humphrey, but LBJ did not wish to be pinned down by timetables, and he surely wanted tougher conditions than Humphrey's. These conditions had been written into the party platform—one that Humphrey was modifying in his address.

Much more noteworthy in the eyes of those watching on television and those speaking to Humphrey afterward was the way the speech transformed the candidate. "It liberated him internally," Ted Van Dyk told Albert Eisele, author of a dual biography of Humphrey and McCarthy. "The American voter watching the screen that night finally saw that Humphrey was for peace, that he was sincere, and that he meant it. On that night, the onus of the war shifted to Nixon."

"He was a new man from then on," Lawrence O'Brien declared. "It was as if a burden had been lifted from his shoulders. And the impact on the campaign itself was just as great."

Humphrey's assessment was simple: "I feel good inside for the first time."

Others were less enthusiastic about the speech. Eugene McCarthy deemed it "no move at all," while Curtis Gans sniffed that "it was nothing but a reiterance of Johnson's policies under peace rhetoric." "Humphrey either has to be for the bombing halt or he has to support the negotiations in Paris," Richard Nixon said, adding that he was uncertain about which side Humphrey was on. LBJ stated his displeasure to anyone listening in the White House; Humphrey, he complained, had seriously set back the Paris talks. The press, although recognizing Humphrey's move away from Johnson, was generally lukewarm on the effects the speech would have on the war.

The public reacted immediately and positively. The night after the Salt Lake City speech, Humphrey spoke at the University of Tennessee, and rather than having to deal with the hostility he had been seeing at nearly every stop since the convention, he was met by a friendly crowd, many carrying signs with such encouraging messages as STOP THE WAR—HUMPHREY WE TRUST YOU and IF YOU MEAN IT, WE'RE WITH YOU. The chanting stopped—in Tennessee and everywhere else for the remainder of the campaign. Money started coming in, first slowly and in small amounts, but steadily building until the Humphrey campaign no longer suffered from a lack of funds. The speech had kick-started his campaign back to life.

4   On October 3, George Wallace called a press conference in a ballroom in Pittsburgh's Hilton Hotel. After months of deliberation, he was prepared to announce his choice for a running mate.

If truth were known, he wasn't especially enamored with the idea of choosing anyone. He felt no need of balancing a ticket, no need to cloud his campaign with another voice; he was a dynamic persona on his own. Still, state laws required a vice-presidential candidate in the general election.

Wallace was familiar with the requirement; he had run into it during the primary season. He had had a stand-in, former Georgia governor Marvin Griffin, listed as a vice-presidential candidate for the primaries in the states requiring a running mate. Griffin wanted nothing to do with the office, and he only agreed to run when Wallace promised that it would be on an interim basis, until he found a permanent candidate. Griffin was simply a name. His value as a candidate was negligible. He would rather have spent a day at the fishing hole than an hour at a campaign rally.

Over the months, Wallace had thrown together a short list of VP candidates that included, among others, FBI director J. Edgar Hoover, ABC radio personality/commentator Paul Harvey, and, perhaps most bizarre of all, Kentucky Fried Chicken magnate Harland Sanders. He eventually settled on two names: former Kentucky governor and senator and onetime baseball commissioner A. B. "Happy" Chandler, and former commander of the Strategic Air Command General Curtis E. LeMay.

He approached Chandler, a moderate conservative, first. Chandler expressed interest, and Wallace believed he had found his candidate. He ran into opposition, however, when delegates from four Southern states said they would drop their support if Chandler appeared on the ballot. Kentucky in particular objected to the choice. As the state's governor, Chandler had not opposed desegregation of Kentucky's schools, and as commissioner of baseball, he had not opposed Jackie Robinson's breaking the color barrier. Wallace decided to look at his other option.

Curtis LeMay knew politics only as they applied to combat. He would say that he preferred to avoid war, but there was nothing in his background to back his words. He was the ultimate lifer in the armed services, a man whose combined knowledge and courage elevated him to the highest positions in the military. He had flown fighter planes and bombers during World War II and led the firebombing missions in Japan. He had gone on to lead the U.S. Air Force during the Cold War and directed the Berlin Airlift. He was appointed commander of the Strategic Air Command. John Kennedy appointed him Air Force chief of staff, but his tenure at the position was limited; he resigned in 1965. Throughout his career, LeMay was well known for his enthusiasm for bigger and more advanced military technology. He didn't back away from advocating anything at his use, including nuclear weaponry. In his 1968 book, *America in Danger,* he deplored what he felt was American weakness in dealing with the Soviet Union during the Cold War years, and he proposed heavier bombing of North Vietnam as a means of ending the war. His idea of bombing North Vietnam "back to the Stone Age" became a rallying point for those who derided him as "Bombs-Away LeMay."

LeMay rejected Wallace's first offer. He was living a good, retired life in California, and he had no interest in giving it up for a suit in Washington, D.C., though he claimed to have received a number of offers. He believed, when Wallace initially approached him, that Richard Nixon adequately covered the conservative agenda, and the odds of his being elected exceeded those of a third-party candidate. "I believed that if we didn't get a conservative government in power in 1968, that we probably would never have another chance," LeMay explained. "I think that we were just that close to socialism or communism. So, I was in favor of Mr. Nixon being the best choice that we had, and when the Wallace people approached me I gave them the same answer I had given all the other people about going into politics."

LeMay's greatest fear was a moderate's winning the Republican nomination. When Nixon handily defeated Rockefeller in Miami, LeMay thought the conservatives had their man. But doubts set in, first, when Nixon stayed quiet about his positions on issues, and, second, when LeMay heard rumors about possible candidates for a Nixon cabinet. He accepted the explanation that it was safer to say little than to harm a candidacy by saying the wrong thing, but he couldn't abide by some of the moderates dominating cabinet discussions. He was further encouraged to look in Wallace's direction when Wallace made headway in the northern unions. LeMay maintained his belief that Wallace had no chance of winning the election, but he thought some of his ideas might be implemented if the election was thrown into the House of Representatives and Wallace had the power of negotiating with the two major candidates. "My only hope was to get people moved over to the right a little bit," he said.

In a move that he and Wallace would regret, LeMay finally agreed to run as Wallace's vice-presidential candidate.

The press conference announcing LeMay's candidacy was a fiasco to all but black humorists looking for new material. After introducing LeMay as his running mate, Wallace stood off to the side, a stony expression on his face, while LeMay self-destructed and in the process all but brought down the Wallace campaign. LeMay offered sincere, straightforward answers to reporters' questions, leaving no doubt about where he stood. He had been coached by Wallace and his advisors on the necessity of presenting the old war-is-hell attitude—and he made several attempts at this during the press conference—but his answers to questions about the use of nuclear weapons made him look like a character from *Dr. Strangelove*.

He was in trouble from the onset, when he attempted to define his position on nuclear war. "We seem to have a phobia about nuclear weapons," he began, quickly adding that the best policy of all was to avoid war. But, he went on, if a country was going to engage in war, the country had to be dedicated to ending it as soon as possible.

> Use whatever force that's necessary. Maybe use a little more to make sure it's enough to stop the fighting as soon as possible. So this means efficiency in the operation of the military establishment. I think there may be times when it would be most efficient to use nuclear weapons. However, the public opinion in this country and throughout the world throw up their hands in horror when you mention nuclear weapons, just because of the propaganda that's been fed to them.

Reporters glanced nervously at one another. They had expected a tough response from a military man, but did he really mean this? Was it all just tactics to him, without a mention of the loss of human life?

But this was only the beginning. LeMay, who, like Wallace, felt that the war protesters were all a bunch of Communists, wanted everyone to understand that as much as he would prefer to stay out of war, he was fully prepared to employ any means necessary to win it. He was damned if he was going to stand by and watch American casualties mount in Vietnam—not when the country had the ultimate weaponry at its disposal.

The world, he insisted, wasn't going to end if nuclear weapons were deployed. He spoke of a film he had seen, a documentary about the Bikini atoll, where many nuclear tests had been conducted. Life, he assured the astonished reporters, had returned to normal. "The fish are all back in the lagoons; the coconut trees are growing coconuts; the guava bushes have fruit on them. As a matter of fact, everything is about the same except the land crabs. They get their minerals from the soil, I guess, through their shells, and the land crabs were a little bit 'hot,' and there's a little question about whether you should eat a land crab or not."

George Wallace, openly agitated, stepped in to defend his vice-presidential choice. "General LeMay hasn't advocated the use of nuclear weapons," Wallace said. "Not at all. He discussed nuclear weapons with you. He's against the use of nuclear weapons, and so am I."

Had the press conference ended on that note, LeMay might have been able to salvage at least some of his reputation. But the fact was, he *wasn't* against the use of nuclear weapons, and to underscore his point, he repeated his thought about the country's *phobia* over nuclear weapons, and he repeated his preference of not launching them. But he refused to back off his position of using them as a means of ending a war.

"I know I'm going to come out with a lot of misquotes from this campaign," he complained. "I have in the past. And I'll be damned lucky if I don't appear as a drooling idiot whose only solution to any problem is to drop atomic bombs all over the world. I assure you I'm not."

And thus, in the span of a brief press conference, Curtis LeMay nuked George Wallace's campaign. And he wasn't finished: no coaching in the world could convince him to back off the nuclear weapons issue, and try as he might, he could not defuse the bomb he had built. After a few messy press conferences, Wallace addressed the problem in a creative way: rather than allow LeMay to risk further—and perhaps fatal—damage to his candidacy, Wallace sent him on a fact-finding mission to Vietnam.

5   George Wallace was not the only candidate having problems with a running mate's making problematic statements. Spiro Agnew, a man who appeared to relish the sound of his own voice and what he perceived to be a clever phrase, had become a press corps favorite for his sheer unpredictability. He spoke with the authority of someone absolutely convinced of his superior thinking on a topic, only to discover, after his words had made their escape, that he might have fared better if he had said nothing at all. Such was the case on September 10, when he attempted to defend Nixon after Humphrey called

him a "cold warrior." Agnew struck when a reporter asked if Humphrey was implying that Nixon was taking a "hard line" approach in his campaigning.

"If you've been soft on communism, and soft on law and order over the years, I guess other people look hard," Agnew said, showing either his ignorance or disregard for the truth. Humphrey's anti-Communist stance was well known in government circles, and the phrase "soft on communism" was straight out of Joseph McCarthy's red-baiting playbook. Rather than let it go at that, Agnew decided to double down on his statement with a bit of a history lesson in his retort. "After you see the similarities between now and before the war," he continued, "Humphrey is beginning to look a lot like Neville Chamberlain. Maybe that makes Mr. Nixon look more like Winston Churchill."

Agnew's remarks drew a storm of criticism from outraged Democrats, the press, and even such high-ranking Republicans as Senate Minority Leader Everett Dirksen and House Minority Leader Gerald Ford. When over the next few days, Agnew tried to explain his statement, he only dug himself a deeper hole. He hadn't been consciously invoking McCarthyism in his statement, he said; that would have been an overreaction. But he added, "When you see communist involvement all over the world, it is pretty unrealistic to say it can't happen here. A certain measure of it is happening here." As for comparing Humphrey to the British prime minister who had capitulated to Hitler before World War II, Agnew said he was merely referring to Humphrey's "squishy soft," "peace at any price" position on Vietnam.

This tempest might have had little impact on average voters, who were more apt to notice some of Agnew's more boneheaded lines, offered when his tongue was working faster than his brain, such as the time, two days later in Chicago, when he was addressing his attitudes toward racial and ethnic backgrounds, and he uttered, "Very frankly, when I am moving in a crowd, I don't look and say, 'Well, there's a Negro, there's an Italian, there's a Greek, and there's a Polack." Or the time he was talking to a *Washington Post* reporter and referred to a Japanese American reporter as a "fat Jap." Or this, from the Agnew Hall of Fame, spoken when he declined an opportunity to tour an inner city: "When you've seen one city slum, you've seen them all." He could try to clarify a comment such as the ones he made on Humphrey ("If I left the impression that I think the vice president is not a loyal American, I want to rectify that. I think he is a man of great integrity and I have a high respect for him."), but he—and Nixon—had to live with the embarrassments. The press loved it.

Agnew's misfirings became all the more noticeable when compared to the statements offered by his Democratic counterpart. Ed Muskie was proving to be one of the best decisions made by Humphrey; he came across so smooth, natural, thoughtful, and honest on the campaign trail that some pundits regarded him as the stronger half of the Humphrey–Muskie ticket. He even out-Humphreyed Hubert Humphrey when he faced hecklers during an appearance in Washington, Pennsylvania: unlike Humphrey, who had offered a heckler time to speak his piece during his debacle in Seattle, only to lose control of his appearance, Muskie did the same during his Pennsylvania speech, only to defang his abuser and win the day. Compared to Agnew, Muskie stood tall and respected.

Nixon tried to stay free of Agnew's negative publicity. He rarely mentioned him on the campaign trail, and he only appeared with him on one occasion. He had much more on his mind than a flare-up in the news, and in fact, Agnew played well in the South and border states, which Nixon desperately wanted to capture. When pressed on Agnew, Nixon was defensive about his running mate. Agnew, he insisted, was a strong, decisive leader, capable of assuming the presidency if something were to happen to him. Nixon, with no more use for the press than Agnew, sent Agnew a note saying: "Dear Ted: When news is concerned, nobody in the press is a friend—they're all enemies."

Agnew's publicity gave Nixon occasion to reevaluate how he, Richard Nixon, was conducting his campaign. From the beginning, he had maintained a distance from the press and the public, and this posture had served him favorably. He had avoided the kind of gaffes that harm a candidacy. His campaign strategy had pushed him to the nomination, and he held a substantial enough lead over Humphrey to conclude that the general election was his as long as he held his course for two more months. His critics, however, doubted if he had any substance. He refused to comment on the two major campaign issues, begging off a discussion of Vietnam for what he claimed was a respect of the peace talk negotiations, and using essentially the same reasoning to avoid addressing the recent violence in Chicago, on the basis that he didn't want to influence or interfere with an appointed panel studying the problem.

"Politicians have often helped themselves by keeping their mouths shut at the appropriate time," the *New York Times* observed, "but Richard Nixon appears to have turned the gift of silence into a major strategic weapon in his campaign."

His advisors were divided on the tactic, some believing that he would do well to withhold his opinions until just before Election Day, others arguing that he looked weak in doing so. His support was evident, if one could judge from his triumphant appearance in Chicago a week after the Democratic convention. In a Democratic town still roiling from the turbulence of the convention, a Nixon motorcade drew four hundred thousand Republican supporters and a flood of confetti raining down from buildings lining the streets. Nixon maintained his neutrality when asked about the recent events in Chicago, noting that it was not his place to offer an opinion on a subject under study. He successfully deflected a law-and-order question by giving a nonanswer to a reporter's query:

> I have often said that you cannot have order unless you have justice, because if you stifle dissent, if you just stifle the process, you're going to have an explosion and you're going to have disorder. On the other hand, you can't progress without order, because you have disorder and revolution, you destroy all the progress that you have.

Nixon's cautious approach included his references to his opponent. He made certain that those attending his rallies understood that Humphrey was not a candidate for change, that a vote for Humphrey meant a vote for four more years of the status quo.

6 Hubert Humphrey's remarkable return from the dead employed a two-pronged media approach, developed by Lawrence O'Brien and Joseph Napolitan, that took an aggressive and sometimes negative tack not often associated with the perennially upbeat candidate. But these were desperate times. If Humphrey hoped to stand any chance of defeating Nixon, he had to be willing to use every available tool to construct his case.

O'Brien's efforts actually dated back to the end of the Democratic National Convention. According to his original agreement with Humphrey, O'Brien was to leave his campaign manager position at the conclusion of the convention, and with this in mind, he wrote a thirty-page exit memo that, in O'Brien's direct, candid, and detailed manner, addressed the strengths and weaknesses of the Humphrey campaign, including those of the candidate himself. O'Brien intended the August 27 memo to be "the final chapter" of his involvement with Humphrey—analysis he hoped the vice president might find useful in the final two months of his campaign. When Humphrey persuaded him to stay on until the election, O'Brien used the memo as his own guide.

O'Brien planned while Humphrey's campaign teetered at the edge of the abyss. As O'Brien saw it, two major issues—Vietnam and the lack of money—stood between Humphrey and the White House. Humphrey could take giant strides by addressing his position on Vietnam; it would depend upon a break with Johnson, but that had been long in the arriving. The Salt Lake City speech took care of that. The lack of money was an entirely different matter. The

Humphrey campaign required television exposure in the final weeks, and even with an influx of cash following the Salt Lake City speech, the campaign was still financially strapped. Without money, Humphrey would be bowled over by the heavily financed Nixon effort. Nixon's refusal to debate Humphrey underscored the importance of television ads: the TV spots would be Humphrey's only way of simulating a national debate with his opponent.

In his memo, O'Brien placed great emphasis on television's impact on getting Humphrey and his message before the voting public. Newspaper coverage cost no money, but it had severe limitations. After all the months of traveling with candidates and covering the campaign, newspaper reporters and editors had set opinions on the candidates and their messages. Any coverage would be filtered through those opinions. Humphrey had been victimized by these preconceptions in the weeks following the Democratic convention, when the context of his speeches was secondary in reports that concentrated largely on the demonstrations against him. Fairly or not, he was tied to Johnson and the Chicago rioting, and the demonstrators, more often than not McCarthy supporters, diminished Humphrey's attempts to push his message forward.

Television spots eliminated the filter; the message would be delivered directly to the viewer. When money started coming in, the television possibilities improved. There was still not enough to go around, but the Humphrey campaign had something to work with. O'Brien's two-pronged approach focused, first, on presenting Humphrey the candidate, and, second, on attacking Nixon and Agnew. O'Brien placed Napolitan in command of creating the different ads. There were also spots to include Edmund Muskie, who was turning out to be as effective a campaigner—if not more so—as Humphrey.

The pro-Humphrey spots ranged from brief ads to a half-hour documentary. The brief ads gave Humphrey little more than time to touch on a single topic. Humphrey, an excellent on-camera presence, fared well in these spots, though the talkative candidate might have done better in longer ads, in which he would have had more time to stretch out. The documentary, which prominently featured the private side of the candidate, was exceptional, with one large drawback: the Humphrey campaign did not have the money to broadcast it as often as O'Brien and Napolitan would have liked.

O'Brien viewed the Nixon–Agnew attack ads as "equally important" as the Humphrey spots. "I felt both Nixon and Agnew were vulnerable—their leadership qualities or lack of them, deviousness, harking back to the fur coat, the Nixon–Kennedy debates. So I saw a potential for very powerful spots."

Agnew was held up to ridicule, as in the spot that depicted a man watching television when Agnew came on; the viewer chuckled, then laughed, and was finally reduced to hysterical laughter, with the message, "Just Imagine Spiro Agnew Vice President of the United States." In another, titled "Spiro Agnew: A Heartbeat from the Presidency," a beating heart moved across the screen with the message emblazoned on the screen. A few of the ads were shown sparingly—just enough to make an impression before they were pulled—and a couple were judged too mean-spirited to show at all. The group debated about using clips from Nixon's "Checker's speech," but it was considered to be too nasty to pursue.

One spot took aim at George Wallace and Curtis LeMay. Humphrey, with a lot of help from unions in the northern part of the country, had been cutting into Wallace's blue-collar support, a demographic that Humphrey's advisers judged to be vulnerable to change. In the ad, a blue-collar type is standing in a voting line, mumbling to himself. He is a lifelong Democrat, now agonizing about switching his vote. But he wants a change. By the time he reaches the voting booth, he has made up his mind. He pulls the curtain closed behind him, and within a couple of seconds, the booth explodes and disintegrates. The spot, aimed at LeMay's trigger-happy reputation, never ran.

The decisions about whether to run or not run certain spots, O'Brien admitted, were tough calls requiring a final judgment over the ads' contents being hard-hitting versus their being the kind of dangerous, negative campaigning that might draw outrage or sympathy. Humphrey himself was disgusted by one of the ads, and it was dropped. The problem? The ad that skirted the line between hard-hitting and distasteful was very often effective.

"We were playing with some fire," O'Brien said, "but it's an indication of the approach to the problem of climbing that mountain."

7 On October 31, exactly seven months after renouncing another presidential bid, Lyndon Johnson appeared on national television and announced that due to "a new and very much more hopeful phase" in Paris peace negotiations, he was ordering a cessation of all bombing in North Vietnam, effective at 8:00 a.m. the following morning.

I cannot tell you tonight specifically in all detail why there has been progress in Paris. But I can tell you that a series of hopeful events has occurred in South Vietnam. The government of South Vietnam has grown steadily stronger. South Vietnam's armed forces have been substantially increased to the point where a million men are tonight under arms, and the effectiveness of these men has steadily improved.

The superb performance of our men, under the brilliant leadership of General Westmoreland and General Abrams, has produced very truly remarkable results.

Johnson's address, long on generalizations and skimpy on details, might have been the result of his knowledge of Nixon's deceptions, as a means of boosting Humphrey's candidacy in a memorable October surprise. Or it might have been an action taken, late in his presidency, as a means of improving his legacy. These would have been cynical explanations.

Or more optimistically, the announcement might have come at a time when Johnson truly believed that there had been signals that peace officials were moving forward. American casualties in Vietnam had sunk to their lowest numbers in fourteen months, which could have been interpreted in two opposing ways: the North Vietnamese were indicting a willingness to talk peace, or as had happened in the past, the North Vietnamese were scaling back their efforts and using the lull to regroup for another offensive. The Soviet Union, carefully monitoring the developments, believed it to be the former. Dean Rusk had met twice with Soviet ambassador Anatoly Dobrynin, who had indicated that the North Vietnamese might be receptive to negotiation if the bombing stopped. Even General Creighton Abrams admitted that "a bombing halt might now be militarily tolerable."

"All my military advisors shared this view and told me we would not be taking serious risks with the lives of our fighting men," Johnson recalled in his memoirs. "Ambassador Bunker and our field commander in Vietnam both supported this move. I knew we would be in a weaker position in Paris without the South Vietnamese at our side, but I felt that it would be far worse to have the Paris talks collapse completely."

Whatever the reasons, the bombing halt had an unsettling effect on Richard Nixon. More than ever, he needed assurance that South Vietnam would be staying away from the peace talks. Anna Chennault, back from a visit to the South Vietnamese embassy, believed that South Vietnam would hold its position. This proved to be true when, on November 2, President Thieu announced that South Vietnam would not be participating in the talks.

Nixon, however, faced other serious problems: Johnson was aware of his illegal interference with State Department affairs. For Johnson, reaching this conclusion had taken weeks and had involved gathering information from a variety of sources. Johnson had tapped into the South Vietnamese embassy and, through intercepted cables, had learned that South Vietnam believed it would get a better peace settlement with Nixon as president. Further communiqués implicated Nixon, John Mitchell, and Texas Republican senator John Tower. Johnson was able to piece together Chennault's involvement. He had her phone tapped and had operatives watching her movements.

Nixon's treachery bothered Johnson deeply. He had trusted Nixon, at least as far as he trusted most people, and he had briefed Nixon (and Humphrey and Wallace) on the continuing negotiations in Paris. He believed that Nixon's position on the war was closer to his than Humphrey's, and he went so far as to suggest to confidants that Nixon might make a better president. On the day of his bombing-halt speech, he called the three candidates and briefed them on what he intended to say. Nixon's deceit, he averred, was more than a betrayal; it was an act of treason.

The problem was what to do with what he knew. He couldn't expect to flush Nixon out by approaching him directly. He did, however, attempt to let Nixon know that he was on to him through a series of conference calls with all three candidates. In one, on October 16, he took a roundabout approach. It was vital, he told the three men, that they exercise extreme caution in the statements they gave to the press; one misstatement could jeopardize negotiations. There had been rumors of a bombing halt, but as of the moment, the White House position had not changed. "We are anxious to stop the bombing," he admitted, but this would not happen under present conditions. "I'm trying to tell you what my judgment is about how not to play politics with it," he continued, moving closer to the point. "I know all of you want peace at the earliest possible moment, and I will just express the hope that you be awfully sure what you're talking about before you get into the intricacies of these negotiations."

"This is consistent with what my position has been all along," Nixon responded. "I've made it very clear that I will make no statement that would undercut the negotiations."

But Nixon would not remain silent. When he heard that Johnson's position had changed, that the president intended on calling for an end to the bombing, he devised a preventive strike. In a statement issued on October 26, five days before Johnson's speech, Nixon allowed that it was likely that the president was going to stop bombing in North Vietnam. Then he slathered on the praise, as if he endorsed Johnson's position and wanted to work with him. He stated that he did not believe that Johnson was stopping the bombing as a way of boosting Humphrey's chances. He followed that with a pious statement about Johnson's dedication to peace. "At no time in the campaign have I found the president anything but impartial and candid in his dealings with the major presidential contenders about Vietnam," Nixon said. "In every conversation I had with him he has made it clear that he will not play politics with the Vietnam war."

Johnson, one aide noted, was "apoplectic." His initial reaction was to go public with everything he knew. He had documents and transcripts that would have been very damaging to Nixon if they were made public—information that might cost Nixon the election. Going public would have been risky. Johnson's methods of obtaining his information invited questions about the National Security Agency and FBI's wiretapping and surveillance. Clark Clifford, although supportive of Johnson and outraged by the Chennault affair, wondered about the legality of the Chennault wiretap. She was a private citizen and free to call whomever she wished; a wiretap without the attorney general's authorization would have been illegal, and though he could have bypassed the attorney general if he thought she was a security risk, Clifford didn't relish the thought of discussing this in public, if it came to that. In addition, Nixon's involvement was murky: there was no smoking gun, no call between Nixon and the South Vietnamese officials, directly linking him to the accusations. Finally, Dean Rusk believed that LBJ's going public could be disastrous, regardless of the outcome of the election. Public trust might be violated, regardless of Nixon's winning or losing.

"It was an extraordinary dilemma," Clark Clifford said. "On one hand, we had positive evidence that the Little Flower [Chennault] and other people speaking for the Republican candidate were encouraging President Thieu to delay the negotiations for political reasons. On the other, the information had been derived from extremely sensitive intelligence-gathering operations of the FBI, the CIA, and the National Security Agency; these included surveillance of the ambassador of our ally, and an American citizen with strong political ties to the Republicans."

Johnson decided to apply more pressure and leave Nixon guessing about his intentions. In another conference call with the three candidates, in a remark aimed at Nixon, Johnson noted that "some old China hands are going around and implying to some of the embassies and some others that they might get a better deal out of somebody who was not involved in this." Before any of the candidates had the chance to object too strenuously, LBJ added a line intended for Nixon: "I know that none of you candidates are aware of or responsible for it."

If Nixon nursed any doubt that Johnson knew of his involvement, Senate Minority Leader Everett Dirksen put that doubt to rest. The president had called Dirksen four hours before his Vietnam speech and complained bitterly about Nixon's duplicity. He repeatedly mentioned Nixon's name, and he was specific about his misdeeds. Johnson informed Dirksen that he had a transcript in which one of Nixon's "partners" discussed the agreement of a better deal for Vietnam in exchange for nonparticipation in the peace talks. Dirksen, of course, was shocked by these revelations.

"He better keep Mrs. Chennault and all this crowd tied up for a few days," Johnson said of Nixon.

Nixon, who undoubtedly heard from Dirksen about the president's call, hung on. The election was only a few days away. Johnson delivered his speech about the bombing halt, and Nixon, LBJ, and the president's advisors awaited South Vietnam's response. On November 2, three days before the election, President Thieu announced that his country would not be attending the peace talks as long as the Vietcong were represented at the table. Nixon's gamble had paid off.

But Johnson, incensed by Thieu's decision, wasn't finished. At 9:18 on the evening of November 2, he placed another call to Dirksen, during which he minced no words. He would release the Nixon news to the public if necessary. "I don't want to get this in the campaign," he told Dirksen. "They oughtn't be doing this. This is treason."

"I know," Dirksen agreed.

Johnson repeated his reluctance to go public, but he also made certain that Dirksen understood that when the South Vietnamese seemed ready to enter the peace talks and the United States had ceased bombing in North Vietnam, it had been relatively quiet in Vietnam. That could change now. Again, Dirksen agreed, and he told the president that he would talk to Nixon.

"You just tell him that their people are messing around in this thing, and if they don't want it on the front pages, they better quit it," Johnson said.

After hearing from Dirksen, Nixon contacted Johnson to protest the president's allegations. Johnson, veteran of a long line of disagreeable conversations, was prepared for Nixon's denials and conciliatory gestures. But he held the advantages. The more Nixon tried to plead innocence, the more Johnson reeled him in. Nixon struggled to make Johnson believe that he wanted South Vietnam at the peace talks; he even volunteered to go to Paris and assist with the negotiations if Johnson thought it would help. Johnson countered that he just wanted no interference from Nixon and his group. "You just see that your people don't tell the South Vietnamese that they're going to get a better deal out of the United States government than a conference," he told an agitated Nixon.

Johnson was accustomed to dominating encounters of this nature, and while he had Nixon on the defensive, he had reached the limits of his success in the battle if he didn't use his biggest weapon—calling Nixon out in public, and that, he feared, would look too political in an election year. Hubert Humphrey was another matter: if he were to take it to reporters, he risked a backlash, but he also held the political high trump if the public judged Nixon harshly. In any event, it was time to brief him on the situation. He assigned William Bundy of the State Department the task of delivering the news.

According to William Connell, Humphrey did not receive the news well. His old friend, "a very optimistic kind of nice guy all the time," a man who had faced humiliation at the hands of his own party and struggled to come back from what appeared to be an insurmountable lead, the vice president who had been undermined by his own boss throughout the campaign, erupted in a rage when he learned of Nixon's actions.

"He was furious, just furious," Connell reported. "He could see his election going down the tubes. The peace process had begun, Johnson had really got them going there, and all of a sudden the goddam corrupt right-wing government over there in South Vietnam was going to do him in. They were going to give it to Nixon because Nixon would give them a better deal. He was furious, and he was with great difficulty persuaded not to go public. He finally calmed down and said, 'Okay, that's it,' and he went out and campaigned."

Humphrey would second-guess his decision for as long as he lived.

"I wonder if I should have blown the whistle on Anna Chenault and Nixon," he wrote in his journal. "He must have known about that call to Thieu. I wish I could have been sure. . . . Maybe I should have blasted them anyway."

Uncertainty kept him from going forward. The evidence was damning, no doubt about it, but without conclusive proof of Nixon's personally contacting and speaking to Thieu or other South Vietnamese officials, Humphrey felt he should remain silent. And what, he asked himself, would become of the peace talks if he reported Nixon and Nixon were to go out and win the presidency?

His advisors argued over the merits of his disclosing the story, and LBJ, angry that he let it drop, grumbled that it was "the dumbest thing in the world not to do it."

Humphrey disagreed, and thus, knowing that his decision could cost him the election, he chose to say nothing and allow the voters to choose on what they already knew.

18 America Votes

1 As the calendar pages flipped into November and the final days before the election, the polls indicated that Hubert Humphrey had done the impossible: he had resurrected his campaign to where he was now running in a dead heat with Richard Nixon. When the Gallup Poll was issued on Sunday, November 3, two days before the election, Nixon led, 42 to 40 percent. A Harris Poll, released a few days earlier, had Nixon leading, 40 to 37 percent. "Since the results are subject to sampling errors," a Gallup official explained, "the popular vote lead as of Saturday must be regarded as one that could go either to Nixon or Humphrey."

Humphrey had benefited from George Wallace's continued postconvention decline. Voters, convinced that Wallace stood no chance of winning, moved back into the two-party fold, and Humphrey enjoyed a push by labor leaders encouraging Wallace supporters to vote Democratic. The campaign, which had begun nearly a year ago, was down to its final hours, and voters were turning serious. This could be seen in a flow of McCarthy votes, which found the senator's backers, bitter about Humphrey's nomination and McCarthy's treatment by his own party, changing their stance from boycotting the election altogether to voting for Humphrey as a way of keeping Nixon out. The more optimistic Humphrey backers had predicted a Humphrey charge but with reservations. "There is no doubt about the upsurge," Terry Sanford, national chairman of Citizens for Humphrey–Muskie, stated in late October. "The only question is whether it's enough."

Humphrey's cause might have been bolstered if he had received earlier support from Lyndon Johnson and Eugene McCarthy, but neither came through for him until the final week of the campaign. Johnson remained firm on his March 31 promise of staying out of partisan politics while he worked on ending the war. Humphrey had solicited McCarthy's endorsement during the Democratic convention week, but McCarthy had begged off, insisting that doing so would be letting down his supporters. Then he had all but disappeared after the convention. He vacationed in Europe and, in October, wrote about the World Series for *Life* magazine.

When he did get around to endorsing Humphrey, it was on October 29, a week to the day before the election, in what had to amount to one of the most tepid endorsements in the history of U.S. presidential elections. After opening his statement by saying that he believed that most Americans were capable of deciding how to vote without his help, McCarthy announced that he intended to vote for Humphrey, and that "those who have wanted this statement should do the same."

Humphrey's position on the principal issues of his campaign, McCarthy went on, fell "far short of what I think it should be. The choice, however, is between Vice President Humphrey and Richard Nixon." Left with that choice, he was supporting Humphrey, largely because Humphrey was stronger than Nixon on domestic policy, and because he believed Humphrey would be more adept than Nixon in "scaling down the arms race and reducing military tensions in the world." He closed his brief statement by announcing that he would not be running for reelection to the Senate in 1970, or for the presidency in 1972.

In public, Humphrey said he was happy with the endorsement, but in private, he wondered how the statement was going to help him. Five of McCarthy's aides had simultaneously issued a minority statement declaring they would not be voting for Humphrey, and that and McCarthy's weak endorsement were hardly glowing testimonials. In all probability, McCarthy was correct when he stated that voters had made up their minds on their own, but a strong endorsement, offered soon after the convention, might have made a difference in convincing his supporters to back Humphrey's campaign.

"Would a more hearty and earlier endorsement have helped? I think it would have," Humphrey wrote in his autobiography. "Had [McCarthy supporters] been encouraged to early support or at least silence, I might have been able to function better and more effectively."

Lyndon Johnson finally threw his support behind Humphrey in a Texas-style rally in Houston's Astrodome on Sunday, November 3. Forty-eight thousand packed the stadium to see Johnson, their home-state hero, flanked by Texas Democratic luminaries, sing Humphrey's praises in a tribute that must have drawn a comment or two from those who had followed the ambiguous relationship between Humphrey and Johnson over the past four years. Johnson had maintained a personal affection for Humphrey dating back to their time together in the Senate, but Humphrey, the politician, grated on him, especially when Humphrey spoke about Vietnam. Johnson deemed Humphrey to be weak on the war, and he would not forgive him his Salt Lake City speech; this, to Johnson, was a sign of disloyalty and an indication that Humphrey might not have what it took to be president. He was pleased by Humphrey's positions on domestic policies, but as he told Clark Clifford, he would have respected him more if he "showed he had more balls" on the war. He felt so strongly about Humphrey speaking out of turn on Vietnam that he had Humphrey's phone tapped in order to stay abreast of Humphrey's thoughts.

Johnson also conceded that his rocky relationship with Humphrey could be unfavorable in an endorsement. Johnson, trying to salvage his legacy by ending the war, knew that in requiring absolute loyalty, he had become a liability to Humphrey. He would be blamed if Humphrey lost the election, and if Humphrey won and put an end to the war, Humphrey would receive the credit. As a Democrat holding the country's highest elected office, Johnson wanted to see a Democrat follow him to the White House, but he wasn't sure he was in the position to help his vice president along. "I frankly don't know whether I would do him good or harm," he confessed to a reporter.

His appearance at the Texas rally, not totally certain until the last minute, was an enormous victory for Humphrey. Johnson and Humphrey, campaigning together for the first time, received an ear-splitting ovation as they walked, side by side, around the baseball field, the two leaders soaking in approval so absent in recent months. The scoreboard flashed HHH in letters four stories high. Frank Sinatra handled the introductions.

Johnson's endorsement was as powerful as McCarthy's was weak.

"A progressive and compassionate American is seeking the office of President," Johnson called out to the largest Humphrey crowd of the campaign. "That man, my friend and co-worker of twenty years, is a healer and a builder and will represent all the people all the time." Johnson could not resist jabbing at Nixon's fearmongering. "Hubert Humphrey has worked all his life not to generate suspicion, and not to generate fear among the people, but to inspire them with confidence in their ability to live together."

In his address, Humphrey built on the theme Johnson had created.

"I have always believed that freedom was possible," he declared. "I have always believed that the basic decency within this nation would one day enable us to lift the veil from our eyes and see each other for what we are as people—not black or white, not rich or poor, not attending one church or another—but as people standing equally together, free of hate or suspicion."

This was Humphrey the orator, as capable as anyone of patching together the words needed to move the masses to action. The cheers and ovations stirred him more than any time in recent months. He was deeply moved when the president embraced him and spoke so powerfully on his behalf. "That afternoon, at least," he said later, "we seemed to have resolved whatever difficulties we had."

The next day, the final one before the election, the two candidates jousted in separate Los Angeles television studios in nationally broadcast telethons, Humphrey on ABC, Nixon on CBS. Humphrey, with Ed Muskie at his side and former McCarthyites Paul Newman and Joanne Woodward taking calls in the background, turned in a first-rate performance. He and Muskie took questions phoned in from across the United States. By his own assessment, Humphrey still felt energized from his previous day's appearance at the Astrodome, and it was evident in the old, talkative Humphrey image projected on television screens from coast to coast. His questions, covering the gamut of issues raised throughout the campaign, were not screened, and Humphrey and Muskie worked like a tag team in answering them. Eugene McCarthy called unexpectedly and offered his best wishes, saying that he hoped his support would be helpful. The Happy Warrior, purveyor of the politics of joy, approved of the way his final appearance before the nation had gone. "When it was over," he would recall, "I thought that no other television we had done was any better or conveyed as well what we were all about."

The telethon was staged in two, two-hour segments, one for the East Coast, the other for West Coast viewers, its contents boosted by what turned out to be two very effective film clips. The first, a brief clip showing Ted Kennedy walking along the Hyannis Port, Massachusetts, beach with Lawrence O'Brien, found Kennedy endorsing Humphrey as the man most likely to bring peace to Southeast Asia. The second, a brief documentary about Humphrey, on and off the political stage, hit an emotional peak when it showed Humphrey playing with his mentally challenged granddaughter and saying how she had taught him the meaning of love.

The telethon had a chippy moment when Humphrey was advised that Richard Nixon had mentioned during his telethon that the North Vietnamese were taking advantage of the bombing halt by building up their supply line along the Ho Chi Minh Trail. Angered by the report, Humphrey addressed Nixon directly onscreen, saying that "there is no indication of increased infiltration, Mr. Nixon. And let me say that it does not help the negotiations to falsely accuse anyone at this time."

Nixon's words suggested how desperate he had become. The scene at his television studio contrasted the vivacity of the Humphrey set: Nixon, sitting stiffly in a chair and looking tired, spoke in a calm, authoritative voice, but there was little life to him. He would be in control until the bitter end. Bud Wilkinson, the revered football coach and a strong public supporter of Nixon throughout the campaign, acted as the telethon's host. He carefully screened calls from viewers, asking Nixon the most general, easiest to answer questions; there would be no slipups on the final day. The cherry-picked studio audience reacted to Nixon as expected. The telethon resembled Nixon's commercial tapings in New Hampshire eight months earlier: in a controlled atmosphere Nixon looked downright presidential. The New Nixon had been excused from the telethon, but it was too late for the old, familiar Nixon, in such an environment, to do much damage.

Spiro Agnew, the one man who could have inflicted damage in the telethon, was nowhere to be seen. He had been dispatched to Virginia, a state Nixon was certain to win, where he could do no harm. Nixon addressed the Agnew controversy early in the telethon, when he attempted to turn the tables on Humphrey by noting that his opponent had mentioned, several weeks previous, that one in three presidents had failed to live out his term. Agnew, Nixon assured his television audience, was "strong, compassionate, good, [and] firm" enough to assume the job if such a tragedy struck while he was in office.

And just like that, it was over. The cameras shut down, the campaign ended. The next night, when the returns were being counted, Nixon would be in New York and Humphrey in Minnesota. Their faces would be all over television screens everywhere, but in the meantime, there was little more that they could do to solicit votes.

Humphrey celebrated by attending a party thrown at the home of his friend Lloyd Hand, in Beverly Hills. He and Muriel mixed with about three hundred guests comprised of Humphrey friends, campaign officials, celebrities, reporters, and others, all putting an end to a long, trying run. Humphrey loved to dance, and according to Edgar Berman, he "must have danced for two hours with every pretty girl in sight."

His plane departed for Minnesota at 2:30 a.m. Unlike the other passengers, exhausted and asleep by the time the plane reached cruising altitude in the darkened sky, Humphrey was too keyed up to rest. He roamed about the cabin, talking to anyone still awake. He expressed optimism to Berman, though he surprised his physician with an unexpected confession.

"It's funny," he told Berman after saying he thought he would win, "I don't feel it."

2 Reporters were waiting for Humphrey when his plane touched down in the cold rain at Minneapolis–St. Paul International, all awaiting a prediction before the candidate and his wife set out to cast their votes on paper ballots in the Marysville Township Hall near their home.

Humphrey was cautious in offering his assessment. "We've done the best job we could," he said. "The American jury is out now. We hope things come out well. We shall see."

The day offered strong hints that it would be a historic one. Humphrey's late charge had wiped out the predictions of a Nixon landslide. Reporters hustled for new angles to a story that had gone from being very dull to what might turn out to be a photo finish. Nixon still looked to be the favorite, but it wouldn't hurt to have stories about the Electoral College, the unreliability of opinion polls, and the influence of third-party candidates in the editorial well in the event that the election would be decided beyond the ballot box.

An Electoral College debate traditionally broke out every four years, one side arguing that it was an antiquated system that no longer reflected the will of the people, the other concluding that it was still the best means of guaranteeing that voters in the less populated states had a fair voice in deciding the outcome of a presidential race. The closer the race, the more passionate the argument. One had to go back eighty years, to 1888 and Benjamin Harrison, to find an election in which the winner of the popular vote was outvoted by the Electoral College vote. That was a possibility now, in 1968, with a third-party candidate splitting the vote, though it was just as likely that the winner of a close vote would win a huge margin in the Electoral College. Humphrey had seen the projected numbers, and he knew he had to overcome some discouraging numbers to come away victorious. A November 4 *New York Times* survey of the states indicated a close popular vote, but in the winner-take-all Electoral College, the survey predicted a convincing win for Nixon, with twenty-nine states and 299 Electoral College votes, defeating Humphrey, with nine states and 77 Electoral College votes; Humphrey could capture every one of George Wallace's predicted wins (five states, 45 votes) and all of the races judged too close to call (seven states, 117 votes) and still lose in the Electoral College.

Conversely, Humphrey stood a better-than-even chance of winning if no candidate won the minimum in the Electoral College and the outcome were to be decided by the House of Representatives. Each state was permitted one vote—a weighting harshly opposed by critics, who complained that there was nothing fair about Rhode Island's having a say equal to Texas's or California's. In a House ruled by Democrats, Humphrey was almost certain to win. The House had decided the election in this manner in 1824, when Andrew Jackson, the popular vote winner, lost out to John Quincy Adams.

With these possibilities hanging over a very close election, political analysts turned their gaze to opinion polls and their possible influence on an election. The *New York Times,* in a column published the day before the election, pulled no punches: "One baffling problem was more evident this year than ever before. The public opinion polls became a major influence on politics."

The *Times* cited two specific examples—the polls released on the eve of the Republican National Convention, dimming Nelson Rockefeller's hopes of a rally for the nomination, and the polls released immediately following the Democratic convention, which showed Humphrey trailing Nixon so badly as to suggest that a Humphrey victory was impossible. But the argument went beyond this. State and municipality surveys, very popular with readers, had an influence on what could be critical Electoral College votes. California and Pennsylvania, two states coveted by Nixon and Humphrey, provided two examples. In California, the public polls after the Democratic convention gave Nixon an almost insurmountable lead; Humphrey chiseled into that lead over the last month of the race until he trailed Nixon by a single point at the end. In Philadelphia, telephone polls produced similar results. Pundits had to ask: were the polls changing voters' minds?

John Mitchell, Richard Nixon's campaign manager, exploded when the final Harris Poll, published only hours after one of their polls had Nixon leading by two points, suggested that Humphrey had somehow managed to take a one-point lead. Lou Harris, Mitchell thundered, had served as John Kennedy's private pollster in 1960, and his national poll favored Democrats. Harris, Mitchell further charged, could not "con the voters into believing Hubert Humphrey could win the election."

Harris was unmoved. He told his subscribers that he would poll throughout Election Day and publish any significant results.

The *Times* column concluded with an observation that both Humphrey and Nixon could appreciate: "If the pollsters are not merely reporting sentiment but rather are influencing it, the whole idea of measuring public opinion becomes suspect."

3 Richard Nixon stayed overnight in Los Angeles on the evening of his telethon. He felt no urgency to get back to New York. He and his wife had cast absentee ballots, so there would be no formal photography of Dick and Pat Nixon at the voting station, no exit interviews with all the obvious questions. Nixon was free to return whenever he wished, and what he really wanted was a good night's sleep and casual start the next day. He hoped to avoid the frenetic pace he had endured on Election Day in 1960.

The final days of the campaign had trapped him in a sort of psychic limbo, caught between confidence that he would win and fear that he would not. He believed that he had bested Humphrey on the campaign trail, but Humphrey's continuing rise in the polls cast doubts on his certainty. He had had to make some late-hour alterations to his campaign approach, and the press had noticed. Going into the final week of the race, he had sworn that he would stay away from attacking Humphrey personally and fearmongering in general, but Humphrey's charge changed his mind. As always, he backed away from discussion about Vietnam, choosing instead to assail Humphrey's law-and-order position, which he painstakingly connected to that of Lyndon Johnson: a Humphrey victory, he warned, would amount to four more years of Johnson.

Humphrey, Nixon charged, was too soft on crime in these turbulent times. Nixon openly disdained recent Supreme Court decisions that, he claimed, now protected the criminals at the expense of their victims. These decisions, backed by Humphrey's liberal, "Depression-born notions" of law and order, placed Humphrey on the outside, badly out of touch with "a crime wave affecting the most affluent society in history." This was the kind of fearmongering, practiced by Nixon and Wallace throughout their campaigns, that Johnson referred to in his Astrodome speech, but Nixon poured it on in any event. "The abused in our society deserve as much protection as the criminal," he said, sounding as if he had cadged a few lines from the standard Wallace stump speech. Appearance didn't matter: the Wallace voters were the ones Nixon had been hoping to win over in those last few days.

Now there was no campaigning left to do. "The hay's in the barn," Nixon said on his return flight to New York.

When Nixon boarded the *Tricia,* his campaign plane named after his elder daughter, at Los Angeles International Airport, he was in a relaxed but reflective mind. He had spent the early portion of the day on the phone, talking to John Mitchell, Maurice Stans, and others about the election, and thanking them for their support and hard work. On the plane, Nixon holed up in his private compartment in the front of the plane. He received occasional visitors and ignored interview requests from the lone reporter allowed on the flight. Those who saw him reported Nixon as focused, in command, fixated on the election. Even as they flew, voters on the East Coast and in the Midwest were casting their ballots. Bob Ellsworth called Nixon periodically and briefed him on the voter turnout.

Nixon's outward appearance of confidence belied at least some level of concern. During the flight, he called for his family, and when they had assembled in his compartment, he thanked them all for their support and sacrifice over the months. He told his wife, daughters, and David Eisenhower that he expected to win, but he wanted to prepare them for every eventuality.

The Johnson bombing halt had probably cost him several million votes, possibly enough to beat him. He was equally concerned that they understand that there was a remote possibility that the election might be decided by the House of Representatives, a process that would extend beyond that evening. No one wanted to hear Nixon speak of anything but victory, of course, but Nixon offered some optimism in the event that he lost. "If we don't win," he advised them, "we'll simply go on to other projects which, from a personal viewpoint may give us more satisfaction. And we won't have the spotlight of the world on us and on every movement that we make."

The uncertainty of the hour hung in the air of the cabin outside Nixon's compartment. One could sing "Happy Days Are Here Again" or release helium-filled balloons in rallies for months, but in the final hours before the vote, the atmosphere was one of a wake more than a celebration.

"It was kind of a very dramatic time," said Leonard Garment of the flight back to New York, "great anxiety, not much talking. A lot of reflecting on what had happened, what was going to happen. Little bit of a quality of a church meeting."

Nixon's plane landed in Newark shortly after 6:00 p.m. EST. By then, all of the continental United States had been voting for hours, and the early East Coast returns were only a couple hours away. This was the way Nixon preferred it: less time for anxiety. The 1960 election had been agonizingly close, and if this one proved to be as close as predicted, Nixon wanted no repetition of the tense hours of waiting. He had shortened his day by flying from west to east, through three time zones, and when he finally arrived at the Waldorf Towers in Manhattan, he had only five hours left to Election Day. He might tack a couple more hours onto his day if the election was tight, but at least it was manageable.

Nixon had no interest in watching the early returns. He had aides totaling the reported voting numbers and calling him with the results. His family, friends, and campaign officials crowded into the main room of his suite, but rather than sit with them, Nixon retreated to his room, where when the time came, he could watch the results in solitude. He kicked off his evening with a long, hot soak in the tub. He shaved, dressed, and prepared himself for the hours ahead. Every so often, one of his campaign officials would check in with him, but he spent most of his time alone. He kept track of the voting on a legal pad.

The early results produced no surprises. Nixon enjoyed a slight lead in the overall popular vote, and he won the Carolinas and Virginia, as expected. He held narrow leads in New Jersey and Pennsylvania, battleground states that both candidates felt they needed to win. Humphrey won New Hampshire and New York. He slowly crept up in the overall tally, until he was nearly even with Nixon by midevening. Although concerned, Nixon was not alarmed.

Looking back, some of his staff confessed plenty of anxiety while watching the returns roll in. Leonard Garment feared a Nixon loss "that whole night." One had to go back twenty years, to 1948, to recall the shocking results of the Truman–Dewey election. It could have easily gone this way in this election, with Humphrey, the underdog, inching past Nixon. "It was very close," said Garment, "and just sort of hung there like a post-term baby."

4   Hubert Humphrey had his own worries. George Wallace was not performing as well as predicted, and it looked as if Nixon was picking up a considerable percentage of Wallace's lost voters. Wallace captured five Southern states (Alabama, Arkansas, Georgia, Mississippi, and Louisiana), but if one could judge by the early returns, Nixon stood to win Florida and maybe Texas. Despite the efforts of Richard Hughes, New Jersey appeared to be lost.

Humphrey fought off conflicting emotions. He was aware of the projected state-by-state numbers, he understood the long odds against his winning, and he was being truthful when he told Edgar Berman that he hadn't *felt* a victory. He needed, as he wrote in his journal, "a few more days." And here he was, on a day he had anticipated his entire adult life, competing against a man with similar dreams and a somewhat similar background, exhausted beyond what he believed to be possible, angry at those who had failed him, depressed for those who had worked so hard for him, sentimental as always, trying to step over the self-pity blocking his path, struggling to convince himself that there really was some measure of hope:

> I've climbed that damned ladder of politics, and every step has been tough. I've slipped so many times and almost fallen back. I wonder what it would have been like with money enough and money early, when it really counts? That top rung is never going to be mine. My fingernails are scraping it, but I don't have a grip. Yet maybe, maybe we can make it. It's so damn close. I am so tired.

He had slept for a few hours after voting and returning to his home in Waverly, Minnesota. He and Muriel wandered about the house, saying very little to each other, trying to kill the hours that stood between the present and the first voting results. Humphrey, growing maudlin, wrote in his journal about how beautiful

Muriel was, how he loved dancing with her, how she had given everything to his campaign, how good she would have been as First Lady.

At seven thirty, Hubert and Muriel Humphrey arrived at the Lake Minnetonka residence of their friends Dwayne and Inez Andreas. They were joined by the Humphrey children, and all tried to take their minds off their anxieties and eat. Hubert's appetite had vanished, and he couldn't sit still. The earliest returns were trickling in, and it looked like Humphrey was going to carry New England. It was a great, though anticipated, start: there was something to be said about banking the first Electoral College votes. On the negative side, he wasn't taking any states projected for Nixon, and Nixon's Southern strategy seemed to have worked. The popular vote stayed tight.

At ten thirty, the Humphreys were taken to the Humphrey headquarters at the Leamington Hotel in Minneapolis. A loud, enthusiastic crowd, still confident of a victory, greeted them. Humphrey usually fed off the energy of such exhibitions of affection but not on this night. The celebratory mood only served to remind him that, in losing, he would be letting down a lot of people—and unless things turned around unexpectedly, he was going to lose. He had taken Maryland (Spiro Agnew's home state) in a surprise vote, but Nixon was winning the border states. In another mild surprise, Humphrey appeared to have won Michigan, but Nixon would be gaining strength as the vote counts from the Plains states and the West were finalized. Humphrey was reaching the point where he absolutely needed the states with large Electoral College numbers. He had a good chance in Texas, LBJ's state, and California, but Illinois was a huge question. Downstate Illinois would probably vote for Nixon, which was likely to offset Cook County (and Chicago). Humphrey wasn't sure that Richard Daley, in the aftermath of the convention, would be able to deliver the state to him.

Humphrey concealed his fears from his supporters. John Bartlow Martin, who had written speeches for Robert Kennedy in Indiana, now employed to write speeches for Humphrey, had been assigned the task of writing three speeches—one for victory, one for losing, and one for the event that the winner would be determined in the House of Representatives—and by midnight, Humphrey was all but certain which one he would be delivering, Humphrey retired to his fourteenth-floor suite, surrounded by his wife, children, two sisters, and closest friends; in time, he escaped to his own room, where, like Nixon in New York, he would deal with the final results on his own.

A little earlier in the evening, when he was projected the winner in Pennsylvania and Michigan and remained slightly ahead of Nixon in the overall national vote, Humphrey, surrounded by a throng of supporters, allowed himself a sliver of hope. His top aides were estimating a victory, but with Nixon on a roll in the western states, Humphrey feared he had to win the key states of California, Illinois, Ohio, Texas, New Jersey, and Missouri to stand any chance—and even then, he was probably fighting to keep Nixon from winning the Electoral College. Those hopes disappeared. Nixon led in all but Texas, and by two o'clock Humphrey had lost New Jersey, Missouri, Ohio, and Missouri. Lawrence O'Brien called and confirmed Humphrey's suspicion: the race was over.

Humphrey dreaded the prospects of facing his supporters downstairs. Nothing was official, and they wouldn't accept anything until it was. The press would be waiting. Ted Van Dyk tried to talk him out of heading down to the hall, but Humphrey insisted.

"The people need a pep talk," he wrote in his journal. "Can't tell them it'll take a miracle to pull this out. Can't tell them it's over. They want hope, not facts. So do I."

So, he fed them hope. Several key states were undecided, he told them. "As you know, this is at best, as we put it, a donnybrook. Anything can happen." He tried to smile. "I feel that by the time that the turn of the day comes tomorrow, that you and I are going to be a lot happier and much more cheerful than we are now."

It was one of the most difficult things he had ever done in his political life. He wasn't yet ready to make a concession speech or call Nixon with his congratulations. He would save that for the next day. He returned to his suite, took a sleeping pill, and tried to get some rest.

■ ■ ■ ■ ■

George Wallace's election night ended before they started counting votes of the states west of the Mississippi River. As expected, he won in Alabama, Mississippi, Georgia, and Louisiana, all Wallace strongholds from the beginning, and he rose above Nixon and Humphrey in Arkansas. The rest was a disappointment. He washed out in the other Southern and border states, although he was runner-up in North Carolina, South Carolina, and Tennessee. He ran third in Florida, a state he needed if he were to have any chance to barter with the other two candidates in the event that neither won the minimum number of Electoral College votes necessary for a win. He won forty-one Electoral College votes—a respectable number for a third party but little more. Wallace watched the results with friends and family gathered in his house. He had hoped to gain 20 percent of the national vote; he barely managed 13 percent.

The final two weeks of his campaign had been a combination of highs and lows. His poll numbers dropped steadily. Immediately following the Democratic convention, Wallace looked as if he might challenge or even pass Humphrey, but that hope was short-lived. In just a one-week period in mid-October, Wallace fell five percentage points to Humphrey in the Gallup Poll. He would not recover. Humphrey's numbers rose significantly in the North, where he was campaigning vigorously among blue-collar, union voters. Humphrey and Nixon took turns at battering Wallace in their campaign ads, both candidates suggesting that a vote for Wallace was a wasted vote, and Nixon going so far as to say that a vote for Wallace was a vote for Humphrey. "Don't play their game. Don't divide your vote," a Nixon ad cautioned, urging voters to vote for "the only team that can provide the new leadership that America needs, the Nixon-Agnew team."

The Wallace campaign was further weakened by internal disagreement and bickering over how and where to spend the campaign funds. One argument stated that in light of the fact that Wallace could not win the election, the money might be best spent on advertising and appearances in regions where the election was still in doubt. Wallace rejected the argument. His campaign, he declared, would continue to be a national one.

Wallace closed out the final two weeks of his campaign at an exhaustive clip. He would appear in as many as four or five rallies a day, giving his standard high-energy talk with all the crowd-pleasing snarls about shooting brick throwers and running over anyone lying down in front of his car. He was greeted by overflow crowds wherever he went, as if in defiance of his shrinking poll numbers. In New York, at a rally in Madison Square Garden on October 24, he stood before the most highly attended political rally there since a Roosevelt appearance in 1936. It was enough to make him hope that the polls were mistaken.

Election night brought him back to reality. On CBS, Walter Cronkite declared that Wallace had "gone down to ignominious defeat" while the voting booths were still open on the West Coast. Wallace reacted angrily to Cronkite's statement, but he knew as well as anyone that he was underperforming. The best he could say was that he had run a tough race and had received more votes than any third-party candidate in U.S. history.

■ ■ ■ ■ ■

Richard Nixon did not allow himself the luxury of sleep. The brutality of 1960—the agony of watching the presidency slip away when, for so long, it seemed within his reach—haunted him as he watched the returns in the solitude of his hotel room. He couldn't have slept if he tried. He worked and reworked the voting figures he entered on his legal pad. He refused all calls outside his tightest inner circle, and he forbade himself the acceptance of the probability, becoming more evident with each passing hour, that he was going to be the next president of the United States. He felt confident, but victory was not a certainty. For Nixon, it had to be official.

His campaign team labored at their assignments throughout the night. John Mitchell, in a room down the hall from Nixon's, manned the phones alongside Robert Finch and Murray Chotiner, confirming reports from Republican organizations across the country. Mitchell, ever sober and in steely command, reported his findings to H. R. Haldeman, who occupied a suite next to Nixon's. Gathered in Haldeman's room, monitoring the results on televisions, were John Ehrlichman, Dwight Chapin, and others, all guarding the candidate's privacy, with Haldeman checking in with Nixon only when he had urgent news to report. The communications group—William Safire, Pat Buchanan, Leonard Garment, Raymond Price, and others coming and going—huddled in another room. The division of labor, so rigidly maintained throughout the campaign, handled tasks in a workmanlike way, assuring their boss of up-to-the-minute information. Those who had been with Nixon in 1960 understood the anxieties of still another incredibly close election.

In the early morning hours of Wednesday, November 6, it became clear to all that a winner would not be announced until after daybreak. When Humphrey took a nationwide popular vote lead of more than a half million, Nixon began to fret that his opponent was gaining momentum that might topple him in the end. Two crucial states—Texas and Illinois—were not issuing final totals, Dallas because there had been a snafu in tabulating results, Illinois because Richard Daley refused to turn over the Cook County totals. While Humphrey was holding on to hope in his Minnesota headquarters, Nixon felt aggravation in New York. Illinois, he thought, was his; Daley was just playing mind games. Texas, on the other hand, was still wide-open. Johnson's last-minute rally might have swayed Texans to vote for Humphrey. Texas was not essential to a Nixon victory, but losing the state meant he would have to win almost all of the other vital states.

Which he did, by the unofficial tallies. California and Ohio went to Nixon, as did Missouri. It was now impossible for Humphrey to win the Electoral College votes needed to win. The best he would be able to do is deny Nixon the minimal requirement, and that was highly unlikely.

"Just before 3 a.m., for the first time in that long night, I allowed myself the luxury of self-assurance," Nixon wrote in his memoirs. "I had won the presidency."

Two more hours passed before he could be talked into trying to get some rest. He called Spiro Agnew and Nelson Rockefeller, awakening the latter.

Both had called earlier in the evening, but Nixon hadn't spoken to them. Nixon's campaign team grouped around him, partly to celebrate, partly to confirm that they all agreed on the status of the different states' totals. Nixon tried—and failed—to sleep. Watching the television news was nerve-racking: none of the three major networks wanted to announce a winner as long as Illinois was uncertain. Finally, at eight-thirty, ABC declared Illinois—and the election—in Nixon's favor.

5 The morning after Election Day, Humphrey rose at eight, cleaned up, and turned on the television to hear the final returns. He was alone, literally and figuratively. Nixon had steamrolled the western states, taking everything but Washington. Richard Daley called and insisted that it wasn't final in Illinois, but both men knew that it was. Humphrey wanted no one's pity, and he certainly wasn't going to hold on to any hope.

The vote count wouldn't be official for several weeks, but when the sun rose on November 6, one fact was clear to all: Richard Nixon would be the next president of the United States. When the official popular vote count was released, Nixon had garnered 31,785,480 (43.4 percent), Humphrey 31,275,166 (42.7 percent), and Wallace 9,906,473 (13.5 percent) of the votes in the second-narrowest election in American history to that point. Only 510,314 votes separated Nixon and Humphrey. Nixon won thirty-two states, Humphrey carried thirteen states (plus the District of Columbia), and Wallace five states. The Electoral College awarded Nixon 302 votes, Humphrey 191, and Wallace 45, but these numbers failed to indicate just how close the race really was: if Humphrey had pulled 2,500 more votes in Missouri, 90,000 in Ohio, and 53,000 in Wisconsin and had won or split Illinois and California, he would have either won the election or sent it to the House of Representatives. Humphrey could walk away with the satisfaction of knowing that he exceeded expectations and had thrown a scare into media projections chirping about a huge Nixon win, but the bottom line remained the same.

Humphrey called Nixon to concede. The president-elect accepted his congratulations gracefully, but Humphrey, after hanging up, couldn't expel the bitterness that led him to call Nixon "a papier-mache man" the night before, or see him any differently when he conceded defeat:

To lose to Nixon. Ye gods! No warmth, no strength, no emotion, no spirit. Politics of the computer. Probably if I had more of it, I'd be President.

Historians and political analysts would spend years sharpening their pencils and trying to understand the election. Nixon, by his own count, had addressed 167 topics on the campaign trail, yet he was so guarded in his speeches and interviews that he was judged to be lacking in substance. Humphrey, who had constructed his career on the foundation of decisive, courageous speeches and actions, had been indecisive and weak at the worst imaginable time. One could argue that Humphrey brought a better breadth of experience and knowledge of the legislative process, but he was outmaneuvered by Nixon at almost every turn. The toughest weakness he would have to face was the fact that he had run a mediocre campaign and was defeated by a man he should have beaten.

Muriel and his aides wandered in, joining him on what was going to be a joyless day. He worked on his concession speech with Ted Van Dyk, and at 10:55 a.m., he ventured down to the Hall of States, where his most faithful supporters awaited. He fought back tears as he formally conceded and read from a telegram he had sent Nixon:

> According to unofficial returns, you are the winner in this election. My congratulations. Please know you will have my support in unifying and leading the nation. This has been a difficult year for the American people and I am confident that if constructive leaders in both our parties join together, we shall be able to go on with the business of building the better America we all seek in the spirit of peace and harmony.

Humphrey ticked out a list of acknowledgments, thanking his wife, family, friends, and campaign workers.

"I shall continue my commitment to the cause of human rights, of peace, and to the betterment of man," he promised. "If I have helped in the campaign to move these causes forward, I feel rewarded. I have done my best. I have lost. Mr. Nixon has won. The democratic process has worked its will, so let us get on with the urgent task of uniting our country."

He started to leave, but his supporters demanded a curtain call. He stood before them, taking in the last love he would receive in the campaign, tears filling his eyes. He encouraged them to continue the work, begun on the campaign, to build a better country. He was feeling relief after all the hard work, and he wasn't looking for sympathy. "I would like for you to feel a little happy," he instructed them. "It is not easy, but quite frankly, this was an uphill fight all the way."

This was vintage Humphrey, absent in the final months of the campaign, when he was confronted at every stop by those who refused to listen. One could be frustrated by his refusal to adapt to the new politics of the times, but in the end he was true to his nature. "It was entirely in character for Vice President Humphrey to admonish his supporters to 'be of good cheer' in his first public words after conceding to Nixon's victory," noted one editorial writer. "He admitted this would not be easy, but on his record there can be no doubt that he set a superb example."

In a column titled "Farewell to the Gentleman from Minnesota," *New York Times* writer James Reston, an open critic of Humphrey throughout the days of the vice president's refusal to split from Lyndon Johnson, offered the type of praise usually reserved for winners:

> Like many other illustrious American political figures—from Henry Clay to Adlai Stevenson—he was the right man at the wrong time. It may very well be that the country needed precisely his remarkable human qualities of fighting and reconciling at the same time, of opposing men but retaining their respect and affection, but it was clearly a time for change and the country didn't quite understand that Hubert Humphrey was a change of a very special kind.

■ ■ ■ ■ ■

And what did the future promise? Win or lose, the long, grueling run concluded so suddenly that it seemed to ridicule the effort. It dated back to months of personal sacrifice; of enduring the cruelty of standing outdoors, in shopping centers, at the gates of factories, and on the backs of flatbed trucks and convertibles, trying but often failing to stay warm in the winter and cool in the summer; of facing the indignities thrust in your direction by demonstrators and other vocal opponents exercising their constitutionally protected rights with chants, slogans, and shouts designed to use hyperbole as a weapon; of eating meals that filled but rarely satisfied; of breathing in air saturated with the smells of excessive perfume and sweat; of delivering speech after speech, usually written by someone else but required to sound as if it burst spontaneously from your heart; of the constant bickering over, adjusting, worrying about, and compromising of ideas and thoughts so they would appeal to general audiences with specific interests; of the constraints of time and schedule; of the relentless fund-raising that established, come what may, allegiances that one might someday regret; of the necessity of appearing upbeat, even when exhaustion, sickness, sleep deprivation, and ill temper attempted to weaken beyond function. All became routine over the course of a presidential race, only to end after the voting hours of a single day. What was the future after all this?

Hubert Humphrey would remain in public service, even though in the immediate future, he would be facing time out of office for the first time in more than two decades. Over the next two months, he would complete his term as vice president. As promised, he would attempt to unite a bitterly divided country, ease the transition between the outgoing Johnson administration and the incoming Nixon administration, and plan for life again in Minnesota. But he would not leave politics. At one point near the end of his campaign, he had ruminated about what he might do in the event of his losing the election. He had decided that if that happened, he would run again for the Senate. He felt that he still had much to contribute to compelling, unfinished business. He would run, and he would win. He would devote the remainder of his days to that august body of the legislative branch.

The presidency would always be a reach that exceeded his grasp. He would run again in 1972, but he never came close to the nomination. Four years into the future after 1968, Humphrey would be an antiquated relic, a political dinosaur, the symbol of an effective past but an irrelevant future. Vietnam was still raging, and young soldiers were still being shipped back to the United States in coffins, but law and order had changed the nature of demonstrations against the war. On May 4, 1970, four young students were murdered by the National Guard dispatched to Kent State University to quell a demonstration at the university. The Democratic Party, still badly divided, nominated George McGovern, a peace candidate, as its 1972 presidential candidate.

Richard Nixon embarked on an inglorious destiny. His inauguration signaled a more conservative leadership that the country was seeking; Republicans would occupy the White House for twenty of the next twenty-four years, though Nixon, working with two bodies of Congress ruled by Democrats, would be more moderate than those who followed him. He had no solution to Vietnam, though he wasn't held as accountable as Lyndon Johnson. Spiro Agnew, whose stern judgment in law-and-order issues had been a calling card during his campaign with Nixon, would resign in disgrace after accounts of his malfeasance while governor of Maryland drew national attention and disapproval. Nixon would replace him with Gerald Ford, whose integrity and political savvy were never in question.

Nixon's integrity turned out to be another matter.

Acknowledgments

I was eighteen years old when the events of the 1968 election transpired. I followed politics as closely as I could, and the immensity of that year was not lost on me. When a friend and I stayed up and watched the California primary returns and learned that Bobby Kennedy had been shot, I turned to my friend and said, "This country has gone mad." It was an obvious and pathetic statement, but it was all I could think to say. There was nothing worse than feeling angry and helpless at the same time, and that particular election elicited these emotions more than anything I had experienced to that point.

I thought about this a lot while I was researching this book, as I thought about two individuals who influenced me time and again over the years. I kept it in mind throughout the writing of the book. These friends were, in a sense, my conscience, and, most definitely, the readers for whom I was writing. I met both in 1968. We were all starting at the same university; we were passionate about our politics. We got together almost every day and discussed and argued about the events that seemed to be sweeping over the United States like a tsunami.

I met Ken Ade, to whom this book is rightfully dedicated, shortly after he returned to the States following a stint in the air force. He was four years older than I, and he had been a few places and seen a few things. We worked together at the Spot, a wonderful drive-in restaurant, and we stood next to each other at the grill, flipping burgers and arguing politics. I had some consistency, but I didn't know why; he filled in the blanks. We remained close over the years, and even now, a half century later, he is a voice of calm reason when my emotional temperature starts to rise.

Jeff Parry, the other friend from those early days, was the biggest political animal I had ever met. He was a conservative, a Nixon backer and Ayn Rand fanatic, who offered a significant balance to our arguments. He was very excited when he learned that I was writing this book, and he would pedal his bike—he never learned to drive—to Franks Diner, my morning headquarters for decades, where we talked and talked. I was very interested in how he would regard this book. Sadly, nature had its own designs, and he passed away before I had completed the writing of this book. Perhaps it is vanity, but I like to believe that he would have liked it.

My thanks and love to both of you.

■ ■ ■ ■ ■

While researching *The Contest,* I had no preconceptions about what I hoped to write, other than the desire to include as much information about the election and its two main issues—the Vietnam War and civil rights/law and order—as possible. I read every book I could find about the election, the candidates, and the times. I scoured countless newspapers and magazine clippings, examined thousands of pages of oral history transcripts, and delved into seemingly endless FBI documents. I watched videos of events and campaign speeches. I even spent months listening exclusively to the music of the times.

The bibliography herein lists books consulted for this volume, and while all contributed to the whole, the really important works can get lost in the list and not receive the credit they deserve. So, in no particular order of overall importance, I would like to recognize books of special significance. Hubert Humphrey's autobiography, *The Education of a Public Man,* a heartfelt guide through the life of a public servant and a detailed account of the election he came so close to winning, started me on the path. Carl Solberg's biography *Hubert Humphrey* remains the benchmark work on Humphrey and his times. Edgar Berman's *Hubert,* while unapologetically slanted in favor of his close friend, offers an insider's interpretation of Humphrey's 1968 presidential run. Albert Eisele's *Almost to the Presidency* is a joint biography of Humphrey and Eugene McCarthy, comparing and contrasting the two Minnesotans in a way that other writers did not and analytically sorting through some of the complexities of their campaigns. Eugene McCarthy's *The Year of the People* recalls the election cycle through the eyes of a candidate and is a remarkable dissertation on the making of a grassroots candidacy. Robert Kennedy's memory has been blessed by more exceptional biographies than one can imagine, but two books—Arthur Schlesinger's monumental *Robert Kennedy and His Times,* and Evan Thomas's *Robert Kennedy: His Life*—are achievements that stand at the head of the class. Jack Newfield, a journalist and friend of Bobby Kennedy, in *Robert Kennedy: A Memoir,* offers a moving, wonderfully anecdotal account of Kennedy's run for the White House. *Mutual Contempt: Lyndon Johnson, Robert Kennedy, and the Feud That Defined a Decade,* by Jeff Shesol, details one of the most notable rivalries in American history. George Wallace, with his segregationist policies and hyperbolic personality, was too easily dismissed as a serious political figure by the press and public, as three books, studying Wallace from different angles, illustrate: Stephan Lesher provides a straight-forward biography in *George Wallace: American Populist,* while Dan T. Carter takes a more analytical approach to Wallace's political life in *The Politics of Rage;* in *Wallace,* Marshall Frady offers a book-length profile, complete with detailed anecdotes that define the man's character and politics. Jules Witcover, a reporter who traveled with the candidates throughout the primaries, author of *85 Days,* a compelling account of Kennedy's pursuit of the presidency, may portray the rise of Richard Nixon the best in *The Resurrection of Richard Nixon,* while Patrick J. Buchanan's *The Greatest Comeback* serves up an out-standing insider's viewpoint. Rick Perlstein, author of several books tracing the establishment of conservatism from Barry Goldwater on out, contributed *Nixonland,* a book as much fun to read as it was informative.

Richard Nixon's *RN* and Lyndon Johnson's *The Vantage Point* offer the ultimate insider views of the workings of the nation's highest office, as well as in-depth views of the issues that drove the 1968 election.

A number of books have been written about the 1968 election, including these notables: Lewis Chester, Godfrey Hodgson, and Bruce Page's *An American Melodrama: The Presidential Campaign of 1968*; *The Making of the President 1968,* the third book of Theodore White's series on presidential elections; Michael Cohen's *American Maelstrom: The 1968 Election and the Politics of Division*; and Lawrence O'Donnell's *Playing with Fire.* Ben Stavis, who worked for McCarthy throughout the campaign, provides a strong narrative on the workings of the McCarthy campaign, from primary to primary through the Chicago convention, in *We Were the Campaign.* Richard Goodwin's *Remembering America* covers the author's work with the McCarthy and, later, Kennedy campaigns. Norman Mailer's *Miami and the Siege of Chicago* remains the vital account of the Republican and Democratic conventions, and Joe McGinniss's *The Selling of the President, 1968* is a groundbreaking examination of how the media shape political campaigns.

There are too many memoirs, biographies, and books about the issues to mention here, but all were important and are included in the bibliography. I owe a debt to all.

■ ■ ■ ■ ■

I relied heavily on oral history interviews not only for research for events taking place in this book but also for a way to include voices from the past—most interviewees are no longer alive to share their stories. My gratitude, then, goes out to all the libraries and institutions housing these oral history collections.

Some of the transcripts were available online; others were not, requiring some travel. Either way, the oral histories were well worth the effort of obtaining and reading them.

The Minnesota Historical Society in St. Paul houses the bulk of the Hubert Humphrey and Eugene McCarthy papers, and in addition to oral histories, speeches, notes, and news clippings about the men and their campaigns, the library contains notes and transcriptions of memoirs by Orville Freeman and Dr. Edgar Berman, two of Humphrey's closest confidants. (My thanks to Roberta Walburn, author of *Miles Lord,* for her assistance in locating the Humphrey collection.) The University of Minnesota in Minneapolis holds a Eugene McCarthy oral history collection not available elsewhere. The Lyndon Baines Johnson Presidential Library in Austin, Texas, is the mother lode of all things LBJ and also includes a wealth of information about the Vietnam War and the events leading to Johnson's decision to forsake a second term as president; the Miller Center of Public Affairs at the University of Virginia provided transcripts to oral history interviews not available at the LBJ Library. The John F. Kennedy Presidential Library in Washington, D.C., contains oral history collections for both John and Robert Kennedy. The Richard Nixon Library and Museum in Yorba Linda, California, houses a substantial oral history collection.

Other libraries, with smaller collections, from which I used a single interview, are acknowledged in the notes section of this book.

■ ■ ■ ■ ■

Finally, I would like to thank individuals whose assistance and support helped make this book (and some of my other books) a reality. In no particular order: Al and Diane Schumacher, Susan Schumacher, Gary and Vicki Schumacher, Mark and Mary Ellen Schumacher, the late Anne Swaim, Sue and Mark Stegbauer, Jim Schumacher and Mary Sullivan, Mary Kay and Jonny Sherman, Teresa and Javi Villanueva, Jim Sieger, Steve Paura, Chris Baher and Bethany Wise, Greg Bonofiglio, Peter Spielmann and Judy Hansen, Mike Gordon, the late John Gilmore, Cheryl and Mark Travanty, Lesleigh Luttrell, and Karen Pynaker Ade.

I feel blessed to have the University of Minnesota Press as my publisher for this and other books. I am grateful for the professionalism and dedication that I find there—a marked contrast to some of my past experiences with larger, New York–based publishers—and their work on this book was exceptional. For me, it always begins and ends with my editor, Erik Anderson, and his assistant, Kristian Tvedten; aside from their considerable skills in their positions, they both possess vision and patience that exceed anything I had experienced prior to working with them. Mary Keirstead did an exceptional job in copyediting this book, not only in suggestions for tightening up the prose but in picking up a few errors that would have proven to be embarrassing if they had been published. Thanks, also, to Douglas Armato, Emily Hamilton, Heather Skinner, Laura Westlund, Daniel Ochsner, and Matt Smiley. I am pleased to work for you.

Last but certainly not least, all my love to Adam Michael, Emily Joy, and Jack Henry. You give me every good reason.

Chronology of the Election

1967

SUMMER AND FALL Allard Lowenstein, Curtis Gans, and others begin a national "Dump Johnson" campaign, with a goal of finding a candidate to challenge the president's reelection.

NOVEMBER 30 Eugene McCarthy officially announces his candidacy for the Democratic Party nomination, with his campaign focusing on ending the war in Vietnam.

DECEMBER 31 Abbie Hoffman, Jerry Rubin, Paul Krassner, and others form the Youth International Party and discuss plans for the Democratic National Convention in Chicago in 1968.

1968

JANUARY 30 The Tet Offensive begins, with North Vietnamese and Vietcong troops invading South Vietnam and waging fierce battles with American and South Vietnamese troops. For the American people, the offensive exposed the gulf between the official reports on the war and what was really taking place.

FEBRUARY 1 Richard Nixon formally announces his candidacy for the Republican Party nomination.

FEBRUARY 29 The National Advisory Committee on Civil Disorders releases its findings on the race rioting of 1967 in what came to be known as the Kerner Report, setting the stage for the arguments over law and order in the months to come. The report declared that "our nation is moving toward two societies, one black, one white—separate and unequal."

MARCH 12 New Hampshire primary. Lyndon Johnson, a write-in candidate, narrowly defeats Eugene McCarthy. The Minnesota senator conducted an effective grassroots campaign, and his run against Johnson establishes him as a serious candidate. Richard Nixon easily wins the Republican vote.

MARCH 16 After painstaking deliberations, Robert Kennedy enters the race for the Democratic nomination.

APRIL 2 Wisconsin primary. With LBJ no longer in the running and Robert Kennedy not on the ballot, Eugene McCarthy wins his party's vote. Nixon cruises on the Republican side.

APRIL 3 The United States and North Vietnam reach an agreement to engage in diplomatic talks on a way to end the Vietnam War. As the months ahead would show, agreeing to talk and actually engaging in meaningful discussion were a long way off.

APRIL 4 Rev. Dr. Martin Luther King Jr. is assassinated in Memphis. Violence breaks out in inner cities throughout the United States.

APRIL 23 Students at Columbia University, angered by the university's defense contracts and plans to build a gym on land used by Harlem residents, take over several buildings and hold them until police physically drive them out. Eugene McCarthy, essentially running alone, wins the nonbinding primary in Pennsylvania.

APRIL 27 Hubert Humphrey enters the race for the Democratic Party nomination.

MAY 7 Robert Kennedy defeats Eugene McCarthy in the Indiana primary, the first confrontation between the two candidates.

MAY 14 Robert Kennedy tallies his second impressive primary victory in Nebraska, though McCarthy fares well enough to continue as a candidate. Hubert Humphrey is trounced as a write-in candidate. Richard Nixon wins the Republican vote, but Ronald Reagan, with his name on the ballot for the first time, scores a surprising 21 percent of the vote.

MAY 28 Oregon primary. Eugene McCarthy wins a shocking victory over Robert Kennedy, marking the first time a Kennedy has lost a primary or general election.

JUNE 4 California primary. Robert Kennedy wins but is shot shortly after giving his victory address. He dies in the early hours of June 6.

JUNE 18 McCarthy wins the New York primary, but with Kennedy out of the race, it is becoming clear that McCarthy has a long uphill battle to gain the Democratic Party nomination over Hubert Humphrey, who has amassed a large number of delegate votes in nonprimary states.

AUGUST 8 Richard Nixon wins the Republican nomination for the presidency. He names Maryland governor Spiro Agnew as his running mate.

AUGUST 10 George McGovern announces his candidacy for the Democratic nomination.

AUGUST 26 The Democratic National Convention officially opens in Chicago. No event in the history of U.S. electoral politics has seen violence as ensues over the following five days. Demonstrators fight with police, troops, and National Guardsmen in parks and streets, with hundreds of arrests and injuries resulting from beatings that unarmed protesters and innocent bystanders receive from Mayor Richard Daley's minions. Hubert Humphrey wins the nomination and names Maine senator Edmund Muskie as his running mate.

SEPTEMBER 30 In a speech in Salt Lake City, Hubert Humphrey breaks with Lyndon Johnson over Vietnam War policy. Humphrey's campaign immediately benefits from the split, and he gains significant ground throughout the month of October.

NOVEMBER 5 In one of the narrowest popular vote margins of victory in presidential election history, Richard Nixon defeats Hubert Humphrey in the general election. He becomes the country's thirty-seventh president.

Notes

ABBREVIATIONS

EMOH	Eugene McCarthy Oral History
HHH	Hubert Horatio Humphrey
HHHOH	Hubert H. Humphrey Oral History
JFK	John Fitzgerald Kennedy
JFKL	John F. Kennedy Presidential Library
JFKOH	John F. Kennedy Oral History
LBJ	Lyndon Baines Johnson
LBJOH	Lyndon B. Johnson Oral History
LBJPL	Lyndon Baines Johnson Presidential Library
MHS	Minnesota Historical Society
RFK	Robert Francis Kennedy
RFKOH	Robert F. Kennedy Oral History

INTRODUCTION

page 1 Gallup Poll: Witcover, *The Year the Dream Died,* 139; Dallek, *Flawed Giant,* 528.

page 2 Tet Offensive: Don Oberdorfer's *Tet!* is the best, most detailed published account of the Tet Offensive and its aftermath. Mark Bowden's *Hue 1968* offers superb, in-depth reportage of the bloodiest battle of the Tet Offensive and the turning point of the Vietnam War. For more, see *Reporting Vietnam, Part I,* 557–81; Karnow, *Vietnam,* 523–55; LaFeber, *The Deadly Bet,* 23–31; Schandler, *Lyndon Johnson and Vietnam,* 74–91.

page 2 "Only a few months . . .": Chester, Hodgson, and Page, *An American Melodrama,* 93; Gould, *1968,* 36.

page 3 "It became necessary . . .": Gelb and Betts, *The Irony of Vietnam,* 171. In a March 18, 1968, speech at the University of Kansas, Robert Kennedy spoke extensively about the Vietnam War and of the urgency to negotiate an ending to it. A military victory, he said, was not the solution; the Johnson policies were a failure. During his talk, Kennedy brought up the remarks about Ben Tre: "I don't think it's up to us here in the United States to say that we're going to destroy all of South Vietnam because we have a commitment there. The commander of the American forces at Ben Tre said we had to destroy that city in order to save it. So, 38,000 people were wiped out or made refugees." He was even more direct earlier that same day in a speech delivered at the University of Kentucky: "If it becomes necessary to destroy all of Vietnam to save it, will we do that, too? And if we care so little about South Vietnam that we are willing to see its land destroyed, and its people dead, then why are we there in the first place?"

page 3 "Many Americans . . .": C. Kaiser, *1968 in America,* 69.

pages 3–4 "The enemy's . . .": ibid., 66.

page 4 "They lost . . .": Wainstock, *The Turning Point,* 28.

page 4 "the greatest victory . . .": Maxwell D. Taylor, oral history interview by Dorothy Pierce, February 10, 1969, LBJOH; Wainstock, *The Turning Point,* 28.

page 4 "Vietnam had become . . .": McPherson, *A Political Education,* 420.

page 4 "The credibility of . . .": Halberstam, *The Best and the Brightest,* 648.

page 4 "What the hell . . .": Oberdorfer, *Tet!,* 158; Brinkley, *Cronkite,* 367.

page 4 "I proposed . . .": Cronkite, *A Reporter's Life,* 256.

page 5 "one of [Johnson's] . . .": Miller, *Lyndon,* 619.

page 5 "the best thing . . .": Solberg, *Hubert Humphrey,* 321.

page 6 "Mr. President . . .": ibid.

page 6 "I've got to become . . .": Witcover, *The Year the Dream Died,* 140.

page 6 "Even if I should . . .": Humphrey, *The Education of a Public Man,* 267.

page 6 "He looked at her . . .": Caro, *The Passage of Power,* 112.

page 7 "His eyes . . .": White, *The Making of the President 1968,* 114.

page 7 "a question of how . . .": Johnson, *The Vantage Point,* 425–26.

page 7 "He found something . . .": D. K. Goodwin, *Lyndon Johnson and the American Dream,* 342.

page 8 "If you're going to run . . .": Solberg, *Hubert Humphrey,* 322.

page 8 "His mind . . .": Valenti, *This Time, This Place,* 34.

page 8 "gave new meaning . . .": Califano, *The Triumph and Tragedy of Lyndon Johnson,* 10.

page 11 Cronkite in Vietnam: Brinkley, *Cronkite,* 366–86; Cronkite, *A Reporter's Life,* 254–58.

page 11 "It seems now . . .": Brinkley, *Cronkite,* 377.

page 11 "My decision . . .": Cronkite, *Reporter's Life,* 257.

page 11 "speculative, personal . . .": Walter Cronkite, "We Are Mired in Stalemate . . ."; text from the CBS television special "Report from Vietnam: Who, What, When, Why," broadcast on February 27, 1968; reprinted in *Reporting Vietnam, Part I,* 581. See also Lawrence Laurent, "Walter Cronkite Speaks Out on Vietnam," *Washington Post,* March 8, 1968.

page 11 "It is increasingly . . .": ibid., 582.

page 12 "If I've lost . . .": ibid., 258. The variations of this quotation were published in Brinkley, *Cronkite,* 379.

page 12 "astonishing political upset": Perlstein, *Nixonland,* 232.

page 12 "New Hampshire . . .": ibid.

page 13 "the thing I had . . .": Caro, *Passage of Power,* 580.

page 13 "I think Al . . .": Newfield, *Robert Kennedy,* 185.

page 13 "How is it possible . . .": D. K. Goodwin, *Lyndon Johnson and the American Dream,* 340–41.

page 14 November 2, 1967, meeting with the Wise Men: McNamara, *In Retrospect,* 306; Isaacson and Thomas, *The Wise Men,* 678–81.

page 14 March 1968 meeting with the Wise Men: Clifford, *Counsel to the President,* 511–19; Ball, *The Past Has Another Pattern,* 407–9; Johnson, *The Vantage Point,* 416–18; Isaacson and Thomas, *The Wise Men,* 696–706; Shesol, *Mutual Contempt,* 433–35; Miller, *Lyndon,* 612–13; Perlstein, *Nixonland,* 248–49; Wainstock, *The Turning Point,* 53–54.

page 14 McNamara's memo to LBJ: McNamara, *In Retrospect,* 307–9; Johnson, *The Vantage Point,* 372–76, 600–601; Clifford, *Counsel to the President,* 456–60.

page 15 "continuation of our present . . .": McNamara, *In Retrospect,* 307.

page 15 "studied McNamara's . . .": Johnson, *The Vantage Point,* 373.

page 15 "thoughtful attention": ibid.

page 15 "I do not know . . .": McNamara, *In Retrospect,* 311.

page 16 "Seven to one . . .": Halberstam, *The Best and Brightest,* 653.

page 16 "What would you do . . .": Clifford, *Counsel to the President,* 514.

page 17 "significant shift": ibid., 516.

page 17 "Your whole group . . .": Ball, *The Past Has Another Pattern,* 409.

page 17 "Let's get one thing . . .": Halberstam, *The Best and Brightest,* 654.

page 17 "I thanked the advisers . . .": Johnson, *The Vantage Point,* 418.

page 17 "If they had been . . .": ibid.

page 18 "hard-nosed": Clark M. Clifford, oral history interview by Paige Mulhollan, July 14, 1969, LBJOH.

page 18 "stern . . . facing up . . .": ibid. The other citations in this passage are from this source. Clifford's change in position on the bombing of North Vietnam—and of the war in Vietnam in general—can be seen in a memo he sent Lyndon Johnson in immediate response to Robert McNamara's memo to LBJ in November 1967. In addressing McNamara's thoughts on halting the bombing, Clifford took the president's position:

> I am at a loss to understand this logic. Would the unconditional suspension of the bombing, without any effort to extract a quid pro quo persuade Hanoi that we were firm and unyielding in our conviction to force them to desist from their aggressive designs?
>
> The answer is a loud and resounding "no."
>
> It would be interpreted by Hanoi as (a) evidence of our discouragement and frustration, and (b) admission of the wrongness and immorality of our bombing of the North, and (c) the first step in our ultimate total disengagement from the conflict. (Johnson, *The Vantage Point,* 375)

page 18 "Bobby Kennedy . . .": Califano, *The Triumph and Tragedy of Lyndon Johnson,* 268.

page 19 "What do you think . . .": Shesol, *Mutual Contempt,* 434–35.

page 19 "murderous": McPherson, *A Political Education,* 428.

page 20 "That's O.K. . . .": ibid., 437.

page 21 "He told me . . .": Miller, *Lyndon,* 602.

page 21 "You know, Johnson's . . .": Berman, *Hubert,* 154.

page 22 "such pain . . .": Lady Bird Johnson, *A White House Diary,* 642.

page 22 "Good evening . . .": Lyndon Baines Johnson: speech, March 31, 1968, LBJPL. All other citations from this speech are from this source.

page 24 "In forty-five minutes . . .": Johnson, *The Vantage Point,* 435.

page 24 "Why didn't . . .": Berman, *Hubert,* 155.

page 25 "As he began . . .": R.N. Goodwin, *Remembering America,* 522.

page 25 "I feel as if . . .": Witcover, *The Year the Dream Died,* 142.

page 25 "clear[ing] the way . . .": ibid.

page 25 "I took no . . .": E. McCarthy, *The Year of the People,* 104.

page 26 "I was genuinely . . .": A. McCarthy, *Private Faces/Public Places,* 256.

page 26 "suppressed triumph": ibid., 257. All other citations in this passage are from this source.

page 26 "I wonder . . .": Homer Bigart, "Kennedy, Told the News on a Plane, Sits in Silence amid the Hubbub," *New York Times,* April 1, 1968; Jimmy Breslin, "Kennedy Gets the News," *New York Post,* April 1, 1968.

page 26 "the year of . . .": Nixon, *RN,* 300.

page 27 "While the dropout . . .": ibid.

page 27 "proved the sincerity . . .": Mann, *The Walls of Jericho,* 488.

page 27 "an act of . . .": Dallek, *Flawed Giant,* 530.

page 27 "Lyndon Johnson's . . .": "What It Means—Some Views from the Top," *New York Post,* April 1, 1968.

page 27 "By removing himself . . .": Tom Wicker, "In the Nation: The First and the Last," *New York Times,* April 2, 1968.

page 27 Gallup Poll: "Poll Finds Johnson's Popularity Has Soared to 49% since March," *New York Times,* April 17, 1968.

page 27 "Mr. Johnson is . . .": Max Frankel, "The Liberation of Lyndon Johnson," *New York Times,* April 14, 1968.

1. HUBERT HUMPHREY

page 32 "I said . . .": Hubert Humphrey, oral history interview by Larry J. Hackman, March 30, 1970, RFKOH/JFKL.

pages 32–38 HHH bio: D. Cohen, *Undefeated,* 19–73; Humphrey, *The Education of a Public Man,* 3–74; William H. Rudy, "Hubert Humphrey: Father and Son," *New York Post,* July 16, 1968; Charles Hyneman, oral history interview by Arthur Naftalin, August 16, 1978, HHHOH/MHS; Julian Hartt, oral history interview by Norman Sherman, July 7, 1978, HHHOH/MHS; Frances Howard, oral history interview by Arthur Naftalin, February 20, 1978, HHHOH/MHS.

page 32 "The kind of . . .": Humphrey, *The Education of a Public Man,* 3.

page 32 "He, according to . . .": Howard, oral history interview.

page 33 "I finally yelled . . .": Hartt, oral history interview.

page 34 "My father . . .": Humphrey, *The Education of a Public Man,* 15.

page 35 "There was . . .": Hyneman, oral history interview.

page 36 "My abstract . . .": Humphrey, *The Education of a Public Man,* 42.

page 36 "If we gave . . .": ibid.

page 38 "capital of . . .": Solberg, *Hubert Humphrey,* 106.

page 38 "He would come . . .": Orville L. Freeman and Everon Kirkpatrick, oral history interview by Arthur Naftalin, January 16, 1978, HHHOH/MHS.

page 39 "action . . .": ibid.

pages 39–48 Truman and civil rights: Dallek, *Harry S. Truman*, 80–86; Gardner, *Truman and Civil Rights*, 95–97; McCullough, *Truman*, 586–92; Pietrusza, *1948*, 212–14.

page 40 "a disgrace . . .": Pietrusza, *1948*, 212.

page 40 "One of the . . .": ibid., 212–13.

page 41 "racial and religious . . .": Gardner, *Truman and Civil Rights*, 96–97.

pages 39–48 Humphrey and 1948 convention: Caro, *Master of the Senate*, 439–45; Clifford, *Counsel to the President*, 217–20; D. Cohen, *Undefeated*, 140–44; Eisele, *Almost to the Presidency*, 66–70; Frost, *The Presidential Debate, 1968*, 53–55; Griffith, *Humphrey*, 150–60; Humphrey, *The Education of a Public Man*, 75–79; Mann, *The Walls of Jericho*, 1–21; McCullough, *Truman*, 638–40; Solberg, *Hubert Humphrey*, 1–20; "The Line Squall," *Time*, July 26, 1948; "Education of a Senator," *Time*, January 17, 1949.

page 41 "the Republicans . . .": Humphrey, *The Education of a Public Man*, 76.

page 41 "sellout to . . .": Solberg, *Hubert Humphrey*, 4.

page 41 "redo Franklin . . .": Griffith, *Humphrey*, 151.

page 41 "Who does this pipsqueak . . .": Solberg, *Hubert Humphrey*, 4.

page 42 "Joe . . .": ibid., 6.

page 42 "crackpots": McCullough, *Truman*, 640.

page 42 "Her strong faith . . .": Humphrey, *The Education of a Public Man*, 77.

page 42 "This may tear . . .": Mann, *The Walls of Jericho*, 5.

page 42 "If there is . . .": Eisele, *Almost to the Presidency*, 69.

page 42 "very courageous . . .": D. Cohen, *Undefeated*, 144.

page 44 "I'm sure . . .": Humphrey, *The Education of a Public Man*, 78.

page 44 "Let them . . .": Eisele, *Almost to the Presidency*, 68.

page 44 "It was the greatest . . .": Caro, *Master of the Senate*, 445.

page 45 "I realize that . . .": Hubert Humphrey, untitled speech delivered at Democratic National Convention in Philadelphia on July 14, 1948, Hubert Humphrey Papers, MHS.

page 47 "I am Hubert . . .": Mann, *The Walls of Jericho*, 20.

page 47 "They all plodded . . .": "The Line Squall," *Time*, July 26, 1948.

page 48 "I think that . . .": Frost, *The Presidential Debate, 1968*, 54.

page 48 "I figured . . .": Griffith, *Humphrey*, 164.

page 49 "I visited . . .": "Education of a Senator," *Time*, January 17, 1949.

page 49 "It's like . . .": ibid.

page 50 "giant killer": Griffith, *Humphrey*, 163.

page 50 "He was all over . . .": ibid.

page 50 "Can you imagine . . .": Solberg, *Hubert Humphrey*, 136.

page 51 "glib, jaunty . . .": *Time*, January 17, 1949.

page 51 "Never in my life . . .": Humphrey, *The Education of a Public Man*, 88.

page 52 "Senator . . .": ibid., 92.

page 52 "to encourage . . .": Humphrey, *The Education of a Public Man*, 143.

pages 53–55 Humphrey and Khrushchev: D. Cohen, *Undefeated*, 197–207; Eisele,

Almost to the Presidency, 105–7; Humphrey, *The Education of a Public Man,* 143–48; Solberg, *Hubert Humphrey,* 188–94; Zehnpfennig, *Hubert H. Humphrey,* 139–45; "Foreign Relations," *Time,* December 15, 1958; "What Khrushchev Wants," *Time,* December 15, 1958; Hubert H. Humphrey, "My Marathon Talk with Russia's Boss," *Life,* January 12, 1959.

page 53 "as if to take . . .": Humphrey, *The Education of a Public Man,* 145.

page 53 "reaction of . . .": ibid.

page 53 "a bone . . .": ibid.

page 54 "Look, Winston . . .": ibid., 147.

page 54 "They are old-fashioned . . .": Solberg, *Hubert Humphrey,* 194.

page 57 "In politics . . .": White, *The Making of the President 1960,* 33.

page 57 "You'd better . . .": Hubert H. Humphrey, oral history interview by Max Kampelman, December 14, 1964, JFKOH/JFKL.

page 57 "it was simply . . .": Humphrey, *The Education of a Public Man,* 150.

pages 57–58 "It was quite obvious . . .": Humphrey, interview by Kampelman.

pages 58–61 Wisconsin primary: D. Cohen, *Undefeated,* 211–17; Eisele, *Almost to the Presidency,* 143–44; R. N. Goodwin, *Remembering America,* 80–84; Griffith, Humphrey, 245–46; Humphrey, *The Education of a Public Man,* 150–55; O'Brien, *John F. Kennedy,* 444–48; Ryskind, *Hubert,* 236–45; Schlesinger, *Robert Kennedy and His Times,* 211–12; Solberg, *Humphrey,* 200–208; Tye, *Bobby Kennedy,* 105–6; White, *The Making of the President 1960,* 80–95; "Strategic Warpath in Wisconsin," *Life,* March 28, 1960; Humphrey, interview by Kampelman; Geraldine Joseph, oral history interview by Arthur Naftalin, July 14, 1978, HHHOH/MHS.

page 58 "Come down here . . .": Humphrey, *The Education of a Public Man,* 151.

page 58 "I cannot win . . .": "Plenty of Jack," *Time,* March 23, 1960.

page 58 "I feel like . . .": Solberg, *Hubert Humphrey,* 205.

page 59 "Kennedy might figure . . .": "Pivotal Primary," *Time,* February 1, 1960.

page 61 "a little intoxicated . . .": Humphrey, interview by Kampelman.

page 61 "It means . . .": O'Brien, *John F. Kennedy,* 448.

pages 61–67 West Virginia primary: Berman, *Hubert,* 259; Caro, *The Passage of Power,* 84–87, 246; D. Cohen, *Undefeated,* 217–23; Eisele, *Almost to the Presidency,* 144–48; R. N. Goodwin, *Remembering America,* 84–89; Griffith, *Humphrey,* 17–24, 246–47; Humphrey, *The Education of a Public Man,* 156–62, 363; Mann, *The Walls of Jericho,* 267; O'Brien, *John F. Kennedy,* 449–55; Ryskind, *Hubert,* 246–50; Schlesinger, *A Thousand Days,* 22, 26–27; Schlesinger, *Robert Kennedy and His Times,* 212–17; Solberg, *Hubert Humphrey,* 208–12; Stein and Plimpton, *American Journey,* 68–71; Strober and Strober, *"Let Us Begin Anew,"* 3–4; Tye, *Bobby Kennedy,* 106–10; White, *The Making of the President 1960,* 90–114; "Stop Signs," *Time,* April 25, 1960; "Tough as Boiled Owls," *Time,* May 9, 1960; "Tough Testing Ground," *Time,* March 20, 1960; "The Religion Issue (Contd.)," *Time,* May 2, 1960; "Vote Getter's Victory," *Time,* May 23, 1960; David S. Broder, "How the 1960 West Virginia Election Made History," *Washington Post,* May 16, 2010; Robert Walters, "Kennedy Drive Enters West Virginia Coalfields," *Washington Star,* n.d., HHH papers, MHS; John A. Blatnik, oral history interview by Joseph E. O'Connor, February 4, 1966, JFKOH/JFKL; Humphrey, interview by Kampelman,; Geraldine Joseph, interview by Naftalin, HHHOH/MHS.

page 61 "Politics in West Virginia . . .": White, *The Making of the President 1960,* 99.

page 61 "West Virginia had . . .": O'Brien, *John F. Kennedy,* 449.

page 62 "I always told . . .": White, *The Making of the President 1960,* 95.

page 62 "Every town . . .": Humphrey, interview by Kampelman.

page 63 "Is anyone . . .": "The Religion Issue."

page 63 "West Virginia . . .": Schlesinger, *Robert Kennedy and His Times,* 213.

page 64 "He didn't believe . . .": O'Brien, *John F. Kennedy,* 454.

page 64 "I can't afford . . .": Eisele, *Almost to the Presidency,* 148.

page 64 "Don't buy . . .": Solberg, *Hubert Humphrey,* 210.

page 64 "I never expected . . .": Mann, *The Walls of Jericho,* 267.

page 65 "He's a good . . .": Ryskind, *Hubert,* 247.

page 65 "Frank Roosevelt . . .": Broder, "How the 1960 West Virginia Election Made History."

page 65 "It was a dishonest . . .": Humphrey, *The Education of a Public Man,* 363.

pages 68–78 1964 VP: Berman, *Hubert,* 90–91; Chester, Hodgson, and Page. *An American Melodrama,* 75, 197–223; D. Cohen, *Undefeated,* 251–52, 255–57; Dallek, *Flawed Giant,* 157–61; R. N. Goodwin, *Remembering America,* 295–98; Herzog, *McCarthy for President,* 65–68; Humphrey, *The Education of a Public Man,* 223–26; Johnson, *The Vantage Point,* 101; Larner, *Nobody Knows,* 22–24; Mann, *The Walls of Jericho,* 436–41; A. McCarthy, *Private Faces/Public Places,* 264–76; E. J. McCarthy, *Up 'Til Now,* 154–65; Solberg, *Hubert Humphrey,* 243–54; White, *The Making of the President 1964,* 282–87, 300–304; Woods, *LBJ,* 528–30; "Dying to Tell," *Time,* August 20, 1964; "The Man Who Quit Kicking the Wall," *Time,* September 4, 1964; Humphrey, interview by Hackman; Eugene McCarthy, oral history interview by Michael L. Gillette, December 12, 1980, LBJOH.

page 69 "Give me a minute . . .": Humphrey, *The Education of a Public Man,* 225.

page 69 "cut his balls . . .": Woods, *LBJ,* 529–30.

page 69 "You'll be surprised . . .": Berman, *Hubert,* 90.

page 74 "Johnson had no . . .": R. N. Goodwin, *Remembering America,* 295.

page 75 "When we got . . .": McCarthy, interview by Gillette.

page 76 "matter of obligation . . .": White, *The Making of the President 1964,* 210.

page 77 "The mounting suspense . . .": "Dying to Tell."

page 77 "This is ridiculous . . .": Solberg, *Hubert Humphrey,* 247.

page 77 "Hubert . . .": ibid.

page 78 "Hubert, do you . . .": Humphrey, *The Education of a Public Man,* 224.

page 78 "like a marriage . . .": ibid.

page 78 "Hubert's was probably . . .": Berman, *Hubert,* 90.

pages 79–81 Pleiku attack: D. Cohen, *Undefeated,* 269–72; Halberstam, *The Best and the Brightest,* 520–22, 531–36; Humphrey, *The Education of a Public Man,* 236–42; Johnson, *The Vantage Point,* 124–30; Solberg, *Hubert Humphrey,* 270–75.

page 79 "They are killing . . .": Johnson, *The Vantage Point,* 125.

page 81 "trigger-happy . . .": Hubert Humphrey, "Memo to Lyndon B. Johnson," February 15, 1965; reprinted in Humphrey, *The Education of a Public Man,* 239–41. All citations in this passage are from this source.

2. EUGENE McCARTHY

pages 85–89 Allard Lowenstein background: Viorst, *Fire in the Streets,* 383–420; Cummings, *The Pied Piper*; Chafe, *Never Stop Running*; Allard Lowenstein oral history interview, McCarthy Historical Project, Oral History Interview Series, University of Minnesota (no interviewer or date provided).

page 85 "The hard-driving . . .": Gitlin, *The Sixties,* 295.

page 86 "the most effective . . .": quoted in Herzog, *McCarthy for President,* 22.

page 87 "I think Bobby . . .": Sandbrook, *Eugene McCarthy,* 68.

page 87 "honor and direction": Chafe, *Never Stop Running,* 270–71.

page 88 "We're going to . . .": ibid.

page 88 "you need . . .": Herzog, *McCarthy for President,* 21.

page 88 "Basically, Gene . . .": Humphrey, *The Education of a Public Man,* 281.

page 88 "Mary, I know . . .": A. McCarthy, *Private Faces/Public Places,* 294.

page 89 "Meeting with . . .": E. J. McCarthy, *The Year of the People,* 54.

page 89 "I'm not worried . . .": Eisele, *Almost to the Presidency,* 284.

page 89 "I guess . . .": Chester, Hodgson, and Page, *An American Melodrama,* 75.

page 89 "did not look . . .": Mailer, *Miami and the Siege of Chicago,* 99.

page 90 "I didn't say . . .": as quoted in R. N. Goodwin, *Remembering America,* 491.

page 90 "He spoke . . .": Humphrey, *The Education of a Public Man,* 281.

page 90 "This is the wildest . . .": LaFeber, *The Deadly Bet,* 37.

page 91 "If I have to run . . .": O'Donnell, *Playing with Fire,* 22.

page 91 "has never been . . .": Eisele, *Almost to the Presidency,* 285.

page 92 "I intend . . .": "McCarthy Statement on Entering the 1968 Primaries, Intention to Escalate Areas of Responsibility, Sees No Great Threat," *New York Times,* December 1, 1967. All other citations from this speech are from this source.

page 92 "Our first plan . . .": E. McCarthy, *Up 'Til Now,* 184–85.

page 93 "Within the political . . .": Kenneth Crawford, "The McCarthy Bomb," *Newsweek,* December 4, 1967.

page 93 "his entry may channel . . .": editorial, *Washington Post,* December 1, 1967.

page 93 "thoughtful, responsible . . .": editorial, *New York Times,* December 1, 1967.

page 93 "none of the punchiness . . ." and "If McCarthy . . .": Larner, *Nobody Knows,* 15–16.

page 93 "When a President . . .": E. McCarthy, *The Year of the People,* 58.

page 94 "as soon as . . .": quoted in Witcover, *The Year the Dream Died,* 39.

page 94 "Al was confused . . .": Chafe, *Never Stop Running,* 280.

page 94 "dull and uninspired": David C. Hoeh, *1968, McCarthy, New Hampshire,* 97.

page 94 "flat": Witcover, *The Year the Dream Died,* 40.

page 94 "the speech . . .": Herzog, *McCarthy for President,* 76.

page 94 "rather a good . . .": E. J. McCarthy, *The Year of the People,* 57.

page 94 "It was not . . .": ibid.

page 94 "test the mood . . .": Eisele, *Almost to the Presidency,* 288.

page 95 "I saw him . . .": Cummings, *The Pied Piper,* 359.

page 95 "I would have . . .": Warren Weaver, "M'Carthy to Fight Johnson Policies in 5 or 6 Primaries," *New York Times,* December 1, 1967.

page 96 "What is your . . .": *Meet the Press,* aired December 3, 1967, on NBC, as quoted in Cummings, *The Pied Piper,* 360. All other citations from this program are from this source.

page 97 "At each step . . .": Hoeh, *1968, McCarthy, New Hampshire,* 108.

page 97 Blair Clark appointment: "New Yorker Heads M'Carthy Campaign," *New York Times,* December 13, 1967; A. McCarthy, *Private Faces/Public Places,* 307–8; White, *The Making of the President 1968,* 80–82.

page 97 "It is impossible . . .": White, *The Making of the President 1968,* 80.

3. RICHARD NIXON

page 99 "Just think . . .": Witcover, *The Resurrection of Richard Nixon,* 22,

page 100 "I was convinced . . .": Frost, *The Presidential Debate, 1968,* 21.

page 100 "I have never . . .": Nixon, *RN,* 246.

page 100 "Barring a miracle . . .": "California: Career's End," *Time,* November 16, 1962.

page 101 "inevitable": Buchanan, *The Greatest Comeback,* 25.

page 101 "Their hesitancy . . .": ibid., 21.

page 102 "You're not . . .": ibid., 27.

page 102 "a more or less . . .": Leonard Garment, oral history interview by Timothy Naftali, April 6, 2007, Richard M. Nixon Presidential Library and Museum.

page 102 *Hill v. Time Inc.*: Garment, *Crazy Rhythm,* 79–91.

page 103 "reading and virtually . . .": ibid., 84.

page 103 "The net effect . . .": Garment, interview by Naftali.

pages 104–5 Haldeman memo: Ambrose, *Nixon,* 137–39; Buchanan, *The Greatest Comeback,* 198–201; Nixon, *RN,* 303–4; White, *The Making of the President 1968,* 132–33.

page 104 "We started . . .": White, *The Making of the President 1968,* 133.

page 104 "The time has come . . .": as quoted in Nixon, *RN,* 303.

page 105 "Nothing can happen . . .": as quoted in McGinniss, *The Selling of the President,* 35. All other citations from this letter are from this source.

page 106 "an illuminating . . .": Garment, *Crazy Rhythm,* 130.

page 106 "surprisingly congenial": ibid.

page 106 "It's not the man . . .": ibid., 139.

page 107 "We can turn . . .": McGinniss, *The Selling of the President,* 45.

page 107 "[devising] a theme . . .": ibid., 46.

page 107 "it's a shame . . .": ibid., 65.

page 107 "I don't even know . . .": Chafets, *Roger Ailes,* 32.

page 108 "I'm his campaign . . .": Rosen, *The Strong Man,* 41.

page 108 "Within a few . . .": Nixon, *RN,* 279.

page 109 "critical influence": White, *The Making of the President 1968,* 46.

page 109 "the heavyweight": "The Administration: Nixon's Heavyweight." *Time,* July 25, 1969.

page 109 "I was impressed . . .": H. R. Haldeman, oral history interview by Raymond H. Geselbracht, April 11, 1988, Richard M. Nixon Presidential Library and Museum.

page 109 "There was no . . .": ibid.

page 110 "I never felt . . .": ibid.

page 110 "feeling an itch": Ehrlichman, *Witness to Power,* 3.

page 111 "it didn't take . . .": ibid., 21.

page 111 "Nixon had begun . . .": ibid., 17.

page 111 "the best . . .": ibid., 22. In *Witness to Power,* Ehrlichman recalled another exceedingly uncomfortable incident in which a very intoxicated Richard Nixon made "some clumsy passes" at an unwilling young woman, who managed to extricate herself from his grip and leave the Nixon suite before he embarrassed himself any further. By his own admission, Ehrlichman was, as a rule, "offended" by this kind of behavior, whether it was coming from Nixon or the Kennedys, known for their womanizing, and it bothered him enough that he concluded that "Nixon's drinking could cost him any chance of a return to public life."

page 112 "big-league pitching": Ambrose, *Nixon,* 105.

page 112 "He was particularly . . .": Witcover, *The Year the Dream Died,* 14.

page 112 "a public impression . . .": ibid., 15.

page 113 "the greatest brainwashing . . .": "Romney Asserts He Underwent 'Brainwashing' on Vietnam Trip," *New York Times,* September 5, 1967.

page 113 "How long . . .": as quoted in Wicker, *One of Us,* 297.

page 113 "I think . . .": Chester, Hodgson, and Page, *An American Melodrama,* 101.

page 113 "I was not . . .": "The Brainwashed Candidate," *Time,* September 15, 1967.

page 115 "Nixon today . . .": as quoted in Chester, Hodgson, and Page, *An American Melodrama,* 218.

page 115 "crime, drugs . . .": Perlstein, *Nixonland,* 92.

page 116 "Reagan's views were . . .": Nixon, *RN,* 263.

page 116 "tentative plans" and "to assure . . .": ibid., 286.

page 116 "enough potential . . .": "Anchors Aweigh," *Time,* October 20, 1967.

page 117 "Now we can run . . .": ibid.

page 117 "dream ticket": ibid.

page 117 "I wouldn't be . . .": Witcover, *The Resurrection of Richard Nixon,* 219.

page 118 "a touchstone . . .": Steve Vogel, "Once More to the Pentagon," *Washington Post,* March 16, 2007.

page 119 "Phil thought . . .": Schumacher, *There But for Fortune,* 147.

page 119 "news manipulation . . .": Witcover, *The Resurrection of Richard Nixon,* 221.

pages 120–21 Nixon's self-doubts: Nixon, *RN,* 290–94.

page 121 "I have decided . . .": Nixon, *RN,* 291. All other citations in this passage are from this source.

page 121 "Had I come . . .": ibid., 292.

page 121 "I think it is . . .": ibid., 293.

page 121 "charade": Ambrose, *Nixon,* 132.

page 121 "a secure home front": ibid.

4. GEORGE WALLACE

page 122 *"Can a former . . .":* Ray Jenkins, "George Wallace Figures to Win Even If He Loses," *New York Times,* April 7, 1968.

pages 123–29 University of Alabama confrontation: Carter, *The Politics of Rage,* 133–55; Frady, *Wallace,* 152–75; Lesher, *George Wallace,* 201–36; Schlesinger, *Robert*

Kennedy and His Times, 362–68; Nicholas Katzenbach, oral history interview by Paige E. Mulhollan, November 12, 1968, LBJOH; George Wallace, oral history interview by T. H. Baker, May 15, 1969, LBJOH.

pages 124–25 James Meredith and Ole Miss: Carter, *Politics of Rage,* 110–11; Lesher, *George Wallace,* 164–66; Mann, *The Walls of Jericho,* 328–34; Schlesinger, *Robert Kennedy and His Times,* 341–62; Nicholas Katzenbach, oral history interview by Anthony Lewis, November 29, 1964, JFKOH; Wallace, interview by Baker.

page 124 "I had been . . .": Katzenbach, interview by Mulhollan.

page 125 "I, like Governor . . .": Lesher, *George Wallace.* 165.

page 125 "John Patterson . . .": Chester, Hodgson, and Page, *An American Melodrama,* 269. Wallace would deny saying this.

page 125 "In the name . . .": Frady, *Wallace,* 145.

page 126 "If we went . . .": Katzenbach, interview by Mulhollan.

page 128 "I have President Kennedy's . . .": Carter, *The Politics of Rage,* 148.

page 128 "Well, you make . . .": ibid.

page 128 "a frightful example . . .": Lesher, *George Wallace,* 229. All other citations from this speech are from this source.

page 128 "thousands of other . . .": ibid.

page 129 "we are awakening . . .": Carter, *The Politics of Rage,* 150.

page 130 "stop and examine . . .": John F. Kennedy, speech, June 11, 1963. All citations in this passage are from this source.

page 131 "It will probably . . .": Lesher, *George Wallace,* 237–38.

page 132 "I was the instrument . . .": "Democrats: I Was the Instrument," *Time,* July 31, 1964.

page 132 "backlash" White, *The Making of the President 1964,* 245.

page 133 "in total command . . .": Carter, *The Politics of Rage,* 136.

page 133 "Hold your temper . . .": ibid.

page 133 "All they wanted . . .": ibid., 138.

pages 134–41 Selma: Carson, *The Autobiography of Martin Luther King, Jr.,* 270–90; Carter, *The Politics of Rage,* 240–59; Combs, *From Selma to Montgomery;* Garrow, *Protest at Selma;* Hampton and Fayer, *Voices of Freedom,* 209–40; King, *My Life with Martin Luther King, Jr.,* 235–50; Lesher, *George Wallace,* 316–39; Lewis, *Walking with the Wind,* 300–363; John Lewis, "Rep. John Lewis: An Oral History of Selma and the Struggle for the Voting Rights Act," Time.com, December 25, 2014.

page 134 Marion: Martin Luther King very briefly considered starting the march in Marion, a small city thirty miles northwest of Selma. Marion had been the site of mounting trouble, when protests and marches were staged by black groups frustrated over the voter registration issue. Each event grew more belligerent and violent, culminating with a police riot on February 18. The trouble had begun after a church service, when an estimated four hundred black churchgoers marched in protest of the arrest of a civil rights worker. Black frustration had reached a boiling point. The courts had ordered the city to register one hundred blacks per day, but it wasn't happening. On February 18, the marchers encountered a large phalanx of local police, state troopers, and local volunteers shortly after the march began. The police ordered the marchers to break up and disperse, and when they didn't, law enforcement personnel charged into the assembly, using their batons on anyone in their path. The news media were beaten ruthlessly as well, and their camera equipment was destroyed. Two marchers, Jimmie Lee Jackson, a twenty-six-year-old pulpwood cutter and Vietnam War veteran, and his mother, Viola Jackson, sought refuge with others in a nearby café, but police burst in and beat any African American in the building. Jackson, seeing his mother brutalized, tried to intervene and was shot in the stomach. He died eight days later. The powers that be, including Nicholas Katzenbach and George Wallace, condemned the violence and announced that they would be conducting investigations into the riot, but nothing significant ever came of it. Two days after the riot, Alabama's state legislature adopted a resolution condemning anyone suggesting that the police had acted improperly toward the media. Wallace paid lip service to deploring any violence during the demonstrations, and he made a point of personally avoiding rallies and demonstrations that might incite violence, but as the events in Marion escalated, he assigned Albert Lingo, head of the state troopers and an avowed segregationist, the task of keeping order. Lingo was not inclined to stand down during demonstrations of this nature, nor was Jim Clark, sheriff of Alabama's Dallas County, whose brutality was legend in the region, and who traveled to Marion on February 18 to be in on the action. When planning the march to Montgomery, Martin Luther King decided that Selma, a larger city and one of Alabama's commercial centers, would be a better starting point for the march.

page 136 "whatever methods . . .": Lesher, *George Wallace,* 320.

page 137 "a mean, vicious man": Lewis, "Rep. John Lewis."

page 137 "John, can you swim?" ibid. All other citations in this conversation are from this source.

page 137 "I still don't . . .": ibid.

page 137 "March . . .": King, *My Life with Martin Luther King, Jr.,* 242.

page 137 "The last thing . . .": Combs, *From Selma to Montgomery,* 37.

page 137 "I remember . . .": Hampton, *Voices of Freedom,* 228.

page 138 "I saw people . . .": ibid.

page 138 "I shall never forget . . .": Carson, *The Autobiography of Martin Luther King, Jr.,* 239.

page 139 "He has written . . .": "Incident at Selma," *New York Times,* March 9, 1965.

page 139 "The brutality is . . .": "Outrage at Selma," *Washington Post,* March 9, 1965.

page 139 "The Selma bridge . . .": George Wallace, oral history interview by Jack Bass and Walter DeVries, July 15, 1974, Southern Oral History Program Collection.

pages 141–43 Wallace meeting with LBJ: Garrow, *Protest at Selma,* 100–102; R. N. Goodwin, *Remembering America,* 321–24; Johnson, *The Vantage Point,* 162–63; Mann, *Walls of Jericho,* 456–58.

page 142 "he's a lot . . .": R. N. Goodwin, *Remembering America,* 320.

page 142 "might have been . . .": ibid., 321.

page 143 "Don't shit me . . .": ibid., 323. All other citations from this conversation are from this source.

page 144 "I knew . . .": Johnson, *The Vantage Point,* 162.

page 144 "unmitigated falsehood": Carter, *The Politics of Rage,* 254.

pages 144–46 LBJ speech: See R. N. Goodwin, *Remembering America,* 325–39. Goodwin takes the reader through the entire process of his writing the speech to Johnson's delivery of it. For Johnson's perspective, see Johnson, *The Vantage Point*, 163–66.

page 145 "At times . . .": Lyndon Johnson speech, March 15, 1965. All other citations from this speech are from this source.

page 145 "victory like none other . . .": Hampton, *Voices of Freedom*, 236.

page 146 "a part of . . ." R. N. Goodwin, *Remembering America*, 334.

page 146 "I looked over . . .": Hampton, *Voices of Freedom*, 236.

page 146 "I remember the ride . . .": Johnson, *The Vantage Point*, 166.

page 148 "an obscure . . .": Frady, *Wallace*, 190–91.

page 148 "brilliantine": Synon, *George Wallace*, 32.

page 148 "Politics was something . . .": Frady, *Wallace*, 84.

page 149 "she was able . . .": Lesher, *George Wallace*, 357.

page 149 "You came into office . . .": Carter, *The Politics of Rage*, 253.

page 150 "the Alabama Movement": Roy Reed, "Wallace Already Campaigning for 1968," *New York Times*, October 16, 1966.

page 150 "An Alabaman . . .": ibid.

page 150 "It's the working man . . .": Roy Reed, "Wallace's Drive Stirs GOP Fears," *New York Times*, November 6, 1966.

page 150 "You can put . . .": Nicholas von Hoffman, "Mississippians Accept the 'Magic' of Wallace," *Washington Post*, October 15, 1966.

page 151 "The law was written . . .": Synon, *George Wallace*, 111.

5. ROBERT KENNEDY

page 152 "He was a divided . . .": Schlesinger, *Robert Kennedy and His Times*, 861.

page 152 "He was not . . .": Newfield, *Robert Kennedy*, 32.

page 152 "The inescapable truth . . .": Caro, *The Passage of Power*, 242.

page 152 "a constellation . . .": R. N. Goodwin, *Remembering America*, 444.

page 152 "Kennedys don't cry": ibid.

page 153 "runt": Caro, *The Passage of Power*, 64.

page 153 "The assassination . . .": Newfield, *Robert Kennedy*, 29.

page 153 "I suppose . . .": Frost, *The Presidential Debate, 1968*, 118.

page 154 "From the neck down . . .": Witcover, *85 Days*, 32.

page 155 "Lyndon Johnson . . .": Newfield, *Robert Kennedy*, 171.

page 155 "in fevered language": Theodore S. Sorensen, oral history interview by Larry J. Hackman, March 24, 1969, RFKOH/JFKL.

page 155 "bemused smile . . .": Newfield, *Robert Kennedy*, 185.

page 155 "How do you . . .": ibid., 185–86.

page 156 "I think Al . . .": Schlesinger, *Robert Kennedy and His Times*, 887.

page 156 "He was probably . . .": John E. Nolan, oral history interview by Roberta W. Greene, July 24, 1970. RFKOH/JFKL.

pages 156–59 RFK/LBJ: The Kennedy–Johnson feud was probably the worst kept secret in a town known for its secrets and gossip. The interpretation of the feud was another matter. Kennedy wisely chose to avoid the issue in public, whenever possible, while Johnson was kind to Bobby in his public statements. In his memoirs of his presidency, he was also gentle. The problem, he asserted, was a matter of chemistry. "I doubt that [Bobby Kennedy] and I would have arrived at genuine friendship if we had worked together," he wrote. "Too much separated us—too much history, too many differences in temperament. But we had, I believe, a regard for each other's abilities." Others witnessing the behind-the-scenes interactions or hearing the two men speak about each other had different assessments. Bobby Baker, Johnson's close friend and advisor, had this to say: "I've never seen two human beings hate the way Lyndon Johnson and Bobby did. Bobby had Lyndon's telephone lines tapped." Johnson told John Connally, governor of Texas, "When this fellow [RFK] looks at me, he looks at me like he's going to look a hole right through me, like I'm a spy or something."

page 156 "It was as if . . .": Shesol, *Mutual Contempt*, 3.

page 157 "Bobby, you do not . . .": Schlesinger, *Robert Kennedy and His Times*, 672.

page 157 "He's not telling . . .": Caro, *The Passage of Power*, 229.

page 158 "Bobby's relationship . . .": Stein and Plimpton, *American Journey*, 198.

page 159 "There was a deep . . .": Frank Mankiewicz, oral history interview by Stephen Goodell, May 5, 1969. LBJOH.

page 159 "one of the greatest . . .": Witcover, *85 Days*, 42.

page 160 "Gene McCarthy . . .": ibid.

page 160 "on the side . . .": ibid., 43.

page 160 "If someone . . .": Chester, Hodgson, and Page, *An American Melodrama*, 106.

page 160 "If I ran . . .": Witcover, *85 Days*, 42.

page 160 "under any conceivable . . .": ibid., 44.

page 162 "Our enemy . . .": Robert F. Kennedy speech, as quoted in Witcover, *85 Days*, 48. All other citations from this speech are from this source.

page 164 "I wanted to say . . .": Newfield, *Robert Kennedy*, 208–9; Schlesinger, *Robert Kennedy and His Times*, 907.

page 164 "I wanted to remind . . .": Newfield, *Robert Kennedy*, 208.

page 165 "Our nation . . .": National Advisory Commission on Civil Disorders, *The Kerner Report*, 1. This is the twentieth anniversary edition of the book, with new introductions by Tom Wicker and Fred R. Harris.

page 165 "Great sustained . . .": ibid., x.

page 165 "Unemployment and underemployment . . .": ibid., 413.

page 166 "constructive and helpful": Johnson, *The Vantage Point*, 172.

page 166 "analysis reflected . . .": ibid.

page 166 "erupt": Califano, *The Triumph and Tragedy of Lyndon Johnson*, 260.

page 167 "ignore or demean . . .": ibid., 261.

page 167 "blames everybody . . .": Lesher, *George Wallace*, 403.

page 167 "Let us maintain . . .": "At Least They Are Trying—and Moving," *Durham (N.C.) Sun*, March 26, 1968.

page 167 "dangerously close . . .": "Humphrey and City Disorders," *Boston Globe*, March 26, 1968.

page 167 "part of the picture . . .": "'Two Society' Picture Wrong Says Humphrey," *Washington Star*, March 25, 1968.

page 167 "the backwash . . .": "HHH Challenges Report on Riots," *Washington Daily News,* March 25, 1968.

page 167 "This means . . .": Witcover, *85 Days,* 53.

pages 168–70 Vietnam Commission: Sorensen, *Counselor,* 455; Witcover, *85 Days,* 62–64; Frederick G. Dutton, oral history interview by Larry J. Hackman, November 18, 1969, RFKOH/JFKL; Sorensen, interview by Hackman.

page 168 "That was Bob . . .": Dutton, interview by Hackman.

page 169 "a five-minute thing . . .": Sorensen, interview by Hackman.

page 169 "I had no idea . . .": ibid.

page 169 "wide-ranging": Sorensen, *Counselor,* 455.

page 169 "To me . . ." ibid.

page 170 "If it could be . . .": Sorensen, interview by Hackman.

6. NEW HAMPSHIRE

pages 173–75 Nixon in New Hampshire: Nixon, *RN,* 297–99; Perlstein, *Nixonland,* 232–41; Witcover, *The Year the Dream Died,* 66–70.

page 173 "greater than ever": Witcover, *The Year the Dream Died,* 67.

page 173 "I believe . . .": ibid.

page 174 "with an old-timer's ease": Garment, *Crazy Rhythm,* 133.

page 175 "There were different . . .": Leonard Garment, oral history interview by Timothy Naftali, April 6, 2007, RNPL.

page 175 "You can't handshake . . .": as quoted in Perlstein, *Nixonland,* 233.

pages 175–77 Romney in New Hampshire: Chester, Hodgson, and Page, *An American Melodrama,* 100–101; Hoeh, *1968, McCarthy, New Hampshire,* 206–14; Perlstein, *Nixonland,* 235–36; Wainstock, *The Turning Point,* 39–40; Witcover, *The Year the Dream Died,* 14–15, 54–57; John H. Fenton, "Nixon Rules Out Debating Romney, *New York Times,* February 3, 1968; John H. Fenton, "Primary Pot Boils in New Hampshire," *New York Times,* March 3, 1968; Jerry M. Fling, "Romney Terms War in Vietnam His Key Issue in New Hampshire," *New York Times,* February 16, 1968; Roy Reed, "Johnson Advisors Express Worry," *New York Times,* March 15, 1968.

page 175 "I've never had . . .": Perlstein, *Nixonland,* 236.

page 176 "outside of a factory . . .": Hoeh, *1968, McCarthy, New Hampshire,* 209.

page 177 "The great debate . . .": Fenton, "Nixon Rules Out Debating Romney."

page 177 "When all this . . .": Hoeh, *1968, McCarthy, New Hampshire,* 211.

page 177 "NEW HAMPSHIRE IS . . .": ibid., 212.

page 177 "I was disappointed . . .": Nixon, *RN,* 299.

pages 178–81 McCarthy in New Hampshire: Boomhower, *Robert Kennedy and the 1968 Indiana Primary,* 21–25; Eisele, *Almost to the Presidency,* 293–95; R. N. Goodwin, *Remembering America,* 511–14; Herzog, *McCarthy for President,* 4–23, 84–99; Hoeh, *1968, McCarthy, New Hampshire,* 239–488; Larner, *Nobody Knows;* A. McCarthy, *Private Places/Faces,* 319–53; E. J. McCarthy, *Up 'til Now,* 185–86; E. J. McCarthy, *The Year of the People,* 67–75, 78–87; Perlstein, *Nixonland,* 229–32; Stavis, *We Were the Campaign,* 22–30; White, *The Making of the President 1968,* 88–90; Witcover, *The Day the Dream Died,* 99–100; "Johnson Margin Cut to 230

Votes," *New York Times,* March 16, 1968; "Unforeseen Eugene," *Time,* March 22, 1968; Tom Wicker, "Effects of Primary," *New York Times,* March 13, 1968; Tom Wicker, "McCarthy and St. Crispin," *New York Times,* March 14, 1968.

page 178 "was essentially anyone . . .": Stavis, *We Were the Campaign,* 4.

page 179 "students were thought . . .": ibid., 5.

page 179 "That's like choosing . . .": Chester, Hodgson, and Page, *An American Melodrama,* 96.

page 180 "ostentatious": Herzog, *McCarthy for President,* 97.

page 180 "I didn't come . . .": Boomhower, *Robert F. Kennedy and the 1968 Indiana Primary,* 22.

page 181 "With these two . . .": Chester, Hodgson, and Page, *An American Melodrama,* 93.

page 181 "My campaign . . .": Eisele, *Almost to the Presidency,* 295.

page 182 "not at all . . .": Boomhower, *Robert F. Kennedy and the 1968 Indiana Primary,* 22.

page 182 "might have cost . . .": Herzog, *McCarthy for President,* 89.

page 182 "intensive and intemperate": "New Hampshire Primary," *New York Times,* March 13, 1968.

page 183 "a champion of . . .": Eisele, *Almost to the Presidency,* 297.

page 183 "To vote . . .": Boomhower, *Robert F. Kennedy and the 1968 Indiana Primary,* 23.

page 183 "let American . . .": E. J. McCarthy, *Up 'til Now,* 186.

page 183 "a gross misinterpretation . . .": ibid.

page 183 "Think how it . . .": Eisele, *Almost to the Presidency,* 298.

page 183 "euphoric": A. McCarthy, *Private Faces/Public Places,* 351.

page 183 "a welcome signal . . .": R. N. Goodwin, *Remembering America,* 511.

page 184 "every vacant space . . .": ibid.

page 184 "Reporters and political . . .": E. J. McCarthy, *Up 'til Now,* 186.

page 184 "People have remarked . . .": Witcover, *The Year the Dream Died,* 100.

page 185 "Clearly . . .": "Unforeseen Eugene," *Time,* March 22, 1968.

page 185 "McCarthy's big vote . . .": Wainstock, *The Turning Point,* 25.

page 185 "Senator McCarthy . . .": "New Hampshire Primary."

page 185 "The least . . .": Wicker, "McCarthy and St. Crispin."

page 185 "Here is your chance . . .": Warren Weaver Jr., "Johnson and Nixon Given Big New Hampshire Edge," *New York Times,* March 10, 1968.

page 185 "hardly be taken . . .": "New Hampshire Primary."

page 186 "actively reassessing": Schlesinger, *Robert Kennedy and His Times,* 912. In his memoir about Robert Kennedy, Jack Newfield labeled Kennedy's "impulsive airport comment" "a classical blooper that he would never live down, or adequately explain away."

pages 187–88 RFK–McCarthy meeting: Chester, Hodgson, and Page, *An American Melodrama,* 124–25; Eisele, *Almost to the Presidency,* 300–301; E. J. McCarthy, *The Year of the People,* 88–89; Schlesinger, *Robert Kennedy and His Times,* 912–13.

page 187 "I did not ask . . .": E. J. McCarthy, *The Year of the People,* 89.

pages 188–89 RFK–Clark Clifford meeting: Clifford, *Counsel to the President,* 502–5;

Clark Clifford, oral history interview by Paige Mulhollan, July 14, 1969, LBJOH/ LBJL; Theodore C. Sorensen, oral history interview by Larry J. Hackman, March 21, 1969, RFKOH/JFKL; Theodore C. Sorensen, oral history interview by Larry J. Hackman, March 24, 1969, RFKOH/JFKL.

page 188 "Ending the bloodshed . . .": Clifford, *Counsel to the President,* 503.

page 188 "The statement . . .": ibid., 503–4.

page 189 "felt that if . . .": Clifford, interview by Mulhollan.

page 189 "a confrontation . . .": Clifford, *Counsel to the President,* 504.

page 189 "to talk about . . .": Sorensen, interview by Hackman, March 21, 1969.

pages 191–92 Ted Kennedy–Eugene McCarthy meeting: A. McCarthy, *Private Face/ Public Places,* 369–74; E. J. McCarthy, *The Year of the People,* 92–93; Schlesinger, *Robert Kennedy and His Times,* 918–19.

page 191 "the campaign . . .": McCarthy, *The Year of the People,* 92–93.

page 192 "From all the indications . . .": A. McCarthy, *Private Face/Public Places,* 373.

page 192 "I am announcing . . .": "The New Context of '68," *Time,* March 22, 1968.

page 193 "It is important . . .": Tom Wicker, "Kennedy to Make 3 Primary Races; Attacks Johnson," *New York Times,* March 17, 1968.

page 193 "an Irishman . . .": ibid.

page 193 "Very terrible . . .": Black, *Richard M. Nixon,* 518.

page 193 "one problem": Clarke, *The Last Campaign,* 114.

page 194 "rioting blacks . . .": Dallek, *Flawed Giant,* 528.

7. WISCONSIN

pages 195–99 McCarthy in Wisconsin: Boomhower, *Robert F. Kennedy and the 1968 Indiana Primary,* 49–50; Chester, Hodgson, and Page, *An American Melodrama,* 132–37; Eisele, *Almost to the Presidency,* 303–9; Herzog, *McCarthy for President,* 110–24; Larner, *Nobody Knows,* 46–49, 61–64; E. J. McCarthy, *The Year of the People,* 89–105; Perlstein, *Nixonland,* 247–48, 252–53; Stavis, *We Were the Campaign,* 43–50; Witcover, *The Year the Dream Died* 136–38; Patrick Anderson, "They Chant, 'We Want Gene!' (but Don't Forget Bobby)," *New York Times,* March 31, 1968; Paul Hope, "Wisconsin Primary Fails to Clarify Democratic Picture," *Evening Star* (Washington), April 3, 1968; Donald Janson, "M'Carthy to Tour Milwaukee Slum," *New York Times,* March 30, 1968; Saul Pett, "Gene McCarthy: Cool Candidate," *St. Paul Pioneer Press,* April 7, 1968; Steven V. Roberts, "M'Carthy Urges Leaders to Wait," *New York Times,* April 3, 1968; "Excerpts from News Conference Held by McCarthy," *New York Times,* March 17, 1968; "Victorious Gene Eyes RFK Match," *Charlotte Observer,* April 4, 1968; Sy [Seymour] Hersh, oral history interview, September 9, 1969 (no interviewer attributed), McCarthy Historical Project, Oral History Interview Series, University of Minnesota; Jay Sykes, oral history interview (no interviewer or date attributed), McCarthy Historical Project, Oral History Interview Series, University of Minnesota.

page 197 "pointless": Eisele, *Almost to the Presidency,* 307.

page 197 "I couldn't get . . .": ibid.

page 197 "highly technical . . .": Stavis, *We Were the Campaign,* 45.

page 198 "I couldn't say . . .": Eisele, *Almost to the Presidency,* 306.

page 198 "tremendous power fight": Hersh, oral history interview.

page 198 "I was dying . . .": ibid.

page 199 "for all its intelligence . . .": *Time,* "The Inner Circle," March 29, 1968.

page 199 "What had happened": Chester, Hodgson, and Page, *An American Melodrama,* 136.

page 200 "If Rocky reaches . . .": "Rocky's Dilemma," *Time,* February 9, 1968.

page 200 "I am not . . .": "The New Rules of Play," *Time,* March 8, 1968.

page 201 "the New Yorker's . . .": Witcover, *White Knight,* 4.

page 201 "I have decided . . .": Morin, *The Associated Press Story of Election 1968,* 75.

page 202 "tremendously surprised . . .": Witcover, *White Knight,* 7.

page 203 "If it goes . . .": Synon, *George Wallace,* 87.

page 203 "spoiler": Warren Weaver Jr., "Wallace Pictures Himself a 'Spoiler' in the 1968 Campaign," *New York Times,* April 27, 1967.

page 203 "That's exactly . . .": ibid.

page 203 "I believe . . .": Frost, *The Presidential Debate, 1968,* 20.

page 203 "it'll be the *last* . . .": Ray Jenkins, "George Wallace Figures to Win Even If He Loses," *New York Times,* April 7, 1968.

page 204 "isolationist state": Jay Sykes, oral history interview, June 25, 1969, for the McCarthy Historical Project (no interviewer attributed). All Sykes citations from this segment come from this source.

page 207 "We have months . . .": Paul Hope, "Wisconsin Primary Fails to Clarify Democratic Picture," *Washington Star,* April 3, 1968.

page 207 "We have demonstrated . . .": Steven V. Roberts, "M'Carthy Urges Leaders to Wait," *New York Times,* April 3, 1968.

page 207 "I think that . . .": "Victorious Gene Eyes RFK Match," *Charlotte Observer,* April 4, 1968.

page 207 "If you're in politics . . .": Pett, "Gene McCarthy."

page 208 "a major transfer . . .": Johnson, *The Vantage Point,* 494.

page 208 "I don't know . . .": Miller, *Lyndon,* 630.

8. TORRENTS OF RAGE AND SORROW

pages 209–11 Martin Luther King Jr. assassination: Clarke, *The Last Campaign,* 91–96; R. N. Goodwin, *Remembering America* 505–6; Isserman and Kazin, *America Divided,* 225–28; C. Kaiser, *1968 in America,* 143–49; Nixon, *RN,* 301; Perlstein, *Nixonland,* 254–63; Schlesinger, *Robert Kennedy and His Times,* 88–90, 938–40; Stein and Plimpton, *American Journey,* 252–61; White, *The Making of the President 1968,* 206–10; Witcover, *The Year the Dream Died,* 151–53, 155–61.

page 210 "Maybe we just . . .": White, *The Making of the President 1968,* 143–44.

page 210 "I don't know . . .": Martin Luther King Jr., speech: "I've Been to the Mountaintop," delivered at the Bishop Charles Mason Temple in Memphis, Tennessee on April 3, 1968.

page 212 "spiritual leader": Schlesinger, *Robert Kennedy and His Times,* 88.

page 212 "I went out . . .": Walter Sheridan, oral history interview by Roberta Greene, August 5, 1969, RFKOH/JFKL.

page 212 "Oh, God . . .": Schlesinger, *Robert Kennedy and His Times,* 88.

page 213 "I have some . . .": Robert F. Kennedy, untitled speech, Indianapolis, on the occasion of Martin Luther King's death. The text of this speech has been published in numerous sources, and a video of RFK delivering the address can be found on a number of online video sites, including YouTube.

page 213 "Martin Luther King . . .": ibid.

page 214 "It was an amazing . . .": Lewis, *Walking with the Wind*, 407.

page 214 "Bob gave . . .": Stein and Plimpton, *American Journey*, 255–56.

page 215 "There was some . . .": ibid., 256.

page 216 "Martin Luther King's . . .": Newfield, *Robert Kennedy*, 250.

page 216 "We can achieve . . .": Perlstein, *Nixonland*, 255–56.

page 217 "If you don't have . . .": C. Kaiser, *1968 in America*, 145.

page 218 "crouched over . . .": "8 Held in the Wake of Panther Shootout," *Oakland Tribune*, April 8, 1968.

pages 217–18 Eldridge Cleaver's account of the shootout: Cleaver's first admission that he was guilty of instigating the shootout with the Oakland police can be found in Kate Coleman's article "Souled Out" in *New West*, May 19, 1980. He went into greater detail in a PBS *Frontline* interview with Henry Louis Gates Jr.: "This shootout that we had took place on the sixth and the seventh of April. So we saw it coming while the police were acting so we decided to get down first. So we started the fight. There were 14 of us. We went down into the area of Oakland where the violence was the worst. . . . We were well armed, and we had a shootout that lasted an hour and a half."

page 219 "I said to him . . .": Cohen and Taylor, *American Pharaoh*, 455.

page 219 "when we began . . .": C. Kaiser, *1968 in America*, 257.

page 219 "mindless menace . . .": Witcover, *85 Days*, 142.

page 220 "If you get . . .": C. Kaiser, *1968 in America*, 147.

page 220 "No coffin . . .": Witcover, *The Year the Dream Died*, 160.

9. INDIANA

page 221 "I do not believe . . .": Tom Wicker, "Kennedy among the Hoosiers," *New York Times*, April 18, 1968.

page 221 "A large majority . . .": Warren Weaver Jr., "Branigin's Appeal in Indiana Is Strong on Surface," *New York Times*, April 22, 1968.

page 221 "a selfish . . .": Boomhower, *Robert Kennedy and the 1968 Indiana Primary*, 34.

page 222 "I believe . . .": Weaver, "Branigin's Appeal in Indiana Is Strong on Surface."

page 222 "trying to put words . . .": Chester, Hodgson, and Page, *An American Melodrama*, 167.

page 222 "The *Indianapolis Star* . . .": Lawrence O'Brien, oral history interview by Michael L. Gillette, June 19, 1987. LBJOH.

page 223 "enjoyed the McCarthy . . .": R. N. Goodwin, *Remembering America*, 527.

page 223 "McCarthy would be . . .": ibid.

page 223 "I can't say . . .": O'Brien, *No Final Victories*, 237–38.

pages 222–27 Kennedy in Indiana: Boomhower, *Robert F. Kennedy and the 1968 Indiana Primary*. This book is an essential source to any study of the 1968 Indiana primary. See also Chester, Hodgson, and Page, *An American Melodrama*, 162–66; Clarke, *The Last Campaign*, 80–83, 185–89; R. N. Goodwin, *Remembering America*, 526–32; Newfield, *Robert Kennedy*, 252–65; O'Brien, *No Final Victories*, 237–39; Schlesinger, *Robert Kennedy and His Times*, 947–49; Tye, *Bobby Kennedy*, 410–24; White, *The Making of the President 1968*, 170–72; Witcover, *85 Days*, 146–82; "'It is Much Better to Win,'" *Newsweek*, May 19, 1968; John Herbers, "Kennedy Outspends Rivals as Staff and Students Step Up the Drive for Crucial Indiana Vote May 7," *New York Times*, April 26, 1968; Hal Higdon, "Indiana: A Test for Bobby Kennedy," *New York Times Magazine*, May 5, 1968; Donald Janson, "Campaign Starts in Indiana Today," *New York Times*, April 3, 1968; Godfrey Sperling Jr., "Kennedy Gains among Democrats," *Christian Science Monitor*, April 6, 1968; Warren Weaver Jr., "Kennedy: Meet the Conservative," *New York Times*, April 28, 1968; Wicker, "Kennedy among the Hoosiers"; Tom Wicker, "Kennedy's 'Jigsaw' Victory," *New York Times*, May 9, 1968; Tom Wicker, "Three Campaigners," *New York Times*, April 21, 1968; Gerald F. Doherty, oral history interview by Larry J. Hackman, February 3, 1972, RFKOH/JFKL; John W. Douglas, oral history interview by Larry J. Hackman, June 24, 1969, RFKOH.JFKL; Frederick G. Dutton, oral history interview by Larry J. Hackman, November 18, 1969, RFKOH/JFKL; O'Brien, interview by Gillette; Walter Sheridan, oral history interview by Roberta Greene, August 5, 1969, RFKOH/JFKL.

page 225 "I was the nation's . . .": Weaver, "Kennedy: Meet the Conservative."

page 226 "the welfare system, the handout system . . .": ibid.

page 226 "The welfare system in . . .": Higdon, "Indiana."

page 226 "making noises . . .": Weaver, "Kennedy: Meet the Conservative."

page 226 "It was a matter . . .": Schlesinger, *Robert Kennedy and His Times*, 946.

page 226 "the most explicit . . .": ibid.

page 227 "It's our own . . .": "Tarot Cards, Hoosier Style," *Time*, May 17, 1968.

page 227 "Some men . . .": Boomhower, *Robert Kennedy and the 1968 Indiana Primary*, 79.

pages 227–31 McCarthy in Indiana: Boomhower, *Robert Kennedy and the 1968 Indiana Primary*, 9–10; Herzog, *McCarthy for President*, 127–31, 139–42; C. Kaiser, *1968 in America*, 173–76; Larner, *Nobody Knows*, 66–68, 75–76; A. McCarthy, *Private Faces/Public Places*, 402–4; E. J. McCarthy, *The Year of the People*, 127–38; E. J. McCarthy, *Up 'Til Now*, 192–96; Witcover, *The Year the Dream Died*, 200–203; "Explaining McCarthy," *Time*, April 18, 1969; E. W. Kenworthy, "Kennedy and McCarthy Square Off," *New York Times*, May 5, 1968; E. W. Kenworthy, "M'Carthy Calls Indiana Crucial," *New York Times*, May 3, 1968; E. W. Kenworthy, "M'Carthy Themes Given New Stress," *New York Times*, May 5, 1968; E. W. Kenworthy, "McCarthy Looking Ahead, Says He Won't 'Dismiss the Troops,'" *New York Times*, May 8, 1968; James Reston, "The Peace Talks and the Presidential Elections," *New York Times*, April 19, 1968; Tom Wicker, "McCarthy after Wisconsin," *New York Times*, April 4, 1968; Tom Wicker, "The Impact of Indiana," *New York Times*, May 8, 1968.

page 228 "For all its style . . .": Herzog, *McCarthy for President*, 139.

page 229 "a fear of . . .": "Explaining McCarthy," *Time*, April 18, 1969.

page 229 "perpetual identity . . .": Larner, *Nobody Knows*, 68.

page 230 "The experience . . .": McCarthy, *Up 'Til Now,* 195.

page 230 "We started auctioning . . .": C. Kaiser, *1968 in America,* 175.

page 230 "It was somewhat . . .": ibid.

page 231 "The dangers are . . .": Reston, "The Peace Talks and the Presidential Elections."

page 231 "I hesitate . . .": Kenworthy, "M'Carthy Calls Indiana Crucial."

page 231 "popularity contest": McCarthy, *The Year of the People,* 113.

page 231 "If I win . . .": Kenworthy, "M'Carthy Calls Indiana Crucial."

pages 232–37 Columbia takeover: Caute, *The Year of the Barricades,* 165–80; Gitlin, *The Sixties,* 306–9; Hayden, *Reunion,* 172–83; Isserman and Kazin, *America Divided,* 228–30; C. Kaiser, *1968 in America,* 155–66; Kurlansky, *1968,* 192–208; Witcover, *The Year the Dream Died,* 186–91; "Mutiny at a Great University," *Life,* May 10, 1968; "Spring '68," *Columbia College Today,* May-June 2008; Richard Goldstein, "The Groovy Revolution: Fold, Spindle, Mutilate," *Village Voice,* May 2, 1968; Marvin Harris, "Big Bust on Morningside Heights," *Nation,* June 10, 1868; Robert D. McFadden, "Remembering Columbia, 1968," *New York Times,* April 25, 2008.

page 233 "Our young people . . .": Caute, *The Year of the Barricades,* 165.

page 233 "fired up . . .": Kurlansky, *1968,* 193.

page 233 "action faction": Hayden, *Reunion,* 273.

page 233 "We will take . . .": Kurlansky, *1968,* 193.

page 233 "There is only one . . .": Caute, *The Year of the Barricades,* 166.

page 235 "We were still . . .": Kurlansky, *1968,* 200.

page 236 "I had never . . .": Hayden, *Reunion,* 274.

page 237 "In the end . . .": "Mutiny at a Great University," *Life,* May 10, 1968.

page 237 "national tragedy . . .": Buchanan, *The Greatest Comeback,* 255.

page 237 "the first major . . .": ibid.

page 237 "We want Bobby! . . .": Schlesinger, *Robert Kennedy and His Times,* 948. All citations from this speech, except where indicated otherwise, are from this source.

page 238 "Let me say . . .": "Kennedy Crosses Words with Student Audience," *Toledo Blade,* April 27, 1968.

page 239 "I want you . . .": R. N. Goodwin, *Remembering America,* 531.

page 239 "Well, it can't . . .": ibid.

pages 239–44 HHH announces candidacy: Chester, Hodgson, and Page, *An American Melodrama,* 142–53; Eisele, *Almost to the Presidency,* 327–30; "Humphrey Declares Candidacy," *Washington Post,* April 28, 1968; "Humphrey Enters the Race," *Washington Star,* April 28, 1968; "Mr. Humphrey Marches to Battle, Pledges Fighting, Unifying Campaign," *National Observer,* April 29, 1968; Robert L. Asher, "Humphrey's Entry Gives District Slate a Candidate," *Washington Post,* April 28, 1968; Jack Bell, "HHH Entering Race under Unity Flag," *New Orleans Times-Picayune,* April 28, 1968; Paul Hope, "Humphrey Launches Candidacy," *Washington Evening Star,* April 27, 1968; James Reston, "Humphrey as a Symbol of Change," *New York Times,* April 28, 1968.

pages 240–41 Humphrey staff issues: While putting together a list of tentative staffers for his campaign, HHH considered Orville Freeman, the secretary of agriculture, a fellow Minnesotan, and longtime friend, for the position of campaign manager. Freeman, however, had reservations about the position, which would require his resigning from the cabinet. When running for office, one of Humphrey's biggest weaknesses was his inability to assemble a strong staff. Freeman noted as much in an April 16, 1968, diary entry, written when Freeman heard rumors of Humphrey's intentions but before he had spoken to Humphrey: "I expect if he asks there's nothing I can do but go ahead, but I want some clearly understood conditions. The Humphrey operation is always a disorganized mess and I want some conditions by way of consultation, planning and policy establishment as well as a clear understanding of my responsibility and authority."

page 240 "*Time* magazine . . .": Fred Harris, oral history interview by Julie Ferdon, May 9, 2000, Morris K. Udall Oral History Project, University of Arizona Library, Special Collections.

page 241 "He had great . . .": Mondale, *The Good Fight,* 75.

page 242 "the ideal outcome . . .": David Broder, "Humphrey Success Tied to Foes' fight," *Washington Post,* April 28, 1968.

page 242 "unmatched in . . .": Ward Just, "Stresses Unity and Peace," *Washington Post,* April 28, 1968.

page 242 "Here we are . . .": Hubert H. Humphrey speech, April 27, 1968. A typescript of the rough draft of the speech, along with the finished version, is available at the Minnesota Historical Society. All other citations from this speech are from this source.

page 242 "You bet . . .": Roy Reed, "Humphrey Is Stung by Attacks on His 'Politics of Happiness,'" *New York Times,* May 25, 1968.

page 243 "an unfortunate statement": Humphrey, *The Education of a Public Man,* 276.

page 244 "safe": Mary McGrory, "An Old Radical Runs as 'Safe' Candidate," *Washington Star,* April 28, 1968.

page 244 "By saying . . .": "Humphrey Takes Responsible Course," *Fort Worth Star-Telegram,* April 30, 1968.

page 244 "I wouldn't think . . .": Carroll Kilpatrick, "Johnson's Politics Ban for Officials Spelled Out," *Washington Post,* April 30, 1968.

page 245 "We've tested . . .": Kenworthy, "McCarthy, Looking Ahead."

page 245 "Senator McCarthy . . .": "It Is Much Better to Win," *Newsweek,* May 19, 1968.

page 246 "bowled over": Witcover, *The Year the Dream Died,* 203.

10. NEBRASKA

page 248 "The dramatic . . .": Witcover, *The Resurrection of Richard Nixon,* 291.

pages 248–49 Lurleen Wallace: Carter, *The Politics of Rage,* 317–20; Lesher, *George Wallace,* 382–84.

page 249 "I feel . . .": Lesher, *George Wallace,* 384.

pages 249–51 McCarthy in Nebraska: Herzog, *McCarthy for President,* 142–43; E. J. McCarthy, *The Year of the People,* 139–44.

page 250 "Although I hoped . . .": E. J. McCarthy, *The Year of the People,* 139.

page 250 "poisoning the well . . .": Witcover, *85 Days,* 185.

page 250 "of a growing bitterness . . .": ibid.

page 250 "These workers . . .": Stavis, *We Were the Campaign,* 85.

page 250 "Nebraska was Indiana . . .": Herzog, *McCarthy for President,* 142.

page 251 "the next best . . .": McCarthy, *The Year of the People,* 142.

page 251 "tired, dispirited . . .": E. W. Kenworthy, "McCarthy Revives Sagging Spirits, and Aides Now Expect a Strong Showing in California," *New York Times,* May 13, 1968.

page 251 "His speeches . . .": Kenworthy, "McCarthy Revives Sagging Spirits."

pages 251–54 Kennedy in Nebraska: Tye, *Bobby Kennedy,* 424–35; Witcover, *85 Days,* 183–99; Witcover, *The Year the Dream Died,* 205–10; "Kennedy Spending High in Nebraska," *New York Times,* April 21, 1968; Tom Wicker, "Poll-Watching in Both Parties," *New York Times,* May 14, 1968; Richard Witkin, "Nebraska's Wide Open Spaces Pose Campaign Problems for the Democratic Presidential Candidates," *New York Times,* May 12, 1968; Peter B. Edelman, oral history interview by Larry Hackman, August 5, 1969, RFKOH/JFKL.

page 253 "With a huge . . .": Edelman, interview by Hackman.

page 253 "the plain . . .": John H. Glenn Jr., oral history interview by Roberta Greene, June 30, 1968, RFKOH/JFKL.

page 253 "one way . . .": Witcover, *85 Days,* 193.

page 253 "Look around you . . .": ibid., 194.

page 254 "significant victory": Warren Weaver Jr., "Nebraska Gives 53% to Kennedy," *New York Times,* May 15, 1968.

page 254 "I don't know . . .": ibid.

page 255 "If this home-spun . . .": Wicker, "Poll-Watching in Both Parties."

page 255 "a credible candidate": Eisele, *Almost to the Presidency,* 314.

page 255 "the McCarthy campaign . . .": Herzog, *McCarthy for President,* 143.

11. OREGON

pages 256–58 Kennedy in Oregon: Clarke, *The Last Campaign,* 227–30; R. N. Goodwin, *Remembering America,* 532–33; Heymann, *RFK,* 481–83; Newfield, *Robert Kennedy,* 270, 272, 274–75; Schlesinger, *Robert Kennedy and His Times* 973–74; Thomas, *Robert Kennedy,* 377–82; Tye, *Bobby Kennedy,* 427–29; Witcover, *85 Days,* 200–225; "R.F.K.: What This Country Is For," *Time,* May 24, 1968; Warren Weaver Jr., "Kennedy: A Crucial Test in Oregon," *New York Times,* May 26, 1968; Warren Weaver Jr., "Kennedy and McCarthy: Two More Rounds to Go," *New York Times,* May 19, 1968; Warren Weaver Jr. "Stiffest Test for Kennedy Is Due in Oregon Tuesday," *New York Times,* May 26, 1968; Peter B. Edelman, oral history interview by Larry Hackman, August 5, 1969, RFKOH/JFKL; Edith Green, oral history interview by Roberta W. Greene, February 27, 1974, RFKOH/JFKL; Lawrence F. O'Brien, oral history interviews by Michael L. Gillette, June 19, 1987, July 21, 1987, LBJOH; Pierre Salinger, oral history interview by Larry Hackman, April 18, 1970, RFKOH/JFKL.

page 256 "If I get beaten . . .": "In the New Politics," *Time,* June 7, 1968.

page 257 "It was understood . . .": Green, interview by Greene.

page 258 "The first twenty-four . . .": Pierre Salinger, interview by Hackman.

page 258 "Let's face it . . .": Clarke, *The Last Campaign,* 228.

page 258 "I'm just absolutely . . .": Green, interview by Greene.

pages 259–62 McCarthy in Oregon: Chester, Hodgson, and Page, *An American Melo-drama,* 297–300; Eisele, *Almost to the Presidency,* 317–19; Herzog, *McCarthy for President,* 144–72; Larner, *Nobody Knows,* 91–103; E. J. McCarthy, *The Year of the People,* 145–51; Stavis, *We Were the Campaign,* 95–118; E. W. Kenworthy, "An Undaunted McCarthy Looks to Oregon and California Races," *New York Times,* May 16, 1968; E. W. Kenworthy, "McCarthy Asserts Neutrality on Rivals," *New York Times,* May 22, 1968; E. W. Kenworthy, "M'Carthy Gibes at Both Rivals," *New York Times,* May 23, 1968; E. W. Kenworthy, "M'Carthy Hails Staff in Oregon," *New York Times,* May 26, 1968; E. W. Kenworthy, "M'Carthy Urges a Wiretap Guide," *New York Times,* May 28, 1968; Tom Wicker, "McCarthy after Oregon," *New York Times,* May 30, 1968.

page 259 "It's all up . . .": Chester, Hodgson, and Page, *An American Melodrama,* 299.

page 260 "It became clear . . .": Allard K. Lowenstein, oral history interview, no interviewer or date provided, McCarthy Historical Project, Oral History Interview Series, University of Minnesota.

page 261 "no preference . . .": Eisele, *Almost to the Presidency,* 317.

page 261 "It was a . . .": Larner, *Nobody Knows,* 92.

page 262 "disastrous adventures": Kenworthy, "M'Carthy Gibes at Both Rivals."

page 262 "These policies . . .": "Democrats Getting Tough," *Time,* May 31, 1968.

pages 262–64 Nixon in Oregon: Ambrose, *Nixon* 153–56; Buchanan, *The Greatest Comeback,* 256–61; Safire, *Before the Fall,* 49–51; Wicker, *One of Us,* 328–30; Witcover, *The Resurrection of Richard Nixon,* 295–308; Tom Wicker, "On the Stump in Oregon," *New York Times,* May 26, 1968; Tom Wicker, "The Long-Distance Runner," *New York Times,* May 28, 1968.

page 263 "new majority": Richard Nixon speech, "A New Alignment for American Unity," as quoted in Ambrose, *Nixon,* 154–55. All other citations from this speech are from this source.

page 264 "This was hardly . . .": Safire, *Before the Fall,* 50.

page 264 "bad reaction": Drew Pearson and Jack Anderson, "Bobby Kennedy and Wiretap Controversy," *San Francisco Chronicle,* May 24, 1968.

page 264 "very important . . .": ibid.

page 264 "Drew got it . . .": Thomas, *Robert Kennedy,* 379.

page 265 "electronic eavesdropping": ibid. Thomas's account is the most detailed report of the Kennedy wiretap and the Pearson column. Thomas determined, through interviews with black leaders, that Kennedy's actions, while disappointing, were not regarded too seriously. "Politics is politics," was Reverend Ralph Abernathy's response to the news. The report might have been true, but it didn't wash away all the positive actions Kennedy had taken on the behalf of African Americans.

page 265 "Senator Kennedy . . .": Kenworthy, "M'Carthy Urges a Wiretap Guide."

page 265 "Everybody knows . . .": ibid.

page 265 "I used to be . . .": Thomas, *Robert Kennedy,* 380.

page 265 "We didn't publish . . .": "Publisher Denies Gag Put on Anti-HHH Book," *Washington Post,* April 25, 1968.

page 266 "Humphrey is a very . . .": Sherrill and Ernst, *The Drugstore Liberal,* back cover copy.

page 267 "Each of them . . .": E. W. Kenworthy, "McCarthy and Kennedy within 15 Yards of Meeting in Oregon," *New York Times,* May 27, 1968.

page 267 "He just had . . .": Edelman, interview by Hackman.

page 268 "This is a serious . . .": O'Brien, interview by Gillette, June 19, 1987.

page 268 "Those fellows need . . .": ibid.

page 268 "somewhat troubling": ibid.

page 268 "I was really . . .": Edelman, interview by Hackman.

page 268 "He didn't feel . . .": Milton Gwirtzman, oral history interview by Roberta W. Greene, April 28, 1972, RFKOH/JFKL.

page 269 "small but significant . . .": ibid.

page 269 "unlike so many . . .": RFK speech, as reported in Witcover, *The Year the Dream Died,* 223. All other citations from this speech are from this source.

page 269 "Sometimes I wish . . .": "In the New Politics," *Time.*

page 270 "My chances . . .": *New York Times,* May 29, 1966.

page 270 "must be America's . . .": Buchanan, *The Greatest Comeback,* 261.

page 271 "That about summed . . .": O'Brien, *No Final Victories,* 242.

page 272 "There were two . . .": O'Brien, oral history interview by Gillette, July 21, 1987.

page 272 "take some satisfaction . . .": Witcover, *85 Days,* 222.

page 272 "Every wagon train . . .": ibid.

page 273 "Our campaign . . .": ibid.

page 273 "the most radical . . .": Wicker, "McCarthy after Oregon."

12. CALIFORNIA

page 274 "I am not . . .": "In the New Politics," *Time,* June 7, 1968.

page 274 "Once defeated . . .": Newfield, *Robert Kennedy,* 272.

page 274 "Oregon was . . .": Walter Sheridan, oral history interview by Roberta W. Greene, August 13, 1969, RFKOH/JFKL.

pages 274–77 Kennedy in California: Clarke, *The Last Campaign,* 260–64; R. N. Goodwin, *Remembering America,* 533–38; Heymann, *RFK,* 483–96; Newfield, *Robert Kennedy,* 272–88; Schlesinger, *Robert Kennedy and His Times,* 977–79; Stein and Plimpton, *American Journey,* 298–309; Thomas, *Robert Kennedy,* 384–90; Tye, *Bobby Kennedy,* 429–36; Witcover, *85 Days,* 226–64; Witcover, *The Year the Dream Died*; Lawrence E. Davies, "Candidates End California Drive; Primary Is Today," *New York Times,* June 4, 1968; Lawrence E. Davies, "Coast Tally Slow," *New York Times,* June 5, 1968; Tom Wicker, "Bobby in the Ghetto," *New York Times,* June 2, 1968; Tom Wicker, "The Trouble with Kennedy," *New York Times,* June 4, 1968; Fred G. Dutton, oral history interview by Larry Hackman, November 18, 1969, RFKOH/JFKL; Peter B. Edelman, oral history interview by Larry Hackman, August 5, 1969, RFKOH/JFKL; Milton S. Gwirtzman, oral history interview by Roberta W. Greene, April 2, 1972, RFKOH/JFKL; Frank Mankiewicz, oral history interview by Larry J. Hackman, December 16, 1969, RFKOH/JFKL; John E. Nolan, oral history interview by Roberta W. Greene, April 12, 1970, RFKOH/JFKL; Walter Sheridan, oral history interview.

page 275 "If I died . . .": Witcover, *The Year the Dream Died,* 235.

page 276 "a lot of hostility . . .": Schlesinger, *Robert Kennedy and His Times,* 975–76.

page 277 "What the goddamned hell . . .": ibid., 976.

page 277 "utmost respect": Stein and Plimpton, *American Journey,* 307.

page 277 "We thought . . .": ibid.

pages 277–80 McCarthy in California: Herzog, *McCarthy for President,* 173–89; Larner, *Nobody Knows,* 102–10, 118–23; E. J. McCarthy, *The Year of the People,* 52–173; Stavis, *We Were the Campaign,* 118–31; E. W. Kenworthy, "Assails Kennedy Slum Plan," *New York Times,* May 29, 1968; E. W. Kenworthy, "M'Carthy Backs Black Power Bid," *New York Times,* May 21, 1968; E. W. Kenworthy, "M'Carthy Invites Votes from Rival," *New York Times,* May 12, 1968; E. W. Kenworthy, "McCarthy Asks Californians to Help Cut Humphrey Lead," *New York Times,* May 30, 1968; E. W. Kenworthy, "McCarthy Calls Rivals Ill-Equipped to Avoid Future Vietnams," *New York Times,* May 24, 1968.

page 278 "I think . . .": Kenworthy, "M'Carthy Leads in Poll," *New York Times,* May 11, 1968.

page 278 "I'm of the opinion . . .": as quoted in Eisele, *Almost to the Presidency,* 309.

page 278 "Only in California . . .": Herzog, *McCarthy for President,* 176.

page 278 "It was a . . .": ibid.

page 279 "rather small . . .": Kenworthy, "M'Carthy Backs Black Power Bid."

page 279 "The question . . .": ibid.

page 279 "He was light," Larner, *Nobody Knows,* 104.

page 279 "McCarthy was smarter . . .": Sheridan, interview by Greene.

pages 280–85 Kennedy–McCarthy debate: Chester, Hodgson, and Page, *An American Melodrama,* 337–49; Eisele, *Almost to the Presidency,* 319–20; Larner, *Nobody Knows,* 110–17; Newfield, *Robert Kennedy,* 276–78; Schlesinger, *Robert Kennedy,* 977–79; Stein and Plimpton, *American Journey,* 310–14; Wainstock, *The Turning Point,* 80–84; R. W. Apple Jr., "Kennedy Disputes M'Carthy on War in TV Discussion," *New York Times,* June 2, 1968; E. W. Kenworthy, "M'Carthy Calls Debate Standoff," *New York Times,* June 3, 1968; Tom Wicker, "California Vote to Test Impact of Video Debate," *New York Times,* June 3, 1968; Edelman, interview by Hackman.

page 280 "in excellent form . . .": Schlesinger, *Robert Kennedy and His Times,* 977.

page 281 "was more like . . .": Weinstock, *The Turning Point,* 82.

page 281 "If, in fact . . .": Apple, "Kennedy Disputes M'Carthy on War in TV Discussion."

page 282 "You say . . .": Clarke, *Last Campaign,* 258.

page 283 "The ghetto may . . .": Kenworthy, "Assails Kennedy Slum Plan."

page 283 "Senator McCarthy . . .": as quoted in Newfield, *Robert Kennedy,* 277–78.

page 284 "neither candidate . . .": Wainstock, *The Turning Point,* 84.

page 284 "He flubbed it!" Eisele, *Almost to the Presidency,* 326.

page 285 "kind of a . . .": Apple, "Kennedy Disputes M'Carthy on War in TV Discussion."

page 285 "I thought . . .": Edelman, interview by Hackman.

page 286 "in a state . . .": Newfield, *Robert Kennedy,* 286.

page 287 "Kennedy ran strongly . . .": Donald Janson, "Kennedy Triumphs in Dakota Primary," *New York Times,* June 5, 1968.

page 287 "remarkable": Heymann, *RFK,* 489.

page 287 "I'm going to chase . . .": Newfield, *Robert Kennedy,* 20.

page 287 "Even if McCarthy . . .": R. N. Goodwin, *Remembering America,* 537.

page 288 "liberated": Newfield, *Robert Kennedy,* 293.

page 288 "It appears, though . . .": Robert Kennedy, interview by Roger Mudd, June 4, 1968, CBS Television. A transcript of this interview has been reprinted extensively, and online videos of the interview are available.

page 290 "My determination . . .": Moldea, *The Killing of Robert F. Kennedy,* photo section, not paginated. A similar reproduction from Sirhan's notebook can be found in R. B. Kaiser, *"R.F.K. Must Die!,"* 383.

page 291 "I hope . . .": RFK victory speech, June 4, 1968, Los Angeles. The text of this speech can be found in numerous sources, and the video of the speech can be found online, including YouTube.

pages 292–93 RFK assassination: Clarke, *The Last Campaign,* 271–75; Heymann, *RFK,* 496–509; R. B. Kaiser, *"R.F.K. Must Die!,"* 1–32; Moldea, *The Killing of Robert F. Kennedy,* 23–73; Stein and Plimpton, *American Journey,* 335–39; Thomas, *Robert Kennedy,* 390–93; Witcover, *85 Days,* 265–91; "Everything Was Not Enough," *Time,* June 14, 1968.

page 293 "If anyone wants . . .": "A Life on the Way to Death," *Time,* June 14, 1968.

page 293 Struggle with Sirhan Sirhan: While those around Robert Kennedy struggled with the gunman, Mutual Radio broadcaster Andrew West described the bedlam in chilling detail and immediacy, his account becoming instant history. "I am right here," he said in a tense half shout, "and Rafer Johnson has hold of the man who apparently has fired the shot! He has fired the shot. . . . He still has the gun! The gun is pointed at me right at this moment! I hope they can get the gun out of his hand. Be very careful. Get the gun . . . get the gun . . . get the gun . . . stay away from the gun . . . his hand is frozen . . . get his thumb! Get his thumb . . . get his thumb . . . get his thumb . . . get his thumb. . . . Take hold of his thumb . . . and break it if you have to . . . get his thumb. Get away from the barrel! Get away from the barrel, man! Look out for the gun! Okay, all right. That's it, Rafer, get it! Get the gun, Rafer! Okay, now hold on to the gun. Hold on to him. Hold on to him. Ladies and gentlemen, they have the gun away from the man."

page 293 "Gently, gently . . .": Witcover, *85 Days,* 273.

page 293 "Don't lift me . . .": ibid.

page 294 "Maybe . . .": Herzog, *McCarthy for President,* 190.

page 295 "If he wins . . .": Eisele, *Almost to the Presidency,* 331.

page 295 "Mr. Vice President . . .": D. Cohen, *Undefeated,* 310.

page 296 "I am . . .": Humphrey, *The Education of a Public Man,* 278.

page 296 "It's the manly . . .": ibid., 279.

page 296 "Brown emphasized . . .": Berman, *Hubert,* 175.

page 296 "General . . .": D. Cohen, *Undefeated,* 311.

page 297 "extremely critical": "Everything Was Not Enough," *Time,* June 14, 1968.

page 297 "stabilized pretty well": ibid.

page 298 "It appears . . .": R. B. Kaiser, *"R.F.K. Must Die!,"* 60.

page 298 "The mayor . . .": ibid.

page 298 "The team of physicians . . .": quoted in Witcover, *85 Days,* 289.

page 299 "Senator Robert . . .": Gladwin Hill, "Kennedy Is Dead; Victim of Assassin," *New York Times,* June 6, 1968.

page 300 "People in Harlem . . .": Richard Reeves, "Campaign Comes to a Halt in Wake of Shooting," *New York Times,* June 6, 1968.

page 300 "I hope . . .": ibid.

page 300 "It is not enough . . .": Roy Reed, "Candidates Halt Drives; Voice Shock and Sympathy," *New York Times,* June 6, 1968.

page 300 "My brother . . .": J. Anthony Lukas, "Thousands in Last Tribute to Kennedy; Service at Arlington Is Held at Night," *New York Times,* July 9, 1968.

13. SUMMER DOLDRUMS

page 302 "I think . . .": Hubert H. Humphrey, oral history interview by Larry J. Hackman, March 30, 1970, RFKOH/JFKL.

page 302 "The bullet that killed . . .": Solberg, *Hubert Humphrey,* 339.

page 302 "Everything in politics . . .": Humphrey, interview by Hackman.

page 303 "It's not going . . .": Eisele, *Almost to the Presidency,* 321.

page 303 "In the days . . .": A. McCarthy, *Private Faces/Public Places,* 407.

page 303 "What kind of nation . . .": Tom Wicker, "American Tragedy: The Terrible Toll of Violence," *New York Times,* June 9, 1968.

page 303 "Is it, finally . . .": ibid.

pages 304–5 New York primary: Chester, Hodgson, and Page, *An American Melodrama,* 405–9; Larner, *Nobody Knows,* 133–35; Stavis, *We Were the Campaign,* 132–49.

page 305 "responsible delegates": Larner, *Nobody Knows,* 131.

page 305 "I just ask . . .": ibid.

page 305 "a limited campaign": ibid., 130.

page 306 "a man of unlimited . . .": Walter Pincus, "H. H. Humphrey's 3 Horses," *Washington Post,* July 14, 1968.

page 306 "One does not . . .": Laurence Stern, "HHH Sees Himself a 'Man of Change,'" *Washington Post,* June 21, 1968.

page 306 "Humphrey as . . .": Mary McGrory, "Humphrey Looks to Election," *Washington Evening Star,* June 23, 1968.

page 306 "This relationship . . .": ibid.

page 306 "There have been . . .": Stern, "HHH Sees Himself a 'Man of Change.'"

page 306 "The great hope . . .": Mary McGrory, "Humphrey Runs Scared," *Washington Evening Star,* June 30, 1968.

page 307 "an enthusiasm gap": "Humphrey Reviews Lagging Campaign," *Christian Science Monitor,* July 8, 1968.

page 308 "He may have to . . .": ibid.

page 308 "a grippy condition": Edgar Berman, diary entry, July 8, 1968, Edgar Berman papers, MHS.

page 308 "a fresh symbol . . .": William F. Buckley Jr., "Politics of Joy, Moscow Included," *Washington Evening Star,* July 19, 1968.

page 308 "both are out . . .": Patrick Anderson, "Fancy-Stepping Pragmatist," *New York Times Book Review,* July 21, 1968.

page 309 "Lyndon Johnson's boy": Frederick Taylor, "Humphrey's Burden: Vice President Tries, but Can't Shake Image as the President's Boy," *Wall Street Journal,* July 31, 1968.

page 309 "We got rid . . .": Robert B. Semple Jr., "Nixon's the Happy One," *New York Times,* June 2, 1968.

page 310 "a contest . . .": ibid.

page 310 "I do not . . .": R. W. Apple Jr., "Rockefeller Links His Goals to Those of Kennedy," *New York Times,* June 12, 1968.

page 310 "a man who cared": ibid.

page 311 "The only chance . . .": "Rockefeller Urged by Laird to Give Up," *New York Times,* June 5, 1968.

page 311 "indicat[ing] that . . .": as quoted in Buchanan, *The Greatest Comeback,* 267.

page 311 "because that's the reason . . .": ibid.

page 312 "a jail sentence . . .": ibid.

page 313 "The only Wallace . . .": Lesher, *George Wallace,* 432.

page 314 "His handlers . . .": Carter, *The Politics of Rage,* 335.

page 315 *Meet the Press: Meet the Press,* aired June 30, 1968, on NBC. This program is available in its entirety on YouTube.

page 315 "A racist . . .": Synon, *George Wallace,* 58.

page 316 "They're frightened . . .": Woods, *LBJ,* 856.

page 316 "were pushing . . .": Halberstam, *The Best and the Brightest,* 659.

page 316 "The goal . . .": Miller, *Lyndon,* 636.

page 317 "It became clear . . .": Johnson, *The Vantage Point,* 510.

page 317 "significant": ibid.

page 318 "between 300 and 400 . . .": Clifford, *Counsel to the President,* 551.

page 318 "I recommended . . .": Ellsworth Bunker, oral history interview by Michael L. Gillette, October 12, 1983, LJBOH.

page 318 "Our position never . . .": Rusk, *As I Saw It,* 486.

page 319 "a misguided venture . . .": Clifford, *Counsel to the President,* 553.

pages 320–21 Chennault–Nixon meeting: Chennault, *The Education of Anna,* 173–76; Chester, Hodgson, and Page, *An American Melodrama,* 732–33; Clifford, *Counsel to the President,* 581–82; M. A. Cohen, *American Maelstrom,* 321–23; Gould, *1968,* 98–99; Safire, *Before the Fall,* 88–90; Solberg, *Hubert Humphrey,* 394–95; Weiner, *One Man against the World,* 19; Witcover, *The Year the Dream Died,* 286–87; Robert Parry, "LBJ's 'X' File on Nixon's 'Treason,'" *Consortiumnews,* March 3, 2012; David Taylor, "The Lyndon Johnson Tapes: Richard Nixon's 'Treason,'" *BBC News,* n.d.

page 320 "flattered by . . .": Chennault, *The Education of Anna,* 170.

page 321 "Anna is . . .": ibid., 176.

14. MIAMI

page 325 "a coronation": Witcover, *The Resurrection of Richard Nixon,* 337.

pages 326–28 Rockefeller–Reagan alliance: Tom Wicker, "Nixon's 2 Rivals Striving to Block Him on First Vote," *New York Times,* August 4, 1968; Tom Wicker,

"Rockefeller and Reagan Struggle to Deny Nixon Victory on First Ballot," *New York Times,* August 7, 1968; Tom Wicker, "Twisting Path to the G.O.P. Convention," *New York Times,* August 5, 1968.

page 327 "a leading and bona fide . . .": Witcover, *The Resurrection of Richard Nixon,* 339.

pages 328–31 Republican platform: "Republican Party Platform of 1968," August 5, 1968. A complete copy of the platform is available in numerous online sites. I used the American Presidency Project website for my source. All citations from the platform document are from this source.

pages 331–33 Nixon nomination: For an overall view of the convention, Norman Mailer's *Miami and the Siege of Chicago,* 11–82, is probably the best, most detailed account available. See also Ambrose, *Nixon,* 169–72; Kurlansky, *1968,* 264–68; Nixon, *RN,* 308–11; O'Donnell, *Playing with Fire,* 275–315; Perlstein, *Nixonland,* 295–302; White, *The Making of the President 1968,* 224–56; Wicker, *One of Us,* 340–45; Witcover, *Resurrection,* 337–49; Tom Wicker, "Nixon Is Nominated on the First Ballot," *New York Times,* August 8, 1968.

page 332 "Our country needs . . .": as quoted in Perlstein, *Nixonland,* 298.

page 333 "a man who will . . .": Tom Wicker, "Nixon Is Nominated on the First Ballot."

page 334 "whatever force . . .": Mailer, *Miami and the Siege of Chicago,* 81.

page 334 "the average delegate . . .": "Average Delegate a White Protestant and a College Man," *New York Times,* August 4, 1968.

page 334 "If the Republican Party . . .": Mailer, *Miami and the Siege of Chicago,* 54.

page 334 "Poor people . . .": ibid., 55.

pages 335–39 Agnew selection: Chester, Hodgson, and Page, *An American Melodrama,* 482–94; Nixon, *RN,* 311–13; Perlstein, *Nixonland,* 302–4; Wainstock, *The Turning Point,* 109–12; White, *The Making of the President 1968,* 249–53; Witcover, *Resurrection,* 349–57; Witcover, *White Knight,* 216–33; Witcover, *Very Strange Bedfellows,* 21–30; "Choice of Agnew as Mate Proves Chief Convention Surprise," *Christian Science Monitor,* August 8, 1968.

page 335 "rimland states": Nixon, *RN,* 316.

page 336 "my closest friend": ibid., 312.

page 336 "Maybe you would be . . .": ibid.

page 337 "Could you live . . .": Witcover, *White Knight,* 227.

page 338 "The selection . . .": Farrell, *Richard Nixon,* 333.

page 339 "If the sore . . .": Wainstock, *The Turning Point,* 112.

page 339 "I can't analyze . . .": Witcover, *White Knight,* 230.

page 339 "They're talking . . .": Ben A. Franklin, "Wallace Says He Influenced G.O.P. on Agnew," *New York Times,* August 10, 1968.

page 341 "improbability": Witcover, *The Year the Dream Died,* 306.

page 341 "Tonight I see . . .": Richard Nixon, "Acceptance Speech," Nixon, *RN,* 315. All other citations from this speech are from this source.

15. RESISTANCE

page 346 "a clash . . .": Krassner, *Confessions of a Raving, Unconfined Nut,* 166.

page 346 "How many other . . .": Jack Mabley, *Chicago American,* August 25, 1968.

page 346 "True, there would . . .": Hoffman, *Soon to be a Major Motion Picture*, 144–45.

page 347 "Conspiracy?" Sloman, *Steal This Dream*, 187.

pages 347–50 Beginnings of the Youth International Party: Farber, *Chicago '68*, 3–27; Jezer, *Abbie Hoffman*, 121–26; Krassner, *Confessions of a Raving, Unconfined Nut*, 161–63; Sloman, *Steal This Dream*, 107–12; Krassner, interview by author, 1995; Jerry Rubin, interview by author, 1995.

page 347 "revolutionary trust": Krassner, *Confessions of a Raving, Unconfined Nut*, 161.

page 348 "The conspiracy . . .": ibid., 162.

page 348 "This would go along . . .": Jezer, *Abbie Hoffman*, 125.

page 349 "an effective . . .": ibid.

page 349 "The life . . .": "Yippie Press Release," reprinted in Sloman, *Steal This Dream*, 109.

page 349 "The Yippies . . .": David Kupfer, "In the Jester's Court," *The Sun*, February 2009.

page 350 "bring bells . . .": Sanders, *1968*, 62; Farber, *Chicago '68*, 31.

pages 350–51 Grand Central Station violence: Gitlin, *The Sixties*, 237–38; Jezer, *Abbie Hoffman*, 130–33; Sanders, *1968*, 61–65; Sloman, *Steal This Dream*, 113–17; "3,000 Hippies Sing and Hurl Objects in Grand Central," *New York Times*, March 23, 1968.

page 351 "the worst example . . .": Jezer, *Abbie Hoffman*, 132.

pages 351–55 Hoffman biography: Farber, *Chicago '68*, 5–8; Hoffman, *Soon to Be a Major Motion Picture*, 2–136; Jezer, *Abbie Hoffman*, 1–70; Sloman, *Steal This Dream*, 7–87; Abbie Hoffman, oral history interview by Elli Wohlgelernter, February 24, 1981, February 25, 1981, William F. Wiener Oral History Library of the American Jewish Committee, New York Public Library.

page 352 "Not exactly prime . . .": Hoffman, *Soon to Be a Major Motion Picture*," 20.

page 352 "I think I've been . . .": Hoffman, interview by Wohlgelernter.

page 352 "generation-shaking . . .": Hoffman, *Soon to Be a Major Motion Picture*, 39.

page 353 "It was exhilarating . . .": ibid., 54.

page 354 "Throughout all this . . .": ibid., 66.

page 354 "It was kind of . . .": Hoffman, interview by Wohlgelernter.

page 355 "I'm only interested . . .": ibid.

page 355 "We decided . . .": Sloman, *Steal This Dream*, 87.

pages 355–56 Media coverage of Wall Street protest: Abbie Hoffman learned a valuable lesson about the media as a result of the Wall Street episode: news coverage was good, but one had to live with the mistakes. Since the press was barred from the stock exchange, reporters had to rely on the accounts from witnesses, including Hoffman, and the resulting accounts varied wildly. The coverage angered Hoffman. "I watched every news report about what we did at the stock exchange," he told a radio interviewer. "On one report I heard that we threw out Monopoly money. On another report I heard that we threw out fake money. Another report I heard that we threw out at the most twenty or thirty dollars. Now, what the hell happened down there? There's no source out there for checking reality. The only reality is in your head." This was only the beginning. As the Yippies earned a certain status in the eyes of the news media, they also paid the consequences of preconceptions, as Hoffman would learn when the Yippies traveled to Chicago for the Democratic National Convention.

page 356 "We were two . . .": Hoffman, *Soon to Be a Major Motion Picture,* 128.

pages 356–61 Rubin biography: Farber, *Chicago '68,* 8–12; Lukas, *Don't Shoot—We Are Your Children!,* 343–92; Viorst, *Fire in the Streets,* 423–62; Jerry Rubin, oral history interview by Ron Chepesiuk, n.d., Louise Pettus Archive and Special Collection, Oral History Project, Winthrop University.

page 357 "My whole life . . .": Lukas, *Don't Shoot—We Are Your Children!,* 361.

page 357 "He tried . . .": Rubin, *Do It!,* 17.

page 357 "a lot of . . .": Lukas, *Don't Shoot—We Are Your Children!,* 362.

page 358 "So here . . .": ibid., 374.

page 359 "At first . . .": Jack Fincher, "'The University Has Become a Factory,'" *Life,* February 16, 1965.

page 359 "We were putting . . .": Rubin, *Do It!,* 38.

page 360 "A movement . . .": ibid., 42.

page 361 "I learned . . .": ibid., 51.

pages 362–66 Dellinger biography: Dellinger, *From Yale to Jail,* 11–185; Michael Carlson, "David Dellinger," *Guardian,* May 27, 2004; Michael T. Kaufman, "David Dellinger, of Chicago 7, Dies at 88," *New York Times,* May 27, 2004; Patricia Sullivan, "Lifelong Protester David Dellinger Dies," *Washington Post,* May 27, 2004; David Dellinger, oral history interview by Ted Gittinger, December 10, 1982, LBJOH.

page 362 "I shall never . . .": Dellinger, *From Yale to Jail,* 39.

page 362 "sadness, shame . . .": ibid.

page 362 "the single most . . .": Kaufman, "David Dellinger, of Chicago 7, Dies at 88."

page 363 "For no reason . . .": Dellinger, *From Yale to Jail,* 84.

page 363 "I went from . . .": Sullivan, "Lifelong Protester David Dellinger Dies."

page 365 "I wanted . . .": Dellinger, *From Yale to Jail,* 298–99.

page 366 "just a beginning . . .": Douglas Robinson, "Many Draft Cards Burned— Eggs Tossed at Parade," *New York Times,* April 16, 1967.

pages 366–68 Pentagon march: Norman Mailer's award-winning book *The Armies of the Night* is still the finest and most detailed account of the march and the events surrounding it. See also Dellinger, *From Yale to Jail,* 298–301; Farber, *Chicago '68,* 56–59; Hoffman, *Soon to Be a Major Motion Picture,* 126–36; Rubin, *Do It!,* 66–80; John Kifner, "Marchers See a Shift from Dissent to Resistance; Leaders Say Capital Protest Marks an End of Parades in Drive against War," *New York Times,* October 23, 1967; Richard Kreitner, "October 21, 1967: March against the Vietnam War," *Nation,* October 21, 1967; Jeff Leen, "The Vietnam Protests: When Worlds Collided," *Washington Post,* September 27, 1999; Steve Vogel, "Once More to the Pentagon," *Washington Post,* March 16, 2007.

pages 367–68 Crowd size: Crowd estimates for events like this would always vary greatly, with the marchers inflating their numbers, and those opposing them deflating them. In the Pentagon march, with such a large, spread-out area and protesters moving about freely, it was difficult to even approximate. Published numbers varied from a low of twenty thousand to a high of well over one hundred thousand. The latter seems more realistic. The most common estimate placed one hundred thousand at the Lincoln Memorial.

page 367 "It was a concern . . .": Vogel, "Once More to the Pentagon."

page 368 "a cultural touchstone . . .": Leen, "The Vietnam Protests."

pages 368–69 *The Port Huron Statement*: This document is available in many places, from books and online. I used the copy in Albert and Albert, *The Sixties Papers*, 176–96. See also "The Port Huron Statement: Still Radical at 50," *In These Times*, April 25, 2012; Julian Brookes, "Tom Hayden on Port Huron at 50," *Rolling Stone*, July 30, 2112; Sam Roberts, "The Port Huron Statement at 50," *New York Times*, March 3, 2012.

page 369 "We are people . . .": Hayden, *The Port Huron Statement*, Albert and Albert, *The Sixties Papers*, 176.

pages 369–78 Hayden biography: Hayden, *Reunion*; Viorst, *Fire in the Streets*, 163–96; Tim Findley, "Tom Hayden: The Rolling Stone Interview (Part One)," *Rolling Stone*, April 28–May 7, 1973; Robert D. McFadden, "Tom Hayden, Civil Rights and Antiwar Activist Turned Lawmaker, Dies at 76," *New York Times*, October 24, 2016; Elaine Woo, "Tom Hayden, Preeminent 1960s Political Radical and Antiwar Protester, Dies at 76," *Washington Post*, October 24, 2016.

page 370 "students who were . . .": Hayden, *Reunion*, 28.

page 371 "summer of transformation": Woo, "Tom Hayden."

page 371 "utopian spirit": Hayden, *Reunion*, 33.

page 371 "better to be . . .": ibid., 34.

page 372 "Ultimately . . .": Woo, "Tom Hayden."

page 372 "As I left . . .": Hayden, *Reunion*, 35–36.

page 372 "The divisions . . .": Findley, "Tom Hayden."

page 373 "It wasn't until . . .": ibid.

page 374 "In Pike . . .": Hayden, *Reunion*, 54.

page 374 "In other words . . .": Viorst, *Fire in the Streets*, 182.

page 375 "agenda . . .": Brookes, "Tom Hayden on Port Huron at 50."

page 375 "grass-roots democracy": ibid.

page 375 "I don't know . . .": ibid.

page 376 "In the beginning . . .": Hayden, *Reunion*, 102.

pages 376–77 "Americans have to . . .": Woo, "Tom Hayden."

16. CHICAGO

page 379 "They give soldiers . . .": Royko, *Boss*, 11.

pages 380–86 Democratic National Convention: I relied on several book-length accounts of the convention and the violence in the streets as the backbone of my research: Farber, *Chicago '68*; Mailer, *Miami and the Siege of Chicago*; Schultz, *No One Was Killed*; Schneir, *Telling It Like It Was*; Walker, *Rights in Conflict*. See also Chester, Hodgson, and Page, *An American Melodrama*, 503–604; Cohen and Taylor, *American Pharaoh*, 459–82; M. A. Cohen, *American Maelstrom*, 261–84; Dellinger, *From Yale to Jail*, 325–37; Eisele, *Almost to the Presidency*, 344–64; Hayden, *Reunion*, 291–326; Herzog, *McCarthy for President*, 240–81; Hoffman, *Soon to be a Major Motion Picture*, 147–61; Jezer, *Abbie Hoffman*, 149–71; Humphrey, *The Education of a Public Man*, 288–98; Krassner, *Confessions of a Raving, Unconfined Nut*, 170–76; E. J. McCarthy, *The Year of the People*, 197–225;

O'Donnell, *Playing with Fire,* 316–74; Jerry Rubin, *Do It!,* 168–94; Schumacher, *Dharma Lion,* 509–17; Schumacher, *There But for Fortune,* 193–203; Sloman, *Steal This Dream,* 119–60; Solberg, *Hubert Humphrey,* 355–71; White, *The Making of the President 1968,* 257–313; Witcover, *The Year the Dream Died,* 309–45; "Yippies Arrested with Pig 'Candidate' at Chicago Center," *New York Times,* August 24, 1968; "300 Demonstrators Hurt Battling Chicago Police," *Toledo Blade,* August 29, 1968; "Dem Dove Assails Humphrey Victory," *Chicago American,* August 30, 1968; "Democrats: The Penultimate Round," *Time,* August 34, 1968; "Strong-Arm Tactics Praised, Condemned," *Washington Post,* August 30, 1968; John Berendt, "Hog-Wild in the Streets," *Esquire,* November 1968; David S. Broder, "Chicago Has a Day of Political Swirls," *Washington Post,* August 24, 1968; Paul Carroll, "The Playboy Interview: Allen Ginsberg," *Playboy,* April 1969; Christopher Chandler, "Protest Groups Split on Aims, Tactics," *Chicago Sun-Times,* August 19, 1968; George Jenks, "Humphrey Wins Nomination on First Ballot, Prepared to Select His Running Mate," *Toledo Blade,* August 29, 1968; Tom Joyce, "HHH Toughens on Vietnam," *Detroit News,* August 26, 1968; Frank Lynn, "Chicago: Before the Turmoil," *Newsday,* n.d.; William McGaffin, "How Hubert Got the Green Light," *Chicago Daily News,* August 30, 1968; Richard Stewart, "Hubert All Smiles at TV Set," *Boston Globe,* August 29, 1968; Witcover, "HHH's Viet Vow Assures Floor Fight," *Long Island Press,* August 26, 1968. I also consulted the massive FBI files on the individual participants and Chicago convention for a different perspective on the convention and the activities taking place during convention week.

page 381 "new Counterintelligence . . .": U.S. Government Memorandum, C. D. Brennan to W. C. Sullivan, May 9, 1968, FBI.

page 381 "It is believed . . .": U.S. Government Memorandum, SAC Newark to Director, FBI [J. Edgar Hoover], May 27, 1968, FBI.

pages 382–83 Security precautions: Cohen and Taylor, *American Pharaoh,* 462–64; Farber, *Chicago '68,* 148–51; Walker, *Rights,* 95–127; White, *The Making of the President 1968,* 260–61; "Chicago Builds a Convention Fortress," *National Observer,* August 19, 1968; Steven V. Roberts, "5,000 Troops Flown to Convention Duty," *New York Times,* August 26, 1968.

pages 383–84 Pigasus: Hoffman, *Soon to be a Major Motion Picture,* 153–54; Jezer, *Abbie Hoffman,* 156; Krassner, *Confessions of a Raving, Unconfined Nut,* 174; Mark Kurlansky, *1968,* 274–75; Rubin, *Do It!,* 176–80; Schumacher, *There But for Fortune,* 195–97; Sloman, *Steal This Dream,* 132–134. In his autobiography, Paul Krassner recalled the group's running into Beat Generation writer William S. Burroughs in Chicago and asking him what he thought of the idea of running a pig for president. Replied Burroughs, "Well, that's a pretty good idea, but it would be more interesting if you ran a tape recorder."

page 383 "Why take . . .": Rubin, *Do It!,* 176.

page 384 "It looked like . . .": Sloman, *Steal This Dream,* 134.

page 384 "Boys . . .": Schumacher, *There But for Fortune,* 197, from author interview with Stew Albert.

page 384 "From that point . . .": Jezer, *Abbie Hoffman,* 156.

page 385 "The scene seemed . . .": Walker, *Rights in Conflict,* 134.

page 385 "Sleeping in Lincoln Park . . .": ibid., 137.

pages 386–89 McCarthy at convention: Chester, Hodgson, and Page, *An American Melodrama,* 550–63; Herzog, *McCarthy for President,* 240–81; Larner, *Nobody Knows,* 174–82; A. McCarthy, *Private Faces/Public Places,* 420–34; E. J. McCarthy, *The Year of the People,* 197–225; Stavis, *We Were the Campaign,* 171–94; "The Government in Exile," *Time,* September 6, 1968.

pages 387–89 Democratic Platform: "Connally Statement to the Platform Committee," *New York Times,* August 23, 1968; "HHH Asks Free Elections in Vietnam—Would Include Cong," *Boston Globe,* August 1, 1968; David S. Broder, "HHH Rejects McCarthy Plank," *Washington Post,* August 19, 1968; Tom Littlewood, "Symbols of Division," *Chicago Sun-Times,* August 25, 1968; Bob Lundergaard, "HHH Pledges No Sellout of South Vietnam," *Minneapolis Tribune,* August 8, 1968; Dan Tomasson, "Peace Plank Skirmish," *Washington Daily News,* August 19, 1968.

page 386 "reliance on . . .": Tom Wicker, "The Trouble with McCarthy," *New York Times,* July 18, 1968.

page 387 "In exercising . . .": Larner, *Nobody Knows,* 175.

page 387 "We hoped . . .": E. J. McCarthy, *The Year of the People,* 198.

page 388 "We are willing . . .": Johnson, *The Vantage Point,* 513.

page 388 "[h]e has pretty . . .": Wainstock, *The Turning Point,* 130.

page 388 "using the Communist . . .": McCarthy, *The Year of the People,* 208.

page 390 "I think . . .": as quoted in Solberg, *Hubert Humphrey,* 356.

page 390 "He entered . . .": Berman, *Hubert,* 183.

page 390 "lousy candidate": Solberg, *Hubert Humphrey,* 352.

page 391 "It isn't all . . .": Humphrey, *The Education of a Public Man,* 291.

page 392 "I've been a Truman . . .": Roy Reed, "Humphrey Likens Campaign to Underdog Truman's 1948 Run," *New York Times,* August 27, 1968.

page 392 "Any man . . .": ibid.

page 392 "Great surging feeling": Farber, *Chicago '68,* 183.

page 392 "100% victory . . .": ibid.

page 394 "After the curfew . . .": Hoffman, *Soon to Be a Major Motion Picture,* 158.

page 394 "We're not here . . .": Walker, *Rights in Conflict,* 167.

page 395 "Monday, August 26 . . .": ibid., 309.

page 395 "The counterrevolution . . .": Mailer, *Miami and the Siege of Chicago,* 149.

page 395 "added smoke . . .": Tom Wicker, "The Man Who Isn't Here," *New York Times,* August 27, 1968.

page 395 "enormous pressure . . .": ibid.

page 396 "I do not intend . . .": "Excerpts from the Debate," *New York Times,* August 28, 1968. All other citations from the debate are from this source.

page 396 "passive and inactive": as quoted in Eisele, *Almost to the Presidency,* 353.

page 396 "I think a little . . ." "Excerpts from the Debate," *New York Times,* August 28. All other citations from this debate are from this source.

page 398 "The meeting . . .": Wallace Turner, "3 Rivals Meet in Debate; McGovern Wins Ovations," *New York Times,* August 28, 1968.

page 398 "Stop all bombing . . .": "Democratic Party Platform of 1968," August 26, 1968. A complete copy of the platform is available in numerous online sites. I used the American Presidency Project website for my source.

page 399 "I should not . . .": Humphrey, *The Education of a Public Man,* 292.

page 399 "What about . . .": Chester, Hodgson, and Page, *An American Melodrama,*
   571.

page 400 "While I'm doing . . .": ibid., 573.

page 401 "It must have been . . .": Hayden, *Reunion,* 309.

page 401 "If a pig . . .": Walker, *Rights in Conflict,* 187.

page 402 "It's always the old . . .": Phil Ochs, "I Ain't Marching Anymore," Appleseed
   Music, Inc. 1964.

page 402 "This is the highlight . . .": Schumacher, *There But for Fortune,* 200, from
   Krassner, interview by author.

page 403 "but with restraint": Walker, *Rights in Conflict,* 193.

page 403 "There seemed to be . . .": ibid., 195.

page 404 "gone underground: ibid., 214.

page 404 "We have found . . .": Farber, *Chicago '68,* 192.

page 404 "by any force necessary": ibid.

page 405 "thugs": Hayden, *Reunion,* 312.

page 405 "The news profession . . .": Cohen and Taylor, *American Pharaoh,* 474. As
   one might expect, the authorities had a different interpretation of the clashes between the police and members of the press. This report, dated September 5, 1968,
   and found in the Abbie Hoffman FBI files, indicates an attitude that the media were
   obstructing the police as they tried to do their jobs: " [NAME BLACKED OUT] observed numerous instances during those demonstrations when the members of the
   Press covering those demonstrations disobeyed Police instruction and were generally very uncooperative at all times. In spite of Police requests and protests, TV
   cameramen continuously blinded Policemen on duty with their television camera
   lights. It was very hard to distinguish members of the Press from other individuals
   because so many people had cameras and professed members of the Press without
   having proper identification. In some instances, when ordered to get behind the
   Police skirmish line, the Press would make verbal insults to the Police such as 'who
   the hell do you think you are?' and 'we have a right to be here.'"

page 406 "Humphrey, who wanted . . .": Kampelman, *Entering New Worlds,* 169.

page 407 "We Democrats . . .": McCarthy, *The Year of the People,* 213.

page 407 "when the people . . .": ibid., 214.

page 408 "They don't represent . . .": Chester, Hodgson, and Page, *An American Melodrama,* 584.

page 408 "Fuck you . . .": M. A. Cohen, *American Maelstrom,* 281. These exact words
   are reported extensively elsewhere, and while Daley refused to repeat what he supposedly shouted at Ribicoff, calling it "immaterial," he always denied using these
   words. "I never used that kind of language in my life," he insisted during a September 9, 1968, press conference, when questioned about what he had shouted at
   Ribicoff. It is quoted here because there is an enormous consensus agreeing that
   these were precisely his words, as indicated by lip readers.

page 409 "It was something . . .": Peggy McCarthy, "Ribicoff and Daley Head to
   Head," *New York Times,* August 25, 1996. At a 1996 reunion of the radicals and
   protesters at the 1968 Democratic National Convention, Daley's son, Richard M.
   Daley, then mayor of Chicago, offered a moving opening speech, in which he noted

that many of those present had not been welcome at the '68 convention, but that they were welcome now.

page 409 "the government . . .": Witcover, *The Year the Dream Died*, 339.

page 409 "There she is . . .": White, *The Making of the President 1968*, 303.

page 410 "The police moved . . .": Hoffman, *Soon to Be a Major Motion Picture*, 160.

page 411 "especially nervous": Dellinger, *From Yale to Jail*, 331.

page 411 "You are doing . . .": Walker, *Rights in Conflict*, 220.

page 412 "heavy chunks . . .": ibid., 223.

page 412 "Rennie Davis . . .": Dellinger, *From Yale to Jail*, 333.

page 413 "We fell through . . .": Hayden, *Reunion*, 319,

page 414 "They attacked . . .": Mailer, *Miami and the Siege of Chicago*, 169.

page 414 "I feel that . . .": Frost, *The Presidential Debate, 1968*, 59.

page 415 "of deep spiritual . . .": ibid.

pages 414–19 Muskie selection: Berman, *Hubert*, 177–78, 193–94; Chester, Hodgson, and Page, *An American Melodrama*, 590–91; Eisele, *Almost to the Presidency*, 359–61; Humphrey, *The Education of a Public Man*, 293–95; Solberg, *Hubert Humphrey*, 366–67; Wainstock, *The Turning Point*, 142–43; White, *The Making of the President 1968*, 304–5; Edmund Muskie, oral history interview by Arthur Naftalin, August 4, 1978, MHS; Lawrence O'Brien, oral history interview by Michael L. Gillette, July 21, 1987, LBJOH. In a 1978 interview, Muskie offered a detailed timeline of the events leading to his being chosen as Humphrey's running mate. According to Muskie, Humphrey initially broached the subject when they were traveling together to the Maine Democratic convention. Muskie, believing the conversation was intended to be confidential, said nothing about it to anyone, including his wife. Hoping to help Humphrey, Muskie ran as a favorite son in Maine, all but assuring Humphrey of all the state's delegate votes. Humphrey hinted at the vice presidency on several occasions over the ensuing months, though the two men never discussed it in depth. Muskie had grown skeptical by the time the Democratic National Convention opened in Chicago, when he had still heard nothing from Humphrey or other leading Democrats. His name was listed on the lists of possibilities, but he heard nothing encouraging. He began to wonder if he had been played. He was surprised, therefore, on the day after Humphrey accepted the nomination, when Humphrey called him to his suite. "I never really believed it," Muskie told his interviewer. "Even that morning it came as a shock to me—I mean all this that Hubert was talking about was real and I suspect I was the most skeptical guy in the city about the possibilities of my being there, being on the ticket. I was looking at this big problem that Hubert faced and I said—God, he's got to do something about that big problem and I don't know how I'm going to contribute to the solution of it. I wasn't reluctant at all. I was fully up to meeting the challenge."

pages 415–16 "intrigued . . .": O'Brien, interview by Gillette.

page 416 "I know I talk . . .": Solberg, *Hubert Humphrey*, 366.

page 416 "He apparently had . . .": Muskie, interview by Naftalin.

page 417 "In an equal . . .": Solberg, *Hubert Humphrey*, 369.

page 417 "His selection . . .": Wainstock, *The Turning Point*, 143.

page 417 "the troubles and . . .": Hubert Humphrey, "Acceptance Speech," delivered in

Chicago, Illinois, on August 29, 1968, reprinted in Engelmayer and Wagman, *Hubert Humphrey,* 294–96. All other citations from the speech are from this source.

page 419 "If no one . . .": Edmund Muskie, "Acceptance Speech," delivered in Chicago, Illinois, on August 29, 1968. All other citations from the speech are from this source.

page 419 "I think . . .": as quoted in Solberg, *Hubert Humphrey,* 370.

page 419 "devotion to duty . . .": as quoted in Cohen and Taylor, *American Pharaoh,* 481.

page 420 "The policeman isn't . . .": Wiener, *Conspiracy in the Streets,* 51.

page 420 "insensitive": Tom Wicker, "The Question at Chicago," *New York Times,* September 1, 1968.

page 420 "The cops had . . .": Jimmy Breslin, "Police Riot," reprinted in Schneir, *Telling It Like It Was,* 65.

page 420 "riot of the police": Walker, *Rights in Conflict,* viii.

pages 421–22 Hotel raid on McCarthy workers: Cohen and Taylor, *American Pharaoh,* 480–81; Eisele, *Almost to the Presidency,* 363–64; Herzog, *McCarthy for President,* 279–80; McCarthy, *The Year of the People,* 218–23; Schultz, *No One Was Killed,* 276–77.

page 422 "The young people . . .": E. J. McCarthy, *The Year of the People,* 219.

page 422 "a massive . . .": ibid., 222.

page 422 "We are leaving . . .": ibid.

17. THE FINAL LAP

page 427 "smooth as . . .": "Scent of Victory," *Time,* September 27, 1968.

pages 428–29 Haldeman memo: Safire, *Before the Fall,* 63–65. All citations from this memo are from this source.

page 429 "Richard the Chicken-Hearted" and "Richard the Careful": Witcover, *The Resurrection of Richard Nixon,* 416.

page 429 "Wallace's campaign . . .": ibid.

pages 431–36 HHH Salt Lake City speech: Ball, *The Past Has Another Pattern,* 444–48; Berman, *Hubert,* 213–25; Clifford, *Counsel to the President,* 572–73; D. Cohen, *Undefeated,* 371–75; Dallek, *Flawed Giant,* 579–81; Eisele, *Almost to the Presidency,* 377–79; Humphrey, *The Education of a Public Man,* 299–303; Johnson, *The Vantage Point,* 548–49; O'Brien, *No Final Victories,* 259–62; Solberg, *Hubert Humphrey,* 379–86; White, *The Making of the President 1968,* 353–56; Witcover, *The Year the Dream Died,* 372–77; Lawrence O'Brien, oral history interview by Michael L. Gillette, July 33, 1987, LBJOH.

page 431 "I thought . . .": Eisele, *Almost to the Presidency,* 373.

page 432 "In Vietnam . . .": ibid., 374.

page 432 "the loudest . . .": Robert B. Semple Jr., "In Pace, Mood and Tone, Rivals Are Worlds Apart," *New York Times,* September 30, 1968.

page 432 "I went back . . .": Humphrey, *The Education of a Public Man,* 300.

page 432 "I'm probably going . . .": ibid.

page 433 "I don't care . . .": White, *The Making of the President 1968,* 354.

page 434 "I don't think . . .": D. Cohen, *Undefeated,* 372.

page 434 "As president," Hubert Humphrey, Speech, Salt Lake City, October 30, 1968.

page 435 "It liberated him . . .": Eisele, *Almost to the Presidency,* 379.

page 435 "He was a new . . .": O'Brien, *No Final Victories,* 261.

page 435 "I feel good . . .": Solberg, *Hubert Humphrey,* 385.

page 435 "no move . . .": Wainstock, *The Turning Point,* 161.

page 435 "It was nothing . . .": ibid.

page 435 "Humphrey either has . . .": Gould, *1968,* 146.

pages 436–39 LeMay vice-presidential candidacy: Carter, *The Politics of Rage,* 354–62; Chester, Hodgson, and Page, *An American Melodrama,* 692–701; M.A. Cohen, *American Maelstrom,* 299–304; Lesher, *George Wallace,* 424–26; White, *The Making of the President 1968,* 366–68; Witcover, *The Resurrection of Richard Nixon,* 409–15; Witcover, *The Year the Dream Died,* 384–89; Curtis LeMay, oral history interview by Joe B. Frentz, June 28, 1971, LBJOH.

page 437 "back to the Stone Age": M. A. Cohen, *American Maelstrom,* 300.

page 437 "I believed . . .": LeMay, interview by Frentz.

page 438 "My only hope . . .": ibid.

page 438 "We seem to have . . .": "Excerpts from the Comments by Wallace and LeMay on the War and Segregation," *New York Times,* October 4, 1968. All other citations from this press conference are from this source.

page 440 "If you've been . . .": as quoted in Witcover, *Very Strange Bedfellows,* 98–99.

page 440 Agnew gaffes: In the strictest sense, Agnew was not a racist. His overall civil rights record was solid, and he had nothing in his past to suggest, as one who dealt with his own Greek heritage, subject to some bias, that he was racially or ethnically challenged. He would never be known for his sensitivity, and his use of "Polock" or "Jap" was a strong indication of his insensitivity. After the two incidents, he issued a statement that was surely sincere, apologizing "to any who might have read in my words an insult to the Japanese heritage, or to any who might have read into my words an insult to the Polish Heritage. . . . Those who have misread my words, I can only say you've misread my heart."

page 441 "Dear Ted . . .": Safire, *Before the Fall,* 75.

page 441 "Politicians have often . . .": Robert B. Semple Jr., "Nixon's Policy of Silence," *New York Times,* September 7, 1968.

page 442 "I have often . . .": Robert B. Semple Jr., "400,000 Welcome Nixon during a Tour of Chicago," *New York Times,* September 5, 1968.

page 442 "the final chapter": O'Brien, interview by Gillette.

page 443 "equally important": ibid.

page 444 "We were playing . . .": ibid.

page 444 "a new and very much . . .": Lyndon Johnson, Speech: "The President's Address to the Nation upon Announcing His Decision to Halt the Bombing of North Vietnam," October 31, 1968, LBJL. All other citations from this speech are from this source.

page 445 "a bombing halt . . .": "The Bombing Halt: Johnson's Gamble for Peace," *Time,* November 8, 1968.

page 445 "All my military . . .": Johnson, *The Vantage Point,* 525.

page 446 "We are anxious . . .": Telephone conversation between Lyndon Johnson and Richard Nixon, Hubert Humphrey, and George Wallace, October 16, 1968,

Presidential Recordings, Miller Center of Public Affairs, University of Virginia. All other citations from this call are from this source.

page 446 "At no time . . .": Nixon, *RN,* 250.

page 447 "apoplectic": Valenti, *This Time, This Place,* 250.

page 447 "It was an extraordinary . . .": Clifford, *Counsel to the President,* 583.

page 447 "some old China . . .": ibid.

page 447 "partners": Robert Parry, "LBJ's 'X' File on Nixon's 'Treason,'" *Consortiumnews,* March 3, 2012.

page 448 "He better keep . . .": ibid. All other citations from these LBJ calls are from this source.

page 449 "a very optimistic . . .": William Connell, oral history interview by Arthur Naftalin, February 15, 1978, HHHOH/MHS.

page 449 "I wonder if . . .": Humphrey, *The Education of a Public Man,* xix.

page 449 "the dumbest thing . . .": Califano, *The Triumph and Tragedy of Lyndon Johnson,* 328.

18. AMERICA VOTES

page 450 "Since the results . . .": "Nixon Ahead, 42–40, in Final Gallup Poll," *New York Times,* November 4, 1968.

page 450 "There is no . . .": Tom Wicker, "Humphrey Surge Is Offering Aides Hope for an Upset," *New York Times,* October 27, 1968.

page 451 "those who have . . .": Eugene McCarthy, "Statement Backing Humphrey," Washington, D.C., October 29, 1968, reprinted in *New York Times,* October 30, 1968.

page 451 "Would a more . . .": Humphrey, *The Education of a Public Man,* 282. Humphrey and McCarthy, once good friends, would never be the same after the election. According to biographer Roberta Walburn, Miles Lord, a Minnesota judge and influential friend of both Humphrey and McCarthy, attempted to broker a Humphrey–McCarthy ticket, and for a while, earlier in the campaign, both men seemed intrigued by the idea; see Walburn, *Miles Lord.* However, the two were unable to reconcile their respective positions on the Vietnam War, and any thought of their working together evaporated. "[I would] go to the Waldorf in New York and have breakfast with Humphrey, fly up to Washington, have lunch with McCarthy, come back and have dinner with Humphrey that night. [I was trying] to get them together," Lord told Arthur Naftalin in a 1978 oral history interview. "To some extent I did. Gene would lay down ultimatums. He must do this. He must declare amnesty for the draft evaders. He must agree not to bomb. I've forgotten all the particulars. He'd lay those conditions down. I'd take them back to Humphrey and Humphrey would say—Let me study them. I think I can do them, if it's at all possible. By the time Humphrey would get back and agree to it, Gene and his friends would have increased the penalty, raised the ante, the ransom? It was very difficult."

page 452 "showed he had . . .": Dallek, *Flawed Giant,* 577.

page 452 "I frankly don't know . . .": ibid., 575.

page 452 "A progressive . . .": as quoted in Solberg, *Hubert Humphrey,* 399. All other citations from this rally are from this source.

pages 452–53 "That afternoon . . .": Humphrey, *The Education of a Public Man*, 314.

page 453 "When it was over . . .": ibid., 305.

page 453 "there is no . . .": as quoted in Witcover, *The Year the Dream Died*, 433.

page 454 "strong, compassionate . . .": ibid., 432.

page 454 "must have danced . . .": Berman, *Hubert*, 227.

page 454 "It's funny . . ." ibid.

page 455 "We've done . . .": R. W. Apple, "Humphrey Ends Campaign Journey," *New York Times*, November 6, 1968.

page 456 "One baffling problem . . .": Tom Wicker, "Salvaging Something for '68," *New York Times*, November 5, 1968.

page 456 "con the voters . . .": Tom Wicker, "Nation Will Vote Today; Close Presidential Race Predicted in Late Polls," *New York Times*, November 5, 1968.

page 456 "If the pollsters . . .": Wicker, "Salvaging Something for '68."

page 457 "Depression-born . . .": E. W. Kenworthy, "Nixon, in Texas, Sharpens His Attack," *New York Times*, November 3, 1968.

page 457 "The hay's . . .": Witcover, *The Resurrection of Richard Nixon*, 450.

page 458 "If we don't . . .": Nixon, *RN*, 330–31.

page 458 "It was kind of . . .": Leonard Garment, oral history interview by Timothy Naftali, April 6, 2007, Richard M. Nixon Presidential Library and Museum.

page 459 "that whole night . . .": ibid.

page 459 "a few more days": Humphrey, *The Education of a Public Man*, xvi.

page 459 "I've climbed . . .": ibid.

page 461 "The people need . . ." ibid., xxii.

page 461 "As you know . . .": as quoted in Eisele, *Almost to the Presidency*, 392.

page 463 "Just before . . .": Nixon, *RN*, 333.

page 464 "papier-mache man": Eisele, *Almost to the Presidency*, 392.

page 464 "To lose . . .": Humphrey, *The Education of a Public Man*, xxii.

page 465 "According to . . .": D. Cohen, *Undefeated*, 383.

page 465 "I shall continue . . .": Solberg, *Hubert Humphrey*, 406.

page 466 "It was entirely . . .": "A Loser Stands Tall," *New York Times*, November 7, 1968.

page 466 "Like many other . . .": James Reston, "Farewell to the Gentleman from Minnesota," *New York Times*, November 8, 1968.

Bibliography

Albert, Judith Clavir, and Stewart Edward Albert. *The Sixties Papers: Documents of a Rebellious Decade*. Westport, Conn.: Praeger, 1984.

Ambrose, Stephen E. *Nixon: The Triumph of a Politician, 1962–1972*. New York: Simon and Schuster, 1989.

Ball, George W. *The Past Has Another Pattern: Memoirs*. New York: W. W. Norton, 1982.

Berman, Edgar. *Hubert: The Triumph and Tragedy of the Humphrey I Knew*. New York: G. P. Putnam's Sons, 1979.

Black, Conrad. *Richard M. Nixon: A Life in Full*. New York: Public Affairs, 2007.

Boomhower, Ray E. *Robert F. Kennedy and the 1968 Indiana Primary*. Bloomington: Indiana University Press, 2008.

Bowden, Mark. *Hue 1968: A Turning Point of the American War in Vietnam*. New York: Atlantic Monthly Press, 2017.

Brinkley, Douglas. *Cronkite*. New York: HarperCollins, 2012.

Buchanan, Patrick J. *The Greatest Comeback*. New York: Crown Forum, 2014.

Bundy, McGeorge. *Danger and Survival*. New York: Random House, 1988.

Califano, Joseph A., Jr. *The Triumph and Tragedy of Lyndon Johnson*. New York: Simon and Schuster, 1991.

Caro, Robert. *Master of the Senate*. The Years of Lyndon Johnson, vol. 3. New York: Alfred A. Knopf, 2003.

———. *Means of Ascent*. The Years of Lyndon Johnson, volume 2. New York: Alfred A. Knopf, 1990.

———. *The Passage of Power*. The Years of Lyndon Johnson, vol. 4. New York: Alfred A. Knopf, 2012.

Carson, Clayborne, ed. *The Autobiography of Martin Luther King, Jr.* New York: Warner, 1998.

Carter, Dan T. *The Politics of Rage*. New York: Simon and Schuster, 1995. Reprint, Baton Rouge: Louisiana State University Press, 2000.

Caute, David. *The Year of the Barricades*. New York: Harper and Row, 1988.

Chafe, William H. *Never Stop Running: Allard Lowenstein and the Struggle to Save American Liberalism*. New York: Basic Books, 1993.

Chafets, Zev. *Roger Ailes*. New York: Sentinel, 2013.

Charters, Ann, ed. *The Portable Sixties Reader*. New York: Penguin Books, 2003.

Chennault, Anna. *The Education of Anna*. New York: Times Books, 1980.

Chester, Lewis, Godfrey Hodgson, and Bruce Page. *An American Melodrama: The Presidential Campaign of 1968*. New York: Viking Press, 1969.

Clarke, Thurston. *The Last Campaign: Robert F. Kennedy and 82 Days That Inspired America.* New York: Henry Holt, 2008.

Clifford, Clark, with Richard Holbrooke. *Counsel to the President: A Memoir.* New York: Random House, 1991.

Cohen, Adam, and Elizabeth Taylor. *American Pharaoh: Mayor Richard J. Daley: His Battle for Chicago and the Nation.* Boston: Little Brown, 2000.

Cohen, Dan. *Undefeated: The Life of Hubert H. Humphrey.* Minneapolis: Lerner Publications Company, 1978.

Cohen, Michael A. *American Maelstrom: The 1968 Election and the Politics of Division.* New York: Oxford University Press, 2016.

Combs, Barbara Harris. *From Selma to Montgomery.* New York: Routledge, 2014.

Cronkite, Walter. *A Reporter's Life.* New York: Alfred A. Knopf, 1996.

Cummings, Richard. *The Pied Piper: Allard K. Lowenstein and the Liberal Dream.* New York: Grove Press, 1985.

Dallek, Robert. *Camelot's Court: Inside the Kennedy White House.* New York: HarperCollins, 2013.

———. *Flawed Giant: Lyndon Johnson and His Times, 1961–1973.* New York: Oxford University Press, 1998.

———. *Harry S. Truman.* New York: Times Books, 2008.

Dellinger, David. *From Yale to Jail.* New York: Pantheon, 1993.

Edelman, Peter. *Searching for America's Heart: RFK and the Renewal of Hope.* Boston: Houghton Mifflin, 2001.

Ehrlichman, John. *Witness to Power.* New York: Pocketbooks, 1982.

Eisele, Albert. *Almost to the Presidency.* Blue Earth, Minn.: Piper, 1972.

Engelmayer, Sheldon D., and Robert J. Wagman, eds. *Hubert Humphrey: The Man and His Dream, 1911–1978.* New York: Methuen, 1978.

Farber, David R. *Chicago '68.* Chicago: University of Chicago Press, 1988.

Farrell, John A. *Richard Nixon: The Life.* New York: Doubleday, 2017.

Frady, Marshall. *Wallace.* New York: Random House, 1996.

Frost, David. *The Presidential Debate, 1968.* New York: Stein and Day, 1968.

Gardner, Michael T. *Truman and Civil Rights.* Carbondale: Southern Illinois University Press, 2002.

Garment, Leonard. *Crazy Rhythm.* New York: Da Capo, 2001.

Garrow, David J. *Protest at Selma.* New Haven, Conn.: Yale University Press, 1978.

Gelb, Leslie H., and Richard K. Betts, *The Irony of Vietnam.* Washington, D.C.: Brookings Institution Press, 1979.

Gentry, Curt. *J. Edgar Hoover: The Man and the Secrets.* New York: W. W. Norton, 1991.

Ginsberg, Allen. *The Fall of America.* San Francisco: City Lights Books, 1973.

———. *Planet News.* San Francisco: City Lights Books, 1967.

Gitlin, Todd. *The Sixties: Years of Hope, Days of Rage.* New York: Bantam, 1987.

Goodman, Mitchell. *The Movement toward a New America: The Beginnings of a Long Revolution.* Philadelphia: Pilgrim Press, 1970.

Goodwin, Doris Kearns. *Lyndon Johnson and the American Dream.* New York: St. Martin's Press, 1976.

Goodwin, Richard N. *Remembering America.* Boston: Little, Brown, 1988.

Gould, Lewis L. *1968: The Election That Changed America.* Chicago: Ivan R. Dee, 1993.

Greenberg, David. *Nixon's Shadow.* New York: W. W. Norton, 2003.

Greenfield, Jeff. *Then Everything Changed.* New York: G. P. Putnam's, 2011.

Griffith, Winthrop. *Humphrey: A Candid Biography.* New York: William Morrow and Co., 1965.

Halberstam, David. *The Best and the Brightest.* New York: Ballantine Books, 1992.

Haldeman, H. R., with Joseph DiMona. *The Ends of Power.* New York: New York Times Books, 1978.

Hampton, Henry, and Steve Fayer, with Sarah Flynn. *Voices of Freedom: An Oral History of the Civil Rights Movement from the 1950s through the 1980s.* New York: Bantam, 1990.

Hayden, Tom. *The Long Sixties.* Boulder, Colo.: Paradigm Press, 2009.

———. *Reunion.* New York: Random House, 1988.

Hersh, Seymour M. *The Dark Side of Camelot.* Boston: Little, Brown, 1997.

Herzog, Arthur. *McCarthy for President.* New York: Viking Press, 1969.

Heymann, C. David. *RFK.* New York: Dutton, 1998.

Hoeh, David C. *1968, McCarthy, New Hampshire: "I Hear America Singing."* Rochester, Minn.: Lone Oak Press, 1994.

Hoffman, Abbie. *Soon to Be a Major Motion Picture.* New York: Perigee, 1980.

Humphrey, Hubert H. *The Cause Is Mankind.* New York: Frederick A. Praeger, 1964.

———. *The Education of a Public Man: My Life and Politics.* Minneapolis: University of Minnesota Press, 1991.

———, ed. *Integration vs. Segregation.* New York: Thomas Y. Crowell, 1964.

Hung, Nguyen Tien, and Jerold L. Scheeter. *The Palace File.* New York: Harper & Row, 1986.

Isaacson, Walter, and Evan Thomas. *The Wise Men.* New York: Simon & Schuster, 1986.

Isserman, Maurice, and Michael Kazin. *America Divided: The Civil War of the 1960s.* New York: Oxford University Press, 2000.

Jezer, Marty. *Abbie Hoffman: American Rebel.* New Brunswick, N.J.: Rutgers University Press, 1992.

Johnson, Lady Bird. *A White House Diary.* New York: Holt, Rinehart, and Winston, 1970.

Johnson, Lyndon Baines. *The Vantage Point: Perspectives of the Presidency 1963–1969.* New York: Holt, Rinehart and Winston, 1971.

Kaiser, Charles. *1968 in America.* New York: Weidenfeld & Nicolson, 1988.

Kaiser, Robert Blair. *"R.F.K. Must Die!,"* Woodstock, N.Y.: The Overlook Press, 2008.

Kampelman, Max M. *Entering New Worlds: The Memoirs of a Private Man in Public Life.* New York: HarperCollins, 1991.

Karnow, Stanley. *Vietnam: A History.* New York: Viking Press, 1983.

Keogh, James. *President Nixon and the Press.* New York: Funk & Wagnall's, 1972.

King, Coretta Scott. *My Life with Martin Luther King, Jr.* Rev. ed. New York: H. Holt, 1993.

Kornbluth, Jesse, ed. *Notes from the New Underground.* New York: Ace Books, 1968.

Kramer, Michael, and Sam Roberts. *"I Never Wanted to Be Vice–President of Any-thing!": An Investigative Biography of Nelson Rockefeller.* New York: Basic Books, 1976.

Krassner, Paul. *Confessions of a Raving, Unconfined Nut.* Berkeley, Calif.: Soft Skull, 2012.

Kurlansky, Mark. *1968: The Year That Rocked the World.* New York: Random House, 2004.

LaFeber, Walter. *The Deadly Bet: LBJ, Vietnam, and the 1968 Election.* Lanham, Md.: Rowman & Littlefield, 2005.

Larner, Jeremy. *Nobody Knows: Reflections on the McCarthy Campaign of 1968.* New York: Macmillan, 1969.

Lasky, Victor. *It Didn't Start with Watergate.* New York: Dial Press, 1977.

Lee, Martin A., and Bruce Shlain. *Acid Dreams: The CIA, LSD, and the Sixties Rebel-lion.* New York: Grove Press, 1985.

Lesher, Stephan. *George Wallace: American Populist.* Reading, Mass.: Addison-Wesley, 1994.

Levine, Mark L., George C. McNamee, and Daniel Greenberg, eds. *The Tales of Hoff-man.* New York: Bantam, 1970.

Lewis, John. *Across That Bridge: Life Lessons and a Vision for Change.* New York: Hyperion, 2012.

———. *Walking with the Wind: A Memoir of the Movement.* New York: Simon & Schuster, 1998.

Lukas, J. Anthony. *Don't Shoot—We Are Your Children!* New York: Random House, 1971.

Mailer, Norman. *The Armies of the Night.* New York: New American Library, 1968.

———. *Miami and the Siege of Chicago.* New York: New American Library, 1968.

Mann, Robert. *The Walls of Jericho.* New York: Harcourt Brace & Company, 1996.

Matthews, Chris. *Bobby Kennedy: A Raging Spirit.* New York: Simon & Schuster. 2017.

———. *Kennedy & Nixon.* New York: Simon & Schuster, 1996.

McCarthy, Abigail. *Private Faces/Public Places.* New York: Curtis Books, 1972.

McCarthy, Eugene J. *The Year of the People.* Garden City, N.Y.: Doubleday, 1969.

———. *Up 'Til Now.* New York: Harcourt Brace Jovanovich, 1987.

McCullough, David. *Truman.* New York: Simon & Schuster, 1992.

McGinniss, Joe. *The Selling of the President, 1968.* New York: Penguin, 1988.

McNamara, Robert S. *In Retrospect: The Tragedy and Lessons of Vietnam.* New York: Vintage Books, 1995.

McPherson, Harry. *A Political Education.* Austin: University of Texas Press, 1995.

Miller, Merle. *Lyndon: An Oral Biography.* New York: Ballantine, 1980.

Moldea, Dan E. *The Killing of Robert F. Kennedy.* New York: W. W. Norton, 1995.

Mondale, Walter, with David Hage. *The Good Fight: A Life in Liberal Politics.* New York: Scribner, 2010. Reprint, Minneapolis: University of Minnesota Press, 2014.

Morin, Relman. *The Associated Press Story of Election 1968.* New York: Pocket Books, 1969.

National Advisory Commission on Civil Disorders. *The Kerner Report: The 1968 Re-port of the National Advisory Commission on Civil Disorders.* New York: Pantheon Books, 1988.

Nelson, Candice J. *Grant Park: The Democratization of Presidential Elections 1968–2008*. Washington, D.C.: Brookings Institute Press, 2011.

Newfield, Jack. *Robert Kennedy: A Memoir*. New York: Dutton, 1969.

Nixon, Richard. *RN: The Memoirs of Richard Nixon*. New York: Grosset and Dunlap, 1978.

———. *Six Crises*. New York: Doubleday & Company, 1962.

Oberdorfer, Don. *Tet!* New York: Avon, 1971.

O'Brien, Lawrence F. *No Final Victories: A Life in Politics*. Garden City, N.Y.: Doubleday & Company, 1974.

O'Brien, Michael. *John F. Kennedy: A Biography*. New York: St. Martin's Press, 2005.

O'Donnell, Lawrence. *Playing with Fire: The 1968 Election and the Transformation of American Politics*. New York: Penguin Press, 2017.

Perlstein, Rick. *Nixonland*. New York: Scribner, 2008.

Pietrusza, David. *1948*. New York: Union Square Press, 2011.

Powers, Richard. *Secrecy and Power: The Life of J. Edgar Hoover*. New York: Free Press, 1987.

Reedy, George. *Lyndon B. Johnson: A Memoir*. Kansas City: Andrews and McMeel, 1982.

Reporting Vietnam, Part I. American Journalism, 1959–1969. New York: The Library of America, 1998.

Reporting Vietnam, Part II. American Journalism, 1969–1975. New York: The Library of America, 1998.

Richardson, Darcy G. *A Nation Divided*. San Jose, Calif.: Writers Club Press, 2002.

Rosen, James. *The Strong Man*. New York: Doubleday, 2008.

Rosenthal, Seth. *Subversives*. New York: Farrar, Straus and Giroux, 2012.

Royko, Mike. *Boss: Richard J. Daley of Chicago*. New York: Dutton, 1971.

Rubin, Jerry. *Do It!* New York: Simon and Schuster, 1970.

Rusk, Dean. *As I Saw It*. New York: Penguin, 1991.

Ryskind, Allan H. *Hubert*. New Rochelle, N.Y.: Arlington House, 1968.

Safire, William. *Before the Fall: An Inside View of the Pre-Watergate White House*. Garden City, N.Y.: Doubleday & Co, 1975.

Salinger, Pierre, Edwin Guthman, Frank Mankiewicz, and John Seigenthaler, eds. *"An Honorable Profession": A Tribute to Robert F. Kennedy*. New York: Doubleday, 1968.

Sandbrook, Dominic. *Eugene McCarthy*. New York: Knopf, 2004.

Sanders, Edward. *1968*. Santa Barbara, Calif.: Black Sparrow Press, 1997.

Schandler, Herbert Y. *Lyndon Johnson and Vietnam: The Unmaking of a President*. Princeton, N.J.: Princeton University Press, 1977.

Schlesinger, Arthur M., Jr. *Robert Kennedy and His Times*. Boston: Houghton Mifflin, 1978.

———. *A Thousand Days: John F. Kennedy in the White House*. Boston: Houghton Mifflin Company, 1965.

Schmitt, Edward R. *President of the Other America: Robert Kennedy and the Politics of Poverty*. Amherst, Mass.: University of Massachusetts Press, 2010.

Schneir, Walter, ed. *Telling It Like It Was: The Chicago Riots*. New York: Signet, 1969.

Schultz, John. *No One Was Killed: The Democratic National Convention, August 1968.* Chicago: University of Chicago Press, 2000.

Schumacher, Michael. *Dharma Lion: A Biography of Allen Ginsberg.* Minneapolis: University of Minnesota Press, 2016 [1992].

———. *There But for Fortune: The Life of Phil Ochs.* Minneapolis: University of Minnesota Press, 2018 [1995].

Sherman, Norman. *From Nowhere to Somewhere: My Political Journey.* Minneapolis: First Avenue Editions, 2016.

Sherrill, Robert, and Harry W. Ernst. *The Drugstore Liberal.* New York: Grossman, 1968.

Shesol, Jeff. *Mutual Contempt: Lyndon Johnson, Robert Kennedy, and the Feud That Defined a Decade.* New York: W. W. Norton, 1997.

Skolnick, Jerome H. *The Politics of Protest.* New York: Ballantine, 1969.

Sloman, Larry. *Steal This Dream.* New York: Doubleday 1998.

Solberg, Carl. *Hubert Humphrey.* New York: W. W. Norton, 1984.

Sorensen, Ted. *Counselor: A Life at the Edge of History.* New York: HarperCollins, 2008.

Stavis, Ben. *We Were the Campaign: New Hampshire to Chicago for McCarthy.* Boston: Beacon Press, 1969.

Stein Jean, and George Plimpton. *American Journey: The Times of Robert Kennedy.* New York: Harcourt Brace Jovanovich, 1970.

Strober, Gerald S., and Deborah H. Strober. *"Let Us Begin Anew": An Oral History of the Kennedy Presidency.* New York: HarperCollins, 1993.

Synon, John J., ed. *George Wallace: Profile of a Presidential Candidate.* Klimarnork, Va.: Ms Inc., 1968.

Terkel, Studs. *Chicago.* New York: Pantheon, 1986.

Thomas, Evan. *Robert Kennedy: His Life.* New York: Simon & Schuster, 2000.

Thomas, Pat, and Jerry Rubin. *Did It!* Seattle: Fantagraphics, 2017.

Tye, Larry. *Bobby Kennedy: The Making of a Liberal Icon.* New York: Random House, 2016.

Valenti, Jack. *This Time, This Place.* New York: Harmony, 2007.

Viorst, Milton. *Fire in the Streets: America in the 1960s.* New York: Simon & Schuster, 1979.

Wainstock, Dennis. *The Turning Point.* Jefferson, N.C.: McFarland & Company, 1988.

Walburn, Roberta. *Miles Lord: The Maverick Judge Who Brought Corporate America to Justice.* Minneapolis: University of Minnesota Press, 2017.

Walker, Daniel, director. *Rights in Conflict: The Walker Report to the National Commission on the Causes and Prevention of Violence.* New York: Bantam, 1968.

Weiner, Tim. *One Man against the World: The Tragedy of Richard Nixon.* New York: Henry Holt and Company, 2015.

Whalen, Charles, and Barbara Whalen. *The Longest Debate: A Legislative History of the 1964 Civil Rights Act.* New York: New American Library, 1985.

White, Theodore H. *America in Search of Itself.* New York: Harper and Row, 1982.

———. *In Search of History: A Personal Adventure.* New York: Harper and Row, 1978.

———. *The Making of the President 1960.* New York: Atheneum, 1961.

————. *The Making of the President 1964.* New York: Atheneum, 1965.

————. *The Making of the President 1968.* New York: Atheneum, 1969.

Wicker, Tom. *One of Us: Richard Nixon and the American Dream.* New York: Random House, 1991.

Wiener, Jon, ed. *Conspiracy in the Streets.* New York: The New Press, 2006.

Wilentz, Sean. *The Age of Reagan.* New York: HarperCollins, 2008.

Wills, Garry. *Nixon Agonistes: The Crisis of the Self-Made Man.* Boston: Houghton Mifflin, 1969.

Witcover, Jules. *85 Days: The Last Campaign of Robert Kennedy.* New York: Quill Books, 1988.

————. *The Resurrection of Richard Nixon.* New York: G. P. Putnam's Sons, 1970.

————. *Very Strange Bedfellows: The Short and Unhappy Marriage of Richard Nixon and Spiro Agnew.* New York: Public Affairs, 2007.

————. *White Knight: The Rise of Spiro Agnew.* New York: Random House, 1972.

————. *The Year the Dream Died: Revisiting 1968 in America.* New York: Warner Books, 1997.

Woods, Randall B. *LBJ: Architect of American Ambition.* New York: Free Press, 2006.

Zehnpfennig, Gladys. *Hubert H. Humphrey: Champion of Human Rights.* Minneapolis: T. S. Denison, 1966.

Zellar, Brad, Brian Horrigan, and Elizabeth Ault. *The 1968 Project: A Nation Coming of Age.* St. Paul: Minnesota Historical Society Press, 2011.

Index

MICHAEL SCHUMACHER is the author of eighteen books, including *Dharma Lion: A Biography of Allen Ginsberg* and *There But for Fortune: The Life of Phil Ochs,* also published by the University of Minnesota Press. He lives in Wisconsin.